Bradley L. Jones and
Peter Aitken

SAMS
Teach Yourself

C

in 21 Days

SIXTH EDITION

SAMS

800 East 96th St., Indianapolis, Indiana, 46240 USA

Sams Teach Yourself C in 21 Days, Sixth Edition

Copyright © 2003 by Sams Publishing

International Standard Book Number: 0-672-32448-2

Library of Congress Catalog Number: 2002106120

Printed in the United States of America

First Printing: September 2002

06   05   04   6   5   4

Trademarks

Warning and Disclaimer

Bulk Sales

Sams Publishing offers excellent discounts on this book when ordered in quantity for bulk purchases or special sales. For more information, please contact

> **U.S. Corporate and Government Sales**
> **1-800-382-3419**
> corpsales@pearsontechgroup.com

For sales outside of the U.S., please contact

> **International Sales**
> international@pearsoned.com

ASSOCIATE PUBLISHER
Michael Stephens

MANAGING EDITOR
Charlotte Clapp

PROJECT EDITORS
Elizabeth Finney
Katelyn Cozatt

INDEXER
Bruce Clingaman
Lisa Wilson

PROOFREADER
Abby VanHuss

TECHNICAL EDITOR
Mark Cashman

TEAM COORDINATOR
Lynne Williams

INTERIOR DESIGN
Gary Adair

COVER DESIGN
Aren Howell

LAYOUT TECHNICIAN
Juli Cook

Contents at a Glance

Table of Contents

About the Authors

BRADLEY L. JONES works with internet.com overseeing the EarthWeb software development channel. This includes overseeing sites such as Developer.com, CodeGuru.com, and Gamelan.com. He has directed the development of systems, both small scale and distributed as well as on a variety of platforms from the Palm OS to mainframe systems. He has developed systems using such tools as C, C#, C++, XML, SQL Server, PowerBuilder, Visual Basic, Active Server Pages (ASP), Satellite Forms, and more. Jones's other authoring credits include *Sams Teach Yourself Advanced C in 21 Days* (Sams Publishing) and *Sams Teach Yourself C# in 21 Days* (Sams Publishing).

PETER AITKEN has been writing about computers and programming for over 10 years, with some 30 books and hundreds of magazine and trade publication articles to his credit. His recent book titles include *Visual Basic .NET Programming With Peter Aitken*, *Office XP Development With VBA*, *XML the Microsoft Way*, *Windows Script Host*, and *Sams Teach Yourself Visual Basic .NET Internet Programming in 21 Days*. For several years he was a Contributing Editor at *Visual Developer* magazine where he wrote a popular Visual Basic column, and he is a regular contributor to *Microsoft OfficePro* magazine and the DevX Web site. Peter is the proprietor of PGA Consulting, providing custom application and Internet development to business, academia, and government since 1994. You can reach him at `peter@pgacon.com`.

Acknowledgments

First and foremost, my thanks go to my co-author, Brad Jones, for his hard work and dedication. I am also greatly indebted to all the people at Sams Publishing, unfortunately too many to mention by name, who helped bring this book from concept to completion. The text and programs in this book have been thoroughly edited and tested, and we believe this book to be largely, if not completely, error-free. Should you encounter an error, we would like to know about it. You can contact me through the publisher, at the address on the CD order form at the back of the book, or via email at `peter@pgacon.com`.

—Peter Aitken

I'd first like to thank my wife for her continued understanding and patience as I take on such projects as the writing of books.

A good book is the result of the symbiosis achieved by a number of people working together. I would like to acknowledge all the people—readers, editors, and others—who have taken the time to provide comments and feedback on this book. By incorporating much of their feedback, I believe that Peter and I have made this the best book for easily learning to program C.

—Bradley L. Jones
`jones@iquest.net`

We Want to Hear from You!

As the reader of this book, *you* are our most important critic and commentator. We value your opinion and want to know what we're doing right, what we could do better, what areas you'd like to see us publish in, and any other words of wisdom you're willing to pass our way.

As an associate publisher for Sams Publishing, I welcome your comments. You can email or write me directly to let me know what you did or didn't like about this book—as well as what we can do to make our books better.

Please note that we cannot help you with technical problems related to the topic of this book. We do have a User Services group, however, where I will forward specific technical questions related to the book.

When you write, please be sure to include this book's title and authors as well as your name, email address, and phone number. I will carefully review your comments and share them with the authors and editors who worked on the book.

Email: feedback@samspublishing.com

Mail: Michael Stephens
          Associate Publisher
          Sams Publishing
          800 East 96th Street
          Indianapolis, IN 46240 USA

For more information about this book or another Sams Publishing title, visit our Web site at www.samspublishing.com. Type the ISBN (excluding hyphens) or the title of a book in the Search field to find the page you're looking for.

Introduction

As you can guess from the title, this book is set up so that you can teach yourself the C programming language in 21 days. Despite stiff competition from languages such as C++, Java, and C#, C remains the language of choice for people who are just learning programming. For reasons we detail on Day 1, you can't go wrong in selecting C as your programming language.

We think you've made a wise decision selecting this book as your means of learning C. Although there are many books on C, we believe this book presents C in the most logical and easy-to-learn sequence. The fact that the five previous editions have been on best-seller lists indicates that readers agree with us! We designed this book for you to work through the chapters in order on a daily basis. We don't assume any previous programming experience on your part, although experience with another language, such as BASIC, might help you learn faster. We also make no assumptions about your computer or compiler; this book concentrates on teaching the C language, regardless of whether you're using a PC, a Mac, or a UNIX system.

As an added bonus, we have included seven extra days in this book. The added bonus days provide you with a primer on object-oriented programming and an introduction to the most popular object-oriented languages, C++, Java and C#. Although these extra chapters won't teach you everything about these topics, they will get you started.

This Book's Special Features

This book contains some special features to aid you on your path to C enlightenment. Syntax boxes show you how to use specific C concepts. Each box provides concrete examples and a full explanation of the C command or concept. To get a feel for the style of the syntax boxes, look at the following example. (Don't try to understand the material; you haven't even reached Day 1!)

▼ SYNTAX

```
#include <stdio.h>
printf( format-string[,arguments,...]);
```

`printf()` is a function that accepts a series of *arguments,* each applying to a conversion specifier in the given format string. It prints the formatted information to the standard output device, usually the display screen. When using `printf()`, you need to include the standard input/output header file, stdio.h.

The *format-string* is required; however, *arguments* are optional. For each argument, there must be a conversion specifier. The format string can also contain escape

▼ sequences. The following are examples of calls to `printf()` and their output:

▼ **Example 1**

```
#include <stdio.h>
int main( void )
{
    printf( "This is an example of something printed!");
}
```

Example 1 Output

```
This is an example of something printed!
```

Example 2

```
printf( "This prints a character, %c\na number, %d\na floating point,
%f", 'z', 123, 456.789 );
```

Example 2 Output

```
This prints a character, z
a number, 123
▲ a floating point, 456.789
```

Another feature of this book is DO/DON'T boxes, which give you pointers on what to do and what not to do.

Do	**DON'T**
DO read the rest of this section. It explains the Workshop sections that appear at the end of each day.	**DON'T** skip any of the quiz questions or exercises. If you can finish the day's workshop, you're ready to move on to new material.

You'll encounter Tip, Note, and Caution boxes as well. Tips provide useful shortcuts and techniques for working with C. Notes provide special details that enhance the explanations of C concepts. Cautions help you avoid potential problems.

Numerous sample programs illustrate C's features and concepts so that you can apply them in your own programs. Each program's discussion is divided into three components: the program itself, the input required and the output generated by it, and a line-by-line analysis of how the program works. These components are indicated by special icons.

Each day ends with a Q&A section containing answers to common questions relating to that day's material. There is also a Workshop at the end of each day. It contains quiz questions and exercises. The quiz tests your knowledge of the concepts presented on that day. If you want to check your answers, or if you're stumped, the answers are provided in Appendix F.

You won't learn C by just reading this book, however. If you want to be a programmer, you must write programs. Following each set of quiz questions is a set of exercises. We recommend that you attempt each exercise. Writing C code is the best way to learn C.

We consider the BUG BUSTER exercises most beneficial. A bug is a program error in C. BUG BUSTER exercises are code listings that contain common problems (bugs). It's your job to locate and fix these errors. If you have trouble busting the bugs, these answers also are given in Appendix F.

As you progress through this book, some of the exercise answers tend to get long. Other exercises have a multitude of answers. As a result, later days don't always provide answers for all the exercises.

Making a Better Book

Nothing is perfect, but we do believe in striving for perfection. This is the sixth edition of *Sams Teach Yourself C in 21 Days*. In preparing this edition, we have gone to even greater lengths to make the code 100 percent compatible with a wider variety of C compilers. This book has been checked several times to ensure an extremely high level of technical accuracy. We have also incorporated the numerous corrections that have been pointed out by the alert readers of the previous editions.

 Note

> The source code in this book has been compiled and tested on the following platforms; DOS, Windows, Macintosh, UNIX, Linux, and OS/2. In addition, readers of previous editions of this book have used the code on virtually every platform that supports C!

Another feature of this edition is the Type & Run sections. You'll find six of these throughout the book. Each Type & Run contains a short C program that does something fun or useful while it illustrates C programming techniques. You can type these listings in and run them. After you've entered them, you can also play with the code to see what else you can make it do. The Type & Runs are for you to experiment with. We hope you have fun playing with these additional code listings!

The CD-Rom and the Book's Code

For your convenience, the code listings in this book are available on the included CD-ROM. As a bonus, the CD-ROM includes a couple of compilers. Appendix G, "Getting Started with Dev-C++" shows you how to use the Bloodshed Dev-C++ compiler which is also included on the CD-Rom.

Errata and updates to the source code, if any, will be placed on the Internet for you to access at `http://samspublishing.com`.

Conventions Used in This Book

This book uses different typefaces to help you differentiate between C code and regular English, and also to help you identify important concepts. Actual C code appears in a special `monospace` font. In the examples of a program's input and output, what the user types appears in **`bold monospace`**. Placeholders—terms that represent what you actually type within the code—appear in *`italic monospace`*. New or important terms appear in *italic*.

WEEK 1

At a Glance

As you prepare for your first week of learning how to program in C, you need a few things: a compiler, an editor, and this book. In this edition we have included all of this for you. On the CD that comes with this book you will find that there are two editors, Bloodshed Dev-C++ and DJGPP. These editors both include compilers. Appendix G, "The Bloodshed Dev-C++ Compiler" will tell you how to install the Bloodshed compiler for Windows. The readme files on the CD will provide you information on the DJGPP. If you have your own editor and compiler, you don't need to use the tools included on the CD. In fact, because this book is written with the ANSI standard in mind, you can use any standard C compiler and editor.

The best way to learn a computer language involves more than just reading a book; it involves entering and running a number of programs. The many C programs included in this book offer hands-on training. If you are interested in cutting corners, you will find most of the complete listings on the book's CD. While you can simply copy and run these programs from the CD, we recommend that you actually type the programs into your editor instead. This will take more time; however, it will help you to understand the code by giving you a closer look at it.

Where You're Going

The first week covers basic material that you need to know to fully understand C. On Day 1, "Getting Started with C," and Day 2, "The Components of a C Program," you'll learn how to create a C program and recognize the basic elements of a

1

2

3

4

5

6

7

simple program. Day 3, "Storing Information: Variables and Constants," builds on the first two days by defining the variable types. Day 4, "Statements, Expressions, and Operators," takes the variables and adds simple expressions so that new values can be created. This day also provides information on how to make decisions and change program flow using if statements. Day 5, "Functions: The Basics" covers C functions and structured programming. Day 6, "Controlling Your Programs Order of Execution," introduces more commands that enable you to control the flow of your programs. The week ends on Day 7, "Fundamentals of Reading and Writing Information," with a discussion of printing information and helpful suggestions to make your programs interact with the keyboard and screen.

In addition to all this material, you will also find several Type & Runs. These are located between Days 1 and 2 and between Days 4 and 5. The program in the first Type & Run will print your program listings with line numbers. The second Type & Run contains a listing that will let you play a number-guessing game.

You will also find that each day ends with a workshop containing a quiz and some exercises. At the end of each day, you should be able to answer all the quiz questions and complete the exercises. Answers to the questions and exercises in the earlier days are provided in Appendix F, "Answers." For later days, answers are not provided for all exercises because there are so many possible solutions. It is strongly suggested that you take advantage of the exercises and check your answers.

You will cover a large amount of material in just one week; but if you take the information one day—chapter—at a time, you should have no problem.

Note

This book covers ANSI Standard C defined by ISO/IEC 9899:1999. It doesn't matter which C compiler you use, as long as it follows this ANSI Standard.

DAY 1

Getting Started with C

Welcome to the sixth edition of *Sams Teach Yourself C in 21 Days!* Today's lesson starts you toward becoming a proficient C programmer. Today you will learn:

- Why C is a great choice among programming languages
- The steps in the program development cycle
- How to write, compile, and run your first C program
- About error messages generated by the compiler and linker

A Brief History of the C Language

You might be wondering about the origin of the C language and where it got its name. C was created by Dennis Ritchie at the Bell Telephone Laboratories in 1972. The language wasn't created for the fun of it, but for a specific purpose: to design the UNIX operating system (which is used on many computers). From the beginning, C was intended to be useful—to allow busy programmers to get things done.

Because C is such a powerful and flexible language, its use quickly spread beyond Bell Labs. Programmers everywhere began using it to write all sorts of programs. Soon, however, different organizations began utilizing their own versions of C, and subtle differences between implementations started to cause programmers headaches. In response to this problem, the American National Standards Institute (ANSI) formed a committee in 1983 to establish a standard definition of C, which became known as ANSI Standard C. With few exceptions, every modern C compiler has the ability to adhere to this standard.

Note

> Although C rarely changes, the most recent changes occurred in 1999 with the ANSI C-99 standard. This standard added a few new features to the language that will be covered in this book. You will find, however, that older compilers may not support these most recent standards.

Now, what about the name? The C language is so named because its predecessor was called B. The B language was developed by Ken Thompson of Bell Labs. You should be able to guess why it was called B.

Why Use C?

In today's world of computer programming, there are many high-level languages to choose from, such as C, Perl, BASIC, Java, and C#. These are all excellent languages suited for most programming tasks. Even so, there are several reasons why many computer professionals feel that C is at the top of the list:

- C is a powerful and flexible language. What you can accomplish with C is limited only by your imagination. The language itself places no constraints on you. C is used for projects as diverse as operating systems, word processors, graphics, spreadsheets, and even compilers for other languages.

- C is a popular language preferred by professional programmers. As a result, a wide variety of C compilers and helpful accessories are available.

- C is a portable language. *Portable* means that a C program written for one computer system (an IBM PC, for example) can be compiled and run on another system (a DEC VAX system, perhaps) with little or no modification. Additionally, a program written with the Microsoft Windows operating system can be moved to a machine running Linux with little or no modification. Portability is enhanced by the ANSI standard for C, the set of rules for C compilers.

- C is a language of few words, containing only a handful of terms, called *keywords,* which serve as the base on which the language's functionality is built. You might think that a language with more keywords (sometimes called *reserved words*) would be more powerful. This isn't true. As you program with C, you will find that it can be programmed to do any task.

- C is modular. C code can (and should) be written in routines called *functions*. These functions can be reused in other applications or programs. By passing pieces of information to the functions, you can create useful, reusable code.

As these features show, C is an excellent choice for your first programming language. What about C++? You might have heard about C++ and the programming technique called *object-oriented programming*. Perhaps you're wondering what the differences are between C and C++ and whether you should be teaching yourself C++ instead of C.

Not to worry! C++ is a superset of C, which means that C++ contains everything C does, plus new additions for object-oriented programming. If you do go on to learn C++, almost everything you learn about C will still apply to the C++ superset. In learning C, you are not only learning one of today's most powerful and popular programming languages, but you are also preparing yourself for object-oriented programming.

Another language that has gotten lots of attention is Java. Java, like C++, is based on C. If later you decide to learn Java, you will find that almost everything you learned about C can be applied.

The newest of these languages is C# (pronounced "*see-sharp*"). Like C++ and Java, C# is an object-oriented language that is derived from C. Once again, you will find that a lot of what you learn about C will directly apply to C# programming.

Note

> Many people who learn C later choose to learn C++, Java, or C#. As a bonus, we have added several additional days to this edition of the book that will provide you with a quick primer to C++, Java, and C#. These additional days assume that you have first learned C.

Preparing to Program

You should take certain steps when you're solving a problem. First, you must define the problem. If you don't know what the problem is, you can't find a solution! Once you know what the problem is, you can devise a plan to fix it. Once you have a plan, you can usually implement it. Once the plan is implemented, you must test the results to see whether the problem is solved. This same logic can be applied to many other areas, including programming.

When creating a program in C (or for that matter, a computer program in any language), you should follow a similar sequence of steps:

1. Determine the objective(s) of the program.
2. Determine the methods you want to use in writing the program.
3. Create the program to solve the problem.
4. Run the program to see the results.

An example of an objective (see step 1) might be to write a word processor or database program. A much simpler objective is to display your name on the screen. If you didn't have an objective, you wouldn't be writing a program, so you already have the first step done.

The second step is to determine the method you want to use to write the program. Do you need a computer program to solve the problem? What information needs to be tracked? What formulas will be used? During this step, you should try to determine what you need to know and in what order the solution should be implemented.

As an example, assume that someone asks you to write a program to determine the area inside a circle. Step 1 is complete, because you know your objective: determine the area inside a circle. Step 2 is to determine what you need to know to ascertain the area. In this example, assume that the user of the program will provide the radius of the circle. Knowing this, you can apply the formula pr2 to obtain the answer. Now you have the pieces you need, so you can continue to steps 3 and 4, which are called the Program Development Cycle.

The Program Development Cycle

The Program Development Cycle has its own steps. In the first step, you use an editor to create a disk file containing your source code. In the second step, you compile the source code to create an object file. In the third step, you link the compiled code to create an executable file. The fourth step is to run the program to see whether it works as originally planned.

Creating the Source Code

NEW TERM   *Source code* is a series of statements or commands that are used to instruct the computer to perform your desired tasks. As mentioned, the first step in the Program Development Cycle is to enter source code into an editor. For example, here is a line of C source code:

```
printf("Hello, Mom!");
```

This statement instructs the computer to display the message Hello, Mom! on-screen. (For now, don't worry about how this statement works.)

Using an Editor

Most compilers come with a built-in editor that can be used to enter source code; however, some don't. Consult your compiler manuals to see whether your compiler came with an editor. If it didn't, many alternative editors are available.

Most computer systems include a program that can be used as an editor. If you're using a Linux or UNIX system, you can use such editors as ed, ex, edit, emacs, or vi. If you're using Microsoft Windows, Notepad or WordPad is available. If you're using MS/DOS 5.0 or later, you can use Edit. If you're using a version of DOS before 5.0, you can use Edlin. If you're using PC/DOS 6.0 or later, you can use E. If you're using OS/2, you can use the E and EPM editors.

Most word processors use special codes to format their documents. These codes can't be read correctly by other programs. The American Standard Code for Information Interchange (ASCII) has specified a standard text format that nearly any program, including C, can use. Many word processors, such as WordPerfect, Microsoft Word, WordPad, and WordStar, are capable of saving source files in ASCII form (as a text file rather than a document file). When you want to save a word processor's file as an ASCII file, select the ASCII or text option when saving.

If none of these editors is what you want to use, you can always buy a different editor. There are packages, both commercial and shareware, that have been designed specifically for entering source code.

Note

To find alternative editors, you can check your local computer store or computer mail-order catalogs. Another place to look is in the ads in computer programming magazines. This book includes on its CD two compilers that also include editors. These are the Bloodshed Dev-C++ and DJGPP. Check the files on the CD and Appendix G, "Bloodshed Dev-C++," for more information on these programs.

When you save a source file, you must give it a name. The name should describe what the program does. In addition, when you save C program source files, give the file a .c extension. Although you could give your source file any name and extension, .c is recognized as the appropriate extension to use.

Compiling the Source Code

 Although you might be able to understand C source code (at least after reading this book you will be able to), your computer can't. A computer requires digital, or *binary,* instructions in what is called *machine language.* Before your C program can run on a computer, it must be translated from source code to machine language. This translation, the second step in program development, is performed by a program called a *compiler.* The compiler takes your source code file as input and produces a disk file containing the machine language instructions that correspond to your source code statements. The machine language instructions created by the compiler are called *object code,* and the disk file containing them is called an *object file.*

> **Note**
>
> This book covers ANSI Standard C. This means that it doesn't matter which C compiler you use, as long as it follows the ANSI Standard. Note that not all compilers support the standards. The specific name of the current standard for C is ISO/IEC 9899:1999. Rather than using this complex name, we will refer to the standard as C-99 throughout this book.

Each compiler needs its own command to be used to create the object code. To compile, you typically use the command to run the compiler followed by the source filename. The following are examples of the commands issued to compile a source file called radius.c using various DOS/Windows compilers:

Compiler	Command
Microsoft C	cl radius.c
Borland's Turbo C	tcc radius.c
Borland C	bcc radius.c

To compile radius.c on a UNIX machine, use the following command:

cc radius.c

On a machine using the GCC compiler, you enter:

gcc radius.c

You would also use gcc if you are using the DJ Delorie port to DOS of the GNU C/C++ compiler that is included on the CD accompanying this book. Consult your compiler's manual to determine the exact command to run your compiler.

If you're using a graphical, integrated development environment, compiling is even simpler. In most graphical environments, you can compile a program listing by selecting the compile icon or selecting something from a menu. Once the code is compiled, selecting the run icon or selecting something from a menu will execute the program. You should check your compiler's manuals for specifics on compiling and running a program. The Bloodshed Dev-C++ program that comes on this book's CD is an example of a graphical development environment that can be used on Microsoft Windows. There are graphical development environments for almost every possible platform.

After you compile, you have an object file. If you look at a list of the files in the directory or folder in which you compiled, you should find a file that has the same name as your source file, but with an .obj (rather than a .c) extension. The .obj extension is recognized as an object file and is used by the linker. On a Linux or UNIX system, the compiler creates object files with an extension of .o instead of .obj.

Linking to Create an Executable File

NEW TERM   One more step is required before you can run your program. Part of the ANSI C language definition is a function library that contains *object code* (code that has already been compiled) for predefined functions. A *predefined function* contains C code that has already been written and is supplied in a ready-to-use form with your compiler package.

NEW TERM   The printf() function used in the previous example is a *library function*. These library functions perform frequently needed tasks, such as displaying information on-screen and reading data from disk files. If your program uses any of these functions (and hardly a program exists that doesn't use at least one), the object file produced when your source code was compiled must be combined with object code from the function library to create the final executable program. (*Executable* means that the program can be run, or executed, on your computer.) This process is called *linking,* and it's performed by a program called (you guessed it) a *linker*.

Figure 1.1 shows the progression from source code to object code to executable program.

Completing the Development Cycle

Once your program is compiled and linked to create an executable file, you can run it by entering its name at the system prompt or just like you would run any other program. If you run the program and receive results different from what you thought you would, you need to go back to the first step. You must identify what caused the problem and correct it in the source code. When you make a change to the source code, you need to recompile and relink the program to create a corrected version of the executable file. You keep following this cycle until you get the program to execute exactly as you intended.

FIGURE 1.1

*The C source code
that you write is con-
verted to object code
by the compiler and
then to an executable
file by the linker.*

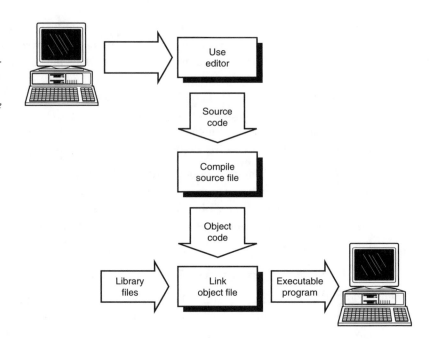

One final note on compiling and linking: Although compiling and linking are mentioned
as two separate steps, many compilers, such as the DOS compilers mentioned earlier, do
both as one step. Most graphical development environments will give you the option of
doing the compiling and linking together or separately. Regardless of the method by
which compiling and linking are accomplished, understand that these two processes,
even when done with one command, are two separate actions.

The C Development Cycle

▼ SYNTAX

Step 1	Use an editor to write your source code. By tradition, C source code files have the extension .c (for example, myprog.c, database.c, and so on).
Step 2	Compile the program using a compiler. If the compiler does-n't find any errors in the program, it produces an object file. The compiler produces object files with an .obj or .o exten-sion and the same name as the source code file (for example, myprog.c compiles to either myprog.obj or myprog.o). If the compiler finds errors, it reports them. You must return to step 1 to make corrections in your source code.
Step 3	Link the program using a linker. If no errors occur, the linker produces an executable program located in a disk file with

▼

▼

1

an .exe extension and the same name as the object file (for example, myprog.obj is linked to create myprog.exe).

Step 4   Execute the program. You should test to determine whether it functions properly. If not, start again with step 1 and make modifications and additions to your source code.

▲

Figure 1.2 shows the program development steps. For all but the simplest programs, you might go through this sequence many times before finishing your program. Even the most experienced programmers can't sit down and write a complete, error-free program in just one step! Because you'll be running through the edit-compile-link-test cycle many times, it's important to become familiar with your tools: the editor, compiler, and linker.

FIGURE 1.2

The steps involved in C program develop-ment.

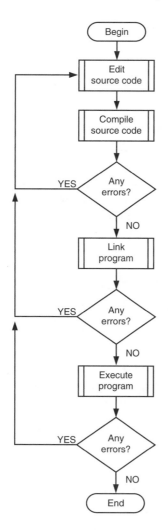

Your First C Program

You're probably eager to try your first program in C. To help you become familiar with your compiler, Listing 1.1 contains a quick program for you to work through. You might not understand everything at this point, but you should get a feel for the process of writing, compiling, and running a real C program.

This demonstration uses a program named hello.c, which does nothing more than display the words Hello, World! on-screen. This program, a traditional introduction to C programming, is a good one for you to learn. The source code for hello.c is in Listing 1.1. When you type in this listing, you won't include the line numbers on the left or the colons.

LISTING 1.1   HELLO.C

```
1:  #include <stdio.h>
2:
3:  int main(void)
4:  {
5:      printf("Hello, World!\n");
6:      return 0;
7:  }
```

Be sure that you have installed your compiler as specified in the installation instructions provided with the software. Whether you are working with Linux, UNIX, DOS, Windows, or any other operating system, make sure you understand how to use the compiler and editor of your choice. Once your compiler and editor are ready, follow these steps to enter, compile, and execute HELLO.C.

Entering and Compiling hello.c

To enter and compile the hello.c program, follow these steps:

1. Start your editor in the directory where your C program will be. As mentioned previously, any text editor can be used, but most C compilers (such as Borland's Turbo C++ and Microsoft's Visual C++) come with an integrated development environment (IDE) that lets you enter, compile, and link your programs in one convenient setting. Check your manuals to see whether your compiler has an IDE available.

2. Use the keyboard to type the hello.c source code exactly as shown in Listing 1.1. Press Enter at the end of each line.

Note | Don't enter the line numbers or colons. These are for reference only.

3. Save the source code. You should name the file hello.c.

4. Verify that hello.c is on disk by listing the files in the directory or folder. You should see hello.c within this listing.

5. Compile and link hello.c. Execute the appropriate command specified by your compiler's manuals. You should get a message stating that there were no errors or warnings.

6. Check the compiler messages. If you receive no errors or warnings, everything should be okay.

   If you made an error typing the program, the compiler will catch it and display an error message. For example, if you misspelled the word printf as prntf, you would see a message similar to the following:

   ```
   Error: undefined symbols:_prntf in hello.c (hello.OBJ)
   ```

7. Go back to step 2 if this or any other error message is displayed. Open the hello.c file in your editor. Compare your file's contents carefully with Listing 1.1, make any necessary corrections, and continue with step 3.

8. Your first C program should now be compiled and ready to run. If you display a directory listing of all files named hello (with any extension), you should see the following:

   > hello.c, the source code file you created with your editor

   > hello.obj or hello.o, which contains the object code for hello.c

   > hello.exe, the executable program created when you compiled and linked hello.c

9. To *execute,* or run, hello.exe, simply enter hello. The message Hello, World! is displayed on-screen.

Congratulations! You have just entered, compiled, and run your first C program. Admittedly, hello.c is a simple program that doesn't do anything useful, but it's a start. In fact, most of today's expert C programmers started learning C in this same way—by compiling HELLO.C—so you're in good company.

Note | If you choose to use the Bloodshed Dev-C++ compiler included on the CD with this book, then you can review Appendix G, "Bloodshed Dev-C++." This appendix covers installing and creating a program with Dev-C++. This compile is for Windows 95 or later.

Compilation Errors

A compilation error occurs when the compiler finds something in the source code that it can't compile. A misspelling, typographical error, or any of a dozen other things can cause the compiler to choke. Fortunately, modern compilers don't just choke; they tell you what they're choking on and where the problem is! This makes it easier to find and correct errors in your source code.

This point can be illustrated by introducing a deliberate error into the hello.c program you entered earlier. If you worked through that example (and you should have), you now have a copy of hello.c on your disk. Using your editor, move the cursor to the end of the line containing the call to printf(), and erase the terminating semicolon. hello.c should now look like Listing 1.2.

LISTING 1.2   hello2.c - hello.c with an error

```
1:  #include <stdio.h>
2:
3:  int main(void)
4:  {
5:      printf("Hello, World!")
6:      return 0;
7:  }
```

Next, save the file. You're now ready to compile it. Do so by entering the command for your compiler. Because of the error you introduced, the compilation is not completed. Rather, the compiler displays a message similar to the following:

```
hello.c(6) : Error: ';' expected
```

Looking at this line, you can see that it has three parts:

hello.c	The name of the file where the error was found
(6) :	The line number where the error was found
Error: ';' expected	A description of the error

This message is quite informative, telling you that in line 6 of hello.c the compiler expected to find a semicolon but didn't. However, you know that the semicolon was actually omitted from line 5, so there is a discrepancy. You're faced with the puzzle of why the compiler reports an error in line 6 when, in fact, a semicolon was omitted from line 5. The answer lies in the fact that C doesn't care about things like breaks between lines. The semicolon that belongs after the printf() statement could have been placed on the next line (although doing so would look confusing and thus be a bad programming practice). Only after encountering the next command (return) in line 6 is the compiler sure that the semicolon is missing. Therefore, the compiler reports that the error is in line 6.

This points out an undeniable fact about C compilers and error messages. Although the compiler is very clever about detecting and localizing errors, it's no Einstein. Using your knowledge of the C language, you must interpret the compiler's messages and determine the actual location of any errors that are reported. They are often found on the line reported by the compiler, but if not, they are almost always on the preceding line. You might have a bit of trouble finding errors at first, but you should soon get better at it.

Note The errors reported might differ depending on the compiler. In most cases, the error message should give you an idea of what or where the problem is.

Before leaving this topic, let's look at another example of a compilation error. Load hello.c into your editor again and make the following changes:

1. Replace the semicolon at the end of line 5.
2. Delete the double quotation mark just before the word Hello.

Save the file to disk and compile the program again. This time, the compiler should display error messages similar to the following:

```
hello.c(5) : Error: undefined identifier 'Hello'
hello.c(7) : Lexical error: unterminated string
Lexical error: unterminated string
Lexical error: unterminated string

Fatal error: premature end of source file
```

The first error message finds the error correctly, locating it in line 5 at the word Hello. The error message undefined identifier means that the compiler doesn't know what to make of the word Hello, because it is no longer enclosed in quotes. However, what about the other four errors that are reported? These errors, the meaning of which you don't need to worry about now, illustrate the fact that a single error in a C program can sometimes cause multiple error messages.

The lesson to learn from all this is as follows: If the compiler reports multiple errors, and you can find only one, go ahead and fix that error and recompile. You might find that your single correction is all that's needed, and the program will compile without errors.

Linker Error Messages

Linker errors are relatively rare and usually result from misspelling the name of a C library function. In this case, you get an Error: undefined symbols: error message, followed by the misspelled name (preceded by an underscore). Once you correct the spelling, the problem should go away.

Summary

After reading today's lesson, you should feel confident that selecting C as your programming language is a wise choice. C offers an unparalleled combination of power, popularity, and portability. These factors, together with C's close relationship to the C++ object-oriented language as well as Java and C#, make C unbeatable.

Today's lesson explained the various steps involved in writing a C program—the process known as program development. You should have a clear grasp of the edit-compile-link-test cycle, as well as the tools to use for each step.

Errors are an unavoidable part of program development. Your C compiler detects errors in your source code and displays an error message, giving both the nature and the location of the error. Using this information, you can edit your source code to correct the error. Remember, however, that the compiler can't always accurately report the nature and location of an error. Sometimes you need to use your knowledge of C to track down exactly what is causing a given error message.

Q&A

Q If I want to give someone a program I wrote, which files do I need to give him?

A One of the nice things about C is that it is a compiled language. This means that after the source code is compiled, you have an executable program. This executable program is a stand-alone program. If you wanted to give hello to all your friends with computers, you could. All you need to give them is the executable program, hello.exe. They don't need the source file, hello.c, or the object file, hello.obj. They don't need to own a C compiler, either. Your friends or those people you give the executable will need to be using the same type of machine as you—such as an PC, a Macintosh, Linux machine, etc.

Q After I create an executable file, do I need to keep the source file (.c) or object file (.obj)?

A If you get rid of the source file, you have no way to make changes to the program in the future, so you should keep this file. The object files are a different matter. There are reasons to keep object files, but they are beyond the scope of what you're doing now. For now, you can get rid of your object files once you have your executable file. If you need the object file, you can recompile the source file.

Most integrated development environments create files in addition to the source file (.c), the object file (.obj or .o), and the executable file. As long as you keep the source file (.c), you can always re-create the other files.

Q If my compiler came with an editor, do I have to use it?

A Definitely not. You can use any editor, as long as it saves the source code in text format. If the compiler came with an editor, you should try to use it. If you like a different editor better, use it. I use an editor that I purchased separately, even though all my compilers have their own editors. The editors that come with compilers are getting better. Some of them automatically format your C code. Others color-code different parts of your source file to make it easier to find errors.

Q What do I do if I only have a C++ compiler and not a C compiler?

A As mentioned in today's lesson, C++ is a superset of C. This means that you can use a C++ compiler to compile C programs. Most people use Microsoft's Visual C++ to compile their C programs on Windows and GNU's compiler on Linux and UNIX. The compilers included with this book's CD will compile both C and C++ programs.

Q Can I ignore warning messages?

A Some warning messages don't affect how the program runs, and some do. If the compiler gives you a warning message, it's a signal that something isn't right. Most compilers let you set the warning level. By setting the warning level, you can get only the most serious warnings, or you can get all the warnings, including the most minute. Some compilers even offer various levels in-between. In your programs, you should look at each warning and make a determination. It's always best to try to write all your programs with absolutely no warnings or errors. (With an error, your compiler won't create the executable file.)

Workshop

The Workshop provides quiz questions to help you solidify your understanding of the material covered and exercises to provide you with experience in using what you've learned. Try to understand the quiz and exercise answers before continuing to tomorrow's lesson. Answers are provided in Appendix F, "Answers."

Quiz

1. Give three reasons why C is the best choice of a programming language.
2. What does the compiler do?
3. What are the steps in the Program Development Cycle?
4. What command do you need to enter in order to compile a program called program1.c with your compiler?

5. Does your compiler do both the linking and compiling with just one command, or do you have to enter separate commands?

6. What extension should you use for your C source files?

7. Is FILENAME.TXT a valid name for a C source file?

8. If you execute a program that you have compiled and it doesn't work as you expected, what should you do?

9. What is machine language?

10. What does the linker do?

Exercises

1. Use your text editor to look at the object file created by Listing 1.1. Does the object file look like the source file? (Don't save this file when you exit the editor.)

2. Enter the following program and compile it. What does this program do? (Don't include the line numbers or colons.)

```
 1:  #include <stdio.h>
 2:
 3:  int radius, area;
 4:
 5:  int main( void )
 6:  {
 7:      printf( "Enter radius (i.e. 10): " );
 8:      scanf( "%d", &radius );
 9:      area = (int) (3.14159 * radius * radius);
10:      printf( "\n\nArea = %d\n", area );
11:      return 0;
12:  }
```

3. Enter and compile the following program. What does this program do?

```
 1:  #include <stdio.h>
 2:
 3:  int x, y;
 4:
 5:  int main( void )
 6:  {
 7:      for ( x = 0; x < 10; x++, printf( "\n" ) )
 8:          for ( y = 0; y < 10; y++ )
 9:              printf( "X" );
10:
11:      return 0;
12:  }
```

4. **BUG BUSTER:** The following program has a problem. Enter it in your editor and compile it. Which lines generate error messages?

```
1:  #include <stdio.h>
2:
3:  int main( void );
4:  {
5:     printf( "Keep looking!" );
6:     printf( "You\'ll find it!\n" );
7:     return 0;
8:  }
```

5. **BUG BUSTER:** The following program has a problem. Enter it in your editor and compile it. Which lines generate problems?

```
1:  #include <stdio.h>
2:
3:  int main( void )
4:  {
5:     printf( "This is a program with a " );
6:     do_it( "problem!");
7:     return 0;
8:  }
```

6. Make the following change to the program in exercise 3. Recompile and rerun this program. What does the program do now?

```
9:  printf( "%c", 1 );
```

Type & Run 1

Printing Your Listings

Throughout this book you will find a number of Type & Run sections. These sections present a listing that is a little longer than the listings within the chapters. The purpose of these listings is to give you a program to type in and run. The listings might contain elements not yet explained in the book.

These programs will generally do something either fun or practical. For instance, the program included here is called print_it. In addition to printing the source code, print_it adds line numbers just like those included in this book. This program can be used to print your listings as you work through the rest of this book.

We suggest that after you type in and run these programs, you take the time to experiment with the code. Make changes, recompile, and then rerun the programs. See what happens. There won't be explanations on how the code works, only what it does. Don't fret, though. By the time you complete this book, you should understand everything within these earlier listings. In the meantime, you will have had the chance to enter and run some listings that are a little more fun or practical!

The First Type & Run

Enter and compile the following program. If you get any errors, make sure you entered the program correctly.

The usage for this program is print_it *filename.ext*, where *filename.ext* is the source filename along with the extension. Note that this program adds line numbers to the listing. (Don't let this program's length worry you; you're not expected to understand it yet. It's included here to help you compare printouts of your programs with the ones given in the book.)

LISTING T&R 1   print_it.c

```
1:  /* print_it.c—This program prints a listing with line numbers! */
2:  #include <stdlib.h>
3:  #include <stdio.h>
4:
5:  void do_heading(char *filename);
6:
7:  int line = 0, page = 0;
8:
9:  int main( int argv, char *argc[] )
10: {
11:    char buffer[256];
12:    FILE *fp;
13:
14:    if( argv < 2 )
15:    {
16:      fprintf(stderr, "\nProper Usage is: " );
17:      fprintf(stderr, "\n\nprint_it filename.ext\n" );
18:      return(1);
19:    }
20:
21:    if (( fp = fopen( argc[1], "r" )) == NULL )
22:    {
23:        fprintf( stderr, "Error opening file, %s!", argc[1]);
24:        return(1);
25:    }
26:
27:    page = 0;
28:    line = 1;
29:    do_heading( argc[1]);
30:
31:    while( fgets( buffer, 256, fp ) != NULL )
32:    {
33:      if( line % 55 == 0 )
34:        do_heading( argc[1] );
35:
```

Listing T&R 1   continued

```
36:      fprintf( stdprn, "%4d:\t%s", line++, buffer );
37:    }
38:
39:    fprintf( stdprn, "\f" );
40:    fclose(fp);
41:    return 0;
42: }
43:
44: void do_heading( char *filename )
45: {
46:    page++;
47:
48:    if ( page > 1)
49:        fprintf( stdprn, "\f" );
50:
51:    fprintf( stdprn, "Page: %d, %s\n\n", page, filename );
52: }
```

Note

This listing uses a value that is available within many PC compilers, but not necessarily in all other compilers. Although stdout is an ANSI-defined value, stdprn is not. You need to check your compiler for specifics on sending output to the printer.

One option for getting around this is to change the stdprn statements to stdout statements. This causes the output to go to the screen. Using your operating system's redirection features (or by piping if you're using UNIX or Linux), you should be able to redirect the output from the screen to the printer.

On Day 14, "Working with the Screen, Printer, and Keyboard," you will learn more about how this program works.

DAY 2

The Components of a C Program

Every C program consists of several components combined in a certain way. Most of this book is devoted to explaining these various program components and how you use them. To help illustrate the overall picture, you should begin by reviewing a complete (though small) C program with all its components identified. Today you will learn:

- About a short C program and its components
- The purpose of each program component
- How to compile and run a sample program

A Short C Program

Listing 2.1 presents the source code for multiply.c. This is a very simple program. All it does is accept two numbers that are entered from the keyboard and calculate their product. At this stage, don't worry about understanding the details of how the program works. The point is for you to gain some familiarity with the parts of a C program so that you can better understand the listings presented later in this book.

NEW TERM   Before looking at the sample program, you need to know what a function is, because functions are central to C programming. A *function* is an independent section of program code that performs a certain task and has been assigned a name. By referencing a function's name, your program can execute the code in the function. The program also can send information, called *arguments,* to the function, and the function can return information to the main part of the program. The two types of C functions are *library functions,* which are a part of the C compiler package, and *user-defined functions,* which you, the programmer, create. You will learn about both types of functions in this book.

Note that, as with all the listings in this book, the line numbers in Listing 2.1 are not part of the program. They are included only for identification purposes, so don't type them.

 List 2.1 is available on the CD-Rom included with this book. You will find it in the Day02 directory.

LISTING 2.1   multiply.c—A program that multiplies two numbers

```
1:    /* Program to calculate the product of two numbers. */
2:    #include <stdio.h>
3:
4:    int val1, val2, val3;
5:
6:    int product(int x, int y);
7:
8:    int main( void )
9:    {
10:       /* Get the first number */
11:       printf("Enter a number between 1 and 100: ");
12:       scanf("%d", &val1);
13:
14:       /* Get the second number */
15:       printf("Enter another number between 1 and 100: ");
16:       scanf("%d", &val2);
17:
18:       /* Calculate and display the product */
19:       val3 = product(val1, val2);
20:       printf ("%d times %d = %d\n", val1, val2, val3);
21:
22:       return 0;
23: }
24:
```

LISTING 2.1 continued

```
25: /* Function returns the product of the two values provided */
26: int product(int x, int y)
27: {
28:     return (x * y);
29: }
```

INPUT/
OUTPUT

```
Enter a number between 1 and 100: 35
Enter another number between 1 and 100: 23

35 times 23 = 805
```

The Program's Components

The following sections describe the various components of the preceding sample program. Line numbers are included so that you can easily identify the program parts being discussed.

The `main()` Function (Lines 8 Through 23)

The only component that is required in every executable C program is the `main()` function. In its simplest form, the `main()` function consists of the name `main` followed by a pair of parentheses containing the word `void` (`(void)`) and a pair of braces (`{}`). You can leave the word `void` out and the program will still work with most compilers. The ANSI standard states that you should include the word `void` so that you know there is nothing being sent to the `main` function.

Within the braces are statements that make up the main body of the program. Under normal circumstances, program execution starts at the first statement in `main()` and terminates at the last statement in `main()`. Per the ANSI standard, the only statement that you need to include is this example is the `return` statement in line 22.

The `#include` Directive (Line 2)

NEW TERM   The `#include` directive instructs the C compiler to add the contents of an include file into your program during compilation. An *include file* is a separate disk file that contains information that can be used by your program or the compiler. Several of these files (sometimes called *header files*) are supplied with your compiler. You rarely need to modify the information in these files; that's why they're kept separate from your source code. Include files should all have an .h extension (for example, stdio.h).

You use the `#include` directive to instruct the compiler to add a specific include file to your program during compilation. In Listing 2.1, the `#include` directive is interpreted to mean "Add the contents of the file stdio.h." You will almost always include one or more include files in your C programs. More information about include files is presented on Day 21, "Advanced Compiler Use."

The Variable Definition (Line 4)

NEW TERM   A *variable* is a name assigned to a location in memory used to store information. Your program uses variables to store various kinds of information during program execution. In C, a variable must be defined before it can be used. A variable definition informs the compiler of the variable's name and the type of information the variable is to hold. In the sample program, the definition on line 4, int val1, val2, val3;, defines three variables—named val1, val2, and val3—that will each hold an integer value. More information about variables and variable definitions is presented on Day 3, "Storing Information: Variables and Constants."

The Function Prototype (Line 6)

NEW TERM   A *function prototype* provides the C compiler with the name and arguments of the functions contained in the program. It appears before the function is used. A function prototype is distinct from a *function definition*, which contains the actual statements that make up the function. (Function definitions are discussed in more detail later today.)

Program Statements (Lines 11, 12, 15, 16, 19, 20, 22, and 28)

The real work of a C program is done by its statements. C statements display information on-screen, read keyboard input, perform mathematical operations, call functions, read disk files, and all the other operations that a program needs to perform. Most of this book is devoted to teaching you the various C statements. For now, remember that in your source code, C statements are generally written one per line and always end with a semicolon. The statements in multiply.c are explained briefly in the following sections.

The printf() Statement

The printf() statement (lines 11, 15, and 20) is a library function that displays information on-screen. The printf() statement can display a simple text message (as in lines 11 and 15) or a message and the value of one or more program variables (as in line 20).

The scanf() Statement

The scanf() statement (lines 12 and 16) is another library function. It reads data from the keyboard and assigns that data to one or more program variables.

The program statement on line 19 calls the function named product(). In other words, it executes the program statements contained in the function product(). It also sends the arguments val1 and val2 to the function. After the statements in product() are completed, product() returns a value to the program. This value is stored in the variable named val3.

The return Statement

Lines 22 and 28 contain return statements. The return statement on line 28 is part of the function product(). It calculates the product of the variables x and y and returns the result to the program that called product(). The return statement on line 22 returns a value of 0 to the operating system just before the program ends.

The Function Definition (Lines 26 Through 29)

NEW TERM   A *function* is an independent, self-contained section of code that is written to perform a certain task. Every function has a name, and the code in each function is executed by including that function's name in a program statement. This execution is known as *calling* the function.

The function named product(), in lines 26 through 29, is a user-defined function. As the name implies, user-defined functions are written by the programmer during program development. This function, which is included in lines 26 to 29, is simple. All it does is multiply two values and return the answer to the program that called it. On Day 5, "Functions: The Basics," you will learn that the proper use of functions is an important part of good C programming practice.

Note that in a real C program, you probably wouldn't use a function for a task as simple as multiplying two numbers. It has been done here for demonstration purposes only.

C also includes library functions that are a part of the C compiler package. Library functions perform most of the common tasks (such as screen, keyboard, and disk input/output) your program needs. In the sample program, printf() and scanf() are library functions.

Program Comments (Lines 1, 10, 14, 18, and 25)

NEW TERM   Any part of your program that starts with /* and ends with */ is called a *comment*. The compiler ignores all comments, so they have absolutely no effect on how a program works. You can put anything you want into a comment, and it won't modify the way your program operates. A comment can span part of a line, an entire line, or multiple lines. Here are three examples:

```
/* A single-line comment */

int a,b,c; /* A partial-line comment */

/* a comment
spanning
multiple lines */
```

You should not use nested comments. A *nested* comment is a comment that has been put into another comment. Most compilers will not accept the following:

```
/*
/* Nested comment */
*/
```

Some compilers do allow nested comments. Although this feature might be tempting to use, you should avoid doing so. Because one of the benefits of C is portability, using a feature such as nested comments might limit the portability of your code. Nested comments also might lead to hard-to-find problems.

Many beginning programmers view program comments as unnecessary and a waste of time. This is a mistake! The operation of your program might be quite clear when you're writing the code; however, as your programs become larger and more complex, or when you need to modify a program you wrote six months ago, you'll find comments invaluable. Now is the time to develop the habit of using comments liberally to document all your programming structures and operations.

The newest ANSI standard added the ability to use single line comments. Single line comments have been available in C++ and Java so it is only natural that C has implemented them.

Single line comments use double forward slashes to signal a comment. Here are two examples:

```
// This entire line is a comment
int x;   // Comment starts with slashes.
```

The two forward slashes signal that the rest of the line is a comment. The ANSI C-99 standard added this feature to C.

Using Braces (Lines 9, 23, 27, and 29)

NEW TERM You use braces ({}) to enclose the program lines that make up every C function—including the main() function. A group of one or more statements enclosed within braces is called a *block*. As you will see in later days, C has many uses for blocks.

Do	**Don't**
DO add abundant comments to your program's source code, especially near statements or functions that could be unclear to you or to someone who might have to modify it later.	**DON'T** add unnecessary comments to statements that are already clear. For example, entering

	`/* The following prints Hello World!`
	`on the screen */`
	`printf("Hello World!");`

DO learn to develop a style that will be helpful. A style that's too lean or cryptic doesn't help. A style that is verbose may cause you to spend more time commenting than programming.	might be going a little too far, at least once you're completely comfortable with the `printf()` function and how it works.

Running the Program

Take the time to enter, compile, and run multiply.c. It provides additional practice in using your editor and compiler. Recall these steps from Day 1, "Getting Started with C":

1. Make your programming directory current.

2. Start your editor.

3. Enter the source code for multiply.c exactly as shown in Listing 2.1, but be sure to omit the line numbers and colons.

4. Save the program file.

5. Compile and link the program by entering the appropriate command(s) for your compiler. If no error messages are displayed, you can run the program by entering `multiply` at the command prompt.

6. If any error messages are displayed, return to step 2 and correct the errors.

 Note   If you are using the Dev-C++, you can see Appendix G for instructions on entering and compiling a program.

A Note on Accuracy

A computer is fast and accurate, but it also is completely literal. It doesn't know enough to correct your simplest mistake; it takes everything you enter exactly as you entered it, not as you meant it!

This goes for your C source code as well. A simple typographical error in your program can cause the C compiler to choke, gag, and collapse. Fortunately, although the compiler isn't smart enough to correct your errors (and you'll make errors—everyone does!), it *is* smart enough to recognize them as errors and report them to you. (You saw in yesterday's material how the compiler reports error messages and how you interpret them.)

A Review of the Parts of a Program

Now that all the parts of a program have been described, you should be able to look at any program and find some similarities. Look at Listing 2.2 and see whether you can identify the different parts.

LISTING 2.2   list_it.c—A program to list a code listing

```
 1:  /* list_it.c__This program displays a listing with line numbers! */
 2:  #include <stdio.h>
 3:  #include <stdlib.h>
 4:
 5:  void display_usage(void);
 6:  int line;
 7:
 8:  int main( int argc, char *argv[] )
 9:  {
10:    char buffer[256];
11:    FILE *fp;
12:
13:    if( argc < 2 )
14:    {
15:       display_usage();
16:       return 1;
17:    }
18:
19:    if (( fp = fopen( argv[1], "r" )) == NULL )
20:    {
21:        fprintf( stderr, "Error opening file, %s!", argv[1] );
22:        return(1);
23:    }
24:
25:    line = 1;
26:
27:    while( fgets( buffer, 256, fp ) != NULL )
28:       fprintf( stdout, "%4d:\t%s", line++, buffer );
29:
30:    fclose(fp);
31:    return 0;
32: }
33:
34: void display_usage(void)
35: {
36:        fprintf(stderr, "\nProper Usage is: " );
37:        fprintf(stderr, "\n\nlist_it filename.ext\n" );
38: }
```

```
C:\>list_it list_it.c
 1:     /* list_it.c - This program displays a listing with line numbers!
*/
 2:     #include <stdio.h>
 3:     #include <stdlib.h>
 4:
 5:     void display_usage(void);
 6:     int line;
 7:
 8:     int main( int argc, char *argv[] )
 9:     {
10:         char buffer[256];
11:         FILE *fp;
12:
13:         if( argc < 2 )
14:         {
15:             display_usage();
16:             return 1;
17:         }
18:
19:         if (( fp = fopen( argv[1], "r" )) == NULL )
20:         {
21:             fprintf( stderr, "Error opening file, %s!", argv[1] );
22:             return(1);
23:         }
24:
25:         line = 1;
26:
27:         while( fgets( buffer, 256, fp ) != NULL )
28:             fprintf( stdout, "%4d:\t%s", line++, buffer );
29:
30:         fclose(fp);
31:         return 0;
32:     }
33:
34:     void display_usage(void)
35:     {
36:         fprintf(stderr, "\nProper Usage is: " );
37:         fprintf(stderr, "\n\nlist_it filename.ext\n" );
38:     }
```

ANALYSIS   The list_it.c program in Listing 2.2 displays C program listings that you have saved. These listings are displayed on the screen with line numbers added.

Looking at this listing, you can summarize where the different parts are. The required main() function is in lines 8 through 32. Lines 2 and 3 have #include directives. Lines 6, 10, and 11 have variable definitions. A function prototype, void display_usage(void), is in line 5. This program has many statements (lines 13, 15, 16, 19, 21, 22, 25, 27, 28, 30, 31, 36, and 37). A function definition for display_usage()

fills lines 34 through 38. Braces enclose blocks throughout the program. Finally, only line 1 has a comment. In most programs, you should probably include more than one comment line.

LIST_IT.C calls many functions. It calls only one user-defined function, `display_usage()`. The library functions that it uses are `fopen()` in line 19; `fprintf()` in lines 21, 28, 36, and 37; `fgets()` in line 27; and `fclose()` in line 30. These library functions are covered in more detail throughout this book.

Summary

Today's lesson was short, but it's important, because it introduced you to the major components of a C program. You learned that the single required part of every C program is the `main()` function. You also learned that a program's real work is done by program statements that instruct the computer to perform your desired actions. You were also introduced to variables and variable definitions, and you learned how to use comments in your source code.

In addition to the `main()` function, a C program can use two types of subsidiary functions: library functions, supplied as part of the compiler package, and user-defined functions, created by the programmer. The next few lessons will go into much more detail on many of the parts of a C program that you saw today.

Q&A

Q What effect do comments have on a program?

A Comments are for programmers. When the compiler converts the source code to object code, it throws the comments and the white space away. This means that they have no effect on the executable program. A program with a lot of comments will execute just as fast as a program with very few comments. Comments do make your source file bigger, but this is usually of little concern. To summarize, you should use comments and white space to make your source code as easy to understand and maintain as possible.

Q What is the difference between a statement and a block?

A A block is a group of statements enclosed in braces (`{}`). A block can be used in most places that a statement can be used.

Q How can I find out what library functions are available?

A Many compilers come with a manual dedicated specifically to documenting the library functions. They are usually in alphabetical order. Another way to find out what library functions are available is to buy a book that lists them. Appendix E, "Common C Functions," lists many of the available functions. After you begin to understand more of C, it would be a good idea to read these appendixes so that you don't rewrite a library function. (There's no use reinventing the wheel!)

Workshop

The Workshop provides quiz questions to help you solidify your understanding of the material covered and exercises to provide you with experience in using what you've learned.

Quiz

1. What is the term for a group of one or more C statements enclosed in braces?

2. What is the one component that must be present in every C program?

3. How do you add program comments, and why are they used?

4. What is a function?

5. C offers two types of functions. What are they, and how are they different?

6. What is the #include directive used for?

7. Can comments be nested?

8. Can comments be longer than one line?

9. What is another name for an include file?

10. What is an include file?

Exercises

1. Write the smallest program possible.

2. Consider the following program:

```
1:  /* ex02-02.c */
2:  #include <stdio.h>
3:
4:  void display_line(void);
5:
6:  int main(void)
7:  {
8:      display_line();
9:      printf("\n Teach Yourself C In 21 Days!\n");
10:     display_line();
11:
12:      return 0;
13: }
```

```
14:
15: /* print asterisk line */
16: void display_line(void)
17: {
18:     int counter;
19:
20:     for( counter = 0; counter < 30; counter++ )
21:         printf("*" );
22: }
23: /* end of program */
```

    a. What line(s) contain statements?

    b. What line(s) contain variable definitions?

    c. What line(s) contain function prototypes?

    d. What line(s) contain function definitions?

    e. What line(s) contain comments?

3. Write an example of a comment.

4. What does the following program do? (Enter, compile, and run it.)

```
1:  /* ex02-04.c */
2:  #include <stdio.h>
3:
4:  int main(void)
5:  {
6:     int ctr;
7:
8:     for( ctr = 65; ctr < 91; ctr++ )
9:         printf("%c", ctr );
10:
11:     return 0;
12: }
13: /* end of program */
```

5. What does the following program do? (Enter, compile, and run it.)

```
1:  /* ex02-05.c */
2:  #include <stdio.h>
3:  #include <string.h>
4:  int main(void)
5:  {
6:     char buffer[256];
7:
8:     printf( "Enter your name and press <Enter>:\n");
9:     gets( buffer );
10:
11:     printf( "\nYour name has %d characters and spaces!",
12                     strlen( buffer ));
13:
14:     return 0;
15: }
```

DAY **3**

Storing Information: Variables and Constants

Computer programs usually work with different types of data and need a way to store the values being used. These values can be numbers or characters. C has two ways of storing number values—variables and constants—with many options for each. A variable is a data storage location that has a value that can change during program execution. In contrast, a constant has a fixed value that can't change. Today you will learn:

- How to store information using variables in C
- Ways to efficiently store different types of numeric values
- The differences and similarities between character and numeric values
- How to declare and initialize variables
- C's two types of numeric constants

Before you get to variables, however, you need to know a little about the operation of your computer's memory.

Understanding Your Computer's Memory

If you already know how a computer's memory operates, you can skip this section. If you're not sure, read on. Understanding your computer's memory and how it works will help you better understand certain aspects of C programming.

A computer uses random-access memory (RAM) to store information while it is operating. RAM is generally located inside your computer. RAM is volatile, which means that it is erased and replaced with new information as often as needed. Being volatile also means that RAM "remembers" only while the computer is turned on and loses its information when you turn the computer off.

Each computer has a certain amount of RAM installed. The amount of RAM in a system is usually specified in megabytes (MB), such as 2MB, 4MB, 8MB, 32MB or more. One megabyte of memory is 1,024 kilobytes. One kilobyte of memory consists of 1,024 bytes. Thus, a system with 4MB of memory actually has 4×1,024 kilobytes, or 4,096 kilobytes of RAM. This would be 4,096KB×1,024 bytes for a total of 4,194,304 bytes of RAM.

A *byte* is the fundamental unit of computer data storage. Day 20, "Working with Memory," has more information about bytes. For now, Table 3.1 provides you with an idea of how many bytes it takes to store certain kinds of data.

TABLE 3.1 Memory space required to store data

Data	Bytes Required
The letter x	1
The number 500	2
The number 241.105	4
The phrase *Sams Teach Yourself C*	22
One typewritten page	Approximately 3,000

The RAM in your computer is organized sequentially, one byte following another. Each byte of memory has a unique address that can be used to identify it. This address can be used to distinguishes the byte of memory from all other bytes. Addresses are assigned to memory locations in order, starting at zero and increasing to the system limit. For now, you don't need to worry about addresses; it's all handled automatically by the C compiler.

What is your computer's RAM used for? It has several uses, but only data storage need concern you as a programmer. Data is the information with which your C program works. Whether your program is maintaining an address list, monitoring the stock market, keeping a household budget, or tracking the price of hog bellies, the information (names, stock prices, expense amounts, or hog futures) is kept in your computer's RAM while the program is running.

Now that you understand a little about the nuts and bolts of memory storage, you can get back to C programming and how C uses memory to store information.

Storing Information with Variables

NEW TERM A *variable* is a named data storage location in your computer's memory. By using a variable's name in your program, you are, in effect, referring to the data stored there.

Variable Names

To use variables in your C programs, you must know how to create variable names. In C, variable names must adhere to the following rules:

- The name can contain letters (a to z and A to Z), digits (0 to 9), and the underscore character (_).
- The first character of the name must be a letter. The underscore is also a legal first character, but its use is not recommended at the beginning of a name. A digit (0 to 9) cannot be used as the first character.
- Case matters (that is, upper- and lowercase letters). C is case-sensitive, thus, the names `count` and `Count` refer to two different variables.
- C keywords can't be used as variable names. A keyword is a word that is part of the C language. (A complete list of the C keywords can be found in Appendix B, "Reserved Words.")

The following list contains some examples of legal and illegal C variable names:

Variable Name	Legality
Percent	Legal
y2x5__fg7h	Legal
annual_profit	Legal
_1990_tax	Legal but not advised
savings#account	Illegal: Contains the illegal character #
double	Illegal: Is a C keyword
4sale	Illegal: First character is a digit

Because C is case-sensitive, the names `percent`, `PERCENT`, and `Percent` would be considered three different variables. C programmers commonly use only lowercase letters in variable names, although this isn't required. Using all-uppercase letters is usually reserved for the names of constants (which are covered later today).

For many compilers, a C variable name can be up to 31 characters long. (It can actually be longer than that, but the compiler looks at only the first 31 characters of the name.) With this flexibility, you can create variable names that reflect the data being stored. For example, a program that calculates loan payments could store the value of the prime interest rate in a variable named `interest_rate`. The variable name helps make its usage clear. You could also have created a variable named x or even `ozzy_osborne`; it doesn't matter to the C compiler. The use of the variable, however, wouldn't be nearly as clear to someone else looking at the source code. Although it might take a little more time to type descriptive variable names, the improvements in program clarity make it worthwhile.

Many naming conventions are used for variable names created from multiple words. You've seen one style: `interest_rate`. Using an underscore to separate words in a variable name makes it easy to interpret. The second style is called *camel notation*. Instead of using spaces, the first letter of each word is capitalized. Instead of `interest_rate`, the variable would be named `InterestRate`. Camel notation is gaining popularity, because it's easier to type a capital letter than an underscore. The underscore is used in this book because it's easier for most people to read. You should decide which style you want to adopt.

Do	Don't
DO use variable names that are descriptive.	**DON'T** start your variable names with an underscore unnecessarily.
DO adopt and stick with a style for naming your variables.	**DON'T** name your variables with all capital letters unnecessarily.

Numeric Variable Types

C provides several different types of numeric variables. You need different types of variables because different numeric values have varying memory storage requirements and differ in the ease with which certain mathematical operations can be performed on them. Small integers (for example, 1, 199, and –8) require less memory to store, and your computer can perform mathematical operations (addition, multiplication, and so on) with such numbers very quickly. In contrast, large integers and floating-point values

(123,000,000, 3.14, or 0.000000871256, for example) require more storage space and more time for mathematical operations. By using the appropriate variable types, you ensure that your program runs as efficiently as possible.

C's numeric variables fall into the following two main categories:

- Integer variables hold values that have no fractional part (that is, whole numbers only). Integer variables come in two flavors: signed integer variables can hold positive or negative values, whereas unsigned integer variables can hold only positive values (and 0).

- Floating-point variables hold values that have a fractional part (that is, real numbers).

Within each of these categories are two or more specific variable types. These are summarized in Table 3.2, which also shows the amount of memory, in bytes, generally required to hold a single variable of each type.

TABLE 3.2 C's numeric data types

Variable Type	Keyword	Bytes Required	Range
Character	`char`	1	−128 to 127
Short integer	`short`	2	−32767 to 32767
Integer	`int`	4	−2,147,483,647 to 2,147,438,647
Long integer	`long`	4	−2,147,483,647 to 2,147,438,647
Long long integer	`long long`	8	−9,223,372,036,854,775,807 to 9,223,372,036,854,775,807
Unsigned character	`unsigned char`	1	0 to 255
Unsigned short integer	`unsigned short`	2	0 to 65535
Unsigned integer	`unsigned int`	4	0 to 4,294,967,295
Unsigned long integer	`unsigned long`	4	0 to 4,294,967,295
Unsigned long long integer	`unsigned long long`	8	0 to 18,446,744,073,709,551,615
Single-precision floating-point	`float`	4	1.2E–38 to 3.4E38[1]
Double-precision floating-point	`double`	8	2.2E–308 to 1.8E308[2]

[1]Approximate range; precision = 7 digits.

[2]Approximate range; precision = 19 digits.

Note

Approximate range means the highest and lowest values a given variable can hold. (Space limitations prohibit listing exact ranges for the values of these variables.) *Precision* is the accuracy with which a variable is stored. (For example, if you evaluate 1/3, the answer is 0.33333... with 3s going to infinity. A variable with a precision of 7 stores seven 3s.)

Caution

Compilers that don't support the C-99 standard may not support long long and an unsigned long long values.

Looking at Table 3.2, you might notice that the variable types int and short are identical. Why are two different types necessary? The int and short variable types are indeed identical on 32-bit Intel systems (PCs), but they might be different on other types of hardware. For example, on a VAX system, a short and an int aren't the same size. Instead, a short is 2 bytes, whereas an int is 4 bytes. Remember that C is a flexible, portable language, so it provides different keywords for the two types. If you're working on a PC, you can use int and short interchangeably.

No special keyword is needed to make an integer variable signed; integer variables are signed by default. You can, however, include the signed keyword if you wish. The keywords shown in Table 3.2 are used in variable declarations, which are discussed in the next section.

Listing 3.1 will help you determine the size of variables on your particular computer. Don't be surprised if your output doesn't match the output presented after the listing.

LISTING 3.1   sizeof.c—A program that displays the size of variable types

```
 1:  /* sizeof.c—Program to tell the size of the C variable */
 2:  /*           type in bytes */
 3:
 4:  #include <stdio.h>
 5:
 6:  int main(void)
 7:  {
 8:      printf( "\nA char      is %d bytes", sizeof( char ));
 9:      printf( "\nAn int      is %d bytes", sizeof( int ));
10:      printf( "\nA short     is %d bytes", sizeof( short ));
11:      printf( "\nA long      is %d bytes", sizeof( long ));
12:      printf( "\nA long long is %d bytes\n", sizeof( long long));
13:      printf( "\nAn unsigned char  is %d bytes", sizeof( unsigned char ));
```

LISTING 3.1 continued

```
14:    printf( "\nAn unsigned int   is %d bytes", sizeof( unsigned int ));
15:    printf( "\nAn unsigned short is %d bytes", sizeof( unsigned short ));
16:    printf( "\nAn unsigned long  is %d bytes", sizeof( unsigned long ));
17:    printf( "\nAn unsigned long long is %d bytes\n",
18:                                   sizeof( unsigned long long));
19:    printf( "\nA float    is %d bytes", sizeof( float ));
20:    printf( "\nA double   is %d bytes\n", sizeof( double ));
21:    printf( "\nA long double is %d bytes\n", sizeof( long double ));
22:
23:    return 0;
24:  }
```

OUTPUT

```
A char     is 1 bytes
An int     is 4 bytes
A short    is 2 bytes
A long     is 4 bytes
A long long is 8 bytes

An unsigned char  is 1 bytes
An unsigned int   is 4 bytes
An unsigned short is 2 bytes
An unsigned long  is 4 bytes
An unsigned long long is 8 bytes

A float    is 4 bytes
A double   is 8 bytes
A long double is 12 bytes
```

ANALYSIS As the preceding output shows, Listing 3.1 tells you exactly how many bytes each variable type on your computer takes. If you're using a standard 32-bit PC, your numbers should match those in Table 3.2.

Don't worry about trying to understand all the individual components of the program. Although some items are new, such as `sizeof`, others should look familiar. Lines 1 and 2 are comments about the name of the program and a brief description. Line 4 includes the standard input/output header file to help print the information on-screen. This is a simple program, in that it contains only a single function, `main()` (lines 7 through 24). Lines 8 through 21 are the bulk of the program. Each of these lines prints a textual description with the size of each of the variable types, which is done using the `sizeof` operator. Line 23 of the program returns the value 0 to the operating system before ending the program.

Although I said the size of the data types can vary depending on your computer platform, C does make some guarantees. There are five things you can count on:

3

- The size of a char is one byte.
- The size of a short is less than or equal to the size of an int.
- The size of an int is less than or equal to the size of a long.
- The size of an unsigned is equal to the size of an int.
- The size of a float is less than or equal to the size of a double.

Note

> Table 3.2 listed the common keyword used to identify the different variable types. The following table (Table 3.3) lists the full name of each of the data types.
>
> As you can see from this table, short and long types are really just variations on the int type. Most programmers don't use the full name of the variable types, rather thy use the shorter version.

TABLE 3.3   Full names of data types

Full name	commonly used keyword
char	signed char
short	signed short int
int	signed int
long	signed long int
long long	signed long long int
unsigned char	unsigned char
unsigned short	unsigned short int
unsigned int	unsigned int
unsigned long	unsigned long int
unsigned long long	unsigned long long int

Variable Declarations

Before you can use a variable in a C program, it must be declared. A variable declaration tells the compiler the name and type of a variable. The declaration may also initialize the variable to a specific value. If your program attempts to use a variable that hasn't been declared, the compiler generates an error message. A variable declaration has the following form:

typename varname;

typename specifies the variable type and must be one of the keywords listed in Table 3.2. *varname* is the variable name, which must follow the rules mentioned earlier. You can declare multiple variables of the same type on one line by separating the variable names with commas:

```
int count, number, start;    /* three integer variables */
float percent, total;        /* two float variables */
```

On Day 12, "Understanding Variable Scope," you'll learn that the location of variable declarations in the source code is important, because it affects the ways in which your program can use the variables. For now, you can place all the variable declarations together just before the start of the main() function.

The typedef Keyword

The typedef keyword is used to create a new name for an existing data type. In effect, typedef creates a synonym. For example, the statement

```
typedef int integer;
```

creates integer as a synonym for int. You then can use integer to define variables of type int, as in this example:

```
integer count;
```

Note that typedef doesn't create a new data type; it only lets you use a different name for a predefined data type. The most common use of typedef concerns aggregate data types, as explained on Day 11, "Structures." An aggregate data type consists of a combination of data types presented today.

Initializing Variables

When you declare a variable, you instruct the compiler to set aside storage space for the variable. However, the value stored in that space—the value of the variable—isn't defined. It might be zero, or it might be some random "garbage" value. Before using a variable, you should always initialize it to a known value. You can do this independently of the variable declaration by using an assignment statement, as in this example:

```
int count;   /* Set aside storage space for count */
count = 0;   /* Store 0 in count */
```

Note that this statement uses the equal sign (=), which is C's assignment operator and is discussed further on Day 4, "Statements, Expressions, and Operators." For now, you need to be aware that the equal sign in programming is not the same as the equal sign in algebra. If you write

```
x = 12
```

in an algebraic statement, you are stating a fact: "x equals 12." In C, however, it means something quite different. In C it means "Assign the value 12 to the variable named x."

You can also initialize a variable when it's declared. To do so, follow the variable name in the declaration statement with an equal sign and the desired initial value:

```
int count = 0;
double percent = 0.01, taxrate = 28.5;
```

The first statement declares a variable called count as an integer and initializes it to zero. The second statement declares two variables as doubles and initializes them. The first, percent, is initialized to 0.01. The second, taxrate, is initialized to 28.5.

Be careful not to initialize a variable with a value outside the allowed range. Here are two examples of out-of-range initializations:

```
int weight = 100000;
unsigned int value = -2500;
```

The C compiler may not catch such errors. Your program might compile and link, but you might get unexpected results when the program is run.

Do	Don't
DO understand the number of bytes that variable types take for your computer.	**DON'T** use a variable that hasn't been initialized. Results can be unpredictable.
DO use typedef to make your programs more readable.	**DON'T** use a float or double variable if you're only storing integers. Although they will work, using them is inefficient.
DO initialize variables when you declare them whenever possible.	**DON'T** try to put numbers that are too big or too small into a variable if its type won't hold them.
	DON'T put negative numbers into variables with an unsigned type.

Constants

Like a variable, a *constant* is a data storage location used by your program. Unlike a variable, the value stored in a constant can't be changed during program execution. C has two types of constants, each with its own specific uses:

- Literal Constants
- Symbolic Constants

Literal Constants

 A *literal constant* is a value that is typed directly into the source code wherever it is needed. Here are two examples:

```
int count = 20;
float tax_rate = 0.28;
```

The 20 and the 0.28 are literal constants. The preceding statements store these values in the variables count and tax_rate. Note that one of these constants contains a decimal point, whereas the other does not. The presence or absence of the decimal point distinguishes floating-point constants from integer constants.

A literal constant written with a decimal point is a floating-point constant and is represented by the C compiler as a double-precision number. Floating-point constants can be written in standard decimal notation, as shown in these examples:

```
123.456
0.019
100.
```

Note that the third constant, 100., is written with a decimal point even though it's an integer (that is, it has no fractional part). The decimal point causes the C compiler to treat the constant as a double-precision value. Without the decimal point, it is treated as an integer constant.

Floating-point constants also can be written in scientific notation. You might recall from high school math that scientific notation represents a number as a decimal part multiplied by 10 to a positive or negative power. Scientific notation is particularly useful for representing extremely large and extremely small values. In C, scientific notation is written as a decimal number followed immediately by an E or e and the exponent:

1.23E2	1.23 times 10 to the 2nd power, or 123
4.08e6	4.08 times 10 to the 6th power, or 4,080,000
0.85e–4	0.85 times 10 to the –4th power, or 0.000085

A constant written without a decimal point is represented by the compiler as an integer number. Integer constants can be written in three different notations:

- A constant starting with any digit other than 0 is interpreted as a decimal integer (that is, the standard base-10 number system). Decimal constants can contain the digits 0 through 9 and a leading minus or plus sign. (Without a leading minus or plus, a constant is assumed to be positive.)

- A constant starting with the digit 0 is interpreted as an octal integer (the base-8 number system). Octal constants can contain the digits 0 through 7 and a leading minus or plus sign.

- A constant starting with 0x or 0X is interpreted as a hexadecimal constant (the base-16 number system). Hexadecimal constants can contain the digits 0 through 9, the letters A through F, and a leading minus or plus sign.

> **Note**   See Appendix C, "Working with Binary and Hexadecimal Numbers," for a more complete explanation of decimal and hexadecimal notation.

Symbolic Constants

NEW TERM   A *symbolic constant* is a constant that is represented by a name (symbol) in your program. Like a literal constant, a symbolic constant can't change. Whenever you need the constant's value in your program, you use its name as you would use a variable name. The actual value of the symbolic constant needs to be entered only once, when it is first defined.

Symbolic constants have two significant advantages over literal constants, as the following example shows. Suppose that you're writing a program that performs a variety of geometrical calculations. The program frequently needs the value π (3.14) for its calculations. (You might recall from geometry class that π is the ratio of a circle's circumference to its diameter.) For example, to calculate the circumference and area of a circle with a known radius, you could write

```
circumference = 3.14 * (2 * radius);
area = 3.14 * (radius)*(radius);
```

The asterisk (*) is C's multiplication operator and is covered on Day 4. Thus, the first of these statements means "Multiply 2 times the value stored in the variable radius, and then multiply the result by 3.14. Finally, assign the result to the variable named circumference."

If, however, you define a symbolic constant with the name PI and the value 3.14, you could write

```
circumference = PI * (2 * radius);
area = PI * (radius)*(radius);
```

The resulting code is clearer. Rather than puzzling over what the value 3.14 is for, you can see immediately that the constant PI is being used.

The second advantage of symbolic constants becomes apparent when you need to change a constant. Continuing with the preceding example, you might decide that for greater accuracy your program needs to use a value of PI with more decimal places: 3.14159 rather than 3.14. If you had used literal constants for PI, you would have to go through your source code and change each occurrence of the value from 3.14 to 3.14159. With a symbolic constant, you need to make a change only in the place where the constant is defined. The rest of your code would not need to be changed.

Defining Symbolic Constants

C has two methods for defining a symbolic constant: the #define directive and the const keyword. The #define directive is used as follows:

```
#define CONSTNAME literal
```

This creates a constant named *CONSTNAME* with the value of *literal*. *literal* represents a literal constant, as described earlier. *CONSTNAME* follows the same rules described earlier for variable names. By convention, the names of symbolic constants are uppercase. This makes them easy to distinguish from variable names, which by convention are lowercase. For the previous example, the required #define directive for a constant called PI would be

```
#define PI 3.14159
```

Note that #define lines don't end with a semicolon (;). #defines can be placed anywhere in your source code, but the defined constant is in effect only for the portions of the source code that follow the #define directive. Most commonly, programmers group all #defines together, near the beginning of the file and before the start of the main() function.

How a #define Works

The precise action of the #define directive is to instruct the compiler as follows: "In the source code, replace *CONSTNAME* with *literal*." The effect is exactly the same as if you had used your editor to go through the source code and make the changes manually. Note that #define doesn't replace instances of its target that occur as parts of longer names, within double quotes, or as part of a program comment. For example, in the following code, the instances of PI in the second and third lines would not get changed:

```
#define PI 3.14159
/* You have defined a constant for PI. */
#define PIPETTE 100
```

Note

The #define directive is one of C's preprocessor directives, and it is discussed more fully on Day 21, "Advanced Compiler Use."

Defining Constants with the const Keyword

The second way to define a symbolic constant is with the const keyword. const is a modifier that can be applied to any variable declaration. A variable declared to be const can't be modified when the program is executed. A value is initialized at the time of declaration and is then prohibited from being changed. Here are some examples:

```
const int count = 100;
const float pi = 3.14159;
const long debt = 12000000, float tax_rate = 0.21;
```

const affects all variables on the declaration line. In the last line, debt and tax_rate are symbolic constants. As a side note, you should notice that in this example, debt was declared as a long and tax_rate was declared as a float.

If your program tries to modify a const variable, the compiler generates an error message. The following code would generate an error:

```
const int count = 100;
count = 200;       /* Does not compile! Cannot reassign or alter */
                   /* the value of a constant. */
```

What are the practical differences between symbolic constants created with the #define directive and those created with the const keyword? The differences have to do with pointers and variable scope. Pointers and variable scope are two very important aspects of C programming, and you will learn about them on Day 9, "Understanding Pointers," and Day 12.

Now take a look at a program that demonstrates variable declarations and the use of literal and symbolic constants. Listing 3.2 prompts the you to enter your weight and year of birth. It then calculates and displays the your weight in grams and your age in the year 2010. You can enter, compile, and run this program using the procedures explained on Day 1, "Getting Started with C."

 Note   Most C programmers today use const instead of #define when declaring constants.

LISTING 3.2   const.c—A program that demonstrates the use of variables and constants

```
1:    /* Demonstrates variables and constants */
2:    #include <stdio.h>
3:
4:    /* Define a constant to convert from pounds to grams */
5:    #define GRAMS_PER_POUND 454
6:
7:    /* Define a constant for the start of the next century */
8:    const int TARGET_YEAR = 2010;
9:
```

LISTING 3.2   continued

```
10:     /* Declare the needed variables */
11:     long weight_in_grams, weight_in_pounds;
12      int year_of_birth, age_in_2010;
13:
14:     int main( void )
15:     {
16:         /* Input data from user */
17:
18:         printf("Enter your weight in pounds: ");
19:         scanf("%d", &weight_in_pounds);
20:         printf("Enter your year of birth: ");
21:         scanf("%d", &year_of_birth);
22:
23:         /* Perform conversions */
24:
25:         weight_in_grams = weight_in_pounds * GRAMS_PER_POUND;
26:         age_in_2010 = TARGET_YEAR - year_of_birth;
27:
28:         /* Display results on the screen */
29:
30:         printf("\nYour weight in grams = %ld", weight_in_grams);
31:         printf("\nIn 2010 you will be %d years old\n", age_in_2010);
32:
33:         return 0;
34:     }
```

INPUT/ OUTPUT

```
Enter your weight in pounds: 175
Enter your year of birth: 1965

Your weight in grams = 79450
In 2010 you will be 45 years old
```

ANALYSIS   This program declares the two types of symbolic constants in lines 5 and 8. In line 5, a constant is used to make the value 454 more understandable. Because it uses GRAMS_PER_POUND, line 25 is easy to understand. Lines 11 and 12 declare the variables used in the program. Notice the use of descriptive names such as weight_in_grams. You can tell what this variable is used for. Lines 18 and 20 print prompts on-screen. The printf() function is covered in greater detail later. To allow the user to respond to the prompts, lines 19 and 21 use another library function, scanf(), which is covered later. scanf() gets information from the screen. For now, accept that this works as shown in the listing. Later, you will learn exactly how it works. Lines 25 and 26 calculate the user's weight in grams and his or her age in the year 2010. These statements and others are covered in detail in tomorrow's chapter. To finish the program, lines 30 and 31 display the results for the user.

Do	**Don't**
DO use constants to make your programs easier to read.	**DON'T** try to assign a value to a constant after it has already been initialized.

Summary

Today's lesson explored numeric variables, which are used by a C program to store data during program execution. You've seen that there are two broad classes of numeric variables, integer and floating-point. Within each class are specific variable types. Which variable type—such as int, long, float, or double—you use for a specific application depends on the nature of the data to be stored in the variable. You've also seen that in a C program, you must declare a variable before it can be used. A variable declaration informs the compiler of the name and type of a variable.

You also learned about C's two constant types, literal and symbolic. Unlike variables, the value of a constant can't change during program execution. You type literal constants into your source code whenever the value is needed. Symbolic constants are assigned a name that is used wherever the constant value is needed. Symbolic constants can be created with the #define directive or with the const keyword.

Q&A

Q long int variables hold bigger numbers, so why not always use them instead of int variables?

A A long int variable takes up more RAM than the smaller int. In smaller programs, this doesn't pose a problem. As programs get bigger, however, you should try to be efficient with the memory you use.

Q What happens if I assign a number with a decimal to an integer?

A You can assign a number with a decimal to an int variable. If you're using a constant variable, your compiler probably will give you a warning. The value assigned will have the decimal portion truncated. For example, if you assign 3.14 to an integer variable called pi, pi will only contain 3. The .14 will be chopped off and thrown away.

Q What happens if I put a number into a type that isn't big enough to hold it?

A Many compilers will allow this without signaling any errors. The number is wrapped to fit and therefore won't be correct. For example, if you assign 32768 to a two-byte signed variable of type short, the variable would really contain the value

-32768. If you assign the value 65535 to this variable, it really contains the value -1. Subtracting the maximum value that the field will hold generally gives you the value that will be stored.

Q What happens if I put a negative number into an unsigned variable?

A As the preceding answer indicated, your compiler might not signal any errors if you do this. The compiler does the same wrapping as if you assigned a number that was too big. For instance, if you assign -1 to an unsigned `int` variable that is two bytes long, the compiler will put the highest number possible in the variable (65535).

Q What are the practical differences between symbolic constants created with the `#define` directive and those created with the `const` keyword?

A The differences have to do with pointers and variable scope. Pointers and variable scope are two very important aspects of C programming and are covered on Days 9 and 12.

Workshop

The Workshop provides quiz questions to help you solidify your understanding of the material covered and exercises to provide you with experience in using what you've learned.

Quiz

1. What's the difference between an integer variable and a floating-point variable?

2. Give two reasons for using a double-precision floating-point variable (type `double`) instead of a single-precision floating-point variable (type `float`).

3. What are five rules that the you know are always true when allocating size for variables?

4. What are the two advantages of using a symbolic constant instead of a literal constant?

5. Show two methods for defining a symbolic constant named MAXIMUM that has a value of 100.

6. What characters are allowed in C variable names?

7. What guidelines should you follow in creating names for variables and constants?

8. What's the difference between a symbolic and a literal constant?

9. What's the minimum value that a type `int` variable can hold?

Exercises

1. In what variable type would you best store the following values?

    a. A person's age to the nearest year.

    b. A person's weight in pounds.

    c. The radius of a circle.

    d. Your annual salary.

    e. The cost of an item.

    f. The highest grade on a test (assume it is always 100).

    g. The temperature.

    h. A person's net worth.

    i. The distance to a star in miles.

2. Determine appropriate variable names for the values in exercise 1.

3. Write declarations for the variables in exercise 2.

4. Which of the following variable names are valid?

    a. `123variable`

    b. `x`

    c. `total_score`

    d. `Weight_in_#s`

    e. `one`

    f. `gross-cost`

    g. `RADIUS`

    h. `Radius`

    i. `radius`

    j. `this_is_a_variable_to_hold_the_width_of_a_box`

DAY **4**

The Pieces of a C Program: Statements, Expressions, and Operators

C programs consist of statements, and most statements are composed of expressions and operators. In order to be able to write C programs, you need to understand statements, expressions, and operators. Today you will learn:

- What a statement is
- What an expression is
- How to use C's mathematical, relational, and logical operators
- What "operator precedence" is
- The `if` statement

Statements

NEW TERM   A *statement* is a complete instruction that directs the computer to carry out some task. In C, statements are usually written one per line, although some statements span multiple lines. C statements always end with a semicolon (except for preprocessor directives such as #define and #include, which are discussed on Day 21, "Advanced Compiler Use"). You've already been introduced to some of C's statement types. For example:

```
x = 2 + 3;
```

is an assignment statement. It instructs the computer to add 3 to 2 and assign the result to the variable x. Other types of statements will be introduced as needed throughout this book.

The Impact of Whitespace on Statements

NEW TERM   The term *white space* refers to spaces, horizontal tabs, vertical tabs, and blank lines in your source code. The C compiler isn't sensitive to white space. When the compiler reads a statement in your source code, it looks for the characters in the statement and for the terminating semicolon, but it ignores white space. Thus, the statement

```
x=2+3;
```

is equivalent to this statement:

```
x = 2 + 3;
```

It is also equivalent to this:

```
x         =
2
     +
3   ;
```

This gives you a great deal of flexibility in formatting your source code. You shouldn't use formatting like the previous example. Statements should be entered one per line with a standardized scheme for spacing around variables and operators. If you follow the formatting conventions used in this book, you should be in good shape. As you become more experienced, you might discover that you prefer slight variations. The point is to keep your source code readable.

The rule that C doesn't care about white space has one exception. Within literal string constants, tabs and spaces aren't ignored; they are considered part of the string. A *string* is a series of characters. Literal string constants are strings that are enclosed within quotes and interpreted literally by the compiler, space for space. An example of a literal string is

```
"How now brown cow"
```

This literal string is different from the following:

```
"How    now    brown    cow"
```

The difference is a result of the additional spaces. With a literal string, C keeps track of the white space.

Although it's extremely bad form, the following is legal code in C:

```
printf(
"Hello, world!"
);
```

This, however, is not legal:

```
printf("Hello,
world!");
```

To break a literal string constant line, you must use the backslash character (\) just before the break. Thus, the following is legal:

```
printf("Hello,\
world!");
```

Creating a Null Statements

NEW TERM If you place a semicolon by itself on a line, you create a *null statement.* A null statement is one that doesn't perform any action. This is perfectly legal in C. Later in this book, you will learn how the null statement can be useful.

Working with Compound Statements

NEW TERM A *compound statement,* also called a *block,* is a group of two or more C statements enclosed in braces. Here's an example of a block:

```
{
    printf("Hello, ");
    printf("world!");
}
```

In C, a block can be used anywhere a single statement can be used. Many examples of this appear throughout this book. Note that the enclosing braces can be positioned in different ways. The following is equivalent to the preceding example:

```
{printf("Hello, ");
printf("world!");}
```

It's a good idea to place braces on their own lines, making the beginning and end of blocks clearly visible. Placing braces on their own lines also makes it easier to see whether you've left one out.

Do	Don't
DO stay consistent with how you use white space in statements.	**DON'T** spread a single statement across multiple lines if there's no need to do so. Limit statements to one line if possible.
DO put block braces on their own lines. This makes the code easier to read.	**DON'T** forget to use a forward slash to continue a string of characters onto a second line.
DO line up block braces so that it's easy to find the beginning and end of a block.	

Understanding Expressions

NEW TERM   In C, an *expression* is anything that evaluates to a numeric value. C expressions come in all levels of complexity.

Simple Expressions

The simplest C expression consists of a single item: a simple variable, literal constant, or symbolic constant. Here are four expressions:

Expression	Description
PI	A symbolic constant (defined in the program)
20	A literal constant
rate	A variable
-1.25	Another literal constant

NEW TERM   A *literal constant* evaluates to its own value. A *symbolic constant* evaluates to the value it was given when you created it using the #define directive. A variable evaluates to the current value assigned to it by the program.

Complex Expressions

NEW TERM   *Complex expressions* consist of simpler expressions connected by operators. For example:

```
2 + 8
```

is an expression consisting of the sub-expressions 2 and 8 and the addition operator +. The expression 2 + 8 evaluates, as you should know, to 10. You can write C expressions of great complexity:

```
1.25 / 8 + 5 * rate + rate * rate / cost
```

When an expression contains multiple operators, the evaluation of the expression depends on operator precedence. The concept of operator precedence is covered later in today, as are details about all of C's operators.

C expressions can get even more interesting. Look at the following assignment statement:

```
x = a + 10;
```

This statement evaluates the expression a + 10 and assigns the result to x. In addition, the entire statement x = a + 10 is itself an expression that evaluates to the value of the variable on the left side of the equal sign. This is illustrated in Figure 4.1.

FIGURE 4.1

An assignment statement is itself an expression.

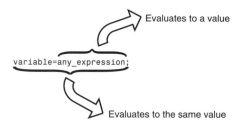

Evaluates to a value

variable=any_expression;

Evaluates to the same value

4

Thus, you can write statements such as the following, which assigns the value of the expression a + 10 to both variables, x and y:

```
y = x = a + 10;
```

You can also write statements such as this:

```
x = 6 + (y = 4 + 5);
```

The result of this statement is that y has the value 9 and x has the value 15. Note the parentheses, which are required in order for the statement to compile. The use of parentheses is covered later today.

Note

With just a few exceptions that will be noted throughout this book, assignment statements should not be nested within other expressions.

Operators

NEW TERM   An *operator* is a symbol that instructs C to perform some operation, or action, on
one or more operands. An *operand* is something that an operator acts on. In C,
all operands are expressions. C operators fall into several categories:

- The assignment operator
- Mathematical operators
- Relational operators
- Logical operators

The Assignment Operator

The *assignment operator* is the equal sign (=). Its use in programming is somewhat different from its use in regular math. If you write

```
x = y;
```

in a C program, it doesn't mean "x is equal to y." Instead, it means "assign the value of y
to x." In a C assignment statement, the right side can be any expression, and the left side
must be a variable name. Thus, the form is as follows:

```
variable = expression;
```

When executed, `expression` is evaluated, and the resulting value is assigned to
`variable`.

The Mathematical Operators

C's mathematical operators perform mathematical operations such as addition and subtraction. C has two unary mathematical operators and five binary mathematical operators.

The Unary Mathematical Operators

The *unary* mathematical operators are so named because they take a single operand. C
has two unary mathematical operators, which are listed in Table 4.1.

TABLE 4.1   C's unary mathematical operators

Operator	Symbol	Action	Examples
Increment	++	Increments the operand by one	++x, x++
Decrement	- -	Decrements the operand by one	- -x, x - -

The increment and decrement operators can be used only with variables, not with constants. The operation performed is to add one to or subtract one from the operand. In other words, the statements

```
++x;
--y;
```

are the equivalent of these statements:

```
x = x + 1;
y = y - 1;
```

You should note from Table 4.1 that either unary mathematical operator can be placed before its operand (*prefix* mode) or after its operand (*postfix* mode). These two modes are not equivalent. They differ in terms of when the increment or decrement is performed:

- When used in prefix mode, the increment and decrement operators modify their operand before the operand is used in the enclosing expression.
- When used in postfix mode, the increment and decrement operators modify their operand after the operand is used in the enclosing expression.

An example should make this clearer. Look at these two statements:

```
x = 10;
y = x++;
```

After these statements are executed, x has the value 11, and y has the value 10. The value of x was assigned to y, and then x was incremented. In contrast, the following statements result in both y and x having the value 11. x is incremented, and then its value is assigned to y.

```
x = 10;
y = ++x;
```

Remember that = is the assignment operator, not a statement of equality. As an analogy, think of = as the "photocopy" operator. The statement y = x means to copy x into y. Subsequent changes to x, after the copy has been made, have no effect on y.

The program in Listing 4.1 illustrates the difference between prefix mode and postfix mode.

LISTING 4.1   unary.c: Demonstrates prefix and postfix modes

```
1:    /* Demonstrates unary operator prefix and postfix modes */
2:
3:    #include <stdio.h>
4:
5:    int a, b;
```

LISTING 4.1 continued

```
6:
7:    int main( void )
8:    {
9:        /* Set a and b both equal to 5 */
10:
11:        a = b = 5;
12:
13:        /* Print them, decrementing each time. */
14:        /* Use prefix mode for b, postfix mode for a */
15:
16:        printf("\nPost  Pre");
17:        printf("\n%d    %d", a--, --b);
18:        printf("\n%d    %d", a--, --b);
19:        printf("\n%d    %d", a--, --b);
20:        printf("\n%d    %d", a--, --b);
21:        printf("\n%d    %d\n", a--, --b);
22:
23:        return 0;
24:    }
```

OUTPUT
```
Post  Pre
5     4
4     3
3     2
2     1
1     0
```

ANALYSIS This program declares two variables, a and b, in line 5. In line 11, the variables are set to the value of 5. With the execution of each `printf()` statement (lines 17 through 21), both a and b are decremented by 1. After a is printed, it is decremented, whereas b is decremented before it is printed.

 Note

> On Day 2, "The Components of a C Program," you learned about another unary operator, `sizeof`. While you might be inclined to think that operators should look like symbols, the `sizeof` keyword is actually considered an operator.

The Binary Mathematical Operators

C's binary operators take two operands. The binary operators, which include the common mathematical operations found on a calculator, are listed in Table 4.2.

TABLE 4.2 C's binary mathematical operators

Operator	Symbol	Action	Example
Addition	+	Adds two operands	x + y
Subtraction	-	Subtracts the second operand from the first operand	x - y
Multiplication	*	Multiplies two operands	x * y
Division	/	Divides the first operand by the second operand	x / y
Modulus	%	Gives the remainder when the first operand is divided by the second operand	x % y

The first four operators listed in Table 4.2 should be familiar to you, and you should have little trouble using them. The fifth operator, modulus, might be new. Modulus returns the remainder when the first operand is divided by the second operand. For example, 11 modulus 4 equals 3 (that is, 4 goes into 11 two times with 3 left over). Here are some more examples:

```
100 modulus 9 equals 1
10 modulus 5 equals 0
40 modulus 6 equals 4
```

Listing 4.2 illustrates how you can use the modulus operator to convert a large number of seconds into hours, minutes, and seconds.

LISTING 4.2 seconds.c: Demonstrates the modulus operator

```
 1:  /* Illustrates the modulus operator. */
 2:  /* Inputs a number of seconds, and converts to hours, */
 3:  /* minutes, and seconds. */
 4:
 5:  #include <stdio.h>
 6:
 7:  /* Define constants */
 8:
 9:  #define SECS_PER_MIN 60
10:  #define SECS_PER_HOUR 3600
11:
12:  unsigned seconds, minutes, hours, secs_left, mins_left;
13:
14:  int main( void )
```

4

LISTING 4.2 continued

```
15:   {
16:         /* Input the number of seconds */
17:
18:         printf("Enter number of seconds (< 65000): ");
19:         scanf("%d", &seconds);
20:
21:         hours = seconds / SECS_PER_HOUR;
22:         minutes = seconds / SECS_PER_MIN;
23:         mins_left = minutes % SECS_PER_MIN;
24:         secs_left = seconds % SECS_PER_MIN;
25:
26:         printf("%u seconds is equal to ", seconds);
27:         printf("%u h, %u m, and %u s\n", hours, mins_left, secs_left);
28:
29:         return 0;
30:   }
```

| INPUT/ |
| OUTPUT |

```
Enter number of seconds (< 65000): 60
60 seconds is equal to 0 h, 1 m, and 0 s

Enter number of seconds (< 65000): 10000
10000 seconds is equal to 2 h, 46 m, and 40 s
```

ANALYSIS The seconds.c program follows the same format that all the previous programs have followed. Lines 1 through 3 provide some comments to state what the program does. Line 4 is white space to make the program more readable. Just like the white space in statements and expressions, blank lines are ignored by the compiler. Line 5 includes the necessary header file for this program. Lines 9 and 10 define two constants, SECS_PER_MIN and SECS_PER_HOUR, that are used to make the statements in the program easier to read. Line 12 declares all the variables that will be used. Some people choose to declare each variable on a separate line rather than all on one. As with many elements of C, this is a matter of style. Either method is correct.

Line 14 is the main() function, which contains the bulk of the program. To convert seconds to hours and minutes, the program must first get the values it needs to work with. To do this, line 18 uses the printf() function to display a statement on-screen, followed by line 19, which uses the scanf() function to get the number that the user entered. The scanf() statement then stores the number of seconds to be converted into the variable seconds. The printf() and scanf() functions are covered in more detail on Day 7, "Fundamentals of Reading and Writing Information." Line 21 contains an expression to determine the number of hours by dividing the number of seconds by the constant SECS_PER_HOUR. Because hours is an integer variable, the remainder value is ignored. Line 22 uses the same logic to determine the total number of minutes for the seconds entered. Because the total number of minutes figured in line 22 also contains minutes for the hours, line 23 uses the modulus operator to divide the hours and keep the remaining minutes. Line 24 carries out a similar calculation for determining the number of seconds that are left. Lines 26 and 27 are similar to what you have seen before. They take the values that have been calculated in the expressions and display them. Line 29 finishes the program by returning 0 to the operating system before exiting.

Operator Precedence and Parentheses

In an expression that contains more than one operator, what is the order in which operations are performed? The importance of this question is illustrated by the following assignment statement:

```
x = 4 + 5 * 3;
```

Performing the addition first results in the following, and x is assigned the value 27:

```
x = 9 * 3;
```

In contrast, if the multiplication is performed first, you have the following, and x is assigned the value 19:

```
x = 4 + 15;
```

Clearly, some rules are needed about the order in which operations are performed. This order, called *operator precedence,* is strictly spelled out in C. Each operator has a specific precedence. When an expression is evaluated, operators with higher precedence are performed first. Table 4.3 lists the precedence of C's mathematical operators. Number 1 is the highest precedence and thus is evaluated first.

TABLE 4.3 The precedence of C's mathematical operators

Operators	Relative Precedence
++ --	1
* / %	2
+ -	3

Looking at Table 4.3, you can see that in any C expression, operations are performed in the following order:

- Unary increment and decrement
- Multiplication, division, and modulus
- Addition and subtraction

If an expression contains more than one operator with the same precedence level, the operators are generally performed in left-to-right order as they appear in the expression. For example, in the following expression, the % and * have the same precedence level, but the % is the leftmost operator, so it is performed first:

```
12 % 5 * 2
```

The expression evaluates to 4 (12 % 5 evaluates to 2; 2 times 2 is 4).

Returning to the previous example, you see that the statement x = 4 + 5 * 3; assigns the value 19 to x because the multiplication is performed before the addition.

What if the order of precedence doesn't evaluate your expression as needed? Using the previous example, what if you wanted to add 4 to 5 and then multiply the sum by 3? C uses parentheses to modify the evaluation order. A sub-expression enclosed in parentheses is evaluated first, without regard to operator precedence. Thus, you could write

```
x = (4 + 5) * 3;
```

The expression 4 + 5 inside parentheses is evaluated first, so the value assigned to x is 27.

You can use multiple and nested parentheses in an expression. When parentheses are nested, evaluation proceeds from the innermost expression outward. Look at the following complex expression:

```
x = 25 - (2 * (10 + (8 / 2)));
```

The evaluation of this expression proceeds as follows:

1. The innermost expression, 8 / 2, is evaluated first, yielding the value 4:

   ```
   25 - (2 * (10 + 4))
   ```

2. Moving outward, the next expression, 10 + 4, is evaluated, yielding the value 14:

   ```
   25 - (2 * 14)
   ```

3. The last, or outermost, expression, 2 * 14, is evaluated, yielding the value 28:

   ```
   25 - 28
   ```

4. The final expression, 25 - 28, is evaluated, assigning the value -3 to the variable x:

   ```
   x = -3
   ```

You might want to use parentheses in some expressions for the sake of clarity, even when they aren't needed for modifying operator precedence. Parentheses must always be in pairs, or the compiler generates an error message.

Order of Sub-expression Evaluation

As was mentioned in the previous section, if C expressions contain more than one operator with the same precedence level, they are evaluated left to right. For example, in the expression

```
w * x / y * z
```

w is first multiplied by x, the result of the multiplication is then divided by y, and the result of the division is then multiplied by z.

Across precedence levels, however, there is no guarantee of left-to-right order. Look at this expression:

```
w * x / y + z / y
```

Because of precedence, the multiplication and division are performed before the addition. However, C doesn't specify whether the sub-expression w * x / y is to be evaluated before or after z / y. It might not be clear to you why this matters. Look at another example:

```
w * x / ++y + z / y
```

If the left sub-expression is evaluated first, y is incremented when the second expression is evaluated. If the right expression is evaluated first, y isn't incremented, and the result is different. Therefore, you should avoid this sort of indeterminate expression in your programming.

Near the end of today's lesson, the section "Operator Precedence Revisited" lists the precedence of all of C's operators.

Do	Don't
DO use parentheses to make the order of expression evaluation clear.	DON'T overload an expression. It is often more clear to break an expression into two or more statements. This is especially true when you're using the unary operators (- -) or (++).

The Relational Operators

C's relational operators are used to compare expressions, asking questions such as, "Is x greater than 100?" or "Is y equal to 0?" An expression containing a relational operator evaluates to either true (1) or false (0). C's six relational operators are listed in Table 4.4.

Table 4.5 shows some examples of how relational operators might be used. These examples use literal constants, but the same principles hold with variables.

Note | "True" is considered the same as "yes," which is also considered the same as 1. "False" is considered the same as "no," which is considered the same as 0.

TABLE 4.4 C's relational operators

Operator	Symbol	Question Asked	Example
Equal	==	Is operand 1 equal to operand 2?	x == y
Greater than	>	Is operand 1 greater than operand 2?	x > y
Less than	<	Is operand 1 less than operand 2?	x < y
Greater than or equal to	>=	Is operand 1 greater than or equal to operand 2?	x >= y
Less than or	<=	Is operand 1 less than or equal to operand 2?	x <= y
Not equal	!=	Is operand 1 not equal to operand 2?	x != y

TABLE 4.5 Relational operators in use

Expression	How It Reads	What It Evaluates To
5 == 1	Is 5 equal to 1?	0 (false)
5 > 1	Is 5 greater than 1?	1 (true)
5 != 1	Is 5 not equal to 1?	1 (true)
(5 + 10) == (3 * 5)	Is (5 + 10) equal to (3 * 5)?	1 (true)

Do	**Don't**
DO learn how C interprets true and false. When working with relational operators, true is equal to 1, and false is equal to 0.	**DON'T** confuse ==, the relational operator, with =, the assignment operator. This is one of the most common errors that C programmers make.

The `if` Statement

Relational operators are used mainly to construct the relational expressions used in `if` and `while` statements, covered in detail on Day 6, "Basic Program Control." For now, you will learn the basics of the `if` statement to show how relational operators are used to make *program control statements*.

You might be wondering what a program control statement is. Statements in a C program normally execute from top to bottom, in the same order as they appear in your source code file. A program control statement modifies the order of statement execution. Program control statements can cause other program statements to execute multiple times or to not execute at all, depending on the circumstances. The `if` statement is one of C's program control statements. Others, such as `do` and `while`, are covered on Day 6.

In its basic form, the `if` statement evaluates an expression and directs program execution depending on the result of that evaluation. The form of an `if` statement is as follows:

```
if (expression)
{
    statement;
}
```

If *expression* evaluates to true, *statement* is executed. If *expression* evaluates to false, *statement* is not executed. In either case, execution then passes to whatever code follows the `if` statement. You can say that execution of *statement* depends on the result of *expression*. Note that both the line `if (expression)` and the line *statement*; are considered to make up the complete `if` statement; they are not separate statements.

An `if` statement can control the execution of multiple statements through the use of a compound statement, or block. As defined earlier in today's lesson, a block is a group of two or more statements enclosed in braces. A block can be used anywhere a single statement can be used. Therefore, you could write an `if` statement as follows:

```
if (expression)
{
    statement1;
    statement2;
    /* additional code goes here */
    statementn;
}
```

4

Do	**Don't**
DO remember that if you program too much in one day, you'll get C sick.	
DO indent statements within a block to make them easier to read. This includes the statements within a block in an `if` statement.	

Caution

Don't make the mistake of putting a semicolon at the end of an `if` statement's expression. An `if` statement should end with the conditional statement that follows it. In the following,due to the semicolon *statement1* executes whether or not x equals 2. The semicolon causes each line to be evaluated as a separate statement, not together as intended:

```
if( x == 2);          /* semicolon does not belong!  */
statement1;
```

The compiler will generally not produce an error for this mistake.

In your programming, you will find that `if` statements are used most often with relational expressions; in other words, "Execute the following statement(s) only if such-and-such a condition is true." Here's an example:

```
if (x > y)
    y = x;
```

This code assigns the value of x to y only if x is greater than y. If x is not greater than y, no assignment takes place. Listing 4.3 illustrates the use of `if` statements.

LISTING 4.3   List0403.c: Demonstrates `if` statements

```
1:   /* Demonstrates the use of if statements */
2:
3:   #include <stdio.h>
4:
5:   int x, y;
6:
7:   int main( void )
8:   {
9:       /* Input the two values to be tested */
10:
11:      printf("\nInput an integer value for x: ");
12:      scanf("%d", &x);
```

LISTING 4.3   continued

```
13:        printf("\nInput an integer value for y: ");
14:        scanf("%d", &y);
15:
16:        /* Test values and print result */
17:
18:        if (x == y)
19:            printf("x is equal to y\n");
20:
21:        if (x > y)
22:            printf("x is greater than y\n");
23:
24:        if (x < y)
25:            printf("x is smaller than y\n");
26:
27:        return 0;
28:    }
```

INPUT/
OUTPUT

```
Input an integer value for x: 100

Input an integer value for y: 10
x is greater than y

Input an integer value for x: 10

Input an integer value for y: 100
x is smaller than y

Input an integer value for x: 10

Input an integer value for y: 10
x is equal to y
```

4

ANALYSIS   List0403.c shows three if statements in action (lines 18 through 25). Many of the lines in this program should be familiar. Line 5 declares two variables, x and y, and lines 11 through 14 prompt the user for values to be placed into these variables. Lines 18 through 25 use if statements to determine whether x is greater than, less than, or equal to y. Note that line 18 uses an if statement to see whether x is equal to y. Remember ==, the equal operator, means "is equal to" and should not be confused with =, the assignment operator. After the program checks to see whether the variables are equal, in line 21 it checks to see whether x is greater than y, followed by a check in line 24 to see whether x is less than y. If you think this is inefficient, you're right. In the next program, you will see how to avoid this inefficiency. For now, run the program with different values for x and y to see the results.

The else Clause

An if statement can optionally include an else clause. The else clause is included as
follows:

```
if (expression)
    statement1;
else
    statement2;
```

If *expression* evaluates to true, *statement1* is executed. If *expression* evaluates to
false, control goes to the else statement, *statement2,* which is then executed. Both
statement1 and *statement2* can be compound statements or blocks.

Listing 4.4 shows the program in Listing 4.3 rewritten to use an if statement with an
else clause.

LISTING 4.4   List0404.c. An if statement with an else clause

```
1:   /* Demonstrates the use of if statement with else clause */
2:
3:   #include <stdio.h>
4:
5:   int x, y;
6:
7:   int main( void )
8:   {
9:       /* Input the two values to be tested */
10:
11:      printf("\nInput an integer value for x: ");
12:      scanf("%d", &x);
13:      printf("\nInput an integer value for y: ");
14:      scanf("%d", &y);
15:
16:      /* Test values and print result */
17:
18:      if (x == y)
19:          printf("x is equal to y\n");
20:      else
21:          if (x > y)
22:              printf("x is greater than y\n");
23:          else
24:              printf("x is smaller than y\n");
```

LISTING 4.4   continued

```
25:
26:      return 0;
27: }
```

INPUT/
OUTPUT

```
Input an integer value for x: 99

Input an integer value for y: 8
x is greater than y

Input an integer value for x: 8

Input an integer value for y: 99

x is smaller than y

Input an integer value for x: 99
Input an integer value for y: 99
x is equal to y
```

ANALYSIS   Lines 18 through 24 are slightly different from the previous listing. Line 18 still checks to see whether x equals y. If x does equal y, x is equal to y appears on-screen, just as in Listing 4.3 (List0403.C). However, the program then ends, and lines 20 through 24 aren't executed. Line 21 is executed only if x is not equal to y, or, to be more accurate, if the expression "x equals y" is false. If x does not equal y, line 21 checks to see whether x is greater than y. If so, line 22 prints x is greater than y; otherwise (else), line 24 is executed.

Listing 4.4 uses a nested if statement. Nesting means to place (nest) one or more C statements inside another C statement. In the case of Listing 4.4, an if statement is part of the first if statement's else clause.

The if Statement

▼ SYNTAX

Form 1

```
if( expression )
{
    statement1;
}
next_statement;
```

This is the if statement in its simplest form. If expression is true, statement1 is executed. If expression is not true, statement1 is ignored.

Form 2

```
if( expression )
▼ {
```

```
▼        statement1;
    }
    else
    {
        statement2;
    }
    next_statement;
```

This is the most common form of the if statement. If *expression* is true, *statement1* is executed; otherwise, *statement2* is executed.

Form 3

```
if( expression1 )
    statement1;
else if( expression2 )
    statement2;
else
    statement3;
next_statement;
```

This is a nested if. If the first expression, *expression1*, is true, *statement1* is executed before the program continues with the *next_statement*. If the first expression is not true, the second expression, *expression2*, is checked. If the first expression is not true, and the second is true, *statement2* is executed. If both expressions are false, *statement3* is executed. Only one of the three statements is executed.

Example 1

```
if( salary > 45,0000 )
{
    tax = .30;
}
else
{
    tax = .25;
}
```

Example 2

```
if( age < 18 )
    printf("Minor");
else if( age < 65 )
    printf("Adult");
else
▲    printf( "Senior Citizen");
```

Evaluating Relational Expressions

Remember that expressions using relational operators are true C expressions that evaluate, by definition, to a value. Relational expressions evaluate to a value of either false (0) or true (1). Although the most common use of relational expressions is within `if` statements and other conditional constructions, they can be used as purely numeric values. This is illustrated in Listing 4.5.

LISTING 4.5 List0405.c. Evaluating relational expressions

```
 1:  /* Demonstrates the evaluation of relational expressions */
 2:
 3:  #include <stdio.h>
 4:
 5:  int a;
 6:
 7:  int main()
 8:  {
 9:      a = (5 == 5);          /* Evaluates to 1 */
10:      printf("\na = (5 == 5)\na = %d", a);
11:
12:      a = (5 != 5);          /* Evaluates to 0 */
13:      printf("\na = (5 != 5)\na = %d", a);
14:
15:      a = (12 == 12) + (5 != 1); /* Evaluates to 1 + 1 */
16:      printf("\na = (12 == 12) + (5 != 1)\na = %d\n", a);
17:      return 0;
18:  }
```

4

OUTPUT
```
a = (5 == 5)
a = 1
a = (5 != 5)
a = 0
a = (12 == 12) + (5 != 1)
a = 2
```

ANALYSIS The output from this listing might seem a little confusing at first. Remember, the most common mistake people make when using the relational operators is to use a single equal sign—the assignment operator—instead of a double equal sign. The following expression evaluates to 5 (and also assigns the value 5 to x):

```
x = 5
```

In contrast, the following expression evaluates to either 0 or 1 (depending on whether x is equal to 5) and doesn't change the value of x:

```
x == 5
```

If by mistake you write

```
if (x = 5)
   printf("x is equal to 5");
```

the message always prints because the expression being tested by the `if` statement always evaluates to true, no matter what the original value of x happens to be.

Looking at Listing 4.5, you can begin to understand why a takes on the values that it does. In line 9, the value 5 does equal 5, so true (1) is assigned to a. In line 12, the statement "5 does not equal 5" is false, so 0 is assigned to a.

To reiterate, the relational operators are used to create relational expressions that ask questions about relationships between expressions. The answer returned by a relational expression is a numeric value of either 1 (representing true) or 0 (representing false).

The Precedence of Relational Operators

Like the mathematical operators discussed earlier in today's lesson, the relational operators each have a precedence that determines the order in which they are performed in a multiple-operator expression. Similarly, you can use parentheses to modify precedence in expressions that use relational operators. The section "Operator Precedence Revisited" near the end of today's lesson lists the precedence of all of C's operators.

First, all the relational operators have a lower precedence than the mathematical operators. Thus, if you write the following, 2 is added to x, and the result is compared to y:

```
if (x + 2 > y)
```

This is the equivalent of the following line, which is a good example of using parentheses for the sake of clarity:

```
if ((x + 2) > y)
```

Although they aren't required by the C compiler, the parentheses surrounding (x + 2) make it clear that it is the sum of x and 2 that is to be compared with y.

There is also a two-level precedence within the relational operators, as shown in Table 4.6.

TABLE 4.6   The order of precedence of C's relational operators

Operators	Relative Precedence
< <= > >=	1
!= ==	2

Thus, if you write

```
x == y > z
```

it is the same as

```
x == (y > z)
```

because C first evaluates the expression y > z, resulting in a value of 0 or 1. Next, C determines whether x is equal to the 1 or 0 obtained in the first step. You will rarely, if ever, use this sort of construction, but you should know about it.

Do	Don't
	DON'T put assignment statements in the expression block of an if statement. This can be confusing to other people who look at your code. They might think it's a mistake and change your assignment to the logical equal statement.
	DON'T use the "not equal to" operator (!=) in an if statement containing an else. It's almost always clearer to use the "equal to" operator (==) with an else. For instance, the following code:

```
if ( x != 5 )
    statement1;
else
    statement2;
```

would be better written as this:

```
if (x == 5 )
    statement2;
else
    statement1;
```

4

The Logical Operators

Sometimes you might need to ask more than one relational question at once. For example, "If it's 7:00 a.m. and a weekday and not my vacation, then ring the alarm." C's logical operators let you combine two or more relational expressions into a single expression that evaluates to either true or false. Table 4.7 lists C's three logical operators.

TABLE 4.7 C's logical operators

Operator	Symbol	Example
AND	&&	exp1 && exp2
OR	||	exp1 || exp2
NOT	!	!exp1

The way these logical operators work is explained in Table 4.8.

TABLE 4.8 C's logical operators in use

Expression	What It Evaluates To
(exp1 && exp2)	True (1) only if both exp1 and exp2 are true; false (0) otherwise.
(exp1 || exp2)	True (1) if either exp1 or exp2 is true; false (0) only if both are false.
(!exp1)	False (0) if exp1 is true; true (1) if exp1 is false.

You can see that expressions that use the logical operators evaluate to either true or false depending on the true/false value of their operand(s). Table 4.9 shows code examples.

TABLE 4.9 Code examples of C's logical operators

Expression	What It Evaluates To
(5 == 5) && (6 != 2)	True (1), because both operands are true
(5 > 1) || (6 < 1)	True (1), because one operand is true
(2 == 1) && (5 == 5)	False (0), because one operand is false
!(5 == 4)	True (1), because the operand is false

You can create expressions that use multiple logical operators. For example, to ask the question "Is x equal to 2, 3, or 4?" you could write

```
(x == 2) || (x == 3) || (x == 4)
```

The logical operators often provide more than one way to ask a question. If x is an integer variable, the preceding question also could be written in either of the following ways:

```
(x > 1) && (x < 5)
```

```
(x >= 2) && (x <= 4)
```

More on True/False Values

You've seen that C's relational expressions evaluate to 0 to represent false and to 1 to represent true. It's important to be aware, however, that any numeric value is interpreted as either true or false when it is used in a C expression or statement that is expecting a logical value (that is, a true or false value). The rules for this are as follows:

- A value of zero represents false.
- Any nonzero value represents true.

This is illustrated by the following example, in which the value of x is printed:

```
x = 125;
if (x)
    printf("%d", x);
```

Because x has a nonzero value, the if statement interprets the expression (x) as true. You can further generalize this because, for any C expression, writing

(*expression*)

is equivalent to writing

(*expression* != 0)

Both evaluate to true if *expression* is nonzero and to false if *expression* is 0. Using the not (!) operator, you can also write

(!*expression*)

which is equivalent to

(*expression* == 0)

The Precedence of Operators

As you might have guessed, C's logical operators also have a precedence order, both among themselves and in relation to other operators. The ! operator has a precedence equal to the unary mathematical operators ++ and --. Thus, ! has a higher precedence than all the relational operators and all the binary mathematical operators.

In contrast, the && and || operators have much lower precedence, lower than all the mathematical and relational operators, although && has a higher precedence than ||. As with all of C's operators, parentheses can be used to modify the evaluation order when using the logical operators. Consider the following example:

You want to write a logical expression that makes three individual comparisons:

1. Is a less than b?

2. Is a less than c?

3. Is c less than d?

You want the entire logical expression to evaluate to true if condition 3 is true and if either condition 1 or condition 2 is true. You might write

a < b || a < c && c < d

However, this won't do what you intended. Because the && operator has higher precedence than ||, the expression is equivalent to

a < b || (a < c && c < d)

and evaluates to true if (a < b) is true, whether or not the relationships (a < c) and (c < d) are true. You need to write

(a < b || a < c) && c < d

which forces the || to be evaluated before the &&. This is shown in Listing 4.6, which evaluates the expression written both ways. The variables are set so that, if written correctly, the expression should evaluate to false (0).

LISTING 4.6 List0406.c. Logical operator precedence

```
1:    #include <stdio.h>
2:
3:    /* Initialize variables. Note that c is not less than d, */
4:    /* which is one of the conditions to test for. */
5:    /* Therefore, the entire expression should evaluate as false.*/
6:
7:    int a = 5, b = 6, c = 5, d = 1;
8:    int x;
9:
10:   int main( void )
11:   {
12:       /* Evaluate the expression without parentheses */
13:
14:       x = a < b || a < c && c < d;
15:       printf("\nWithout parentheses the expression evaluates as %d", x);
16:
17:       /* Evaluate the expression with parentheses */
18:
19:       x = (a < b || a < c) && c < d;
20:       printf("\nWith parentheses the expression evaluates as %d\n", x);
21:       return 0;
22:   }
```

OUTPUT
```
Without parentheses the expression evaluates as 1
With parentheses the expression evaluates as 0
```

ANALYSIS Enter and run this listing. Note that the two values printed for the expression are different. This program initializes four variables, in line 7, with values to be used in the comparisons. Line 8 declares x to be used to store and print the results. Lines 14 and 19 use the logical operators. Line 14 doesn't use parentheses, so the results are determined by operator precedence. In this case, the results aren't what you wanted. Line 19 uses parentheses to change the order in which the expressions are evaluated.

Compound Assignment Operators

C's compound assignment operators provide a shorthand method for combining a binary mathematical operation with an assignment operation. For example, say you want to increase the value of x by 5, or, in other words, add 5 to x and assign the result to x. You could write

```
x = x + 5;
```

Using a compound assignment operator, which you can think of as a shorthand method of assignment, you would write

```
x += 5;
```

In more general notation, the compound assignment operators have the following syntax (where op represents a binary operator):

exp1 op= *exp2*

This is equivalent to writing

exp1 = exp1 op *exp2*;

You can create compound assignment operators using the five binary mathematical operators discussed earlier in this chapter. Table 4.10 lists some examples.

TABLE 4.10   Examples of compound assignment operators

When You Write This	It Is Equivalent To This
x *= y	x = x * y
y -= z + 1	y = y - z + 1
a /= b	a = a / b
x += y / 8	x = x + y / 8
y %= 3	y = y % 3

The compound operators provide a convenient shorthand, the advantages of which are particularly evident when the variable on the left side of the assignment operator has a long name. As with all other assignment statements, a compound assignment statement is an expression and evaluates to the value assigned to the left side. Thus, executing the following statements results in both x and z having the value 14:

```
x = 12;
z = x += 2;
```

The Conditional Operator

The conditional operator is C's only *ternary* operator, meaning that it takes three operands. Its syntax is

```
exp1 ? exp2 : exp3;
```

If *exp1* evaluates to true (that is, nonzero), the entire expression evaluates to the value of *exp2*. If *exp1* evaluates to false (that is, zero), the entire expression evaluates as the value of *exp3*. For example, the following statement assigns the value 1 to x if y is true and assigns 100 to x if y is false:

```
x = y ? 1 : 100;
```

Likewise, to make z equal to the larger of x and y, you could write

```
z = (x > y) ? x : y;
```

Perhaps you've noticed that the conditional operator functions somewhat like an if statement. The preceding statement could also be written like this:

```
if (x > y)
z = x;
else
z = y;
```

The conditional operator can't be used in all situations in place of an if...else construction, but the conditional operator is more concise. The conditional operator can also be used in places you can't use an if statement, such as inside a call to another function such as a single printf() statement:

```
printf( "The larger value is %d", ((x > y) ? x : y) );
```

The Comma Operator

The comma is frequently used in C as a simple punctuation mark, serving to separate variable declarations, function arguments, and so on. In certain situations, the comma acts as an operator rather than just as a separator. You can form an expression by separating two sub-expressions with a comma. The result is as follows:

- Both expressions are evaluated, with the left expression being evaluated first.
- The entire expression evaluates to the value of the right expression.

For example, the following statement assigns the value of b to x, then increments a, and then increments b:

```
x = (a++ , b++);
```

Because the ++ operator is used in postfix mode, the value of b—before it is incremented—is assigned to x. Using parentheses is necessary because the comma operator has low precedence, even lower than the assignment operator.

As you'll learn in tomorrow's lesson, the most common use of the comma operator is in for statements.

Do	**Don't**
DO use the logical operators && and || instead of nesting if statements.	**DON'T** confuse the assignment operator (=) with the equal to (==) operator.

Operator Precedence Revisited

Table 4.11 lists the C operators in order of decreasing precedence. Operators on the same line have the same precedence.

TABLE 4.11   C Operator Precedence

Level	Operators
1	() [] -> .
2	! ~ ++ -- * *(indirection)* & *(address of)* (type)
	sizeof + *(unary)* - *(unary)*
3	* *(multiplication)* / %
4	+ -
5	<< >>
6	< <= > >=
7	== !=
8	& *(bitwise* AND*)*
9	^
10	|

TABLE 4.11 continued

Level	Operators
11	&&
12	||
13	?:
14	= += -= *= /= %= &= ^= |= <<= >>=
15	,

( ) *is the function operator;* [ ] *is the array operator.*

Tip

> This is a good table to keep referring to until you become familiar with the order of precedence. You might find that you need it later.

Summary

Today's lessons covered a lot of material. You learned what a C statement is, that white space doesn't matter to a C compiler, and that statements always end with a semicolon. You also learned that a compound statement (or block), which consists of two or more statements enclosed in braces, can be used anywhere a single statement can be used.

Many statements are made up of some combination of expressions and operators. Remember that an expression is anything that evaluates to a numeric value. Complex expressions can contain many simpler expressions, which are called sub-expressions.

Operators are C symbols that instruct the computer to perform an operation on one or more expressions. Some operators are unary, which means that they operate on a single operand. Most of C's operators are binary, however, operating on two operands. One operator, the conditional operator, is ternary. C's operators have a defined hierarchy of precedence that determines the order in which operations are performed in an expression that contains multiple operators.

The C operators covered in today's lesson fall into three categories:

- Mathematical operators perform arithmetic operations on their operands (for example, addition).

- Relational operators perform comparisons between their operands (for example, greater than).

- Logical operators operate on true/false expressions. Remember that C uses 0 and 1 to represent false and true, respectively, and that any nonzero value is interpreted as being true.

You've also been introduced to C's `if` statement, which lets you control program execution based on the evaluation of relational expressions.

Q&A

Q What effect do spaces and blank lines have on how a program runs?

A White space (lines, spaces, tabs) makes the code listing more readable. When the program is compiled, white space is stripped and thus has no effect on the executable program. For this reason, you should use white space to make your program easier to read.

Q Is it better to code a compound `if` statement or to nest multiple `if` statements?

A You should make your code easy to understand. If you nest `if` statements, they are evaluated as shown in this chapter. If you use a single compound statement, the expressions are evaluated only until the entire statement evaluates to false.

Q What is the difference between unary and binary operators?

A As the names imply, unary operators work with one variable, and binary operators work with two.

Q Is the subtraction operator (`-`) binary or unary?

A It's both! The compiler is smart enough to know which one you're using. It knows which form to use based on the number of variables in the expression that is used. In the following statement, it is unary:

```
x = -y;
```

versus the following binary use:

```
x = a - b;
```

Q Are negative numbers considered true or false?

A Remember that `0` is false, and any other value is true. This includes negative numbers.

Workshop

The Workshop provides quiz questions to help you solidify your understanding of the material covered and exercises to provide you with experience in using what you've learned.

Quiz

1. What is the following C statement called, and what is its meaning?

   ```
   x = 5 + 8;
   ```

2. What is an expression?

3. In an expression that contains multiple operators, what determines the order in which operations are performed?

4. If the variable x has the value 10, what are the values of x and a after each of the following statements is executed separately?

   ```
   a = x++;
   a = ++x;
   ```

5. To what value does the expression 10 % 3 evaluate?

6. To what value does the expression 5 + 3 * 8 / 2 + 2 evaluate?

7. Rewrite the expression in question 6, adding parentheses so that it evaluates to 16.

8. If an expression evaluates to false, what value does the expression have?

9. In the following list, which has higher precedence?

   a. == or <

   b. * or +

   c. != or ==

   d. >= or >

10. What are the compound assignment operators, and how are they useful?

Exercises

1. The following code is not well-written. Enter and compile it to see whether it works.

   ```
   #include <stdio.h>
   int x,y;int main(){ printf(
   "\nEnter two numbers");scanf(
   "%d %d",&x,&y);printf(
   "\n\n%d is bigger",(x>y)?x:y);return 0;}
   ```

2. Rewrite the code in exercise 1 to be more readable.

3. Change Listing 4.1 to count upward instead of downward.

4. Write an if statement that assigns the value of x to the variable y only if x is between 1 and 20. Leave y unchanged if x is not in that range.

5. Use the conditional operator to perform the same task as in exercise 4.

6. Rewrite the following nested `if` statements using a single `if` statement and logical operators.

```
if (x < 1)
   if ( x > 10 )
      statement;
```

7. To what value do each of the following expressions evaluate?

    a. `(1 + 2 * 3)`

    b. `10 % 3 * 3 - (1 + 2)`

    c. `((1 + 2) * 3)`

    d. `(5 == 5)`

    e. `(x = 5)`

8. If `x = 4`, `y = 6`, and `z = 2`, determine whether each of the following evaluates to true or false.

    a. `if( x == 4)`

    b. `if(x != y - z)`

    c. `if(z = 1)`

    d. `if(y)`

9. Write an `if` statement that determines whether someone is legally an adult (age 21), but not a senior citizen (age 65).

10. **BUG BUSTER:** Fix the following program so that it runs correctly:

```
/* a program with problems... */
#include <stdio.h>
int x= 1:
int main( void )
{
   if( x = 1);
      printf(" x equals 1" );
   otherwise
      printf(" x does not equal 1");
   return 0;
}
```

4

Type & Run 2

Find the Number

This is the second Type & Run section. Remember, the purpose of the listings in these sections is to give you something a little more functional than what you are getting in the chapters. This listing contains elements not yet explained in the book; however, we believe you will find the listing easy to follow. After you type in and run this program, take the time to experiment with the code. Make changes, recompile, and then rerun the program to see what happens. If you get any errors, make sure you entered it correctly.

LISTING T&R 2   find_nbr.c

```
 1:  /* Name:     find_nbr.c
 2:   * Purpose:  This program picks a random number and then
 3:   *           lets the user try to guess it
 4:   * Returns:  Nothing
 5:   */
 6:
 7:  #include <stdio.h>
 8:  #include <stdlib.h>
 9:  #include <time.h>
10:
11:  #define NO    0
12:  #define YES   1
```

LISTING T&R 2   continued

```
13:
14: int main( void )
15: {
16:     int guess_value = -1;
17:     int number;
18:     int nbr_of_guesses;
19:     int done = NO;
20:
21:     printf("\n\nGetting a Random number\n");
22:
23:     /* use the time to seed the random number generator */
24:     srand( (unsigned) time( NULL ) );
25:     number = rand();
26:
27:     nbr_of_guesses = 0;
28:     while ( done == NO )
29:     {
30:         printf("\nPick a number between 0 and %d> ", RAND_MAX);
31:         scanf( "%d", &guess_value );   /* Get a number */
32:
33:         nbr_of_guesses++;
34:
35:         if ( number == guess_value )
36:         {
37:             done = YES;
38:         }
39:         else
40:         if ( number < guess_value )
41:         {
42:             printf("\nYou guessed high!");
43:         }
44:         else
45:         {
46:             printf("\nYou guessed low!");
47:         }
48:     }
49:
50:     printf("\n\nCongratulations! You guessed right in %d Guesses!",
51:             nbr_of_guesses);
52:     printf("\n\nThe number was %d\n\n", number);
53:
54:     return 0;
55: }
```

This program is a simple guessing game. You're trying to find the number that the computer randomly generates. After each guess, the program will tell you if your guess was high or low. When you guess correctly, you will be congratulated and told how many guesses it took you.

If you want to cheat, you can add a line to the program that prints the answer after the program generates it. You might want to add this cheat into the program after you first compile it:

```
26:  printf( "The random number (answer) is: %d", number ); /* cheat */
```

This will let you see that the program works correctly. If you decide to give the running program to your friends, make sure to take the cheat line out!

DAY 5

Packaging Code in Functions

Functions are central to C programming and to the philosophy of C program design. You've already been introduced to some of C's library functions, which are complete functions supplied as part of your compiler. Today's lesson covers user-defined functions, which, as the name implies, are functions defined and created by you, the programmer. Today you will learn:

- What a function is and what its parts are
- About the advantages of structured programming with functions
- How to create a function
- How to declare local variables in a function
- How to return a value from a function to the program
- How to pass arguments to a function

What Is a Function?

Today you will learn the answer to the question "What is a function?" in two ways. First, you will learn what functions are, and then you will learn how they are used.

A Function Defined

NEW TERM   First the definition: A *function* is a named, independent section of C code that performs a specific task and optionally returns a value to the calling program. Now take a look at the parts of this definition:

- *A function is named.* Each function has a unique name. By using that name in another part of the program, you can execute the statements contained in the function. This is known as *calling* the function. A function can be called from within another function.

- *A function is independent.* A function can perform its task without interference from or interfering with other parts of the program.

- *A function performs a specific task.* This is the easy part of the definition. A task is a discrete job that your program must perform as part of its overall operation, such as sending a line of text to a printer, sorting an array into numerical order, or calculating a cube root.

- *A function can return a value to the calling program.* When your program calls a function, the statements it contains are executed. If you want them to, these statements can pass information back to the calling program.

That's all there is in regard to defining a function. Keep the previous definition in mind as you look at the next section.

A Function Illustrated

Listing 5.1 contains a user-defined function.

LISTING 5.1   cube.c. A program that uses a function to calculate the cube of a number

```
1:   /* Demonstrates a simple function */
2:   #include <stdio.h>
3:
4:   long cube(long x);
5:
6:   long input, answer;
7:
8:   int main( void )
9:   {
```

LISTING 5.1 continued

```
10:     printf("Enter an integer value: ");
11:     scanf("%d", &input);
12:     answer = cube(input);
13:     /* Note: %ld is the conversion specifier for */
14:     /* a long integer */
15:     printf("\nThe cube of %ld is %ld.\n", input, answer);
16:
17:     return 0;
18:  }
19:
20:  /* Function: cube() - Calculates the cubed value of a variable */
21:  long cube(long x)
22:  {
23:     long x_cubed;
24:
25:     x_cubed = x * x * x;
26:     return x_cubed;
27:  }
```

INPUT/ OUTPUT

```
Enter an integer value: 100

The cube of 100 is 1000000.

Enter an integer value: 9

The cube of 9 is 729.

Enter an integer value: 3

The cube of 3  is 27.
```

Note

The following analysis focuses on the components of the program that relate directly to the function rather than explaining the entire program.

ANALYSIS

NEW TERM

Line 4 contains the *function prototype,* a model for a function that will appear later in the program. A function's prototype contains the name of the function, a list of variables that must be passed to it, and the type of variable it returns, if any. Looking at line 4, you can tell that the function is named cube, that it requires a variable of the type long, and that it will return a value of type long. The variables to be passed to the function are called *arguments,* and they are enclosed in parentheses following the function's name. In this example, the function has a single argument: long x. The keyword before the name of the function indicates the type of variable the function returns. In this case, a variable of type long is returned.

Line 12 calls the function `cube` and passes the variable `input` to it as the function's argument. The function's return value is assigned to the variable `answer`. Notice that both `input` and `answer` are declared on line 6 as variables of type `long`. This matches the types used in the function prototype on line 4.

NEW TERM The function itself is called the *function definition*. In this case, the function is called `cube` and it is contained in lines 21 through 27. Like the prototype, the function definition has several parts. The function starts out with a function header on line 21. The *function header* is at the start of a function, and it gives the function's name (in this case, the name is `cube`). The header also gives the function's return type and describes its arguments. Note that the function header is identical to the function prototype (minus the semicolon).

The body of the function, lines 22 through 27, is enclosed in braces. The body contains statements, such as on line 25, that are executed whenever the function is called. Line 23 is a variable declaration that looks like the declarations you have seen before, with one difference: it's local. *Local* variables are declared within a function body. (Local declarations are discussed further on Day 12, "Understanding Variable Scope.") Finally, the function concludes with a `return` statement on line 26, which signals the end of the function. A `return` statement also passes a value back to the calling program. In this case, the value of the variable `x_cubed` is returned.

If you compare the structure of the `cube()` function with that of the `main()` function, you'll see that they are the same. `main()` is also a function. Other functions that you already have used are `printf()` and `scanf()`. Although `printf()` and `scanf()` are library functions (as opposed to user-defined functions), they are functions that can take arguments and return values just like the functions you create.

How a Function Works

NEW TERM A C program doesn't execute the statements in a function until the function is called by another part of the program. When a function is called, the program can send the function information in the form of one or more arguments. An *argument* is program data sent to the function. This data can be used by the function to perform its task. The statements in the function then execute, performing whatever task each was designed to do. When the function's statements have finished, execution passes back to the same location in the program that called the function. Functions can send information back to the program in the form of a return value.

Figure 5.1 shows a program with three functions, each of which is called once. Each time a function is called, execution passes to that function. When the function is finished, execution passes back to the place from which the function was called. A function can be called as many times as needed, and functions can be called in any order.

FIGURE 5.1

When a program calls a function, execution passes to the function and then back to the calling program.

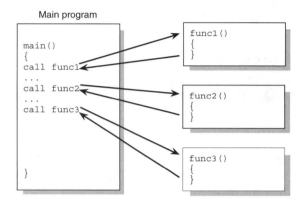

You now know what a function is and the importance of functions. Lessons on how to create and use your own functions follow.

▼ SYNTAX

Functions

Function Prototype

```
return-type function_name( arg-type name-1,...,arg-type name-n);
```

Function Definition

```
return-type function_name( arg-type name-1,...,arg-type name-n)
{
    /* statements; */
}
```

A *function prototype* provides the compiler with a description of a function that will be defined at a later point in the program. The prototype includes a return type indicating the type of variable that the function will return. It also includes the function name, which should describe what the function does. The prototype also contains the variable types of the arguments (`arg-type`) that will be passed to the function. Optionally, it can contain the names of the variables that will be passed. A prototype should always end with a semicolon.

A *function definition* is the actual function. The definition contains the code that will be executed. If the prototype contains the names of the variables, the first line of a function definition, called the *function header,* should be identical to the function prototype, with the exception of the semicolon. A function header shouldn't end with a semicolon. In

▼ addition, although the argument variable names were optional in the prototype, they must

5

▼ be included in the function header. Following the header is the function body, containing the statements that the function will perform. The function body should start with an opening bracket and end with a closing bracket. If the function return type is anything other than void, a return statement should be included, returning a value matching the return type.

Function Prototype Examples

```
double squared( double number );
void print_report( int report_number );
int get_menu_choice( voi
```

Function Definition Examples

```
double squared( double number )          /* function header */
{                                        /* opening bracket */
    return(  number * number );          /* function body   */
}                                        /* closing bracket */
void print_report( int report_number )
{
    if( report_number == 1 )
        puts( "Printing Report 1" );
    else
        puts( "Not printing Report 1" );
▲ }
```

Functions and Structured Programming

NEW TERM   By using functions in your C programs, you can practice *structured program-ming,* in which individual program tasks are performed by independent sections of program code. "Independent sections of program code" sounds just like part of the definition of functions given earlier, doesn't it? Functions and structured programming are closely related.

The Advantages of Structured Programming

Why is structured programming so great? There are two important reasons:

- It's easier to write a structured program, because complex programming problems are broken into a number of smaller, simpler tasks. Each task is performed by a function in which code and variables are isolated from the rest of the program. You can progress more quickly by dealing with these relatively simple tasks one at a time.

- It's easier to debug a structured program. If your program has a *bug* (something that causes it to work improperly), a structured design makes it easy to isolate the problem to a specific section of code (such as a specific function).

A related advantage of structured programming is the time you can save. If you write a function to perform a certain task in one program, you can quickly and easily use it in another program that needs to execute the same task. Even if the new program needs to accomplish a slightly different task, you'll often find that modifying a function you created earlier is easier than writing a new one from scratch. Consider how much you've used the two functions `printf()` and `scanf()` even though you probably haven't seen the code they contain. If your functions have been created to perform a single task, using them in other programs is much easier.

Planning a Structured Program

If you're going to write a structured program, you need to do some planning first. This planning should take place before you write a single line of code, and it usually can be done with nothing more than pencil and paper. Your plan should be a list of the specific tasks your program performs. Begin with a global idea of the program's function. If you were planning a program to manage your contacts (a list of names and addresses), what would you want the program to do? Here are some obvious things:

- Enter new names and addresses.
- Modify existing entries.
- Sort entries by last name.
- Print mailing labels.

With this list, you've divided the program into four main tasks, each of which can be assigned to a function. Now you can go a step further, dividing these tasks into subtasks. For example, the "Enter new names and addresses" task can be subdivided into these subtasks:

- Read the existing address list from disk.
- Prompt the user for one or more new entries.
- Add the new data to the list.
- Save the updated list to disk.

Likewise, the "Modify existing entries" task can be subdivided as follows:

- Read the existing address list from disk.
- Modify one or more entries.
- Save the updated list to disk.

You might have noticed that these two lists have two subtasks in common—the ones dealing with reading from and saving to disk. You can write one function to "Read the existing address list from disk," and that function can be called by both the "Enter new names and addresses" function and the "Modify existing entries" function. The same is true for "Save the updated list to disk."

Already you should see at least one advantage of structured programming. By carefully dividing the program into tasks, you can identify parts of the program that share common tasks. You can write "double-duty" disk access functions, saving yourself time and making your program smaller and more efficient.

This method of programming results in a *hierarchical,* or layered, program structure. Figure 5.2 illustrates hierarchical programming for the address list program.

FIGURE 5.2

A structured program is organized hierarchically.

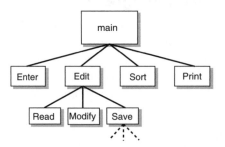

When you follow this planned approach, you quickly make a list of discrete tasks that your program needs to perform. Then you can tackle the tasks one at a time, giving all your attention to one relatively simple task. When that function is written and working properly, you can move on to the next task. Before you know it, your program starts to take shape.

The Top-Down Approach

By using structured programming, C programmers take the *top-down approach.* You saw this illustrated in Figure 5.2, where the program's structure resembles an inverted tree. Many times, most of the real work of the program is performed by the functions at the tips of the "branches." The functions closer to the "trunk" primarily direct program execution among these functions.

As a result, many C programs have a small amount of code in the main body of the program—that is, in main(). The bulk of the program's code is found in functions. In main(), all you might find are a few dozen lines of code that direct program execution among the functions. Often, a menu is presented to the person using the program. Program execution is branched according to the user's choices. Each branch of the menu uses a different function.

Note Using menus is a good approach to program design. Day 13, "Advanced Program Control," shows how you can use the `switch` statement to create a versatile menu-driven system.

Now that you know what functions are and why they're so important, the time has come for you to learn how to write your own.

Do	Don't
DO plan before starting to code. By determining your program's structure ahead of time, you can save time writing the code and debugging it.	**DON'T** try to do everything in one function. A single function should perform a single task, such as reading information from a file.

Writing a Function

The first step in writing a function is to know what you want the function to do. Once you know that, the actual mechanics of writing the function aren't particularly difficult.

The Function Header

The first line of every function is the function header, which has three components, each serving a specific function. They are shown in Figure 5.3 and explained in the following sections.

FIGURE 5.3

The three components of a function header.

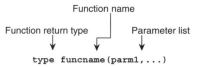

```
type funcname(parm1,...)
```

Function return type — Function name — Parameter list

The Function Return Type

The return type of a function specifies the data type that the function returns to the calling program. The function return type can be any of C's data types. This includes `char`, `int`, `long`, `float`, or `double`. You can also define a function that doesn't return a value by using a return type of `void`. Here are some examples:

```
int func1(...)      /* Returns a type int.   */
float func2(...)    /* Returns a type float. */
void func3(...)     /* Returns nothing.      */
```

In these examples, you can see that *func1* returns an integer, *func2* returns a floating-point number, and *func3* doesn't return anything.

The Function Name

You can name a function anything you like, as long as you follow the rules for C variable names (given in Day 3, "Storing Data: Variables and Constants"). In C programs, a function name must be unique (not assigned to any other function or variable). It's a good idea to assign a name that reflects what the function does.

The Parameter List

Many functions use *arguments*, which are values passed to the function when it's called. A function needs to know what kinds of arguments to expect—the data type of each argument. You can pass to a function any of C's data types. Argument type information is provided in the function header by a parameter list.

For each argument that is passed to the function, the parameter list must contain one entry. This entry specifies the data type and the name of the parameter. For example, here's the header from the function in Listing 5.1:

```
long cube(long x)
```

The parameter list consists of `long x`, specifying that this function takes one type `long` argument, represented by the parameter x. If there is more than one parameter, each must be separated by a comma. The function header

```
void func1(int x, float y, char z)
```

specifies a function with three arguments: a type `int` named x, a type `float` named y, and a type `char` named z. Some functions take no arguments, in which case the parameter list should consist of `void`, like this:

```
int func2(void)
```

Note You do not place a semicolon at the end of a function header. If you mistakenly include one, the compiler will generate an error message.

Sometimes confusion arises about the distinction between a parameter and an argument. A *parameter* is an entry in a function header; it serves as a "placeholder" for an argument. A function's parameters are fixed; they do not change during program execution.

An *argument* is an actual value passed to the function by the calling program. Each time a function is called, it can be passed different arguments. In C, a function must be passed the same number and type of arguments each time it's called, but the argument values can be different. In the function, the argument is accessed by using the corresponding parameter name.

An example will make this clearer. Listing 5.2 presents a very simple program with one function that is called twice.

LISTING 5.2   List0502.c. The difference between arguments and parameters

```
1:    /* Illustrates the difference between arguments and parameters. */
2:
3:    #include <stdio.h>
4:
5:    float x = 3.5, y = 65.11, z;
6:
7:    float half_of(float k);
8:
9:    int main( void )
10:   {
11:       /* In this call, x is the argument to half_of(). */
12:       z = half_of(x);
13:       printf("The value of z = %f\n", z);
14:
15:       /* In this call, y is the argument to half_of(). */
16:       z = half_of(y);
17:       printf("The value of z = %f\n", z);
18:
19:       return 0;
20:   }
21:
22:   float half_of(float k)
23:   {
24:       /* k is the parameter. Each time half_of() is called, */
25:       /* k has the value that was passed as an argument. */
26:
27:       return (k/2);
28:   }
```

OUTPUT
```
The value of z = 1.750000
The value of z = 32.555000
```

Figure 5.4 shows the relationship between arguments and parameters.

ANALYSIS   Looking at Listing 5.2, you can see that the half_of() function prototype is declared on line 7. Lines 12 and 16 call half_of(), and lines 22 through 28 contain the actual function. Lines 12 and 16 each send a different argument to half_of(). Line 12 sends x, which contains a value of 3.5, and line 16 sends y, which contains a value of 65.11. When the program runs, it prints the correct number for each. The values in x and y are passed into the argument k of half_of(). This is like copying the values from x to k, and then from y to k. half_of() then returns this value after dividing it by 2 (line 27).

FIGURE 5.4

Each time a function is called, the arguments are passed to the function's parameters.

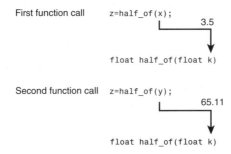

First function call   `z=half_of(x);`

3.5

`float half_of(float k)`

Second function call   `z=half_of(y);`

65.11

`float half_of(float k)`

Do	**Don't**
DO use a function name that describes the purpose of the function.	**DON'T** pass values to a function that it doesn't need.
DO make sure that the data type of the arguments you pass to a function match the data types of the parameters of the function.	**DON'T** try to pass fewer (or more) arguments to a function than there are parameters. In C programs, the number of arguments passed much match the number of parameters.

The Function Body

The *function body* is enclosed in braces, and it immediately follows the function header. It's in the function body that the real work is done. When a function is called, execution begins at the start of the body and terminates (returns to the calling program) when a return statement is encountered or when execution reaches the closing brace.

Local Variables

NEW TERM   You can declare variables within the body of a function. Variables declared in a function are called *local variables*. The term *local* means that the variables are private to that particular function and are distinct from other variables of the same name declared elsewhere in the program. This will be explained shortly; for now, you should learn how to declare local variables.

A local variable is declared like any other variable, using the same variable types and rules for names that you learned on Day 3. Local variables can also be initialized when they are declared. You can declare any of C's variable types in a function. Here is an example of four local variables being declared within a function:

```
int func1(int y)
{
    int a, b = 10;
    float rate;
    double cost = 12.55;
    /* function code goes here... */
}
```

The preceding declarations create the local variables a, b, rate, and cost, which can be used by the code in the function. Note that the function parameters are considered to be variable declarations, so the variables, if any, in the function's parameter list also are available.

When you declare and use a variable in a function, it is totally separate and distinct from any other variables that are declared elsewhere in the program. This is true even if the variables have the same name. Listing 5.3 demonstrates this independence.

LISTING 5.3   var.c. A demonstration of local variables

```
 1:   /* Demonstrates local variables. */
 2:
 3:   #include <stdio.h>
 4:
 5:   int x = 1, y = 2;
 6:
 7:   void demo(void);
 8:
 9:   int main( void )
10:   {
11:     printf("\nBefore calling demo(), x = %d and y = %d.", x, y);
12:     demo();
13:     printf("\nAfter calling demo(), x = %d and y = %d\n.", x, y);
14:
15:     return 0;
16:   }
17:
18:   void demo(void)
19:   {
20:       /* Declare and initialize two local variables. */
21:
22:       int x = 88, y = 99;
23:
24:       /* Display their values. */
25:
26:       printf("\nWithin demo(), x = %d and y = %d.", x, y);
27:   }
```

5

OUTPUT
```
Before calling demo(), x = 1 and y = 2.
Within demo(), x = 88 and y = 99.
After calling demo(), x = 1 and y = 2.
```

ANALYSIS Listing 5.3 is similar to the previous programs you have seen today. Line 5 declares variables x and y. These are declared outside of any functions and therefore are considered global. Line 7 contains the prototype for the demonstration function, named demo(). It doesn't take any parameters, so it has void in the prototype. It also doesn't return any values, giving it a return type of void. Line 9 starts the main() function, which is very simple. First, printf() is called on line 11 to display the values of x and y, and then the demo() function is called. Notice that demo() declares its own local versions of x and y on line 22. Line 26 shows that the local variables take precedence over any others. After the demo function is called, line 13 again prints the values of x and y. Because you are no longer in demo(), the original global values are printed.

As you can see, local variables x and y in the function are totally independent from the global variables x and y declared outside the function. Three rules govern the use of variables in functions:

- To use a variable in a function, you must declare it in the function header or the function body (except for global variables, which are covered on Day 12).

- In order for a function to obtain a value from the calling program, the value must be passed as an argument.

- In order for a calling program to obtain a value from a function, the value must be explicitly returned from the function.

To be honest, these "rules" are not strictly applied, because you'll learn how to get around them later in this book. However, follow these rules for now, and you should stay out of trouble.

Keeping the function's variables separate from other program variables is one way in which functions are independent. A function can perform any sort of data manipulation you want, using its own set of local variables. There's no worry that these manipulations will have an unintended effect on another part of the program.

Function Statements

There is essentially no limitation on the statements that can be included within a function. The only thing you can't do inside a function is to define another function. You can, however, use all other C statements, including loops (these are covered on Day 6, "Controlling Your Program's Order of Execution"), if statements, and assignment statements. You can call library functions and other user-defined functions.

What about function length? C places no length restriction on functions, but as a matter of practicality, you should keep your functions relatively short. Remember that in structured programming, each function is supposed to perform a relatively simple task. If you find that a function is getting long, perhaps you're trying to perform a task too complex for one function alone. It probably can be broken into two or more smaller functions.

How long is too long? There's no definite answer to that question, but in practical experience it's rare to find a function longer than 25 or 30 lines of actual code. Functions with more lines of actual code will generally be doing more than one thing. You have to use your own judgment. Some programming tasks require longer functions, whereas many functions are only a few lines long. As you gain programming experience, you will become more adept at determining what should and shouldn't be broken into smaller functions.

Returning a Value

To return a value from a function, you use the `return` keyword, followed by a C expression. When execution reaches a `return` statement, the expression is evaluated, and execution passes the value back to the calling program. The return value of the function is the value of the expression. Consider this function:

```
int func1(int var)
{
    int x;
    /* Function code goes here... */
    return x;
}
```

When this function is called, the statements in the function body execute up to the `return` statement. The `return` terminates the function and returns the value of x to the calling program. The expression to the right of the `return` keyword can be any valid C expression.

A function can contain multiple `return` statements. The first `return` executed is the only one that has any effect. Multiple `return` statements can be an efficient way to return different values from a function, as demonstrated in Listing 5.4.

LISTING 5.4   returns.c. Using multiple `return` statements in a function

```
1:   /* Demonstrates using multiple return statements in a function. */
2:
3:   #include <stdio.h>
4:
5:   int x, y, z;
6:
7:   int larger_of( int a, int b);
```

LISTING **5.4**   continued

```
 8:
 9:  int main( void )
10:  {
11:      puts("Enter two different integer values: ");
12:      scanf("%d%d", &x, &y);
13:
14:      z = larger_of(x,y);
15:
16:      printf("\nThe larger value is %d.", z);
17:
18:      return 0;
19:  }
20:
21:  int larger_of( int a, int b)
22:  {
23:      if (a > b)
24:          return a;
25:      else
26:          return b;
27:  }
```

OUTPUT
Enter two different integer values:
200 300

The larger value is 300.

INPUT/
OUTPUT
Enter two different integer values:
300
200

The larger value is 300.

 ANALYSIS As in other examples, Listing 5.4 starts with a comment to describe what the program does (line 1). The stdio.h header file is included for the standard input/output functions that allow the program to display information to the screen and get user input. Line 7 is the function prototype for larger_of(). Notice that larger_of() takes two int variables for parameters and returns an int. Line 14 calls larger_of() with x and y. This function contains the multiple return statements. Using an if statement, the function checks to see whether a is bigger than b on line 23. If it is, line 24 executes a return statement, and the function immediately ends. Lines 25 and 26 are ignored in this case. If a isn't bigger than b, line 24 is skipped, the else clause is instigated, and the return on line 26 executes. You should be able to see that, depending on the arguments passed to the function larger_of(), either the first or the second return statement is executed, and the appropriate value is passed back to the calling function.

One final note on this program. Line 11 is a new function that you haven't seen before. puts() —meaning *put string*—is a simple function that displays a string to the standard output, usually the computer screen. (Strings are covered on Day 10, "Working with Characters and Strings." For now, know that they are just quoted text.)

Remember that a function's return value has a type that is specified in the function header and function prototype. The value returned by the function must be of the same type, or the compiler generates an error message.

> **Note**
>
> Structured programming suggests that you have only one entry and one exit in a function. This means that you should try to have only one return statement within your function. At times, however, a program might be much easier to read and maintain with more than one return statement. In such cases, maintainability should take precedence.

The Function Prototype

A program should include a prototype for each function it uses. You saw an example of a function prototype on line 4 of Listing 5.1, and there have been function prototypes in the other listings as well. What is a function prototype, and why is it needed?

You can see from the earlier examples that the prototype for a function is identical to the function header, with a semicolon added at the end. Like the function header, the function prototype includes information about the function's return type, name, and parameters. The prototype's job is to tell the compiler about the function. By providing information on the function's return type, name, and parameters, the compiler can check every time your source code calls the function and verify that you're passing the correct number and type of arguments and using the return value correctly. If there's a mismatch, the compiler generates an error message.

Strictly speaking, a function prototype doesn't need to exactly match the function header. The parameter names can be different, as long as they are the same type, number, and in the same order. There's no reason for the header and prototype not to match; having them identical makes source code easier to understand. Matching the two also makes writing a program easier. When you complete a function definition, use your editor's cut-and-paste feature to copy the function header and create the prototype. Be sure to add a semicolon at the end of the prototype.

Where should function prototypes be placed in your source code? They should be placed before the start of the first function. For readability, it's best to group all prototypes in one location.

5

Do	**Don't**
DO use local variables whenever possible. **DO** limit each function to a single task.	**DON'T** try to return a value that has a type different from the function's type. **DON'T** let functions get too long. If a function starts getting long, try to break it into separate, smaller tasks. **DON'T** have multiple return statements if they aren't needed. You should try to have one return when possible; however, sometimes having multiple return statements is easier and clearer.

Passing Arguments to a Function

To pass arguments to a function, you list them in parentheses following the function name. The number of arguments and the type of each argument must match the parameters in the function header and prototype. For example, if a function is defined to take two type int arguments, you must pass it exactly two int arguments—no more, no less—and no other type. If you try to pass a function an incorrect number and/or type of argument, the compiler will detect it, based on the information in the function prototype.

If the function takes multiple arguments, the arguments listed in the function call are assigned to the function parameters in order: the first argument to the first parameter, the second argument to the second parameter, and so on, as shown in Figure 5.5.

FIGURE 5.5

Multiple arguments are assigned to function parameters in order.

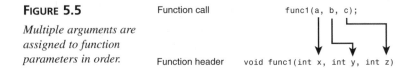

Function call   `func1(a, b, c);`

Function header   `void func1(int x, int y, int z)`

Each argument can be any valid C expression: a constant, a variable, a mathematical or logical expression, or even another function (one with a return value). For example, if `half()`, `square()`, and `third()` are all functions with return values, you could write

`x = half(third(square(half(y))));`

The program first calls `half()`, passing it `y` as an argument. When execution returns from `half()`, the program calls `square()`, passing `half()`'s return value as an argument. Next, `third()` is called with `square()`'s return value as the argument. Then, `half()` is called again, this time with `third()`'s return value as an argument. Finally, `half()`'s return value is assigned to the variable x. The following is an equivalent piece of code:

```
a = half(y);
b = square(a);
c = third(b);
x = half(c);
```

Calling Functions

There are two ways to call a function. Any function can be called by simply using its name and argument list alone in a statement, as in the following example. If the function has a return value, it is discarded.

```
wait(12);
```

The second method can be used only with functions that have a return value. Because these functions evaluate to a value (that is, their return value), they are valid C expressions and can be used anywhere a C expression can be used. You've already seen an expression with a return value used as the right side of an assignment statement. Here are some more examples.

In the following example, `half_of()` is a parameter of a function:

```
printf("Half of %d is %d.", x, half_of(x));
```

First, the function `half_of()` is called with the value of x, and then `printf()` is called using the values `"Half of %d is %d."`, x, and `half_of(x)`.

In this second example, multiple functions are being used in an expression:

```
y = half_of(x) + half_of(z);
```

Although `half_of()` is used twice, the second call could have been any other function. The following code shows the same statement, but not all on one line:

```
a = half_of(x);
b = half_of(z);
y = a + b;
```

The following final two examples show effective ways to use the return values of functions. Here, a function is being used with the `if` statement:

```
if ( half_of(x) > 10 )
{
    /* statements; */        /* these could be any statements! */
}
```

5

If the return value of the function meets the criteria (in this case, if `half_of()` returns a value greater than 10), the `if` statement is true, and its statements are executed. If the returned value doesn't meet the criteria, the statements in the `if` are not executed.

The following example is even better:

```
if ( do_a_process() != OKAY )
{
    /* statements; */          /* do error routine */
}
```

Again, actual statements are not provided, nor is `do_a_process()` a real function; however, this is an important example. The return value of a process is checked to see whether it ran correctly. If it didn't, the statements take care of any error handling or cleanup. This is commonly used with accessing information in files, comparing values, and allocating memory.

> **Caution**
>
> If you try to use a function with a `void` return type as an expression, the compiler generates an error message.

Do	**Don't**
DO pass parameters to functions in order to make the function generic and thus reusable.	**DON'T** make an individual statement confusing by putting a bunch of functions in it. You should put functions into your statements only if they don't make the code more confusing.
DO take advantage of the ability to put functions into expressions.	

Recursion

NEW TERM The term *recursion* refers to a situation in which a function calls itself either directly or indirectly. *Indirect recursion* occurs when one function calls another function that then calls the first function. C allows recursive functions, and they can be useful in some situations.

For example, recursion can be used to calculate the factorial of a number. The factorial of a number x is written x! and is calculated as follows:

```
x! = x * (x-1) * (x-2) * (x-3) * ... * (2) * 1
```

However, you can also calculate x! like this:

x! = x * (x-1)!

Going one step further, you can calculate (x-1)! using the same procedure:

(x-1)! = (x-1) * (x-2)!

You continue calculating recursively until you're down to a value of 1, in which case you're finished. The program in Listing 5.5 uses a recursive function to calculate factorials. Because the program uses unsigned integers, it's limited to an input value of 8; the factorial of 9 and larger values are outside the allowed range for integers.

LISTING 5.5   recurse.c. Using a recursive function to calculate factorials

```
 1:    /* Demonstrates function recursion. Calculates the */
 2:    /* factorial of a number. */
 3:
 4:    #include <stdio.h>
 5:
 6:    unsigned int f, x;
 7:    unsigned int factorial(unsigned int a);
 8:
 9:    int main( void )
10:    {
11:        puts("Enter an integer value between 1 and 8: ");
12:        scanf("%d", &x);
13:
14:        if( x > 8 || x < 1)
15:        {
16:            printf("Only values from 1 to 8 are acceptable!");
17:        }
18:        else
19:        {
20:            f = factorial(x);
21:            printf("%u factorial equals %u\n", x, f);
22:        }
23:
24:        return 0;
25:    }
26:
27:    unsigned int factorial(unsigned int a)
28:    {
29:        if (a == 1)
30:            return 1;
31:        else
32:        {
33:            a *= factorial(a-1);
34:            return a;
35:        }
36:    }
```

5

**INPUT/
OUTPUT**
```
Enter an integer value between 1 and 8:
6
6 factorial equals 720
```

ANALYSIS The first half of this program is like many of the other programs you have worked with so far. It starts with comments on lines 1 and 2. On line 4, the appropriate header file is included for the input/output routines. Line 6 declares a couple of unsigned integer values. Line 7 is a function prototype for the factorial function. Notice that it takes an unsigned int as its parameter and returns an unsigned int. Lines 9 through 25 are the main() function. Lines 11 and 12 print a message asking for a value from 1 to 8 and then accept an entered value.

Lines 14 through 22 show an interesting if statement. Because a value greater than 8 causes a problem, this if statement checks the value. If it's greater than 8, an error message is printed; otherwise, the program figures the factorial on line 20 and prints the result on line 21. When you know there could be a problem, such as a limit on the size of a number, add code to detect the problem and prevent it.

The recursive function, factorial(), is located on lines 27 through 36. The value passed is assigned to a. On line 29, the value of a is checked. If it's 1, the program returns the value of 1. If the value isn't 1, a is set equal to itself times the value of factorial(a-1). The program calls the factorial function again, but this time the value of a is (a-1). If (a-1) isn't equal to 1, factorial() is called again with ((a-1)-1), which is the same as (a-2). This process continues until the if statement on line 29 is true. If the value of the factorial is 3, the factorial is evaluated to the following:

```
3 * (3-1) * ((3-1)-1)
```

Do	Don't
DO understand and work with recursion before you use it in a program you are going to distribute.	DON'T use recursion if there will be several iterations. (An iteration is the repetition of a program statement.) Recursion uses many resources because the function has to remember where it is.

Where the Functions Belong

You might be wondering where in your source code you should place your function definitions. For now, they should go in the same source code file as main() and after the end of main(). Figure 5.6 shows the basic structure of a program that uses functions.

FIGURE 5.6

Place your function prototypes before your function definitions. Generally the proto-types are near the top of your listing.

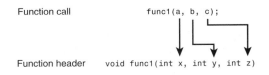

You can keep your user-defined functions in a separate source-code file, apart from main(). This technique is useful with large programs and when you want to use the same set of functions in more than one program. This technique is discussed on Day 21, "Advanced Compiler Use."

Working with Inline Functions

There is a special type of function that can be created in C. These are inline functions. Older versions of C will most likely not support inline functions; however, compilers that support the C-99 standard should have support.

Inline functions are generally small functions. When the compiler executes, it will try to execute an inline function in the fastest manner possible. This may be done by copying the function's code into the calling function. Because execution of this code would be placed right into the calling function's code it is called "inline."

A function is made inline by using the inline keyword. The following declares an inline function called toInches:

```
inline int toInches( int Feet )
{
    return (Feet/12);
}
```

When the toInches() function is used, the compiler will do its best to optimize it to be fast. Be aware that although the general assumption is that the code will simply be moved into the calling function, this is not a guarantee. The only guarantee is that the compiler will do its best to optimize the use of the code in this function. You will use inline functions the same way as any other function.

Summary

Today's lesson introduced you to functions, an important part of C programming. Functions are independent sections of code that perform specific tasks. When your pro-gram needs a task performed, it calls the function that performs that task. The use of functions is essential for structured programming—a method of program design that emphasizes a modular, top-down approach. Structured programming creates more efficient programs and also is much easier for you, the programmer, to use.

You also learned that a function consists of a header and a body. The header includes information about the function's return type, name, and parameters. The body contains local variable declarations and the C statements that are executed when the function is called. Finally, you saw that local variables—those declared within a function—are totally independent of any other program variables declared elsewhere.

Q&A

Q What if I need to return more than one value from a function?

A Many times you will need to return more than one value from a function, or, more commonly, you will want to change a value you send to the function and keep the change after the function ends. This process is covered on Day 18, "Getting More from Functions."

Q How do I know what a good function name is?

A A good function name describes as specifically as possible what the function does.

Q When variables are declared at the top of the listing, before `main()`, they can be used anywhere, but local variables can be used only in the specific function. Why not just declare everything before `main()` as global?

A Variable scope is discussed in more detail on Day 12. You will learn at that time why it is better to declare variables locally within functions instead of globally before `main()`.

Q What other ways are there to use recursion?

A The factorial function is a prime example of using recursion. The factorial number is needed in many statistical calculations. Recursion is just a loop; however, it has one difference from other loops. With recursion, each time a recursive function is called, a new set of variables is created. This is not true of the other loops that you will learn about in the next chapter.

Q Does `main()` have to be the first function in a program?

A No. It is a standard in C that the `main()` function is the first function to execute; however, it can be placed anywhere in your source file. Most people place it either first or last so that it's easy to locate.

Q What are member functions?

A Member functions are special functions used in object-oriented languages such as C#, C++, and Java. They are part of a class—which is a special type of structure used in object-oriented languages. You'll learn more about member functions in the bonus week.

Workshop

The Workshop provides quiz questions to help you solidify your understanding of the material covered and exercises to provide you with experience in using what you've learned.

Quiz

1. Will you use structured programming when writing your C programs?
2. How does structured programming work?
3. How do C functions fit into structured programming?
4. What must be the first line of a function definition, and what information does it contain?
5. How many values can a function return?
6. If a function doesn't return a value, what type should it be declared?
7. What's the difference between a function definition and a function prototype?
8. What is a local variable?
9. How are local variables special?
10. Where should the main() function be placed?

Exercises

1. Write a header for a function named do_it() that takes three type char arguments and returns a type float to the calling program.
2. Write a header for a function named print_a_number() that takes a single type int argument and doesn't return anything to the calling program.
3. What type value do the following functions return?

   a. int print_error(float err_nbr);

   b. long read_record(int rec_nbr, int size);

4. **BUG BUSTER:** What's wrong with the following listing?

   ```
   #include <stdio.h>
   ```

5

```
void print_msg( void );
int main( void )
{
    print_msg( "This is a message to print" );
    return 0;
}
void print_msg( void )
{
    puts( "This is a message to print" );
    return 0;
}
```

5. **BUG BUSTER:** What's wrong with the following function definition?

```
int twice(int y);
{
    return (2 * y);
}
```

6. Rewrite Listing 5.4 so that it needs only one `return` statement in the `larger_of()` function.

7. Write a function that receives two numbers as arguments and returns the value of their product.

8. Write a function that receives two numbers as arguments. The function should divide the first number by the second. Don't divide by the second number if it's zero. (Hint: Use an `if` statement.)

9. Write a function that calls the functions in exercises 7 and 8.

10. Write a program that uses a function to find the average of five type `float` values entered by the user.

11. Write a recursive function to take the value 3 to the power of another number. For example, if 4 is passed, the function will return 81.

DAY **6**

Basic Program Control

Day 4, "Statements, Expressions, and Operators," covered the `if` statement, which gives you some control over the flow of your programs. Many times, though, you need more than just the ability to make true and false decisions. Today's lesson introduces three new ways to control the flow of the program. Today you will learn:

- How to use simple arrays
- How to use `for`, `while`, and `do...while` loops to execute statements multiple times
- How you can nest program control statements

This is not intended to be a complete treatment of these topics, but rather, today's lesson provides enough information for you to be able to start writing real programs. These topics are covered in greater detail on Day 13, "Advanced Program Control."

Arrays: The Basics

Before we cover the `for` statement, you should take a short detour to learn about the basics of arrays. (See Day 8, "Using Numeric Arrays," for a complete treatment of arrays.) The `for` statement and arrays are closely linked in C, so it's difficult to define one without explaining the other. To help you understand the arrays used in the `for` statement examples to come, a quick treatment of arrays follows.

 An *array* is an indexed group of data storage locations that have the same name and are distinguished from each other by a *subscript,* or *index*—a number following the variable name, enclosed in brackets. (This will become clearer as you continue.) Like other C variables, arrays must be declared. An array declaration includes both the data type and the size of the array (the number of elements in the array). For example, the following statement declares an array named `data` that is type `int` and has 1,000 elements:

```
int data[1000];
```

The individual elements are referred to by subscript as `data[0]` through `data[999]`. The first element is `data[0]`, not `data[1]`. In other languages, such as BASIC, the first element of an array may be 1; this is not true in C. In C, the first element is indexed with zero.

> **Note**
>
> One way to look at the index number is as an offset. For the first item in the array, you want to be offset by nothing (or zero). For the second item you are offset by one item so the index is one.

Each element of this array is equivalent to a normal integer variable and can be used the same way. The subscript of an array can be another C variable, as in this example:

```
int data[1000];
int index;
index = 100;
data[index] = 12;      /* The same as data[100] = 12 */
```

This has been a quick introduction to arrays. However, you should now be able to understand how arrays are used in the program examples later in this chapter. If every detail of arrays isn't clear to you, don't worry. You will learn more about arrays on Day 8.

Do	DON'T
	DON'T declare arrays with subscripts larger than you will need. It wastes memory.
	DON'T forget that in C, arrays are referenced starting with subscript 0, not 1.

Controlling Program Execution

The default order of execution in a C program is top-down. Execution starts at the beginning of the `main()` function and progresses, statement by statement, until the end of `main()` is reached. However, this sequential order is rarely encountered in real C programs. The C language includes a variety of program control statements that let you control the order of program execution. You have already learned how to use C's fundamental decision operator, the `if` statement, so now it's time to explore three additional control statements you will find useful:

- The `for` statement
- The `while` statement
- The `do...while` statement

The `for` Statement

The `for` statement is a C programming construct that executes a block of one or more statements a certain number of times. It is sometimes called the `for` *loop* because program execution typically loops through the statement more than once. You've seen a few `for` statements used in programming examples earlier in this book. Now you're ready to see how the `for` statement works.

A `for` statement has the following structure:

```
for ( initial; condition; increment )
    statement;
```

initial, *condition*, and *increment* are all C expressions, and *statement* is a single or compound C statement. When a `for` statement is encountered during program execution, the following events occur:

1. The expression *initial* is evaluated. *initial* is usually an assignment statement that sets a variable to a particular value.

2. The expression *condition* is evaluated. *condition* is typically a relational expression.

6

3. If *condition* evaluates to false (that is, it is equal to zero), the for statement terminates and execution passes to the first statement following *statement*.

4. If *condition* evaluates to true (that is, it is equal to a nonzero value), the C statement(s) in *statement* are executed.

5. The expression *increment* is evaluated, and execution returns to step 2.

Figure 6.1 shows the operation of a for statement. Note that *statement* never executes if *condition* is false the first time it's evaluated.

FIGURE 6.1

A schematic representation of a for *statement.*

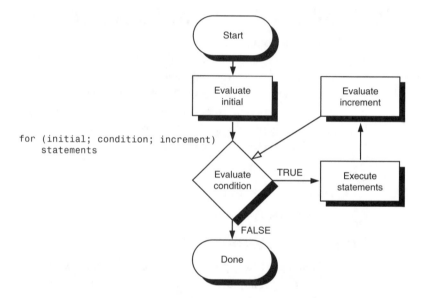

```
for (initial; condition; increment)
        statements
```

Listing 6.1 presents a simple example by using a for statement to print the numbers 1 through 20. You can see that the resulting code is much more compact than it would be if a separate printf() statement were used for each of the 20 values.

LISTING 6.1   forstate.c. A simple for statement

```
1:    /* Demonstrates a simple for statement */
2:
3:    #include <stdio.h>
4:
5:    int count;
6:
7:    int main( void )
8:    {
9:        /* Print the numbers 1 through 20 */
```

LISTING 6.1 continued

```
10:
11:        for (count = 1; count <= 20; count++)
12:            printf("%d\n", count);
13:
14:        return 0;
15:   }
```

OUTPUT
```
1
2
3
4
5
6
7
8
9
10
11
12
13
14
15
16
17
18
19
20
```

Figure 6.2 illustrates the operation of the `for` loop in Listing 6.1.

FIGURE 6.2

How the `for` loop in Listing 6.1 operates.

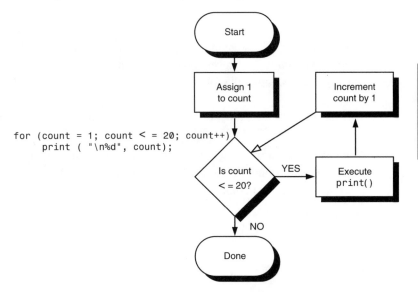

```
for (count = 1; count < = 20; count++)
        print ( "\n%d", count);
```

6

ANALYSIS Line 3 includes the standard input/output header file. Line 5 declares a type `int` variable, named `count`, that will be used in the `for` loop. Lines 11 and 12 are the `for` loop. When the `for` statement is reached, the initial statement is executed first. In this listing, the initial statement is `count = 1`. This initializes `count` so that it can be used by the rest of the loop. The second step in executing this `for` statement is the evaluation of the condition `count <= 20`. Because `count` was just initialized to 1, you know that it is less than 20, so the statement in the `for` command, the `printf()`, is executed. After executing the printing function, the increment expression, `count++`, is evaluated. This adds 1 to `count`, making it 2. Now the program loops back and checks the condition again. If it is true, the `printf()` reexecutes, the increment adds to `count` (making it 3), and the condition is checked. This loop continues until the condition evaluates to false, at which point the program exits the loop and continues to the next line (line 14), which returns 0 before ending the program.

The `for` statement is frequently used, as in the previous example, to "count up," incrementing a counter from one value to another. You also can use it to "count down," decrementing (rather than incrementing) the counter variable.

```
for (count = 100; count > 0; count--)
```

You can also "count by" a value other than 1, as in this example which counts by 5:

```
for (count = 0; count < 1000; count += 5)
```

The `for` statement is quite flexible. For example, you can omit the initialization expression if the test variable has been initialized previously in your program. (You still must use the semicolon separator as shown, however.)

```
count = 1;
for ( ; count < 1000; count++)
```

The initialization expression doesn't need to be an actual initialization; it can be any valid C expression. Whatever it is, it is executed once when the `for` statement is first reached. For example, the following prints the statement `Now sorting the array...`:

```
count = 1;
for (printf("Now sorting the array...") ; count < 1000; count++)
    /* Sorting statements here */
```

You can also omit the increment expression, performing the updating in the body of the `for` statement. Again, the semicolon must be included. To print the numbers from 0 to 99, for example, you could write

```
for (count = 0; count < 100; )
    printf("%d", count++);
```

The test expression that terminates the loop can be any C expression. As long as it evaluates to true (nonzero), the `for` statement continues to execute. You can use C's logical operators to construct complex test expressions. For example, the following `for` statement prints the elements of an array named `array[]`, stopping when all elements have been printed or an element with a value of 0 is encountered:

```
for (count = 0; count < 1000 && array[count] != 0; count++)
    printf("%d", array[count]);
```

You could simplify this `for` loop even further by writing it as follows. (If you don't understand the change made to the test expression, you need to review Day 4.)

```
for (count = 0; count < 1000 && array[count]; )
    printf("%d", array[count++]);
```

You can follow the `for` statement with a null statement, allowing all the work to be done in the `for` statement itself. Remember, the null statement is a semicolon alone on a line. For example, to initialize all elements of a 1,000-element array to the value `50`, you could write

```
for (count = 0; count < 1000; array[count++] = 50)
    ;
```

In this `for` statement, `50` is assigned to each member of the array by the increment part of the statement. A better way to write this statement is

```
for (count = 0; count < 1000; array[count++] = 50)
{
    ;
}
```

Putting the semicolon into a block (the two brackets) makes it more obvious that there is no work being done in the body of the `for` statement.

Day 4 mentioned that C's comma operator is most often used in `for` statements. You can create an expression by separating two sub-expressions with the comma operator. The two sub-expressions are evaluated (in left-to-right order), and the entire expression evaluates to the value of the right sub-expression. By using the comma operator, you can make each part of a `for` statement perform multiple duties.

Imagine that you have two 1,000-element arrays, `a[]` and `b[]`. You want to copy the contents of `a[]` to `b[]` in reverse order so that after the copy operation, `b[0]` = `a[999]`, `b[1]` = `a[998]`, and so on. The following `for` statement does the trick:

```
for (i = 0, j = 999; i < 1000; i++, j--)
    b[j] = a[i];
```

The comma operator is used to initialize two variables, `i` and `j`. It is also used to increment part of these two variables with each loop.

6

▼ SYNTAX

The for Statement

```
for (initial; condition; increment)
    statement(s)
```

initial is any valid C expression. It is usually an assignment statement that sets a variable to a particular value.

condition is any valid C expression. It is usually a relational expression. When *condition* evaluates to false (zero), the for statement terminates, and execution passes to the first statement following *statement(s)*; otherwise, the C statement(s) in *statement(s)* are executed.

increment is any valid C expression. It is usually an expression that increments a variable initialized by the initial expression.

statement(s) are the C statements that are executed as long as the condition remains true.

A for statement is a looping statement. It can have an initialization, test condition, and increment as parts of its command. The for statement executes the initial expression first. It then checks the condition. If the condition is true, the statements execute. Once the statements are completed, the increment expression is evaluated. The for statement then rechecks the condition and continues to loop until the condition is false.

Example 1

```
/* Prints the value of x as it counts from 0 to 9 */
int x;
for (x = 0; x <10; x++)
    printf( "\nThe value of x is %d", x );
```

Example 2

```
/*Obtains values from the user until 99 is entered */
int nbr = 0;
for ( ; nbr != 99; )
    scanf( "%d", &nbr );
```

Example 3

```
/* Lets user enter up to 10 integer values       */
/* Values are stored in an array named value. If 99 is */
/* entered, the loop stops                         */
int value[10];
int ctr,nbr=0;
for (ctr = 0; ctr < 10 && nbr != 99; ctr++)
{
    puts("Enter a number, 99 to quit ");
    scanf("%d", &nbr);
    value[ctr]  = nbr;
▲ }
```

Nesting for Statements

A for statement can be executed within another for statement. This is called *nesting*. (You saw nesting on Day 4 with the if statement.) By nesting for statements, you can do some complex programming. Listing 6.2 is not a complex program, but it illustrates the nesting of two for statements.

LISTING 6.2   nestfor.c. Nested for statements

```
1:    /* Demonstrates nesting two for statements */
2:
3:    #include <stdio.h>
4:
5:    void draw_box( int, int);
6:
7:    int main( void )
8:    {
9:        draw_box( 8, 35 );
10:
11:       return 0;
12:   }
13:
14:   void draw_box( int row, int column )
15:   {
16:       int col;
17:       for ( ; row > 0; row--)
18:       {
19:           for (col = column; col > 0; col--)
20:               printf("X");
21:
22:           printf("\n");
23:       }
24:   }
```

OUTPUT
```
XXXXXXXXXXXXXXXXXXXXXXXXXXXXXXXXXXX
XXXXXXXXXXXXXXXXXXXXXXXXXXXXXXXXXXX
XXXXXXXXXXXXXXXXXXXXXXXXXXXXXXXXXXX
XXXXXXXXXXXXXXXXXXXXXXXXXXXXXXXXXXX
XXXXXXXXXXXXXXXXXXXXXXXXXXXXXXXXXXX
XXXXXXXXXXXXXXXXXXXXXXXXXXXXXXXXXXX
XXXXXXXXXXXXXXXXXXXXXXXXXXXXXXXXXXX
XXXXXXXXXXXXXXXXXXXXXXXXXXXXXXXXXXX
```

6

ANALYSIS   The main work of this program is accomplished on line 20. When you run this program, 280 Xs are printed on-screen, forming an 8×35 square. The program has only one command to print an X, but it is nested in two loops.

In this listing, a function prototype for draw_box() is declared on line 5. This function takes two type int variables, row and column, which contain the dimensions of the box of Xs to be drawn. In line 9, main() calls draw_box() and passes the value 8 as the row and the value 35 as the column.

Looking closely at the draw_box() function, you might see a couple things you don't readily understand. The first is why the local variable col was declared. The second is why the second printf() in line 22 was used. Both of these will become clearer after you look at the two for loops.

Line 17 starts the first for loop. The initialization is skipped because the initial value of row was passed to the function. Looking at the condition, you see that this for loop is executed until the row is 0. On first executing line 17, row is 8; therefore, the program continues to line 19.

Line 19 contains the second for statement. Here the passed parameter, column, is copied to a local variable, col, of type int. The value of col is 35 initially (the value passed via column), and column retains its original value. Because col is greater than 0, line 20 is executed, printing an X. col is then decremented, and the loop continues. When col is 0, the for loop ends, and control goes to line 22. Line 22 causes the on-screen printing to start on a new line. (Printing is covered in detail on Day 7, "Fundamentals of Reading and Writing Information.") After moving to a new line on the screen, control reaches the end of the first for loop's statements, thus executing the increment expression, which subtracts 1 from row, making it 7. This puts control back at line 19. Notice that the value of col was 0 when it was last used. If column had been used instead of col, it would fail the condition test, because it will never be greater than 0. Only the first line would be printed. Take the initializer out of line 19 and change the two col variables to column to see what actually happens.

Do	Don't

DO remember the semicolon if you use a for with a null statement. Put the semicolon placeholder on a separate line, or place a space between it and the end of the for statement. It's clearer to put it on a separate line.
 	
``
for (count = 0; count < 1000;
        array[count] = 50) ;
            /* note space! */
``
	DON'T put too much processing in the for statement. Although you can use the comma separator, it is often clearer to put some of the functionality into the body of the loop.

The while Statement

The while statement, also called the while *loop,* executes a block of statements as long as a specified condition is true. The while statement has the following form:

```
while (condition)
    statement
```

condition is any C expression, and statement is a single or compound C statement. When program execution reaches a while statement, the following events occur:

1. The expression condition is evaluated.

2. If condition evaluates to false (that is, zero), the while statement terminates, and execution passes to the first statement following statement.

3. If condition evaluates to true (that is, nonzero), the C statement(s) in statement are executed.

4. Execution returns to step 1.

The operation of a while statement is shown in Figure 6.3.

FIGURE 6.3

The operation of a while *statement.*

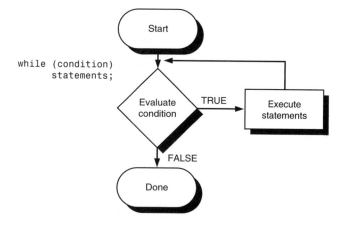

Listing 6.3 is a simple program that uses a while statement to print the numbers 1 through 20. (This is the same task that is performed by a for statement in Listing 6.1.)

LISTING 6.3   whilest.c. A simple while statement

```
1:    /* Demonstrates a simple while statement */
2:
3:    #include <stdio.h>
4:
5:    int count;
```

LISTING 6.3 continued

```
 6:
 7:    int main( void )
 8:    {
 9:        /* Print the numbers 1 through 20 */
10:
11:        count = 1;
12:
13:        while (count <= 20)
14:        {
15:            printf("%d\n", count);
16:            count++;
17:        }
18:    return 0;
19:    }
```

OUTPUT

```
1
2
3
4
5
6
7
8
9
10
11
12
13
14
15
16
17
18
19
20
```

ANALYSIS Examine Listing 6.3 and compare it with Listing 6.1, which uses a `for` statement to perform the same task. In line 11, `count` is initialized to 1. Because the `while` statement doesn't contain an initialization section, you must take care of initializing any variables before starting the `while`. Line 13 is the actual `while` statement, and it contains the same condition statement from Listing 6.1, `count <= 20`. In the `while` loop, line 16 takes care of incrementing `count`. What do you think would happen if you forgot to put line 16 in this program? Your program wouldn't know when to stop, because `count` would always be 1, which is always less than 20.

You might have noticed that a `while` statement is essentially a `for` statement without the initialization and increment components. Thus,

```
for ( ; condition ; )
```

is equivalent to

```
while (condition)
```

Because of this equality, anything that can be done with a `for` statement can also be done with a `while` statement. When you use a `while` statement, any necessary initialization must first be performed in a separate statement, and the updating must be performed by a statement that is part of the `while` loop.

When initialization and updating are required, most experienced C programmers prefer to use a `for` statement rather than a `while` statement. This preference is based primarily on source code readability. When you use a `for` statement, the initialization, test, and increment expressions are located together and are easy to find and modify. With a `while` statement, the initialization and update expressions are located separately and might be less obvious.

The `while` Statement

▼ SYNTAX

```
while (condition)
    statement(s)
```

condition is any valid C expression, usually a relational expression. When *condition* evaluates to false (zero), the `while` statement terminates, and execution passes to the first statement following *statement(s)*; otherwise, the first C statement in *statement(s)* is executed.

statement(s) is the C statement(s) that is executed as long as *condition* remains true.

A `while` statement is a C looping statement. It allows repeated execution of a statement or block of statements as long as the condition remains true (nonzero). If the condition is not true when the `while` command is first executed, the *statement(s)* is never executed.

6

Example 1

```
int x = 0;
while (x < 10)
{
    printf("\nThe value of x is %d", x );
    x++;
}
```

▼ **Example 2**

```
/* get numbers until you get one greater than 99 */
int nbr=0;
while (nbr <= 99)
    scanf("%d", &nbr );
```

Example 3

```
/* Lets user enter up to 10 integer values      */
/* Values are stored in an array named value. If 99 is */
/* entered, the loop stops                      */
int value[10];
int ctr = 0;
int nbr;
while (ctr < 10 && nbr != 99)
{
    puts("Enter a number, 99 to quit ");
    scanf("%d", &nbr);
    value[ctr] = nbr;
    ctr++;
▲ }
```

Nesting while Statements

Just like the for and if statements, while statements can also be nested. Listing 6.4 shows an example of nested while statements. Although this isn't the best use of a while statement, the example does present some new ideas.

LISTING 6.4   whiles.c. Nested while statements

```
 1:    /* Demonstrates nested while statements */
 2:
 3:    #include <stdio.h>
 4:
 5:    int array[5];
 6:
 7:    int main( void )
 8:    {
 9:       int ctr = 0,
10:           nbr = 0;
11:
12:        printf("This program prompts you to enter 5 numbers\n");
13:        printf("Each number should be from 1 to 10\n");
14:
15:        while ( ctr < 5 )
16:        {
17:            nbr = 0;
18:            while (nbr < 1 || nbr > 10)
19:            {
```

LISTING 6.4   continued

```
20:                 printf("\nEnter number %d of 5: ", ctr + 1 );
21:                 scanf("%d", &nbr );
22:             }
23:
24:         array[ctr] = nbr;
25:         ctr++;
26:     }
27:
28:     for (ctr = 0; ctr < 5; ctr++)
29:         printf("Value %d is %d\n", ctr + 1, array[ctr] );
30:
31:     return 0;
32: }
```

**INPUT/
OUTPUT**

```
This program prompts you to enter 5 numbers
Each number should be from 1 to 10

Enter number 1 of 5: 3

Enter number 2 of 5: 6

Enter number 3 of 5: 3

Enter number 4 of 5: 9

Enter number 5 of 5: 2

Value 1 is 3
Value 2 is 6
Value 3 is 3
Value 4 is 9
Value 5 is 2
```

ANALYSIS   As in previous listings, line 1 contains a comment with a description of the program, and line 3 contains an #include statement for the standard input/output header file. Line 5 contains a declaration for an array (named array) that can hold five integer values. The function main() contains two additional local variables, ctr and nbr (lines 9 and 10). Notice that these variables are initialized to zero at the same time they are declared. Also notice that the comma operator is used as a separator at the end of line 9, allowing nbr to be declared as an int without restating the int type command. Stating declarations in this manner is a common practice for many C programmers. Lines 12 and 13 print messages stating what the program does and what is expected of the user. Lines 15 through 26 contain the first while command and its statements. Lines 18 through 22 also contain a nested while loop with its own statements that are all part of the outer while.

6

This outer loop continues to execute while ctr is less than 5 (line 15). As long as ctr is less than 5, line 17 sets nbr to 0, lines 18 through 22 (the nested while statement) gather a number in variable nbr, line 24 places the number in array, and line 25 increments ctr. Then the loop starts again. Therefore, the outer loop gathers five numbers and places each into array, indexed by ctr.

The inner loop is a good use of a while statement. Only the numbers from 1 to 10 are valid, so until the user enters a valid number, there is no point continuing the program. Lines 18 through 22 prevent continuation. This while statement states that while the number is less than 1 or greater than 10, the program should print a message to enter a number, and then get the number.

Lines 28 and 29 print the values that are stored in array. Notice that because the while statements are done with the variable ctr, the for command can reuse it. Starting at zero and incrementing by one, the for loops five times, printing the value of ctr plus one (because the count started at zero) and printing the corresponding value in array.

For additional practice, there are two things you can change in this program. The first is the values that the program accepts. Instead of 1 to 10, try making it accept from 1 to 100. You can also change the number of values that it accepts. Currently, it allows for five numbers. Try making it accept 10.

Do	**Don't**

DO use the for statement instead of the while statement if you need to initialize and increment within your loop. The for statement keeps the initialization, condition, and increment statements all together. The while statement does not.	**DON'T** use the following convention if it isn't necessary:
	
	`while (x)`
	
	Instead, use this convention:
	
	`while (x != 0)`
	
	Although both work, the second is clearer when you're debugging (trying to find problem in the code). When compiled, these produce virtually the same code.

The do...while Loop

C's third loop construct is the do...while loop, which executes a block of statements as long as a specified condition is true. The do...while loop tests the condition at the end of the loop rather than at the beginning, as is done by the for loop and the while loop.

The structure of the do...while loop is as follows:

```
do
    statement
while (condition);
```

condition is any C expression, and *statement* is a single or compound C statement. When program execution reaches a do...while statement, the following events occur:

1. The statements in *statement* are executed.

2. *condition* is evaluated. If it's true, execution returns to step 1. If it's false, the loop terminates.

The operation of a do...while loop is shown in Figure 6.4.

FIGURE 6.4

The operation of a do...while *loop.*

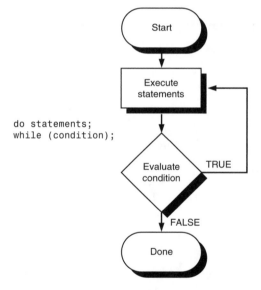

```
do statements;
while (condition);
```

The statements associated with a do...while loop are always executed at least once. This is because the test condition is evaluated at the end, instead of the beginning, of the loop. In contrast, for loops and while loops evaluate the test condition at the start of the loop, so the associated statements are not executed at all if the test condition is initially false.

The do...while loop is used less frequently than while and for loops. It is most appropriate when the statement(s) associated with the loop must be executed at least once. You could, of course, accomplish the same thing with a while loop by making sure that the test condition is true when execution first reaches the loop. A do...while loop probably would be more straightforward, however.

6

Listing 6.5 shows an example of a do...while loop.

LISTING 6.5   do.c. A simple do...while loop

```
1:   /* Demonstrates a simple do...while statement */
2:
3:   #include <stdio.h>
4:
5:   int get_menu_choice( void );
6:
7:   int main( void )
8:   {
9:       int choice;
10:
11:      choice = get_menu_choice();
12:
13:      printf("You chose Menu Option %d\n", choice );
14:
15:      return 0;
16:  }
17:
18:  int get_menu_choice( void )
19:  {
20:      int selection = 0;
21:
22:      do
23:      {
24:          printf("\n" );
25:          printf("\n1 - Add a Record" );
26:          printf("\n2 - Change a record");
27:          printf("\n3 - Delete a record");
28:          printf("\n4 - Quit");
29:          printf("\n" );
30:          printf("\nEnter a selection: " );
31:
32:          scanf("%d", &selection );
33:
34:      }while ( selection < 1 || selection > 4 );
35:
36:      return selection;
37:  }
```

INPUT/
OUTPUT

```
1 - Add a Record
2 - Change a record
3 - Delete a record
4 - Quit

Enter a selection: 8
```

```
1 - Add a Record
2 - Change a record
3 - Delete a record
4 - Quit

Enter a selection: 4
You chose Menu Option 4
```

ANALYSIS This program provides a menu with four choices. You can select one of the four choices. The program then prints the number selected. Programs later in this book use and expand on this concept. For now, you should be able to follow most of the listing. The main() function (lines 7 through 16) adds nothing to what you already know.

Note

The body of main() could have been written into one line, like this:

```
printf( "You chose Menu Option %d", get_menu_option() );
```

If you were to expand this program and act on the selection, you would need the value returned by get_menu_choice(), so it is wise to assign the value to a variable (such as choice).

Lines 18 through 37 contain get_menu_choice(). This function displays a menu on-screen (lines 24 through 30) and then gets a selection. Because you have to display a menu at least once to get an answer, it is appropriate to use a do...while loop. In the case of this program, the menu is displayed until a valid choice is entered. Line 34 contains the while part of the do...while statement and validates the value of the selection, appropriately named selection. If the value entered is not between 1 and 4, the menu is redisplayed, and the user is prompted for a new value. When a valid selection is entered, the program continues to line 36, which returns the value in the variable selection.

The do...while Statement

▼ SYNTAX

```
do
{
    statement(s)
}while (condition);
```

condition is any valid C expression, usually a relational expression. When *condition* evaluates to false (zero), the while statement terminates, and execution passes to the first statement following the while statement; otherwise, the program loops back to the do, and the C statement(s) in *statement(s)* is executed.

▼ *statement(s)* is either a single C statement or a block of statements that are executed the first time through the loop and then as long as *condition* remains true.

6

▼ A do...while statement is a C looping statement. It allows repeated execution of a statement or block of statements as long as the condition remains true (nonzero). Unlike the while statement, a do...while loop executes its statements at least once.

Example 1

```
/* prints even though condition fails! */
int x = 10;
do
{
    printf("\nThe value of x is %d", x );
}while (x != 10);
```

Example 2

```
/* gets numbers until the number is greater than 99 */
int nbr;
do
{
    scanf("%d", &nbr );
}while (nbr <= 99);
```

Example 3

```
/* Enables user to enter up to 10 integer values    */
/* Values are stored in an array named value. If 99 is */
/* entered, the loop stops                          */
int value[10];
int ctr = 0;
int nbr;
do
{
    puts("Enter a number, 99 to quit ");
    scanf( "%d", &nbr);
    value[ctr] = nbr;
    ctr++;
▲ }while (ctr < 10 && nbr != 99);
```

Nested Loops

The term *nested loop* refers to a loop that is contained within another loop. You have seen examples of some nested statements. C places no limitations on the nesting of loops, except that each inner loop must be enclosed completely in the outer loop; you can't have overlapping loops. Thus, the following is not allowed:

```
for ( count = 1; count < 100; count++)
{
    do
    {
        /* the do...while loop */
```

```
} /* end of for loop */
   }while (x != 0);
```

If the do...while loop is placed entirely in the for loop, there is no problem:

```
for (count = 1; count < 100; count++)
{
    do
    {
        /* the do...while loop */
    }while (x != 0);
} /* end of for loop */
```

When you use nested loops, remember that changes made in the inner loop might affect the outer loop as well. Note, however, that the inner loop might be independent from any variables in the outer loop; in this example, they are not. In the previous example, if the inner do...while loop modifies the value of count, the number of times the outer for loop executes is affected.

Good indenting style makes code with nested loops easier to read. Each level of loop should be indented one step further than the last level. This clearly labels the code associated with each loop.

Do	Don't
DO use the do...while loop when you know that a loop should be executed at least once.	**DON'T** try to overlap loops. You can nest them, but they must be entirely within each other.

Summary

After today's lesson, you are almost ready to start writing real C programs on your own.

C has three loop statements that control program execution: for, while, and do...while. Each of these constructs lets your program execute a block of statements zero times, one time, or more than one time, based on the condition of certain program variables. Many programming tasks are well-served by the repetitive execution allowed by these loop statements.

Although all three can be used to accomplish the same task, each is different. The for statement lets you initialize, evaluate, and increment all in one command. The while statement operates as long as a condition is true. The do...while statement always executes its statements at least once and continues to execute them until a condition is false.

6

Nesting is the placing of one command within another. C allows for the nesting of any of its commands. Nesting the `if` statement was demonstrated on Day 4. In today's lesson, the `for`, `while`, and `do...while` statements were nested.

Q&A

Q How do I know which programming control statement to use—the `for`, the `while`, or the `do...while`?

A If you look at the syntax boxes provided, you can see that any of the three can be used to solve a looping problem. Each has a small twist to what it can do, however. The `for` statement is best when you know that you need to initialize and increment in your loop. If you only have a condition that you want to meet, and you aren't dealing with a specific number of loops, `while` is a good choice. If you know that a set of statements needs to be executed at least once, a `do...while` might be best. Because all three can be used for most problems, the best course is to learn them all and then evaluate each programming situation to determine which is best.

Q How deep can I nest my loops?

A You can nest as many loops as you want. If your program requires you to nest more than two loops deep, consider using a function instead. You might find sorting through all those braces difficult, so perhaps a function would be easier to follow in code.

Q Can I nest different loop commands?

A You can nest `if`, `for`, `while`, `do...while`, or any other command. You will find that many of the programs you try to write will require that you nest at least a few of these.

Workshop

The Workshop provides quiz questions to help you solidify your understanding of the material covered, and exercises to provide you with experience in using what you've learned.

Quiz

1. What is the index value of the first element in an array?
2. What is the difference between a `for` statement and a `while` statement?
3. What is the difference between a `while` statement and a `do...while` statement?

4. Is it true that a `while` statement can be used and still get the same results as coding a `for` statement?

5. What must you remember when nesting statements?

6. Can a `while` statement be nested in a `do...while` statement?

7. What are the four parts of a `for` statement?

8. What are the two parts of a `while` statement?

9. What are the two parts of a `do...while` statement?

Exercises

1. Write a declaration for an array that will hold 50 type `long` values.

2. Show a statement that assigns the value of `123.456` to the 50th element in the array from exercise 1.

3. What is the value of x when the following statement is complete?

   ```
   for (x = 0; x < 100, x++) ;
   ```

4. What is the value of `ctr` when the following statement is complete?

   ```
   for (ctr = 2; ctr < 10; ctr += 3) ;
   ```

5. How many Xs does the following print?

   ```
   for (x = 0; x < 10; x++)
       for (y = 5; y > 0; y--)
           puts("X");
   ```

6. Write a `for` statement to count from 1 to 100 by 3s.

7. Write a `while` statement to count from 1 to 100 by 3s.

8. Write a `do...while` statement to count from 1 to 100 by 3s.

9. **BUG BUSTER:** What is wrong with the following code fragment?

   ```
   record = 0;
   while (record < 100)
   {
       printf( "\nRecord %d ", record );
       printf( "\nGetting next number..." );
   }
   ```

10. **BUG BUSTER:** What is wrong with the following code fragment? (`MAXVALUES` is not the problem!)

    ```
    for (counter = 1; counter < MAXVALUES; counter++);
        printf("\nCounter = %d", counter );
    ```

6

DAY 7

Fundamentals of Reading and Writing Information

In most programs you create, you will need to display information on the screen or read information from the keyboard. Many of the programs presented in earlier lessons have performed these tasks, but you might not have understood exactly how. Today you will learn:

- The basics of C's input and output statements
- How to display information on-screen with the printf() and puts() library functions
- How to format the information that is displayed on-screen
- How to read data from the keyboard with the scanf() library function

Today's lesson isn't intended to be a complete treatment of these topics, but it provides enough information so that you can start writing real programs. These topics are covered in greater detail later in this book.

Displaying Information On-Screen

You will want most of your programs to display information on-screen. Two of the most frequently used ways to do display information are with C's library functions `printf()` and `puts()`.

The `printf()` Function

The `printf()` function is part of the standard C library and is included as a part of the ANSI standard. It is perhaps the most versatile way for a program to display data on the screen. You've already seen `printf()` used in many of the examples in this book. Now you will to see how `printf()` works.

Printing a text message on the screen is simple. You call the `printf()` function, passing the desired message enclosed in double quotation marks. For example, to display How Now Brown Cow! On the screen, you write

```
printf("How Now Brown Cow!");
```

In addition to text messages, however, you frequently need to display the value of program variables. This is a little more complicated than displaying only a message. For example, suppose you want to display the value of the numeric variable myNumber on the screen, along with some identifying text. Furthermore, you want the information to start at the beginning of a new line. You could use the `printf()` function as follows:

```
printf("\nThe value of myNumber is %d", myNumber);
```

The resulting screen display, assuming that the value of myNumber is 12, would be

```
The value of myNumber is 12
```

In this example, two arguments are passed to `printf()`. The first argument is enclosed in double quotation marks and is called the *format string*. The second argument is the name of the variable (myNumber) containing the value to be printed.

The `printf()` Format Strings

A `printf()` format string specifies how the output is to be formatted. Here are the three possible components of a format string:

- *Literal text* is displayed exactly as entered in the format string. In the preceding example, the characters starting with the T (in The) and up to, but not including, the % comprise a literal string.

- An *escape sequence* provides special formatting control. An escape sequence consists of a backslash (\) followed by a single character. In the preceding example, \n is an escape sequence. It is called the *newline character*, and it means "move to the start of the next line." Escape sequences are also used to print certain characters. Common escape sequences are listed in Table 7.1.

- A *conversion specifier* consists of the percent sign (%) followed by a character. In the example, the conversion specifier is %d. A conversion specifier tells the printf() function how to interpret the variable(s) being printed. The %d tells printf() to interpret the variable myNumber as a signed decimal integer.

TABLE 7.1 The most frequently used escape sequences

Sequence	Meaning
\a	Bell (alert)
\b	Backspace
\f	Form feed
\n	New line
\r	Carriage return
\t	Horizontal tab
\v	Vertical tab
\\	Backslash
\?	Question mark
\'	Single quotation
\"	Double quotation

The printf() Escape Sequences

Escape sequences are used to control the location of output by moving the screen cursor. They are also used to print characters that would otherwise have a special meaning to printf(). For example, to print a single backslash character, you include a double back-slash (\\) in the format string. The first backslash tells printf() that the second back-slash is to be interpreted as a literal character, not as the start of an escape sequence. In general, the backslash tells printf() to interpret the next character in a special manner. Here are some examples:

Sequence	Meaning
n	The character n
\n	Newline
\"	The double quotation character
"	The start or end of a string

7

Table 7.1 lists C's most commonly used escape sequences. Listing 7.1 demonstrates some of the frequently used escape sequences.

LISTING 7.1   escape.c. Using `printf()` escape sequences

```
1:    /* Demonstration of frequently used escape sequences */
2:
3:    #include <stdio.h>
4:
5:    #define QUIT  3
6:
7:    int  get_menu_choice( void );
8:    void print_report( void );
9:
10:   int main( void )
11:   {
12:       int choice = 0;
13:
14:       while (choice != QUIT)
15:       {
16:          choice = get_menu_choice();
17:
18:          if (choice == 1)
19:              printf("\nBeeping the computer\a\a\a" );
20:          else
21:          {
22:              if (choice == 2)
23:                  print_report();
24:          }
25:       }
26:       printf("You chose to quit!\n");
27:
28:       return 0;
29:   }
30:
31:   int get_menu_choice( void )
32:   {
33:       int selection = 0;
34:
35:       do
36:       {
37:           printf( "\n" );
38:           printf( "\n1 - Beep Computer" );
39:           printf( "\n2 - Display Report");
40:           printf( "\n3 - Quit");
41:           printf( "\n" );
42:           printf( "\nEnter a selection:" );
43:
44:           scanf( "%d", &selection );
```

LISTING 7.1 continued

```
45:
46:        }while ( selection < 1 || selection > 3 );
47:
48:        return selection;
49: }
50:
51: void print_report( void )
52: {
53:        printf( "\nSAMPLE REPORT" );
54:        printf( "\n\nSequence\tMeaning" );
55:        printf( "\n=========\t=======" );
56:        printf( "\n\\a\t\tbell (alert)" );
57:        printf( "\n\\b\t\tbackspace" );
58:        printf( "\n...\t\t...");
59: }
```

```
1 - Beep Computer
2 - Display Report
3 - Quit

Enter a selection:1

Beeping the computer

1 - Beep Computer
2 - Display Report
3 - Quit

Enter a selection:2

SAMPLE REPORT
Sequence        Meaning
=========       =======
\a              bell (alert)
\b              backspace
...             ...
1 - Beep Computer
2 - Display Report
3 - Quit

Enter a selection:3
You chose to quit!
```

ANALYSIS Listing 7.1 seems long compared with previous examples, but it offers some additions that are worth noting. The stdio.h header was included in line 3 because printf() is used in this listing. In line 5, a constant named QUIT is defined. From Day 3, "Storing Information: Variables and Constants," you know that #define makes using the constant QUIT equivalent to using the value 3. Lines 7 and 8 are function prototypes. This program has two functions: get_menu_choice() and print_report().

7

The get_menu_choice() function is defined in lines 31 through 49. This is similar to the menu function in Listing 6.5. Lines 37 and 41 contain calls to printf() that print the new line escape sequence. Lines 38, 39, 40, and 42 also use the new line escape character, and they print text. Line 37 could have been eliminated by changing line 38 to the following:

```
printf( "\n\n1 - Beep Computer" );
```

However, leaving line 37 makes the program easier to read.

Looking at the main() function, you see the start of a while loop on line 14. The while loop's statements will keep looping as long as choice is not equal to QUIT. Because QUIT is a constant, you could have replaced it with 3; however, the program wouldn't be as clear. Line 16 gets the variable choice, which is then analyzed in lines 18 through 25 in an if statement. If the user chooses 1, line 19 prints the new line character, a message, and then three beeps. If the user selects 2, line 23 calls the function print_report().

The print_report() function is defined on lines 51 through 59. This simple function shows the ease of using printf() and the escape sequences to print formatted information to the screen. You've already seen the new line character. Lines 54 through 58 also use the tab escape character, \t. The tab character aligns the columns of the report vertically. Lines 56 and 57 might seem confusing at first, but if you start at the left and work to the right, they make sense. Line 56 prints a new line (\n), then a backslash (\), then the letter a, and then two tabs (\t\t). The line ends with some descriptive text, (bell (alert)). Line 57 follows the same format.

This program prints the first two lines of Table 7.1, along with a report title and column headings. In exercise 9 at the end of today's lesson, you will complete this program by making it print the rest of the table.

The printf() Conversion Specifiers

The format string must contain one conversion specifier for each printed variable. The printf() function then displays each variable as directed by its corresponding conversion specifier. You'll learn more about this process on Day 15. For now, be sure to use the conversion specifier that corresponds to the type of variable being printed.

Exactly what does this mean? If you're printing a variable that is a signed decimal integer (types int and long), use the %d conversion specifier. For an unsigned decimal integer (types unsigned int and unsigned long), use %u. For a floating-point variable (types float and double), use the %f specifier. The conversion specifiers you need most often are listed in Table 7.2.

TABLE 7.2   The most commonly needed conversion specifiers

Specifier	Meaning	Types Converted
%c	Single character	char
%d	Signed decimal integer	int, short
%ld	Signed long decimal integer	long
%f	Decimal floating-point number	float, double
%s	Character string	char arrays
%u	Unsigned decimal integer	unsigned int, unsigned short
%lu	Unsigned long decimal integer	unsigned long

Note   Any program that uses `printf()` should include the header file stdio.h.

The literal text of a format specifier is anything that doesn't qualify as either an escape sequence or a conversion specifier. Literal text is simply printed as is, including all spaces.

What about printing the values of more than one variable? A single `printf()` statement can print an unlimited number of variables, but the format string must contain one conversion specifier for each variable. The conversion specifiers are paired with variables in left-to-right order. If you write

```
printf("Rate = %f, amount = %d", rate, amount);
```

the variable `rate` is paired with the `%f` specifier, and the variable `amount` is paired with the `%d` specifier. The positions of the conversion specifiers in the format string determine the position of the output. If there are more variables passed to `printf()` than there are conversion specifiers, the unmatched variables aren't printed. If there are more specifiers than variables, the unmatched specifiers print "garbage."

You aren't limited to printing the value of variables with `printf()`. The arguments can be any valid C expression. For example, to print the sum of x and y, you could write

```
total = x + y;
printf("%d", total);
```

You also could write

```
printf("%d", x + y);
```

7

Listing 7.2 demonstrates the use of `printf()`. Day 15 gives more details on `printf()`.

LISTING 7.2   nums.c. Using `printf()` to display numerical values

```
 1:    /* Demonstration using printf() to display numerical values. */
 2:
 3:    #include <stdio.h>
 4:
 5:    int a = 2, b = 10, c = 50;
 6:    float f = 1.05, g = 25.5, h = -0.1;
 7:
 8:    int main( void )
 9:    {
10:        printf("\nDecimal values without tabs: %d %d %d", a, b, c);
11:        printf("\nDecimal values with tabs: \t%d \t%d \t%d", a, b, c);
12:
13:        printf("\nThree floats on 1 line: \t%f\t%f\t%f", f, g, h);
14:        printf("\nThree floats on 3 lines: \n\t%f\n\t%f\n\t%f", f, g, h);
15:
16:        printf("\nThe rate is %f%%", f);
17:        printf("\nThe result of %f/%f = %f\n", g, f, g / f);
18:
19:        return 0;
20:    }
```

OUTPUT
```
Decimal values without tabs: 2 10 50
Decimal values with tabs:       2         10         50
Three floats on 1 line:        1.050000        25.500000
➥0.100000
Three floats on 3 lines:
          1.050000
          25.500000
          -0.100000
The rate is 1.050000%
The result of 25.500000/1.050000 = 24.285715
```

ANALYSIS   Listing 7.2 prints six lines of information. Lines 10 and 11 each print three decimals: a, b, and c. Line 10 prints them without tabs, and line 11 prints them with tabs. Lines 13 and 14 each print three `float` variables: f, g, and h. Line 13 prints them on one line, and line 14 prints them on three lines. Line 16 prints a `float` variable, f, followed by a percent sign. Because a percent sign is normally a message to print a variable, you must place two in a row to print a single percent sign. This is exactly like the backslash escape character. Line 17 shows one final concept. When printing values in conversion specifiers, you don't have to use variables. You can also use expressions such as g / f, or even constants.

▼ SYNTAX

Do	Don't
DO remember to use the new line escape character when printing multiple lines of information in separate `printf()` statements.	**DON'T** try to put multiple lines of text into one `printf()` statement. In most instances, it's clearer to print multiple lines with multiple print statements than to use just one with several new line (\n) escape characters. **DON'T** misspell `stdio.h`. Many C programmers accidentally type `studio.h`; however, there is no u.

The `printf()` Function

```
#include <stdio.h>
printf( format-string[,arguments,...]);
```

`printf()` is a function that accepts a series of *arguments*, each applying to a conversion specifier in the given format string. `printf()` prints the formatted information to the standard output device, usually the display screen. When using `printf()`, you need to include the standard input/output header file, STDIO.H.

The *format-string* is required; however, arguments are optional. For each argument, there must be a conversion specifier. Table 7.2 lists the most commonly used conversion specifiers.

The *format-string* can also contain escape sequences. Table 7.1 lists the most frequently used escape sequences.

The following are examples of calls to `printf()` and their output:

Example 1 Input

```
#include <stdio.h>
int main( void )
{
    printf("This is an example of something printed!");
    return 0;
}
```

Example 1 Output

```
This is an example of something printed!
```

Example 2 Input

```
printf("This prints a character, %c\na number, %d\na floating \
point, %f", 'z', 123, 456.789 );
```

7

▼ **Example 2 Output**

```
This prints a character, z
a number, 123
a floating point, 456.789
```
▲

Tip

> You may notice in the second example, that the printf() function is using a string that wraps to a second line. At the end of the first line a forward slash (\) is used to indicate that the string continues to the next line. The compiler will treat the two lines as one.

Displaying Messages with puts()

The puts() function can also be used to display text messages on the screen, but it can't display numeric variables. The puts() function takes a single string as its argument and displays it, automatically adding a new line at the end. For example, the statement

```
puts("Hello, world.");
```

performs the same action as

```
printf("Hello, world.\n");
```

You can include escape sequences (including \n) in a string passed to puts(). They have the same effect as when they are used with printf() (see Table 7.1 for the most common escape sequences).

Just like printf(), any program that uses puts() should include the header file stdio.h. Note that stdio.h should be included only once in a program.

Do	**Don't**
DO use the puts() function instead of the printf() function whenever you want to print text but don't need to print any variables.	**DON'T** try to use conversion specifiers with the puts() statement.

The puts() Function

```
#include <stdio.h>
puts( string );
```

puts() is a function that copies a string to the standard output device, usually the display screen. When you use puts(), include the standard input/output header file (stdio.h).

▼ `puts()` also appends a new line character to the end of the string that is printed. The format string can contain escape sequences. Table 7.1 lists the most frequently used escape sequences.

The following are examples of calls to `puts()` and their output:

Example 1 Input

```
puts("This is printed with the puts() function!");
```

Example 1 Output

```
This is printed with the puts() function!
```

Example 2 Input

```
puts("This prints on the first line. \nThis prints on the second line.");
puts("This prints on the third line.");
puts("If these were printf()s, all four lines would be on two lines!");
```

Example 2 Output

```
This prints on the first line.
This prints on the second line.
This prints on the third line.
```
▲ `If these were printf()s, all four lines would be on two lines!`

Inputting Numeric Data with `scanf()`

Just as most programs need to output data to the screen, they also need to input data from the keyboard. The most flexible way your program can read numeric data from the keyboard is by using the `scanf()` library function.

The `scanf()` function reads data from the keyboard according to a specified format and assigns the input data to one or more program variables. Like `printf()`, `scanf()` uses a format string to describe the format of the input. The format string utilizes the same conversion specifiers as the `printf()` function. For example, the statement

```
scanf("%d", &x);
```

reads a decimal integer from the keyboard and assigns it to the integer variable x. Likewise, the following statement reads a floating-point value from the keyboard and assigns it to the variable rate:

```
scanf("%f", &rate);
```

What is that ampersand (&) before the variable's name? The & symbol is C's *address of* operator, which is fully explained on Day 9, "Understanding Pointers." For now, all you need to remember is that `scanf()` requires the & symbol before each numeric variable name in its argument list.

7

A single scanf() can input more than one value if you include multiple conversion specifiers in the format string and variable names (again, each preceded by & in the argument list). The following statement inputs an integer value and a floating-point value and assigns them to the variables x and rate, respectively:

```
scanf("%d %f", &x, &rate);
```

When multiple variables are entered, scanf() uses white space to separate input into fields. White space can be spaces, tabs, or new lines. Each conversion specifier in the scanf() format string is matched with an input field; the end of each input field is identified by white space.

This gives you considerable flexibility. In response to the preceding scanf(), you could enter

```
10 12.45
```

You also could enter this:

```
10                      12.45
```

or this:

```
10
12.45
```

As long as there's some white space between values, scanf() can assign each value to its variable.

 Caution Caution should be used with scanf(). If you are looking for a character and the user enters a number, or if you are looking for a number and the user enters a character, then your user may see unexpected results.

As with the other functions discussed in today's lesson, programs that use scanf() must include the stdio.h header file. Although Listing 7.3 gives an example of using scanf(), a more complete description is presented on Day 15.

LISTING 7.3   scanit.c. Using scanf() to obtain numerical values

```
1:   /* Demonstration of using scanf() */
2:
3:   #include <stdio.h>
4:
5:   #define QUIT 4
6:
```

LISTING 7.3   continued

```
 7:    int get_menu_choice( void );
 8:
 9:    int main( void )
10:    {
11:        int   choice   = 0;
12:        int   int_var  = 0;
13:        float float_var = 0.0;
14:        unsigned unsigned_var = 0;
15:
16:        while (choice != QUIT)
17:        {
18:            choice = get_menu_choice();
19:
20:            if (choice == 1)
21:            {
22:                puts("\nEnter a signed decimal integer (i.e. -123)");
23:                scanf("%d", &int_var);
24:            }
25:            if (choice == 2)
26:            {
27:                puts("\nEnter a decimal floating-point number\
28:                    (e.g. 1.23)");
29:                scanf("%f", &float_var);
30:            }
31:            if (choice == 3)
32:            {
33:                puts("\nEnter an unsigned decimal integer \
34:                (e.g. 123)" );
35:                scanf( "%u", &unsigned_var );
36:            }
37:        }
38:        printf("\nYour values are: int: %d  float: %f  unsigned: %u \n",
39:                                int_var, float_var, unsigned_var );
40:
41:        return 0;
42:    }
43:
44:    int get_menu_choice( void )
45:    {
46:        int selection = 0;
47:
48:        do
49:        {
50:            puts( "\n1 - Get a signed decimal integer" );
51:            puts( "2 - Get a decimal floating-point number" );
52:            puts( "3 - Get an unsigned decimal integer" );
53:            puts( "4 - Quit" );
54:            puts( "\nEnter a selection:" );
55:
```

7

LISTING 7.3   continued

```
56:            scanf( "%d", &selection );
57:
58:        }while ( selection < 1 || selection > 4 );
59:
60:        return selection;
61:    }
```

INPUT/
OUTPUT

```
1 - Get a signed decimal integer
2 - Get a decimal floating-point number
3 - Get an unsigned decimal integer
4 - Quit

Enter a selection:
1

Enter a signed decimal integer (e.g. -123)
-123

1 - Get a signed decimal integer
2 - Get a decimal floating-point number
3 - Get an unsigned decimal integer
4 - Quit

Enter a selection:
3

Enter an unsigned decimal integer (e.g. 123)
321

1 - Get a signed decimal integer
2 - Get a decimal floating-point number
3 - Get an unsigned decimal integer
4 - Quit

Enter a selection:
2

Enter a decimal floating point number (e.g. 1.23)
1231.123

1 - Get a signed decimal integer
2 - Get a decimal floating-point number
3 - Get an unsigned decimal integer
4 - Quit

Enter a selection:
4

Your values are: int: -123  float: 1231.123047 unsigned: 321
```

Listing 7.3 uses the same menu concepts that were used in Listing 7.1. The differences in get_menu_choice() (lines 44 through 61) are minor but should be noted. First, puts() is used instead of printf(). Because no variables are printed, there is no need to use printf(). Because puts() is being used, the new line escape characters have been removed from lines 51 through 53. Line 58 was also changed to allow values from 1 to 4 because there are now four menu options. Notice that line 56 has not changed; however, now it should make a little more sense. scanf() gets a decimal value and places it in the variable selection. The function returns selection to the calling program in line 60.

Listings 7.1 and 7.3 use the same main() structure. An if statement evaluates choice, the return value of get_menu_choice(). Based on choice's value, the program prints a message, asks for a number to be entered, and reads the value using scanf(). Notice the difference between lines 23, 29, and 35. Each is set up to get a different type of variable. Lines 12 through 14 declare variables of the appropriate types.

When the user selects Quit, the program prints the last-entered number for all three types. If the user didn't enter a value, 0 is printed, because lines 12, 13, and 14 initialized all three types. One final note on lines 20 through 36: The if statements used here are not structured well. If you're thinking that an if...else structure would have been better, you're correct. Day 14, "Working with the Screen, Printer, and Keyboard," introduces a new control statement, switch. This statement offers an even better option.

Do	Don't
DO use printf() or puts() in conjunction with scanf(). Use the printing functions to display a prompting message for the data you want scanf() to get.	DON'T forget to include the address of operator (&) when using scanf() variables.

The scanf() Function

▼ SYNTAX

```
#include <stdio.h>
scanf( format-string[,arguments,...]);
```

scanf() is a function that uses a conversion specifier in a given format-string to place values into variable arguments. The arguments should be the addresses of the variables rather than the actual variables themselves. For numeric variables, you can pass the address by putting the address of (&) operator at the beginning of the variable name. When using scanf(), you should include the stdio.h header file.

▼

scanf() reads input fields from the standard input stream, usually the keyboard. It places each of these read fields into an argument. When it places the information, it converts it

▼ to the format of the corresponding specifier in the format string. For each argument, there must be a conversion specifier. Table 7.2 lists the most commonly needed conversion specifiers.

Example 1

```
int x, y, z;
scanf( "%d %d %d", &x, &y, &z);
```

Example 2

```
#include <stdio.h>
int main( void )
{
    float y;
    int x;
    puts( "Enter a float, then an int" );
    scanf( "%f %d", &y, &x);
    printf( "\nYou entered %f and %d ", y, x );
    return 0;
▲ }
```

Using Trigraph Sequences

You have now learned the basics of reading and writing information using functions such as printf() and scanf(). There is one additional topic that will be covered in today's lesson. This is not about reading and writing information, rather it is about special sequences of characters in your source file that will be interpreted to mean something else. These special sequences are called *trigraph sequences.*

Note You will most likely never use trigraph sequences. It is included here in case you inadvertently use a trigraph sequence in your code and find that it automatically gets converted as described below.

Trigraph sequences are similar to the escape sequences you learned about earlier. The biggest difference is that trigraph sequences are interpreted at the time the compiler looks at your source code. Anywhere in your source file that a trigraph sequence is found, it will be converted.

Trigraph sequences starts with two question marks (??). Table 7.3 lists the trigraph sequences listed in the ANSI standard. Per the standards, no other trigraph sequences should exist.

TABLE 7.3 The Trigraph Sequences

Code	Character equivalent
??=	#
??(	[
??/	\
??)	]
??'	^
??<	{
??!	|
??>	}
??-	~

If a trigraph sequence codes—one of the values in Table 7.3—is present in your source file, it will be changed to the character equivalent. It will be changed even if it is part of a string. For example,

```
printf("??[WOW??]");
```

Will be changed to

```
printf("[WOW]");
```

If extra question marks are included, they are not changed. For example,

printf("???-");

will be changed to

printf("?~");

Summary

With the completion of today's lesson, you are ready to write your own C programs. By combining the printf(), puts(), and scanf() functions and the programming control statements you learned about in earlier days, you have the tools needed to write simple programs.

Screen display is performed with the printf() and puts() functions. The puts() function can display text messages only, whereas printf() can display text messages and variables. Both functions use escape sequences for special characters and printing controls.

7

The scanf() function reads one or more numeric values from the keyboard and interprets each one according to a conversion specifier. Each value is assigned to a program variable.

At the end of today's lesson you learned about the trigraph sequences. You learned that trigraph sequences are special codes that are converted to character equivalents.

Q&A

Q **Why should I use puts() if printf() does everything puts() does and more?**

A Because printf() does more, it has additional overhead. When you're trying to write a small, efficient program, or when your programs get big and resources are valuable, you will want to take advantage of the smaller overhead of puts(). In general, you should use the simplest available resource.

Q **Why do I need to include stdio.h when I use printf(), puts(), or scanf()?**

A stdio.h contains the prototypes for the standard input/output functions. printf(), puts(), and scanf() are three of these standard functions. Try running a program without the stdio.h header and see the errors and warnings you get.

Q **What happens if I leave the address of operator (&) off a scanf() variable?**

A This is an easy mistake to make. Unpredictable results can occur if you forget the address of operator. When you read about pointers on Days 9 and 13, you will understand this better. For now, know that if you omit the address of operator, scanf() doesn't place the entered information in your variable, but in some other place in memory. This could do anything from apparently having no effect to locking up your computer so that you must reboot.

Workshop

The Workshop provides quiz questions to help you solidify your understanding of the material covered, and exercises to provide you with experience in using what you've learned.

Quiz

1. What is the difference between puts() and printf()?

2. What header file should you include when you use printf()?

3. What do the following escape sequences do?

    a. \\

    b. \b

    c. \n

    d. \t

    e. \a

4. What conversion specifiers should be used to print the following?

    a. A character string

    b. A signed decimal integer

    c. A decimal floating-point number

5. What is the difference between using each of the following in the literal text of `puts()`?

    a. b

    b. \b

    c. \

    d. \\

Exercises

Note

Starting with today's lesson, some of the exercises ask you to write complete programs that perform a particular task. Because there is always more than one way to do things in C, the answers provided at the back of the book shouldn't be interpreted as the only correct ones. If you can write your own code that performs what's required, great! If you have trouble, refer to the answer for help. The answers are presented with minimal comments because it's good practice for you to figure out how they operate.

1. Write both a `printf()` and a `puts()` statement to start a new line.

2. Write a `scanf()` statement that could be used to get a character, an unsigned decimal integer, and another single character.

3. Write the statements to get an integer value and print it.

4. Modify exercise 3 so that it accepts only even values (2, 4, 6, and so on).

5. Modify exercise 4 so that it returns values until the number 99 is entered, or until six even values have been entered. Store the numbers in an array. (Hint: You need a loop.)

7

6. Turn exercise 5 into an executable program. Add a function that prints the values, separated by tabs, in the array on a single line. (Print only the values that were entered into the array.)

7. **BUG BUSTER:** Find the error(s) in the following code fragment:

```
printf( "Jack said, "Peter Piper picked a peck of pickled peppers."");
```

8. **BUG BUSTER:** Find the error(s) in the following program:

```
int get_1_or_2( void )
{
    int answer = 0;
    while (answer < 1 || answer > 2)
    {
        printf(Enter 1 for Yes, 2 for No);
        scanf( "%f", answer );
    }
    return answer;
}
```

9. Using Listing 7.1, complete the `print_report()` function so that it prints the rest of Table 7.1.

10. Write a program that inputs two floating-point values from the keyboard and then displays their product.

11. Write a program that inputs 10 integer values from the keyboard and then displays their sum.

12. Write a program that inputs integers from the keyboard, storing them in an array. Input should stop when a zero is entered or when the end of the array is reached. Then, find and display the array's largest and smallest values. (Note: This is a tough problem, because arrays haven't been completely covered in this book yet. If you have difficulty, try solving this problem again after reading Day 8, "Using Numeric Arrays.")

WEEK 1

In Review

You have finished your first week of learning how to program in C. You should feel comfortable entering programs and using your editor and compiler. The following program pulls together many of the topics you have learned over the previous seven days' lessons.

You will find that this section is different from the Type & Run programs you have done before. After you look through the listing, you will see that analysis has been included. You will find that every topic in this listing has been covered in the preceding week's lessons. You will see similar Weeks in Review after Weeks 2 and 3.

1

2

3

4

5

6

7

Note   The numbers in the left margin indicate the day that covers the concept presented on that line. If you are confused by a particular line, refer to that day for more information.

LISTING R1.1   week1.c. Week 1's review listing

```
CH 02      1: /* Program Name: week1.c                              */
           2: /* Purpose:     Program to enter the ages and incomes of up */
           3: /*              to 100 people.  The program prints a report */
           4: /*              based on the numbers entered.               */
           5: /*----------------------------------------------------------*/
           6: /*-------------------*/
           7: /* included files    */
           8: /*-------------------*/
CH 02      9: #include <stdio.h>
          10:
CH 02     11: /*-------------------*/
          12: /* defined constants */
          13: /*-------------------*/
          14:
CH 03     15: #define MAX    100
          16: #define YES    1
          17: #define NO     0
          18:
CH 02     19: /*-------------------*/
          20: /* variables         */
          21: /*-------------------*/
          22:
CH 03     23: long   income[MAX]; /* to hold incomes     */
          24: int    month[MAX], day[MAX], year[MAX]; /* to hold birthdays */
          25: int    x, y, ctr;   /* For counters         */
          26: int    cont;  /* For program control */
          27: long   month_total, grand_total; /* For totals     */
          28:
CH 02     29: /*-------------------*/
          30: /* function prototypes*/
          31: /*-------------------*/
          32:
CH 05     33: int main(void);
          34: int display_instructions(void);
          35: void get_data(void);
          36: void display_report(void);
          37: int continue_function(void);
          38:
          39: /*-------------------*/
          40: /* start of program  */
          41: /*-------------------*/
          42:
CH 02     43: int main(void)
```

LISTING R1.1   continued

```
44: {
```
CH 05
```
45:     cont = display_instructions();
```
```
46:
```
CH 04
```
47:     if ( cont == YES )
```
```
48:     {
```
CH 05
```
49:         get_data();
```
CH 05
```
50:         display_report();
```
```
51:     }
```
CH 04
```
52:     else
```
CH 07
```
53:         printf( "\nProgram Aborted by User!\n\n");
```
```
54:
```
```
55:     return 0;
```
```
56: }
```
CH 02
```
57: /*----------------------------------------------------------------*
```
```
58:  *  Function:   display_instructions()                            *
```
```
59:  *  Purpose:    This function displays information on how to       *
```
```
60:  *              use this program and asks the user to enter 0      *
```
```
61:  *              to quit, or 1 to continue.                         *
```
```
62:  *  Returns:    NO  - if user enters 0                             *
```
```
63:  *              YES - if user enters any number other than 0       *
```
```
64:  *----------------------------------------------------------------*/
```
CH 05
```
65: int display_instructions( void )
```
```
66: {
```
CH 07
```
67:     printf("\n\n");
```
```
68:     printf("\nThis program enables you to enter up to 99 people\'s ");
```
```
69:     printf("\nincomes and birthdays.  It then prints the incomes by");
```
```
70:     printf("\nmonth along with the overall income and overall average.");
```
```
71:     printf("\n");
```
```
72:
```
CH 05
```
73:     cont = continue_function();
```
CH 05
```
74:     return( cont );
```
```
75: }
```
CH 02
```
76: /*-------------------------------------------------------------*
```
```
77:  *  Function:  get_data() *
```
```
78:  *  Purpose: This function gets the data from the user. It       *
```
```
79:  *            continues to get data until either 100 people are *
```
```
80:  *            entered, or until the user enters 0 for the month.*
```
```
81:  *  Returns: nothing *
```
```
82:  *  Notes:    This allows 0/0/0 to be entered for birthdays in   *
```
```
83:  *            case the user is unsure.  It also allows for 31     *
```
```
84:  *            days in each month.                                 *
```
```
85:  *-------------------------------------------------------------*/
```
```
86:
```
CH 05
```
87: void get_data(void)
```
```
88: {
```
CH 06
```
89:     for ( cont = YES, ctr = 0; ctr < MAX && cont == YES; ctr++ )
```
```
90:     {
```
CH 07
```
91:         printf("\nEnter information for Person %d.", ctr+1 );
```
```
92:         printf("\n\tEnter Birthday:");
```
```
93:
```

LISTING R1.1   continued

```
CH 06      94:          do
           95:          {
CH 07      96:              printf("\n\tMonth (0 - 12): ");
CH 07      97:              scanf("%d", &month[ctr]);
CH 06      98:          }while (month[ctr] < 0 || month[ctr] > 12 );
           99:
CH 06     100:          do
          101:          {
CH 07     102:              printf("\n\tDay (0 - 31): ");
CH 07     103:              scanf("%d", &day[ctr]);
CH 06     104:          }while ( day[ctr] <  0 || day[ctr] > 31 );
          105:
CH 06     106:          do
          107:          {
CH 07     108:              printf("\n\tYear (0 - 2002): ");
CH 07     109:              scanf("%d", &year[ctr]);
CH 06     110:          }while ( year[ctr] < 0 || year[ctr] > 2002 );
          111:
CH 07     112:          printf("\nEnter Yearly Income (whole dollars): ");
CH 07     113:          scanf("%ld", &income[ctr]);
          114:
CH 05     115:          cont = continue_function();
          116:      }
CH 07     117:      /* ctr equals the number of people that were entered.    */
          118: }
CH 02     119: /*-------------------------------------------------------------*
          120:  *  Function: display_report()                                 *
          121:  *  Purpose:  This function displays a report to the screen *
          122:  *  Returns:  nothing                                          *
          123:  *  Notes:    More information could be printed.               *
          124:  *-------------------------------------------------------------*/
          125:
CH 05     126: void display_report()
          127: {
CH 04     128:      grand_total = 0;
CH 07     129:      printf("\n\n\n");                      /* skip a few lines   */
          130:      printf("\n        SALARY SUMMARY");
          131:      printf("\n        ==============");
          132:
CH 06     133:      for( x = 0; x <= 12; x++ )  /* for each month, including 0*/
          134:      {
          135:          month_total = 0;
CH 04     136:          for( y = 0; y < ctr; y++ )
CH 06     137:          {
          138:              if( month[y] == x )
CH 04     139:                  month_total += income[y];
CH 04     140:          }
          141:          printf("\nTotal for month %d is %ld", x, month_total);
CH 07     142:          grand_total += month_total;
CH 04     143:      }
```

LISTING **R1.1**   continued

```
CH 07   144:     printf("\n\nReport totals:");
        145:     printf("\nTotal Income is %ld", grand_total);
        146:     printf("\nAverage Income is %ld", grand_total/ctr );
        147:
        148:     printf("\n\n* * * End of Report * * *\n");
        149: }
CH 02   150: /*----------------------------------------------------------------*
        151:  * Function: continue_function()                                 *
        152:  * Purpose:  This function asks the user if they wish to continue.*
        153:  * Returns:  YES - if user wishes to continue                    *
        154:  *           NO - if user wishes to quit                         *
        155:  *----------------------------------------------------------------*/
        156:
CH 05   157: int continue_function( void )
        158: {
CH 07   159:     printf("\n\nDo you wish to continue? (0=NO/1=YES): ");
        160:     scanf( "%d", &x );
        161:
CH 06   162:     while( x < 0 || x > 1 )
        163:     {
CH 07   164:         printf("\n%d is invalid!", x);
        165:         printf("\nPlease enter 0 to Quit or 1 to Continue: ");
        166:         scanf("%d", &x);
        167:     }
CH 04   168:     if(x == 0)
CH 05   169:         return(NO);
CH 04   170:     else
CH 05   171:         return(YES);
        172: }
```

ANALYSIS   After completing the quizzes and exercises on Day 1, "Getting Started with C," and Day 2, "The Components of a C Program," you should be able to enter and compile this program. This program contains more comments than any other listing throughout this book. These comments are typical of a "real-world" C program. In particular, you should notice the comments at the beginning of the program and before each major function. The comments on lines 1 to 5 give an overview of the entire program, including the program name. Some programmers also include information such as the author of the program, the compiler used, its version number, the libraries linked into the program, and the date on which the program was created. The comments before each function describe the purpose of the function, possible return values, the function's calling conventions, and anything relating specifically to that function.

The comments on lines 1 to 5 specify that you can enter information in this program for up to 100 people. Before you can enter the data, the program calls display_instructions() on line 45. This function displays instructions for using the program and asks you whether you want to continue or quit. On lines 67–71, you can see that this function uses the `printf()` function from Day 7, "Fundamentals of Reading and Writing Information," to display the instructions.

On lines 157 to 172, `continue_function()` uses some of the features covered at the end of the week. This function asks whether you want to continue (line 159). Using the `while` control statement from Day 6, "Basic Program Control," the function verifies that the answer entered was a `0` or a `1`. As long as the answer isn't one of these two values, the function keeps prompting for a response. After the program receives an appropriate answer, an `if...else` statement (covered on Day 4, "Statements, Expressions, and Operators") returns a constant variable of either `YES` or `NO`.

The heart of this program lies in two functions: `get_data()` and `display_report()`. The `get_data()` function prompts you to enter data, placing the information into the arrays declared near the beginning of the program. Using a `for` statement on line 89, you are prompted to enter data until `cont` is not equal to the defined constant `YES` (returned from `continue_function()`) or until the counter, `ctr`, is greater than or equal to the maximum number of array elements, `MAX`. The program checks each piece of information entered to ensure that it is appropriate. For example, lines 94–98 prompt you to enter a month. The only values that the program accepts are `0` to `12`. If you enter a number greater than `12`, the program again prompts for the month. Line 115 calls `continue_function()` to check whether you want to continue adding data.

When the user responds to the continue function with a `0`, or the maximum number of sets of information is entered (`MAX` sets), the program returns to line 50 in `main()`, where it calls `display_report()`. The `display_report()` function, on lines 119 to 149, prints a report to the screen. This report uses a nested `for` loop to total incomes for each month and give a grand total for all the months. This report might seem complicated; if so, review Day 6 for coverage of nested statements. Many of the reports you will create as a programmer are more complicated than this one.

This program uses what you learned during your first week of teaching yourself C. There was a large amount of material to cover in just one week, but you did it! If you use everything you learned this week, you can write your own programs in C. However, there are still limits to what you can do.

WEEK 2

At a Glance

You have finished your first week of learning how to program in C. By now you should feel comfortable entering programs and using your editor and compiler.

Where You're Going

This week covers a large amount of material. You will learn about many of the features that make up the heart of C. You will learn how to use numeric and character arrays, expand character variable types into arrays and strings, and group different variable types by using structures.

The second week builds on subjects you learned in the first week. It introduces additional program control statements, provides detailed explanations of functions, and presents alternative functions.

Day 9, "Understanding Pointers," and Day 12, "Understanding Variable Scope," focus on concepts that are extremely important to capitalizing on C's assets. You should spend extra time working with pointers and their basic functions.

In addition to the critical topics of scope and pointers, on Day 8, "Using Numeric Arrays" and Day 11, "Implementing Structures, Unions, and TypeDefs" you will learn new ways to store information by using arrays, structures, unions, and more. You will also learn more about working with characters and strings on Day 10, "Working with Characters and Strings." On Day 14, "Working with the Screen, Printer, and Keyboard," you will take more control of printing and displaying information.

8

9

10

11

12

13

14

At the end of the first week, you learned to write many simple C programs. By the time you finish the second week, you should be able to write complex programs that can accomplish almost any task.

DAY 8

Using Numeric Arrays

Arrays are a type of data storage that you often use in C programs. You had a brief introduction to arrays on Day 6, "Controlling Your Program's Order of Execution." Today you will learn:

- What an array is
- The definition of single- and multidimensional numeric arrays
- How to declare and initialize arrays

What Is an Array?

NEW TERM An *array* is a collection of data storage locations, each storing the same type of data and having the same name. Each storage location in an array is called an *array element*. Why do you need arrays in your programs? This question can be answered with an example.

If you're keeping track of your business expenses for 2003 and filing your receipts by month, you could have a separate folder for each month's receipts, but it would be more convenient to have a single folder with 12 compartments.

Extend this example to computer programming. Imagine that you're designing a program to keep track of your business expenses. The program could declare 12 separate variables, one for each month's expense total. This approach is analogous to having 12 separate folders for your receipts. Good programming practice, however, would utilize an array with 12 elements, storing each month's total in the corresponding array element. This approach is comparable to filing your receipts in a single folder with 12 compartments. Figure 8.1 illustrates the difference between using individual variables and an array.

FIGURE 8.1

Variables are like individual folders, whereas an array is like a single folder with many compartments.

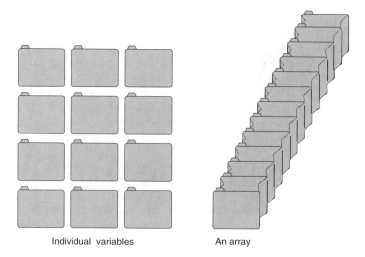

Individual variables   An array

Using Single-Dimensional Arrays

NEW TERM A *single-dimensional array* has only a single subscript. A *subscript* is a number in brackets that follows an array's name. This number can identify the number of individual elements in the array. An example should make this clear. For the business expenses program, you could use the following line to declare an array of type `float`:

```
float expenses[12];
```

The array is named `expenses`, and it contains 12 elements. Each of the 12 elements is the exact equivalent of a single `float` variable.

All of C's data types can be used for arrays. C array elements are always numbered starting at 0, so the 12 elements of expenses are numbered 0 through 11. In the preceding example, January's expense total would be stored in `expenses[0]`, February's in `expenses[1]`, and so on. The expense total for December would be in `expenses[11]`.

When you declare an array, the compiler sets aside a block of memory large enough to hold the entire array. Individual array elements are stored in sequential memory locations, as shown in Figure 8.2.

FIGURE 8.2

Array elements are stored in sequential memory locations.

Where you declare an array in your source code is important. As with variables that are not a part of an array, the declaration's location affects how your program can use the array. The effect of a declaration's location is covered in more detail on Day 12, "Understanding Variable Scope." For now, place your array declarations with other variable declarations.

An array element can be used in your program anywhere a nonarray variable of the same type can be used. Individual elements of the array are accessed by using the array name followed by the element subscript enclosed in square brackets. For example, the following statement stores the value 89.95 in the second array element (remember, the first array element is expenses[0], not expenses[1]):

```
expenses[1] = 89.95;
```

Likewise, the statement

```
expenses[10] = expenses[11];
```

assigns a copy of the value that is stored in array element expenses[11] into array element expenses[10]. When you refer to an array element, the array subscript can be a literal constant, as in these examples. However, your programs might often use a subscript that is a C integer variable or expression, or even another array element. Here are some examples:

```
float expenses[100];
int a[10];
/* additional statements go here */
expenses[i] = 100;      // i is an integer variable
expenses[2 + 3] = 100;  // equivalent to expenses[5]
expenses[a[2]] = 100;   // a[] is an integer array
```

That last example might need an explanation. If, for instance, you have an integer array named a[] and the value 8 is stored in element a[2], writing

```
expenses[a[2]]
```

has the same effect as writing

```
expenses[8];
```

When you use arrays, keep the element numbering scheme in mind: In an array of *n* elements, the allowable subscripts range from 0 to *n*–1. If you use the subscript value *n*, you might get program errors. The C compiler doesn't recognize whether your program uses an array subscript that is out of bounds. Your program compiles and links, but out-of-range subscripts generally produce erroneous results.

> **Caution**
>
> Remember that array elements start with 0, not 1. Also remember that the last element is one less than the number of elements in the array. For example, an array with 10 elements contains elements 0 through 9.

Sometimes you might want to treat an array of n elements as if its elements were numbered 1 through *n*. For instance, in the previous example, a more natural method might be to store January's expense total in `expenses[1]`, February's in `expenses[2]`, and so on. The simplest way to do this is to declare the array with one more element than needed, and ignore element 0. In this case, you would declare the array as follows. You could also store some related data in element 0 (the yearly expense total, perhaps).

```
float expenses[13];
```

The program expenses.c in Listing 8.1 demonstrates the use of an array. This is a simple program with no real practical use; however, it helps demonstrate the use of an array.

LISTING 8.1   expenses.c. Using an array

```
 1:    /* expenses.c - Demonstrates use of an array */
 2:
 3:    #include <stdio.h>
 4:
 5:    /* Declare an array to hold expenses, and a counter variable */
 6:
 7:    float expenses[13];
 8:    int count;
 9:
10:    int main( void )
11:    {
12:        /* Input data from keyboard into array */
13:
14:        for (count = 1; count < 13; count++)
15:        {
16:            printf("Enter expenses for month %d: ", count);
17:            scanf("%f", &expenses[count]);
```

LISTING 8.1 continued

```
18:    }
19:
20:    /* Print array contents */
21:
22:    for (count = 1; count < 13; count++)
23:    {
24:        printf("Month %d = $%.2f\n", count, expenses[count]);
25:    }
26:    return 0;
27: }
```

**INPUT/
OUTPUT**

```
Enter expenses for month 1: 100
Enter expenses for month 2: 200.12
Enter expenses for month 3: 150.50
Enter expenses for month 4: 300
Enter expenses for month 5: 100.50
Enter expenses for month 6: 34.25
Enter expenses for month 7: 45.75
Enter expenses for month 8: 195.00
Enter expenses for month 9: 123.45
Enter expenses for month 10: 111.11
Enter expenses for month 11: 222.20
Enter expenses for month 12: 120.00
Month 1 = $100.00
Month 2 = $200.12
Month 3 = $150.50
Month 4 = $300.00
Month 5 = $100.50
Month 6 = $34.25
Month 7 = $45.75
Month 8 = $195.00
Month 9 = $123.45
Month 10 = $111.11
Month 11 = $222.20
Month 12 = $120.00
```

ANALYSIS When you run expenses.c, the program prompts you to enter expenses for months 1 through 12. The values you enter are stored in an array. You must enter a value for each month. After the 12th value is entered, the array contents are displayed on-screen.

The flow of the program is similar to listings you've seen before. Line 1 starts with a comment that describes what the program does. Notice that the name of the program, expenses.c, is included. When the name of the program is included in a comment, you know which program you're viewing. This is helpful when you're reviewing printouts of a listing.

Line 5 contains an additional comment explaining the variables that are being declared. In line 7, an array of 13 elements is declared. In this program, only 12 elements are needed, one for each month, but 13 have been declared. The `for` loop in lines 14 through 18 ignores element `0`. This lets the program use elements `1` through `12`, which relate directly to the 12 months. Going back to line 8, a variable, `count`, is declared and is used throughout the program as a counter and an array index.

The program's `main()` function begins on line 10. As stated earlier, this program uses a `for` loop to print a message and accept a value for each of the 12 months. Notice that in line 17, the `scanf()` function uses an array element. In line 7, the `expenses` array was declared as `float`, so `%f` is used. The address-of operator (`&`) also is placed before the array element, just as if it were a regular type `float` variable and not an array element.

Lines 22 through 25 contain a second `for` loop that prints the values just entered. An additional formatting command has been added to the `printf()` function so that the expenses values print in a more orderly fashion. For now, know that `%.2f` prints a floating number with two digits to the right of the decimal. Additional formatting commands are covered in more detail on Day 14, "Working with the Screen, Printer, and Keyboard."

DO use arrays instead of creating several variables that store the same thing. For example, if

Do	Don't
you want to store total sales for each month of the year, create an array with 12 elements to hold sales rather than creating a sales variable for each month. **DON'T** forget that array subscripts start at element 0.	**Using Multidimensional**

Arrays

A multidimensional array has more than one subscript. A two-dimensional array has two subscripts, a three-dimensional array has three subscripts, and so on. There is no limit to the number of dimensions a C array can have. (There *is* a limit on total array size, as discussed later in today's lesson.)

For example, you might write a program that plays checkers. The checkerboard contains 64 squares arranged in eight rows and eight columns. Your program could represent the board as a two-dimensional array, as follows:

```
int checker[8][8];
```

The resulting array has 64 elements: `checker[0][0]`, `checker[0][1]`, `checker[0][2]...checker[7][6]`, `checker[7][7]`. The structure of this two-dimensional array is illustrated in Figure 8.3.

FIGURE 8.3

A two-dimensional array has a row-and-column structure.

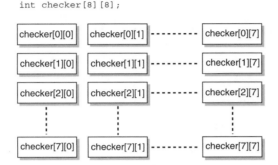

```
int checker[8][8];
```

Similarly, a three-dimensional array could be thought of as a cube. Four-dimensional arrays (and higher) are probably best left to your imagination. All arrays, no matter how many dimensions they have, are stored sequentially in memory. More detail on array storage is presented on Day 15, "Pointers: Beyond the Basics."

Naming and Declaring Arrays

The rules for assigning names to arrays are the same as for variable names, covered on Day 3, "Storing Information: Variables and Constants." An array name must be unique. It can't be used for another array or for any other identifier (variable, constant, and so on). As you have probably realized, array declarations follow the same form as declarations of nonarray variables, except that the number of elements in the array must be enclosed in square brackets immediately following the array name.

When you declare an array, you can specify the number of elements with a literal constant (as was done in the earlier examples) or with a symbolic constant created with the `#define` directive. Thus the following:

```
#define MONTHS 12
int array[MONTHS];
```

is equivalent to this statement:

```
int array[12];
```

With most compilers, however, you can't declare an array's elements with a symbolic constant created with the `const` keyword:

```
const int MONTHS = 12;
int array[MONTHS];              /* Wrong! */
```

Listing 8.2, grades.c, is another program demonstrating the use of a single-dimensional array. The grades.c program uses an array to store 10 grades.

LISTING 8.2   grades.c. Storing 10 grades in an array

```
1:    /*grades.c - Sample program with array */
2:    /* Get 10 grades and then average them */
3:
4:    #include <stdio.h>
5:
6:    #define MAX_GRADE 100
7:    #define STUDENTS  10
8:
9:    int grades[STUDENTS];
10:
11:   int idx;
12:   int total = 0;            /* used for average */
13:
14:   int main( void )
15:   {
16:       for( idx=0;idx< STUDENTS;idx++)
17:       {
18:           printf( "Enter Person %d's grade: ", idx +1);
19:           scanf( "%d", &grades[idx] );
20:
21:           while ( grades[idx] > MAX_GRADE )
22:           {
23:               printf( "\nThe highest grade possible is %d",
24                        MAX_GRADE );
25:               printf( "\nEnter correct grade: " );
26:               scanf( "%d", &grades[idx] );
27:           }
28:
29:           total += grades[idx];
30:       }
31:
32:       printf( "\n\nThe average score is %d\n", ( total / STUDENTS) );
33:
34:       return (0);
35:   }
```

OUTPUT
```
Enter Person 1's grade: 95
Enter Person 2's grade: 100
Enter Person 3's grade: 60
Enter Person 4's grade: 105

The highest grade possible is 100
Enter correct grade: 100
Enter Person 5's grade: 25
```

8

```
Enter Person 6's grade: 0
Enter Person 7's grade: 85
Enter Person 8's grade: 85
Enter Person 9's grade: 95
Enter Person 10's grade: 85

The average score is 73
```

Like expenses.c, this listing prompts the user to enter values. It prompts for the grades from 10 people. Instead of printing each grade, the program prints the average score.

As you learned earlier, arrays are named like regular variables. On line 9, the array for this program is named grades. It should be safe to assume that this array holds grades. On lines 6 and 7, two constants, MAX_GRADE and STUDENTS, are defined. These constants can be changed easily. Knowing that STUDENTS is defined as 10, you then know that the grades array has 10 elements. Two other variables are declared, idx and total. An abbreviation of *index,* idx is used as a counter and array subscript. A running total of all of the grades is kept in total.

The heart of this program is the for loop in lines 16 through 30. The for statement initializes idx to 0, the first subscript for an array. It then loops as long as idx is less than the number of students. Each time it loops, it increments idx by 1. For each loop, the program prompts for a person's grade (lines 18 and 19). Notice that in line 18, 1 is added to idx in order to count the people from 1 to 10 instead of from 0 to 9. Because arrays start with subscript 0, the first grade is put in grade[0]. Instead of confusing users by asking for Person 0's grade, they are asked for Person 1's grade.

Lines 21 through 27 contain a while loop nested within the for loop. This is an edit check that ensures that the grade isn't higher than the maximum grade, MAX_GRADE. Users are prompted to enter a correct grade if they enter a grade that is too high. You should check program data whenever you can.

Line 29 adds the entered grade to a total counter. In line 32, this total is used to print the average score (total/STUDENTS).

Do	**Don't**
DO use #define statements to create constants that can be used when declaring arrays. Then you can easily change the number of elements in the array. In grades.c, for example, you could change the number of students in the #define, and you wouldn't have to make any other changes in the program.	**DON'T** use multidimensional arrays with more than three dimensions if you can avoid them. Remember, multidimensional arrays can get very big very quickly.

Initializing Arrays

You can initialize all or part of an array when you first declare it. Follow the array declaration with an equal sign and a list of values enclosed in braces and separated by commas. The listed values are assigned in order to array elements starting at number 0.

Consider the following code:

```
int array[4] = { 100, 200, 300, 400 };
```

For this example, the value 100 is assigned to array[0], the value 200 is assigned to array[1], the value 300 is assigned to array[2], and the value 400 is assigned to array[3].

If you omit the array size, the compiler creates an array just large enough to hold the initialization values. Thus, the following statement would have exactly the same effect as the previous array declaration statement:

```
int array[] = { 100, 200, 300, 400 };
```

You can, however, include too few initialization values, as in this example:

```
int array[10] = { 1, 2, 3 };
```

If you don't explicitly initialize an array element, you can't be sure what value it holds when the program runs. If you include too many initializers (more initializers than array elements), the compiler detects an error. According to the ANSI standard, the elements that are not initialized will be set to zero.

Tip

> Don't rely upon the compiler to automatically initialize values. It is best to
> make sure you know what a value is initialized to by setting it yourself.

Initializing Multidimensional Arrays

Multidimensional arrays can also be initialized. The list of initialization values is assigned to array elements in order, with the last array subscript changing first. For example:

```
int array[4][3] = { 1, 2, 3, 4, 5, 6, 7, 8, 9, 10, 11, 12 };
```

results in the following assignments:

```
array[0][0] is equal to 1
array[0][1] is equal to 2
array[0][2] is equal to 3
array[1][0] is equal to 4
```

```
array[1][1] is equal to 5
array[1][2] is equal to 6
array[2][0] is equal to 7
array[2][1] is equal to 8
array[2][2] is equal to 9
array[3][0] is equal to 10
array[3][1] is equal to 11
array[3][2] is equal to 12
```

When you initialize multidimensional arrays, you can make your source code clearer by using extra braces to group the initialization values and also by spreading them over several lines. The following initialization is equivalent to the one just given:

```
int array[4][3] = { { 1, 2, 3 } , { 4, 5, 6 } ,
{ 7, 8, 9 } , { 10, 11, 12 } };
```

Remember, initialization values must be separated by a comma—even when there is a brace between them. Also, be sure to use braces in pairs—a closing brace for every opening brace—or the compiler becomes confused.

Now look at an example that demonstrates the advantages of arrays. Listing 8.3, random.c, creates a 1,000-element, three-dimensional array and fills it with random numbers. The program then displays the array elements on-screen. Imagine how many lines of source code you would need to perform the same task with nonarray variables.

You see a new library function, getchar(), in this program. The getchar() function reads a single character from the keyboard. In Listing 8.3, getchar() pauses the program until the user presses the Enter key. The getchar() function is covered in detail on Day 14.

LISTING 8.3   random.c. Creating a multidimensional array

```
1:   /* random.c - Demonstrates using a multidimensional array */
2:
3:   #include <stdio.h>
4:   #include <stdlib.h>
5:   /* Declare a three-dimensional array with 1000 elements */
6:
7:   int random_array[10][10][10];
8:   int a, b, c;
9:
10:  int main( void )
11:  {
12:      /* Fill the array with random numbers. The C library */
13:      /* function rand() returns a random number. Use one */
14:      /* for loop for each array subscript. */
15:
16:      for (a = 0; a < 10; a++)
```

LISTING 8.3   continued

```
17:     {
18:         for (b = 0; b < 10; b++)
19:         {
20:             for (c = 0; c < 10; c++)
21:             {
22:                 random_array[a][b][c] = rand();
23:             }
24:         }
25:     }
26:
27:     /* Now display the array elements 10 at a time */
28:
29:     for (a = 0; a < 10; a++)
30:     {
31:         for (b = 0; b < 10; b++)
32:         {
33:             for (c = 0; c < 10; c++)
34:             {
35:                 printf("\nrandom_array[%d][%d][%d] = ", a, b, c);
36:                 printf("%d", random_array[a][b][c]);
37:             }
38:             printf("\nPress Enter to continue, CTRL-C to quit.");
39:
40:             getchar();
41:         }
42:     }
43:     return 0;
44: }   /* end of main() */
```

OUTPUT

```
random_array[0][0][0] = 346
random_array[0][0][1] = 130
random_array[0][0][2] = 10982
random_array[0][0][3] = 1090
random_array[0][0][4] = 11656
random_array[0][0][5] = 7117
random_array[0][0][6] = 17595
random_array[0][0][7] = 6415
random_array[0][0][8] = 22948
random_array[0][0][9] = 31126
Press Enter to continue, CTRL-C to quit.

random_array[0][1][0] = 9004
random_array[0][1][1] = 14558
random_array[0][1][2] = 3571
random_array[0][1][3] = 22879
random_array[0][1][4] = 18492
random_array[0][1][5] = 1360
random_array[0][1][6] = 5412
```

8

```
random_array[0][1][7] = 26721
random_array[0][1][8] = 22463
random_array[0][1][9] = 25047
Press Enter to continue, CTRL-C to quit
  ...          ...
random_array[9][8][0] = 6287
random_array[9][8][1] = 26957
random_array[9][8][2] = 1530
random_array[9][8][3] = 14171
random_array[9][8][4] = 6951
random_array[9][8][5] = 213
random_array[9][8][6] = 14003
random_array[9][8][7] = 29736
random_array[9][8][8] = 15028
random_array[9][8][9] = 18968
Press Enter to continue, CTRL-C to quit.

random_array[9][9][0] = 28559
random_array[9][9][1] = 5268
random_array[9][9][2] = 20182
random_array[9][9][3] = 3633
random_array[9][9][4] = 24779
random_array[9][9][5] = 3024
random_array[9][9][6] = 10853
random_array[9][9][7] = 28205
random_array[9][9][8] = 8930
random_array[9][9][9] = 2873
Press Enter to continue, CTRL-C to quit.
```

ANALYSIS On Day 6 you saw a program that used a nested `for` statement; this program has two nested `for` loops. Before you look at the `for` statements in detail, note that lines 7 and 8 declare four variables. The first is an array named `random_array`, used to hold random numbers. `random_array` is a three-dimensional type `int` array that is 10-by-10-by-10, giving a total of 1,000 type `int` elements (10[ts]10[ts]10). Imagine coming up with 1,000 unique variable names if you couldn't use arrays! Line 8 then declares three variables, a, b, and c, used to control the `for` loops.

This program also includes the header file stdlib.h (for standard library) on line 4. It is included to provide the prototype for the `rand()` function used on line 22.

The bulk of the program is contained in two nests of `for` statements. The first is in lines 16 through 25, and the second is in lines 29 through 42. Both `for` nests have the same structure. They work just like the loops in Listing 6.2, but they go one level deeper. In the first set of `for` statements, line 22 is executed repeatedly. Line 22 assigns the return value of a function, `rand()`, to an element of the `random_array` array, where `rand()` is a library function that returns a random number.

Going backward through the listing, you can see that line 20 changes variable c from 0 to 9. This loops through the farthest right subscript of the random_array array. Line 18 loops through b, the middle subscript of the random array. Each time b changes, it loops through all the c elements. Line 16 increments variable a, which loops through the farthest left subscript. Each time this subscript changes, it loops through all 10 values of subscript b, which in turn loop through all 10 values of c. This loop initializes every value in the random array to a random number.

Lines 29 through 42 contain the second nest of for statements. These work like the previous for statements, but these loops print each of the values assigned previously. After 10 are displayed, line 38 prints a message and waits for Enter to be pressed. Line 40 takes care of the keypress using getchar(). If Enter hasn't been pressed, getchar() waits until it is. Run this program and watch the displayed values.

Maximum Array Size

Because of the way memory models work, you shouldn't try to create more than 64KB of data variables for now. An explanation of this limitation is beyond the scope of this book, but there's no need to worry: none of the programs in this book exceed this limitation. To understand more, or to get around this limitation, consult your compiler manuals. Generally, 64KB is enough data space for programs, particularly the relatively simple programs you will write as you work through this book. A single array can take up the entire 64KB of data storage if your program uses no other variables. Otherwise, you need to apportion the available data space as needed.

 Note Some operating systems don't have a 64KB limit. DOS does; Windows doesn't.

The size of an array in bytes depends on the number of elements it has, as well as each element's size. Element size depends on the data type of the array and your computer. The sizes for each numeric data type, given in Table 3.2, are repeated in Table 8.1 for your convenience. These are the data type sizes for many PCs.

TABLE 8.1 Storage space requirements for numeric data types for many PCs

Element Data Type	Element Size (Bytes)
int	4
short	2
long	4

TABLE 8.1 continued

Element Data Type	Element Size (Bytes)
long long	8
float	4
double	8

8

To calculate the storage space required for an array, multiply the number of elements in the array by the element size. For example, a 500-element array of type `float` requires storage space of 500 [ts] 4 = 2000 bytes.

As you saw earlier in this book, you can determine storage space within a program by using C's `sizeof` operator; `sizeof` is a unary operator, not a function. It takes as its argument a variable name or the name of a data type and returns the size, in bytes, of its argument. The use of `sizeof` is illustrated in Listing 8.4.

LISTING 8.4 arraysize.c. Using the `sizeof()` operator to determine storage space requirements for an array

```
 1:   /* Demonstrates the sizeof() operator */
 2:
 3:   #include <stdio.h>
 4:
 5:   /* Declare several 100-element arrays */
 6:
 7:   int intarray[100];
 8:   float floatarray[100];
 9:   double doublearray[100];
10:
11:   int main()
12:   {
13:       /* Display the sizes of numeric data types */
14:
15:       printf("\n\nSize of int = %d bytes", sizeof(int));
16:       printf("\nSize of short = %d bytes", sizeof(short));
17:       printf("\nSize of long = %d bytes", sizeof(long));
18:       printf("\nSize of long long = %d bytes", sizeof(long long));
19:       printf("\nSize of float = %d bytes", sizeof(float));
20:       printf("\nSize of double = %d bytes", sizeof(double));
21:
22:       /* Display the sizes of the three arrays */
23:
24:       printf("\nSize of intarray = %d bytes", sizeof(intarray));
25:       printf("\nSize of floatarray = %d bytes",
26:               sizeof(floatarray));
27:       printf("\nSize of doublearray = %d bytes\n",
```

LISTING 8.4   continued

```
28:               sizeof(doublearray));
29:
30:       return 0;
31:  }
```

The following output is from a 32-bit Windows 3.1 machine:

OUTPUT
```
Size of int = 2 bytes
Size of short = 2 bytes
Size of long = 4 bytes
Size of long long = 8 bytes
Size of float = 4 bytes
Size of double = 8 bytes
Size of intarray = 200 bytes
Size of floatarray = 400 bytes
Size of doublearray = 800 bytes
```

You would see the following output on a 32-bit Windows NT machine, as well as a 32-bit Linux or UNIX machine:

OUTPUT
```
Size of int = 4 bytes
Size of short = 2 bytes
Size of long = 4 bytes
Size of long long = 8 bytes
Size of float = 4 bytes
Size of double = 8 bytes
Size of intarray = 400 bytes
Size of floatarray = 400 bytes
Size of doublearray = 800 bytes
```

ANALYSIS   Enter and compile the program in this listing by using the procedures you learned on Day 1, "Getting Started with C." When the program runs, it displays the sizes—in bytes—of the three arrays and six numeric data types.

On Day 3 you ran a similar program; however, this listing uses sizeof() to determine the storage size of arrays. Lines 7, 8, and 9 declare three arrays, each of different types. Lines 23 through 27 print the size of each array. The size should equal the size of the array's variable type times the number of elements. For example, if an int is 4 bytes, intarray should be 4 × 100, or 400 bytes. Run the program and check the values. As you can see from the output, different machines or operating systems might have different sized data types.

8

> **Tip**
>
> You can determine the number of elements in an array by dividing the size of the array by the size of a single array element. For the doublearray in Listing 18.4, you could determine the number of elements with the following line of code:
>
> ```
> ArraySize = sizeof(doublearray) / sizeof(double);
> ```

Summary

Today's lesson introduced numeric arrays, a powerful data storage method that lets you group a number of same-type data items under the same group name. Individual items, or elements, in an array are identified using a subscript after the array name. Computer programming tasks that involve repetitive data processing lend themselves to array storage.

Like nonarray variables, arrays must be declared before they can be used. Optionally, array elements can be initialized when the array is declared.

Q&A

Q What happens if I use a subscript on an array that is larger than the number of elements in the array?

A If you use a subscript that is out of bounds with the array declaration, the program will probably compile and even run. However, the results of such a mistake can be unpredictable. This can be a difficult error to find once it starts causing problems, so make sure you're careful when initializing and accessing array elements.

Q What happens if I use an array without initializing it?

A This mistake doesn't produce a compiler error. If you don't initialize an array, there can be any value in the array elements. You might get unpredictable results. You should always initialize variables and arrays so that you know exactly what's in them. Day 12 introduces you to one exception to the need to initialize. For now, play it safe.

Q How many dimensions can an array have?

A As stated in today's lesson, you can have as many dimensions as you want. As you add more dimensions, you use more data storage space. You should declare an array only as large as you need to avoid wasting storage space.

Q Is there an easy way to initialize an entire array at once?

A Each element of an array must be initialized. The safest way for a beginning C programmer to initialize an array is either with a declaration, as shown in this chapter, or with a `for` statement. There are other ways to initialize an array, but they are beyond the scope of this book.

Q Can I add two arrays together (or multiply, divide, or subtract them)?

A If you declare two arrays, you can't add the two together. Each element must be added individually. Exercise 10 illustrates this point. You could, however, create a function that could add the two arrays together. Such a function will still be required to add the individual elements.

Q Why is it better to use an array instead of individual variables?

A With arrays, you can group like values with a single name. In Listing 8.3, 1,000 values were stored. Creating 1,000 variable names and initializing each to a random number would have taken a tremendous amount of typing. By using an array, you made the task easy.

Q What do you do if you don't know how big the array needs to be when you're writing the program?

A There are functions within C that let you allocate space for variables and arrays on-the-fly. These functions are covered on Day 15.

Workshop

The Workshop provides quiz questions to help you solidify your understanding of the material covered, and exercises to provide you with experience in using what you've learned.

Quiz

1. Which of C's data types can be used in an array?

2. If an array is declared with 10 elements, what is the subscript of the first element?

3. In a one-dimensional array declared with n elements, what is the subscript of the last element?

4. What happens if your program tries to access an array element with an out-of-range subscript?

5. How do you declare a multidimensional array?

6. An array is declared with the following statement. How many total elements does the array have?

   ```
   int array[2][3][5][8];
   ```

7. What would be the name of the tenth element in the array in question 6?

8. How would you determine the number of elements in the array xyz if it were of type long?

Exercises

1. Write a C program line that would declare three one-dimensional integer arrays, named one, two, and three, with 1,000 elements each.

2. Write the statement that would declare a 10-element integer array and initialize all its elements to 1.

3. Given the following array, write code to initialize all the array elements to 88:

```
int eightyeight[88];
```

4. Given the following array, write code to initialize all the array elements to 0:

```
int stuff[12][10];
```

5. **BUG BUSTER:** What is wrong with the following code fragment?

```
int x, y;
int array[10][3];
int main( void )
{
    for ( x = 0; x < 3; x++ )
        for ( y = 0; y < 10; y++ )
            array[x][y] = 0;
    return 0;
}
```

6. **BUG BUSTER:** What is wrong with the following?

```
int array[10];
int x = 1;

int main( void )
{
    for ( x = 1; x <= 10; x++ )
        array[x] = 99;
    .
    return 0;
}
```

7. Write a program that puts random numbers into a two-dimensional array that is 5 by 4. Print the values in columns on-screen. (Hint: Use the rand() function from Listing 8.3.)

8. Rewrite Listing 8.3 to use a single-dimensional array. Print the average of the 1,000 variables before printing the individual values. Note: Don't forget to pause after every 10 values are printed.

9. Write a program that initializes an array of 10 elements. Each element should be equal to its subscript. The program should then print each of the 10 elements.

10. Modify the program from exercise 9. After printing the initialized values, the program should copy the values to a new array and add 10 to each value. The new array values should be printed.

WEEK 2

DAY 9

Understanding Pointers

Today's lesson introduces you to pointers, an important part of the C language. Pointers provide a powerful and flexible method of manipulating data in your programs. Today you will learn:

- The definition of a pointer
- The uses of pointers
- How to declare and initialize pointers
- How to use pointers with simple variables and arrays
- How to use pointers to pass arrays to functions

As you read through today's lesson, the advantages of using pointers might not be immediately clear. The advantages fall into two categories: things that can be done better with pointers than without, and things that can be done only with pointers. The specifics should become clear as you read this and subsequent days' lessons. At present, just know that you must understand pointers if you want to be a proficient C programmer.

What Is a Pointer?

To understand pointers, you need a basic knowledge of how your computer stores information in memory. The following is a somewhat simplified account of PC memory storage.

Your Computer's Memory

A PC's memory (RAM) consists of many thousands if not millions of sequential storage locations, and each location is identified by a unique address. The memory addresses in a given computer range from zero to a maximum value that depends on the amount of memory installed.

When you're using your computer, the operating system uses some of the system's memory. When you're running a program, the program's code (the machine-language instructions for the program's various tasks) and data (the information the program is using) also use some of the system's memory. This section examines the memory storage for program data.

When you declare a variable in a C program, the compiler sets aside a memory location with a unique address to store that variable. The compiler associates that address with the variable's name. When your program uses the variable name, it automatically accesses the proper memory location. The location's address is used, but it is hidden from you, and you need not be concerned with it.

Figure 9.1 shows this schematically. A variable named `rate` has been declared and initialized to `100`. The compiler has set aside storage at address `1004` for the variable and has associated the name `rate` with the address `1004`.

FIGURE 9.1

A program variable is stored at a specific memory address.

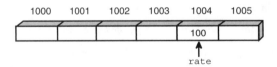

Creating a Pointer

You should note that the address of the variable `rate` (or any other variable) is a number and can be treated like any other number in C. If you know a variable's address, you can create a second variable in which to store the address of the first. The first step is to declare a variable to hold the address of `rate`. Give it the name `p_rate`, for example. At first, `p_rate` is uninitialized. Storage has been allocated for `p_rate`, but its value is undetermined, as shown in Figure 9.2.

FIGURE 9.2

Memory storage space has been allocated for the variable p_rate.

The next step is to store the address of the variable rate in the variable p_rate. Because p_rate now contains the address of rate, it indicates the location where rate is stored in memory. In C parlance, p_rate *points* to rate, or is a pointer to rate. This is shown in Figure 9.3.

FIGURE 9.3

The variable p_rate contains the address of the variable rate and is therefore a pointer to rate.

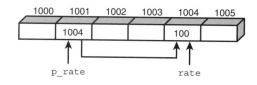

To summarize, a pointer is a variable that contains the address of another variable. Now you can get down to the details of using pointers in your C programs.

Pointers and Simple Variables

In the example just given, a pointer variable pointed to a simple (that is, nonarray) variable. This section shows you how to create and use pointers to simple variables.

Declaring Pointers

A pointer is a numeric variable and, like all variables, must be declared before it can be used. Pointer variable names follow the same rules as other variables and must be unique. Today's lesson uses the convention that a pointer to the variable name is called p_name. This isn't necessary, however; you can name pointers anything you want as long as they follow C's naming rules.

A pointer declaration takes the following form:

typename *ptrname;

where *typename* is any of C's variable types and indicates the type of the variable that the pointer points to. The asterisk (*) is the indirection operator, and it indicates that *ptrname* is a pointer to type *typename* and not a variable of type *typename*. Pointers can be declared along with nonpointer variables. Here are some more examples:

```
char *ch1, *ch2;        /* ch1 and ch2 both are pointers to type char */
float *value, percent;  /* value is a pointer to type float, and
                        /* percent is an ordinary float variable */
```

Note

> The * symbol is used as both the indirection operator and the multiplication operator. Don't worry about the compiler becoming confused. The context in which * is used always provides enough information for the compiler to figure out whether you mean indirection or multiplication.

Initializing Pointers

Now that you've declared a pointer, what can you do with it? You can't do anything with it until you make it point to something. Like regular variables, uninitialized pointers can be used, but the results are unpredictable and potentially disastrous. Until a pointer holds the address of a variable, it isn't useful. The address doesn't get stored in the pointer by magic; your program must put it there by using the address-of operator, the ampersand (&). When placed before the name of a variable, the address-of operator returns the address of the variable. Therefore, you initialize a pointer with a statement of the form

```
pointer = &variable;
```

Look back at the example in Figure 9.3. The program statement to initialize the variable p_rate to point at the variable rate would be

```
p_rate = &rate;    /* assign the address of rate to p_rate */
```

This statement assigns the address of rate to p_rate. Before the initialization, p_rate didn't point to anything in particular. After the initialization, p_rate is a pointer to rate.

Using Pointers

Now that you know how to declare and initialize pointers, you're probably wondering how to use them. The indirection operator (*) comes into play again. When the * precedes the name of a pointer, it refers to the variable pointed to.

Consider the previous example, in which the pointer p_rate has been initialized to point to the variable rate. If you write *p_rate, it refers to the variable rate. If you want to print the value of rate (which is 100 in the example), you could write

```
printf("%d", rate);
```

or you could write this statement:

```
printf("%d", *p_rate);
```

NEW TERM In C, these two statements are equivalent. Accessing the contents of a variable by using the variable name is called *direct access*. Accessing the contents of a variable by using a pointer to the variable is called *indirect access* or *indirection*. Figure 9.4 shows that a pointer name preceded by the indirection operator refers to the value of the pointed-to variable.

FIGURE 9.4

Use of the indirection operator with pointers.

Pause a minute and think about this material. Pointers are an integral part of the C language, and it's essential that you understand them. Pointers have confused many people, so don't worry if you're feeling a bit puzzled. If you need to review, that's fine. Maybe the following summary can help.

If you have a pointer named ptr that has been initialized to point to the variable var, the following are true:

- *ptr and var both refer to the contents of var (that is, whatever value the program has stored there).
- ptr and &var refer to the address of var.

As you can see, a pointer name without the indirection operator accesses the pointer value itself, which is, of course, the address of the variable pointed to.

Listing 9.1 demonstrates basic pointer use. You should enter, compile, and run this program.

LISTING 9.1 ptr.c. Basic pointer use

```
 1:  /* Demonstrates basic pointer use. */
 2:
 3:  #include <stdio.h>
 4:
 5:  /* Declare and initialize an int variable */
 6:
 7:  int var = 1;
 8:
 9:  /* Declare a pointer to int */
10:
11:  int *ptr;
12:
13:  int main( void )
14:  {
```

LISTING 9.1   continued

```
15:     /* Initialize ptr to point to var */
16:
17:     ptr = &var;
18:
19:     /* Access var directly and indirectly */
20:
21:     printf("\nDirect access, var = %d", var);
22:     printf("\nIndirect access, var = %d", *ptr);
23:
24:     /* Display the address of var two ways */
25:
26:     printf("\n\nThe address of var = %d", &var);
27:     printf("\nThe address of var = %d\n", ptr);
28:
29:     return 0;
30: }
```

OUTPUT
```
Direct access, var = 1
Indirect access, var = 1

The address of var = 4202504
The address of var = 4202504
```

Note   The address reported for var might not be 4202504 on your system.

ANALYSIS   In this listing, two variables are declared. In line 7, var is declared as an int and initialized to 1. In line 11, a pointer to a variable of type int is declared and named ptr. In line 17, the pointer ptr is assigned the address of var using the address-of operator (&). The rest of the program prints the values from these two variables to the screen. Line 21 prints the value of var, whereas line 22 prints the value stored in the location pointed to by ptr. In this program, this value is 1. Line 26 prints the address of var using the address-of operator. This is the same value printed by line 27 using the pointer variable, ptr.

This listing is good to study. It shows the relationship between a variable, its address, a pointer, and the dereferencing of a pointer.

DO	**DON'T**
DO understand what pointers are and how they work. The mastering of C requires mastering pointers.	**DON'T** use an uninitialized pointer until an address has been assigned. Results can be disastrous if you do.

Pointers and Variable Types

The previous discussion ignores the fact that different variable types occupy different amounts of memory. For the more common PC operating systems, an short takes two bytes, a float takes four bytes, and so on. Each individual byte of memory has its own address, so a multibyte variable actually occupies several addresses.

How, then, do pointers handle the addresses of multibyte variables? Here's how it works: The address of a variable is actually the address of the first (lowest) byte it occupies. This can be illustrated with an example that declares and initializes three variables:

```
short vshort = 12252;
char vchar = 90;
float vfloat = 1200.156004;
```

These variables are stored in memory as shown in Figure 9.5. In this figure, the short variable occupies two bytes, the char variable occupies one byte, and the float variable occupies four bytes.

FIGURE 9.5

Different types of numeric variables occupy different amounts of storage space in memory.

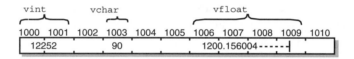

Now declare and initialize pointers to these three variables:

```
int *p_vshort;
char *p_vchar;
float *p_vfloat;
/* additional code goes here */
p_vshort = &vshort;
p_vchar = &vchar;
p_vfloat = &vfloat;
```

Each pointer is equal to the address of the first byte of the pointed-to variable. Thus, p_vshort equals 1000, p_vchar equals 1003, and p_vfloat equals 1006. Remember, however, that each pointer was declared to point to a certain type of variable. The compiler knows that a pointer to type short points to the first of two bytes, a pointer to type float points to the first of four bytes, and so on. This is illustrated in Figure 9.6.

FIGURE 9.6

The compiler knows the size of the variable that a pointer points to.

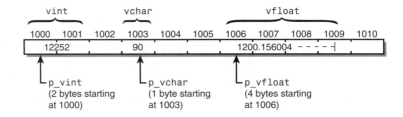

Figures 9.5 and 9.6 show some empty memory storage locations among the three variables. This is for the sake of visual clarity. In actual practice, most C compilers store the three variables in adjacent memory locations with no unused bytes between them. You shouldn't count on either being the case.

Pointers and Arrays

Pointers can be useful when you're working with simple variables, but they are more helpful with arrays. There is a special relationship between pointers and arrays in C. In fact, when you use the array subscript notation that you learned on Day 8, "Using Numeric Arrays," you're really using pointers without knowing it. The following sections explain how this works.

The Array Name as a Pointer

An array name without brackets is a pointer to the array's first element. Thus, if you've declared an array `data[]`, `data` is the address of the first array element.

"Wait a minute," you might be saying. "Don't you need the address-of operator to get an address?" Yes. You can also use the expression `&data[0]` to obtain the address of the array's first element. In C, the relationship (`data == &data[0]`) is true.

You've seen that the name of an array is a pointer to the array. The name of an array is a pointer constant; it can't be changed and remains fixed for the entire time the program executes. This makes sense: If you changed its value, it would point elsewhere and not to the array (which remains at a fixed location in memory).

You can, however, declare a pointer variable and initialize it to point at the array. For example, the following code initializes the pointer variable `p_array` with the address of the first element of `array[]`:

```
int array[100], *p_array;
/* additional code goes here */
p_array = array;
```

Because p_array is a pointer variable, it can be modified to point elsewhere. Unlike the array name (array), p_array isn't locked into pointing at the first element of array[]. For example, it could be changed to point at other elements of array[]. How would you do this? First, you need to look at how array elements are stored in memory.

Array Element Storage

As you might remember from Day 8, the elements of an array are stored in sequential memory locations with the first element in the lowest address. Subsequent array elements (those with an index greater than 0) are stored in higher addresses. How much higher depends on the array's data type (char, int, float, and so forth).

Take an array of type short. As you learned on Day 3, "Storing Data: Variables and Constants," a single short variable can occupy two bytes of memory. Each array element is therefore located two bytes above the preceding element, and the address of each array element is two higher than the address of the preceding element. A type float, on the other hand, can occupy four bytes. In an array of type float, each array element is located four bytes above the preceding element, and the address of each array element is four higher than the address of the preceding element.

Figure 9.7 illustrates the relationship between array storage and addresses for a six-element short array and a three-element float array.

FIGURE 9.7

Array storage for different array types.

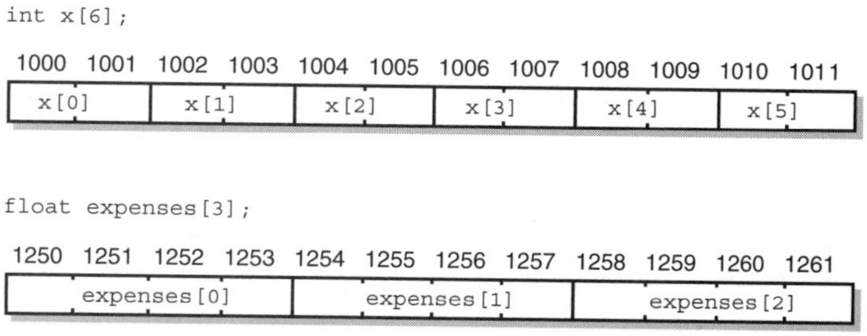

```
int x[6];

1000  1001  1002  1003  1004  1005  1006  1007  1008  1009  1010  1011
 x[0]         x[1]         x[2]         x[3]         x[4]         x[5]


float expenses[3];

1250  1251  1252  1253  1254  1255  1256  1257  1258  1259  1260  1261
    expenses[0]            expenses[1]            expenses[2]
```

By looking at Figure 9.7, you should be able to see why the following relationships are true:

```
1: x == 1000
2: &x[0] == 1000
3: &x[1] = 1002
4: expenses == 1250
5: &expenses[0] == 1250
6: &expenses[1] == 1254
```

x without the array brackets is the address of the first element (x[0]). You can also see that x[0] is at the address of 1000. Line 2 shows this too. It can be read like this: "The address of the first element of the array x is equal to 1000." Line 3 shows that the address of the second element (subscripted as 1 in an array) is 1002. Again, Figure 9.7 can confirm this. Lines 4, 5, and 6 are virtually identical to 1, 2, and 3, respectively. They vary in the difference between the addresses of the two array elements. In the type short array x, the difference is two bytes, and in the type float array, expenses, the difference is four bytes.

How do you access these successive array elements using a pointer? You can see from these examples that a pointer must be increased by 2 to access successive elements of a type short array, and by 4 to access successive elements of a type float array. You can generalize and say that to access successive elements of an array of a particular data type, a pointer must be increased by sizeof(datatype). Remember from Day 3 that the sizeof() operator returns the size in bytes of a C data type.

Listing 9.2 illustrates the relationship between addresses and the elements of different type arrays by declaring arrays of type short, float, and double and by displaying the addresses of successive elements.

LISTING 9.2   asize.c. Displaying the addresses of successive array elements

```
1:  /* Demonstrates the relationship between addresses and */
2:  /* elements of arrays of different data types. */
3:
4:  #include <stdio.h>
5:
6:  /* Declare a counter and three arrays. */
7:  int ctr;
8:  short array_s[10];
9:  float array_f[10];
10: double array_d[10];
11:
12: int main( void )
13: {
14:     /* Print the table heading */
15:
16:     printf("\t\tShort\t\tFloat\t\tDouble");
17:
18:     printf("\n=================================");
19:     printf("========================");
20:
21:     /* Print the addresses of each array element. */
22:
23:     for (ctr = 0; ctr < 10; ctr++)
24:         printf("\nElement %d:\t%ld\t\t%ld\t\t%ld", ctr,
25:             &array_s[ctr], &array_f[ctr], &array_d[ctr]);
26:
```

LISTING 9.2 continued

```
27:     printf("\n=================================");
28:     printf("========================\n");
29:
30:     return 0;
31: }
```

OUTPUT

```
                Short           Float           Double
        ====================================================
Element 0:      4206736         4206608         4206656
Element 1:      4206738         4206612         4206664
Element 2:      4206740         4206616         4206672
Element 3:      4206742         4206620         4206680
Element 4:      4206744         4206624         4206688
Element 5:      4206746         4206628         4206696
Element 6:      4206748         4206632         4206704
Element 7:      4206750         4206636         4206712
Element 8:      4206752         4206640         4206720
Element 9:      4206754         4206644         4206728
        ====================================================
```

ANALYSIS The exact addresses that your system displays will be different from these, but the relationships are the same. In this output, there are two bytes between short elements, four bytes between float elements, and eight bytes between double elements.

Note Some machines use different sizes for variable types. If your machine differs, the preceding output might have different-size gaps; however, they will be consistent gaps.

This listing takes advantage of the escape characters discussed on Day 7, "Fundamentals of Reading and Writing Information." The printf() calls in lines 16 and 24 use the tab escape character (\t) to help format the table by aligning the columns.

Looking more closely at Listing 9.2, you can see that three arrays are created in lines 8, 9, and 10. Line 8 declares array array_s of type short, line 9 declares array array_f of type float, and line 10 declares array array_d of type double. Line 16 prints the column headers for the table that will be displayed. Lines 18 and 19, along with lines 27 and 28, print dashed lines across the top and bottom of the table data. This is a nice touch for a report. Lines 23, 24, and 25 are a for loop that prints each of the table's rows. The number of the element ctr is printed first. This is followed by the address of the element in each of the three arrays.

Pointer Arithmetic

You have a pointer to the first array element; the pointer must increment by an amount equal to the size of the data type stored in the array. How do you access array elements using pointer notation? You use *pointer arithmetic*.

"Just what I don't need," you might be thinking, "another kind of arithmetic to learn!" Don't worry. Pointer arithmetic is simple, and it makes using pointers in your programs much easier. You have to be concerned with only two pointer operations: incrementing and decrementing.

Incrementing Pointers

When you *increment* a pointer, you are increasing its value. For example, when you increment a pointer by 1, pointer arithmetic automatically increases the pointer's value so that it points to the next array element. In other words, C knows the data type that the pointer points to (from the pointer declaration) and increases the address stored in the pointer by the size of the data type.

Suppose that `ptr_to_short` is a pointer variable to some element of an `short` array. If you execute the statement

```
ptr_to_short++;
```

the value of `ptr_to_short` is increased by the size of type `short` (usually 2 bytes), and `ptr_to_short` now points to the next array element. Likewise, if `ptr_to_float` points to an element of a type `float` array, the statement

```
ptr_to_float++;
```

increases the value of `ptr_to_float` by the size of type `float` (usually 4 bytes).

The same holds true for increments greater than 1. If you add the value n to a pointer, C increments the pointer by n array elements of the associated data type. Therefore,

```
ptr_to_short += 4;
```

increases the value stored in `ptr_to_short` by 8 (assuming that a short is 2 bytes), so it points four array elements ahead. Likewise,

```
ptr_to_float += 10;
```

increases the value stored in `ptr_to_float` by 40 (assuming that a float is 4 bytes), so it points 10 array elements ahead.

Decrementing Pointers

The same concepts that apply to incrementing pointers hold true for decrementing pointers. *Decrementing* a pointer is actually a special case of incrementing by adding a negative value. If you decrement a pointer with the `--` or `-=` operators, pointer arithmetic automatically adjusts for the size of the array elements.

Listing 9.3 presents an example of how pointer arithmetic can be used to access array elements. By incrementing pointers, the program can step through all the elements of the arrays efficiently.

LISTING 9.3   ptr_math.c. Using pointer arithmetic and pointer notation to access array elements

```
 1:   /* Demonstrates using pointer arithmetic to access */
 2:   /* array elements with pointer notation. */
 3:
 4:   #include <stdio.h>
 5:   #define MAX 10
 6:
 7:   /* Declare and initialize an integer array. */
 8:
 9:   int i_array[MAX] = { 0,1,2,3,4,5,6,7,8,9 };
10:
11:   /* Declare a pointer to int and an int variable. */
12:
13:   int *i_ptr, count;
14:
15:   /* Declare and initialize a float array. */
16:
17:   float f_array[MAX] = { .0, .1, .2, .3, .4, .5, .6, .7, .8, .9 };
18:
19:   /* Declare a pointer to float. */
20:
21:   float *f_ptr;
22:
23:   int main( void )
24:   {
25:       /* Initialize the pointers. */
26:
27:       i_ptr = i_array;
28:       f_ptr = f_array;
29:
30:       /* Print the array elements. */
31:
32:       for (count = 0; count < MAX; count++)
33:           printf("%d\t%f\n", *i_ptr++, *f_ptr++);
34:
35:       return 0;
36:   }
```

```
0      0.000000
1      0.100000
2      0.200000
3      0.300000
4      0.400000
5      0.500000
6      0.600000
7      0.700000
8      0.800000
9      0.900000
```

ANALYSIS In this program, a defined constant named MAX is set to 10 in line 5; it is used throughout the listing. In line 9, MAX is used to set the number of elements in an array of ints named i_array. The elements in this array are initialized at the same time that the array is declared. Line 13 declares two additional int variables. The first is a pointer named i_ptr. You know this is a pointer because an indirection operator (*) is used. The other variable is a simple type int variable named count. In line 17, a second array is defined and initialized. This array is of type float, contains MAX values, and is initialized with float values. Line 21 declares a pointer to a float named f_ptr.

The main() function is on lines 23 through 36. The program assigns the beginning address of the two arrays to the pointers of their respective types in lines 27 and 28. Remember, an array name without a subscript is the same as the address of the array's beginning. A for statement in lines 32 and 33 uses the int variable count to count from 0 to the value of MAX. For each count, line 33 dereferences the two pointers and prints their values in a printf() function call. The increment operator then increments each of the pointers so that each points to the next element in the array before continuing with the next iteration of the for loop.

You might be thinking that this program could just as well have used array subscript notation and dispensed with pointers altogether. This is true, and in simple programming tasks like this, the use of pointer notation doesn't offer any major advantages. As you start to write more complex programs, however, you should find the use of pointers advantageous.

Remember that you can't perform incrementing and decrementing operations on pointer constants. (An array name without brackets is a *pointer constant*.) Also remember that when you're manipulating pointers to array elements, the C compiler doesn't keep track of the start and finish of the array. If you're not careful, you can increment or decrement the pointer so that it points somewhere in memory before or after the array. Something is stored there, but it isn't an array element. You should keep track of pointers and where they're pointing.

Other Pointer Manipulations

The other pointer arithmetic operation that you will want to use is called *differencing,* which refers to subtracting two pointers. If you have two pointers to different elements of the same array, you can subtract them and find out how far apart they are. Again, pointer arithmetic automatically scales the answer so that it refers to the number of array elements. Thus, if `ptr1` and `ptr2` point to elements of an array (of any type), the following expression tells you how far apart the elements are:

```
ptr1 - ptr2
```

You can also compare pointers. Pointer comparisons are valid only between pointers that point to the same array. Under these circumstances, the relational operators ==, !=, >, <, >=, and <= work properly. Lower array elements (that is, those having a lower subscript) always have a lower address than higher array elements. Thus, if `ptr1` and `ptr2` point to elements of the same array, the comparison

```
ptr1 < ptr2
```

is true if `ptr1` points to an earlier member of the array than `ptr2` does.

This covers all allowed pointer operations. Many arithmetic operations that can be performed with regular variables, such as multiplication and division, don't make sense with pointers. The C compiler doesn't allow them. For example, if `ptr` is a pointer, the statement

```
ptr *= 2;
```

generates an error message. Table 9.1 indicates all of the operations you can do with a pointer, all of which have been covered in today's lesson.

TABLE 9.1 Pointer operations

Operation	Description
Assignment	You can assign a value to a pointer. The value should be an address, obtained with the address-of operator (&) or from a pointer constant (array name).
Indirection	The indirection operator (*) gives the value stored in the pointed-to location (often called dereferencing).
Address of	You can use the address-of operator to find the address of a pointer, so you can have pointers to pointers. This is an advanced topic and is covered on Day 15, "Pointers: Beyond the Basics."
Incrementing	You can add an integer to a pointer in order to point to a different memory location.

TABLE 9.1 continued

Operation	Description
Decrementing	You can subtract an integer from a pointer in order to point to a different memory location.
Differencing	You can subtract one pointer from another pointer in order to determine how far apart they are.
Comparison	Valid only with two pointers that point to the same array.

Pointer Cautions

When you're writing a program that uses pointers, you must avoid one serious error: using an uninitialized pointer on the left side of an assignment statement. For example, the following statement declares a pointer to type `int`:

```
int *ptr;
```

This pointer isn't yet initialized, so it doesn't point to anything. To be more exact, it doesn't point to anything *known*. An uninitialized pointer has some value; you just don't know what it is. In many cases, it is zero. If you use an uninitialized pointer in an assignment statement, this is what happens:

```
*ptr = 12;
```

The value `12` is assigned to whatever address `ptr` points to. That address can be almost anywhere in memory—where the operating system is stored or somewhere in the program's code. The `12` that is stored there might overwrite some important information, and the result can be anything from strange program errors to a full system crash.

The left side of an assignment statement is the most dangerous place to use an uninitialized pointer. Other errors, although less serious, can also result from using an uninitialized pointer anywhere in your program, so be sure your program's pointers are properly initialized before you use them. You must do this yourself; don't assume that the compiler will do this for you.

Do	Don't
DO remember that subtracting from or adding to a pointer changes the pointer based on the size of the data type it points to. It doesn't change it by 1 or by the number being added (unless it's a pointer to a one-byte character). **DO** understand the size of variable types on your computer. As you can begin to see, you need to know variable sizes when working with pointers and memory.	**DON'T** try to perform mathematical operations such as division, multiplication, and modulus on pointers. Adding (incrementing) and subtracting (differencing) pointers are acceptable. **DON'T** try to increment or decrement an array variable. Assign a pointer to the beginning address of the array and increment it (see Listing 9.3).

Array Subscript Notation and Pointers

An array name without brackets is a pointer to the array's first element. Therefore, you can access the first array element using the indirection operator. If `array[]` is a declared array, the expression `*array` is the array's first element, `*(array + 1)` is the array's second element, and so on. If you generalize for the entire array, the following relationships hold true:

```
*(array) == array[0]
*(array + 1) == array[1]
*(array + 2) == array[2]
...
*(array + n) == array[n]
```

This illustrates the equivalence of array subscript notation and array pointer notation. You can use either in your programs; the C compiler sees them as two different ways of accessing array data using pointers.

Passing Arrays to Functions

Today's lesson has already discussed the special relationship that exists in C between pointers and arrays. This relationship comes into play when you need to pass an array as an argument to a function. The only way you can pass an array to a function is by using a pointer.

As you learned on Day 5, "Functions: The Basics," an argument is a value that the calling program passes to a function. It can be an `int`, a `float`, or any other simple data type, but it must be a single numerical value. It can be a single array element, but it can't be an entire array. What if you need to pass an entire array to a function? Well, you can have a pointer to an array, and that pointer is a single numeric value (the address of the array's first element). If you pass that value to a function, the function knows the address of the array and can access the array elements using pointer notation.

Consider another problem. If you write a function that takes an array as an argument, you want a function that can handle arrays of different sizes. For example, you could write a function that finds the largest element in an array of integers. The function wouldn't be much use if it were limited to dealing with arrays of one fixed size.

How does the function know the size of the array whose address it was passed? Remember, the value passed to a function is a pointer to the first array element. It could be the first of 10 elements or the first of 10,000. There are two methods of letting a function know an array's size.

You can identify the last array element by storing a special value there. As the function processes the array, it looks for that value in each element. When the value is found, the end of the array has been reached. The disadvantage of this method is that it forces you to reserve a value as the end-of-array indicator, reducing the flexibility you have for storing real data in the array.

The other method is more flexible and straightforward, and it's the one used in this book: Pass the function the array size as an argument. This can be a simple type int argument. Thus, the function is passed two arguments: a pointer to the first array element, and an integer specifying the number of elements in the array.

Listing 9.4 accepts a list of values from the user and stores them in an array. It then calls a function named largest(), passing the array (both pointer and size). The function finds the largest value in the array and returns it to the calling program.

LISTING 9.4   passing.c. Passing an array to a function

```
1:  /* Passing an array to a function. */
2:
3:  #include <stdio.h>
4:
5:  #define MAX 10
6:
7:  int array[MAX], count;
8:
9:  int largest(int num_array[], int length);
10:
11: int main( void )
12: {
13:     /* Input MAX values from the keyboard. */
14:
```

LISTING 9.4   continued

```
15:        for (count = 0; count < MAX; count++)
16:        {
17:            printf("Enter an integer value: ");
18:            scanf("%d", &array[count]);
19:        }
20:
21:        /* Call the function and display the return value. */
22:        printf("\n\nLargest value = %d\n", largest(array, MAX));
23:
24:        return 0;
25: }
26: /* Function largest() returns the largest value */
27: /* in an integer array */
28:
29: int largest(int num_array[], int length)
30: {
31:        int count, biggest = -12000;
32:
33:        for ( count = 0; count < length; count++)
34:        {
35:            if (num_array[count] > biggest)
36:                biggest = num_array[count];
37:        }
38:
39:        return biggest;
40: }
```

OUTPUT

```
Enter an integer value: 1
Enter an integer value: 2
Enter an integer value: 3
Enter an integer value: 4
Enter an integer value: 5
Enter an integer value: 10
Enter an integer value: 9
Enter an integer value: 8
Enter an integer value: 7
Enter an integer value: 6

Largest value = 10
```

ANALYSIS   The function used in this example to accept a pointer to an array is called
largest(). The function prototype is in line 9 and with the exception of the
semicolon, it is identical to the function header in line 29.

Most of what is presented in the function header in line 29 should make sense to you:
largest() is a function that returns an int to the calling program; its second argument is
an int represented by the parameter length. The only thing new is the first parameter,

`int num_array[]`, which indicates that the first argument is a pointer to type `int`, represented by the parameter `num_array`. You also could write the function declaration and header as follows:

```
int largest(int *num_array, int length);
```

This is equivalent to the first form; both `int num_array[]` and `int *num_array` mean "pointer to `int`." The first form might be preferable, because it reminds you that the parameter represents a pointer to an array. Of course, the pointer doesn't know that it points to an array, but the function uses it that way.

Now look at the function `largest()`. When it is called, the parameter `num_array` holds the value of the first argument and is therefore a pointer to the first element of the array. You can use x anywhere an array pointer can be used. In `largest()`, the array elements are accessed using subscript notation in lines 35 and 36. You also could use pointer notation, rewriting the `if` loop like this:

```
for (count = 0; count < length; count++)
{
    if (*(num_array+count) > biggest)
        biggest = *(num_array+count);
}
```

Listing 9.5 shows the other way of passing arrays to functions.

LISTING 9.5 passing2.c. An alternative way of passing an array to a function

```
 1:  /* Passing an array to a function. Alternative way. */
 2:
 3:  #include <stdio.h>
 4:
 5:  #define MAX 10
 6:
 7:  int array[MAX+1], count;
 8:
 9:  int largest(int num_array[]);
10:
11:  int main( void )
12:  {
13:      /* Input MAX values from the keyboard. */
14:
15:      for (count = 0; count < MAX; count++)
16:      {
17:          printf("Enter an integer value: ");
18:          scanf("%d", &array[count]);
19:
20:          if ( array[count] == 0 )
21:              count = MAX;                    /* will exit for loop */
```

LISTING 9.5   continued

```
22:      }
23:      array[MAX] = 0;
24:
25:      /* Call the function and display the return value. */
26:      printf("\n\nLargest value = %d\n", largest(array));
27:
28:      return 0;
29: }
30: /* Function largest() returns the largest value */
31: /* in an integer array */
32:
33: int largest(int num_array[])
34: {
35:      int count, biggest = -12000;
36:
37:      for ( count = 0; num_array[count] != 0; count++)
38:      {
39:          if (num_array[count] > biggest)
40:              biggest = num_array[count];
41:      }
42:
43:      return biggest;
44: }
```

INPUT/
OUTPUT

```
Enter an integer value: 1
Enter an integer value: 2
Enter an integer value: 3
Enter an integer value: 4
Enter an integer value: 5
Enter an integer value: 10
Enter an integer value: 9
Enter an integer value: 8
Enter an integer value: 7
Enter an integer value: 6

Largest value = 10
```

Here is the output from running the program a second time:

INPUT/
OUTPUT

```
Enter an integer value: 10
Enter an integer value: 20
Enter an integer value: 55
Enter an integer value: 3
Enter an integer value: 12
Enter an integer value: 0

Largest value = 55
```

ANALYSIS This program uses a `largest()` function that has the same functionality as Listing 9.4. The difference is that only the array tag is needed. The `for` loop in line 37 continues looking for the largest value until it encounters a `0`, at which point it knows it is done.

Looking at the early parts of this program, you can see the differences between Listing 9.4 and Listing 9.5. First, in line 7 you need to add an extra element to the array to store the value that indicates the end. In lines 20 and 21, an `if` statement is added to see whether the user entered `0`, thus signaling that he is done entering values. If `0` is entered, `count` is set to its maximum value so that the `for` loop can be exited cleanly. Line 23 ensures that the last element is `0` in case the user entered the maximum number of values (`MAX`).

By adding the extra commands when entering the data, you can make the `largest()` function work with any size of array; however, there is one catch. What happens if you forget to put a `0` at the end of the array? `largest()` continues past the end of the array, comparing values in memory until it finds a `0`.

As you can see, passing an array to a function is not particularly difficult. You simply pass a pointer to the array's first element. In most situations, you also need to pass the number of elements in the array. In the function, the pointer value can be used to access the array elements with either subscript or pointer notation.

> **Caution**
>
> Recall from Day 5 that when a simple variable is passed to a function, only a copy of the variable's value is passed. The function can use the value but can't change the original variable because it doesn't have access to the variable itself. When you pass an array to a function, things are different. A function is passed the array's address, not just a copy of the values in the array. The code in the function works with the actual array elements and can modify the values stored in the array.

Summary

Today's lesson introduced you to pointers, a central part of C programming. A pointer is a variable that holds the address of another variable; a pointer is said to "point to" the variable whose address it holds. The two operators needed with pointers are the address-of operator (`&`) and the indirection operator (`*`). When placed before a variable name, the address-of operator returns the variable's address. When placed before a pointer name, the indirection operator returns the contents of the pointed-to variable.

Pointers and arrays have a special relationship. An array name without brackets is a pointer to the array's first element. The special features of pointer arithmetic make it easy to access array elements using pointers. Array subscript notation is in fact a special form of pointer notation.

You also learned to pass arrays as arguments to functions by passing a pointer to the array. Once the function knows the array's address and length, it can access the array elements using either pointer notation or subscript notation.

9

Q&A

Q Why are pointers so important in C?

A Pointers give you more control over the computer and your data. When used with functions, pointers let you change the values of variables that were passed, regardless of where they originated. On Day 15, you will learn additional uses for pointers.

Q How does the compiler know the difference between * for multiplication, for dereferencing, and for declaring a pointer?

A The compiler interprets the different uses of the asterisk based on the context in which it is used. If the statement being evaluated starts with a variable type, it can be assumed that the asterisk is for declaring a pointer. If the asterisk is used with a variable that has been declared as a pointer, but not in a variable declaration, the asterisk is assumed to dereference. If it is used in a mathematical expression, but not with a pointer variable, the asterisk can be assumed to be the multiplication operator.

Q What happens if I use the address-of operator on a pointer?

A You get the address of the pointer variable. Remember, a pointer is just another variable that holds the address of the variable to which it points.

Q Are variables always stored in the same location?

A No. Each time a program runs, its variables can be stored at different addresses within the computer. You should never assign a constant address value to a pointer.

Workshop

The Workshop provides quiz questions to help you solidify your understanding of the material covered and exercises to provide you with experience in using what you've learned.

Quiz

1. What operator is used to determine the address of a variable?

2. What operator is used to determine the value at the location pointed to by a pointer?

3. What is a pointer?

4. What is indirection?

5. How are the elements of an array stored in memory?

6. Show two ways to obtain the address of the first element of the array data[].

7. If an array is passed to a function, what are two ways to know where the end of that array is?

8. What are the six operations covered in this chapter that can be accomplished with a pointer?

9. Assume that you have two pointers. If the first points to the third element in an array of ints and the second points to the fourth element, what value is obtained if you subtract the first pointer from the second? (Assume that the size of an integer is 2 bytes.)

10. Assume that the array in question 9 is of float values. What value is obtained if the two pointers are subtracted? (Assume that the size of a float is two bytes.)

Exercises

1. Show a declaration for a pointer to a type char variable. Name the pointer char_ptr.

2. If you have a type int variable named cost, how would you declare and initialize a pointer named p_cost that points to that variable?

3. Continuing with exercise 2, how would you assign the value 100 to the variable cost using both direct access and indirect access?

4. Continuing with exercise 3, how would you print the value of the pointer, plus the value being pointed to?

5. Show how to assign the address of a float value called radius to a pointer.

6. Show two ways to assign the value 100 to the third element of data[].

7. Write a function named sumarrays() that accepts two arrays as arguments, totals all values in both arrays, and returns the total to the calling program.

8. Use the function created in exercise 7 in a simple program.

9. Write a function named addarrays() that accepts two arrays that are the same size. The function should add each element in the arrays together and place the values in a third array.

TYPE & RUN 3

Pausing for a Second or Two

This is the third Type & Run section. Remember, the purpose of the listings in the Type & Run sections is to give you something a little more functional than what you are getting in the daily lessons. This listing contains only a few elements not already explained, thus making it an easy listing to follow. After you type in and run this program, take the time to experiment with the code. Make changes, recompile, and then rerun the program and see what happens. If you get any errors, make sure you entered the program correctly.

LISTING T&R 3   seconds.c. A program with a sleep function

```
1:  /* seconds.c */
2:  /* Program that pauses. */
3:
4:  #include <stdio.h>
5:  #include <stdlib.h>
6:  #include <time.h>
7:
8:  void sleep( int nbr_seconds );
9:
```

LISTING T&R 3   continued

```
10:  int main( void )
11:  {
12:      int ctr;
13:      int wait = 13;
14:
15:      /* Pause for a number of seconds. Print a *
16:       * dot each second waited.                */
17:
18:      printf("Delay for %d seconds\n", wait );
19:      printf(">");
20:
21:      for (ctr=1; ctr <= wait; ctr++)
22:      {
23:         printf(".");        /* print a dot */
24:         fflush(stdout);     /* force dot to print on buffered machines */
25:         sleep( (int) 1 );   /* pause 1 second */
26:      }
27:      printf( "Done!\n");
28:      return (0);
29:  }
30:
31:  /* Pauses for a specified number of seconds */
32:  void sleep( int nbr_seconds )
33:  {
34:      clock_t goal;
35:
36:      goal = ( nbr_seconds * CLOCKS_PER_SEC ) + clock();
37:
38:      while( goal > clock() )
39:      {
40:          ; /* loop */
41:      }
42:  }
```

This program contains a function you might find useful in other programs you write. The
sleep() function pauses the computer for a number of seconds. During this time, the
computer simply checks to see if it has waited long enough. Once the specified number
of seconds has elapsed, the function returns control. You'll find that this function, or variations of this function, can be used in a number of ways. Because of the speed of computers, you will often want to pause the computer so that the reader has time to read
information you display. For example, you might want to display a copyright screen
when you first start an application.

As a simple illustration, the main part of this program prints dots. Between each dot, the
program pauses for one second by using the sleep() function just described. For fun,

you can increase the pause time and then use a stop watch to see how accurate the computer's pause time is.

You can also modify this listing to print dots (or some other value) for a specified amount of time rather than pausing for a specified amount of time. Try replacing line 40 with the following:

```
printf("x");
```

 Caution | If your operating system has a program named sleep, you may need to give this program a different name to avoid conflicts.

DAY 10

Working with Characters and Strings

NEW TERM   A *character* is a single letter, numeral, punctuation mark, or other such symbol. A *string* is any sequence of characters. Strings are used to hold text data, which is comprised of letters, numerals, punctuation marks, and other symbols. Clearly, characters and strings are extremely useful in many programming applications. Today you will learn:

- How to use C's char data type to hold single characters
- How to create arrays of type char to hold multiple-character strings
- How to initialize characters and strings
- How to use pointers with strings
- How to print and input characters and strings

The char Data Type

C uses the char data type to hold characters. You saw on Day 3, "Storing Information: Variables and Constants," that char is one of C's numeric integer data types. If char is a numeric type, how can it be used to hold characters?

The answer lies in how C stores characters. Your computer's memory stores all data in numeric form. There is no direct way to store characters. However, a numeric code exists for each character. This is called the *ASCII code* or the *ASCII character set*. (*ASCII* stands for American Standard Code for Information Interchange.) The code assigns values between 0 and 255 for uppercase and lowercase letters, numeric digits, punctuation marks, and other symbols. The ASCII character set is listed in Appendix A.

 Note

> The ASCII codes and ASCII character set is targeted towards systems using a single byte character set. On systems using multi-byte character sets, you would use a different character set. This is, however, beyond the scope of this book.

For example, 97 is the ASCII code for the letter a. When you store the character a in a type char variable, you're really storing the value 97. Because the allowable numeric range for type char matches the standard ASCII character set, char is ideally suited for storing characters.

At this point, you might be a bit puzzled. If C stores characters as numbers, how does your program know whether a given type char variable is a character or a number? As you'll learn later, declaring a variable as type char is not enough; you must do something else with the variable:

- If a char variable is used somewhere in a C program where a character is expected, it is interpreted as a character.
- If a char variable is used somewhere in a C program where a number is expected, it is interpreted as a number.

This gives you some understanding of how C uses a numeric data type to store character data. Now you can go on to the details.

Using Character Variables

Like other variables, you must declare chars before using them, and you can initialize them at the time of declaration. Here are some examples:

```
char a, b, c;        /* Declare three uninitialized char variables */
char code = 'x';     /* Declare the char variable named code */
                     /* and store the character x there */
code = '!';          /* Store ! in the variable named code */
```

To create literal character constants, you enclose a single character in single quotation marks. The compiler automatically translates literal character constants into the corresponding ASCII codes, and the numeric code value is assigned to the variable.

You can create symbolic character constants by using either the #define directive or the const keyword:

```
#define EX 'x'

char code = EX;      /* Sets code equal to 'x' */
const char A = 'Z';
```

Now that you know how to declare and initialize character variables, it's time for a demonstration. Listing 10.1 illustrates the numeric nature of character storage using the printf() function you learned on Day 7, "Fundamentals of Reading and Writing Information." The function printf() can be used to print both characters and numbers. The format string %c instructs printf() to print a character, whereas %d instructs it to print a decimal integer. Listing 10.1 initializes two type char variables and prints each one, first as a character, and then as a number.

LISTING 10.1   chars.c. The numeric nature of type char variables

```
 1:  /* Demonstrates the numeric nature of char variables */
 2:
 3:  #include <stdio.h>
 4:
 5:  /* Declare and initialize two char variables */
 6:
 7:  char c1 = 'a';
 8:  char c2 = 90;
 9:
10:  int main( void )
11:  {
12:      /* Print variable c1 as a character, then as a number */
13:
14:      printf("\nAs a character, variable c1 is %c", c1);
15:      printf("\nAs a number, variable c1 is %d", c1);
16:
17:      /* Do the same for variable c2 */
18:
19:      printf("\nAs a character, variable c2 is %c", c2);
20:      printf("\nAs a number, variable c2 is %d\n", c2);
21:
22:      return 0;
23:  }
```

10

OUTPUT
```
As a character, variable c1 is a
As a number, variable c1 is 97
As a character, variable c2 is Z
As a number, variable c2 is 90
```

ANALYSIS You learned on Day 3 that the allowable range for a variable of type char goes only to 127, whereas the ASCII codes go to 255. The ASCII codes are actually divided into two parts. The standard ASCII codes go only to 127; this range includes all letters, numbers, punctuation marks, and other keyboard symbols. The codes from 128 to 255 are the extended ASCII codes and represent special characters such as foreign letters and graphics symbols (see Appendix A for a full list). Thus, for standard text data, you can use type char variables; if you want to print the extended ASCII characters, you must use an unsigned char.

Listing 10.2 prints some of the extended ASCII characters.

LISTING 10.2   ascii.c. Printing extended ASCII characters

```
 1:  /* Demonstrates printing extended ASCII characters */
 2:
 3:  #include <stdio.h>
 4:
 5:  unsigned char mychar;      /* Must be unsigned for extended ASCII */
 6:
 7:  int main( void )
 8:  {
 9:      /* Print extended ASCII characters 180 through 203 */
10:
11:      for (mychar = 180; mychar < 204; mychar++)
12:      {
13:          printf("ASCII code %d is character %c\n", mychar, mychar);
14:      }
15:
16:      return 0;
17:  }
```

OUTPUT
```
ASCII code 180 is character '
ASCII code 181 is character µ
ASCII code 182 is character ¶
ASCII code 183 is character ·
ASCII code 184 is character ‚
ASCII code 185 is character ¹
ASCII code 186 is character °
ASCII code 187 is character »
ASCII code 188 is character 1/4
ASCII code 189 is character 1/2
ASCII code 190 is character 3/4
```

```
ASCII code 191 is character ¿
ASCII code 192 is character À
ASCII code 193 is character Á
ASCII code 194 is character Â
ASCII code 195 is character Ã
ASCII code 196 is character Ä
ASCII code 197 is character Å
ASCII code 198 is character Æ
ASCII code 199 is character Ç
ASCII code 200 is character È
ASCII code 201 is character É
ASCII code 202 is character Ê
ASCII code 203 is character Ë
```

ANALYSIS   Looking at this program, you see that line 5 declares an `unsigned` character variable, `mychar`. This gives a range of 0 to 255. As with other numeric data types, you must not initialize a `char` variable to a value outside the allowed range, or you might get unexpected results. In line 11, `mychar` is not initialized outside the range; instead, it is initialized to 180. In the `for` statement, `mychar` is incremented by 1 until it reaches 204. Each time `mychar` is incremented, line 13 prints the value of `mychar` and the character value of `mychar`. Remember that `%c` prints the character, or ASCII, value of `mychar`.

Do	Don't
DO use `%c` to print the character value of a number.	**DON'T** use double quotations when initializing a character variable.
DO use single quotations when initializing a variable.	**DON'T** try to put extended ASCII character values into a signed `char` variable.
DO look at the ASCII chart in Appendix A to see the interesting characters that can be printed.	

> **Caution**
>
> Some computer systems might use a different character set; however, most use the same ASCII values for 0 to 127.

Using Strings

Variables of type `char` can hold only a single character, so they have limited usefulness. You also need a way to store *strings*. A string is simply a sequences of characters. A person's name and address are examples of strings. Although there is no special data type for strings, C handles this type of information with arrays of characters.

Arrays of Characters

To hold a string of six characters, for example, you need to declare an array of type `char` with seven elements. Arrays of type `char` are declared like arrays of other data types. For example, the statement

```
char string[10];
```

declares a 10-element array of type `char`. This array could be used to hold a string of nine or fewer characters.

"But wait," you might be saying. "It's a 10-element array, so why can it hold only nine characters? In C, a string is defined as a sequence of characters ending with the null character. The null character is a special character represented by `\0`. Although it's represented by two characters (backslash and zero), the null character is interpreted as a single character and has the ASCII value of `0`. It's one of C's escape sequences.

> **Note**
>
> Escape sequences were covered on Day 7.

When a C program stores the string `Alabama`, for example, it stores the seven characters A, l, a, b, a, m, and a, followed by the null character `\0`, for a total of eight characters. Thus, a character array can hold a string of characters numbering one less than the total number of elements in the array.

Initializing Character Arrays

Like other C data types, character arrays can be initialized when they are declared. Character arrays can be assigned values element by element, as shown here:

```
char string[10] = { 'A', 'l', 'a', 'b', 'a', 'm', 'a', '\0' };
```

 NEW TERM It's more convenient, however, to use a *literal string,* which is a sequence of characters enclosed in double quotes:

```
char string[10] = "Alabama";
```

When you use a literal string in your program, the compiler automatically adds the terminating null character at the end of the string. If you don't specify the number of subscripts when you declare an array, the compiler calculates the size of the array for you. Thus, the following line creates and initializes an eight-element array:

```
char string[] = "Alabama";
```

Remember that strings require a terminating null character. The C functions that manipulate strings (covered in Day 17, "Manipulating Strings") determine string length by looking for the null character. These functions have no other way of recognizing the end of the string. If the null character is missing, your program thinks that the string extends until the next null character in memory. Pesky program bugs can result from this sort of error.

Strings and Pointers

You've seen that strings are stored in arrays of type char, with the end of the string (which might not occupy the entire array) marked by the null character. Because the end of the string is marked, all you need in order to define a given string is something that points to its beginning. (Is *points* the right word? Indeed it is!)

With that hint, you might be leaping ahead of the game. From Day 9, "Understanding Pointers," you know that the name of an array is a pointer to the first element of the array. Therefore, for a string that's stored in an array, you need only the array name in order to access it. In fact, using the array's name is C's standard method of accessing strings.

To be more precise, using the array's name to access strings is the method the C library functions expect. The C standard library includes a number of functions that manipulate strings. (These functions are covered in Day 17.) To pass a string to one of these functions, you pass the array name. The same is true of the string display functions printf() and puts(), discussed later in today's lesson.

You might have noticed that I mentioned "strings stored in an array" a moment ago. Does this imply that some strings aren't stored in arrays? Indeed it does, and the next section explains why.

Strings Without Arrays

From the preceding section, you know that a string is defined by the character array's name and a null character. The array's name is a type char pointer to the beginning of the string. The null marks the string's end. The actual space occupied by the string in an array is incidental. In fact, the only purpose the array serves is to provide allocated space for the string.

What if you could find some memory storage space without allocating an array? You could then store a string with its terminating null character there instead. A pointer to the first character could serve to specify the string's beginning just as if the string were in an allocated array. How do you go about finding memory storage space? There are two

10

methods: One allocates space for a literal string when the program is compiled, and the other uses the `malloc()` function to allocate space while the program is executing, a process known as *dynamic allocation*.

Allocating String Space at Compilation

The start of a string, as mentioned earlier, is indicated by a pointer to a variable of type `char`. You might recall how to declare such a pointer:

```
char *message;
```

This statement declares a pointer to a variable of type `char` named `message`. It doesn't point to anything now, but what if you changed the pointer declaration to read:

```
char *message = "Great Caesar\'s Ghost!";
```

When this statement executes, the string `Great Caesar's Ghost!` (with a terminating null character) is stored somewhere in memory, and the pointer `message` is initialized to point to the first character of the string. Don't worry where in memory the string is stored; it's handled automatically by the compiler. Once defined, `message` is a pointer to the string and can be used as such.

The preceding declaration/initialization is equivalent to the following, and the two notations `*message` and `message[]` also are equivalent; they both mean "a pointer to."

```
char message[] = "Great Caesar\'s Ghost!";
```

This method of allocating space for string storage is fine when you know what you string you need when writing the program. What if the program has varying string storage needs, depending on user input or other factors that are unknown when you're writing the program? You use the `malloc()` function, which lets you allocate storage space on-the-fly.

The `malloc()` Function

The `malloc()` function is one of C's *memory allocation* functions. When you call `malloc()`, you pass it the number of bytes of memory needed. `malloc()` finds and reserves a block of memory of the required size and returns the address of the first byte in the block. You don't need to worry about where the memory is found; it's handled automatically.

The `malloc()` function returns an address, and its return type is a pointer to type `void`. Why `void`? A pointer to type `void` is compatible with all data types. Because the memory allocated by `malloc()` can be used to store any of C's data types, the `void` return type is appropriate.

The `malloc()` Function

```
#include <stdlib.h>
void *malloc(size_t size);
```

`malloc()` allocates a block of memory that is the number of bytes stated in *size*. By allocating memory as needed with `malloc()` instead of all at once when a program starts, you can use a computer's memory more efficiently. When using `malloc()`, you need to include the STDLIB.H header file. Some compilers have other header files that can be included; for portability, however, it's best to include stdlib.h.

`malloc()` returns a pointer to the allocated block of memory. If `malloc()` was unable to allocate the required amount of memory, it returns null. Whenever you try to allocate memory, you should always check the return value, even if the amount of memory to be allocated is small.

Example 1

```
#include <stdlib.h>
#include <stdio.h>
int main( void )
{
    /* allocate memory for a 100-character string */
    char *str;
    str = (char *) malloc(100);
    if (str == NULL)
    {
        printf( "Not enough memory to allocate buffer\n");
        exit(1);
    }
    printf( "String was allocated!\n" );
    return 0;
}
```

Example 2

```
/* allocate memory for an array of 50 integers */
int *numbers;
numbers = (int *) malloc(50 * sizeof(int));
```

Example 3

```
/* allocate memory for an array of 10 float values */
float *numbers;
numbers = (float *) malloc(10 * sizeof(float));
```

Using the `malloc()` Function

You can use `malloc()` to allocate memory to store a single type char. First, declare a pointer to type char:

```
char *ptr;
```

Next, call `malloc()` and pass the size of the desired memory block. Because a type `char` usually occupies one byte, you need a block of one byte. The value returned by `malloc()` is assigned to the pointer:

```
ptr = malloc(1);
```

This statement allocates a memory block of one byte and assigns its address to `ptr`. Unlike variables that are declared in the program, this byte of memory has no name. Only the pointer can reference the variable. For example, to store the character `'x'` there, you would write

```
*ptr = 'x';
```

Allocating storage for a string with `malloc()` is almost identical to using `malloc()` to allocate space for a single variable of type `char`. The main difference is that you need to know the amount of space to allocate—the maximum number of characters in the string. This maximum depends on the needs of your program. For this example, say you want to allocate space for a string of 99 characters, plus one for the terminating null character, for a total of 100. First you declare a pointer to type `char`, and then you call `malloc()`:

```
char *ptr;
ptr = malloc(100);
```

Now `ptr` points to a reserved block of 100 bytes that can be used for string storage and manipulation. You can use `ptr` just as though your program had explicitly allocated that space with the following array declaration:

```
char ptr[100];
```

Using `malloc()` lets your program allocate storage space as needed in response to demand. Of course, available space is not unlimited; it depends on the amount of memory installed in your computer and on the program's other storage requirements. If not enough memory is available, `malloc()` returns null (`0`). Your program should test the return value of `malloc()` so that you'll know the memory requested was allocated successfully. You always should test `malloc()`'s return value against the symbolic constant `NULL`, which is defined in stdlib.h. Listing 10.3 illustrates the use of `malloc()`. Any program using `malloc()` must #include the header file stdlib.h.

> **Tip**
>
> Literal values were used to allocate space for characters in the above examples. You should always multiply the size of the data type you are allocating space for by the amount of space you want. The above allocations assumed that a character was stored in just one byte. If a character is stored in more than one byte, then the above examples will overwrite other areas of memory. For example:
>
> ```
> ptr = malloc(100);
> ```
>
> should really be declared as
>
> ```
> ptr = malloc( 100 * sizeof(char));
> ```

LISTING 10.3 memalloc.c. Using the `malloc()` function to allocate storage space for string data

10

```
 1:  /* Demonstrates the use of malloc() to allocate storage */
 2:  /* space for string data. */
 3:
 4:  #include <stdio.h>
 5:  #include <stdlib.h>
 6:
 7:  char count, *ptr, *p;
 8:
 9:  int main( void )
10:  {
11:      /* Allocate a block of 35 bytes. Test for success. */
12:      /* The exit() library function terminates the program. */
13:
14:      ptr = malloc(35 * sizeof(char));
15:
16:      if (ptr == NULL)
17:      {
18:          puts("Memory allocation error.");
19:          return 1;
20:      }
21:
22:      /* Fill the string with values 65 through 90, */
23:      /* which are the ASCII codes for A-Z. */
24:
25:      /* p is a pointer used to step through the string. */
26:      /* You want ptr to remain pointed at the start */
27:      /* of the string. */
28:
29:      p = ptr;
30:
31:      for (count = 65; count < 91 ; count++)
32:          *p++ = count;
```

LISTING 10.3 continued

```
33:
34:     /* Add the terminating null character. */
35:
36:     *p = '\0';
37:
38:     /* Display the string on the screen. */
39:
40:     puts(ptr);
41:
42:     free(ptr);
43:
44:     return 0;
45: }
```

OUTPUT

ABCDEFGHIJKLMNOPQRSTUVWXYZ

ANALYSIS This program uses `malloc()` in a simple way. Although the program seems long, it's filled with comments. Lines 1, 2, 11, 12, 22 through 27, 34, and 38 are all comments that detail everything the program does. Line 5 includes the stdlib.h header file needed for `malloc()`, and line 4 includes the stdio.h header file for the `puts()` functions. Line 7 declares two pointers and a character variable used later in the listing. None of these variables is initialized, so they shouldn't be used—yet!

The `malloc()` function is called in line 14 with a parameter of 35 multiplied by the *size* of a `char`. Could you have just used 35? Yes, but you're assuming that everyone running this program will be using a computer that stores `char` type variables as one byte in size. Remember from Day 3 that different compilers can use different-size variables. Using the `sizeof` operator is an easy way to create portable code.

Never assume that `malloc()` gets the memory you tell it to get. In fact, you aren't *telling* it to get memory—you're *asking* it. Line 16 shows the easiest way to check whether `malloc()` provided the memory. If the memory was allocated, `ptr` points to it; otherwise, `ptr` is null. If the program failed to get the memory, lines 18 and 19 display an error message and gracefully exit the program.

Line 29 initializes the other pointer declared in line 7, p. It is assigned the same address value as `ptr`. A `for` loop uses this new pointer to place values into the allocated memory. Looking at line 31, you see that `count` is initialized to `65` and incremented by 1 until it reaches `91`. For each loop of the `for` statement, the value of `count` is assigned to the address pointed to by p. Notice that each time `count` is incremented, the address pointed to by p is also incremented. This means that each value is placed one after the other in memory.

You should have noticed that numbers are being assigned to `count`, which is a type `char` variable. Remember the discussion of ASCII characters and their numeric equivalents? The number 65 is equivalent to A, 66 equals B, 67 equals C, and so on. The `for` loop ends after the alphabet is assigned to the memory locations pointed to. Line 36 caps off the character values pointed to by putting a null at the final address pointed to by `p`. By appending the null, you can now use these values as a string. Remember that `ptr` still points to the first value, A, so if you use it as a string, it prints every character until it reaches the null. Line 40 uses `puts()` to prove this point and to show the results of what has been done.

You will notice a new function is used in line 42. This is the `free()` function. Whenever you allocate memory dynamically, you should also unallocated it—or return it—when you are done using it. The free function returns allocated memory, so in line 42, the memory allocated and assigned to `ptr` is returned to the system.

10

Do	Don't
	DON'T allocate more memory than you need. Not everyone has a lot of memory, so you should try to use it sparingly.
	DON'T try to assign a new string to a character array that was previously allocated only enough memory to hold a smaller string. For example, in this declaration:
	`char a_string[] = "NO";`
	`a_string` points to "NO". If you try to assign "YES" to this array, you could have serious problems. The array initially could hold only three characters—'N', 'O', and a null. "YES" is four characters—'Y', 'E', 'S', and a null. You have no idea what the fourth character, null, overwrites.

Displaying Strings and Characters

If your program uses string data, it probably needs to display the data on the screen at some time. String display is usually done with either the `puts()` function or the `printf()` function.

The `puts()` Function

You've already seen the `puts()` library function in some of the programs earlier in this book. The `puts()` function puts a string on-screen—hence its name. A pointer to the string to be displayed is the only argument `puts()` takes. Because a literal string evaluates as a pointer to a string, `puts()` can be used to display literal strings as well as string variables. The `puts()` function automatically inserts a new line character at the end of each string it displays, so each subsequent string displayed with `puts()` is on its own line.

Listing 10.4 illustrates the use of `puts()`.

LISTING 10.4 put.c. Using the `puts()` function to display text on-screen

```
1: /* Demonstrates displaying strings with puts(). */
2:
3: #include <stdio.h>
4:
5: char *message1 = "C";
6: char *message2 = "is the";
7: char *message3 = "best";
8: char *message4 = "programming";
9: char *message5 = "language!!";
10:
11: int main( void )
12: {
13:     puts(message1);
14:     puts(message2);
15:     puts(message3);
16:     puts(message4);
17:     puts(message5);
18:
19:     return 0;
20: }
```

OUTPUT
```
C
is the
best
programming
language!!
```

ANALYSIS This is a fairly simple listing to follow. Because `puts()` is a standard output function, the stdio.h header file needs to be included, as done on line 3. Lines 5 through 9 declare and initialize five different message variables. Each of these variables is a character pointer, or string variable. Lines 13 through 17 use the `puts()` function to print each string.

The `printf()` Function

You can also display strings using the `printf()` library function. Recall from Day 7 that `printf()` uses a format string and conversion specifiers to shape its output. To display a string, use the conversion specifier `%s`.

When `printf()` encounters a `%s` in its format string, the function matches the `%s` with the corresponding argument in its argument list. For a string, this argument must be a pointer to the string that you want displayed. The `printf()` function displays the string on-screen, stopping when it reaches the string's terminating null character. For example:

```
char *str = "A message to display";
printf("%s", str);
```

You can also display multiple strings and mix them with literal text and/or numeric variables:

```
char *bank = "First Federal";
char *name = "John Doe";
int balance = 1000;
printf("The balance at %s for %s is %d.", bank, name, balance);
```

The resulting output is

```
The balance at First Federal for John Doe is 1000.
```

For now, this information should be sufficient for you to be able to display string data in your programs. Complete details on using `printf()` are given on Day 14, "Working with the Screen, Printer, and Keyboard."

Reading Strings from the Keyboard

In addition to displaying strings, programs often need to accept inputted string data from the user via the keyboard. The C library has two functions that can be used for this purpose—`gets()` and `scanf()`. Before you can read in a string from the keyboard, however, you must have somewhere to put it. You can create space for string storage using either of the methods discussed earlier—an array declaration or the `malloc()` function.

Inputting Strings Using the `gets()` Function

The `gets()` function gets a string from the keyboard. When `gets()` is called, it reads all characters typed at the keyboard up to the first new line character (which you generate by pressing Enter). This function discards the new line, adds a null character, and gives the string to the calling program. The string is stored at the location indicated by a pointer to type `char` passed to `gets()`. A program that uses `gets()` must `#include` the file stdio.h. Listing 10.5 presents an example.

LISTING 10.5   get.c. Using gets() to input string data from the keyboard

```
1:  /* Demonstrates using the gets() library function. */
2:
3:  #include <stdio.h>
4:
5:  /* Allocate a character array to hold input. */
6:
7:  char input[81];
8:
9:  int main( void )
10: {
11:     puts("Enter some text, then press Enter: ");
12:     gets(input);
13:     printf("You entered: %s\n", input);
14:
15:     return 0;
16: }
```

**INPUT/
OUTPUT**
```
Enter some text, then press Enter:
This is a test
You entered: This is a test
```

ANALYSIS   In this example, the argument to gets() is the expression input, which is the
name of a type char array and therefore a pointer to the first array element. The
array is declared with 257 elements in line 7. Because the maximum line length possible
on most computer screens is 256 characters, this array size provides space for the longest
possible input line (plus the null character that gets() adds at the end).

The gets() function has a return value, which was ignored in the previous example.
gets() returns a pointer to type char with the address where the input string is stored.
Yes, this is the same value that is passed to gets(), but having the value returned to the
program in this way lets your program test for a blank line. Listing 10.6 shows how to do
this.

LISTING 10.6   getback.c. Using the gets() return value to test for input of a blank line

```
1:  /* Demonstrates using the gets() return value. */
2:
3:  #include <stdio.h>
4:
5:  /* Declare a character array to hold input, and a pointer. */
6:
7:  char input[257], *ptr;
8:
9:  int main( void )
10: {
```

LISTING 10.6 continued

```
11:     /* Display instructions. */
12:
13:     puts("Enter text a line at a time, then press Enter.");
14:     puts("Enter a blank line when done.");
15:
16:     /* Loop as long as input is not a blank line. */
17:
18:     while ( *(ptr = gets(input)) != NULL)
19:         printf("You entered %s\n", input);
20:
21:     puts("Thank you and good-bye\n");
22:
23:     return 0;
24: }
```

INPUT/ OUTPUT

```
Enter text a line at a time, then press Enter.
Enter a blank line when done.
First string
You entered First string
Two
You entered Two
Bradley L. Jones
You entered Bradley L. Jones

Thank you and good-bye
```

ANALYSIS Now you can see how the program works. If you enter a blank line (that is, if you simply press Enter) in response to line 18, the string (which contains 0 characters) is still stored with a null character at the end. Because the string has a length of 0, the null character is stored in the first position. This is the position pointed to by the return value of gets(), so if you test that position and find a null character, you know that a blank line was entered.

Listing 10.6 performs this test in the while statement in line 18. This statement is a bit complicated, so look carefully at the details in order. Figure 10.1 illustrates the components of this statement.

Caution

Because it is not always possible to know how many characters gets() will read, and because gets() will continue to store characters past the end of the buffer, it should be used with caution.

10

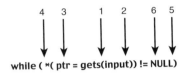

FIGURE **10.1**

The components of a while *statement that tests for input of a blank line.*

1. The gets() function accepts input from the keyboard until it reaches a newline character.

2. The string entered, minus the new line and with a trailing null character, is stored in the memory location pointed to by input.

3. The address of the string (the same value as input) is returned to the pointer ptr.

4. An *assignment statement* is an expression that evaluates to the value of the variable on the left side of the assignment operator. Therefore, the entire expression ptr = gets(input) evaluates to the value of ptr. By enclosing this expression in parentheses and preceding it with the indirection operator (*), you obtain the value stored at the pointed-to address. This is, of course, the first character of the input string.

5. NULL is a symbolic constant defined in the header file stdio.h. It has the value of the null character (0).

6. If the first character of the input string isn't the null character (if a blank line hasn't been entered), the comparison operator returns true, and the while loop executes. If the first character is the null character (if a blank line has been entered), the comparison operator returns false, and the while loop terminates.

When you use gets() or any other function that stores data using a pointer, be sure that the pointer points to allocated space. It's easy to make a mistake such as this:

```
char *ptr;
gets(ptr);
```

The pointer ptr has been declared but not initialized. It points somewhere, but you don't know where. The gets() function doesn't know that ptr hasn't been initialized to point somewhere, so it simply goes ahead and stores the entered string at whatever address is contained in ptr. The string might overwrite something important, such as program code or the operating system. Most compilers won't catch this type of mistakes, so you, the programmer, must be vigilant.

The `gets()` Function

```
#include <stdio.h>
char *gets(char *str);
```

The `gets()` function gets a string, `str`, from the standard input device, usually the keyboard. The string consists of any characters entered until a newline character is read. At that point, a null is appended to the end of the string.

Then the `gets()` function returns a pointer to the string just read. If there is a problem getting the string, `gets()` returns null.

Example

```
/* gets() example */
#include <stdio.h>
char line[256];
void main( void )
{
    printf( "Enter a string:\n");
    gets( line );
    printf( "\nYou entered the following string:\n" );
    printf( "%s\n", line );
}
```

10

Inputting Strings Using the `scanf()` Function

You saw on Day 7 that the `scanf()` library function accepts numeric data input from the keyboard. This function can also input strings. Remember that `scanf()` uses a *format string* that tells it how to read the information entered. To read a string, include the specifier `%s` in `scanf()`'s format string. Like `gets()`, `scanf()` is passed a pointer to the string's storage location.

How does `scanf()` decide where the string begins and ends? The beginning is the first non-whitespace character encountered. The end can be specified in one of two ways. If you use `%s` in the format string, the string runs up to (but not including) the next whitespace character (space, tab, or newline). If you use `%ns` (where n is an integer constant that specifies field width), `scanf()` accepts the next n characters or up to the next whitespace character, whichever comes first.

You can read in multiple strings with `scanf()` by including more than one `%s` in the format string. For each `%s` in the format string, `scanf()` uses the preceding rules to find the requested number of strings in the input. For example

```
scanf("%s%s%s", s1, s2, s3);
```

If in response to this statement you enter `January February March`, `January` is assigned to the string `s1`, `February` is assigned to `s2`, and `March` to `s3`.

What about using the field-width specifier? If you execute the statement

```
scanf("%3s%3s%3s", s1, s2, s3);
```

and in response you enter September, Sep is assigned to s1, tem is assigned to s2, and ber is assigned to s3.

What if you enter fewer or more strings than the scanf() function expects? If you enter fewer strings, scanf() continues to look for the missing strings, and the program doesn't continue until they're entered. For example, if in response to the statement

```
scanf("%s%s%s", s1, s2, s3);
```

you enter January February, the program sits and waits for the third string specified in the scanf() format string. If you enter more strings than requested, the unmatched strings remain pending (waiting in the keyboard buffer) and are read by any subsequent scanf() or other input statements. For example, if in response to the statements

```
scanf("%s%s", s1, s2);
scanf("%s", s3);
```

you enter January February March, the result is that January is assigned to the string s1 and February is assigned to s2 in the first scanf() call. March is then automatically carried over and assigned to s3 in the second scanf() call.

The scanf() function has a return value, an integer value equaling the number of items successfully inputted. The return value is often ignored. When you're reading text only, the gets() function is usually preferable to scanf(). It's best to use the scanf() function when you're reading in a combination of text and numeric data. This is illustrated by Listing 10.7. Remember from Day 7 that you must use the address-of operator (&) when inputting numeric variables with scanf().

LISTING 10.7   input.c. Inputting numeric and text data with scanf()

```
1:  /* Demonstrates using scanf() to input numeric and text data. */
2:
3:  #include <stdio.h>
4:
5:  char lname[257], fname[257];
6:  int count, id_num;
7:
8:  int main( void )
9:  {
10:     /* Prompt the user. */
11:
12:     puts("Enter last name, first name, ID number separated");
13:     puts("by spaces, then press Enter.");
```

LISTING 10.7 continued

```
14:
15:    /* Input the three data items. */
16:
17:    count = scanf("%s%s%d", lname, fname, &id_num);
18:
19:    /* Display the data. */
20:
21:    printf("%d items entered: %s %s %d \n", count, fname, lname, id_num);
22:
23:    return 0;
24: }
```

INPUT/
OUTPUT

```
Enter last name, first name, ID number separated
by spaces, then press Enter.
Jones Bradley 12345
3 items entered: Bradley Jones 12345
```

10

ANALYSIS Remember that `scanf()` requires the addresses of variables for parameters. In Listing 10.7, `lname` and `fname` are pointers (that is, addresses), so they don't need the address-of operator (`&`). In contrast, `id_num` is a regular variable name, so it requires the `&` when passed to `scanf()` on line 17.

Some programmers feel that data entry with `scanf()` is prone to errors. They prefer to input all data, numeric and string, using `gets()`, and then have the program separate the numbers and convert them to numeric variables. Such techniques are beyond the scope of this book, but they would make a good programming exercise. For that task, you need the string manipulation functions covered on Day 17.

Summary

Today's lesson covered C's `char` data type. One use of type `char` variables is to store individual characters. You saw that characters are actually stored as numbers: The ASCII code assigns a numerical code to each character. Therefore, you can use type `char` to store small integer values as well. Both `signed` and `unsigned char` types are available.

A string is a sequence of characters terminated by the null character. Strings can be used for text data. C stores strings in arrays of type `char`. To store a string of length *n*, you need an array of type `char` with *n*+1 elements.

You can use memory allocation functions such as `malloc()` to make your programs more dynamic. By using `malloc()`, you can allocate the right amount of memory for your program. Without such functions, you would have to guess at the amount of memory storage the program needs. Your estimate would probably be high, so you would allocate more memory than needed. When you are done with the memory you have allocated, you should always take the time to return it to the system using the `free()` function.

Q&A

Q What is the difference between a string and an array of characters?

A A string is defined as a sequence of characters ending with the null character. An array is a sequence of characters. A string, therefore, is a null-terminated array of characters.

If you define an array of type `char`, the actual storage space allocated for the array is the specified size, not the size minus 1. You're limited to that size; you can't store a larger string. Here's an example:

```
char state[10]="Minneapolis";  /* Wrong! String longer than array. */
char state2[10]="MN";          /* OK, but wastes space because */
                               /* string is shorter than array. */
```

If, on the other hand, you define a pointer to type `char`, these restrictions don't apply. The variable is a storage space only for the pointer. The actual strings are stored elsewhere in memory (but you don't need to worry about where in memory). There's no length restriction or wasted space. The actual string is stored elsewhere. A pointer can point to a string of any length.

Q Why shouldn't I just declare big arrays to hold values instead of using a memory allocation function such as `malloc()`?

A Although it might seem easier to declare large arrays, this isn't an effective use of memory. When you're writing small programs, such as those in today's lesson, it might seem trivial to use a function such as `malloc()` instead of arrays, but as your programs get bigger, you'll want to be able to allocate memory only as needed. When you're done with memory, you can put it back by *freeing* it. When you free memory, some other variable or array in a different part of the program can use it. (Day 20, "Working with Memory," covers freeing allocated memory.)

Q Do all computers support the extended ASCII character set?

A No. Most PCs support the extended ASCII set. Some older PCs don't, but the number of older PCs lacking this support is diminishing. Most programmers use the line and block characters of the extended set.

Additionally, many international character sets contain more than characters available in ASCII. These characters are usually stored in `wchar_t` type variables instead of variables of type char. `wchar_t` is defined in the stddef.h header file. It can be used to hold larger characters. Check the ANSI documents for more information on using `wchar_t` and other character sets.

Q What happens if I put a string into a character array that is bigger than the array?

A This can cause a hard-to-find error. You can do this in C, but anything stored in the memory directly after the character array is overwritten. This could be an area of memory not used, some other data, or some vital system information. Your results will depend on what you overwrite. Often, nothing happens for a while. You don't want to do this.

Workshop

The Workshop provides quiz questions to help you solidify your understanding of the material covered and exercises to provide you with experience in using what you've learned.

Quiz

1. What is the range of numeric values in the ASCII character set?
2. When the C compiler encounters a single character enclosed in single quotation marks, how is it interpreted?
3. What is C's definition of a string?
4. What is a literal string?
5. To store a string of *n* characters, you need a character array of *n*+1 elements. Why is the extra element needed?
6. When the C compiler encounters a literal string, how is it interpreted?
7. Using the ASCII chart in Appendix A, state the numeric value stored for each of the following:

    a. a

    b. A

    c. 9

    d. a space

    e. ╬

    f. ♠

8. Using the ASCII chart in Appendix A, translate the following numeric values to their equivalent characters:

    a. 73

    b. 32

    c. 99

    d. 97

    e. 110

    f. 0

    g. 2

9. How many bytes of storage are allocated for each of the following variables? (Assume that a character is one byte.)

    a. `char *str1 = { "String 1" };`

    b. `char str2[] = { "String 2" };`

    c. `char string3;`

    d. `char str4[20] = { "This is String 4" };`

    e. `char str5[20];`

10. Using the following declaration:

```
char *string = "A string!";
```

What are the values of the following?

    a. `string[0]`

    b. `*string`

    c. `string[9]`

    d. `string[33]`

    e. `*string+8`

    f. `string`

Exercises

1. Write a line of code that declares a type `char` variable named `letter`, and initialize it to the character $.

2. Write a line of code that declares an array of type `char`, and initialize it to the string `"Pointers are fun!"` Make the array just large enough to hold the string.

3. Write a line of code that allocates storage for the string `"Pointers are fun!"`, as in exercise 2, but without using an array.

4. Write code that allocates space for an 80-character string and then inputs a string from the keyboard and stores it in the allocated space.

5. Write a function that copies one array of characters into another. (Hint: Do this just like the programs you wrote on Day 9.)

6. Write a function that accepts two strings. Count the number of characters in each, and return a pointer to the longer string.

7. **ON YOUR OWN:** Write a function that accepts two strings. Use the `malloc()` function to allocate enough memory to hold the two strings after they have been concatenated (linked). Return a pointer to this new string.

   For example, if I pass `"Hello"` and `"World!"`, the function returns a pointer to `"Hello World!"`. Having the concatenated value be the third string is easiest. (You might be able to use your answers from exercises 5 and 6.)

8. **BUG BUSTER:** Is anything wrong with the following?

   ```
   char a_string[10] = "This is a string";
   ```

9. **BUG BUSTER:** Is anything wrong with the following?

   ```
   char *quote[100] = { "Smile, Friday is almost here!" };
   ```

10. **BUG BUSTER:** Is anything wrong with the following?

    ```
    char *string1;
    char *string2 = "Second";
    string1 = string2;
    ```

11. **BUG BUSTER:** Is anything wrong with the following?

    ```
    char string1[];
    char string2[] = "Second";
    string1 = string2;
    ```

12. **ON YOUR OWN:** Using the ASCII chart, write a program that prints a box on-screen using the double-line characters.

10

Caution

Today's lesson dynamically allocated memory using the `malloc()` function. When you dynamically allocate memory, you should release it back to the computer system when you are done with it. You can put dynamically allocated memory back by *freeing* it. Day 20 will cover freeing allocated memory.

DAY 11

Implementing Structures, Unions, and TypeDefs

Many programming tasks are simplified by the C data constructs called *structures*. A structure is a data storage type designed by you, the programmer, to suit your programming needs exactly. Today you will learn:

- What simple and complex structures are
- How to define and declare structures
- How to access data in structures
- How to create structures that contain arrays and arrays of structures
- How to declare pointers in structures and pointers to structures
- How to pass structures as arguments to functions
- How to define, declare, and use unions
- How to use type definitions with structures

Working with Simple Structures

NEW TERM   A *structure* is a collection of one or more variables grouped under a single name for easy manipulation. The variables in a structure, unlike those in an array, can be of different data types. A structure can contain any of C's data types, including arrays and other structures. Each variable within a structure is called a *member* of the structure. The next section shows a simple example.

You should start with simple structures. Note that the C language makes no distinction between simple and complex structures, but it's easier to explain structures in this way.

Defining and Declaring Structures

If you're writing a graphics program, your code needs to deal with the coordinates of points on the screen. Screen coordinates are written as an x value, giving the horizontal position, and a y value, giving the vertical position. You can define a structure named coord that contains both the x and y values of a screen location as follows:

```
struct coord
{
    int x;
    int y;
};
```

The struct keyword is used to identify identifies the beginning of a structure definition. This struct keyword must be followed immediately by the name of the structure. This is the same rule that applies to the other data types you have created in C. The name of a structure is also known as the structure's *tag* or *type name*. Later you will see how the tag is used.

Following the structure tag is an opening brace. Within the braces following the structure name is a list of the structure's member variables. You must give a variable type and name for each member.

The preceding code statements define a structure type named coord that contains two integer variables, x and y. This declaration of coord and its members, x and y, does not, however, actually create any instances of the structure coord or of the x and y variables. In other words, they don't *declare* (set aside storage for) any structures. There are two ways to declare structures. One is to follow the structure definition with a list of one or more variable names, as is done here:

```
struct coord {
    int x;
    int y;
} first, second;
```

These statements define the structure type coord and declare two structures, first and second, of type coord. first and second are each *instances* of type coord; first contains two integer members named x and y, and so does second.

This method of declaring structures combines the declaration with the definition. The second method is to declare structure variables at a different location in your source code from the definition. The following statements also declare two instances of type coord:

```
struct coord {
    int x;
    int y;
};
/* Additional code may go here */
struct coord first, second;
```

In this example, you can see that the definition of the coord structure is separate from the declaration of variables. When declaring variables separately, you use the struct keyword followed by the structured tag followed by the name of the variable or variables you want to create.

Accessing Members of a Structure

Individual structure members can be used like other variables of the same type. Structure members are accessed using the *structure member operator* (.), also called the *dot operator,* between the structure name and the member name. Thus, to have the structure named first refer to a screen location that has coordinates x=50, y=100, you could write

```
first.x = 50;
first.y = 100;
```

To display the screen locations stored in the structure second, you could write

```
printf("%d,%d", second.x, second.y);
```

At this point, you might be wondering what the advantage is of using structures rather than individual variables. One major advantage is that you can copy information between structures of the same type with a simple equation statement. Continuing with the preceding example, the statement

```
first = second;
```

is equivalent to this statement:

```
first.x = second.x;
first.y = second.y;
```

When your program uses complex structures with many members, this notation can be a great time-saver. Other advantages of structures will become apparent as you learn some advanced techniques. In general, you'll find structures to be useful whenever information of different variable types should be treated as a group. For example, in a mailing list database, each entry could be a structure, and each piece of information (name, address, city, and so on) could be a structure member.

Listing 11.1 pulls together everything that has been covered up to this point. It is not very practical; however, it illustrates the point of a simple structure.

LISTING 11.1   simple.c. Declaring and using a simple structure

```
1:   /* simple.c - Demonstrates the use of a simple structures*/
2:
3:   #include <stdio.h>
4:
5:   int length, width;
6:   long area;
7:
8:   struct coord{
9:       int x;
10      int y;
11: } myPoint;
12:
13: int main( void )
14: {
15:      /* set values into the coordinates */
16:      myPoint.x = 12;
17:      myPoint.y = 14;
18:
19:      printf("\nThe coordinates are: (%d, %d).",
20:             myPoint.x, myPoint.y);
21:
22:      return 0;
23: }
```

INPUT/OUTPUT   The coordinates are: (12, 14).

ANALYSIS   This listing defines a simple structure for holding the coordinates of a point. This is the same structure you've seen illustrated earlier in today's lessons. In line 8 you see that struct keyword is used followed by the tag, coord. The body of the structure is then defined in lines 9 to 11. This structure is declared with two members, x and y which are both variables of type int.

In line 11, a variable called myPoint is also declared as an instance of the coord structure. This declaration could also have been done in a separate line as follows:

```
struct coord myPoint;
```

In lines 16 and 17 you see that the members of `myPoint` are assigned values. As stated earlier values are assigned by using the name of the structure variable, followed by the member operator (`.`), finally followed by the name of the member. In lines 19 and 20 you see these same variables used in a `printf` statement.

The `struct` Keyword

▼ SYNTAX

```
struct tag {
    structure_member(s);
    /* additional statements may go here */
} instance;
```

The `struct` keyword is used to declare structures. A structure is a collection of one or more variables (`structure_members`) that have been grouped under a single name for easy manipulation. The variables don't have to be of the same variable type, nor do they have to be simple variables. Structures also can hold arrays, pointers, and other structures.

The keyword `struct` identifies the beginning of a structure definition. It's followed by a tag that is the name given to the structure. Following the tag are the structure members, enclosed in braces. An *instance*, the actual declaration of a structure, can also be defined. If you define the structure without the instance, it's just a template, or definition, that can be used later in a program to declare structures. Here is a template's format:

```
struct tag {
    structure_member(s);
    /* additional statements may go here */
};
```

To use the template, you use the following format:

```
struct tag instance;
```

To use this format, you must have previously declared a structure with the given tag.

Example 1

```
/* Declare a structure template called SSN */
struct SSN {
    int first_three;
    char dash1;
    int second_two;
    char dash2;
    int last_four;
}
/* Use the structure template */
struct SSN customer_ssn;
```

▼ **Example 2**
```
/* Declare a structure and instance together */
struct date {
    char month[2];
    char day[2];
    char year[4];
} current_date;
```

Example 3
```
/* Declare and initialize a structure */
struct time {
    int hours;
    int minutes;
    int seconds;
} time_of_birth = { 8, 45, 0 };
```
▲

Using Structures That Are More Complex

Now that you have been introduced to simple structures, you can go on to the more interesting and complex types of structures. These are structures that contain other structures as members and structures that contain arrays as members.

Including Structures Within Other Structures

As mentioned earlier, a C structure can contain any of C's data types. For example, a structure can contain other structures. The preceding example can be extended to illustrate this.

Assume that your graphics program has to deal with rectangles. A rectangle can be defined by the coordinates of two diagonally opposite corners. You've already seen how to define a structure that can hold the two coordinates required for a single point. You need two such structures to define a rectangle. You can define a structure as follows (assuming, of course, that you have already defined the type coord structure):

```
struct rectangle {
    struct coord topleft;
    struct coord bottomrt;
};
```

This statement defines a structure of type rectangle that contains two structures of type coord. These two type coord structures are named topleft and bottomrt.

The preceding statement defines only the type rectangle structure. To declare a structure, you must then include a statement such as

```
struct rectangle mybox;
```

You could have combined the definition and declaration, as you did before for the type coord:

```
struct rectangle {
    struct coord topleft;
    struct coord bottomrt;
} mybox;
```

To access the actual data locations (the type int members), you must apply the member operator (.) twice. Thus, the expression

```
mybox.topleft.x
```

refers to the x member of the topleft member of the type rectangle structure named mybox. To define a rectangle with coordinates (0,10),(100,200), you would write

```
mybox.topleft.x = 0;
mybox.topleft.y = 10;
mybox.bottomrt.x = 100;
mybox.bottomrt.y = 200;
```

Maybe this is a bit confusing. You will understand better if you look at Figure 11.1, which shows the relationship between the type rectangle structure, the two type coord structures it contains, and the two type int variables each type coord structure contains. These structures are named as in the preceding example.

FIGURE 11.1

The relationship between a structure, structures within a structure, and the structure members.

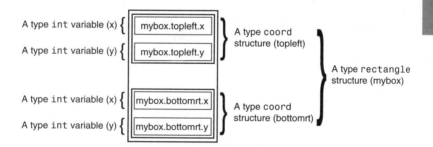

Listing 11.2 presents an example of using structures that contain other structures. This listing takes input from the user for the coordinates of a rectangle and then calculates and displays the rectangle's area. Note the program's assumptions, given in comments near the start of the program (lines 3 through 8).

LISTING 11.2   struct.c. A demonstration of structures that contain other structures

```
1:  /* Demonstrates structures that contain other structures. */
2:
3:  /* Receives input for corner coordinates of a rectangle and
4:     calculates the area. Assumes that the y coordinate of the
5:     lower-right corner is greater than the y coordinate of the
```

LISTING **11.2**   continued

```
 6:     upper-left corner, that the x coordinate of the lower-
 7:     right corner is greater than the x coordinate of the upper-
 8:     left corner, and that all coordinates are positive. */
 9:
10: #include <stdio.h>
11:
12: int length, width;
13: long area;
14:
15: struct coord{
16:     int x;
17:     int y;
18: };
19:
20: struct rectangle{
21:     struct coord topleft;
22:     struct coord bottomrt;
23: } mybox;
24:
25: int main( void )
26: {
27:     /* Input the coordinates */
28:
29:     printf("\nEnter the top left x coordinate: ");
30:     scanf("%d", &mybox.topleft.x);
31:
32:     printf("\nEnter the top left y coordinate: ");
33:     scanf("%d", &mybox.topleft.y);
34:
35:     printf("\nEnter the bottom right x coordinate: ");
36:     scanf("%d", &mybox.bottomrt.x);
37:
38:     printf("\nEnter the bottom right y coordinate: ");
39:     scanf("%d", &mybox.bottomrt.y);
40:
41:     /* Calculate the length and width */
42:
43:     width = mybox.bottomrt.x - mybox.topleft.x;
44:     length = mybox.bottomrt.y - mybox.topleft.y;
45:
46:     /* Calculate and display the area */
47:
48:     area = width * length;
49:     printf("\nThe area is %ld units.\n", area);
50:
51:     return 0;
52: }
```

INPUT/
OUTPUT
```
Enter the top left x coordinate: 1

Enter the top left y coordinate: 1

Enter the bottom right x coordinate: 10

Enter the bottom right y coordinate: 10

The area is 81 units.
```

ANALYSIS The coord structure is defined in lines 15 through 18 with its two members, x and y. Lines 20 through 23 declare and define an instance, called mybox, of the rectangle structure. The two members of the rectangle structure are topleft and bottomrt, both structures of type coord.

Lines 29 through 39 fill in the values in the mybox structure. At first, it might seem that there are only two values to fill because mybox has only two members. However, each of mybox's members has its own members. topleft and bottomrt have two members each, x and y from the coord structure. This gives a total of four members to be filled. After the members are filled with values, the area is calculated using the structure and member names. When using the x and y values, you must include the structure instance name. Because x and y are in a structure within a structure, you must use the instance names of both structures—mybox.bottomrt.x, mybox.bottomrt.y, mybox.topleft.x, and mybox.topleft.y—in the calculations.

The C programming language doesn't have to place a limit on the number of structures that can be nested; however, compliance to the ANSI standard only guarantees support for 63 levels. While memory allows, you can define structures that contain structures that contain structures that contain structures—well, you get the idea! Of course, there's a limit beyond which nesting becomes unproductive. Rarely are more than three levels of nesting used in any C program.

Structures That Contain Arrays

You can define a structure that contains one or more arrays as members. The array can be of any C data type (int, char, and so on). For example, the statements

```
struct data
{
    int  x[4];
    char y[10];
};
```

define a structure of type data that contains a 4-element integer array member named x and a 10-element character array member named y. You can then declare a structure named record of type data as follows:

```
struct data record;
```

The organization of this structure is shown in Figure 11.2. Note that, in this figure, the elements of array x are shown to take up twice as much space as the elements of array y. This is because a type int typically requires two bytes of storage, whereas a type char usually requires only one byte (as you learned on Day 3, "Storing Information: Variables and Constants").

FIGURE 11.2

The organization of a structure that contains arrays as members.

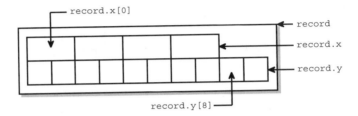

You access individual elements of arrays that are structure members using a combination of the member operator and array subscripts:

```
record.x[2] = 100;
record.y[1] = 'x';
```

You probably remember that character arrays are most frequently used to store strings. You should also remember (from Day 9, "Understanding Pointers") that the name of an array, without brackets, is a pointer to the array. Because this holds true for arrays that are structure members, the expression

```
record.y
```

is a pointer to the first element of array y[] in the structure record. Therefore, you could print the contents of y[] onscreen using the statement

```
puts(record.y);
```

Now look at another example. Listing 11.3 uses a structure that contains a type float variable and two type char arrays.

LISTING 11.3   array.c. A structure that contains array members

```
1:  /* Demonstrates a structure that has array members. */
2:
3:  #include <stdio.h>
4:
5:  /* Define and declare a structure to hold the data. */
6:  /* It contains one float variable and two char arrays. */
7:
```

LISTING 11.3 continued

```
 8:  struct data{
 9:      float amount;
10:      char fname[30];
11:      char lname[30];
12: } rec;
13:
14: int main( void )
15: {
16:     /* Input the data from the keyboard. */
17:
18:     printf("Enter the donor's first and last names,\n");
19:     printf("separated by a space: ");
20:     scanf("%s %s", rec.fname, rec.lname);
21:
22:     printf("\nEnter the donation amount: ");
23:     scanf("%f", &rec.amount);
24:
25:     /* Display the information. */
26:     /* Note: %.2f specifies a floating-point value */
27:     /* to be displayed with two digits to the right */
28:     /* of the decimal point. */
29:
30:     /* Display the data on the screen. */
31:
32:     printf("\nDonor %s %s gave $%.2f.\n", rec.fname, rec.lname,
33:             rec.amount);
34:
35:     return 0;
36: }
```

11

INPUT/
OUTPUT

```
Enter the donor's first and last names,
separated by a space: Bradley Jones

Enter the donation amount: 1000.00

Donor Bradley Jones gave $1000.00.
```

ANALYSIS   This program includes a structure that contains array members named fname[30] and lname[30]. Both are arrays of characters that hold a person's first name and last name, respectively. The structure declared in lines 8 through 12 is called data. It contains the fname and lname character arrays with a type float variable called amount. This structure is ideal for holding a person's name (in two parts, first name and last name) and a value, such as the amount the person donated to a charitable organization.

An instance of the array, called rec, has also been declared in line 12. The rest of the program uses rec to get values from the user (lines 18 through 23) and then print them (lines 32 and 33).

Arrays of Structures

If you can have structures that contain arrays, can you also have arrays of structures? You bet you can! In fact, arrays of structures are very powerful programming tools. Here's how it's done.

You've seen how a structure definition can be tailored to fit the data your program has to work with. Usually a program has to work with more than one instance of the data. For example, in a program to maintain a list of phone numbers, you can define a structure to hold each person's name and number:

```
struct entry
{
    char fname[10];
    char lname[12];
    char phone[8];
};
```

A phone list must hold many entries, so a single instance of the `entry` structure isn't of much use. What you need is an array of structures of type `entry`. After the structure has been defined, you can declare an array as follows:

```
struct entry list[1000];
```

This statement declares an array named `list` that contains 1,000 elements. Each element is a structure of type `entry` and is identified by subscript like other array element types. Each of these structures has three elements, each of which is an array of type `char`. This entire complex creation is diagrammed in Figure 11.3.

FIGURE 11.3

The organization of the array of structures defined in the text.

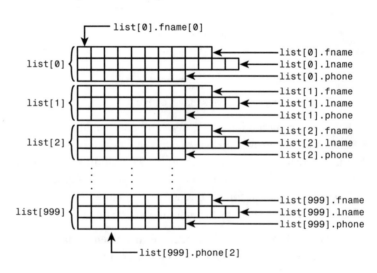

When you have declared the array of structures, you can manipulate the data in many ways. For example, to assign the data in one array element to another array element, you would write

```
list[1] = list[5];
```

This statement assigns to each member of the structure list[1] the values contained in the corresponding members of list[5]. You can also move data between individual structure members. The statement

```
strcpy(list[1].phone, list[5].phone);
```

copies the string in list[5].phone to list[1].phone. (The strcpy() library function copies one string to another string. You'll learn the details of this on Day 17, "Manipulating Strings.") If you want to, you can also move data between individual elements of the structure member arrays:

```
list[5].phone[1] = list[2].phone[3];
```

This statement moves the second character of list[5]'s phone number to the fourth position in list[2]'s phone number. (Don't forget that subscripts start at offset 0.)

Listing 11.4 demonstrates the use of arrays of structures. Moreover, it demonstrates arrays of structures that contain arrays as members.

LISTING 11.4   strucarr.c. Arrays of structures

```
 1: /* Demonstrates using arrays of structures. */
 2:
 3: #include <stdio.h>
 4:
 5: /* Define a structure to hold entries. */
 6:
 7: struct entry {
 8:     char fname[20];
 9:     char lname[20];
10:     char phone[10];
11: };
12:
13: /* Declare an array of structures. */
14:
15: struct entry list[4];
16:
17: int i;
18:
19: int main( void )
20: {
21:
```

11

LISTING 11.4   continued

```
22:     /* Loop to input data for four people. */
23:
24:     for (i = 0; i < 4; i++)
25:     {
26:         printf("\nEnter first name: ");
27:         scanf("%s", list[i].fname);
28:         printf("Enter last name: ");
29:         scanf("%s", list[i].lname);
30:         printf("Enter phone in 123-4567 format: ");
31:         scanf("%s", list[i].phone);
32:     }
33:
34:     /* Print two blank lines. */
35:
36:     printf("\n\n");
37:
38:     /* Loop to display data. */
39:
40:     for (i = 0; i < 4; i++)
41:     {
42:         printf("Name: %s %s", list[i].fname, list[i].lname);
43:         printf("\t\tPhone: %s\n", list[i].phone);
44:     }
45:
46:     return 0;
47: }
```

INPUT/
OUTPUT

```
Enter first name: Bradley
Enter last name: Jones
Enter phone in 123-4567 format: 555-1212

Enter first name: Peter
Enter last name: Aitken
Enter phone in 123-4567 format: 555-3434

Enter first name: Melissa
Enter last name: Jones
Enter phone in 123-4567 format: 555-1212

Enter first name: Kyle
Enter last name: Rinni
Enter phone in 123-4567 format: 555-1234

Name: Bradley Jones          Phone: 555-1212
Name: Peter Aitken           Phone: 555-3434
Name: Melissa Jones          Phone: 555-1212
Name: Kyle Rinni             Phone: 555-1234
```

ANALYSIS This listing follows the same general format as most of the other listings. It starts with the comment in line 1 and, for the input/output functions, the `#include` file stdio.h in line 3. Lines 7 through 11 define a template structure called `entry` that contains three character arrays: `fname`, `lname`, and `phone`. Line 15 uses the template to define an array of four entry structure variables called `list`. Line 17 defines a variable of type `int` to be used as a counter throughout the program. `main()` starts in line 19. The first function of `main()` is to perform a loop four times with a `for` statement. This loop is used to get information for the array of structures. This can be seen in lines 24 through 32. Notice that `list` is being used with a subscript in the same way as the array variables on Day 8, "Using Numeric Arrays," were subscripted.

Line 36 provides a break from the input before starting with the output. It prints two new lines in a manner that shouldn't be new to you. Lines 40 through 44 display the data that the user entered in the preceding step. The values in the array of structures are printed with the subscripted array name followed by the member operator (`.`) and the structure member name.

Familiarize yourself with the techniques used in Listing 11.4. Many real-world programming tasks are best accomplished by using arrays of structures containing arrays as members.

Do	Don't
DO remember to use the `struct` keyword when declaring an instance from a previously defined structure.	**DON'T** forget the structure instance name and member operator (.) when using a structure's members.
DO declare structure instances with the same scope rules as other variables. (Day 12, "Understanding Variable Scope," covers this topic fully.)	**DON'T** confuse a structure's tag with its instances! The tag is used to define the structure's template, or format. The instance is a variable declared using the tag.

Initializing Structures

Like other C variable types, structures can be initialized when they're declared. This procedure is similar to that for initializing arrays. The structure declaration is followed by an equal sign and a list of initialization values separated by commas and enclosed in braces. For example, look at the following statements:

```
1: struct sale {
2:     char customer[20];
3:     char item[20];
4:     float amount;
5: } mysale = {
6:                 "Acme Industries",
7:                 "Left-handed widget",
8:                  1000.00
9:                 };
```

When these statements are executed, they perform the following actions:

1. Define a structure type named `sale` (lines 1 through 5).

2. Declare an instance of structure type `sale` named `mysale` (line 5).

3. Initialize the structure member `mysale.customer` to the string `"Acme Industries"` (lines 5 and 6).

4. Initialize the structure member `mysale.item` to the string `"Left-handed widget"` (line 7).

5. Initialize the structure member `mysale.amount` to the value `1000.00` (line 8).

For a structure that contains structures as members, list the initialization values in order. They are placed in the structure members in the order in which the members are listed in the structure definition. Here's an example that expands on the preceding one:

```
1:   struct customer {
2:       char firm[20];
3:       char contact[25];
4:   }
5:
6:   struct sale {
7:       struct customer buyer;
8:       char item[20];
9:       float amount;
10: } mysale = { { "Acme Industries", "George Adams"},
11:                 "Left-handed widget",
12:                  1000.00
13:                 };
```

These statements perform the following initializations:

1. The structure member `mysale.buyer.firm` is initialized to the string `"Acme Industries"` (line 10).

2. The structure member `mysale.buyer.contact` is initialized to the string `"George Adams"` (line 10).

3. The structure member `mysale.item` is initialized to the string `"Left-handed widget"` (line 11).

4. The structure member `mysale.amount` is initialized to the amount `1000.00` (line 12).

You can also initialize arrays of structures. The initialization data that you supply is applied, in order, to the structures in the array. For example, to declare an array of structures of type `sale` and initialize the first two array elements (that is, the first two structures), you could write

```
1:  struct customer {
2:      char firm[20];
3:      char contact[25];
4:  };
5:
6:  struct sale {
7:      struct customer buyer;
8:      char item[20];
9:      float amount;
10: };
11:
12:
13: struct sale y1990[100] = {
14:     { { "Acme Industries", "George Adams"},
15:         "Left-handed widget",
16:          1000.00
17:     }
18:     { { "Wilson & Co.", "Ed Wilson"},
19:         "Type 12 gizmo",
20:          290.00
21:     }
22: };
```

This is what occurs in this code:

1. The structure member `y1990[0].buyer.firm` is initialized to the string `"Acme Industries"` (line 14).

2. The structure member `y1990[0].buyer.contact` is initialized to the string `"George Adams"` (line 14).

3. The structure member `y1990[0].item` is initialized to the string `"Left-handed widget"` (line 15).

4. The structure member `y1990[0].amount` is initialized to the amount `1000.00` (line 16).

5. The structure member `y1990[1].buyer.firm` is initialized to the string `"Wilson & Co."` (line 18).

6. The structure member `y1990[1].buyer.contact` is initialized to the string `"Ed Wilson"` (line 18).

11

7. The structure member y1990[1].item is initialized to the string "Type 12 gizmo" (line 19).

8. The structure member y1990[1].amount is initialized to the amount 290.00 (line 20).

Structures and Pointers

Given that pointers are such an important part of C, you shouldn't be surprised to find that they can be used with structures. You can use pointers as structure members, and you can also declare pointers to structures. These topics are covered in the following sections.

Including Pointers as Structure Members

You have complete flexibility in using pointers as structure members. Pointer members are declared in the same manner as pointers that aren't members of structures—that is, by using the indirection operator (*). Here's an example:

```
struct data
{
    int *value;
    int *rate;
} first;
```

These statements define and declare a structure whose two members are both pointers to type int. As with all pointers, declaring them is not enough; you must also initialize them to point to something. Remember, this can be done by assigning them the address of a variable. If cost and interest have been declared to be type int variables, you could write

```
first.value = &cost;
first.rate = &interest;
```

Now that the pointers have been initialized, you can use the indirection operator (*), as explained on Day 9, to evaluate the values stored in each. The expression *first.value evaluates to the value of cost, and the expression *first.rate evaluates to the value of interest.

Perhaps the type of pointer most frequently used as a structure member is a pointer to type char. Recall from Day 10, "Working with Characters and Strings," that a *string* is a sequence of characters delineated by a pointer that points to the string's first character and a null character that indicates the end of the string. To refresh your memory, you can declare a pointer to type char and initialize it to point at a string as follows:

```
char *p_message;
p_message = "Teach Yourself C In 21 Days";
```

You can do the same thing with pointers to type char that are structure members:

```
struct msg {
    char *p1;
    char *p2;
} myptrs;
myptrs.p1 = "Teach Yourself C In 21 Days";
myptrs.p2 = "By SAMS Publishing";
```

Figure 11.4 illustrates the result of executing these statements. Each pointer member of the structure points to the first byte of a string, stored elsewhere in memory. Contrast this with Figure 11.3, which shows how data is stored in a structure that contains arrays of type char.

FIGURE 11.4

A structure that contains pointers to type char.

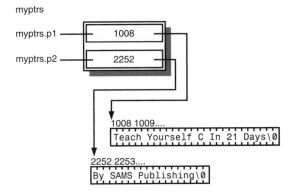

You can use pointer structure members anywhere a pointer can be used. For example, to print the pointed-to strings, you would write

```
printf("%s %s", myptrs.p1, myptrs.p2);
```

What's the difference between using an array of type char as a structure member and using a pointer to type char? These are both methods for "storing" a string in a structure, as shown here in the structure msg, which uses both methods:

```
struct msg
{
    char p1[30];
    char *p2;       /* caution: uninitialized */
} myptrs;
```

Recall that an array name without brackets is a pointer to the first array element. Therefore, you can use these two structure members in similar fashion (note that p2 should be initialized before you copy a value to it):

```
strcpy(myptrs.p1, "Teach Yourself C In 21 Days");
strcpy(myptrs.p2, "By SAMS Publishing");
/* additional code goes here */
puts(myptrs.p1);
puts(myptrs.p2);
```

What's the difference between these methods? It is this: If you define a structure that contains an array of type char, every instance of that structure type contains storage space for an array of the specified size. Furthermore, you're limited to the specified size; you can't store a larger string in the structure. Here's an example:

```
struct msg
{
    char p1[10];
    char p2[10];
} myptrs;
...
strcpy(p1, "Minneapolis"); /* Wrong! String longer than array.*/
strcpy(p2, "MN");          /* Okay, but wastes space because    */
                           /* string shorter than array.        */
```

If, on the other hand, you define a structure that contains pointers to type char, these restrictions don't apply. Each instance of the structure contains storage space for only the pointer. The actual strings are stored elsewhere in memory (but you don't have to worry about *where* in memory). There's no length restriction or wasted space. The actual strings aren't stored as part of the structure. Each pointer in the structure can point to a string of any length. That string becomes part of the structure, even though it isn't stored in the structure.

Caution   If you do not initialize the pointer, you can inadvertently overwrite memory being used for something else. When using a pointer instead of an array, you must remember to initialize the pointer. This can be done by assigning it to another variable or by allocating memory dynamically.

Creating Pointers to Structures

In a C program you can declare and use pointers to structures, just as you can declare pointers to any other data storage type. As you'll see later in today's lesson, pointers to structures are often used when passing a structure as an argument to a function. Pointers to structures are also used in a very powerful data storage method known as *linked lists*. Linked lists are explored on Day 15, "Pointers: Beyond the Basics."

For now, take a look at how your program can create and use pointers to structures. First, define a structure:

```
struct part
{
    short number;
    char name[10];
};
```

Now declare a pointer to type `part`:

```
struct part *p_part;
```

Remember, the indirection operator (*) in the declaration says that `p_part` is a pointer to type `part`, not an instance of type `part`.

Can the pointer be initialized now? No, because even though the structure `part` has been defined, no instances of it have been declared. Remember that it's a declaration, not a definition, which sets aside storage space in memory for a data object. Because a pointer needs a memory address to point to, you must declare an instance of type `part` before anything can point to it. Here's the declaration:

```
struct part gizmo;
```

Now you can perform the pointer initialization:

```
p_part = &gizmo;
```

This statement assigns the address of `gizmo` to `p_part`. (Recall the address-of operator, `&`, from Day 9.) Figure 11.5 shows the relationship between a structure and a pointer to the structure.

FIGURE 11.5

A pointer to a structure points to the structure's first byte.

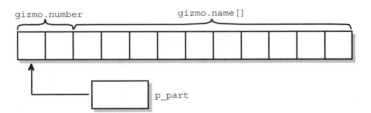

Now that you have a pointer to the structure `gizmo`, how do you make use of it? One method uses the indirection operator (*). Recall from Day 9 that if `ptr` is a pointer to a data object, the expression `*ptr` refers to the object pointed to.

Applying this to the current example, you know that `p_part` is a pointer to the structure `gizmo`, so `*p_part` refers to `gizmo`. You then apply the structure member operator (.) to access individual members of `gizmo`. To assign the value `100` to `gizmo.number`, you could write

```
(*p_part).number = 100;
```

*p_part must be enclosed in parentheses because the structure member operator (.) has a higher precedence than the indirection operator (*).

A second way to access structure members using a pointer to the structure is to use)>)> (indirect membership) operator> the *indirect membership operator,* which consists of the characters -> (a hyphen followed by the greater-than symbol). (Note that when they are used together in this way, C treats them as a single operator, not two.) This symbol is placed between the pointer name and the member name. For example, to access the num- ber member of gizmo with the p_part pointer, you would write

```
p_part->number
```

Looking at another example, if str is a structure, p_str is a pointer to str, and memb is a member of str, you can access str.memb by writing

```
p_str->memb
```

Therefore, there are three ways to access a structure member:

- Using the structure name
- Using a pointer to the structure with the indirection operator (*)
- Using a pointer to the structure with the indirect membership operator (->)

If p_str is a pointer to the structure str, the following three expressions are all equiva- lent:

```
str.memb
```

```
(*p_str).memb
```

```
p_str->memb
```

Note Some people refer to the indirect membership operator as the "structure pointer operator."

Working with Pointers and Arrays of Structures

You've seen that arrays of structures can be a very powerful programming tool, as can pointers to structures. You can combine the two, using pointers to access structures that are array elements.

To illustrate, here is a structure definition from an earlier example:

```
struct part
{
    short number;
    char name[10];
};
```

After the part structure is defined, you can declare an array of type part:

```
struct part data[100];
```

Next you can declare a pointer to type part and initialize it to point to the first structure in the array data:

```
struct part *p_part;
p_part = &data[0];
```

Recall that the name of an array without brackets is a pointer to the first array element, so the second line could also have been written as

```
p_part = data;
```

You now have an array of structures of type part and a pointer to the first array element (that is, the first structure in the array). For example, you could print the contents of the first element using the statement

```
printf("%d %s", p_part->number, p_part->name);
```

What if you wanted to print all the array elements? You would probably use a for loop, printing one array element with each iteration of the loop. To access the members using pointer notation, you must change the pointer p_part so that with each iteration of the loop it points to the next array element (that is, the next structure in the array). How do you do this?

C's pointer arithmetic comes to your aid. The unary increment operator (++) has a special meaning when applied to a pointer: It means "increment the pointer by the size of the object it points to." Put another way, if you have a pointer ptr that points to a data object of type obj, the statement

```
ptr++;
```

has the same effect as

```
ptr += sizeof(obj);
```

This aspect of pointer arithmetic is particularly relevant to arrays because array elements are stored sequentially in memory. If a pointer points to array element n, incrementing the pointer with the (++) operator causes it to point to element n + 1. This is illustrated

11

in Figure 11.6, which shows an array named x[] that consists of 4-byte elements (for example, a structure containing two type short members, each 2 bytes long). The pointer ptr was initialized to point to x[0]; each time ptr is incremented, it points to the next array element.

FIGURE 11.6

With each increment, a pointer steps to the next array element.

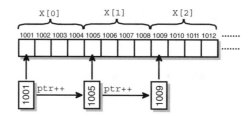

What this means is that your program can step through an array of structures (or an array of any other data type, for that matter) by incrementing a pointer. This sort of notation is usually easier to use and more concise than using array subscripts to perform the same task. Listing 11.5 shows how you do this.

LISTING 11.5   access.c. Accessing successive array elements by incrementing a pointer

```
 1:  /* Demonstrates stepping through an array of structures */
 2:  /* using pointer notation. */
 3:
 4:  #include <stdio.h>
 5:
 6:  #define MAX 4
 7:
 8:  /* Define a structure, then declare and initialize */
 9:  /* an array of 4 structures. */
10:
11: struct part {
12:     short number;
13:     char name[10];
14: } data[MAX] = {1, "Smith",
15:                2, "Jones",
16:                3, "Adams",
17:                4, "Wilson"
18:                };
19:
20: /* Declare a pointer to type part, and a counter variable. */
21:
22: struct part *p_part;
23: int count;
24:
25: int main( void )
```

LISTING 11.5 continued

```
26: {
27:     /* Initialize the pointer to the first array element. */
28:
29:     p_part = data;
30:
31:     /* Loop through the array, incrementing the pointer */
32:     /* with each iteration. */
33:
34:     for (count = 0; count < MAX; count++)
35:     {
36:         printf("At address %d: %d %s\n", p_part, p_part->number,
37:             p_part->name);
38:         p_part++;
39:     }
40:
41:     return 0;
42: }
```

OUTPUT

```
At address 4202504: 1 Smith
At address 4202516: 2 Jones
At address 4202528: 3 Adams
At address 4202540: 4 Wilson
```

ANALYSIS First, in lines 11 through 18, this program declares and initializes an array of part structures called data. A pointer called p_part is then defined in line 22 to be used to point to the data structure. The main() function's first task in line 29 is to set the pointer, p_part, to point to the part structure that was declared. All the elements are then printed using a for loop in lines 34 through 39 that increments the pointer to the array with each iteration. The program also displays the address of each element.

Look closely at the addresses displayed. The precise values might differ on your system, but they are in equal-sized increments—just the size of the structure part. This clearly illustrates that incrementing a pointer increases it by an amount equal to the size of the data object it points to.

Passing Structures as Arguments to Functions

Like other data types, a structure can be passed as an argument to a function. Listing 11.6 shows how to do this. This program is a modification of the program shown in Listing 11.3. It uses a function to display information on the screen from a structure that is passed in, whereas Listing 11.3 uses statements that are part of main().

LISTING 11.6 func.c. Passing a structure as a function argument

```
1:  /* Demonstrates passing a structure to a function. */
2:
3:  #include <stdio.h>
4:
5:  /* Declare and define a structure to hold the data. */
6:
7:  struct data {
8:      float amount;
9:      char fname[30];
10:     char lname[30];
11: } rec;
12:
13: /* The function prototype. The function has no return value, */
14: /* and it takes a structure of type data as its one argument. */
15:
16: void print_rec(struct data diplayRec);
17:
18: int main( void )
19: {
20:     /* Input the data from the keyboard. */
21:
22:     printf("Enter the donor's first and last names,\n");
23:     printf("separated by a space: ");
24:     scanf("%s %s", rec.fname, rec.lname);
25:
26:     printf("\nEnter the donation amount: ");
27:     scanf("%f", &rec.amount);
28:
29:     /* Call the display function. */
30:     print_rec( rec );
31:
32:     return 0;
33: }
34: void print_rec(struct data displayRec)
35: {
36:     printf("\nDonor %s %s gave $%.2f.\n", displayRec.fname,
37:             displayRec.lname, displayRec.amount);
38: }
```

INPUT/OUTPUT

```
Enter the donor's first and last names,
separated by a space: Bradley Jones

Enter the donation amount: 1000.00

Donor Bradley Jones gave $1000.00.
```

ANALYSIS Looking at line 16, you see the function prototype for the function that is to receive the structure. As you would with any other data type that was going to be passed, you must include the proper arguments. In this case, it is a structure of type data.

This is repeated in the header for the function in line 34. When calling the function, you only have to pass the structure instance name—in this case, rec (line 30). That's all there is to it. Passing a structure to a function isn't very different from passing a simple variable.

You can also pass a structure to a function by passing the structure's address (that is, a pointer to the structure). In fact, in older versions of C, this was the only way to pass a structure as an argument. It's not necessary now, but you might see older programs that still use this method. If you pass a pointer to a structure as an argument, remember that you must use the indirect membership operator (->) to access structure members in the function.

Do	Don't
DO take advantage of declaring a pointer to a structure—especially when using arrays of structures. **DO** use the indirect membership operator (->) when working with a pointer to a structure.	**DON'T** confuse arrays with structures. **DON'T** forget that when you increment a pointer, it moves a distance equivalent to the size of the data to which it points. In the case of a pointer to a structure, this is the size of the structure.

Understanding Unions

Unions are similar to structures. A union is declared and used in the same ways that a structure is. A union differs from a structure in that only one of its members can be used at a time. The reason for this is simple. All the members of a union occupy the same area of memory—they are laid on top of one another.

Defining, Declaring, and Initializing Unions

Unions are defined and declared in the same fashion as structures. The only difference in the declarations is that the keyword union is used instead of struct. To define a simple union of a char variable and an integer variable, you would write the following:

```
union shared
{
    char c;
    int i;
};
```

This union, shared, can be used to create instances of a union that can hold either a character value c or an integer value i. This is an OR condition. Unlike a structure that would hold both values, the union can hold only one value at a time. Figure 11.7 illustrates how the shared union would appear in memory.

FIGURE 11.7

The union can hold only one value at a time.

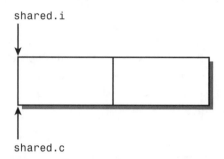

A union can be initialized on its declaration. Because only one member can be used at a time, only one member can be initialized. To avoid confusion, only the first member of the union can be initialized. The following code shows an instance of the shared union being declared and initialized:

```
union shared generic_variable = {'@'};
```

Notice that the generic_variable union was initialized just as the first member of a structure would be initialized.

Accessing Union Members

Individual union members can be used in the same way that structure members can be used—by using the member operator (.). However, there is an important difference in accessing union members. Only one union member should be accessed at a time. Because a union stores its members on top of each other, it's important to access only one member at a time. Listing 11.7 presents an example.

LISTING 11.7 union.c. An example of the wrong use of unions

```
1:    /* Example of using more than one union member at a time */
2:    #include <stdio.h>
3:
4:    int main( void )
5:    {
6:        union shared_tag {
7:            char   c;
8:            int    i;
9:            long   l;
10:           float  f;
11:           double d;
12:       } shared;
```

LISTING 11.7 continued

```
13:
14:        shared.c = '$';
15:
16:        printf("\nchar c   = %c",  shared.c);
17:        printf("\nint i    = %d",  shared.i);
18:        printf("\nlong l   = %ld", shared.l);
19:        printf("\nfloat f  = %f",  shared.f);
20:        printf("\ndouble d = %f",  shared.d);
21:
22:        shared.d = 123456789.8765;
23:
24:        printf("\n\nchar c   = %c",  shared.c);
25:        printf("\nint i    = %d",  shared.i);
26:        printf("\nlong l   = %ld", shared.l);
27:        printf("\nfloat f  = %f",  shared.f);
28:        printf("\ndouble d = %f\n",  shared.d);
29:
30:        return 0;
31:    }
```

OUTPUT

```
char c   = $
int i    = 65572
long l   = 65572
float f  = 0.000000
double d = 0.000000

char c   = 7
int i    = 1468107063
long l   = 1468107063
float f  = 284852666499072.000000
double d = 123456789.876500
```

11

ANALYSIS In this listing, you can see that a union named shared is defined and declared in lines 6 through 12. shared contains five members, each of a different type. Lines 14 and 22 initialize individual members of shared. Lines 16 through 20 and 24 through 28 then present the values of each member, using printf() statements.

Note that, with the exceptions of char c = $ and double d = 123456789.876500, the output might not be the same on your computer. Because the character variable, c, was initialized in line 14, it is the only value that should be used until a different member is initialized. The results of printing the other union member variables (i, l, f, and d) can be unpredictable (lines 16 through 20). Line 22 puts a value into the double variable, d. Notice that the printing of the variables again is unpredictable for all but d. The value entered into c in line 14 has been lost because it was overwritten when the value of d in line 22 was entered. This is evidence that the members all occupy the same space.

▼ SYNTAX

The union Keyword

```
union tag {
    union_member(s);
    /* additional statements may go here */
}instance;
```

The union keyword is used for declaring unions. A union is a collection of one or more variables (*union_members*) that have been grouped under a single name. In addition, each of these union members occupies the same area of memory.

The keyword union identifies the beginning of a union definition. It's followed by a tag that is the name given to the union. Following the tag are the union members, enclosed in braces. An *instance*, the actual declaration of a union, also can be defined. If you define the structure without the instance, it's just a template that can be used later in a program to declare structures. The following is a template's format:

```
union tag {
    union_member(s);
    /* additional statements may go here */
};
```

To use the template, you would use the following format:

```
union tag instance;
```

To use this format, you must have previously declared a union with the given tag.

Example 1

```
/* Declare a union template called tag */
union tag {
    int nbr;
    char character;
}
/* Use the union template */
union tag mixed_variable;
```

Example 2

```
/* Declare a union and instance together */
union generic_type_tag {
    char c;
    int i;
    float f;
    double d;
} generic;
```

Example 3

```
/* Initialize a union. */
union date_tag {
```

▼

```
    ▼       char full_date[9];
            struct part_date_tag {
                char month[2];
                char break_value1;
                char day[2];
                char break_value2;
                char year[2];
            } part_date;
    ▲   }date = {"01/01/97"};
```

Listing 11.8 shows a more practical use of a union. Although this use is simplistic, it's one of the more common uses of a union.

LISTING 11.8   union2.c. A practical use of a union

```
 1:    /* Example of a typical use of a union */
 2:
 3:    #include <stdio.h>
 4:
 5:    #define CHARACTER    'C'
 6:    #define INTEGER      'I'
 7:    #define FLOAT        'F'
 8:
 9:    struct generic_tag{
10:        char type;
11:        union shared_tag {
12:            char   c;
13:            int    i;
14:            float  f;
15:        } shared;
16:    };
17:
18:    void print_function( struct generic_tag generic );
19:
20:    int main( void )
21:    {
22:        struct generic_tag var;
23:
24:        var.type = CHARACTER;
25:        var.shared.c = '$';
26:        print_function( var );
27:
28:        var.type = FLOAT;
29:        var.shared.f = (float) 12345.67890;
30:        print_function( var );
31:
32:        var.type = 'x';
33:        var.shared.i = 111;
34:        print_function( var );
35:        return 0;
```

11

LISTING **11.8**   continued

```
36:    }
37:    void print_function( struct generic_tag generic )
38:    {
39:        printf("\n\nThe generic value is...");
40:        switch( generic.type )
41:        {
42:            case CHARACTER: printf("%c",  generic.shared.c);
43:                            break;
44:            case INTEGER:   printf("%d",  generic.shared.i);
45:                            break;
46:            case FLOAT:     printf("%f",  generic.shared.f);
47:                            break;
48:            default:        printf("an unknown type: %c\n",
49:                                   generic.type);
50:                            break;
51:        }
52:    }
```

OUTPUT

```
The generic value is...$

The generic value is...12345.678711

The generic value is...an unknown type: x
```

ANALYSIS   This program is a very simplistic version of what could be done with a union. This program provides a way of storing multiple data types in a single storage space. The generic_tag structure lets you store either a character, an integer, or a floating-point number within the same area. This area is a union called shared that operates just like the examples in Listing 11.7. Notice that the generic_tag structure also adds an additional field called type. This field is used to store information on the type of variable contained in shared. type helps prevent shared from being used in the wrong way, thus helping to avoid erroneous data such as that presented in Listing 11.7.

A formal look at the program shows that lines 5, 6, and 7 define constants CHARACTER, INTEGER, and FLOAT. These are used later in the program to make the listing more readable. Lines 9 through 16 define a generic_tag structure that will be used later. Line 18 presents a prototype for the print_function(). The structure var is declared in line 22 and is first initialized to hold a character value in lines 24 and 25. A call to print_function() in line 26 lets the value be printed. Lines 28 through 30 and 32 through 34 repeat this process with other values.

The print_function() is the heart of this listing. Although this function is used to print the value from a generic_tag variable, a similar function could have been used to initialize it. `print_function()` will evaluate the `type` variable in order to print a statement with the appropriate variable type. This prevents getting erroneous data such as that in Listing 11.7.

Do	Don't
DO remember which union member is being used. If you fill in a member of one type and then try to use a different type, you can get unexpected results.	**DON'T** try to initialize more than the first union member. **DON'T** forget that the size of a union is equal to its largest member.

Creating Synonyms for Structures with typedef

You can use the `typedef` keyword to create a synonym for a structure or union type. For example, the following statements define `coord` as a synonym for the indicated structure:

```
typedef struct {
    int x;
    int y;
} coord;
```

You can then declare instances of this structure using the `coord` identifier:

```
coord topleft, bottomright;
```

Note that a `typedef` is different from a structure tag, as described earlier in today's lesson. If you write

```
struct coord {
    int x;
    int y;
};
```

the identifier `coord` is a tag for the structure. You can use the tag to declare instances of the structure, but unlike using a `typedef`, you must include the `struct` keyword:

```
struct coord topleft, bottomright;
```

Whether you use `typedef` or a structure tag to declare structures makes little difference. Using `typedef` results in slightly more concise code because the `struct` keyword doesn't have to be used. On the other hand, using a tag and having the `struct` keyword explicit makes it clear that it is a structure being declared.

11

Summary

Today's lesson showed you how to use structures, a data type that you design to meet the needs of your program. A structure can contain any of C's data types, including other structures, pointers, and arrays. Each data item within a structure, called a *member,* is accessed using the structure member operator (.) between the structure name and the member name. Structures can be used individually, and also in arrays.

Unions are similar to structures. The main difference between a union and a structure is that the union stores all its members in the same area. This means that only one member of a union can be used at a time.

Q&A

Q Is there any reason to declare a structure without an instance?

A Today you saw two ways of declaring a structure. The first is to declare a structure body, tag, and instance all at once. The second is to declare a structure body and tag without an instance. An instance can then be declared later by using the `struct` keyword, the tag, and a name for the instance. It's common programming practice to use the second method. Many programmers declare the structure body and tag without any instances. The instances are then declared later in the program. Tomorrow's lesson describes variable scope. Scope will apply to the instance, but not to the tag or structure body.

Q Is it more common to use a `typedef` or a structure tag?

A Many programmers use `typedef`s to make their code easier to read, but it makes little practical difference. Many add-in libraries that contain functions are available for purchase. These add-ins usually have a many `typedef`s to make the product unique. This is especially true of database add-in products.

Q Can I simply assign one structure to another with the assignment operator?

A Yes and no. Newer versions of C compilers let you assign one structure to another, but older versions might not. In older versions of C, you might need to assign each member of the structures individually. This is true of unions, also.

Q How big is a union?

A Because each member in a union is stored in the same memory location, the amount of room required to store the union is equal to that of its largest member.

Workshop

The Workshop provides quiz questions to help you solidify your understanding of the material covered and exercises to provide you with experience in using what you've learned.

Quiz

1. How is a structure different from an array?

2. What is the structure member operator, and what purpose does it serve?

3. What keyword is used in C to create a structure?

4. What is the difference between a structure tag and a structure instance?

5. What does the following code fragment do?

```
struct address
{
    char name[31];
    char add1[31];
    char add2[31];
    char city[11];
    char state[3];
    char zip[11];
} myaddress = { "Bradley Jones",
                "RTSoftware",
                "P.O. Box 1213",
                "Carmel", "IN", "46082-1213"};
```

11

6. If you create a `typedef` called `word`, how would you declare a variable called `myWord` using it?

7. Assume you have declared an array of structures and that `ptr` is a pointer to the first array element (that is, the first structure in the array). How would you change `ptr` to point to the second array element?

Exercises

1. Write code that defines a structure named `time`, which contains three `int` members.

2. Write code that performs two tasks: defines a structure named `data` that contains one type `int` member and two type `float` members, and declares an instance of type `data` named `info`.

3. Continuing with exercise 2, how would you assign the value `100` to the integer member of the structure `info`?

4. Write code that declares and initializes a pointer to `info`.

5. Continuing with exercise 4, show two ways of using pointer notation to assign the value 5.5 to the first float member of info.

6. Write the definition for a structure type named data that can hold a single string of up to 20 characters.

7. Create a structure containing five strings: address1, address2, city, state, and zip. Create a typedef called RECORD that can be used to create instances of this structure.

8. Using the typedef from exercise 7, allocate and initialize an element called myad-dress.

9. **BUG BUSTER:** What is wrong with the following code?

```
struct {
    char zodiac_sign[21];
    int month;
} sign = "Leo", 8;
```

10. **BUG BUSTER:** What is wrong with the following code?

```
/* setting up a union */
union data{
    char a_word[4];
    long a_number;
}generic_variable = { "WOW", 1000 };
```

DAY 12

Understanding Variable Scope

On Day 5, "Functions: The Basics," you saw that a variable defined within a function is different from a variable defined outside a function. Without knowing it, you were being introduced to the concept of *variable scope,* an important aspect of C programming. Today you will learn:

- About variable scope and why it's important
- What external variables are and why you should usually avoid them
- The ins and outs of local variables
- The difference between static and automatic variables
- About local variables and blocks
- How to select a storage class

What Is Scope?

NEW TERM The *scope* of a variable refers to the extent to which different parts of a program have access to the variable—in other words, where the variable is *visible*. When referring to C variables, the terms *accessibility* and *visibility* are used interchangeably. When speaking about scope, the term *variable* refers to all C data types: simple variables, arrays, structures, pointers, and so forth. It also refers to symbolic constants defined with the const keyword.

NEW TERM Scope also affects a variable's *lifetime*: how long the variable persists in memory, or in other words when the variable's storage is allocated and deallocated. After a quick demonstration of scope, today's lesson examines visibility and scope in more detail.

A Demonstration of Scope

Look at the program in Listing 12.1. It defines the variable x in line 5, uses printf() to display the value of x in line 11, and then calls the function print_value() to display the value of x again. Note that the function print_value() is not passed the value of x as an argument; it simply uses x as an argument to printf() in line 19.

LISTING 12.1   scope.c. The variable x is accessible within the function print_value()

```
 1:   /* Illustrates variable scope. */
 2:
 3:   #include <stdio.h>
 4:
 5:   int x = 999;
 6:
 7:   void print_value(void);
 8:
 9:   int main( void )
10:   {
11:       printf("%d\n", x);
12:       print_value();
13:
14:       return 0;
15:   }
16:
17:   void print_value(void)
18:   {
19:       printf("%d\n", x);
20:   }
```

OUTPUT
999
999

This program compiles and runs with no problems. Now make a minor modification in the program, moving the definition of the variable x to a location within the `main()` function. The new source code is shown in Listing 12.2, with the definition of x now on line 9.

LISTING 12.2   scope2.c. The variable x is not accessible within the function `print_value()`

```
 1:  /* Illustrates variable scope. */
 2:
 3:  #include <stdio.h>
 4:
 5:  void print_value(void);
 6:
 7:  int main( void )
 8:  {
 9:      int x = 999;
10:
11:      printf("%d\n", x);
12:      print_value();
13:
14:      return 0;
15: }
16:
17: void print_value(void)
18: {
19:      printf("%d\n", x);
20: }
```

ANALYSIS   If you try to compile Listing 12.2, the compiler generates an error message similar to the following:

```
list1202.c(19) : Error: undefined identifier 'x'.
```

Remember that in an error message, the number in parentheses refers to the program line where the error was found. Line 19 is the call to `printf()` within the `print_value()` function.

This error message tells you that when line 19 was compiled, within the `print_value()` function, the variable x is undefined or, in other words, not visible. Note, however, that the call to `printf()` in line 11 doesn't generate an error message; in this part of the program, outside `print_value()`, the variable x *is* visible.

12

The only difference between Listings 12.1 and 12.2 is where variable x is defined. By moving the definition of x, you change its scope. In Listing 12.1, x is defined outside of main() and is therefore an *external variable,* and its scope is the entire program. It is accessible within both the main() function and the print_value() function. In Listing 12.2, x is defined inside a function, the main() function, and is therefore a *local variable* with its scope limited to within the main() function. As far as print_value() is concerned, x doesn't exist, and this is why the compiler generated an error message. Later in today's lesson, you'll learn more about local and external variables, but first you need to understand the importance of scope.

Why Is Scope Important?

To understand the importance of variable scope, you need to recall the discussion of structured programming on Day 5. The structured approach, you may remember, divides the program into independent functions that each perform a specific task. The key word here is *independent.* For true independence, it's necessary for each function's variables to be isolated from possible interference caused by code in other functions. Only by isolating each function's data can you make sure that the function goes about its job without some other part of the program throwing a monkey wrench into the works. By defining variables within functions, as you will learn soon, you can "hide" those variables from other parts of the program.

If you're thinking that complete data isolation between functions isn't always desirable, you are correct. You will soon realize that by specifying the scope of variables, a programmer has a great deal of control over the degree of data isolation.

Creating External Variables

 An *external variable* is a variable defined outside of any function. This means outside of main() as well because main() is a function, too. Until now, most of the variable definitions in this book have been external, placed in the source code before the start of main(). External variables are sometimes referred to as *global variables.*

> **Note**
>
> If you don't explicitly initialize an external variable (assign a value to it) when it's defined, the compiler initializes it to 0.

External Variable Scope

The scope of an external variable is the entire program. This means that an external variable is visible throughout `main()` and throughout every other function in the program. For example, the variable x in Listing 12.1 is an external variable. As you saw when you compiled and ran the program, x is visible within both functions, `main()` and `print_value()`, and would also be visible in any other functions you might add to the program.

Strictly speaking, it's not accurate to say that the scope of an external variable is the entire program. Instead, the scope is the entire source code file that contains the variable definition. If the entire program is contained in one source code file, the two scope definitions are equivalent. Most small-to-medium-sized C programs are contained in one file, and that's certainly true of the programs you're writing now.

It's possible, however, for a program's source code to be contained in two or more separate files. You'll learn how and why this is done on Day 21, "Advanced Compiler Use," and you'll see what special handling is required for external variables in these situations.

When to Use External Variables

NEW TERM   Although the sample programs to this point have used external variables, in actual practice you should use them rarely. Why? Because when you use external variables, you are violating the principle of *modular independence* that is central to structured programming. Modular independence is the idea that each function, or module, in a program contains all the code and data it needs to do its job. With the relatively small programs you're writing now, this might not seem important, but as you progress to larger and more complex programs, over-reliance on external variables can start to cause problems.

When should you use external variables? Make a variable external only when all or most of the program's functions need access to the variable. Symbolic constants defined with the `const` keyword are often good candidates for external status. If only some of your functions need access to a variable, pass the variable to the functions as an argument rather than making it external.

The `extern` Keyword

When a function uses an external variable, it is good programming practice to declare the variable within the function using the `extern` keyword. The declaration takes the form

```
extern type name;
```

in which *type* is the variable type and *name* is the variable name. For example, you would add the declaration of x to the functions `main()` and `print_value()` in Listing 12.1. The resulting program is shown in Listing 12.3.

LISTING 12.3   extern.c. The external variable x is declared as extern within the functions main() and print_value()

```
 1:  /* Illustrates declaring external variables. */
 2:
 3:  #include <stdio.h>
 4:
 5:  int x = 999;
 6:
 7:  void print_value(void);
 8:
 9:  int main( void )
10:  {
11:      extern int x;
12:
13:      printf("%d\n", x);
14:      print_value();
15:
16:      return 0;
17:  }
18:
19:  void print_value(void)
20:  {
21:      extern int x;
22:      printf("%d\n", x);
23:  }
```

OUTPUT
```
999
999
```

ANALYSIS   This program prints the value of x twice, first in line 13 as a part of main(), and then in line 21 as a part of print_value(). Line 5 defines x as a type int variable equal to 999. Lines 11 and 21 declare x as an extern int. Note the distinction between a variable definition, which sets aside storage for the variable, and an extern declaration. The latter says: "This function uses an external variable with such-and-such a name and type that is defined elsewhere." In this case, the extern declaration isn't needed, strictly speaking—the program will work the same without lines 11 and 21. However, if the function print_value() were in a different code module than the global declaration of the variable x (in line 5), the extern declaration would be required.

If you remove the definition of x in line 5, the listing will still compile. What you'll find, however, is that an error will be given when you run the program. This is because the functions expect x to be defined elsewhere.

Creating Local Variables

NEW TERM   A *local variable* is one that is defined within a function. The scope of a local variable is limited to the function in which it is defined. Day 5 describes local variables within functions, how to define them, and what their advantages are. Local variables aren't automatically initialized to 0 by the compiler. If you don't initialize a local variable when it's defined, it has an undefined or *garbage* value. You must explicitly assign a value to local variables before they're used for the first time.

A variable can be local to the main() function as well. This is the case for x in Listing 12.2. It is defined within main(), and as compiling and executing that program illustrates, it's also only visible within main().

Do	Don't
DO use local variables for items such as loop counters. **DO** use local variables to isolate the values the variables contain from the rest of the program.	**DON'T** use external variables if they aren't needed by a majority of the program's functions.

Static Versus Automatic Variables

Local variables are *automatic* by default. This means that local variables are created anew each time the function is called, and they are destroyed when execution leaves the function. What this means, in practical terms, is that an automatic variable doesn't retain its value between calls to the function in which it is defined.

Suppose your program has a function that uses a local variable x. Also suppose that the first time it is called, the function assigns the value 100 to x. Execution returns to the calling program, and the function is called again later. Does the variable x still hold the value 100? No, it does not. The first instance of variable x was destroyed when execution left the function after the first call. When the function was called again, a new instance of x was created. The old x is gone.

What if the function needs to retain the value of a local variable between calls? For example, a printing function might need to remember the number of lines already sent to the printer to determine when it is necessary to start a new page. In order for a local variable to retain its value between calls, it must be defined as *static* with the static keyword. For example:

12

```
void print(int x)
{
    static int lineCount;
    /* Additional code goes here */
}
```

Listing 12.4 illustrates the difference between automatic and static local variables.

LISTING 12.4   static.c. The difference between automatic and static local variables

```
 1:  /* Demonstrates automatic and static local variables. */
 2:  #include <stdio.h>
 3:  void func1(void);
 4:  int main( void )
 5:  {
 6:      int count;
 7:
 8:      for (count = 0; count < 20; count++)
 9:      {
10:          printf("At iteration %d: ", count);
11:          func1();
12:      }
13:
14:      return 0;
15: }
16:
17: void func1(void)
18: {
19:     static int x = 0;
20:     int y = 0;
21:
22:     printf("x = %d, y = %d\n", x++, y++);
23: }
```

OUTPUT
```
At iteration 0: x = 0, y = 0
At iteration 1: x = 1, y = 0
At iteration 2: x = 2, y = 0
At iteration 3: x = 3, y = 0
At iteration 4: x = 4, y = 0
At iteration 5: x = 5, y = 0
At iteration 6: x = 6, y = 0
At iteration 7: x = 7, y = 0
At iteration 8: x = 8, y = 0
At iteration 9: x = 9, y = 0
At iteration 10: x = 10, y = 0
At iteration 11: x = 11, y = 0
At iteration 12: x = 12, y = 0
At iteration 13: x = 13, y = 0
At iteration 14: x = 14, y = 0
```

```
At iteration 15: x = 15, y = 0
At iteration 16: x = 16, y = 0
At iteration 17: x = 17, y = 0
At iteration 18: x = 18, y = 0
At iteration 19: x = 19, y = 0
```

ANALYSIS This program has a function, func1(), that defines and initializes one static local variable and one automatic local variable. This function is shown in lines 17 through 23. Each time the function is called, both variables are displayed on-screen and incremented (line 22). The main() function in lines 4 through 15 contains a for loop (lines 8 through 12) that prints a message (line 10) and then calls func1() (line 11). The for loop iterates 20 times.

In the output, note that x, the static variable, increases with each iteration because it retains its value between calls. The automatic variable y, on the other hand, is reinitialized to 0 with each call and therefore does not increment.

This program also illustrates a difference in the way explicit variable initialization is handled (that is, when a variable is initialized at the time of definition). A static variable is initialized only the first time the function is called. At later calls, the program remembers that the variable has already been initialized and therefore doesn't reinitialize. Instead, the variable retains the value it had when execution last exited the function. In contrast, an automatic variable is initialized to the specified value every time the function is called.

If you experiment with automatic variables, you might get results that disagree with what you've read here. For example, if you modify Listing 12.4 so that the two local variables aren't initialized when they're defined, the function func1() in lines 17 through 23 reads

```
17: void func1(void)
18: {
19:     static int x;
20:     int y;
21:
22:     printf("x = %d, y = %d\n", x++, y++);
23: }
```

When you run the modified program, you might find that the value of y increases by 1 with each iteration. This means that y is keeping its value between calls to the function even though it is an automatic local variable. Is what you've read here about automatic variables losing their value a bunch of malarkey?

No, what you read is true (Have faith!). If you find that an automatic variable keeps its value during repeated calls to the function, it's only by chance. Here's what happens: Each time the function is called, a new y is created. The compiler might use the same

12

memory location for the new y that was used for y the preceding time the function was called. If y isn't explicitly initialized by the function, the storage location might contain the value that y had during the preceding call. The variable seems to have kept its old value, but it's just a chance occurrence; you definitely can't count on it happening every time. Because you can't always count on it, you should never count on it!

Because automatic is the default for local variables, it doesn't need to be specified in the variable definition. If you want to, you can include the auto keyword in the definition before the type keyword, as shown here:

```
void func1(int y)
{
    auto int count;
    /* Additional code goes here */
}
```

The Scope of Function Parameters

NEW TERM   A variable that is contained in a function heading's parameter list has *local scope*. For example, look at the following function:

```
void func1(int x)
{
    int y;
    /* Additional code goes here */
}
```

Both x and y are local variables with a scope that is the entire function func1(). Of course, x initially contains whatever value was passed to the function by the calling program. Once you've made use of that value, you can use x like any other local variable.

Because parameter variables always start with the value passed as the corresponding argument, it's meaningless to think of them as being either static or automatic.

External Static Variables

You can make an external variable static by including the static keyword in its definition:

```
static float rate;

int main( void )
{
    /* Additional code goes here */
}
```

The difference between an ordinary external variable and a static external variable is one of scope. An ordinary external variable is visible to all functions in the file and can be used by functions in other files. A static external variable is visible only to functions in its own file and below the point of definition.

These distinctions obviously apply mostly to programs with source code that is contained in two or more files. This topic is covered on Day 21.

Register Variables

The `register` keyword is used to suggest to the compiler that an automatic local variable be stored in a *processor register* rather than in regular memory. What is a processor register, and what are the advantages of using it?

The central processing unit (CPU) of your computer contains a few data storage locations called *registers*. It is in the CPU registers that actual data operations, such as addition and division, take place. To manipulate data, the CPU must move the data from memory to its registers, perform the manipulations, and then move the data back to memory. Moving data to and from memory takes a finite amount of time. If a particular variable could be kept in a register to begin with, manipulations of the variable would proceed much faster.

By using the `register` keyword in the definition of an automatic variable, you ask the compiler to store that variable in a register. Look at the following example:

```
void func1(void)
{
    register int x;
    /* Additional code goes here */
}
```

Note that I said *ask*, not *tell*. Depending on the program's needs, a register might not be available for the variable. If no register is available, the compiler treats the variable as an ordinary automatic variable. In other words, the `register` keyword is a suggestion, not an order. The benefits of the `register` storage class are greatest for variables that the function uses frequently, such as the counter variable for a loop.

The `register` keyword can be used only with simple numeric variables, not arrays or structures. Also, it can't be used with either static or external storage classes. You can't define a pointer to a register variable.

12

Do	Don't
DO initialize local variables, or you won't know what values they will contain. **DO** initialize global variables even though they're initialized to <u>0</u> by default. If you always initialize your variables, you'll avoid problems such as forgetting to initialize local variables.	**DON'T** declare all your variables as global if they are only needed in a few functions. It is often better to them as function parameters. **DON'T** use register variables for nonnumeric values, structures, or arrays.

Local Variables and the `main()` Function

Everything said so far about local variables applies to `main()` as well as to all other functions. Strictly speaking, `main()` is a function like any other. The `main()` function is called when the program is started from your operating system, and control is returned to the operating system from `main()` when the program terminates.

This means that local variables defined in `main()` are created when the program begins, and their lifetime is over when the program ends. The notion of a static local variable retaining its value between calls to `main()` really does not make sense: A variable can't remain in existence between program executions. Within `main()`, therefore, there is no difference between automatic and static local variables. You can define a local variable in `main()` as being static, but it has no real effect.

Do	Don't
DO remember that `main()` is a function similar in most respects to any other function.	**DON'T** declare static variables in `main()` because doing so gains nothing.

Which Storage Class Should You Use?

When you're deciding which storage class to use for particular variables in your programs, it might be helpful to refer to Table 12.1, which summarizes the five storage classes available in C.

TABLE 12.1 C's five variable storage classes

Storage Class	Keyword	Lifetime	Where It's Defined	Scope
Automatic	None[1]	Temporary	In a function	Local
Static	static	Temporary	In a function	Local
Register	register	Temporary	In a function	Local
External	None[2]	Permanent	Outside a function	Global (all files)
External	static	Permanent	Outside a function	Global (one file)

[1]*The auto keyword is optional.*

[2]*The extern keyword is used in functions to declare a static external variable that is defined elsewhere.*

When you're deciding on a storage class, you should use an automatic storage class whenever possible and use other classes only when needed. Here are some guidelines to follow:

- Give each variable an automatic local storage class to begin with.
- If the variable will be manipulated frequently, such as a loop counter, add the register keyword to its definition.
- In functions other than main(), make a variable static if its value must be retained between calls to the function.
- If a variable is used by most or all of the program's functions, define it with the external storage class.

Local Variables and Blocks

So far, today's lesson has discussed only variables that are local to a function. This is the primary way local variables are used, but you can define variables that are local to any program block (any section enclosed in braces). When declaring variables within the block, you must remember that the declarations must be first. Listing 12.5 shows an example.

LISTING 12.5 block.c. Defining local variables within a program block

```
1:  /* Demonstrates local variables within blocks. */
2:
3:  #include <stdio.h>
4:
```

12

LISTING 12.5. continued

```
 5:  int main( void )
 6:  {
 7:      /* Define a variable local to main(). */
 8:
 9:      int count = 0;
10:
11:      printf("\nOutside the block, count = %d", count);
12:
13:      /* Start a block. */
14:      {
15:        /* Define a variable local to the block. */
16:
17:        int count = 999;
18:        printf("\nWithin the block, count = %d", count);
19:      }
20:
21:      printf("\nOutside the block again, count = %d\n", count);
22:      return 0;
23:  }
```

OUTPUT
```
Outside the block, count = 0
Within the block, count = 999
Outside the block again, count = 0
```

ANALYSIS   From this program, you can see that the count defined within the block is independent of the count defined outside the block. Line 9 defines count as a type int variable equal to 0. Because it is declared at the beginning of main(), it can be used throughout the entire main() function. The code in line 11 shows that the variable count has been initialized to 0 by printing its value. A block is declared in lines 14 through 19, and within the block, another count variable is defined as a type int variable. This count variable is initialized to 999 in line 17. Line 18 prints the block's count variable value of 999. Because the block ends on line 19, the print statement in line 21 uses the original count initially declared in line 9 of main().

The use of this type of local variable isn't common in C programming, and you may never find a need for it. Its most common use is probably when a programmer tries to isolate a problem within a program. You can temporarily isolate sections of code in braces and establish local variables to assist in tracking down the problem. Another advantage is that the variable declaration/initialization can be placed closer to the point where it's used, which can help in understanding the program.

Do	Don't
DO use variables at the beginning of a block (temporarily) to help track down problems.	DON'T try to put variable definitions anywhere other than at the beginning of a function or at the beginning of a block.
	DON'T define variables at the beginning of a block unless it makes the program clearer.

Summary

Today's lesson covered the concept of scope and lifetime as related to C's variable storage classes. Every C variable, whether a simple variable, an array, a structure, or whatever, has a specific storage class that determines two things: its scope, or where in the program it's visible; and its lifetime, or how long the variable persists in memory.

Proper use of storage classes is an important aspect of structured programming. By keeping most variables local to the function that uses them, you enhance functions' independence from each other. A variable should be given automatic storage class unless there is a specific reason to make it external or static.

Q&A

Q If global variables can be used anywhere in the program, why not make all variables global?

A As your programs get bigger they will contain more and more variables. Global variables take up memory as long as the program is running, whereas automatic local variables take up memory only while the function they are defined in is executing. Hence, use of local variables reduces memory usage. More important, however, is that the use of local variables greatly decreases the chance of unwanted interactions between different parts of the program, hence lessening program bugs and following the principles of structured programming.

Q Day 11, "Implementing Structures, Unions, and TypeDefs" stated that scope affects a structure instance but not a structure tag or body. Why doesn't scope affect the structure tag or body?

A When you declare a structure without instances, you are creating a template, or definition, but not actually declaring any variables. It isn't until you create an instance of the structure that you declare a variable that occupies memory and has

12

scope. For this reason, you can leave a structure body external to any functions with no real effect on memory. Many programmers put commonly used structure bodies with tags into header files and then include these header files when they need to create an instance of the structure. (Header files are covered on Day 21.)

Q How does the computer know the difference between a global variable and a local variable that have the same name?

A The answer to this question is beyond the scope of this book. The important thing to know is that when a local variable is declared with the same name as a global variable, the program temporarily ignores the global variable when the local variable is in scope (inside the function where it is defined). It continues to ignore the global variable until the local variable goes out of scope.

Q Can I declare a local variable and a global variable that have the same name, as long as they have different variable types?

A Yes. When you declare a local variable with the same name as a global variable, it is a completely different variable. This means that you can make it whatever type you want. You should be careful, however, when declaring global and local variables that have the same name. Some programmers prefix all global variable names with "g" (for example, gCount instead of Count). This makes it clear in the source code which variables are global and which are local.

Workshop

The Workshop provides quiz questions to help you solidify your understanding of the material covered, and exercises to provide you with experience in using what you've learned. The answers to the quiz are in Appendix F, "Answers."

Quiz

1. What does scope refer to?
2. What is the most important difference between local storage class and external storage class?
3. How does the location of a variable definition affect its storage class?
4. When defining a local variable, what are the two options for the variable's lifetime?
5. Your program can initialize both automatic and static local variables when they are defined. When do the initializations take place?
6. True or False: A register variable will always be placed in a register.

7. What value does an uninitialized global variable contain?

8. What value does an uninitialized local variable contain?

9. What will line 21 of Listing 12.5 print if lines 9 and 11 are removed? Think about this, and then try the program to see what happens.

10. If a function needs to remember the value of a local type int variable between calls, how should the variable be declared?

11. What does the extern keyword do?

12. What does the static keyword do?

Exercises

1. Write a declaration for a variable to be placed in a CPU register.

2. Change Listing 12.2 to prevent the error. Do this without using any external variables.

3. Write a program that declares a global variable of type int called var. Initialize var to any value. The program should print the value of var in a function (not main()). Do you need to pass var as a parameter to the function?

4. Change the program in exercise 3. Instead of declaring var as a global variable, change it to a local variable in main(). The program should still print var in a separate function. Do you need to pass var as a parameter to the function?

5. Can a program have a global and a local variable with the same name? Write a program that uses a global and a local variable with the same name to prove your answer.

6. **BUG BUSTER:** Can you spot the problem in this code? Hint: It has to do with where a variable is declared.

```
void a_sample_function( void )
{
   int ctr1;

   for ( ctr1 = 0; ctr1 < 25; ctr1++ )
      printf( "*" );

   puts( "\nThis is a sample function" );
   {
      char star = '*';
      puts( "\nIt has a problem\n" );
      for ( int ctr2 = 0; ctr2 < 25; ctr2++ )
      {
```

12

```
          printf( "%c", star);
        }
    }
}
```

7. **BUG BUSTER:** What is wrong with the following code?

```
/*Count the number of even numbers between 0 and 100. */

#include <stdio.h>

int main( void )
{
    int x = 1;
    static int tally = 0;

    for (x = 0; x < 101; x++)
    {
        if (x % 2 == 0)   /*if x is even...*/
        tally++;          /*add 1 to tally.*/

    }

    printf("There are %d even numbers.\n", tally);
    return 0;
}
```

8. **BUG BUSTER:** Is anything wrong with the following program?

```
#include <stdio.h>

void print_function( char star );

int ctr;

int main( void )
{
    char star;

    print_function( star );
    return 0;
}

void print_function( char star )
{
    char dash;

    for ( ctr = 0; ctr < 25; ctr++ )
    {
        printf( "%c%c", star, dash );
    }
}
```

9. What does the following program print? Don't run the program—try to figure it out by reading the code.

```c
#include <stdio.h>
void print_letter2(void);              /* function prototype */

int ctr;
char letter1 = 'X';
char letter2 = '=';

int main( void )
{
   for( ctr = 0; ctr < 10; ctr++ )
   {
      printf( "%c", letter1 );
      print_letter2();
   }
   return 0;
}

void print_letter2(void)
{
   for( ctr = 0; ctr < 2; ctr++ )
      printf( "%c", letter2 );
}
```

10. **BUG BUSTER:** Will the preceding program run? If not, what's the problem? Rewrite it so that it is correct.

12

TYPE & RUN 4

Secret Messages

This is the fourth Type & Run section. Remember, the purpose of the listings in the Type & Run sections is to give you something a little more functional than what you are getting in the daily lessons. This listing contains many elements you have already learned. It also contains a few that you will learn in later lessons. This includes using disk files which you will learn about on Day 16.

The following program enables you to code or decode secret messages. When you run this program, you need to include two command-line parameters:

```
coder filename action
```

The *filename* is either the name of the file you are creating to hold the new secret message or the name of a file that contains a secret message to be decoded. The *action* is either D for decode a secret message or C for encode a secret message. If you run the program without passing any parameters, you are given instructions on how to enter the correct parameters.

Because the program codes and decodes, you can give a copy to your friends or associates. You can then code a secret message and send it to them. Using the same program, they will be able to decode it. People without the program won't know what the message in the file says!

LISTING **T&R 4**   Coder.c

```
 1:    /* Program:   Coder.c
 2:     * Usage:     Coder  [filename] [action]
 3:     *                  where filename = filename for/with coded data
 4:     *                  where action = D for decode anything else for
 5:     *                                   coding
 6:     *-------------------------------------------------------------*/
 7:
 8:    #include <stdio.h>
 9:    #include <stdlib.h>
10:    #include <string.h>
11:
12:    int encode_character( int ch, int val );
13:    int decode_character( int ch, int val );
14:
15:    int main( int argc, char *argv[])
16:    {
17:        FILE *fh;              /* file handle  */
18:        int rv = 1;            /* return value */
19:        int ch = 0;            /* variable to hold a character */
20:        unsigned int ctr = 0;  /* counter */
21:        int val = 5;           /* value to code with */
22:        char buffer[257];      /* buffer */
23:
24:        if( argc != 3 )
25:        {
26:            printf("\nError:  Wrong number of parameters..." );
27:            printf("\n\nUsage:\n  %s filename action", argv[0]);
28:            printf("\n\n  Where:");
29:            printf("\n         filename = name of file to code or decode");
30:            printf("\n         action   = D for decode or C for encode\n\n");
31:            rv = -1;           /* set return error value */
32:        }
33:        else
34:        if(( argv[2][0] == 'D') || (argv [2][0] == 'd' ))  /* to decode */
35:        {
36:            fh = fopen(argv[1], "r");  /* open the file   */
37:            if( fh <= 0 )              /* check for error */
38:            {
39:                printf( "\n\nError opening file..." );
40:                rv = -2;               /* set return error value */
41:            }
42:            else
43:            {
44:                ch = getc( fh );    /* get a character */
45:                while( !feof( fh ) ) /* check for end of file */
46:                {
47:                    ch = decode_character( ch, val );
48:                    putchar(ch); /* write the character to screen */
49:                    ch = getc( fh);
50:                }
```

LISTING T&R 4   continued

```
51:
52:                      fclose(fh);
53:                      printf( "\n\nFile decoded to screen.\n" );
54:              }
55:          }
56:      else   /* assume coding to file. */
57:          {
58:
59:              fh = fopen(argv[1], "w");
60:              if( fh <= 0 )
61:                  {
62:                      printf( "\n\nError creating file..." );
63:                      rv = -3;   /* set return value */
64:                  }
65:              else
66:                  {
67:                      printf("\n\nEnter text to be coded. ");
68:                      printf("Enter a blank line to end.\n\n");
69:
70:                      while( gets(buffer) != NULL )
71:                          {
72:                              if( buffer[0] == 0 )
73:                                  break;
74:
75:                              for( ctr = 0; ctr < strlen(buffer); ctr++ )
76:                                  {
77:                                      ch = encode_character( buffer[ctr], val );
78:                                      ch = fputc(ch, fh);     /* write the character to file
*/
79:                                  }
80:                          }
81:                      printf( "\n\nFile encoded to file.\n" );
82:                      fclose(fh);
83:                  }
84:
85:          }
86:      return (rv);
87: }
88:
89: int encode_character( int ch, int val )
90: {
91:     ch = ch + val;
92:     return (ch);
93: }
94:
95: int decode_character( int ch, int val )
96: {
97:     ch = ch - val;
98:     return (ch);
99: }
```

Here is an example of a secret message:

```
Ymnx%nx%f%xjhwjy%rjxxflj&
```

Decoded, this message says:

```
This is a secret message!
```

This program codes and decodes the information by simply adding and subtracting a value from the characters being entered. This is a pretty easy code to crack. You can make it even harder to crack by replacing lines 91 and 97 with the following:

```
ch = ch ^ val;
```

Suffice it to say that the ^ is a binary math operator that modifies the character at the bit level. It will make your secret messages even more secret!

If you want to give the program to a number of different people, you might want to add a third parameter to the command line. This parameter would accept the value for val. The variable val stores the value to be used to encode or decode.

DAY 13

Advanced Program Control

Day 6, "Controlling Your Program's Order of Execution," introduces several C program control statements that govern the execution of other statements in your program. Today's lesson covers more advanced aspects of program control, including the goto statement and some of the more interesting things you can do with loops. Today you will learn:

- How to use the break and continue statements
- What infinite loops are and why you might use them
- What the goto statement is and why you should avoid it
- How to use the switch statement
- How to control exiting the program
- How to execute functions automatically upon program completion
- How to execute system commands in your program

Ending Loops Early

On Day 6 you learned how the `for` loop, the `while` loop, and the `do...while` loop can control program execution. These loop constructions execute a block of C statements never, once, or more than once, depending on conditions in the program. In all three cases, termination or exit of the loop occurs only when a certain condition occurs.

At times, however, you might want to exert more control over loop execution. The `break` and `continue` statements provide this control.

The `break` Statement

The `break` statement can be placed only in the body of a `for` loop, `while` loop, or `do...while` loop. (It's valid in a `switch` statement, too, but that topic isn't covered until later today.) When a `break` statement is encountered, execution immediately exits the loop. The following is an example:

```
for ( count = 0; count < 10; count++ )
{
    if ( count == 5 )
        break;
}
```

Left to itself, the `for` loop would execute 10 times. On the sixth iteration, however, `count` is equal to 5, and the `break` statement executes, causing the `for` loop to terminate. Execution then passes to the statement immediately following the `for` loop's closing brace. When a `break` statement is encountered inside a nested loop, it causes the program to exit the innermost loop only.

Listing 13.1 demonstrates the use of `break`.

LISTING 13.1   breaking.c. Using the `break` statement

```
1:  /* Demonstrates the break statement. */
2:
3:  #include <stdio.h>
4:
5:  char s[] = "This is a test string. It contains two sentences.";
6:
7:  int main( void )
8:  {
9:      int count;
10:
11:     printf("\nOriginal string: %s", s);
12:
13:     for (count = 0; s[count]!='\0'; count++)
14:     {
```

LISTING 13.1 continued

```
15:            if (s[count] == '.')
16:            {
17:                s[count+1] = '\0';
18:                break;
19:            }
20:        }
21:        printf("\nModified string: %s\n", s);
22:
23:        return 0;
24: }
```

OUTPUT Original string: This is a test string. It contains two sentences.
Modified string: This is a test string.

ANALYSIS This program extracts the first sentence from a string. It searches the string, character by character, for the first period (which should mark the end of a sentence). This is done in the for loop in lines 13 through 20. Line 13 starts the for loop, incrementing count to go from character to character in the string, s. Line 15 checks whether the current character in the string is a period. If it is, a null character is inserted immediately after the period (line 17). This, in effect, trims the string. After you trim the string, you no longer need to continue the loop, so a break statement in line 18 quickly terminates the loop and sends control to the first line after the loop (line 21). If no period is found, the string isn't altered.

A loop can contain multiple break statements, but only the first break executed (if any) has any effect. If no break is executed, the loop terminates normally (according to its test condition). Figure 13.1 shows the operation of the break statement.

FIGURE 13.1

The operation of the break *and* continue *statements.*

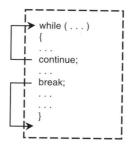

13

The break Statement

```
break;
```

break is used inside a loop or switch statement. It causes the control of a program to immediately exit the current loop (for, while, or do...while) or switch statement. No further iterations of the loop execute; the first statement following the loop or switch statement executes.

Example

```
int x;
printf ( "Counting from 1 to 10\n" );
/* having no condition in the for loop will cause it to loop forever */

for( x = 1; ; x++ )
{
   if( x == 10 )    /* This checks for the value of 10 */
      break;        /* This ends the loop */
   printf( "\n%d", x );
}
```

▲

The continue Statement

Like the break statement, the continue statement can be placed only in the body of a for loop, a while loop, or a do...while loop. When a continue statement executes, the next iteration of the enclosing loop begins immediately. The statements between the continue statement and the end of the loop aren't executed. The operation of continue is also shown in Figure 13.1. Notice how this differs from the operation of a break statement.

Listing 13.2 uses the continue statement. This program accepts a line of input from the keyboard and then displays it with all lowercase vowels removed.

LISTING 13.2   cont.c. Using the continue statement

```
1:    /* Demonstrates the continue statement. */
2:
3:    #include <stdio.h>
4:
5:    int main( void )
6:    {
7:        /* Declare a buffer for input and a counter variable. */
8:
9:        char buffer[81];
10:       int ctr;
11:
12:       /* Input a line of text. */
```

LISTING 13.2 continued

```
13:
14:        puts("Enter a line of text:");
15:        gets(buffer);
16:
17:        /* Go through the string, displaying only those */
18:        /* characters that are not lowercase vowels. */
19:
20:        for (ctr = 0; buffer[ctr] !='\0'; ctr++)
21:        {
22:
23:            /* If the character is a lowercase vowel, loop back */
24:            /* without displaying it. */
25:
26:            if (buffer[ctr] == 'a' || buffer[ctr] == 'e'
27:                || buffer[ctr] == 'i' || buffer[ctr] == 'o'
28:                || buffer[ctr] == 'u')
29:                continue;
30:
31:            /* If not a vowel, display it. */
32:
33:            putchar(buffer[ctr]);
34:        }
35:        return 0;
36: }
```

**INPUT/
OUTPUT**

```
Enter a line of text:
This is a line of text
Ths s  ln f txt
```

ANALYSIS   Although this isn't the most practical program, it does use a `continue` statement
effectively. Lines 9 and 10 declare the program's variables. `buffer[]` holds the
string that the user enters in line 15. The other variable, `ctr`, increments through the elements of the array `buffer[]`, while the `for` loop in lines 20 through 34 searches for vowels. For each letter in the loop, an `if` statement in lines 26 through 28 checks the letter
against lowercase vowels. If there is a match, a `continue` statement executes, sending
control back to line 20, the `for` statement. If the letter isn't a vowel, control passes to the
`if` statement, and line 33 is executed. Line 33 contains a new library function,
`putchar()`, which displays a single character onscreen.

The `continue` Statement

▼ **SYNTAX**

`continue;`

`continue` is used inside a loop. It causes the control of a program to skip the rest of the
current iteration of a loop and start the next iteration.

13

▼ **Example**

```
int x;
printf("Printing only the even numbers from 1 to 10\n");
for( x = 1; x <= 10; x++ )
{
    if( x % 2 != 0 )     /* See if the number is NOT even */
        continue;        /* Get next instance x */
    printf( "\n%d", x );
}
```
▲

The goto Statement

The goto statement is one of C's *unconditional jump,* or *branching,* statements. When program execution reaches a goto statement, execution immediately jumps, or branches, to the location specified by the goto statement. This statement is unconditional because execution always branches when a goto statement is encountered; the branch doesn't depend on any program conditions (unlike if statements, for example).

The target of a goto statement is identified by a text label followed by a colon at the start of a line. A target label can be on a line by itself or at the beginning of a line that contains a C statement. In a program, each target must be unique.

A goto statement and its target must be in the same function, but they can be in different blocks. Take a look at Listing 13.3, a simple program that uses a goto statement.

LISTING 13.3   gotoIt.c. Using the goto statement

```
1:  /* Demonstrates the goto statement */
2:
3:  #include <stdio.h>
4:
5:  int main( void )
6:  {
7:      int n;
8:
9:  start:
10:
11:     puts("Enter a number between 0 and 10: ");
12:     scanf("%d", &n);
13:
14:     if (n < 0 ||n > 10 )
15:         goto start;
16:     else if (n == 0)
17:         goto location0;
18:     else if (n == 1)
19:         goto location1;
```

LISTING 13.3 continued

```
20:      else
21:          goto location2;
22:
23: location0:
24:      puts("You entered 0.\n");
25:      goto end;
26:
27: location1:
28:      puts("You entered 1.\n");
29:      goto end;
30:
31: location2:
32:      puts("You entered something between 2 and 10.\n");
33:
34: end:
35:      return 0;
36: }
```

INPUT/OUTPUT

```
Enter a number between 0 and 10:
1
You entered 1.
```

INPUT/OUTPUT

```
Enter a number between 0 and 10:
9
You entered something between 2 and 10.
```

ANALYSIS This is a simple program that accepts a number between 0 and 10. If the number isn't between 0 and 10, the program uses a goto statement on line 15 to go to start, which is on line 9. Otherwise, the program checks on line 16 to see whether the number equals 0. If it does, a goto statement on line 17 sends control to location0 (line 23), which prints a statement on line 24 and executes another goto. The goto on line 25 sends control to end at the end of the program. The program executes the same logic for the value of 1 and all values between 2 and 10 as a whole.

The target of a goto statement can come either before or after that statement in the code. The only restriction, as mentioned earlier, is that both the goto and the target must be in the same function. They can be in different blocks, however. You can use goto to transfer execution both into and out of loops, such as a for statement, but you should never do this. In fact, we strongly recommend that you never use the goto statement anywhere in your programs. There are two reasons:

13

- You don't need it. No programming task requires the goto statement. You can always write the necessary code using C's other branching statements.

- It's dangerous. The `goto` statement might seem like an ideal solution for certain programming problems, but it's easy to abuse. When program execution branches with a `goto` statement, no record is kept of where the execution came from, so execution can weave through the program willy-nilly. This type of programming is known as *spaghetti code.*

Some careful programmers can write perfectly fine programs that use `goto`. There might be situations in which a judicious use of `goto` is the simplest solution to a programming problem. It's never the only solution, however. If you're going to ignore this warning, at least be careful!

Do	Don't
DO avoid using the `goto` statement if possible (and it's always possible!).	DON'T confuse `break` and `continue`. `break` ends a loop, whereas `continue` starts the next iteration of the loop.

The `goto` Statement

SYNTAX

```
goto location;
```

`location` is a label statement that identifies the program location where execution is to branch. A *label statement* consists of an identifier followed by a colon and, optionally, a C statement:

```
location: a C statement;
```

You can also put a label by itself on a line. When this is done, some programmers like to follow it with the null statement (a semicolon by itself), although this is not required:

▲   `location: ;`

Infinite Loops

What is an infinite loop, and why would you want one in your program? An infinite loop is one that, if left to its own devices, would run forever. It can be a `for` loop, a `while` loop, or a `do...while` loop. For example, if you write

```
while (1)
{
    /* additional code goes here */
}
```

you create an infinite loop. The condition that the `while` tests is the constant 1, which is always true and can't be changed by the program. Because 1 can never be changed on its own, the loop never terminates.

In the preceding section, you saw that the `break` statement can be used to exit a loop. Without the `break` statement, an infinite loop would be useless. With `break`, you can take advantage of infinite loops.

You can also create an infinite `for` loop, as follows:

```
for (;;)
{
    /* additional code goes here */
}
```

or an infinite `do...while` loop, as follows:

```
do
{
    /* additional code goes here */
} while (1);
```

The principle remains the same for all three loop types. In the following examples, the `while` loop is used.

An infinite loop can be used when there are many conditions that need to be tested to determine whether the loop should terminate. It might be difficult to include all the test conditions in parentheses after the `while` statement. It might be easier to test the conditions individually in the body of the loop and then exit by executing a `break` as needed. In general, you should try to avoid infinite loops if there are other alternatives.

An infinite loop can also create a menu system that directs your program's operation. You might remember from Day 5, "Functions: The Basics," that a program's `main()` function often serves as a sort of "traffic cop," directing execution among the various functions that do the real work of the program. This is often accomplished by a menu of some kind: The user is presented with a list of choices and makes an entry by selecting one of them. One of the available choices should be to terminate the program. When a choice is made, one of C's decision statements is used to direct program execution accordingly.

Listing 13.4 demonstrates a menu system.

13

LISTING 13.4   menu.c. Using an infinite loop to implement a menu system

```
1:  /* Demonstrates using an infinite loop to implement */
2:  /* a menu system. */
3:  #include <stdio.h>
4:  #define DELAY  150000        /* Used in delay loop. */
5:
6:  int menu(void);
7:  void delay(void);
8:
9:  int main( void )
10: {
11:    int choice;
12:
13:    while (1)
14:    {
15:
16:     /* Get the user's selection. */
17;
18:     choice = menu();
19:
20:     /* Branch based on the input. */
21:
22;     if (choice == 1)
23:     {
24:         puts("\nExecuting task A.");
25:         delay();
26:     }
27:     else if (choice == 2)
28:         {
29:             puts("\nExecuting task B.");
30:             delay();
31:         }
32;     else if (choice == 3)
33:         {
34:             puts("\nExecuting task C.");
35:             delay();
36:         }
37:     else if (choice == 4)
38:         {
39:             puts("\nExecuting task D.");
40:             delay();
41:         }
42:     else if (choice == 5)        /* Exit program. */
43:         {
44:             puts("\nExiting program now...\n");
45:             delay();
46:             break;
47:         }
48:         else
```

LISTING 13.4 continued

```
49:              {
50:                  puts("\nInvalid choice, try again.");
51:                  delay();
52:              }
53:      }
54:      return 0;
55: }
56:
57: /* Displays a menu and inputs user's selection. */
58: int menu(void)
59: {
60:      int reply;
61:
62:      puts("\nEnter 1 for task A.");
63:      puts("Enter 2 for task B.");
64:      puts("Enter 3 for task C.");
65:      puts("Enter 4 for task D.");
66:      puts("Enter 5 to exit program.");
67:
68:      scanf("%d", &reply);
69:
70:      return reply;
71: }
72:
73: void delay( void )
74: {
75:      long x;
76:      for ( x = 0; x < DELAY; x++ )
77:          ;
78: }
```

**INPUT/
OUTPUT**

```
Enter 1 for task A.
Enter 2 for task B.
Enter 3 for task C.
Enter 4 for task D.
Enter 5 to exit program.
1

Executing task A.

Enter 1 for task A.
Enter 2 for task B.
Enter 3 for task C.
Enter 4 for task D.
Enter 5 to exit program.
6
```

13

```
Invalid choice, try again.

Enter 1 for task A.
Enter 2 for task B.
Enter 3 for task C.
Enter 4 for task D.
Enter 5 to exit program.
5

Exiting program now...
```

ANALYSIS

Caution

> Listing 13.4 does not contain any error checking. If you enter a value other than a number, the results could be unpredictable.

In Listing 13.4, a function named `menu()` is called on line 18 and defined on lines 58 through 71. `menu()` displays a menu onscreen, accepts user input, and returns the input to the main program. In `main()`, a series of nested `if` statements tests the returned value and directs execution accordingly. The only thing this program does is display messages on the screen. In a real program, the code would call various functions to perform the selected task.

This program also uses a second function, named `delay()`. `delay()` is defined on lines 73 through 78 and really doesn't do much. Simply stated, the `for` statement on line 76 loops, doing nothing (line 77). The statement loops `DELAY` times. This is an effective method of pausing the program momentarily. If the delay is too short or too long, the defined value of `DELAY` can be adjusted accordingly.

Many compilers include a function similar to `delay()`, Borland's and Symantec's compilers have a function called `sleep()`. This function pauses program execution for the number of seconds that is passed as its argument. To use `sleep()`, a program must include the header file time.h if you're using the Symantec compiler. You must use dos.h if you're using a Borland compiler. If you're using either of these compilers or a compiler that supports `sleep()`, you could use it instead of `delay()`.

Caution

> There are better ways to pause the computer than what is shown in Listing 13.4. If you choose to use a function such as `sleep()`, as just mentioned, be cautious. The `sleep()` function is not ANSI-compatible. This means that it might not work with other compilers or on all platforms.

The `switch` Statement

C's most flexible program control statement is the `switch` statement, which lets your program execute different statements based on an expression that can have more than two values. Earlier control statements, such as `if`, were limited to evaluating an expression that could have only two values: true or false. To control program flow based on more than two values, you had to use multiple nested `if` statements, as shown in Listing 13.4. The `switch` statement makes such nesting unnecessary.

The general form of the `switch` statement is as follows:

```
switch (expression)
{
    case    template_1: statement(s);
    case    template_2: statement(s);
    ...
    case    template_n: statement(s);
    default: statement(s);
}
```

In this statement, *expression* is any expression that evaluates to an integer value: type `long`, `int`, or `char`. The `switch` statement evaluates *expression* and compares the value against the templates following each `case` label. Then one of the following happens:

- If a match is found between *expression* and one of the templates, execution is transferred to the statement that follows the `case` label.

- If no match is found, execution is transferred to the statement following the optional `default` label.

- If no match is found and no `default` label exists, execution passes to the first statement following the `switch` statement's closing brace.

The `switch` statement is demonstrated in Listing 13.5, which displays a message based on the user's input.

LISTING 13.5 switch.c. Using the `switch` statement

```
 1:  /* Demonstrates the switch statement. */
 2:
 3:  #include <stdio.h>
 4:
 5:  int main( void )
 6:  {
 7:      int reply;
 8:
 9:      puts("Enter a number between 1 and 5:");
10:      scanf("%d", &reply);
```

13

LISTING 13.5   continued

```
11:
12:     switch (reply)
13:     {
14:         case 1:
15:             puts("You entered 1.");
16:         case 2:
17:             puts("You entered 2.");
18:         case 3:
19:             puts("You entered 3.");
20:         case 4:
21:             puts("You entered 4.");
22:         case 5:
23:             puts("You entered 5.");
24:         default:
25:             puts("Out of range, try again.");
26:     }
27:
28:     return 0;
29: }
```

**INPUT/
OUTPUT**

```
Enter a number between 1 and 5:
2
You entered 2.
You entered 3.
You entered 4.
You entered 5.
Out of range, try again.
```

ANALYSIS   Well, that's certainly not right, is it? It looks as though the switch statement finds the first matching template and then executes everything that follows (not just the statements associated with the template). That's exactly what does happen; however, that's how switch is supposed to work. In effect, it performs a goto to the matching template. To ensure that only the statements associated with the matching template are executed, include a break statement where needed. Listing 13.6 shows the program rewritten with break statements. Now it functions properly.

LISTING 13.6   switch2.c. Correct use of switch, including break statements as needed

```
1:  /* Demonstrates the switch statement correctly. */
2:
3:  #include <stdio.h>
4:
5:  int main( void )
6:  {
7:      int reply;
```

LISTING **13.6** continued

```
8:
9:     puts("\nEnter a number between 1 and 5:");
10:    scanf("%d", &reply);
11:
12:    switch (reply)
13:    {
14:      case 0:
15:          break;
16:      case 1:
17:          {
18:             puts("You entered 1.\n");
19:             break;
20:          }
21:      case 2:
22:          {
23:             puts("You entered 2.\n");
24:             break;
25:          }
26:      case 3:
27:          {
28:             puts("You entered 3.\n");
29:             break;
30:          }
31:      case 4:
32:          {
33:             puts("You entered 4.\n");
34:             break;
35:          }
36:      case 5:
37:          {
38:             puts("You entered 5.\n");
39:             break;
40:          }
41:      default:
42:          {
43:             puts("Out of range, try again.\n");
44:          }
45:    }               /* End of switch */
46:    return 0;
47: }
```

**INPUT/
OUTPUT**

```
Enter a number between 1 and 5:
1
You entered 1.
```

INPUT/
OUTPUT
Enter a number between 1 and 5:
6
Out of range, try again.

When you compile and run this version; you'll see that it runs correctly.

One common use of the switch statement is to implement the sort of menu shown in Listing 13.4. Listing 13.7 uses switch instead of if to implement a menu. Using switch is much better than using nested if statements, which were used in the earlier version of the menu program, shown in Listing 13.4.

LISTING 13.7 menu2.c. Using the switch statement to execute a menu system

```
1:  /* Demonstrates using an infinite loop and the switch */
2:  /* statement to implement a menu system. */
3:  #include <stdio.h>
4:  #include <stdlib.h>
5:
6:  #define DELAY 150000
7:
8:  int menu(void);
9:  void delay(void);
10:
11: int main( void )
12: {
13:    int command = 0;
14:    command = menu();
15:
16:    while (command != 5 )
17:    {
18:         /* Get user's selection and branch based on the input. */
19:
20:         switch(command)
21:         {
22:           case 1:
23:              {
24:                 puts("\nExecuting task A.");
25:                 delay();
26:                 break;
27:              }
28:           case 2:
29:              {
30:                 puts("\nExecuting task B.");
31:                 delay();
32:                 break;
33:              }
34:           case 3:
35:              {
36:                 puts("\nExecuting task C.");
```

LISTING 13.7   continued

```
37:                     delay();
38:                     break;
39:                 }
40:             case 4:
41:                 {
42:                     puts("\nExecuting task D.");
43:                     delay();
44:                     break;
45:                 }
46:             case 5:      /* Exit program. */
47:                 {
48:                     puts("\nExiting program now...\n");
49:                 }
50:             default:
51:                 {
52:                     puts("\nInvalid choice, try again.");
53:                 }
54:         }  /* End of switch */
55:         command = menu();
56:     }         /* End of while  */
57:     return 0;
58: }
59:
60: /* Displays a menu and inputs user's selection. */
61: int menu(void)
62: {
63:     int reply;
64:
65:     puts("\nEnter 1 for task A.");
66:     puts("Enter 2 for task B.");
67:     puts("Enter 3 for task C.");
68:     puts("Enter 4 for task D.");
69:     puts("Enter 5 to exit program.");
70:
71:     scanf("%d", &reply);
72:
73:     return reply;
74: }
75:
76: void delay( void )
77: {
78:     long x;
79:     for( x = 0; x < DELAY; x++ )
80:         ;
81: }
```

13

```
Enter 1 for task A.
Enter 2 for task B.
Enter 3 for task C.
Enter 4 for task D.
Enter 5 to exit program.
1

Executing task A.

Enter 1 for task A.
Enter 2 for task B.
Enter 3 for task C.
Enter 4 for task D.
Enter 5 to exit program.
6

Invalid choice, try again.

Enter 1 for task A.
Enter 2 for task B.
Enter 3 for task C.
Enter 4 for task D.
Enter 5 to exit program.
5

Exiting program now...
```

ANALYSIS   This program has one has a switch statement that has cases based on the choices of a menu that is displayed. Line 14 calls the menu the first time and gets a command value from it. If the value is anything other than 5, a while loop is executed. This while loop is primarily a switch statement that executes different code based on the command selected from the menu. Once the appropriate case is executed, the menu is redisplayed and a new command is obtained in line 55.

Having execution "fall through" parts of a switch construction can be useful at times. Say, for example, that you want the same block of statements executed if one of several values is encountered. Simply omit the break statements and list all the case templates before the statements. If the test expression matches any of the case conditions, execution will "fall through" the following case statements until it reaches the block of code you want executed. This is illustrated in Listing 13.8.

LISTING 13.8   fallthru.c. Another way to use the switch statement

```
1:  /* Another use of the switch statement. */
2:
3:  #include <stdio.h>
4:  #include <stdlib.h>
```

LISTING 13.8   continued

```
 5:
 6:  int main( void )
 7:  {
 8:      int reply;
 9:
10:      while (1)
11:      {
12:          puts("\nEnter a value between 1 and 10, 0 to exit: ");
13:          scanf("%d", &reply);
14:
15:          switch (reply)
16:          {
17:              case 0:
18:                  exit(0);
19:              case 1:
20:              case 2:
21:              case 3:
22:              case 4:
23:              case 5:
24:                  {
25:                      puts("You entered 5 or below.\n");
26:                      break;
27:                  }
28:              case 6:
29:              case 7:
30:              case 8:
31:              case 9:
32:              case 10:
33:                  {
34:                      puts("You entered 6 or higher.\n");
35:                      break;
36:                  }
37:              default:
38:                  puts("Between 1 and 10, please!\n");
39:          } /* end of switch */
40:      }     /*end of while */
41:      return 0;
43:  }
```

13

INPUT/
OUTPUT

```
Enter a value between 1 and 10, 0 to exit:
11
Between 1 and 10, please!

Enter a value between 1 and 10, 0 to exit:
1
You entered 5 or less.
```

```
Enter a value between 1 and 10, 0 to exit:
6
You entered 6 or more.

Enter a value between 1 and 10, 0 to exit:
0
```

ANALYSIS This program accepts a value from the keyboard and then states whether the value is 5 or less, 6 or more, or not between 1 and 10. If the value is 0, line 18 executes a call to the exit() function, thus ending the program.

You can't use break in line 18, as you did in Listing 13.4 earlier. Executing a break would merely break out of the switch statement; it wouldn't break out of the infinite while loop. The exit() function terminates the program. You'll learn more about the exit() function in the next section.

The switch Statement

▼ SYNTAX

```
switch  (expression)
{
    case   template_1: statement(s);
    case   template_2: statement(s);
    ...
    case   template_n: statement(s);
    default: statement(s);
}
```

The switch statement allows for multiple branches from a single expression. It's more efficient and easier to follow than a multileveled if statement. A switch statement evaluates an expression and then branches to the case statement that contains the template matching the expression's result. If no value matches the expression's result, control goes to the default statement. If there is no default statement, control goes to the end of the switch statement.

Program flow continues from the case statement down unless a break statement is encountered. If that occurs, control goes to the end of the switch statement.

Example 1

```
switch( letter )
{
   case 'A':
   case 'a':
       printf( "You entered A" );
       break;
   case 'B':
   case 'b':
       printf( "You entered B");
       break;
```

▼
```
        ...
        ...
    default:
        printf( "I don't have a case for %c", letter );
}
```

Example 2

```
switch( number )
{
    case 0:    puts( "Your number is 0 or less.");
    case 1:    puts( "Your number is 1 or less.");
    case 2:    puts( "Your number is 2 or less.");
    case 3:    puts( "Your number is 3 or less.");
    ...
    ...
    case 99:   puts( "Your number is 99 or less.");
               break;
    default:   puts( "Your number is greater than 99.");
}
```

Because there are no break statements for the first case statements, this example finds the case that matches the number and prints every case from that point down to the break in case 99. If the number was 3, you would be told that your number is equal to 3 or less, 4 or less, 5 or less, up to 99 or less. The program continues printing until it reaches the break statement in case 99.

▲

Do	Don't
DO use a default case in a switch statement, even if you think you've covered all possible cases.	**DON'T** forget to use break statements if your switch statements need them.
DO use a switch statement instead of an if statement if more than two conditions are being evaluated for the same variable.	
DO line up your case statements so that they're easy to read.	

13

Exiting the Program

A C program normally terminates when execution reaches the closing brace of the main() function. However, you can terminate a program at any time by calling the library function exit(). You can also specify one or more functions to be automatically executed at termination.

The exit() Function

The exit() function terminates program execution and returns control to the operating system. This function takes a single type int argument that is passed back to the operating system to indicate the program's success or failure. The syntax of the exit() function is

```
exit(status);
```

If status has a value of 0, it indicates that the program terminated normally. A value of 1 indicates that the program terminated with some sort of error. The return value is usually ignored. In a DOS system, you can test the return value with a DOS batch file and the if errorlevel statement. This isn't a book about DOS, so you need to refer to your DOS documentation if you want to use a program's return value. If you're using an operating system other than DOS, you should check its documentation to determine how to use a return value from a program.

To use the exit() function, a program must include the header file stdlib.h. This header file also defines two symbolic constants for use as arguments to the exit() function:

```
#define EXIT_SUCCESS    0
#define EXIT_FAILURE    1
```

Thus, to exit with a return value of 0, call exit(EXIT_SUCCESS); for a return value of 1, call exit(EXIT_FAILURE).

Do	Don't
DO use the exit() command to get out of the program if there's a problem. **DO** pass meaningful values to the exit() function.	

Executing Operating System Commands in a Program

The C standard library includes a function, system(), that lets you execute operating system commands in a running C program. This can be useful, allowing you to read a disk's directory listing or format a disk without exiting the program. To use the system() function, a program must include the header file stdlib.h. The format of system() is

```
system(command);
```

The argument *command* can be either a string constant or a pointer to a string. For example, to obtain a directory listing in DOS, you could write either

```
system("dir");
```

or

```
char *command = "dir";
system(command);
```

After the operating system command is executed, execution returns to the program at the location immediately following the call to system(). If the command you pass to sys-tem() isn't a valid operating system command, you get a Bad command or file name error message before returning to the program. The use of system() is illustrated in Listing 13.9.

LISTING 13.9   system.c. Using the system() function to execute system commands

```
 1:  /* Demonstrates the system() function. */
 2:  #include <stdio.h>
 3:  #include <stdlib.h>
 4:
 5:  int main( void )
 6:  {
 7:      /* Declare a buffer to hold input. */
 8:
 9:      char input[40];
10:
11:      while (1)
12:      {
13:          /* Get the user's command. */
14:
15:          puts("\nInput the desired system command, blank to exit");
16:          gets(input);
17:
18:          /* Exit if a blank line was entered. */
19:
20:          if (input[0] == '\0')
21:              exit(0);
22:
23:          /* Execute the command. */
24:
25:          system(input);
26:      }
27:      return 0;
28: }
```

13

Input the desired system command, blank to exit
dir *.bak

```
Volume in drive E is BRAD_VOL_B
Directory of E:\BOOK\LISTINGS
LIST1414 BAK      1416 05-22-99    5:18p
1 file(s)         1416 bytes
240068096 bytes free
```

Input the desired DOS command, blank to exit

> **Note**
>
> `dir *.bak` is a DOS command that tells the system to list all the files in the
> current directory that have a .BAK extension. This command also works
> under Microsoft Windows. For UNIX machines, you could enter `ls *.bak`
> and get similar results. If you're using System 7 or some other operating
> system, you'll need to enter the appropriate operating system command.

ANALYSIS Listing 13.9 illustrates the use of system(). Using a while loop in lines 11
through 26, this program enables operating system commands. Lines 15 and 16
prompt the user to enter the operating system command. If the user presses Enter without
entering a command, lines 20 and 21 call exit() to end the program. Line 25 calls sys-
tem() with the command entered by the user. If you run this program on your system,
you'll get different output, of course.

The commands you pass to system() aren't limited to simple operating commands, such
as listing directories or formatting disks. You can also pass the name of any executable
file or batch file—and that program is executed normally. For example, if you passed the
argument LIST1308, you would execute the program called LIST1308. When you exit the
program, execution passes back to where the system() call was made.

The only restrictions on using system() have to do with memory. When system() is
executed, the original program remains loaded in your computer's RAM, and a new copy
of the operating system command processor and any program you run are loaded as well.
This works only if the computer has sufficient memory. If not, you get an error message.

> **Note**
>
> If you are using the BloodShed Dev-C++ compiler that was included on the
> CD-ROM with this book, you will find that it uses the system() function
> when you create a new source file. If you select "New Source file" from the
> File menu, a new C source file is created with the following code:

```
#include <iostream.h>
#include <stdlib.h>

int main()
{

    system("PAUSE");
    return 0;
}
```

The system("PAUSE") causes the system to pause until a key is pressed. This allows you to view the output from the listing; otherwise, the window that displays the output is closed before you have a chance to see it.

Summary

Today's lesson covers a variety of topics related to program control. You learned about the goto statement and why you should avoid using it in your programs. You saw that the break and continue statements give additional control over the execution of loops and that these statements can be used in conjunction with infinite loops to perform useful programming tasks. You also learned how to use the exit() function to control program termination. Finally, you saw how to use the system() function to execute system commands from within your program.

Q&A

Q Is it better to use a switch statement or a nested loop?

A If you're checking a variable that can take on more than two values, the switch statement is almost always better. The resulting code is easier to read, too. If you're checking a true/false condition, go with an if statement.

Q Why should I avoid a goto statement?

A When you first see a goto statement, it's easy to believe that it could be useful. However, goto can cause you more problems than it fixes. A goto statement is an unstructured command that takes you to another point in a program. Many *debuggers* (software that helps you trace program problems) can't interrogate a goto properly. goto statements also lead to *spaghetti* code—code that goes all over the place.

13

Q Why don't all compilers have the same functions?

A In today's lesson, you saw that certain C functions aren't available with all compilers or all computer systems. For example, sleep() is available with the Borland C compilers but not with the Microsoft compilers.

Although there are standards that all ANSI compilers follow, these standards don't prohibit compiler manufacturers from adding additional functionality. They do this by creating and including new functions. Each compiler manufacturer usually adds a number of functions that it believes will be helpful to its users.

Q Isn't C supposed to be a standardized language?

A C is, in fact, highly standardized. The American National Standards Institute (ANSI) has developed the ANSI C Standard, which specifies almost all details of the C language, including the functions that are provided. Some compiler vendors have added more functions—ones that aren't part of the ANSI standard—to their C compilers in an effort to one-up the competition. In addition, you sometimes come across a compiler that doesn't claim to meet the ANSI standard. If you limit yourself to ANSI-standard compilers, however, you'll find that 99 percent of program syntax and functions are common among them.

Q Is it good to use the system() function to execute system functions?

A The system() function might appear to be an easy way to do such things as list the files in a directory, but you should be cautious. Most operating system commands are specific to a particular operating system. If you use a system() call, your code probably won't be portable. If you want to run another program (not an operating system command), you shouldn't have portability problems.

Workshop

The Workshop provides quiz questions to help you solidify your understanding of the material covered and exercises to provide you with experience in using what you've learned.

Quiz

1. When is it advisable to use the goto statement in your programs?
2. What's the difference between the break statement and the continue statement?
3. What is an infinite loop, and how do you create one?
4. What two events cause program execution to terminate?
5. To what variable types can a switch evaluate?

6. What does the `default` statement do?

7. What does the `exit()` function do?

8. What does the `system()` function do?

Exercises

1. Write a statement that causes control of the program to go to the next iteration in a loop.

2. Write the statement(s) that send control of a program to the end of a loop.

3. Write a line of code that displays a listing of all the files in the current directory (for a DOS system).

4. **BUG BUSTER:** Is anything wrong with the following code?

```
switch( answer )
{
    case 'Y': printf("You answered yes");
              break;
    case 'N': printf( "You answered no");
}
```

5. **BUG BUSTER:** Is anything wrong with the following code?

```
switch( choice )
{
    default:
        printf("You did not choose 1 or 2");
    case 1:
        printf("You answered 1");
        break;
    case 2:
        printf( "You answered 2");
        break;
}
```

6. Rewrite exercise 5 using `if` statements.

7. Write an infinite `do...while` loop.

Because of the multitude of possible answers for the following exercises, answers are not provided. These are exercises for you to try "on your own."

8. **ON YOUR OWN:** Write a program that works like a calculator. The program should allow for addition, subtraction, multiplication, and division.

9. **ON YOUR OWN:** Write a program that provides a menu with five options. The fifth option should quit the program. Each of the other options should execute a system command using the `system()` function.

13

DAY 14

Working with the Screen, Printer, and Keyboard

Almost every program must perform input and output. How well a program handles input and output is often the best judge of the program's usefulness. You've already learned how to perform some basic input and output. Today you will learn:

- How C uses streams for input and output
- Various ways of accepting input from the keyboard
- Methods of displaying text and numeric data on-screen
- How to send output to the printer
- How to redirect program input and output

Streams and C

Before you get to the details of program input/output, you need to learn about streams. All C input/output is done with streams, no matter where input is coming from or where output is going to. As you will see later, this standard way of handling all input and output has definite advantages for the programmer. Of course, this makes it essential that you understand what streams are and how they work. First, however, you need to know exactly what the terms *input* and *output* mean.

What Exactly Is Program Input/Output?

As you learned earlier in this book, a C program keeps data in random access memory (RAM) while executing. This data is in the form of variables, structures, and arrays that have been declared by the program. Where did this data come from, and what can the program do with it?

- Data can come from some location external to the program. Data moved from an external location into RAM, where the program can access it, is called *input*. The keyboard and disk files are the most common sources of program input.

- Data can also be sent to a location external to the program; this is called *output*. The most common destinations for output are the screen, a printer, and disk files.

Input sources and output destinations are collectively referred to as *devices*. The keyboard is a device, the screen is a device, and so on. Some devices (the keyboard) are for input only, others (the screen) are for output only, and still others (disk files) are for both input and output. This is illustrated in Figure 14.1.

Whatever the device, and whether it's performing input or output, C carries out all input and output operations by means of streams.

FIGURE 14.1

Input and output can take place between your program and a variety of external devices.

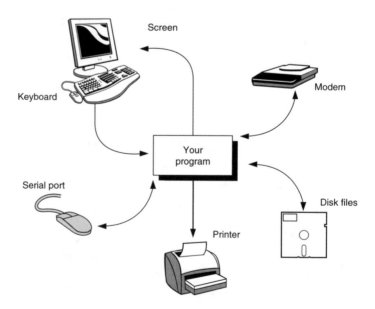

What Is a Stream?

NEW TERM A *stream* is a sequence of characters. More exactly, it is a sequence of bytes of data. A sequence of bytes flowing into a program is an input stream; a sequence of bytes flowing out of a program is an output stream. By focusing on streams, you don't have to worry as much about where they're going or where they originated. The major advantage of streams, therefore, is that input/output programming is *device independent*. Programmers don't need to write special input/output functions for each device (keyboard, disk, and so on). The program sees input/output as a continuous stream of bytes no matter where the input is coming from or going to.

NEW TERM Every C stream is connected to a file. In this context, the term *file* doesn't refer to a disk file. Rather, it is an intermediate step between the stream that your program deals with and the actual physical device being used for input or output. For the most part, the beginning C programmer doesn't need to be concerned with these files, because the details of interactions between streams, files, and devices are taken care of automatically by the C library functions and the operating system.

Text Versus Binary Streams

C streams fall into two modes: text and binary. A text stream consists only of characters, such as text data being sent to the screen. Text streams are organized into lines, which can be up to 255 characters long and are terminated by an end-of-line, or newline, character. Certain characters in a text stream are recognized as having special meaning, such as the newline character. Today's lesson deals with text streams.

NEW TERM A *binary* stream can handle any sort of data, including, but not limited to, text data. Bytes of data in a binary stream aren't translated or interpreted in any special way; they are read and written exactly as-is. Binary streams are used primarily with disk files, which are covered in Day 16, "Using Disk Files."

Predefined Streams

The ANSI standard for C has three predefined streams, also referred to as the *standard input/output files*. If you're programming for an IBM-compatible PC running Windows or DOS, then two additional standard streams may available to you. These streams are automatically opened when a C program starts executing and are closed when the program terminates. The programmer doesn't need to take any special action to make these streams available. Table 14.1 lists the standard streams and the devices they normally are connected with. All five of the standard streams are text-mode streams.

14

TABLE 14.1   The five standard streams

Name	Streams	Device
stdin	Standard input	Keyboard
stdout	Standard output	Screen
stderr	Standard error	Screen
stdprn*	Standard printer	Printer (LPT1:)
stdaux*	Standard auxiliary	Serial port (COM1:)

Supported only under Windows and DOS—Not part of ANSI standard.

You have actually been using two of these streams already. Whenever you have used the printf() or puts() functions to display text on-screen, you have used the stdout stream. Likewise, when you use gets() or scanf() to read keyboard input, you use the stdin stream. The standard streams are opened automatically, but other streams, such as those used to manipulate information stored on disk, must be opened explicitly. You'll learn how to do this on Day 16. The remainder of this chapter deals with the standard streams.

Using C's Stream Functions

The C standard library has a variety of functions that deal with stream input and output. Most of these functions come in two varieties: one that always uses one of the standard streams, and one that requires the programmer to specify the stream. These functions are listed in Table 14.2. This table doesn't list all of C's input/output functions, nor are all of the functions in the table covered in today's lesson.

TABLE 14.2   The standard library's stream input/output functions

Uses One of the Standard Streams	Requires a Stream Name	Description
printf()	fprintf()	Formatted output
vprintf()	vfprintf()	Formatted output with a variable argument list
puts()	fputs()	String output
putchar()	putc(), fputc()	Character output
scanf()	fscanf()	Formatted input
vscanf()	vfscanf()	Formatted input with a variable argument list
gets()	fgets()	String input
getchar()	getc(), fgetc()	Character input
perror()		String output to stderr only

All these functions require that you include stdio.h. The function perror() may also require stdlib.h. The functions vprintf() and vfprintf() also require stdargs.h. On UNIX systems, vprintf() and vfprintf() may also require varargs.h. Your compiler's Library Reference will state whether any additional or alternative header files are needed.

An Example

The short program in Listing 14.1 demonstrates the equivalence of streams.

LISTING 14.1 stream.c. The equivalence of streams

```
1:  /* Demonstrates the equivalence of stream input and output. */
2:  #include <stdio.h>
3:
4:  int main( void )
5:  {
6:      char buffer[256];
7:
8:      /* Input a line, then immediately output it. */
9:
10:     puts(gets(buffer));
11:
12:     return 0;
13: }
```

On line 10, the gets() function is used to input a line of text from the keyboard (stdin). Because gets() returns a pointer to the string, it can be used as the argument to puts(), which displays the string on-screen (stdout). When run, this program inputs a line of text from the user and then immediately displays the string on-screen.

Do	Don't
DO take advantage of the standard input/output streams that C provides.	DON'T rename or change the standard streams unnecessarily. DON'T try to use an input stream such as stdin for an output function such as fprintf().

14

For a beginner learning to program C, using gets() is fine. For a real-world program, however, you should use fgets() (explained later in today's lesson) as gets() poses some risks to program security.

Accepting Keyboard Input

Most C programs require some form of input from the keyboard (that is, from the `stdin` stream). Input functions are divided into a hierarchy of three levels: character input, line input, and formatted input.

Character Input

The character input functions read input from a stream one character at a time. When called, each of these functions returns the next character in the stream, or `EOF` if the end of the file has been reached or an error has occurred. `EOF` is a symbolic constant defined in stdio.h as `-1`. Character input functions differ in terms of buffering and echoing.

- Some character input functions are *buffered*. This means that the operating system holds all characters in a temporary storage space until you press Enter, and then the system sends the characters to the `stdin` stream. Others are *unbuffered,* meaning that each character is sent to `stdin` as soon as the key is pressed.

- Some input functions automatically *echo* each character to `stdout` as it is received. Others don't echo; the character is sent to `stdin` and not `stdout`. Because `stdout` is assigned to the screen, that's where input is echoed.

The uses of buffered, unbuffered, echoing, and nonechoing character input are explained in the following sections.

The `getchar()` Function

The function `getchar()` obtains the next character from the stream `stdin`. It provides buffered character input with echo, and its prototype is

```
int getchar(void);
```

The use of `getchar()` is demonstrated in Listing 14.2. Notice that the `putchar()` function, explained in detail later today, simply displays a single character on-screen.

LISTING **14.2**   getchar.c. The `getchar()` function

```
1: /* Demonstrates the getchar() function. */
2:
3: #include <stdio.h>
4:
5: int main( void )
6: {
7:     int ch;
8:
9:     while ((ch = getchar()) != '\n')
```

LISTING 14.2   continued

```
10:            putchar(ch);
11:
12:     return 0;
13: }
```

INPUT/OUTPUT   **This is what's typed in.**
This is what's typed in.

ANALYSIS   On line 9, the getchar() function is called and waits to receive a character from
stdin. Because getchar() is a buffered input function, no characters are
received until you press Enter. However, each key you press is echoed immediately on
the screen.

When you press Enter, all the characters you entered, including the newline, are sent to
stdin by the operating system. The getchar() function returns the characters one at a
time, assigning each in turn to ch.

Each character is compared to the newline character '\n' and, if not equal, displayed on-
screen with putchar(). When a newline is returned by getchar(), the while loop terminates.

The getchar() function can be used to input entire lines of text, as shown in Listing
14.3. However, other input functions are better suited for this task, as you'll learn later
today.

LISTING 14.3   getchar2.c. Using the getchar() function to input an entire line of text

```
 1:  /* Using getchar() to input strings. */
 2:
 3:  #include <stdio.h>
 4:
 5:  #define MAX 80
 6:
 7:  int main( void )
 8:  {
 9:      char ch, buffer[MAX+1];
10:      int x = 0;
11:
12:      while ((ch = getchar()) != '\n' && x < MAX)
13:          buffer[x++] = ch;
14:
15:      buffer[x] = '\0';
16:
17:      printf("%s\n", buffer);
18:
19:      return 0;
20: }
```

14

OUTPUT

```
This is a string
This is a string
```

ANALYSIS This program is similar to Listing 14.2 in the way that it uses getchar(). An extra condition has been added to the loop. This time the while loop accepts characters from getchar() until either a newline character is reached or 80 characters are read. Each character is assigned to an array called buffer. When the characters have been input, line 15 puts a null on the end of the array so that the printf() function on line 17 can print the entered string.

On line 9, why was buffer declared with a size of MAX + 1 instead of just MAX? If you declare buffer with a size of MAX + 1, the string can be 80 characters plus a null terminator. Don't forget to include a place for the null terminator at the end of your strings.

The getch() Function

The getch() function obtains the next character from the stream stdin. It provides unbuffered character input without echo. The getch() function isn't part of the ANSI standard. This means that it might not be available on every system. Additionally, it might require that different header files be included. Generally, the prototype for getch() is in the header file conio.h, as follows:

```
int getch(void);
```

Because it is unbuffered, getch() returns each character as soon as the key is pressed, without waiting for the user to press Enter. Because getch() doesn't echo its input, the characters aren't displayed on-screen. Listing 14.4 illustrates the use of getch().

 Caution
The following listing uses getch(), which is not ANSI-compliant. You should be careful when using non-ANSI functions, because there is no guarantee that all compilers support them. If you get errors from the following listing, it might be because your compiler doesn't support getch().

LISTING 14.4   getch.c. Using the getch() function

```
1:  /* Demonstrates the getch() function. */
2:  /* Non-ANSI code */
3:  #include <stdio.h>
4:  #include <conio.h>
5:
6:  int main( void )
7:  {
8:      int ch;
9:
```

LISTING **14.4**   continued

```
10:      while ((ch = getch()) != '\r')
11:          putchar(ch);
12:
13:      return 0;
14: }
```

OUTPUT   Testing the getch() function

ANALYSIS   When this program runs, getch() returns each character as soon as you press a key—it doesn't wait for you to press Enter. There's no echo, so the only reason that each character is displayed on-screen is the call to putchar(). To get a better understanding of how getch() works, add a semicolon to the end of line 10 and remove line 11 (putchar(ch)). When you rerun the program, you will find that nothing you type is echoed to the screen. The getch() function gets the characters without echoing them to the screen. You know the characters are being gotten because the original listing used putchar() to display them.

Why does this program compare each character to \r instead of to \n? The code \r is the escape sequence for the carriage return character. When you press Enter, the keyboard device sends a carriage return to stdin. The buffered character input functions automatically translate the carriage return to a newline, so the program must test for \n to determine whether Enter has been pressed. The unbuffered character input functions don't translate, so a carriage return is input as \r, and that's what the program must test for.

Listing 14.5 uses getch() to input an entire line of text. Running this program clearly illustrates that getch() doesn't echo its input. With the exception of substituting getch() for getchar(), this program is virtually identical to Listing 14.3.

LISTING **14.5**   getch2.c. Using the getch() function to input an entire line

```
1:  /* Using getch() to input strings. */
2:  /* Non-ANSI code */
3:  #include <stdio.h>
4:  #include <conio.h>
5:
6:  #define MAX 80
7:
8:  int main( void )
9:  {
10:      char ch, buffer[MAX+1];
11:      int x = 0;
12:
13:      while ((ch = getch()) != '\r' && x < MAX)
```

14

LISTING 14.5 continued

```
14:        buffer[x++] = ch;
15:
16:     buffer[x] = '\0';
17:
18:     printf("%s", buffer);
19:
20:     return 0;
21: }
```

Here's a string
Here's a string

>
> **Caution**
>
> Remember that getch() isn't an ANSI-standard command. This means that your compiler (and other compilers) might or might not support it. getch() is supported by Symantec and Borland. Microsoft supports _getch(). If you have problems using this command, you should check your compiler and see whether it supports getch(). If you're concerned about portability, you should avoid non-ANSI functions. The Bloodshed Dev-C++ compiler included with this book has support for getch(); however, its support is different than described above—another issue with non-ANSI functions.

The getche() Function

This is a short section, because getche() is exactly like getch(), except that it echoes each character to stdout. Modify the program in Listing 14.4 to use getche() instead of getch(). When the program runs, each key you press is displayed on-screen twice—once as echoed by getche(), and once as echoed by putchar().

> **Caution**
>
> getche() is not an ANSI-standard command, but many C compilers support it.

The getc() and fgetc() Functions

The getc() and fgetc() character input functions don't automatically work with stdin. Instead, they let the program specify the input stream. They are used primarily to read characters from disk files. See Day 16 for more details.

Do	Don't
DO understand the difference between echoed and nonechoed input.	**DON'T** use non-ANSI standard functions if portability is a concern.
DO understand the difference between buffered and unbuffered input.	**DON'T** expect non-ANSI standard functions to work the same if you switch compilers.

"Ungetting" a Character with `ungetc()`

What does *ungetting* a character mean? An example should help you understand. Suppose that your program is reading characters from an input stream and can detect the end of input only by reading one character too many. For example, you might be inputting digits only, so you know that input has ended when the first nondigit character is encountered. That first nondigit character might be an important part of subsequent data, but it has been removed from the input stream. Is it lost? No, it can be "ungotten" or returned to the input stream, where it is then the first character read by the next input operation on that stream.

To "unget" a character, you use the `ungetc()` library function. Its prototype is

```
int ungetc(int ch, FILE *fp);
```

The argument `ch` is the character to be returned. The argument `*fp` specifies the stream that the character is to be returned to, which can be any input stream. For now, simply specify `stdin` as the second argument: `ungetc(ch, stdin);`. The notation `FILE *fp` is used with streams associated with disk files; you'll learn about this on Day 16.

You can unget only a single character to a stream between reads, and you can't unget `EOF` at any time. The function `ungetc()` returns `ch` on success and `EOF` if the character can't be returned to the stream.

Line Input

The line-input functions read a line from an input stream—they read all characters up to the next newline character. The standard library has two line input functions, `gets()` and `fgets()`.

The `gets()` Function

You were introduced to the `gets()` function on Day 10, "Working with Characters and Strings." This is a straightforward function, reading a line from `stdin` and storing it in a string. The function prototype is

```
char *gets(char *str);
```

14

You probably can interpret this prototype by yourself. `gets()` takes a pointer to type `char` as its argument and returns a pointer to type `char`. The `gets()` function reads characters from `stdin` until a newline (`\n`) or end-of-file is encountered; the newline is replaced with a null character, and the string is stored at the location indicated by `str`.

The return value is a pointer to the string (the same as `str`). If `gets()` encounters an error or reads end-of-file before any characters are input, a null pointer is returned.

Before calling `gets()`, you must allocate sufficient memory space to store the string, using the methods covered on Day 10. This function has no way of knowing whether space pointed to by `ptr` is allocated; the string is input and stored starting at `ptr` in either case. If the space hasn't been allocated, the string might overwrite other data and cause program errors.

Listings 10.5 and 10.6 used `gets()`

The `fgets()` Function

The `fgets()` library function is similar to `gets()` in that it reads a line of text from an input stream. It's more flexible, because it lets the programmer specify the specific input stream to use and the maximum number of characters to be input. The `fgets()` function is often used to input text from disk files, covered on Day 16. To use it for input from `stdin`, you specify `stdin` as the input stream. The prototype of `fgets()` is

```
char *fgets(char *str, int n, FILE *fp);
```

The last parameter, `FILE *fp`, is used to specify the input stream. For now, simply specify the standard input stream, `stdin`, as the stream argument.

The pointer `str` indicates where the input string is stored. The argument `n` specifies the maximum number of characters to be input. The `fgets()` function reads characters from the input stream until a newline or end-of-line is encountered or `n - 1` characters have been read. The newline is included in the string and terminated with a `\0` before it is stored. The return values of `fgets()` are the same as described earlier for `gets()`.

Strictly speaking, `fgets()` doesn't input a single line of text (if you define a line as a sequence of characters ending with a newline). It can read less than a full line if the line contains more than `n - 1` characters. When used with `stdin`, execution doesn't return from `fgets()` until you press Enter, but only the first `n - 1` characters are stored in the string. The newline is included in the string only if it falls within the first `n - 1` characters. Listing 14.6 demonstrates the `fgets()` function.

LISTING 14.6   fgets.c. Using the `fgets()` function for keyboard input

```
1:  /* Demonstrates the fgets() function. */
2:
3:  #include <stdio.h>
4:
5:  #define MAXLEN 10
6:
7:  int main( void )
8:  {
9:      char buffer[MAXLEN];
10:
11:     puts("Enter text a line at a time; enter a blank to exit.");
12:
13:     while (1)
14:     {
15:         fgets(buffer, MAXLEN, stdin);
16:
17:         if (buffer[0] == '\n')
18:             break;
19:
20:         puts(buffer);
21:     }
22:     return 0;
23: }
```

INPUT/
OUTPUT

```
Enter text a line at a time; enter a blank to exit.
Roses are red
Roses are
 red
Violets are blue
Violets a
re blue

Programming in C
Programmi
ng in C

Is for people like you!
Is for pe
ople like
 you!
```

Line 15 contains the `fgets()` function. When running the program, enter lines of length less than and greater than MAXLEN to see what happens. If a line greater than MAXLEN is entered, the first MAXLEN - 1 characters are read by the first call to `fgets()`; the remaining characters remain in the keyboard buffer and are read by the next call to `fgets()` or any other function that reads from `stdin`. The program exits when a blank line is entered (lines 17 and 18).

14

Working with Formatted Input

The input functions covered up to this point have simply taken one or more characters from an input stream and put them somewhere in memory. No interpretation or formatting of the input has been done, and you still have no way to input numeric variables. For example, how would you input the value 12.86 from the keyboard and assign it to a type float variable? Enter the scanf() and fscanf() functions. You were introduced to scanf() on Day 7, "Fundamentals of Reading and Writing Information." This section explains its use in more detail.

These two functions are identical, except that scanf() always uses stdin, whereas the user can specify the input stream in fscanf(). This section covers scanf(); fscanf() generally is used with disk file input and is covered on Day 16.

The scanf() Function's Arguments

The scanf() function takes a variable number of arguments; it requires a minimum of two. The first argument is a format string that uses special characters to tell scanf() how to interpret the input. The second and additional arguments are the addresses of the variable(s) to which the input data is assigned. Here's an example:

```
scanf("%d", &x);
```

The first argument, "%d", is the format string. In this case, %d tells scanf() to look for one signed integer value. The second argument uses the address-of operator (&) to tell scanf() to assign the input value to the variable x. Now you can look at the format string details.

The scanf() format string can contain the following:

- Spaces and tabs, which are ignored (they can be used to make the format string more readable).
- Characters (but not %), which are matched against non-whitespace characters in the input.
- One or more *conversion specifications,* which consist of the % character followed by special characters. Generally, the format string contains one conversion specification for each variable.

NEW TERM The only required part of the format string is the conversion specifications. Each conversion specification begins with the % character and contains optional and required components in a certain order. The scanf() function applies the conversion specifications in the format string, in order, to the input fields. An *input field* is a sequence of non-whitespace characters that ends when the next white space is encountered or when the field width, if specified, is reached. The conversion specification components include the following:

- The optional assignment suppression flag (*) immediately follows the %. If present, this character tells scanf() to perform the conversion corresponding to the current conversion specifier but to ignore the result (not assign it to any variable).

- The next component, the field width, is also optional. The field width is a decimal number specifying the width, in characters, of the input field. In other words, the field width specifies how many characters from stdin scanf() should examine for the current conversion. If a field width isn't specified, the input field extends to the next white space.

- The next component is the optional precision modifier, a single character that can be h, l, or L. If present, the precision modifier changes the meaning of the type specifier that follows it. Details are given later in this chapter.

- The only required component of the conversion specifier (besides the %) is the type specifier. The type specifier is one or more characters that tell scanf() how to interpret the input. These characters are listed and described in Table 14.3. The Argument column lists the required type of the corresponding variable. For example, the type specifier d requires int * (a pointer to type int).

TABLE 14.3 The type specifier characters used in scanf() conversion specifiers

Type	Argument	Meaning of Type
d	int *	A decimal integer.
i	int *	An integer in decimal, octal (with leading 0), or hexadecimal (with leading 0X or 0x) notation.
o	int *	An integer in octal notation with or without the leading 0.
u	unsigned int *	An unsigned decimal integer.
x	int *	A hexadecimal integer with or without the leading 0X or 0x.
c	char *	One or more characters are read and assigned sequentially to the memory location indicated by the argument. No terminating \0 is added. If a field width argument isn't given, one character is read. If a field width argument is given, that number of characters, including white space (if any), is read.
s	char *	A string of non-whitespace characters is read into the specified memory location, and a terminating \0 is added.

14

TABLE 14.3   continued

Type	Argument	Meaning of Type
a,e,f,g	float *	A floating-point number. Numbers can be input in decimal or scientific notation.
[...]	char *	A string. Only the characters listed between the brackets are accepted. Input ends as soon as a nonmatching character is encountered, the specified field width is reached, or Enter is pressed. To accept the] character, list it first:[]...]. A \0 is added at the end of the string.
[^...]	char *	The same as [...], except that only characters not listed between the brackets are accepted.
%	None	Literal %: Reads the % character. No assignment is made.

Before seeing some examples of scanf(), you need to understand the precision modifiers, which are listed in Table 14.4.

TABLE 14.4   The precision modifiers

Precision Modifier	Meaning
hh	Specifies that a following d, i, o, u, x, X, or n conversion specifier applies to an argument with type pointer to signed char or unsigned char.
hh	When placed before the type specifier d, i, o, u, x, X, or n, the modifier hh specifies that the argument is a pointer to a signed char or unsigned char.
h	When placed before the type specifier d, i, o, u, x, X, or n, the modifier h specifies that the argument is a pointer to type short int or unsigned short int.
l	When placed before the type specifier d, i, o, u, x, X, or n, the modifier l specifies that the argument is a pointer to type long or unsigned long. When placed before the type specifier a, A, e, E, f, F, g, or G, the modifier l specifies that the argument is a pointer to type double.
ll	When placed before type specifier d, i, o, u, x, X, or n, the modifier ll specifies that the argument is a pointer to a long long or unsigned long long.
L	When placed before the type specifier a, A, e, E, f, F, g, or G, the modifier L specifies that the argument is a pointer to type long double.

Handling Extra Characters

Input from scanf() is buffered; no characters are actually received from stdin until the user presses Enter. The entire line of characters then "arrives" from stdin, and is processed, in order, by `scanf()`. Execution returns from `scanf()` only when enough input has been received to match the specifications in the format string. Also, `scanf()` processes only enough characters from `stdin` to satisfy its format string. Extra, unneeded characters, if any, remain waiting in `stdin`. These characters can cause problems. Take a closer look at the operation of `scanf()` to see how.

When a call to `scanf()` is executed and the user has entered a single line, you can have three situations. For these examples, assume that `scanf("%d %d", &x, &y);` is being executed; in other words, `scanf()` is expecting two decimal integers. Here are the possibilities:

- The line the user inputs matches the format string. For example, suppose the user enters 12 14 followed by Enter. In this case, there are no problems. `scanf()` is satisfied, and no characters are left over in `stdin`.

- The line that the user inputs has too few elements to match the format string. For example, suppose the user enters 12 followed by Enter. In this case, `scanf()` continues to wait for the missing input. Once the input is received, execution continues, and no characters are left over in `stdin`.

- The line that the user enters has more elements than required by the format string. For example, suppose the user enters 12 14 16 followed by Enter. In this case, `scanf()` reads the 12 and the 14 and then returns. The extra characters, the 1 and the 6, are left waiting in `stdin`.

It is this third situation (specifically, those leftover characters) that can cause problems. They remain waiting for as long as your program is running, until the next time the program reads input from `stdin`. Then the leftover characters are the first ones read, ahead of any input the user makes at the time. It's clear how this could cause errors. For example, the following code asks the user to input an integer and then a string:

```
puts("Enter your age.");
scanf("%d", &age);
puts("Enter your first name.");
scanf("%s", name);
```

Say, for example, that in response to the first prompt, the user decides to be precise and enters 29.00 and then presses Enter. The first call to `scanf()` is looking for an integer, so it reads the characters 29 from `stdin` and assigns the value 29 to the variable age. The characters .00 are left waiting in `stdin`. The next call to `scanf()` is looking for a string. It goes to `stdin` for input and finds .00 waiting there. The result is that the string .00 is assigned to name.

How can you avoid this problem? If the people who use your programs never make mistakes when entering information, that's one solution—but it's rather impractical.

14

A better solution is to make sure there are no extra characters waiting in stdin before prompting the user for input. You can do this by calling gets(), which reads any remaining characters from stdin, up to and including the end of the line. Rather than calling gets() directly from the program, you can put it in a separate function with the descriptive name of clear_kb(). This function is shown in Listing 14.7.

LISTING 14.7 clearing.c. Clearing stdin of extra characters to avoid errors

```
1:  /* Clearing stdin of extra characters. */
2:
3:  #include <stdio.h>
4:
5:  void clear_kb(void);
6:
7:  int main( void )
8:  {
9:      int age;
10:     char name[20];
11:
12:     /* Prompt for user's age. */
13:
14:     puts("Enter your age.");
15:     scanf("%d", &age);
16:
17:     /* Clear stdin of any extra characters. */
18:
19:     clear_kb();
20:
21:     /* Now prompt for user's name: */
22:
23:     puts("Enter your first name:");
24:     scanf("%s", name);
25:     /* Display the data. */
26:
27:     printf("Your age is %d.\n", age);
28:     printf("Your name is %s.\n", name);
29:
30:     return 0;
31: }
32:
33: void clear_kb(void)
34:
35: /* Clears stdin of any waiting characters. */
36: {
37:     char junk[80];
38:     gets(junk);
39: }
```

INPUT/
OUTPUT

```
Enter your age:
29 and never older!
Enter your first name:
Bradley
Your age is 29.
Your name is Bradley.
```

ANALYSIS When you run Listing 14.7, enter some extra characters after your age, before pressing Enter. Make sure the program ignores them and correctly prompts you for your name. Then modify the program by removing the call to clear_kb(), and run it again. Any extra characters entered on the same line as your age are assigned to name.

Handling Extra Characters with fflush()

There is a second way in which you can clear the extra characters that were typed in. The fflush() function flushes the information in a stream—including the standard input stream. fflush() is generally used with disk files (which are covered on Day 16); however, it can also be used to make Listing 14.7 even simpler. Listing 14.8 uses the fflush() function instead of the clear_kb() function that was created in Listing 14.7.

LISTING 14.8   clear.c. Clearing stdin of extra characters using fflush()

```
1:  /* Clearing stdin of extra characters. */
2:  /* Using the fflush() function         */
3:  #include <stdio.h>
4:
5:  int main( void )
6:  {
7:      int age;
8:      char name[20];
9:
10:     /* Prompt for user's age. */
11:     puts("Enter your age.");
12:     scanf("%d", &age);
13:
14:     /* Clear stdin of any extra characters. */
15:     fflush(stdin);
16:
17:     /* Now prompt for user's name. */
18:     puts("Enter your first name.");
19:     scanf("%s", name);
20:
21:     /* Display the data. */
22:     printf("Your age is %d.\n", age);
23:     printf("Your name is %s.\n", name);
24:
25:     return 0;
26: }
```

14

```
Enter your age.
29 and never older!
Enter your first name.
Bradley
Your age is 29.
Your name is Bradley.
```

ANALYSIS As you can see in line 15, the `fflush()` function is being used. The prototype for the `fflush()` function is as follows:

```
int fflush( FILE *stream);
```

The *stream* is the stream to be flushed. In Listing 14.8, the standard input stream, `stdin`, is being passed for *stream*.

scanf() Examples

The best way to become familiar with the operation of the `scanf()` function is to use it. It's a powerful function, but it can be a bit confusing at times. Try it and see what happens. Listing 14.9 demonstrates some of the unusual ways to use `scanf()`. You should compile and run this program and then experiment by making changes to the `scanf()` format strings.

LISTING 14.9   scanf.c. Some ways to use `scanf()` for keyboard input

```
 1:  /* Demonstrates some uses of scanf(). */
 2:
 3:  #include <stdio.h>
 4:
 5:  int main( void )
 6:  {
 7:      int i1;
 8:      int i2;
 9:      long l1;
10:
11:      double d1;
12:      char buf1[80]
13:      char buf2[80];
14:
15:      /* Using the l modifier to enter long integers and doubles.*/
16:
17:      puts("Enter an integer and a floating point number.");
18:      scanf("%ld %lf", &l1, &d1);
19:      printf("\nYou entered %ld and %lf.\n",l1, d1);
20:      puts("The scanf() format string used the l modifier to store");
21:      puts("your input in a type long and a type double.\n");
22:
23:      fflush(stdin);
24:
```

LISTING 14.9 continued

```
25:    /* Use field width to split input. */
26:
27:    puts("Enter a 5 digit integer (for example, 54321).");
28:    scanf("%2d%3d", &i1, &i2);
29:
30:    printf("\nYou entered %d and %d.\n", i1, i2);
31:    puts("Note how the field width specifier in the scanf() format");
32:    puts("string split your input into two values.\n");
33:
34:    fflush(stdin);
35:
36:    /* Using an excluded space to split a line of input into */
37:    /* two strings at the space. */
38:
39:    puts("Enter your first and last names separated by a space.");
40:    scanf("%[^ ]%s", buf1, buf2);
41:    printf("\nYour first name is %s\n", buf1);
42:    printf("Your last name is %s\n", buf2);
43:    puts("Note how [^ ] in the scanf() format string, by excluding");
44:    puts("the space character, caused the input to be split.");
45:
46:    return 0;
47: }
```

INPUT/ OUTPUT

```
Enter an integer and a floating point number.
123 45.6789

You entered 123 and 45.678900.
The scanf() format string used the l modifier to store
your input in a type long and a type double.

Enter a 5 digit integer (for example, 54321).
54321

You entered 54 and 321.
Note how the field width specifier in the scanf() format
string split your input into two values.

Enter your first and last names separated by a space.
Gayle Johnson

Your first name is Gayle
Your last name is Johnson
Note how [^ ] in the scanf() format string, by excluding
the space character, caused the input to be split.
```

14

ANALYSIS   This listing starts by defining several variables in lines 7 through 13 for data input. The program then walks you through the steps of entering various types of data. Lines 17 through 21 have you enter and print long integers and a `double`. Line 23 calls the `fflush()` function to clear any unwanted characters from the standard input stream. Lines 27 and 28 get the next value, a five-character integer. Because there are width specifiers, the five-digit integer is split into two integers—one that is two characters, and one that is three characters. Line 34 calls `fflush()` to clear the keyboard again. The final example, in lines 36 through 44, uses the exclude character. Line 40 uses `"%[^ ]"`, which tells `scanf()` to get a string but to stop at any spaces. This effectively splits the input.

Take the time to modify this listing and enter additional values to see what the results are.

The `scanf()` function can be used for most of your input needs, particularly those involving numbers (strings can be input more easily with `gets()`). It is often worthwhile, however, to write your own specialized input functions. You can see some examples of user-defined functions on Day 18, "Getting More from Functions."

Do	Don't
DO use the `gets()` and `scanf()` functions instead of the `fgets()` and `fscanf()` functions if you're using the standard input file (`stdin`) only.	**DON'T** forget to check the input stream for extra characters.

Controlling Output to the Screen

Screen output functions are divided into three general categories along the same lines as the input functions: character output, line output, and formatted output. You were introduced to some of these functions in earlier lessons. This section covers them in detail.

Character Output with `putchar()`, `putc()`, and `fputc()`

The C library's character output functions send a single character to a stream. The function `putchar()` sends its output to `stdout` (normally the screen). The functions `fputc()` and `putc()` send their output to a stream specified in the argument list.

Using the `putchar()` Function

The prototype for `putchar`, which is located in stdio.h, is as follows:

```
int putchar(int c);
```

This function writes the character stored in c to stdout. Although the prototype specifies a type int argument, you pass putchar() a type char. You can also pass it a type int as long as its value is appropriate for a character (that is, in the range 0 to 255). The function returns the character that was just written, or EOF if an error has occurred.

You saw putchar() demonstrated in Listing 14.2. Listing 14.10 displays the characters with ASCII values between 14 and 127.

LISTING 14.10 putchar.c. The putchar() function

```
1:  /* Demonstrates putchar(). */
2:
3:  #include <stdio.h>
4:  int main( void )
5:  {
6:      int count;
7:
8:      for (count = 14; count < 128; )
9:              putchar(count++);
10:
11:     return 0;
12: }
```

OUTPUT
```
?¤????¶§?????????? !"#$%&'()*+,-./0123456789:;<=>?@ABCDEF
GHIJKLMNOPQRSTUVWXYZ[\]^_`abcdefghijklmnopqrstuvwxyz{|}~
```

You can also display strings with the putchar() function (as shown in Listing 14.11), although other functions are better suited for this purpose.

LISTING 14.11 putchar2.c. Displaying a string with putchar()

```
1:  /* Using putchar() to display strings. */
2:
3:  #include <stdio.h>
4:
5:  #define MAXSTRING 80
6:
7:  char message[] = "Displayed with putchar().";
8:  int main( void )
9:  {
10:     int count;
11:
12:     for (count = 0; count < MAXSTRING; count++)
13:     {
14:
15:         /* Look for the end of the string. When it's found, */
16:         /* write a newline character and exit the loop. */
```

14

LISTING 14.11 continued

```
17:
18:         if (message[count] == '\0')
19:         {
20:            putchar('\n');
21:            break;
22:         }
23:         else
24:
25:         /* If end of string not found, write the next character. */
26:
27:            putchar(message[count]);
28:      }
29:      return 0;
30: }
```

OUTPUT Displayed with putchar().

Using the `putc()` and `fputc()` Functions

The `putc()` and `fputc()` functions perform the same action—sending a single character to a specified stream. `putc()` is a macro implementation of `fputc()`. You'll learn about macros on Day 21, "Advanced Compiler Use." For now, just stick to `fputc()`. Its prototype is

```
int fputc(int c, FILE *fp);
```

The `FILE *fp` part might puzzle you. You pass `fputc()` the output stream in this argument. (You'll learn more about this on Day 16.) If you specify `stdout` as the stream, `fputc()` behaves exactly the same as `putchar()`. Thus, the following two statements are equivalent:

```
putchar('x');
fputc('x', stdout);
```

Using `puts()` and `fputs()` for String Output

Your programs display strings on-screen more often than they display single characters. The library function `puts()` displays strings. The function `fputs()` sends a string to a specified stream; otherwise, it is identical to `puts()`. The prototype for `puts()` is

```
int puts(char *cp);
```

`*cp` is a pointer to the first character of the string that you want displayed. The `puts()` function displays the entire string up to but not including the terminating null character, adding a new line at the end. Then `puts()` returns a positive value if successful or `EOF` on error. (Remember, `EOF` is a symbolic constant with the value -1; it is defined in stdio.h.)

The puts() function can be used to display any type of string, as demonstrated in Listing 14.12.

LISTING 14.12 puts.c. Using the puts() function to display strings

```
 1:  /* Demonstrates puts(). */
 2:
 3:  #include <stdio.h>
 4:
 5:  /* Declare and initialize an array of pointers. */
 6:
 7:  char *messages[5] = { "This", "is", "a", "short", "message." };
 8:
 9:  int main( void )
10:  {
11:      int x;
12:
13:      for (x=0; x<5; x++)
14:          puts(messages[x]);
15:
16:      puts("And this is the end!");
17:
18:      return 0;
19:  }
```

OUTPUT

```
This
is
a
short
message.
And this is the end!
```

ANALYSIS This listing declares an array of pointers, a subject not covered yet. (It will be covered tomorrow.) Lines 13 and 14 print each of the strings stored in the message array.

Using `printf()` and `fprintf()` for Formatted Output

So far, the output functions have displayed characters and strings only. What about numbers? To display numbers, you must use the C library's formatted output functions, printf() and fprintf(). These functions can also display strings and characters. You were officially introduced to printf() on Day 7, and you've used it in almost every day's lessons since. This section provides the remainder of the details.

The two functions printf() and fprintf() are identical, except that printf() always sends output to stdout, whereas fprintf() specifies the output stream. fprintf() is generally used for output to disk files. It's covered on Day 16.

14

The `printf()` function takes a variable number of arguments, with a minimum of one. The first and only required argument is the format string, which tells `printf()` how to format the output. The optional arguments are variables and expressions whose values you want to display. Take a look at these few simple examples, which give you a feel for `printf()`, before you really get into the nitty-gritty:

- The statement `printf("Hello, world.");` displays the message `Hello, world.` on-screen. This is an example of using `printf()` with only one argument, the format string. In this case, the format string contains only a literal string to be displayed on-screen.

- The statement `printf("%d", i);` displays the value of the integer variable `i` on-screen. The format string contains only the format specifier `%d`, which tells `printf()` to display a single decimal integer. The second argument `i` is the name of the variable whose value is to be displayed.

- The statement `printf("%d plus %d equals %d.", a, b, a+b);` displays `2 plus 3 equals 5` on-screen (assuming that `a` and `b` are integer variables with the values of 2 and 3, respectively). This use of `printf()` has four arguments: a format string that contains literal text as well as format specifiers, and two variables and an expression whose values are to be displayed.

Now look at the `printf()` format string in more detail. It can contain the following:

- Zero, one, or more conversion commands that tell `printf()` how to display a value in its argument list. A conversion command consists of `%` followed by one or more characters.

- Characters that are not part of a conversion command and are displayed as-is.

The third example's format string is `%d plus %d equals %d`. In this case, the three `%d`s are conversion commands, and the remainder of the string, including the spaces, is literal characters that are displayed directly.

Now you can dissect the conversion command. The components of the command are given here and explained next. Components in brackets are optional.

`%[flag][field_width][.[precision]][l]conversion_char`

The *conversion_char* is the only required part of a conversion command (other than the `%`). Table 14.5 lists the conversion characters and their meanings.

TABLE 14.5 The `printf()` and `fprintf()` conversion characters

Conversion Character	Meaning
d, i	Display a signed integer in decimal notation.
u	Display an unsigned integer in decimal notation.
o	Display an integer in unsigned octal notation.
x, X	Display an integer in unsigned hexadecimal notation. Use x for lower-case output and X for uppercase output.
c	Display a single character (the argument gives the character's ASCII code).
e, E	Display a `float` or `double` in scientific notation (for example, `123.45` is displayed as `1.234500e+002`). Six digits are displayed to the right of the decimal point unless another precision is specified with the f specifier. Use e or E to control the case of output.
f	Display a `float` or `double` in decimal notation (for example, `123.45` is displayed as `123.450000`). Six digits are displayed to the right of the decimal point unless another precision is specified.
g, G	Use e, E, or f format. The e or E format is used if the exponent is less than `-3` or greater than the precision (which defaults to 6). f format is used otherwise. Trailing zeros are truncated.
n	Nothing is displayed. The argument corresponding to an n conversion command is a pointer to type `int`. The `printf()` function assigns to this variable the number of characters output so far.
s	Display a string. The argument is a pointer to `char`. Characters are displayed until a null character is encountered or the number of characters specified by precision is displayed. The terminating null character is not output.
%	Display the % character.

You can place the l modifier just before the conversion character. This modifier applies only to the conversion characters o, u, x, X, i, d, and b. When applied, this modifier specifies that the argument is a type `long` rather than a type `int`. If the l modifier is applied to the conversion characters e, E, f, g, or G, it specifies that the argument is a type `double`. If an l is placed before any other conversion character, it is ignored.

In addition to the l specifier there is an ll specifier. The ll specifier works just like the l specifier except that the argument is type `long long` instead of type `long`.

14

The precision specifier consists of a decimal point (.) by itself or followed by a number. A precision specifier applies only to the conversion characters e, E, f, g, G, and s. It specifies the number of digits to display to the right of the decimal point or, when used with s, the number of characters to output. If the decimal point is used alone, it specifies a precision of 0.

The field-width specifier determines the minimum number of characters output. The field-width specifier can be the following:

- A decimal integer not starting with 0. The output is padded on the left with spaces to fill the designated field width.

- A decimal integer starting with 0. The output is padded on the left with zeros to fill the designated field width.

- The * character. The value of the next argument (which must be an int) is used as the field width. For example, if w is a type int with a value of 10, the statement printf("%*d", w, a); prints the value of a with a field width of 10.

If no field width is specified, or if the specified field width is narrower than the output, the output field is just as wide as needed.

The last optional part of the printf() format string is the flag, which immediately follows the % character. There are four available flags:

-	This means that the output is left-justified in its field rather than right-justified, which is the default.
+	This means that signed numbers are always displayed with a leading + or -.
' '	A space means that positive numbers are preceded by a space.
#	This applies only to x, X, and o conversion characters. It specifies that nonzero numbers are displayed with a leading 0X or 0x (for x and X) or a leading 0 (for o).

When you use printf(), the format string can be a string literal enclosed in double quotes in the printf() argument list. It can also be a null-terminated string stored in memory, in which case you pass a pointer to the string to printf(). For example, this statement

```
char *fmt = "The answer is %f.";
printf(fmt, x);
```

is equivalent to this statement

```
printf("The answer is %f.", x);
```

As explained on Day 7, the printf() format string can contain escape sequences that provide special control over the output. Table 14.6 lists the most frequently used escape sequences. For example, including the newline sequence (\n) in a format string causes subsequent output to appear starting on the next screen line.

TABLE 14.6   The most frequently used escape sequences

Sequence	Meaning
\a	Bell (alert)
\b	Backspace
\n	Newline
\t	Horizontal tab
\\	Backslash
\?	Question mark
\'	Single quote
\"	Double quote

printf() is somewhat complicated. The best way to learn how to use it is to look at examples and then experiment on your own. Listing 14.13 demonstrates many of the ways you can use printf().

LISTING 14.13   printf.c. Some ways to use the printf() function

```
 1:  /* Demonstration of printf(). */
 2:
 3:  #include <stdio.h>
 4:
 5:  char *m1 = "Binary";
 6:  char *m2 = "Decimal";
 7:  char *m3 = "Octal";
 8:  char *m4 = "Hexadecimal";
 9:
10:  int main( void )
11:  {
12:      float d1 = 10000.123;
13:      int n, f;
14:
15:
16:      puts("Outputting a number with different field widths.\n");
17:
18:      printf("%5f\n", d1);
19:      printf("%10f\n", d1);
20:      printf("%15f\n", d1);
21:      printf("%20f\n", d1);
```

14

LISTING 14.13   continued

```
22:        printf("%25f\n", d1);
23:
24:        puts("\n Press Enter to continue...");
25:        fflush(stdin);
26:        getchar();
27:
28:        puts("\nUse the * field width specifier to obtain field width");
29:        puts("from a variable in the argument list.\n");
30:
31:        for (n=5;n<=25; n+=5)
32:            printf("%*f\n", n, d1);
33:
34:        puts("\n Press Enter to continue...");
35:        fflush(stdin);
36:        getchar();
37:
38:        puts("\nInclude leading zeros.\n");
39:
40:        printf("%05f\n", d1);
41:        printf("%010f\n", d1);
42:        printf("%015f\n", d1);
43:        printf("%020f\n", d1);
44:        printf("%025f\n", d1);
45:
46:        puts("\n Press Enter to continue...");
47:        fflush(stdin);
48:        getchar();
49:
50:        puts("\nDisplay in octal, decimal, and hexadecimal.");
51:        puts("Use # to precede octal and hex output with 0 and 0X.");
52:        puts("Use - to left-justify each value in its field.");
53:        puts("First display column labels.\n");
54:
55:        printf("%-15s%-15s%-15s", m2, m3, m4);
56:
57:        for (n = 1;n< 20; n++)
58:            printf("\n%-15d%-#15o%-#15X", n, n, n);
59:
60:        puts("\n Press Enter to continue...");
61:        fflush(stdin);
62:        getchar();
63:
64:        puts("\n\nUse the %n conversion command to count characters.\n");
65:
66:        printf("%s%s%s%s%n", m1, m2, m3, m4, &n);
67:
68:        printf("\n\nThe last printf() output %d characters.\n", n);
69:
70:        return 0;
71: }
```

OUTPUT   Outputting a number with different field widths.

```
10000.123047
10000.123047
    10000.123047
        10000.123047
            10000.123047

Press Enter to continue...


Use the * field width specifier to obtain field width
from a variable in the argument list.

10000.123047
10000.123047
    10000.123047
        10000.123047
            10000.123047

Press Enter to continue...


Include leading zeros.

10000.123047
10000.123047
00010000.123047
0000000010000.123047
000000000000010000.123047

Press Enter to continue...


Display in octal, decimal, and hexadecimal.
Use # to precede octal and hex output with 0 and 0X.
Use - to left-justify each value in its field.
First display column labels.

Decimal        Octal          Hexadecimal
1              01             0X1
2              02             0X2
3              03             0X3
4              04             0X4
5              05             0X5
6              06             0X6
7              07             0X7
8              010            0X8
9              011            0X9
10             012            0XA
11             013            0XB
```

14

```
12              014             0XC
13              015             0XD
14              016             0XE
15              017             0XF
16              020             0X10
17              021             0X11
18              022             0X12
19              023             0X13
```

```
Press Enter to continue...

Use the %n conversion command to count characters.

BinaryDecimalOctalHexadecimal

The last printf() output 29 characters.
```

Redirecting Input and Output

A program that uses stdin and stdout can utilize an operating-system feature called *redirection*. Redirection allows you to do the following:

- Output sent to stdout can be sent to a disk file or the printer rather than to the screen.
- Program input from stdin can come from a disk file rather than from the keyboard.

You don't code redirection into your programs; you specify it on the command line when you run the program. In DOS and the Microsoft Windows Command prompt, as in UNIX, the symbols for redirection are < and >. I'll discuss redirection of output first.

Remember your first C program, hello.c? It used the printf() library function to display the message Hello, world on-screen. As you now know, printf() sends output to stdout, so it can be redirected. When you enter the program name at the command-line prompt, follow it with the > symbol and the name of the new destination:

hello > *destination*

Thus, if you enter hello >prn, the program output goes to the printer instead of to the screen (prn is the DOS name for the printer attached to port LPT1:). If you enter hello >hello.txt, the output is placed in a disk file with the name hello.txt.

When you redirect output to a disk file, be careful. If the file already exists, the old copy is deleted and replaced with the new file. If the file doesn't exist, it is created. When redirecting output to a file, you can also use the >> symbol. If the specified destination file already exists, the program output is appended to the end of the file. Listing 14.14 demonstrates redirection.

LISTING 14.14 redirect.c. the redirection of input and output

```
 1:  /* Can be used to demonstrate redirection of stdin and stdout. */
 2:
 3:  #include <stdio.h>
 4:
 5:  int main( void )
 6:  {
 7:     char buf[80];
 8:
 9:     gets(buf);
10:     printf("The input was: %s\n", buf);
11:     return 0;
12:  }
```

ANALYSIS This program accepts a line of input from stdin and then sends the line to std-out, preceding it with The input was:. After compiling and linking the program, run it without redirection (assuming that the program is named redirect) by entering redirect at the command-line prompt. If you then enter I am teaching myself C, the program displays the following on-screen:

```
The input was: I am teaching myself C
```

If you run the program by entering redirect >test.txt and make the same entry, nothing is displayed on-screen. Instead, a file named test.txt is created on the disk. If you use the DOS TYPE (or an equivalent) command to display the contents of the file:

```
type test.txt
```

you'll see that the file contains only the line The input was: I am teaching myself C. Similarly, if you had run the program by entering redirect >prn, the output line would have been printed on the printer (prn is a DOS command name for the printer).

Run the program again, this time redirecting output to TEST.TXT with the >> symbol. Instead of the file's getting replaced, the new output is appended to the end of TEST.TXT.

Redirecting Input

Now let's look at redirecting input. First you need a source file. Use your editor to create a file named INPUT.TXT that contains the single line William Shakespeare. Now run Listing 14.14 by entering the following at the DOS prompt:

```
redirect < INPUT.TXT
```

The program doesn't wait for you to make an entry at the keyboard. Instead, it immediately displays the following message on-screen:

14

```
The input was: William Shakespeare
```

The stream stdin was redirected to the disk file INPUT.TXT, so the program's call to gets() reads one line of text from the file rather than the keyboard.

You can redirect input and output at the same time. Try running the program with the following command to redirect stdin to the file INPUT.TXT and redirect stdout to JUNK.TXT:

```
redirect < INPUT.TXT > JUNK.TXT
```

Redirecting stdin and stdout can be useful in certain situations. A sorting program, for example, could sort either keyboard input or the contents of a disk file. Likewise, a mailing list program could display addresses on-screen, send them to the printer for mailing labels, or place them in a file for some other use.

Note
Remember that redirecting stdin and stdout is a feature of the operating system and not of the C language itself. However, it does provide another example of the flexibility of streams. You can check your operating system documentation for more information on redirection.

When to Use fprintf()

As mentioned earlier, the library function fprintf() is identical to printf(), except that you can specify the stream to which output is sent. The main use of fprintf() involves disk files, as explained on Day 16. There are two other uses, as explained here.

Using stderr

One of C's predefined streams is stderr (standard error). A program's error messages traditionally are sent to the stream stderr and not to stdout. Why is this?

As you just learned, output to stdout can be redirected to a destination other than the display screen. If stdout is redirected, the user might not be aware of any error messages the program sends to stdout. Unlike stdout, stderr can't be redirected and is always connected to the screen (at least in DOS—UNIX systems might allow redirection of stderr). By directing error messages to stderr, you can be sure the user always sees them. You do this with fprintf():

```
fprintf(stderr, "An error has occurred.");
```

You can write a function to handle error messages and then call the function when an error occurs rather than calling fprintf():

```
error_message("An error has occurred.");

void error_message(char *msg)
{
    fprintf(stderr, msg);
}
```

By using your own function instead of directly calling `fprintf()`, you provide additional flexibility (one of the advantages of structured programming). For example, in special circumstances you might want a program's error messages to go to the printer or a disk file. All you need to do is modify the `error_message()` function so that the output is sent to the desired destination.

Printer Output Under DOS and the Windows Command Prompt

On a DOS or Windows system, you send output to your printer by accessing the predefined stream `stdprn`. On IBM PCs and compatibles, the stream `stdprn` is connected to the device LPT1: (the first parallel printer port). Listing 14.15 presents a simple example.

Note

To use `stdprn`, you need to turn ANSI compatibility off in your compiler. Consult your compiler's manuals for more information. Because `stdprn` is not a part of the ANSI standard, your compiler may not support it.

LISTING **14.15**   printer.c. sending output to the printer

```
1:  /* Demonstrates printer output. */
2:  /* stdprn is not ANSI standard   */
3:  #include <stdio.h>
4:
5:  int main( void )
6:  {
7:      float f = 2.0134;
8:
9:      fprintf(stdprn, "\nThis message is printed.\r\n");
10:     fprintf(stdprn, "And now some numbers:\r\n");
11:     fprintf(stdprn, "The square of %f is %f.", f, f*f);
12:
13:     /* Send a form feed. */
14:     fprintf(stdprn, "\f");
15:
16:     return 0;
17: }
```

14

OUTPUT
```
This message is printed.
And now some numbers:
The square of 2.013400 is 4.053780.
```

Note | This output is printed by the printer. It won't appear on-screen.

If your DOS system has a printer connected to port LPT1:, you can compile and run this program. It prints three lines on the page. Line 14 sends an "\f" to the printer. \f is the escape sequence for a form feed, the command that causes the printer to advance a page (or, in the case of a laser printer, to eject the current page).

Do	**Don't**
DO use fprintf() to create programs that can send output to stdout, stderr, stdprn, or any other stream. **DO** use fprintf() with stderr to print error messages to the screen. **DO** create functions such as error_message to make your code more structured and maintainable.	**DON'T** ever try to redirect stderr. **DON'T** use stderr for purposes other than printing error messages or warnings.

Summary

This was a long day full of important information on program input and output. You learned how C uses streams, treating all input and output as a sequence of bytes. You also learned that ASNI C has three predefined streams:

stdin	The keyboard
stdout	The screen
stderr	The screen

Input from the keyboard arrives from the stream stdin. Using C's standard library functions, you can accept keyboard input character by character, a line at a time, or as formatted numbers and strings. Character input can be buffered or unbuffered, echoed or unechoed.

Output to the display screen is normally done with the stdout stream. Like input, program output can be by character, by line, or as formatted numbers and strings. For output to the printer, you use fprintf() to send data to the stream stdprn.

When you use `stdin` and `stdout`, you can redirect program input and output. Input can come from a disk file rather than the keyboard, and output can go to a disk file or to the printer rather than to the display screen.

You learned why error messages should be sent to the stream `stderr` instead of `stdout`. Because `stderr` is usually connected to the display screen, you are assured of seeing error messages even when the program output is redirected.

You also learned about two other streams that are not ANSI standard:

`stdprn`	The printer
`stdaux`	The communications port

Q&A

Q What happens if I try to get input from an output stream?

A You can write a C program to do this, but it won't work. For example, if you try to use `stdprn` with `fscanf()`, the program compiles into an executable file, but the printer is incapable of sending input, so your program doesn't operate as intended.

Q What happens if I redirect one of the standard streams?

A Doing this might cause problems later in the program. If you redirect a stream, you must put it back if you need it again in the same program. Many of the functions described in this chapter use the standard streams. They all use the same streams, so if you change the stream in one place, you change it for all the functions. For example, assign `stdout` equal to `stdprn` in one of the listings from today's lessons and see what happens.

Q Is there any danger in using non-ANSI functions in a program?

A Most compilers come with many useful functions that aren't ANSI-standard. If you plan on always using that compiler and not porting your code to other compilers or platforms, there won't be a problem. If you're going to use other compilers and platforms, you should be concerned with ANSI compatibility.

Q Why shouldn't I always use `fprintf()` instead of `printf()`? Or `fscanf()` instead of `scanf()`?

A If you're using the standard output or input streams, you should use `printf()` and `scanf()`. By using these simpler functions, you don't have to bother with any other streams.

14

Workshop

The Workshop provides quiz questions to help you solidify your understanding of the material covered and exercises to provide you with experience in using what you've learned.

Quiz

1. What is a stream, and what does a C program use streams for?

2. Are the following input devices or output devices?

    a. Printer

    b. Keyboard

    c. Modem

    d. Monitor

    e. Disk drive

3. List the five predefined streams and the devices with which they are associated.

4. What stream do the following functions use?

    a. `printf()`

    b. `puts()`

    c. `scanf()`

    d. `gets()`

    e. `fprintf()`

5. What is the difference between buffered and unbuffered character input from `stdin`?

6. What is the difference between echoed and unechoed character input from `stdin`?

7. Can you "unget" more than one character at a time with `ungetc()`? Can you "unget" the `EOF` character?

8. When you use C's line input functions, how is the end of a line determined?

9. Which of the following are valid type specifiers?

    a. `"%d"`

    b. `"%4d"`

    c. `"%3i%c"`

    d. `"%q%d"`

    e. `"%%%i"`

    f. `"%9ld"`

10. What is the difference between `stderr` and `stdout`?

Exercises

1. Write a statement to print "Hello World" to the screen.

2. Use two different C functions to do the same thing the function in exercise 1 did.

3. Write a statement to print "Hello Auxiliary Port" to the standard auxiliary port.

4. Write a statement that gets a string 30 characters or shorter. If an asterisk is encountered, truncate the string.

5. Write a single statement that prints the following:

```
Jack asked, "What is a backslash?"
Jill said, "It is '\'"
```

   Because of the multitude of possibilities, answers are not provided for the following exercises; however, you should attempt to do them.

6. **ON YOUR OWN:** Write a program that redirects a file to the printer one character at a time.

7. **ON YOUR OWN:** Write a program that uses redirection to accept input from a disk file, counts the number of times each letter occurs in the file, and then displays the results on-screen. (A hint is provided in Appendix F, "Answers.")

8. **ON YOUR OWN:** Write a program that prints your C source files. Use redirection to enter the source file, and use fprintf() to do the printing.

9. **ON YOUR OWN:** Modify the program from exercise 8 to put line numbers at the beginning of the listing when it is printed. (A hint is provided in Appendix F, "Answers.")

10. **ON YOUR OWN:** Write a "typing" program that accepts keyboard input, echoes it to the screen, and then reproduces this input on the printer. The program should count lines and advance the paper in the printer to a new page when necessary. Use a function key to terminate the program.

14

WEEK 2

In Review

You have finished your second week of learning how to program in C. By now you should feel comfortable with the C language. You have covered almost all the basic C statements. The following program pulls together many of the topics from the previous week.

8

9

10

11

12

13

14

Note The numbers to the left of the line numbers indicate the day that covers the concept presented on that line. If you're confused by the line, refer to the referenced day for more information.

LISTING **R2.1**   week2.c. Week 2's review listing

```
 1:  /*----------------------------------------------------*/
 2:  /* Program Name:  week2.c                          */
 3:  /* program to enter information for up to 100      */
 4:  /* people.  The program prints a report            */
 5:  /*          based on the numbers entered.          */
 6:  /*----------------------------------------------------*/
 7:  /*--------------------*/
 8:  /* included files     */
 9:  /*--------------------*/
10:  #include <stdio.h>
11:  #include <stdlib.h>
12:
13:  /*--------------------*/
14:  /* defined constants  */
15:  /*--------------------*/
16:  #define MAX   100
17:  #define YES   1
18:  #define NO    0
19:
20:  /*--------------------*/
21:  /* variables          */
22:  /*--------------------*/
23:
24:  struct record {
25:      char fname[15+1];              /* first name + NULL    */
26:      char lname[20+1];              /* last name + NULL     */
27:      char phone[9+1];               /* phone number + NULL  */
28:      long income;                   /* incomes              */
29:      int  month;                    /* birthday month       */
30:      int  day;                      /* birthday day         */
31:      int  year;                     /* birthday year        */
32:  };
33:
34:  struct record list[MAX];      /* declare actual structure */
35:
36:  int last_entry = 0;           /* total number of entries  */
37:
38:  /*--------------------*/
39:  /* function prototypes */
40:  /*--------------------*/
41:  int main(void);
42:  void get_data(void);
43:  void display_report(void);
```

Line 24: CH 11
Line 26: CH 10
Line 34: CH 11
Line 36: CH 12

LISTING R2.1 continued

CH 14
CH 12
CH 14
CH 14
CH 13
CH 13

```
44:  int  continue_function(void);
45:  void clear_kb(void);
46:
47:  /*--------------------*/
48:  /* start of program   */
49:  /*--------------------*/
50:
51:  int main( void )
52:  {
53:     int cont = YES;
54:     int ch;
55:
56:     while( cont == YES )
57:     {
58:        printf( "\n");
59:        printf( "\n     MENU");
60:        printf( "\n    =======\n");
61:        printf( "\n1.  Enter names");
62:        printf( "\n2.  Print report");
63:        printf( "\n3.  Quit");
64:        printf( "\n\nEnter Selection ==> ");
65:
66:        ch = getchar();
67:
68:        fflush(stdin);  /* remove extra characters from keyboard buffer */
69:
70:        switch( ch )
71:        {
72:          case '1': get_data();
73:                    break;
74:          case '2': display_report();
75:                    break;
76:          case '3': printf("\n\nThank you for using this program!\n");
77:                    cont = NO;
78:                    break;
79:          default:  printf("\n\nInvalid choice, Please select 1 to 3!");
80:                    break;
81:        }
82:     }
83:     return 0;
84:  }
85:  /*-----------------------------------------------------------*
86:   *  Function:  get_data()                                    *
87:   *  Purpose: This function gets the data from the user. It   *
88:   *           continues to get data until either 100 people are *
89:   *           entered, or the user chooses not to continue.   *
90:   *  Returns: nothing                                         *
91:   *  Notes: This allows 0/0/0 to be entered for birthdates in *
92:   *         case the user is unsure.  It also allows for 31 days *
93:   *          in each month.                                   *
94:   *-----------------------------------------------------------*/
```

LISTING R2.1   continued

```
95:
96:   void get_data(void)
97:   {
98:     int cont;
99:
100:     for ( cont = YES; last_entry < MAX && cont == YES;last_entry++ )
101:     {
102:         printf("\n\nEnter information for Person %d.",last_entry+1 );
103:
104:         printf("\n\nEnter first name: ");
105:         gets(list[last_entry].fname);
106:
107:         printf("\nEnter last name: ");
108:         gets(list[last_entry].lname);
109:
110:         printf("\nEnter phone in 123-4567 format: ");
111:         gets(list[last_entry].phone);
112:
113:         printf("\nEnter Yearly Income (whole dollars): ");
114:         scanf("%ld", &list[last_entry].income);
115:
116:         printf("\nEnter Birthday:");
117:
118:         do
119:         {
120:             printf("\n\tMonth (0 - 12): ");
121:             scanf("%d", &list[last_entry].month);
122:         }while ( list[last_entry].month < 0 ||
123:                 list[last_entry].month > 12 );
124:
125:         do
126:         {
127:             printf("\n\tDay (0 - 31): ");
128:             scanf("%d", &list[last_entry].day);
129:         }while ( list[last_entry].day <  0 ||
130:                 list[last_entry].day > 31 );
131:
132:         do
133:         {
134:             printf("\n\tYear (1800 - 1997): ");
135:             scanf("%d", &list[last_entry].year);
136:         }while (list[last_entry].year != 0 &&
137:                 (list[last_entry].year < 1800 ||
138:                 list[last_entry].year > 1997 ));
139:
140:         cont = continue_function();
141:     }
142:
143:     if( last_entry == MAX)
144:         printf("\n\nMaximum Number of Names has been entered!\n");
145: }
```

CH 11 (line 98)

CH 14 (line 105)

CH 14 (line 108)

CH 14 (line 111)

CH 09 (line 114)

CH 09 (line 121)

CH 09 (line 128)

CH 09 (line 135)

LISTING R2.1 continued

```
146:
147: /*-----------------------------------------------------------*
148:  *  Function:   display_report()                            *
149:  *  Purpose:    This function displays a report to the screen *
150:  *  Returns:    nothing                                      *
151:  *  Notes:      More information could be displayed.         *
152:  *              Change stdout to stdprn to Print report      *
153:  *-----------------------------------------------------------*/
154:
155: void display_report()
156: {
157:     long   month_total = 0,
158:            grand_total = 0;        /* For totals */
159:     int    x, y;
160:
161:     fprintf(stdout, "\n\n");         /* skip a few lines */
162:     fprintf(stdout, "\n            REPORT");
163:     fprintf(stdout, "\n            ========");
164:
165:     for( x = 0; x <= 12; x++ )   /* for each month, including 0 */
166:     {
167:        month_total = 0;
168:        for( y = 0; y < last_entry; y++ )
169:        {
170:           if( list[y].month == x )
171:           {
172:              fprintf(stdout,"\n\t%s %s %s %ld",list[y].fname,
173:                     list[y].lname, list[y].phone,list[y].income);
174:              month_total += list[y].income;
175:           }
176:        }
177:        fprintf(stdout, "\nTotal for month %d is %ld",x,month_total);
178:        grand_total += month_total;
179:     }
180:     fprintf(stdout, "\n\nReport totals:");
181:     fprintf(stdout, "\nTotal Income is %ld", grand_total);
182:     fprintf(stdout, "\nAverage Income is %ld", grand_total/last_entry );
183:
184:     fprintf(stdout, "\n\n* * * End of Report * * *");
185: }
186:
187: /*-----------------------------------------------------------*
188:  *  Function:   continue_function()                          *
189:  *  Purpose:    This function asks the user if they wish to continue. *
190:  *  Returns:    YES - if user wishes to continue             *
191:  *              NO  - if user wishes to quit                 *
192:  *-----------------------------------------------------------*/
193:
194: int continue_function( void )
195: {
```

CH 12 (line 157)
CH 12 (line 159)
CH 14 (line 161)
CH 11 (line 173)
CH 14 (line 177)

LISTING R2.1 continued

```
CH 12     196:    int ch;
          197:
          198:    printf("\n\nDo you wish to continue? (Y)es/(N)o: ");
          199:
CH 14     200:    fflush(stdin);
CH 14     201:    ch = getchar();
          202:
          203:    while( ch != 'n' && ch != 'N' && ch != 'y' && ch != 'Y' )
          204:    {
          205:        printf("\n%c is invalid!", ch);
          206:        printf("\n\nPlease enter \'N\' to Quit or \'Y\' to Continue: ");
          207:
CH 14     208:        fflush(stdin);      /* clear keyboard buffer (stdin) */
          209:        ch = getchar();
          210:    }
          211:
          212:
          213:    clear_kb();  /* this function is similar to fflush(stdin) */
          214:
          215:    if(ch == 'n' || ch == 'N')
          216:        return(NO);
          217:    else
          218:        return(YES);
          219: }
          220:
          221: /*------------------------------------------------------------*
          222:  * Function:   clear_kb()                                     *
          223:  * Purpose:    This function clears the keyboard of extra characters. *
          224:  * Returns:    Nothing                                        *
          225:  * Note:       This function could be replaced by fflush(stdin);  *
          226:  *------------------------------------------------------------*/
          227: void clear_kb(void)
          228: {
CH 09     229:     char junk[80];
CH 14     230:     gets(junk);
          231: }
```

ANALYSIS It appears that, as you learn about C, your programs grow larger. Although this program resembles the one presented after your first week of programming in C, it changes a few of the tasks and adds a few more. Like Week 1's review, you can enter up to 100 sets of information. The data entered is information about people. You should notice that this program can display the report while you enter information. With the other program, you couldn't print the report until you had finished entering the data.

You should also notice the addition of a structure used to save the data. The structure is defined on lines 24–32. Structures often are used to group similar data, as discussed on

Day 11, "Implementing Structures, Unions, and TypeDefs." This program groups all the data for each person into a structure named `record`. Much of this data should look familiar; however, a few new items are being tracked. Lines 25–27 contain three arrays, or strings, of characters to hold the first name, last name, and phone number. Notice that each of these strings is declared with a +1 in its array size. You should remember from Day 10, "Working with Characters and Strings," that this extra spot holds the character that signifies the end of a string.

This program demonstrates proper use of variable scope (see Day 12, "Understanding Variable Scope"). Lines 34 and 36 contain two global variables. Line 36 uses an `int` called `last_entry` to hold the number of people who have been entered. This is similar to the variable `ctr` used in Week 1 in Review. The other global variable is `list[MAX]`, an array of record structures. Local variables are used in each of the functions throughout the program. Of special note are the variables `month_total`, `grand_total`, `x`, and `y` on lines 157–159 in `display_report()`. In Week 1 in Review, these were global variables. Because these variables apply only to `display_report()`, they are better placed as local variables.

An additional program control statement, the `switch` statement (see Day 13, "Advanced Program Control"), is used on lines 70 through 81. Using a `switch` statement instead of several `if...else` statements makes the code easier to follow. Lines 72 through 79 execute various tasks based on a menu choice. Notice that the `default` statement is also included in case you enter a value that isn't a valid menu option.

Looking at the `get_data()` function, notice that there are some additional changes from Week 1 in Review. Lines 104 and 105 prompt for a string. Line 105 uses the `gets()` function (see Day 14, "Working with the Screen, Printer, and Keyboard") to accept a person's first name. The `gets()` function gets a string and places the value in `list[last_entry].fname`. You should remember from Day 11 that this places the first name into `fname`, a member of the structure list.

`display_report()` has been modified; it uses `fprintf()` instead of `printf()` to display the information. The reason for this change is simple. If you want the report to go to the printer instead of the screen, on each `fprintf()` statement, change `stdout` to `stdprn`. Day 14 covered `fprintf()`, `stdout`, and `stdprn`. Remember that `stdout` and `stdprn` are streams that output to the screen and the printer, respectively.

`continue_function()`, on lines 194 to 219, has also been modified. You now respond to the question with `Y` or `N` instead of `0` or `1`. This is more user-friendly. Also notice that the `clear_kb()` function from Listing 13.9 has been added on line 213 to remove any extra characters that the user entered. Additionally, the `fflush()` function is used to clear any characters that might have been left in the buffer.

Note You can replace lines 229 and 230 with fflush(stdin); and not change the program. You can't, however, replace all of the fflush() calls with clear_kb(). If you can't see why, you should review Day 14.

This program uses what you learned in your first two weeks of teaching yourself C. As you can see, many of the concepts from the second week make your C programs more functional and coding in C easier. Week 3 continues to build on these concepts.

WEEK 3

At a Glance

By now you have finished your second week of learning how to program in C. You should feel comfortable with C now, having touched on the most important areas of the language. There's more to learn, however, and it will be covered in this third week.

Where You're Going

In the third week, you'll complete your study of C. You'll learn some aspects of C that are new to you, as well as return to some topics from the first and second weeks to cover more advanced techniques.

After you complete the third week, you should have a thorough knowledge of C. Day 15, "Pointers: Beyond the Basics," tackles one of the hardest but most powerful parts of C—advanced pointer use. As on Day 9, "Understanding Pointers," you should dedicate a little extra time to the topics covered. Day 16, "Using Disk Files," covers a subject that is necessary for most applications—disk files. You will learn how to use disk files for data storage and retrieval. Day 17, "Manipulating Strings," discusses all the tools C provides for working with text. Day 18, "Getting More from Functions," explores some advanced aspects of C functions. Day 19, "Exploring the C Function Library," provides details on a variety of useful functions in the C library. Day 20, "Working with Memory," covers memory management in greater detail. Day 21, "Advanced Compiler Use," covers some odds and ends of C, explaining such issues as command-line arguments and preprocessor directives.

18

DAY 15

Pointers: Beyond the Basics

On Day 9, "Understanding Pointers," you were introduced to the basics of pointers, which are an important part of the C programming language. Today you'll go further, exploring some advanced pointer topics that can add flexibility to your programming. Today you will learn

- How to declare a pointer to a pointer
- How to use pointers with multidimensional arrays
- How to declare arrays of pointers
- How to declare pointers to functions
- How to use pointers to create linked lists for data storage

Declaring Pointers to Pointers

As you learned on Day 9, a *pointer* is a numeric variable with a value that is the address of another variable. You declare a pointer using the indirection operator (*). For example, the declaration

```
int *ptr;
```

declares a pointer named `ptr` that can point to a type `int` variable. You then use the address-of operator (&) to make the pointer point to a specific variable of the corresponding type. Assuming that `myVar` has been declared as a type `int` variable, the statement

```
ptr = &myVar;
```

assigns the address of `myVar` to `ptr` and makes `ptr` point to `myVar`. Again, using the indirection operator, you can access the pointed-to variable by using its pointer. Both of the following statements assign the value 12 to `myVar`:

```
myVar = 12;
*ptr = 12;
```

Because a pointer is itself a numeric variable, it is stored in your computer's memory at a particular address. Therefore, you can create a pointer to a pointer, a variable whose value is the address of a pointer. Here's how:

```
int myVar = 12;              /* myVar is a type int variable. */
int *ptr = &myVar;           /* ptr is a pointer to myVar. */
int **ptr_to_ptr = &ptr;     /* ptr_to_ptr is a pointer to a */
                             /* pointer to type int. */
```

Note the use of a double indirection operator (**) when declaring a pointer to a pointer. You also use the double indirection operator when accessing the pointed-to variable with a pointer to a pointer. Thus, the statement

```
**ptr_to_ptr = 12;
```

assigns the value 12 to the variable `myVar`, and the statement

```
printf("%d", **ptr_to_ptr);
```

displays the value of `myVar` on-screen. If you mistakenly use a single indirection operator, you get errors. The statement

```
*ptr_to_ptr = 12;
```

assigns the value 12 to `ptr`, which results in `ptr`'s pointing to whatever happens to be stored at address 12. This clearly is a mistake.

Declaring and using a pointer to a pointer is called *multiple indirection*. Figure 15.1 shows the relationship between a variable, a pointer, and a pointer to a pointer. There's really no limit to the level of multiple indirection possible—you can have a pointer to a pointer to a pointer *ad infinitum,* but there's rarely any advantage to going beyond two levels; the complexities involved are an invitation to mistakes.

FIGURE 15.1

A pointer to a pointer.

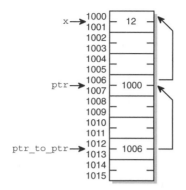

15

How can you use pointers to pointers? The most common use involves arrays of pointers, which are covered later in today's lesson. Listing 19.5 on Day 19, "Exploring the C Function Library," presents an example of using multiple indirection.

Pointers and Multidimensional Arrays

Day 8, "Using Numeric Arrays," covers the special relationship between pointers and arrays. Specifically, the name of an array without its following brackets is a pointer to the first element of the array. As a result, it's easier to use pointer notation when you're accessing certain types of arrays. These earlier examples, however, were limited to single-dimensional arrays. What about multidimensional arrays?

Remember that a multidimensional array is declared with one set of brackets for each dimension. For example, the following statement declares a two-dimensional array that contains eight type `int` variables:

```
int multi[2][4];
```

You can visualize an array as having a row and column structure—in this case, two rows and four columns. There's another way to visualize a multidimensional array, however, and this way is closer to the manner in which C actually handles arrays. You can consider `multi` to be a two-element array, with each of these two elements being an array of four integers.

In case this isn't clear to you, Figure 15.2 dissects the array declaration statement into its component parts.

Here's how to interpret the components of the declaration:

1. Declare an array named `multi`.

FIGURE 15.2

The components of a multidimensional array declaration.

2. The array `multi` contains two elements.

3. Each of these two elements contains four elements.

4. Each of the four elements is of type `int`.

You read a multidimensional array declaration starting with the array name and moving to the right, one set of brackets at a time. When the last set of brackets (the last dimension) has been read, you jump to the beginning of the declaration to determine the array's basic data type.

Under the array-of-arrays scheme, you can visualize a multidimensional array as shown in Figure 15.3.

FIGURE 15.3

A two-dimensional array can be visualized as an array of arrays.

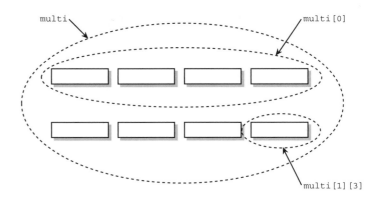

Now, let's get back to the topic of array names as pointers. (Today's lesson is about pointers, after all!) As with a one-dimensional array, the name of a multidimensional array is a pointer to the first array element. Continuing with our example, `multi` is a pointer to the first element of the two-dimensional array that was declared as `int multi[2][4]`. What exactly is the first element of `multi`? It isn't the type `int` variable `multi[0][0]`, as you might think. Remember that `multi` is an array of arrays, so its first element is `multi[0]`, which is an array of four type `int` variables (one of the two such arrays contained in `multi`).

Now, if `multi[0]` is also an array, does it point to anything? Yes, indeed! `multi[0]` points to its first element, `multi[0][0]`. You might wonder why `multi[0]` is a pointer.

Remember that the name of an array without brackets is a pointer to the first array element. The term `multi[0]` is the name of the array `multi[0][0]` with the last pair of brackets missing, so it qualifies as a pointer.

If you're a bit confused at this point, don't worry. This material is difficult to grasp. It might help if you remember the following rules for any array of *n* dimensions used in code:

- The array name followed by *n* pairs of brackets (each pair containing an appropriate index, of course) evaluates as array data (that is, the data stored in the specified array element).

- The array name followed by fewer than *n* pairs of brackets evaluates as a pointer to an array element.

In the example, therefore, `multi` evaluates as a pointer, `multi[0]` evaluates as a pointer, and `multi[0][0]` evaluates as array data.

Now look at what all these pointers actually point to. Listing 15.1 declares a two-dimensional array—similar to those you've been using in the examples—and then prints the values of the associated pointers. It also prints the address of the first array element.

INPUT | **LISTING 15.1**   multi.c. The relationship between a multidimensional array and pointers

```
1:    /* Demonstrates pointers and multidimensional arrays. */
2:
3:    #include <stdio.h>
4:
5:    int multi[2][4];
6:
7:    int main( void )
8:    {
9:        printf("\nmulti = %u", multi);
10:       printf("\nmulti[0] = %u", multi[0]);
11:       printf("\n&multi[0][0] = %u\n", &multi[0][0]);
12:
13:       return 0;
14:   }
```

OUTPUT
```
multi = 4206592
multi[0] = 4206592
&multi[0][0] = 4206592
```

ANALYSIS   The actual value might not be 4206592 on your system, but all three values will be the same. The address of the array `multi` is the same as the address of the array `multi[0]`, and both are equal to the address of the first integer in the array, `multi[0][0]`.

If all three of these pointers have the same value, what is the practical difference between them in terms of your program? Remember from Day 9 that the C compiler knows what a pointer points to. To be more exact, the compiler knows the size of the item a pointer is pointing to.

What are the sizes of the elements you've been using? Listing 15.2 uses the operator `sizeof()` to display the sizes, in bytes, of these elements.

INPUT   **LISTING 15.2**   multsize.c. Determining the sizes of elements

```
1:  /* Demonstrates the sizes of multidimensional array elements. */
2:
3:  #include <stdio.h>
4:
5:  int multi[2][4];
6:
7:  int main( void )
8:  {
9:      printf("\nThe size of multi = %u", sizeof(multi));
10:     printf("\nThe size of multi[0] = %u", sizeof(multi[0]));
11:     printf("\nThe size of multi[0][0] = %u\n", sizeof(multi[0][0]));
12:
13:     return 0;
14: }
```

The output of this program (assuming that your compiler uses four-byte integers) is as follows:

OUTPUT
```
The size of multi = 32
The size of multi[0] = 16
The size of multi[0][0] = 4
```

Note that on different machines the size values may be different.

ANALYSIS
```
The size of multi = 32
The size of multi[0] = 16
The size of multi[0][0] = 4
```

If you're running an a 32-bit operating system, your output will most likely be 32, 16, and 4. This is because a type `int` contains four bytes on these systems. On older 16-bit systems you may get the results of 16, 8, and 2.

Think about these size values. The array `multi` contains two arrays, each of which contains four integers. Each integer requires four bytes of storage. With a total of eight integers, the size of 32 bytes makes sense.

Next, `multi[0]` is an array containing four integers. Each integer takes four bytes, so the size of 16 bytes for `multi[0]` also makes sense.

Finally, `multi[0][0]` is an integer, so its size is, of course, four bytes.

Now, keeping these sizes in mind, recall the discussion on Day 9 about pointer arithmetic. The C compiler knows the size of the object being pointed to, and pointer arithmetic takes this size into account. When you increment a pointer, its value is increased by the amount needed to make it point to the "next" of whatever it's pointing to. In other words, it's incremented by the size of the object to which it points.

When you apply this to the example, `multi` is a pointer to a four-element integer array with a size of 16. If you increment `multi`, its value should increase by 16 (the size of a four-element integer array). If `multi` points to `multi[0]`, therefore, `(multi + 1)` should point to `multi[1]`. Listing 15.3 tests this theory.

INPUT   **LISTING 15.3**   multmath.c. Pointer arithmetic with multidimensional arrays

```
1:   /*  Demonstrates pointer arithmetic with pointers */
2:   /*  to multidimensional arrays. */
3:
4:   #include <stdio.h>
5:
6:   int multi[2][4];
7:
8:   int main( void )
9:   {
10:      printf("\nThe value of (multi) = %u", multi);
11:      printf("\nThe value of (multi + 1) = %u", (multi+1));
12:      printf("\nThe address of multi[1] = %u\n", &multi[1]);
13:
14:      return 0;
15:   }
```

OUTPUT
```
The value of (multi) = 4206592
The value of (multi + 1) = 4206608
The address of multi[1] = 4206608
```

ANALYSIS   The precise values might be different on your system, but the relationships are the same. Incrementing `multi` by one increases its value by 16 (or by eight on an older 16-bit system) and makes it point to the next element of the array, `multi[1]`.

In this example, you've seen that `multi` is a pointer to `multi[0]`. You've also seen that `multi[0]` is itself a pointer (to `multi[0][0]`). Therefore, `multi` is a pointer to a pointer. To use the expression `multi` to access array data, you must use double indirection. To print the value stored in `multi[0][0]`, you could use any of the following three statements:

```
printf("%d", multi[0][0]);
printf("%d", *multi[0]);
printf("%d", **multi);
```

These concepts apply equally to arrays with three or more dimensions. Thus, a three-dimensional array is an array with elements that are each a two-dimensional array; each of these elements is itself an array of one-dimensional arrays.

This material on multidimensional arrays and pointers might seem a bit confusing. When you work with multidimensional arrays, keep this point in mind: An array with n dimensions has elements that are arrays with n-1 dimensions. When n becomes 1, that array's elements are variables of the data type specified at the beginning of the array declaration line.

So far, you've been using array names that are pointer constants and that can't be changed. How would you declare a pointer variable that points to an element of a multidimensional array? Look at the previous example, which declared a two-dimensional array as follows:

```
int multi[2][4];
```

To declare a pointer variable ptr that can point to an element of multi (that is, can point to a four-element integer array), you write

```
int (*ptr)[4];
```

You then make ptr point to the first element of multi by writing

```
ptr = multi;
```

You might wonder why the parentheses are necessary in the pointer declaration. Brackets ([ ]) have a higher precedence than *. If you wrote

```
int *ptr[4];
```

you would be declaring an array of four pointers to type int. Indeed, you can declare and use arrays of pointers. This isn't what you want to do now, however.

How can you use pointers to elements of multidimensional arrays? As with single-dimensional arrays, pointers must be used to pass an array to a function. This is illustrated for a multidimensional array in Listing 15.4, which uses two methods of passing a multidimensional array to a function.

INPUT **LISTING 15.4** ptrmulti.c. Passing a multidimensional array to a function using a pointer

```
1:  /* Demonstrates passing a pointer to a multidimensional */
2:  /* array to a function. */
3:
```

LISTING 15.4   continued

```
 4:  #include <stdio.h>
 5:
 6:  void printarray_1(int (*ptr)[4]);
 7:  void printarray_2(int (*ptr)[4], int n);
 8:
 9:  int main( void )
10:  {
11:      int  multi[3][4] = { { 1, 2, 3, 4 },
12:                           { 5, 6, 7, 8 },
13:                           { 9, 10, 11, 12 } };
14:
15:      /* ptr is a pointer to an array of 4 ints. */
16:
17:      int (*ptr)[4], count;
18:
19:      /* Set ptr to point to the first element of multi. */
20:
21:      ptr = multi;
22:
23:      /* With each loop, ptr is incremented to point to the next */
24:      /* element (that is, the next 4-element integer array) of multi. */
25:
26:      for (count = 0; count < 3; count++)
27:          printarray_1(ptr++);
28:
29:      puts("\n\nPress Enter...");
30:      getchar();
31:      printarray_2(multi, 3);
32:      printf("\n");
33:      return 0;
34:  }
35:
36:  void printarray_1(int (*ptr)[4])
37:  {
38:  /* Prints the elements of a single four-element integer array. */
39:  /* p is a pointer to type int. You must use a type cast */
40:  /* to make p equal to the address in ptr. */
41:
42:      int *p, count;
43:      p = (int *)ptr;
44:
45:      for (count = 0; count < 4; count++)
46:          printf("\n%d", *p++);
47:  }
48:
49:  void printarray_2(int (*ptr)[4], int n)
50:  {
51:  /* Prints the elements of an n by four-element integer array. */
52:
```

LISTING **15.4**   continued

```
53:        int *p, count;
54:        p = (int *)ptr;
55:
56:        for (count = 0; count < (4 * n); count++)
57:            printf("\n%d", *p++);
58: }
```

OUTPUT
```
1
2
3
4
5
6
7
8
9
10
11
12

Press Enter...

1
2
3
4
5
6
7
8
9
10
11
12
```

ANALYSIS On lines 11 through 13, the program declares and initializes an array of integers, multi[3][4]. Lines 6 and 7 are the prototypes for the functions printarray_1() and printarray_2(), which print the contents of the array.

The function printarray_1() (lines 36 through 47) is passed only one argument, a pointer to an array of four integers. This function prints all four elements of the array. The first time main() calls printarray_1() on line 27, it passes a pointer to the first element (the first four-element integer array) in multi. It then calls the function two more times, incrementing the pointer each time to point to the second, and then to the third element of multi. After all three calls are made, the 12 integers in multi are displayed on-screen.

15

The second function, `printarray_2()`, takes a different approach. It too is passed a pointer to an array of four integers, but, in addition, it is passed an integer variable that specifies the number of elements (the number of arrays of four integers) that the multidimensional array contains. With a single call from line 31, `printarray_2()` displays the entire contents of `multi`.

Both functions use pointer notation to step through the individual integers in the array. The notation `(int *)ptr` in both functions (lines 43 and 54) might not be clear. The `(int *)` is a typecast, which temporarily changes the variable's data type from its declared data type to a new one. The typecast is required when assigning the value of `ptr` to `p` because they are pointers to different types (`p` is a pointer to type `int`, whereas `ptr` is a pointer to an array of four integers). C doesn't let you assign the value of one pointer to a pointer of a different type. The typecast tells the compiler, "For this statement only, treat `ptr` as a pointer to type `int`." Day 20, "Working with Memory," covers typecasts in more detail.

Do	Don't

DO remember to use the double indirection operator (`**`) when declaring a pointer to a pointer.
 	
DO remember that a pointer increments by the size of the pointer's type (usually what is being pointed to).
	DON'T forget to use parentheses when declaring pointers to arrays.
	
	To declare a pointer to an array of characters, use this format:
	
	`char (*letters)[26];`
	
	To declare an array of pointers to characters, use this format:
	
	`char *letters[26];`

Working with Arrays of Pointers

Recall from Day 8, "Using Numeric Arrays," that an array is a collection of data storage locations that have the same data type and are referred to by the same name. Because pointers are one of C's data types, you can declare and use arrays of pointers. This type of program construct can be very powerful in certain situations.

Perhaps the most common use of an array of pointers is with strings. A string, as you learned on Day 10, "Working with Characters and Strings," is a sequence of characters stored in memory. The start of the string is indicated by a pointer to the first character (a pointer to type `char`), and the end of the string is marked by a null character. By declaring and initializing an array of pointers to type `char`, you can access and manipulate a large number of strings using the pointer array. Each element in the array points to a different string, and by looping through the array, you can access each of them in turn.

Strings and Pointers: A Review

This is a good time to review some material from Day 10 regarding string allocation and initialization. One way to allocate and initialize a string is to declare an array of type char as follows:

```
char message[] = "This is the message.";
```

You could accomplish the same thing by declaring a pointer to type char:

```
char *message = "This is the message.";
```

Both declarations are equivalent. In each case, the compiler allocates enough space to hold the string along with its terminating null character, and the expression message is a pointer to the start of the string. But what about the following two declarations?

```
char message1[20];
char *message2;
```

The first line declares an array of type char that is 20 characters long, with message1 being a pointer to the first array position. Although the array space is allocated, it isn't initialized, and the array contents are undetermined. The second line declares message2, a pointer to type char. No storage space for a string is allocated by this statement—only space to hold the pointer. If you want to create a string and then have message2 point to it, you must allocate space for the string first. On Day 10, you learned how to use the malloc() memory allocation function for this purpose. Remember that any string must have space allocated for it, whether at compilation in a declaration or at runtime with malloc() or a related memory allocation function.

Declaring an Array of Pointers to Type char

Now that you're done with the review, how would you declare an array of pointers? The following statement declares an array of 10 pointers to type char:

```
char *message[10];
```

Each element of the array message[] is an individual pointer to type char. As you might have guessed, you can combine the declaration with initialization and allocation of storage space for the strings:

```
char *message[10] = { "one", "two", "three" };
```

This declaration does the following:

- It allocates a 10-element array named message; each element of message is a pointer to type char.
- It allocates space somewhere in memory (exactly where doesn't concern you) and stores the three initialization strings, each with a terminating null character.

15

- It initializes message[0] to point to the first character of the string "one", message[1] to point to the first character of the string "two", and message[2] to point to the first character of the string "three".

This is illustrated in Figure 15.4, which shows the relationship between the array of pointers and the strings. Note that in this example, the array elements message[3] through message[9] aren't initialized to point at anything.

FIGURE 15.4

An array of pointers to type char.

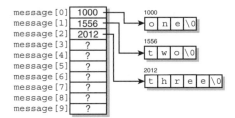

Now look at Listing 15.5, which is an example of using an array of pointers.

INPUT

LISTING 15.5 message.c. Initializing and using an array of pointers to type char

```
1:  /* Initializing an array of pointers to type char. */
2:
3:  #include <stdio.h>
4:
5:  int main( void )
6:  {
7:      char *message[8] = { "Four", "score", "and", "seven",
8:                           "years", "ago,", "our", "forefathers" };
9:      int count;
10:
11:     for (count = 0; count < 8; count++)
12:         printf("%s ", message[count]);
13:     printf("\n");
14:
15:     return 0;
16: }
```

OUTPUT Four score and seven years ago, our forefathers

ANALYSIS This program declares an array of eight pointers to type char and initializes them to point to eight strings (lines 7 and 8). It then uses a for loop on lines 11 and 12 to display each element of the array on-screen.

You probably can see how manipulating the array of pointers is easier than manipulating
the strings themselves. This advantage is obvious in more complicated programs, such as
the one presented later in today's lessons. As you'll see in that program, the advantage is
greatest when you're using functions. It's much easier to pass an array of pointers to a
function than to pass several strings. This can be illustrated by rewriting the program in
Listing 15.5 so that it uses a function to display the strings. The modified program is
shown in Listing 15.6.

INPUT   **LISTING 15.6**   message2.c. Passing an array of pointers to a function

```
1:   /* Passing an array of pointers to a function. */
2:
3:   #include <stdio.h>
4:
5:   void print_strings(char *p[], int n);
6:
7:   int main( void )
8:   {
9:       char *message[8] = { "Four", "score", "and", "seven",
10:                      "years", "ago,", "our", "forefathers" };
11:
12:      print_strings(message, 8);
13:      return 0;
14:  }
15:
16:  void print_strings(char *p[], int n)
17:  {
18:     int count;
19:
20:     for (count = 0; count < n; count++)
21:         printf("%s ", p[count]);
22:     printf("\n");
23:  }
```

OUTPUT   Four score and seven years ago, our forefathers

ANALYSIS   Looking at line 16, you see that the function print_strings() takes two arguments. One is an array of pointers to type char, and the other is the number of
elements in the array. Thus, print_strings() could be used to print the strings pointed
to by any array of pointers.

You might remember that, in the section on pointers to pointers, you were told that you
would see a demonstration later. Well, you've just seen it. Listing 15.6 declared an array
of pointers, and the name of the array is a pointer to its first element. When you pass that
array to a function, you're passing a pointer (the array name) to a pointer (the first array
element).

Pulling Things Together With an Example

Now it's time for a more complicated example. Listing 15.7 uses many of the programming skills you've learned, including arrays of pointers. This program accepts lines of input from the keyboard, allocating space for each line as it is entered and keeping track of the lines by means of an array of pointers to type char. When you signal the end of an entry by entering a blank line, the program sorts the strings alphabetically and displays them on-screen.

If you were writing this program from scratch, you would approach the design of this program from a structured programming perspective. First, make a list of the things the program must do:

1. Accept lines of input from the keyboard one at a time until a blank line is entered.
2. Sort the lines of text into alphabetical order.
3. Display the sorted lines on-screen.

This list suggests that the program should have at least three functions: one to accept input, one to sort the lines, and one to display the lines. Now you can design each function independently. What do you need the input function—called get_lines()—to do? Again, make a list:

1. Keep track of the number of lines entered, and return that value to the calling program after all lines have been entered.
2. Don't allow input of more than a preset maximum number of lines.
3. Allocate storage space for each line.
4. Keep track of all lines by storing pointers to strings in an array.
5. Return to the calling program when a blank line is entered.

Now think about the second function, the one that sorts the lines. It could be called sort(). (Really original, right?) The sort technique used is a simple, brute-force method that compares adjacent strings and swaps them if the second string is less than the first string. More exactly, the function compares the two strings whose pointers are adjacent in the array of pointers and swaps the two pointers if necessary.

To be sure that the sorting is complete, you must go through the array from start to finish, comparing each pair of strings and swapping if necessary. For an array of n elements, you must go through the array $n-1$ times. Why is this necessary?

Each time you go through the array, a given element can be shifted by, at most, one position. For example, if the string that should be first is actually in the last position, the first pass through the array moves it to the next-to-last position, the second pass through the array moves it up one more position, and so on. It requires *n*–1 passes to move it to the first position, where it belongs.

Note that this is a very inefficient and inelegant sorting method. However, it's easy to implement and understand, and it's more than adequate for the short lists that the sample program sorts.

The final function displays the sorted lines on-screen. It is, in effect, already written in Listing 15.6; and it requires only minor modification for use in Listing 15.7.

LISTING 15.7 sort.c. A program that reads lines of text from the keyboard, sorts them alphabetically, and displays the sorted list

INPUT

```
1:   /* Inputs a list of strings from the keyboard, sorts them, */
2:   /* and then displays them on the screen. */
3:   #include <stdlib.h>
4:   #include <stdio.h>
5:   #include <string.h>
6:
7:   #define MAXLINES 25
8:
9:   int get_lines(char *lines[]);
10:  void sort(char *p[], int n);
11:  void print_strings(char *p[], int n);
12:
13:  char *lines[MAXLINES];
14:
15:  int main( void )
16:  {
17:     int number_of_lines;
18:
19:     /* Read in the lines from the keyboard. */
20:
21:     number_of_lines = get_lines(lines);
22:
23:     if ( number_of_lines < 0 )
24:     {
25:        puts(" Memory allocation error");
26:        exit(-1);
27:     }
28:
29:     sort(lines, number_of_lines);
30:     print_strings(lines, number_of_lines);
31:     return 0;
32:  }
33:
34:  int get_lines(char *lines[])
35:  {
36:     int n = 0;
```

LISTING 15.7 continued

```
37:     char buffer[80];   /* Temporary storage for each line. */
38:
39:     puts("Enter one line at time; enter a blank when done.");
40:
41:     while ((n < MAXLINES) && (gets(buffer) != 0) &&
42:             (buffer[0] != '\0'))
43:     {
44:         if ((lines[n] = (char *)malloc(strlen(buffer)+1)) == NULL)
45:             return -1;
46:         strcpy( lines[n++], buffer );
47:     }
48:     return n;
49:
50: } /* End of get_lines() */
51:
52: void sort(char *p[], int n)
53: {
54:     int a, b;
55:     char *tmp;
56:
57:     for (a = 1; a < n; a++)
58:     {
59:         for (b = 0; b < n-1; b++)
60:         {
61:             if (strcmp(p[b], p[b+1]) > 0)
62:             {
63:                 tmp = p[b];
64:                 p[b] = p[b+1];
65:                 p[b+1] = tmp;
66:             }
67:         }
68:     }
69: }
70:
71: void print_strings(char *p[], int n)
72: {
73:     int count;
74:
75:     for (count = 0; count < n; count++)
76:         printf("%s\n", p[count]);
77: }
```

OUTPUT

```
Enter one line at time; enter a blank when done.
dog
apple
zoo
program
merry
```

```
apple
dog
merry
program
zoo
```

ANALYSIS It will be worthwhile for you to examine some of the details of this program. Several new library functions are used for various types of string manipulation. They are explained briefly here and in more detail on Day 17, "Manipulating Strings." The header file string.h must be included in a program that uses these functions.

In the get_lines() function, input is controlled by the while statement on lines 41 and 42, which read as follows (condensed here onto one line):

```
while ((n < MAXLINES) && (gets(buffer) != 0) && (buffer[0] != '\0'))
```

The condition tested by the while has three parts. The first part, n < MAXLINES, ensures that the maximum number of lines has not been input yet. The second part, gets(buffer) != 0, calls the gets() library function to read a line from the keyboard into buffer and verifies that end-of-file or some other error has not occurred. The third part, buffer[0] != '\0', verifies that the first character of the line just input is not the null character, which would signal that a blank line had been entered.

If any of these three conditions isn't satisfied, the while loop terminates, and execution returns to the calling program, with the number of lines entered as the return value. If all three conditions are satisfied, the following if statement on line 44 is executed:

```
if ((lines[n] = (char *)malloc(strlen(buffer)+1)) == NULL)
```

This statement calls malloc() to allocate space for the string that was just input. The strlen() function returns the length of the string passed as an argument; the value is incremented by 1 so that malloc() allocates space for the string plus its terminating null character. The (char *), just before malloc() on line 44, is a *typecast* that specifies the type of pointer to be returned by malloc(), in this case a pointer to type char. You'll learn more about typecasts on Day 20.

The library function malloc(), you might remember, returns a pointer. The statement assigns the value of the pointer returned by malloc() to the corresponding element of the array of pointers. If malloc() returns NULL, the if loop returns execution to the calling program with a return value of -1. The code in main() tests the return value of get_lines() and checks whether a value less than zero is returned; lines 23 through 27 report a memory allocation error and terminate the program.

If the memory allocation was successful, the program uses the strcpy() function on line 46 to copy the string from the temporary storage location buffer to the storage space just allocated by malloc(). The while loop then repeats, getting another line of input.

After execution returns from get_lines() to main(), the following has been accomplished (assuming that a memory allocation error didn't occur):

- A number of lines of text have been read from the keyboard and stored in memory as null-terminated strings.
- The array lines[] contains pointers to all the strings. The order of pointers in the array is the order in which the strings were input.
- The variable number_of_lines holds the number of lines that were input.

Now it's time to sort. Remember, you're not actually going to move the strings around, only the order of the pointers in the array lines[]. Look at the code in the function sort(). It contains one for loop nested inside another (lines 57 through 68). The outer loop executes number_of_lines - 1 times. Each time the outer loop executes, the inner loop steps through the array of pointers, comparing (string n) with (string n+1) for n = 0 to n = number_of_lines - 1. The comparison is performed by the library function strcmp() on line 61, which is passed pointers to two strings. The function strcmp() returns one of the following:

- A value greater than zero if the first string is greater than the second string.
- Zero if the two strings are identical.
- A value less than zero if the second string is greater than the first string.

In the program, a return value from strcmp() that is greater than zero means that the first string is "greater than" the second string, and they must be swapped (that is, their pointers in lines[] must be swapped). This is done using a temporary variable tmp. Lines 63 through 65 perform the swap.

When program execution returns from sort(), the pointers in lines[] are ordered properly: A pointer to the "lowest" string is in lines[0], a pointer to the "next-lowest" is in lines[1], and so on. Suppose, for example, that you entered the following five lines, in this order:

```
dog
apple
zoo
program
merry
```

The situation before calling sort() is illustrated in Figure 15.5, and the situation after the return from sort() is illustrated in Figure 15.6.

Finally, the program calls the function print_strings() to display the sorted list of strings on-screen. This function should be familiar to you from previous examples in this chapter.

FIGURE 15.5

Before sorting, the pointers are in the same order in which the strings were entered.

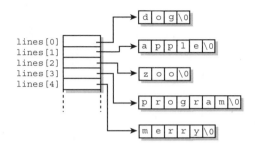

FIGURE 15.6

After sorting, the pointers are ordered according to the alphabetical order of the strings.

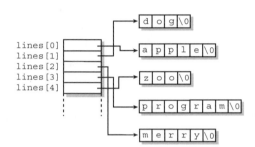

The program in Listing 15.7 is the most complex you have yet encountered in this book. It uses many of the C programming techniques that were covered in previous lessons. With the aid of the preceding explanation, you should be able to follow the program's operation and understand each step. If you find areas that are unclear to you, review the related sections of this book until you understand.

Working with Pointers to Functions

Pointers to functions provide another way of calling functions. "Hold on," you might be thinking. "How can you have a pointer to a function? Doesn't a pointer hold the address where a variable is stored?"

Well, yes and no. It's true that a pointer holds an address, but it doesn't have to be the address where a variable is stored. When your program runs, the code for each function is loaded into memory starting at a specific address. A pointer to a function holds the starting address of a function—its entry point.

Why use a pointer to a function? As I mentioned earlier, it provides a more flexible way of calling a function. It lets the program choose from among several functions, selecting the one that is appropriate for the current circumstances.

Declaring a Pointer to a Function

As with all C variables, you must declare a pointer to a function before using it. The general form of the declaration is as follows:

```
type (*ptr_to_func)(parameter_list);
```

This statement declares `ptr_to_func` as a pointer to a function that returns `type` and is passed the parameters in `parameter_list`. Here are some more concrete examples:

```
int (*func1)(int x);
```

```
void (*func2)(double y, double z);
```

```
char (*func3)(char *p[]);
```

```
void (*func4)();
```

The first line declares `func1` as a pointer to a function that takes one type `int` argument and returns a type `int`. The second line declares `func2` as a pointer to a function that takes two type `double` arguments and has a `void` return type (no return value). The third line declares `func3` as a pointer to a function that takes an array of pointers to type `char` as its argument and returns a type `char`. The final line declares `func4` as a pointer to a function that doesn't take any arguments and has a `void` return type.

Why do you need parentheses around the pointer name? Why can't you write, for the first example:

```
int *func1(int x);
```

The reason has to do with the precedence of the indirection operator, `*`. It has a relatively low precedence, lower than the parentheses surrounding the parameter list. The declaration just given, without the first set of parentheses, declares `func1` as a function that returns a pointer to type `int`. (Functions that return pointers are covered on Day 18, "Getting More from Functions.") When you declare a pointer to a function, always remember to include a set of parentheses around the pointer name and indirection operator, or you will get into trouble.

Initializing and Using a Pointer to a Function

A pointer to a function must not only be declared, but also initialized to point to something. That "something" is, of course, a function. There's nothing special about a function that gets pointed to. The only requirement is that its return type and parameter list match the return type and parameter list of the pointer declaration. For example, the following code declares and defines a function and a pointer to that function:

```
float square(float x);      // The function prototype.
float (*ptr)(float x);      // The pointer declaration.
float square(float x)       // The function definition.
{
  return x * x;
}
```

Because the function square() and the pointer ptr have the same parameter and return types, you can initialize ptr to point to square as follows:

```
ptr = square;
```

You can then call the function using the pointer as follows:

```
answer = ptr(x);
```

It's that simple. For a real example, compile and run Listing 15.8, which declares and initializes a pointer to a function and then calls the function twice, using the function name the first time and the pointer the second time. Both calls produce the same result.

INPUT   **LISTING 15.8**   ptr.c. Using a pointer to a function to call the function

```
1:  /* Demonstration of declaring and using a pointer to a function.*/
2:
3:  #include <stdio.h>
4:
5:  /* The function prototype. */
6:
7:  double square(double x);
8:
9:  /* The pointer declaration. */
10:
11: double (*ptr)(double x);
12:
13: int main( void )
14: {
15:     /* Initialize p to point to square(). */
16:
17:      ptr = square;
18:
19:     /* Call square() two ways. */
20:     printf("%f  %f\n", square(6.6), ptr(6.6));
21:     return 0;
22: }
23:
24: double square(double x)
25: {
26:     return x * x;
27: }
```

OUTPUT   43.560000   43.560000

Note

> Precision of the values might cause some numbers to not display as the
> exact values entered. For example, the correct answer, 43.56, might appear
> as 43.559999.

Line 7 declares the function `square()`, and line 11 declares the pointer `ptr` to a function containing a `double` argument and returning a `double` value, matching the declaration of `square()`. Line 17 sets the pointer `ptr` equal to `square`. Notice that parentheses aren't used with `square` or `ptr`. Line 20 prints the return values from calls to `square()` and `ptr()`.

A function name without parentheses is a pointer to the function (sounds similar to the situation with arrays, doesn't it?). What's the point of declaring and using a separate pointer to the function? Well, the function name itself is a pointer constant and can't be changed (again, a parallel to arrays). A pointer variable, in contrast, can be changed. Specifically, it can be made to point to different functions as the need arises.

Listing 15.9 calls a function, passing it an integer argument. Depending on the value of the argument, the function initializes a pointer to point to one of three other functions and then uses the pointer to call the corresponding function. Each of these three functions displays a specific message on-screen.

INPUT   **LISTING 15.9**   ptr2.c. Using a pointer to a function to call different functions depending on program circumstances

```
1:  /* Using a pointer to call different functions. */
2:
3:  #include <stdio.h>
4:
5:  /* The function prototypes. */
6:
7:  void func1(int x);
8:  void one(void);
9:  void two(void);
10: void other(void);
11:
12:   int main( void )
13: {
14:      int nbr;
15:
```

LISTING **15.9**   continued

```
16:     for (;;)
17:     {
18:         puts("\nEnter an integer between 1 and 10, 0 to exit: ");
19:         scanf("%d", &nbr);
20:
21:         if (nbr == 0)
22:             break;
23:         func1(nbr);
24:     }
25:     return 0;
26: }
27:
28: void func1(int val)
29: {
30:     /* The pointer to function. */
31:
32:     void (*ptr)(void);
33:
34:     if (val == 1)
35:         ptr = one;
36:     else if (val == 2)
37:         ptr = two;
38:     else
39:         ptr = other;
40:
41:     ptr();
42: }
43:
44: void one(void)
45: {
46:     puts("You entered 1.");
47: }
48:
49: void two(void)
50: {
51:     puts("You entered 2.");
52: }
53:
54: void other(void)
55: {
56:     puts("You entered something other than 1 or 2.");
57: }
```

INPUT/
OUTPUT

```
Enter an integer between 1 and 10, 0 to exit:
2
You entered 2.

Enter an integer between 1 and 10, 0 to exit:
9
```

```
You entered something other than 1 or 2.

Enter an integer between 1 and 10, 0 to exit:
0
```

ANALYSIS This program employs an infinite loop starting on line 16 to continue execution until a value of 0 is entered. When a nonzero value is entered, it's passed to func1(). Note that line 32, in func1(), contains a declaration for a pointer ptr to a function. Being declared within a function makes ptr local to func1(), which is appropriate because no other part of the program needs access to it. func1() then uses this value to set ptr equal to the appropriate function (lines 34 through 39). Line 41 then makes a single call to ptr(), which calls the appropriate function.

Of course, this program is for illustration purposes only. You could have easily accomplished the same result without using a pointer to a function.

Now you can learn another way to use pointers to call different functions: passing the pointer as an argument to a function. Listing 15.10 is a revision of Listing 15.9.

INPUT **LISTING 15.10** passptr.c. Passing a pointer to a function as an argument

```
1:  /* Passing a pointer to a function as an argument. */
2:
3:  #include <stdio.h>
4:
5:  /* The function prototypes. The function func1() takes as */
6:  /* its one argument a pointer to a function that takes no */
7:  /* arguments and has no return value. */
8:
9:  void func1(void (*p)(void));
10: void one(void);
11: void two(void);
12: void other(void);
13:
14: int main( void )
15: {
16:     /* The pointer to a function. */
18:     void (*ptr)(void);
19:     int nbr;
20:
21:     for (;;)
22:     {
23:         puts("\nEnter an integer between 1 and 10, 0 to exit: ");
24:         scanf("%d", &nbr);
25:
26:         if (nbr == 0)
27:             break;
28:         else if (nbr == 1)
```

LISTING 15.10   continued

```
29:             ptr = one;
30:         else if (nbr == 2)
31:             ptr = two;
32:         else
33:             ptr = other;
34:         func1(ptr);
35:     }
36:     return 0;
37: }
38:
39: void func1(void (*p)(void))
40: {
41:     p();
42: }
43:
44: void one(void)
45: {
46:     puts("You entered 1.");
47: }
48:
49: void two(void)
50: {
51:     puts("You entered 2.");
52: }
53:
54: void other(void)
55: {
56:     puts("You entered something other than 1 or 2.");
57: }
```

INPUT/
OUTPUT

```
Enter an integer between 1 and 10, 0 to exit:
2
You entered 2.

Enter an integer between 1 and 10, 0 to exit:
11
You entered something other than 1 or 2.

Enter an integer between 1 and 10, 0 to exit:
0
```

ANALYSIS   Notice the differences between Listing 15.9 and Listing 15.10. The declaration of the pointer to a function has been moved to line 18 in main(), where it is needed. Code in main() now initializes the pointer to point to the correct function, depending on the value the user entered (lines 26 through 33), and then passes the initialized pointer to func1(). func1() really serves no purpose in Listing 15.10; all it does is call the function pointed to by ptr. Again, this program is for illustration purposes. The same principles can be used in real-world programs, such as the example in the next section.

One programming situation in which you might use pointers to functions is one in which sorting is required. Sometimes you might want different sorting rules used. For example, you might want to sort in alphabetical order one time and in reverse alphabetical order another time. By using pointers to functions, your program can call the correct sorting function. More precisely, it's usually a different comparison function that's called.

Look back at Listing 15.7. In the sort() function, the actual sort order is determined by the value returned by the strcmp() library function, which tells the program whether a given string is "less than" or "greater than" another string. What if you wrote two comparison functions—one that sorts alphabetically (where A is less than Z), and another that sorts in reverse alphabetical order (where Z is less than A)? The program can ask the user what order he wants and, by using pointers, the sorting function can call the proper comparison function. Listing 15.11 modifies Listing 15.7 to incorporate this feature.

INPUT   **LISTING 15.11**   ptrsort.c. Using pointers to functions to control sort order

```
 1:  /* Inputs a list of strings from the keyboard, sorts them */
 2:  /* in ascending or descending order, and then displays them */
 3:  /* on the screen. */
 4:  #include <stdlib.h>
 5:  #include <stdio.h>
 6:  #include <string.h>
 7:
 8:  #define MAXLINES 25
 9:
10:  int get_lines(char *lines[]);
11:  void sort(char *p[], int n, int sort_type);
12:  void print_strings(char *p[], int n);
13:  int alpha(char *p1, char *p2);
14:  int reverse(char *p1, char *p2);
15:
16:  char *lines[MAXLINES];
17:
18:  int main( void )
19:  {
20:     int number_of_lines, sort_type;
21:
22:     /* Read in the lines from the keyboard. */
23:
24:     number_of_lines = get_lines(lines);
25:
26:     if ( number_of_lines < 0 )
27:     {
28:        puts("Memory allocation error");
29:        exit(-1);
30:     }
31:
```

LISTING **15.11**   continued

```
32:      puts("Enter 0 for reverse order sort, 1 for alphabetical:" );
33:      scanf("%d", &sort_type);
34:
35:      sort(lines, number_of_lines, sort_type);
36:      print_strings(lines, number_of_lines);
37:      return 0;
38:  }
39:
40:  int get_lines(char *lines[])
41:  {
42:      int n = 0;
43:      char buffer[80];  /* Temporary storage for each line. */
44:
45:      puts("Enter one line at time; enter a blank when done.");
46:
47:      while (n < MAXLINES && gets(buffer) != 0 && buffer[0] != '\0')
48:      {
49:          if ((lines[n] = (char *)malloc(strlen(buffer)+1)) == NULL)
50:          return -1;
51:          strcpy( lines[n++], buffer );
52:      }
53:      return n;
54:
55:  } /* End of get_lines() */
56:
57:  void sort(char *p[], int n, int sort_type)
58:  {
59:      int a, b;
60:       char *x;
61:
62:      /* The pointer to function.  */
63:
64:      int (*compare)(char *s1, char *s2);
65:
66:      /* Initialize the pointer to point to the proper comparison */
67:      /* function depending on the argument sort_type. */
68:
69:      compare = (sort_type) ? reverse : alpha;
70:
71:      for (a = 1; a < n; a++)
72:      {
73:          for (b = 0; b < n-1; b++)
74:          {
75:              if (compare(p[b], p[b+1]) > 0)
76:              {
77:                  x = p[b];
78:                  p[b] = p[b+1];
79:                  p[b+1] = x;
80:              }
```

LISTING 15.11   continued

```
81:          }
82:       }
83:  }  /* end of sort() */
84:
85:  void print_strings(char *p[], int n)
86:  {
87:      int count;
88:
89:      for (count = 0; count < n; count++)
90:          printf("%s\n", p[count]);
91:  }
92:
93:  int alpha(char *p1, char *p2)
94:  /* Alphabetical comparison. */
95:  {
96:      return(strcmp(p2, p1));
97:  }
98:
99:  int reverse(char *p1, char *p2)
100: /* Reverse alphabetical comparison. */
101: {
102:      return(strcmp(p1, p2));
103: }
```

**INPUT/
OUTPUT**

```
Enter one line at time; enter a blank when done.
Roses are red
Violets are blue
C has been around,
But it is new to you!

Enter 0 for reverse order sort, 1 for alphabetical:
0

Violets are blue
Roses are red
C has been around,
But it is new to you!
```

ANALYSIS   Lines 32 and 33 in main() prompt the user for the desired sort order. The value entered is placed in sort_type. This value is passed to the sort() function along with the other information described for Listing 15.7. The sort() function contains a couple of changes. Line 64 declares a pointer to a function called compare() that takes two character pointers (strings) as arguments. Line 69 sets compare() equal to one of the two new functions added to the listing based on the value of sort_type. The two new functions are alpha() and reverse(). alpha() uses the strcmp() library function just as it was used in Listing 15.7; reverse() does not. reverse() switches the parameters passed so that a reverse-order sort is done.

Do	**DON'T**

DO remember to use parentheses when declaring pointers to functions.
 	
Here's how you declare a pointer to a function that takes no arguments and returns a character:
 	
`char (*func)();`
 	
Here's how you declare a function that returns a pointer to a character:
 	
`char *func();`
	DON'T use a pointer without first initializing it.
	
	DON'T use a function pointer that has been declared with a different return type or different arguments than you need.

Bonus Section: Understanding Linked Lists

A *linked list* is a useful method of data storage that can easily be implemented in C. Why are we covering linked lists in a chapter on pointers? Because, as you will soon see, pointers are central to linked lists.

There are several kinds of linked lists, including single-linked lists, double-linked lists, and binary trees. Each type is suited for certain types of data storage. The one thing that these lists have in common is that the links between data items are defined by information that is contained in the items themselves, in the form of pointers. This is distinctly different from arrays, in which the links between data items result from the layout and storage of the array. This section explains the most fundamental kind of linked list: the single-linked list (which we refer to as simply a linked list).

Basics of Linked Lists

Each data item in a linked list is contained in a structure. (You learned about structures on Day 11, "Implementing Structures, Unions, and TypeDefs.") The structure contains the data elements needed to hold the data being stored; these depend on the needs of the specific program. In addition, there is one more data element—a pointer. This pointer provides the links in a linked list. Here's a simple example:

```
struct person {
char name[20];
struct person *next;
};
```

This code defines a structure named `person`. For the data, `person` contains only a 20-element array of characters. You generally wouldn't use a linked list for such simple data, but this will serve for an example. The `person` structure also contains a pointer to type

15

person—in other words, a pointer to another structure of the same type. This means that each structure of type `person` can not only contain a chunk of data, but also can point to another `person` structure. Figure 15.7 shows how this lets the structures be linked together in a list.

FIGURE 15.7

Links in a linked list.

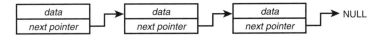

Notice that in Figure 15.7, each `person` structure points to the next `person` structure. The last `person` structure doesn't point to anything. The last element in a linked list is identified by the pointer element being assigned the value of NULL.

> **Note**
>
> The structures that make up a link in a linked list can be referred to as *links, nodes,* or *elements* of a linked list.

You have seen how the last link in a linked list is identified. What about the first link? This is identified by a special pointer (not a structure) called the *head pointer*. The head pointer always points to the first element in the linked list. The first element contains a pointer to the second element; the second element contains a pointer to the third, and so on, until you encounter an element whose pointer is NULL. If the entire list is empty (contains no links), the head pointer is set to NULL. Figure 15.8 illustrates the head pointer before the list is started and after the first list element is added.

FIGURE 15.8

A linked list's head pointer.

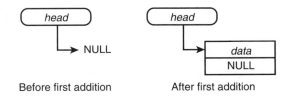

Before first addition   After first addition

> **Note**
>
> The *head pointer* is a pointer to the first element in a linked list. The head pointer is sometimes referred to as the first element pointer or top pointer.

Working with Linked Lists

When you're working with a linked list, you can add, delete, or modify elements or links. Modifying an element presents no real challenge; however, adding and deleting elements can. As we stated earlier, elements in a list are connected with pointers. Much of the work of adding and deleting elements consists of manipulating these pointers. Elements can be added to the beginning, middle, or end of a linked list; this determines how the pointers must be changed.

Later in today's lesson you'll find a simple linked list demonstration, as well as a more complex working program. Before getting into the nitty-gritty of code, however, it's a good idea to examine some of the actions you need to perform with linked lists. For these sections, we will continue using the person structure that was introduced earlier.

Preliminaries

Before you start a linked list, you must define the data structure that will be used for the list, and you also need to declare the head pointer. Because the list starts out empty, the head pointer should be initialized to NULL. You will also need an additional pointer to your list structure type for use in adding records. (You might need more than one pointer, as you'll soon see.) Here's how you do it:

```
struct person {
  char name[20];
  struct person *next;
};
struct person *new;
struct person *head;
head = NULL;
```

Adding an Element to the Beginning of a List

If the head pointer is NULL, the list is empty, and the new element will be its only member. If the head pointer is not NULL, the list already contains one or more elements. In either case, however, the procedure for adding a new element to the start of the list is the same:

1. Create an instance of your structure, allocating memory space using malloc().

2. Set the next pointer of the new element to the current value of the head pointer. This will be NULL if the list is empty, or the address of the current first element otherwise.

3. Make the head pointer point to the new element.

Here is the code to perform this task:

```
new = (person*)malloc(sizeof(struct person));
new->next = head;
head = new
```

Note that malloc() is typecast so that its return value is the proper type—a pointer to the person data structure.

It's important to switch the pointers in the correct order. If you reassign the head pointer first, you will lose the list!

Figure 15.9 illustrates the procedure for adding a new element to an empty list, and Figure 15.10 illustrates adding a new first element to an existing list.

FIGURE 15.9

Adding a new element to an empty linked list.

Before addition

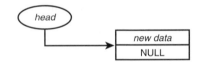

After addition

FIGURE 15.10

Adding a new first element to an existing list.

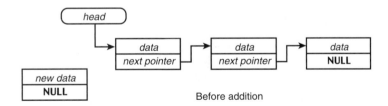

Before addition

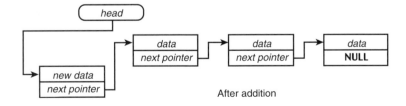

After addition

Notice that malloc() is used to allocate the memory for the new element. As each new element is added, only the memory needed for it is allocated. The calloc() function could also be used. You should be aware of the differences between these two functions. The main difference is that calloc() will initialize the new element; malloc() will not.

 Caution

In these code fragments, the return value of malloc() is not checked to ensure that the memory was successfully allocated. In a real program, you should always check the return value of a memory allocation function.

 Tip

You should always initialize pointers to NULL when you declare them. Never leave a pointer uninitialized. Doing so is just asking for trouble.

Adding an Element to the End of the List

To add an element to the end of a linked list, you start at the head pointer and go through the list until you find the last element. After you've found it, follow these steps:

1. Create an instance of your structure, allocating memory space using malloc().

2. Set the next pointer in the last element to point to the new element (whose address is returned by malloc()).

3. Set the next pointer in the new element to NULL to signal that it is the last item in the list.

Here is the code:

```
person *current;
...
current = head;
while (current->next != NULL)
    current = current->next;
new = (person*)malloc(sizeof(struct person));
current->next = new;
new->next = NULL;
```

Figure 15.11 illustrates the procedure for adding a new element to the end of a linked list.

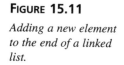

FIGURE 15.11

Adding a new element to the end of a linked list.

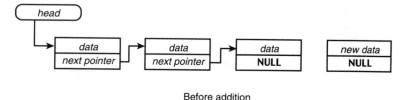

Before addition

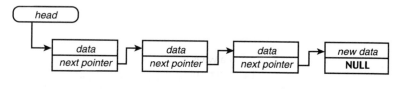

After addition

Adding an Element to the Middle of the List

When you're working with a linked list, most of the time you will be adding elements somewhere in the middle of the list. Exactly where the new element is placed depends on how you're keeping the list—for example, if it is sorted on one or more data elements. This process, then, requires that you first locate the position in the list where the new element will go, and then add it. Here are the steps to follow:

1. In the list, locate the existing element that the new element will be placed after. Let's call this the marker element.

2. Create an instance of your structure, allocating memory space using `malloc()`.

3. Set the next pointer of the marker element to point to the new element (whose address is returned by `malloc()`).

4. Set the next pointer of the new element to point to the element that the marker element used to point to.

Here's how the code might look:

```
person *marker;
/* Code here to set marker to point to the desired list location. */
...
new = (LINK)malloc(sizeof(PERSON));
new->next = marker->next;
marker->next = new;
```

Figure 15.12 illustrates this process.

FIGURE 15.12

Adding a new element to the middle of a linked list.

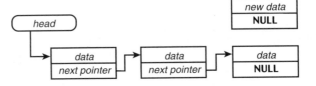

Before addition

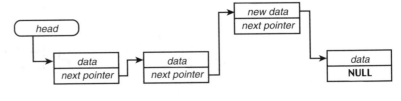

After addition

Deleting an Element from the List

Deleting an element from a linked list is a simple matter of manipulating pointers. The exact process depends on where in the list the element is located:

- To delete the first element, set the head pointer to point to the second element in the list.
- To delete the last element, set the next pointer of the next-to-last element to NULL.
- To delete any other element, set the next pointer of the element before the one being deleted to point to the element after the one being deleted.

In addition, the memory of the element that is removed from the list should be freed so the program does not claim more memory than it needs (this is called a *memory leak*). Freeing memory is done with the free() function, which is explained in detail on Day 20. Here's the code to delete the first element in a linked list:

```
free(head);
head = head->next;
```

This code deletes the last element in the list:

```
person *current1, *current2;
current1 = head;
current2= current1->next;
while (current2->next != NULL)
{
    current1 = current2;
```

```
        current2= current1->next;
}
free(current1->next);
current1->next = null;
if (head == current1)
    head = null;
```

Finally, the following code deletes an element from within the list:

```
person *current1, *current2;
/* Code goes here to have current1 point to the */
/* element just before the one to be deleted. */
current2 = current1->next;
free(current1->next);
current1->next = current2->next;
```

After any of these procedures, the deleted element still exists in memory, but it is removed from the list because there is no pointer in the list pointing to it. In a real-world program, you would want to reclaim the memory occupied by the deleted element. This is accomplished with the free() function. You'll learn about this function in detail on Day 20.

A Simple Linked List Demonstration

Listing 15.12 demonstrates the basics of using a linked list. This program is clearly for demonstration purposes only, because it doesn't accept user input and doesn't do anything useful other than show the code required for the most basic linked list tasks. The program does the following:

1. It defines a structure and the required pointers for the list.

2. It adds the first element to the list.

3. It adds an element to the end of the list.

4. It adds an element to the middle of the list.

5. It displays the list contents on-screen.

INPUT   **LISTING 15.12**   linkdemo.c. The basics of a linked list

```
1:  /* Demonstrates the fundamentals of using */
2:  /* a linked list. */
3:
4:  #include <stdlib.h>
5:  #include <stdio.h>
6:  #include <string.h>
7:
8:  /* The list data structure. */
9:  struct data {
```

LISTING **15.12**   continued

```
10:      char name[20];
11:      struct data *next;
12: };
13:
14: /* Define typedefs for the structure */
15: /* and a pointer to it. */
16: typedef struct data PERSON;
17: typedef PERSON *LINK;
18:
19: int main( void )
20: {
21:    /* Head, new, and current element pointers. */
22:    LINK head = NULL;
23:    LINK new = NULL;
24:    LINK current = NULL;
25:
26:    /* Add the first list element. We do not */
27:    /* assume the list is empty, although in */
28:    /* this demo program it always will be. */
29:
30:    new = (LINK)malloc(sizeof(PERSON));
31:    new->next = head;
32:    head = new;
33:    strcpy(new->name, "Abigail");
34:
35:    /* Add an element to the end of the list. */
36:    /* We assume the list contains at least one element. */
37:
38:    current = head;
39:    while (current->next != NULL)
40:    {
41:      current = current->next;
42:    }
43:
44:    new = (LINK)malloc(sizeof(PERSON));
45:    current->next = new;
46:    new->next = NULL;
47:    strcpy(new->name, "Carolyn");
48:
49:    /* Add a new element at the second position in the list. */
50:    new = (LINK)malloc(sizeof(PERSON));
51:    new->next = head->next;
52:    head->next = new;
53:    strcpy(new->name, "Beatrice");
54:
55:    /* Print all data items in order. */
56:    current = head;
57:    while (current != NULL)
58:    {
```

LISTING 15.12 continued

```
59:     printf("\n%s", current->name);
60:     current = current->next;
61:   }
62:
63:   printf("\n");
64:
65:   return 0;
66: }
```

OUTPUT

```
Abigail
Beatrice
Carolyn
```

ANALYSIS   You can probably figure out at least some of the code. Lines 9 through 12 declare the data structure for the list. Lines 16 and 17 define typedefs for both the data structure and for a pointer to the data structure. Strictly speaking, this isn't necessary, but it simplifies coding by enabling you to write PERSON in place of struct data and LINK in place of struct data *.

Lines 22 through 24 declare a head pointer and a couple of other pointers that will be used when manipulating the list. All of these pointers are initialized to NULL.

Lines 30 through 33 add a new link to the start of the list. Line 30 allocates a new data structure. Note that the successful operation of malloc() is assumed—something you would never do in a real program!

Line 31 sets the next pointer in this new structure to point to whatever the head pointer contains. Why not simply assign NULL to this pointer? That works only if you know that the list is empty. As it is written, the code will work even if the list already contains some elements. The new first element will end up pointing to the element that used to be first, which is just what you want.

Line 32 makes the head pointer point to the new record, and line 33 stores some data in the record.

Adding an element to the end of the list is a bit more complicated. Although in this case you know that the list contains only one element, you can't assume this in a real program. Therefore, it's necessary to loop through the list, starting with the first element, until you find the last element (as indicated by the next pointer's being NULL). Then you know you have found the end of the list. This task is accomplished in lines 38 through 42. After you have found the last element, it is a simple matter to allocate a new data structure, have the old last element point to it, and set the new element's next pointer to NULL, because it is now the last element in the list. This is done in lines 44 through 47.

Note that the return type from malloc() is typecast to be type LINK (you learn more about typecasts on Day 20).

The next task is to add an element to the middle of the list—in this case, at the second position. After a new data structure is allocated (line 50), the new element's next pointer is set to point to the element that used to be second and is now third in the list (line 51), and the first element's next pointer is made to point to the new element (line 52).

Finally, the program prints all the records in the linked list. This is a simple matter of starting with the element that the head pointer points to and then progressing through the list until the last list element is found, as indicated by a NULL pointer. Lines 56 through 61 perform this task.

Implementing a Linked List

Now that you have seen the ways to add links to a list, it's time to see them in action. Listing 15.13 is a rather long program that uses a linked list to hold a list of five characters. The characters are stored in memory using a linked list. These characters just as easily could have been names, addresses, or any other data. To keep the example as simple as possible, only a single character is stored in each link.

What makes this linked list program complicated is the fact that it sorts the links as they are added. Of course, this also is what makes this program so valuable. Each link is added to the beginning, middle, or end, depending on its value. The link is always sorted. If you were to write a program that simply added the links to the end, the logic would be much simpler. However, the program also would be less useful.

INPUT   **LISTING 15.13**   linklist.c. Implementing a linked list of characters

```
 1:  /*=========================================================*
 2:   * Program:  listlist.c                                    *
 3:   * Book:     Sams Teach Yourself C in 21 Days              *
 4:   * Purpose:  Implementing a linked list                    *
 5:   *=========================================================*/
 6:  #include <stdio.h>
 7:  #include <stdlib.h>
 8:
 9:  #ifndef NULL
10:     #define NULL 0
11:  #endif
12:
13:  /* List data structure */
14:  struct list
15:  {
16:     int    ch;      /* using an int to hold a char */
```

LISTING 15.13 continued

15

```
17:    struct list *next_rec;
18: };
19:
20: /* Typedefs for the structure and pointer. */
21: typedef struct list LIST;
22: typedef LIST *LISTPTR;
23:
24: /* Function prototypes. */
25: LISTPTR add_to_list( int, LISTPTR );
26: void show_list(LISTPTR);
27: void free_memory_list(LISTPTR);
28:
29: int main( void )
30: {
31:    LISTPTR first = NULL;   /* head pointer */
32:    int i = 0;
33:    int ch;
34:    char trash[256];        /* to clear stdin buffer. */
35:
36:    while ( i++ < 5 )       /* build a list based on 5 items given */
37:    {
38:       ch = 0;
39:       printf("\nEnter character %d, ", i);
40:
41:       do
42:       {
43:           printf("\nMust be a to z: ");
44:           ch = getc(stdin);  /* get next char in buffer  */
45:           gets(trash);       /* remove trash from buffer */
46:       } while( (ch < 'a' || ch > 'z') && (ch < 'A' || ch > 'Z'));
47:
48:       first = add_to_list( ch, first );
49:    }
50:
51:    show_list( first );            /* Dumps the entire list */
52:    free_memory_list( first );     /* Release all memory */
53:    return 0;
54: }
55:
56: /*=========================================================*
57:  * Function: add_to_list()
58:  * Purpose : Inserts new link in the list
59:  * Entry   : int ch = character to store
60:  *           LISTPTR first = address of original head pointer
61:  * Returns : Address of head pointer (first)
62:  *=========================================================*/
63:
64: LISTPTR add_to_list( int ch, LISTPTR first )
65: {
```

LISTING 15.13   continued

```
66:     LISTPTR new_rec = NULL;        /* Holds address of new rec */
67:     LISTPTR tmp_rec = NULL;        /* Hold tmp pointer         */
68:     LISTPTR prev_rec = NULL;
69:
70:     /* Allocate memory. */
71:     new_rec = (LISTPTR)malloc(sizeof(LIST));
72:     if (!new_rec)       /* Unable to allocate memory */
73:     {
74:         printf("\nUnable to allocate memory!\n");
75:         exit(1);
76:     }
77:
78:     /* set new link's data */
79:     new_rec->ch = ch;
80:     new_rec->next_rec = NULL;
81:
82:     if (first == NULL)    /* adding first link to list */
83:     {
84:         first = new_rec;
85:         new_rec->next_rec = NULL;  /* redundant but safe */
86:     }
87:     else    /* not first record */
88:     {
89:         /* see if it goes before the first link */
90:         if ( new_rec->ch < first->ch)
91:         {
92:             new_rec->next_rec = first;
93:             first = new_rec;
94:         }
95:         else   /* it is being added to the middle or end */
96:         {
97:             tmp_rec = first->next_rec;
98:             prev_rec = first;
99:
100:            /* Check to see where link is added. */
101:
102:            if ( tmp_rec == NULL )
103:            {
104:                /* we are adding second record to end */
105:                prev_rec->next_rec = new_rec;
106:            }
107:            else
108:            {
109:                /* check to see if adding in middle */
110:                while (( tmp_rec->next_rec != NULL))
111:                {
112:                    if( new_rec->ch < tmp_rec->ch )
113:                    {
114:                        new_rec->next_rec = tmp_rec;
```

LISTING 15.13   continued

```
115:                        if (new_rec->next_rec != prev_rec->next_rec)
116:                        {
117:                            printf("ERROR");
118:                            getc(stdin);
119:                            exit(0);
120:                        }
121:                        prev_rec->next_rec = new_rec;
122:                        break;   /* link is added; exit while */
123:                    }
124:                    else
125:                    {
126:                      tmp_rec = tmp_rec->next_rec;
127:                      prev_rec = prev_rec->next_rec;
128:                    }
129:                }
130:
131:                /* check to see if adding to the end */
132:                if (tmp_rec->next_rec == NULL)
133:                {
134:                   if (new_rec->ch < tmp_rec->ch ) /* 1 b4 end */
135:                   {
136:                      new_rec->next_rec = tmp_rec;
137:                      prev_rec->next_rec = new_rec;
138:                   }
139:                   else  /* at the end */
140:                   {
141:                      tmp_rec->next_rec = new_rec;
142:                      new_rec->next_rec = NULL;  /* redundant */
143:                   }
144:               }
145:            }
146:        }
147:    }
148:    return(first);
149: }
150:
151: /*========================================================*
152:  * Function: show_list
153:  * Purpose : Displays the information current in the list
154:  *========================================================*/
155:
156: void show_list( LISTPTR first )
157: {
158:    LISTPTR cur_ptr;
159:    int counter = 1;
160:
161:    printf("\n\nRec addr  Position  Data  Next Rec addr\n");
162:    printf("========  ========  ====  =============\n");
163:
```

LISTING 15.13   continued

```
164:    cur_ptr = first;
165:    while (cur_ptr != NULL )
166:    {
167:       printf("  %X   ", cur_ptr );
168:       printf("     %2i      %c", counter++, cur_ptr->ch);
169:       printf("     %X  \n",cur_ptr->next_rec);
170:       cur_ptr = cur_ptr->next_rec;
171:    }
172: }
173:
174: /*========================================================*
175:  * Function: free_memory_list
176:  * Purpose : Frees up all the memory collected for list
177:  *========================================================*/
178:
179: void free_memory_list(LISTPTR first)
180: {
181:    LISTPTR cur_ptr, next_rec;
182:    cur_ptr = first;                 /* Start at beginning */
183:
184:    while (cur_ptr != NULL)          /* Go while not end of list */
185:    {
186:       next_rec = cur_ptr->next_rec; /* Get address of next record */
187:       free(cur_ptr);                /* Free current record */
188:       cur_ptr = next_rec;           /* Adjust current record*/
189:    }
190: }
```

INPUT/
OUTPUT

Enter character 1,
Must be a to z: **q**

Enter character 2,
Must be a to z: **b**

Enter character 3,
Must be a to z: **z**

Enter character 4,
Must be a to z: **c**

Enter character 5,
Must be a to z: **a**

Rec addr	Position	Data	Next Rec addr
==========	==========	======	===============
2224A0	1	a	222470
222470	2	b	222490

```
222490        3       c       222450
222450        4       q       222480
222480        5       z       0
```

Note   Your output will probably show different address values.

ANALYSIS   This program demonstrates adding a link to a linked list. It isn't the easiest listing to understand; however, if you walk through it, you'll see that it's a combination of the three methods of adding links that were discussed earlier. This listing can be
used to add links to the beginning, middle, or end of a linked list. Additionally, this listing takes into consideration the special cases of adding the first link (the one that gets
added to the beginning) and the second link (the one that gets added to the middle).

Tip   The easiest way to fully understand this listing is to step through it line-by-
line in your compiler's debugger and to read the following analysis. By seeing the logic executed, you will better understand the listing.

Several items at the beginning of Listing 15.13 should be familiar or easy to understand.
Lines 9 through 11 check to see whether the value of NULL is already defined. If it isn't,
line 10 defines it to be 0. Lines 14 through 22 define the structure for the linked list and
also declare the type definitions to make working with the structure and pointers easier.

The main() function should be easy to follow. A head pointer called first is declared in
line 31. Notice that this is initialized to NULL. Remember that you should never let a
pointer go uninitialized. Lines 36 through 49 contain a while loop that is used to get five
characters from the user. Within this outer while loop, which repeats five times, a
do...while is used to ensure that each character entered is a letter. The isalpha() function could have been used just as easily.

After a piece of data is obtained, add_to_list() is called. The pointer to the beginning
of the list and the data being added to the list are passed to the function.

The main() function ends by calling show_list() to display the list's data and then
free_memory_list() to release all the memory that was allocated to hold the links in the
list. Both these functions operate in a similar manner. Each starts at the beginning of the
linked list using the head pointer first. A while loop is used to go from one link to the
next using the next_ptr value. When next_ptr is equal to NULL, the end of the linked
list has been reached, and the functions return.

The most important (and most complicated!) function in this listing is add_to_list() in lines 56 through 149. Lines 66 through 68 declare three pointers that will be used to point to three different links. The new_rec pointer will point to the new link that is to be added. The tmp_rec pointer will point to the current link in the list being evaluated. If there is more than one link in the list, the prev_rec pointer will be used to point to the previous link that was evaluated.

Line 71 allocates memory for the new link that is being added. The new_rec pointer is set to the value returned by malloc(). If the memory can't be allocated, lines 74 and 75 print an error message and exit the program. If the memory is allocated successfully, the program continues.

Line 79 sets the data in the structure to the data passed to this function. This simply consists of assigning the character passed to the function ch to the new record's character field (new_rec->ch). In a more complex program, this could entail the assigning of several fields. Line 80 sets the next_rec in the new record to NULL so that it doesn't point to some random location.

Line 82 starts the "add a link" logic by checking to see whether there are any links in the list. If the link being added is the first link in the list, as indicated by the head pointer first being NULL, the head pointer is simply set equal to the new pointer, and you're done.

If this link isn't the first, the function continues within the else at line 87. Line 90 checks to see whether the new link goes at the beginning of the list. As you should remember, this is one of the three cases for adding a link. If the link does go first, line 92 sets the next_rec pointer in the new link to point to the previous "first" link. Line 93 then sets the head pointer, first, to point to the new link. This results in the new link's being added to the beginning of the list.

If the new link isn't the first link to be added to an empty list, and if it's being added at the first position in an existing list, you know it must be in the middle or at the end of the list. Lines 97 and 98 set up the tmp_rec and prev_rec pointers that were declared earlier. The pointer tmp_rec is set to the address of the second link in the list, and prev_rec is set to the first link in the list.

You should note that if there is only one link in the list, tmp_rec will be equal to NULL. This is because tmp_rec is set to the next_ptr in the first link, which will be equal to NULL. Line 102 checks for this special case. If tmp_rec is NULL, you know that this is the second link being added to the list. Because you know the new link doesn't come before the first link, it can only go at the end. To accomplish this, you simply set prev_rec->next_ptr to the new link, and then you're done.

If the `tmp_rec` pointer isn't NULL, you know that you already have more than two links in your list. The `while` statement in lines 110 through 129 loops through the rest of the links to determine where the new link should be placed. Line 112 checks to see whether the new link's data value is less than the link currently being pointed to. If it is, you know this is where you want to add the link. If the new data is greater than the current link's data, you need to look at the next link in the list. Lines 126 and 127 set the pointers `tmp_rec` and `next_rec` to the next links.

If the character is "less than" the current link's character, you would follow the logic presented earlier in this chapter for adding to the middle of a linked list. This process can be seen in lines 114 through 122. In line 114, the new link's next pointer is set to equal the current link's address (`tmp_rec`). Line 121 sets the previous link's next pointer to point to the new link. After this, you're done. The code uses a `break` statement to get out of the `while` loop.

Note

Lines 115 through 120 contain debugging code that was left in the listing for you to see. These lines could be removed; however, as long as the program is running correctly, they will never be called. After the new link's next pointer is set to the current pointer, it should be equal to the previous link's next pointer, which also points to the current record. If they aren't equal, something went wrong!

The previously covered logic takes care of links being added to the middle of the list. If the end of the list is reached, the `while` loop in lines 110 through 129 will end without adding the link. Lines 132 through 144 take care of adding the link to the end.

If the last link in the list was reached, `tmp_rec->next_rec` will equal NULL. Line 132 checks for this condition. Line 134 checks to see whether the link goes before or after the last link. If it goes after the last link, the last link's `next_rec` is set to the new link (line 132), and the new link's next pointer is set to NULL (line 142).

Improving Listing 15.13

Linked lists are not the easiest thing to learn. As you can see from Listing 15.13, however, they are an excellent way of storing data in a sorted order. Because it's easy to add new data items anywhere in a linked list, the code for keeping a list of data items in sorted order with a linked list is a lot simpler that it would be if you used, say, an array. This listing could easily be converted to sort names, phone numbers, or any other data. Additionally, although this listing sorted in ascending order (A to Z), it just as easily could have sorted in descending order (Z to A).

Deleting from a Linked List

The capability to add information to a linked list is essential, but there will be times when you will want to remove information too. Deleting links, or elements, is similar to adding them. You can delete links from the beginning, middle, or end of linked lists. In each case, the appropriate pointers need to be adjusted. Also, the memory used by the deleted link needs to be freed.

 Note   Don't forget to free memory when deleting links!

Do	Don't
DO understand the difference between `calloc()` and `malloc()`. Most important, remember that `malloc()` doesn't initialize allocated memory—`calloc()` does.	**DON'T** forget to free any memory allocated for links when deleting them.

Summary

Today's lesson covered some of the advanced uses of pointers. As you probably realize by now, pointers are a central part of the C language. C programs that don't use pointers are rare. You saw how to use pointers to pointers and how arrays of pointers can be very useful when dealing with strings. You also learned how C treats multidimensional arrays as arrays of arrays, and you saw how to use pointers with such arrays. You learned how to declare and use pointers to functions, an important and flexible programming tool. Finally, you learned how to implement linked lists, a powerful and flexible data storage method.

This has been a long and involved lesson. Although some of its topics are a bit complicated, they're exciting as well. With this chapter, you're really getting into some of the sophisticated capabilities of the C language. Power and flexibility are among the main reasons C is such a popular language.

Q&A

Q How many levels deep can I go with pointers to pointers?

A You need to check your compiler manuals to determine whether there are any limitations. There is rarely any reason to go more than three levels deep with pointers (pointers to pointers to pointers). Most programs rarely go over two levels.

Q Is there a difference between a pointer to a string and a pointer to an array of characters?

A No. A string can be considered an array of characters.

Q Is it necessary to use the concepts presented in today's lesson to take advantage of C?

A You can use C without ever using any advanced pointer concepts; however, you won't take advantage of the power that C offers. Pointer manipulations such as those shown in today's lesson can make many programming tasks easier and more efficient.

Q Are there other times when function pointers are useful?

A Yes. Pointers to functions also are used with menus. Based on a value returned from a menu, a pointer is set to the function that should be called based on the menu choice.

Q Name two major advantages of linked lists.

A One: The size of a linked list can be increased or decreased while the program is running; it doesn't have to be predefined when you write the code. Two: It's easy to keep a linked list in sorted order, because elements can easily be added or deleted anywhere in the list.

Workshop

The Workshop provides quiz questions to help you solidify your understanding of the material covered and exercises to provide you with experience in using what you've learned.

Quiz

1. Write code that declares a type `float` variable, declares and initializes a pointer to the variable, and declares and initializes a pointer to the pointer.

2. Continuing with the example in question 1, say that you want to use the pointer to a pointer to assign the value `100` to the variable `x`. What, if anything, is wrong with the following assignment statement?

   ```
   *ppx = 100;
   ```

   If it isn't correct, how should it be written?

3. Assume that you have declared an array as follows:

   ```
   int array[2][3][4];
   ```

   What is the structure of this array, as seen by the C compiler?

4. Continuing with the array declared in question 3, what does the expression
   `array[0][0]` mean?

5. Again using the array from question 3, which of the following comparisons is true?

   ```
   array[0][0] == &array[0][0][0];
   array[0][1] == array[0][0][1];
   array[0][1] == &array[0][1][0];
   ```

6. Write the prototype for a function that takes an array of pointers to type `char` as its
   one argument and returns `void`.

7. How would the function that you wrote a prototype for in question 6 know how
   many elements are in the array of pointers passed to it?

8. What is a pointer to a function?

9. Write a declaration of a pointer to a function that returns a type `char` and takes an
   array of pointers to type `char` as an argument.

10. You might have answered question 9 with

    ```
    char *ptr(char *x[]);
    ```

    What is wrong with this declaration?

11. When defining a data structure to be used in a linked list, what is the one element
    that must be included?

12. What does it mean if the head pointer is equal to `NULL`?

13. How are single-linked lists connected?

14. What do the following declare?

    a. `int *var1;`

    b. `int var2;`

    c. `int **var3;`

15. What do the following declare?

    a. `int a[3][12];`

    b. `int (*b)[12];`

    c. `int *c[12];`

16. What do the following declare?

    a. `char *z[10];`

    b. `char *y(int field);`

    c. `char (*x)(int field);`

Exercises

1. Write a declaration for a pointer to a function that takes an integer as an argument and returns a type float variable.

2. Write a declaration for an array of pointers to functions. The functions should all take a character string as a parameter and return an integer. What could such an array be used for?

3. Write a statement to declare an array of 10 pointers to type char.

4. **BUG BUSTER:** Is anything wrong with the following code?

```
int x[3][12];
int *ptr[12];
ptr = x;
```

5. Write a structure that is to be used in a single-linked list. This structure should hold your friends' names and addresses.

Because of the many possible solutions, answers are not provided for the following exercises.

6. **ON YOUR OWN:** Write a program that declares a 12[ts]12 array of characters. Place X's in every other element. Use a pointer to the array to print the values to the screen in a grid format.

7. **ON YOUR OWN:** Write a program that uses pointers to type double variables to accept 10 numbers from the user, sort them, and print them to the screen. (Hint: See Listing 15.10.)

8. **ON YOUR OWN:** Modify the program in exercise 7 to allow the user to specify whether the sort order is ascending or descending.

15

DAY 16

Using Disk Files

Most of the programs you write will use files written to a hard drive. These files will contain information that will serve one purpose or another: data storage, configuration information, and so on. Today you will learn

- How to relate streams to disk files
- About C's two disk file types
- The commands for opening a file
- How to write data to a file
- Reading data from a file
- When to close a file
- Disk file management
- Using temporary files

Relating Streams to Disk Files

As you learned on Day 14, "Working with the Screen, Printer, and Keyboard," C performs all input and output, including disk files, by means of streams. You saw how to use C's predefined streams that are connected to specific devices such as the keyboard, screen, and (on some systems) the printer. Disk file streams work essentially the same way. This is one of the advantages of stream input/output—techniques for using one stream can be used with little or no change for other streams. The major difference with disk file streams is that your program must explicitly create a stream associated with a specific disk file.

Understanding the Types of Disk Files

On Day 14, you saw that C streams come in two flavors: text and binary. You can associate either type of stream with a file, and it's important that you understand the distinction in order to use the proper mode for your files.

Text streams are associated with text-mode files. Text-mode files consist of a sequence of lines. Each line contains zero or more characters and ends with one or more characters that mark the end of the line. It's important to remember that a "line" in a text-mode file is not the same as a C string; there is no terminating NULL character (\0). When you use a text-mode stream, translation occurs between C's newline character (\n) and whatever character or characters the operating system uses to mark end-of-line in disk files. On DOS systems or in Microsoft Windows console, it's a carriage-return linefeed (CR-LF) combination. When data is written to a text-mode file, each \n is translated to a CR-LF; when data is read from a disk file, each CR-LF is translated to a \n. On UNIX systems, no translation is done—newline characters remain unchanged.

Binary streams are associated with binary-mode files. Any and all data is written and read unchanged, with no separation into lines and no use of end-of-line characters. The NULL and end-of-line characters have no special significance and are treated like any other byte of data.

Some file input/output functions are restricted to one file mode, whereas other functions can use either mode. Today's lesson teaches you which mode to use with which functions.

Using Filenames

Every disk file has a name, and you must use filenames when dealing with disk files. Filenames are stored as strings, just like other text data. The rules that establish what is acceptable for filenames (and what is not) differ from one operating system to another. In DOS and Windows 3.x, a complete filename consists of a name that has from one to eight characters, optionally followed by a period and an extension that has from one to three characters. In contrast, the Microsoft Windows 95 and later versions of Microsoft

Windows (including NT, XP, and .NET), as well as most UNIX systems, permit file-names up to 256 characters long.

Operating systems also differ in the characters that are permitted in filenames. In Windows 95/98, for example, the following characters are not permitted:

```
/ \ : * ? " < > |
```

You must be aware of the filename rules of whichever operating system you're writing for.

A filename in a C program also can contain path information. The *path* specifies the drive and/or directory (or folder) where the file is located. If you specify a filename with-out a path, it will be assumed that the file is located at whatever location the operating system currently designates as the default. It's good programming practice to always specify path information as part of your filenames.

Tip

If the path isn't specified for a file, it is recommended that you assume the file is in the same directory as the program being executed. You may want to include programming logic to include the path of the current program.

On PCs, the backslash character is used to separate directory names in a path. For exam-ple, in DOS and Microsoft Windows, the name

```
c:\data\list.txt
```

refers to a file named list.txt in the directory \DATA on drive C. Remember that the back-slash character has a special meaning to C when it's in a string. To represent the back-slash character itself, you must precede it with another backslash. Thus, in a C program, you would represent the filename as follows:

```
char *filename = "c:\\data\\list.txt";
```

However, if when running a program, you enter a filename using the keyboard, enter only a single backslash.

Not all systems use the backslash as the directory separator. For example, UNIX uses the forward slash (/).

Opening a File

The process of creating a stream linked to a disk file is called *opening* the file. When you open a file, it becomes available for reading (meaning that data is input from the file to the program), writing (meaning that data from the program is saved in the file), or both. When you're done using the file, you must close it. Closing a file is covered later today.

To open a file, you use the fopen() library function. The prototype of fopen() is located in stdio.h and reads as follows:

```
FILE *fopen(const char *filename, const char *mode);
```

This prototype tells you that fopen() returns a pointer to type FILE, which is a structure declared in stdio.h. The members of the FILE structure are used by the program in the various file access operations, but you don't need to be concerned about them. However, for each file that you want to open, you must declare a pointer to type FILE. When you call fopen(), that function creates an instance of the FILE structure and returns a pointer to that structure. You use this pointer in all subsequent operations on the file. If fopen() fails, it returns NULL. Such a failure can be caused, for example, by a hardware error or by trying to open a file on a diskette that hasn't been formatted.

The argument filename is the name of the file to be opened. As noted earlier, filename can—and should—contain a path specification. The filename argument can be a literal string enclosed in double quotation marks or a pointer to a string variable.

The argument mode specifies the mode in which to open the file. In this context, mode controls whether the file is binary or text and whether it is for reading, writing, or both. The permitted values for mode are listed in Table 16.1.

TABLE 16.1 Values of mode for the fopen() function

mode	Meaning
r	Opens the file for reading. If the file doesn't exist, fopen() returns NULL.
w	Opens the file for writing. If a file of the specified name doesn't exist, it is created. If a file of the specified name does exist, it is deleted without warning, and a new, empty file is created.
a	Opens the file for appending. If a file of the specified name doesn't exist, it is created. If the file does exist, new data is appended to the end of the file.
r+	Opens the file for reading and writing. If a file of the specified name doesn't exist, it is created. If the file does exist, new data is added to the beginning of the file, overwriting existing data.
w+	Opens the file for reading and writing. If a file of the specified name doesn't exist, it is created. If the file does exist, it is overwritten.
a+	Opens a file for reading and appending. If a file of the specified name doesn't exist, it is created. If the file does exist, new data is appended to the end of the file.

The default file mode is text. To open a file in binary mode, you append a b to the *mode* argument. Thus, a *mode* argument of a would open a text-mode file for appending, whereas ab would open a binary-mode file for appending.

Remember that fopen() returns NULL if an error occurs. Error conditions that can cause a return value of NULL include the following:

- Using an invalid filename.
- Trying to open a file on a disk that isn't ready (the drive door isn't closed or the disk isn't formatted, for example).
- Trying to open a file in a nonexistent directory or on a nonexistent disk drive.
- Trying to open a nonexistent file in mode r.

Whenever you use fopen(), you need to test for the occurrence of an error. There's no way to tell exactly which error occurred, but you can display a message to the user and try to open the file again, or you can end the program. Most C compilers include non-ANSI extensions that let you obtain information about the nature of the error; refer to your compiler documentation for information.

Listing 16.1 demonstrates fopen().

INPUT **LISTING 16.1** fopen.c. Using fopen() to open disk files in various modes

```
1:  /* Demonstrates the fopen() function. */
2:  #include <stdlib.h>
3:  #include <stdio.h>
4:
5:  int main( void )
6:  {
7:     FILE *fp;
8:     char ch, filename[40], mode[4];
9:
10:    while (1)
11:    {
12:
13:        /* Input filename and mode. */
14:
15:        printf("\nEnter a filename: ");
16:        gets(filename);
17:        printf("\nEnter a mode (max 3 characters): ");
18:        gets(mode);
19:
20:        /* Try to open the file. */
21:
22:        if ( (fp = fopen( filename, mode )) != NULL )
23:        {
```

16

LISTING 16.1   continued

```
24:                printf("\nSuccessful opening %s in mode %s.\n",
25:                        filename, mode);
26:                fclose(fp);
27:                puts("Enter x to exit, any other to continue.");
28:                if ( (ch = getc(stdin)) == 'x')
29:                    break;
30:                else
31:                    continue;
32:            }
33:            else
34:            {
35:                fprintf(stderr, "\nError opening file %s in mode %s.\n",
36:                        filename, mode);
37:                puts("Enter x to exit, any other to try again.");
38:                if ( (ch = getc(stdin)) == 'x')
39:                    break;
40:                else
41:                    continue;
42:            }
43:        }
44: return0;
45:}
```

INPUT/ OUTPUT

```
Enter a filename: junk.txt

Enter a mode (max 3 characters): w

Successful opening junk.txt in mode w.
Enter x to exit, any other to continue.
j

Enter a filename: morejunk.txt

Enter a mode (max 3 characters): r

Error opening morejunk.txt in mode r.
Enter x to exit, any other to try again.
x
```

ANALYSIS	This program prompts you for both the filename and the mode specifier on lines 15 through 18. After getting the names, line 22 attempts to open the file and assign its file pointer to fp. As an example of good programming practice, the if statement on line 22 checks to see that the opened file's pointer isn't equal to NULL. If fp isn't equal to NULL, a message is printed stating that the open was successful and that the user can continue. If the file pointer is NULL, the else condition of the if loop executes. The else condition on lines 33 through 42 prints a message stating that there is a problem. It then prompts the user to determine whether the program should continue.

You can experiment with different names and modes to see which ones give you an error. In the output just shown, you can see that trying to open morejunk.txt in mode r resulted in an error because the file didn't exist on the disk. If an error occurs, you're given the choice of entering the information again or quitting the program. To force an error, you could enter an invalid filename such as [ ].

Writing and Reading File Data

A program that uses a disk file can write data to a file, read data from a file, or a combination of the two. You can write data to a disk file in three ways:

- You can use formatted output to save formatted data to a file. You should use formatted output only with text-mode files. The primary use of formatted output is to create files containing text and numeric data to be read by other programs such as spreadsheets or databases. You rarely, if ever, use formatted output to create a file to be read again by a C program.

- You can use character output to save single characters or lines of characters to a file. Although technically it's possible to use character output with binary-mode files, it can be tricky. You should restrict character-mode output to text files. The main use of character output is to save text (but not numeric) data in a form that can be read by C, as well as other programs such as word processors.

- You can use direct output to save the contents of a section of memory directly to a disk file. This method is for binary files only. Direct output is the best way to save data for later use by a C program.

When you want to read data from a file, you have the same three options: formatted input, character input, or direct input. The type of input you use in a particular case depends almost entirely on the nature of the file being read. Generally, you will read data in the same mode that it was saved in, but this is not a requirement. However, reading a file in a mode different from the one it was written in requires a thorough knowledge of C and file formats.

The previous descriptions of the three types of file input and output suggest tasks best suited for each type of output. This is by no means a set of strict rules. The C language is very flexible (this is one of its advantages!), so a clever programmer can make any type of file output suit almost any need. As a beginning programmer, you might find it easier if you follow these guidelines, at least initially.

Formatted File Input and Output

Formatted file input/output deals with text and numeric data that is formatted in a specific way. It is directly analogous to formatted keyboard input and screen output done with the `printf()` and `scanf()` functions, as described on Day 14. We'll discuss formatted output first, followed by input.

Formatted File Output

Formatted file output is done with the library function `fprintf()`. The prototype of `fprintf()` is in the header file stdio.h, and it reads as follows:

```
int fprintf(FILE *fp, char *fmt, ...);
```

The first argument is a pointer to type `FILE`. To write data to a particular disk file, you pass the pointer that was returned when you opened the file with `fopen()`.

The second argument is the format string. You learned about format strings in the discussion of `printf()` on Day 14. The format string used by `fprintf()` follows exactly the same rules as `printf()`. Refer to Day 14 for details.

The final argument is .... What does that mean? In a function prototype, ellipses represent a variable number of arguments. In other words, in addition to the file pointer and the format string arguments, `fprintf()` takes zero, one, or more additional arguments. This is just like `printf()`. These arguments are the names of the variables to be output to the specified stream.

Remember, `fprintf()` works just like `printf()`, except that it sends its output to the stream specified in the argument list. In fact, if you specify a stream argument of `stdout`, `fprintf()` is identical to `printf()`.

Listing 16.2 demonstrates the use of `fprintf()`.

INPUT

LISTING 16.2 fprintf.c. The equivalence of `fprintf()` formatted output to both a file and to `stdout`

```
1:  /* Demonstrates the fprintf() function. */
2:  #include <stdlib.h>
3:  #include <stdio.h>
4:
5:  void clear_kb(void);
6:
7:  int main( void )
8:  {
9:      FILE *fp;
10:     float data[5];
11:     int count;
12:     char filename[20];
13:
14:     puts("Enter 5 floating-point numerical values.");
15:
```

LISTING 16.2   continued

```
16:        for (count = 0; count < 5; count++)
17:            scanf("%f", &data[count]);
18:
19:        /* Get the filename and open the file. First clear stdin */
20:        /* of any extra characters. */
21:
22:        clear_kb();
23:
24:        puts("Enter a name for the file.");
25:        gets(filename);
26:
27:        if ( (fp = fopen(filename, "w")) == NULL)
28:        {
29:            fprintf(stderr, "Error opening file %s.", filename);
30:            exit(1);
31:        }
32:
33:        /* Write the numerical data to the file and to stdout. */
34:
35:        for (count = 0; count < 5; count++)
36:        {
37:            fprintf(fp, "\ndata[%d] = %f", count, data[count]);
38:            fprintf(stdout, "\ndata[%d] = %f", count, data[count]);
39:        }
40:        fclose(fp);
41:        printf("\n");
42:        return 0;
43: }
44:
45: void clear_kb(void)
46: /* Clears stdin of any waiting characters. */
47: {
48:        char junk[80];
49:        gets(junk);
50: }
```

INPUT/ OUTPUT

```
Enter 5 floating-point numerical values.
3.14159
9.99
1.50
3.
1000.0001
Enter a name for the file.
numbers.txt

data[0] = 3.141590
data[1] = 9.990000
data[2] = 1.500000
data[3] = 3.000000
data[4] = 1000.000122
```

16

ANALYSIS You might wonder why the program displays `1000.000122` when the value entered was `1000.0001`. This isn't an error in the program. It's a normal consequence of the way C stores numbers internally. Some floating-point values can't be stored exactly, so minor inaccuracies such as this one sometimes result.

This program uses `fprintf()` on lines 37 and 38 to send some formatted text and numeric data to `stdout` and to the disk file whose name you specified. The only difference between the two lines is the first argument—that is, the stream to which the data is sent. After running the program, use your editor to look at the contents of the file numbers.txt (or whatever name you assigned to it), which will be in the same directory as the program files. You'll see that the text in the file is an exact copy of the text that was displayed on-screen.

Note that Listing 16.2 uses the `clear_kb()` function discussed on Day 14. This is necessary to remove from `stdin` any extra characters that might be left over from the call to `scanf()`. If you don't clear `stdin`, these extra characters (specifically, the newline) are read by the `gets()` that inputs the filename, and the result is a file creation error.

Formatted File Input

For formatted file input, use the `fscanf()` library function, which is used like `scanf()` (see Day 14), except that input comes from a specified stream instead of from `stdin`. The prototype for `fscanf()` is

```
int fscanf(FILE *fp, const char *fmt, ...);
```

The argument `fp` is the pointer to type `FILE` returned by `fopen()`, and `fmt` is a pointer to the format string that specifies how `fscanf()` is to read the input. The components of the format string are the same as for `scanf()`. Finally, the ellipses (`...`) indicate one or more additional arguments, the addresses of the variables where `fscanf()` is to assign the input.

Before getting started with `fscanf()`, you might want to review the section on `scanf()` on Day 14. The function `fscanf()` works exactly the same as `scanf()`, except that characters are taken from the specified stream rather than from `stdin`.

To demonstrate `fscanf()`, you need a text file containing some numbers or strings in a format that can be read by the function. Use your editor to create a file named INPUT.TXT, and enter five floating-point numbers with some space between them (spaces or new lines). For example, your file might look like this:

```
123.45      87.001
100.02
0.00456     1.0005
```

Now, compile and run Listing 16.3.

INPUT

LISTING 16.3 fscanf.c. Using `fscanf()` to read formatted data from a disk file

```
1:  /* Reading formatted file data with fscanf(). */
2:  #include <stdlib.h>
3:  #include <stdio.h>
4:
5:  int main( void )
6:  {
7:      float f1, f2, f3, f4, f5;
8:      FILE *fp;
9:
10:     if ( (fp = fopen("INPUT.TXT", "r")) == NULL)
11:     {
12:         fprintf(stderr, "Error opening file.\n");
13:         exit(1);
14:     }
15:
16:     fscanf(fp, "%f %f %f %f %f", &f1, &f2, &f3, &f4, &f5);
17:     printf("The values are %f, %f, %f, %f, and %f\n.",
18:             f1, f2, f3, f4, f5);
19:
20:     fclose(fp);
21:     return 0;
22: }
```

OUTPUT The values are 123.449997, 87.000999, 100.019997, 0.004560, and 1.000500

Note

> The precision of the values might cause some numbers to not display as the exact values you entered. For example, `100.02` might appear as `100.01999`.

ANALYSIS This program reads the five values from the file you created and then displays them on-screen. The `fopen()` call on line 10 opens the file for read mode. It also checks to see that the file opened correctly. If the file wasn't opened, an error message is displayed on line 12, and the program exits (line 13). Line 16 demonstrates the use of the `fscanf()` function. With the exception of the first parameter, `fscanf()` is identical to `scanf()`, which you have been using throughout this book. The first parameter points to the file that you want the program to read. You can do further experiments with `fscanf()`, creating input files with your programming editor and seeing how `fscanf()` reads the data.

Character Input and Output

When used with disk files, the term *character I/O* refers to single characters as well as lines of characters. Remember, a line is a sequence of zero or more characters terminated by the newline character. Use character I/O with text-mode files. The following sections describe character input/output functions, and then you'll see a demonstration program.

Character Input

There are three character input functions for reading from files: getc(), and fgetc() for single characters, and fgets() for lines.

The getc() and fgetc() Functions   The functions getc() and fgetc() are identical and can be used interchangeably. They input a single character from the specified stream. Here is the prototype of getc(), which is in stdio.h:

```
int getc(FILE *fp);
```

The argument fp is the pointer returned by fopen() when the file was opened. The function returns the character that was input or EOF on error.

You've seen getc() used in earlier programs to input a character from the keyboard. This is another example of the flexibility of C's streams—the same function can be used for keyboard or file input.

If getc() and fgetc() return a single character, why are they prototyped to return a type int? The reason is that, when reading files, you need to be able to read in the end-of-file marker, which on some systems isn't a type char but a type int. You'll see getc() in action later, in Listing 16.10.

 Note   The getchar() function is also used to read characters. It, however, reads from the stdin stream rather than from a file you specify.

The fgets() Function   To read a line of characters from a file, use the fgets() library function. The prototype is

```
char *fgets(char *str, int n, FILE *fp);
```

The argument str is a pointer to a buffer in which the input is to be stored. n is the maximum number of characters to be input. fp is the pointer to type FILE that was returned by fopen() when the file was opened.

When called, fgets() reads characters from fp into memory, starting at the location pointed to by str. Characters are read until a newline is encountered or until n-1 characters have been read, whichever occurs first. By setting n equal to the number of bytes allocated for the buffer str, you prevent input from overwriting memory beyond allocated space. (The n-1 is to allow space for the terminating \0 that fgets() adds to the end of the string.) If successful, fgets() returns str. Two types of errors can occur, as indicated by the return value of NULL:

- If a read error or EOF is encountered before any characters have been assigned to str, NULL is returned, and the memory pointed to by str is unchanged.
- If a read error or EOF is encountered after one or more characters have been assigned to str, NULL is returned, and the memory pointed to by str contains garbage.

You can see that fgets() doesn't necessarily input an entire line (that is, everything up to the next new line character). If n-1 characters are read before a new line is encountered, fgets() stops. The next read operation from the file starts where the last one leaves off. To be sure that fgets() reads in entire strings, stopping only at new lines, be sure that the size of your input buffer and the corresponding value of n passed to fgets() are large enough.

Character Output

You need to know about a few character output functions: putc() fputc(), puts(), and fputs().

The putc() and fputc() Functions   The library functions fputc() and putc() write a single character to a specified stream. The prototype for putc(), in stdio.h, reads

```
int putc(int ch, FILE *fp);
```

The argument ch is the character to output. As with other character functions, it is formally called a type int, but only the lower-order byte is used. The argument fp is the pointer associated with the file (the pointer returned by fopen() when the file was opened). The function putc() returns the character just written (if successful) or EOF (if an error occurs). The symbolic constant EOF is defined in stdio.h, and it has the value -1. Because no "real" character has that numeric value, EOF can be used as an error indicator (with text-mode files only).

Note

> The putchar() function is also used to write characters. It, however, reads from the stdout stream rather than from a file you specify.

The fputs() Function   To write a line of characters to a stream, use the library function fputs(). This function works just like puts(), covered on Day 14. The only difference is that with fputs(), you can specify the output stream. Also, fputs() doesn't add a new line to the end of the string; if you want it, you must explicitly include it. Its prototype in stdio.h is

```
char fputs(char *str, FILE *fp);
```

The argument `str` is a pointer to the null-terminated string to be written, and `fp` is the pointer to type `FILE` returned by `fopen()` when the file was opened. The string pointed to by `str` is written to the file, minus its terminating `\0`. The function `fputs()` returns a nonnegative value if successful or `EOF` on error.

Direct File Input and Output

You use direct file I/O most often when you save data to be read later by the same or a different C program. Direct I/O is used only with binary-mode files. With direct output, blocks of data are written from memory to disk. Direct input reverses the process: A block of data is read from a disk file into memory. For example, a single direct-output function call can write an entire array of type `double` to disk, and a single direct-input function call can read the entire array from disk back into memory. The direct I/O functions are `fread()` and `fwrite()`.

The `fwrite()` Function

The `fwrite()` library function writes a block of data from memory to a binary-mode file. Its prototype, in stdio.h, is

```
int fwrite(void *buf, int size, int count, FILE *fp);
```

The argument `buf` is a pointer to the region of memory holding the data to be written to the file. The pointer type is `void`; it can be a pointer to anything.

The argument `size` specifies the size, in bytes, of the individual data items, and `count` specifies the number of items to be written. For example, if you wanted to save a 100-element integer array, `size` would be 2 (because each `int` occupies 2 bytes), and `count` would be 100 (because the array contains 100 elements). To obtain the `size` argument, you can use the `sizeof()` operator.

The argument `fp` is, of course, the pointer to type `FILE`, returned by `fopen()` when the file was opened. The `fwrite()` function returns the number of items written on success; if the value returned is less than `count`, it means that an error has occurred. To check for errors, you usually program `fwrite()` as follows:

```
if( (fwrite(buf, size, count, fp)) != count)
fprintf(stderr, "Error writing to file.");
```

Here are some examples of using `fwrite()`. To write a single type `double` variable x to a file, use the following:

```
fwrite(&x, sizeof(double), 1, fp);
```

To write an array data[] of 50 structures of type address to a file, you have two choices:

```
fwrite(data, sizeof(address), 50, fp);

fwrite(data, sizeof(data), 1, fp);
```

The first method writes the array as 50 elements, with each element having the size of a single type address structure. The second method treats the array as a single element. The two methods accomplish exactly the same thing.

The following section explains fread() and then presents a program demonstrating fread() and fwrite().

The fread() Function

The fread() library function reads a block of data from a binary-mode file into memory. Its prototype in stdio.h is

```
int fread(void *buf, int size, int count, FILE *fp);
```

The argument *buf* is a pointer to the region of memory that receives the data read from the file. As with fwrite(), the pointer type is void.

The argument *size* specifies the size, in bytes, of the individual data items being read, and *count* specifies the number of items to read. Note how these arguments parallel the arguments used by fwrite(). Again, the sizeof() operator is typically used to provide the *size* argument. The argument fp is (as always) the pointer to type FILE that was returned by fopen() when the file was opened. The fread() function returns the number of items read; this can be less than *count* if end-of-file was reached or an error occurred.

Listing 16.4 demonstrates the use of fwrite() and fread().

INPUT   **LISTING 16.4**   direct.c. Using fwrite() and fread() for direct file access

```
1:    /* Direct file I/O with fwrite() and fread(). */
2:    #include <stdlib.h>
3:    #include <stdio.h>
4:
5:    #define SIZE 20
6:
7:    int main( void )
8:    {
9:        int count, array1[SIZE], array2[SIZE];
10:       FILE *fp;
11:
12:       /* Initialize array1[]. */
13:
```

LISTING **16.4**   continued

```
14:        for (count = 0; count < SIZE; count++)
15:            array1[count] = 2 * count;
16:
17:        /* Open a binary mode file. */
18:
19:        if ( (fp = fopen("direct.txt", "wb")) == NULL)
20:        {
21:            fprintf(stderr, "Error opening file.");
22:            exit(1);
23:        }
24:        /* Save array1[] to the file. */
25:
26:        if (fwrite(array1, sizeof(int), SIZE, fp) != SIZE)
27:        {
28:            fprintf(stderr, "Error writing to file.");
29:            exit(1);
30:        }
31:
32:        fclose(fp);
33:
34:        /* Now open the same file for reading in binary mode. */
35:
36:        if ( (fp = fopen("direct.txt", "rb")) == NULL)
37:        {
38:            fprintf(stderr, "Error opening file.");
39:            exit(1);
40:        }
41:
42:        /* Read the data into array2[]. */
43:
44:        if (fread(array2, sizeof(int), SIZE, fp) != SIZE)
45:        {
46:            fprintf(stderr, "Error reading file.");
47:            exit(1);
48:        }
49:
50:        fclose(fp);
51:
52:        /* Now display both arrays to show they're the same. */
53:
54:        for (count = 0; count < SIZE; count++)
55:            printf("%d\t%d\n", array1[count], array2[count]);
56:        return 0;
57: }
```

OUTPUT
```
0        0
2        2
4        4
```

```
6        6
8        8
10       10
12       12
14       14
16       16
18       18
20       20
22       22
24       24
26       26
28       28
30       30
32       32
34       34
36       36
38       38
```

ANALYSIS   Listing 16.4 demonstrates the use of the `fwrite()` and `fread()` functions. This program initializes an array on lines 14 and 15. It then uses `fwrite()` on line 26 to save the array to disk. The program uses `fread()` on line 44 to read the data into a different array. Finally, it displays both arrays on-screen to show that they now hold the same data (lines 54 and 55).

When you save data with `fwrite()`, not much can go wrong except some type of disk error. With `fread()`, be careful, however. As far as `fread()` is concerned, the data on the disk is just a sequence of bytes. The function has no way of knowing what it represents. For example, on a 16-bit system, a block of 100 bytes could be 100 `char` variables, 50 `int` variables, 25 `long` variables, or 25 `float` variables. If you ask `fread()` to read that block into memory, it obediently does so. However, if the block is saved from an array of type `int` and you retrieve it into an array of type `float`, no error occurs, but you get strange results. When writing programs, you must be sure that `fread()` is used properly, reading data into the appropriate types of variables and arrays. Notice that in Listing 16.4, all calls to `fopen()`, `fwrite()`, and `fread()` are checked to ensure that they worked correctly.

File Buffering: Closing and Flushing Files

When you're finished using a file, you should close it using the `fclose()` function. You saw `fclose()` used in programs presented earlier today. Its prototype is

```
int fclose(FILE *fp);
```

The argument `fp` is the FILE pointer associated with the stream; `fclose()` returns 0 on success or -1 on error. When you close a file, the file's buffer is flushed (written to the file). You can also close all open streams except the standard ones (stdin, stdout, std-prn, stderr, and stdaux) by using the fcloseall() function. Its prototype is

```
int fcloseall(void);
```

This function also flushes any stream buffers and returns the number of streams closed.

When a program terminates (either by reaching the end of main() or by executing the exit() function), all streams are automatically flushed and closed. However, it's a good idea to close streams explicitly—particularly those linked to disk files—as soon as you're finished with them. The reason has to do with stream buffers.

When you create a stream linked to a disk file, a buffer is automatically created and associated with the stream. A buffer is a block of memory used for temporary storage of data being written to and read from the file. Buffers are needed because disk drives are block-oriented devices, which means that they operate most efficiently when data is read and written in blocks of a certain size. The size of the ideal block differs, depending on the specific hardware in use. It's typically on the order of a few hundred to a thousand bytes. You don't need to be concerned about the exact block size, however.

The buffer associated with a file stream serves as an interface between the stream (which is character-oriented) and the disk hardware (which is block-oriented). As your program writes data to the stream, the data is saved in the buffer until the buffer is full, and then the entire contents of the buffer are written, as a block, to the disk. An analogous process occurs when reading data from a disk file. The creation and operation of the buffer is handled by the operating system and is entirely automatic; you don't have to be concerned with it. (C does offer some functions for buffer manipulation, but they are beyond the scope of this book.)

In practical terms, this buffer operation means that, during program execution, data that your program wrote to the disk might still be in the buffer, not on the disk. If your program hangs up, if there's a power failure, or if some other problem occurs, the data that's still in the buffer might be lost, and you won't know what's contained in the disk file.

You can flush a stream's buffers without closing it by using the fflush() or flushall() library functions. Use fflush() when you want a file's buffer to be written to disk while still using the file. Use flushall() to flush the buffers of all open streams. The prototypes of these two functions are as follows:

```
int fflush(FILE *fp);
```

```
int flushall(void);
```

The argument fp is the FILE pointer returned by fopen() when the file was opened. If a file was opened for writing, fflush() writes its buffer to disk. If the file was opened for reading, the buffer is cleared. The function `fflush()` returns 0 on success or EOF if an error occurred. The function `flushall()` returns the number of open streams.

Do	Don't
DO open a file before trying to read or write to it.	**DON'T** assume that a file access is okay. Always check after doing a read, write, or open to ensure that the function worked.
DO use the `sizeof()` operator with the `fwrite()` and `fread()` functions.	
DO close all files that you've opened.	**DON'T** use `fcloseall()` unless you have a reason to close all the streams.

Understanding Sequential Versus Random File Access

Every open file has a file position indicator associated with it. The position indicator specifies where read and write operations take place in the file. The position is always given in terms of bytes from the beginning of the file. When a new file is opened, the position indicator is always at the beginning of the file, position 0. (Because the file is new and has a length of 0, there's no other location to indicate.) When an existing file is opened, the position indicator is at the end of the file if the file is opened in append mode, or at the beginning of the file if the file is opened in any other mode.

The file input/output functions, covered earlier in this chapter, make use of the position indicator, although the manipulations go on behind the scenes. Writing and reading operations occur at the location of the position indicator and update the position indicator as well. For example, if you open a file for reading, and 10 bytes are read, you input the first 10 bytes in the file (the bytes at positions 0 through 9). After the read operation, the position indicator is at position 10, and the next read operation begins there. Thus, if you want to read all the data in a file sequentially or write data to a file sequentially, you don't need to be concerned about the position indicator. The stream I/O functions take care of it automatically.

When you need more control, use the C library functions that let you determine and change the value of the file position indicator. By controlling the position indicator, you can perform random file access. Here, *random* means that you can read data from or write data to any position in a file without reading or writing all the preceding data.

The `ftell()` and `rewind()` Functions

To set the position indicator to the beginning of the file, use the library function
`rewind()`. Its prototype, in stdio.h, is

```
void rewind(FILE *fp);
```

The argument `fp` is the `FILE` pointer associated with the stream. After `rewind()` is called,
the file's position indicator is set to the beginning of the file (byte 0). Use `rewind()` if
you've read some data from a file and you want to start reading from the beginning of
the file again without closing and reopening the file.

To determine the value of a file's position indicator, use `ftell()`. This function's prototype, located in stdio.h, reads

```
long ftell(FILE *fp);
```

The argument `fp` is the `FILE` pointer returned by `fopen()` when the file was opened. The
function `ftell()` returns a type `long` that gives the current file position in bytes from the
start of the file (the first byte is at position 0). If an error occurs, `ftell()` returns `-1L` (a
type `long` `-1`).

To get a feel for the operation of `rewind()` and `ftell()`, look at Listing 16.5.

INPUT   **LISTING 16.5**   ftell.c. Using `ftell()` and `rewind()`

```
 1:  /* Demonstrates ftell() and rewind(). */
 2:  #include <stdlib.h>
 3:  #include <stdio.h>
 4:
 5:  #define BUFLEN 6
 6:
 7:  char msg[] = "abcdefghijklmnopqrstuvwxyz";
 8:
 9:  int main( void )
10:  {
11:      FILE *fp;
12:      char buf[BUFLEN];
13:
14:      if ( (fp = fopen("TEXT.TXT", "w")) == NULL)
15:      {
16:          fprintf(stderr, "Error opening file.");
17:          exit(1);
18:      }
19:
20:      if (fputs(msg, fp) == EOF)
21:      {
22:          fprintf(stderr, "Error writing to file.");
```

LISTING 16.5 continued

```
23:            exit(1);
24:        }
25:
26:        fclose(fp);
27:
28:        /* Now open the file for reading. */
29:
30:        if ( (fp = fopen("TEXT.TXT", "r")) == NULL)
31:        {
32:            fprintf(stderr, "Error opening file.");
33:            exit(1);
34:        }
35:        printf("\nImmediately after opening, position = %ld", ftell(fp));
36:
37:        /* Read in 5 characters. */
38:
39:        fgets(buf, BUFLEN, fp);
40:        printf("\nAfter reading in %s, position = %ld", buf, ftell(fp));
41:
42:        /* Read in the next 5 characters. */
43:
44:        fgets(buf, BUFLEN, fp);
45:        printf("\n\nThe next 5 characters are %s, and position now = %ld",
46:                buf, ftell(fp));
47:
48:        /* Rewind the stream. */
49:
50:        rewind(fp);
51:
52:        printf("\n\nAfter rewinding, the position is back at %ld",
53:                ftell(fp));
54:
55:        /* Read in 5 characters. */
56:
57:        fgets(buf, BUFLEN, fp);
58:        printf("\nand reading starts at the beginning again: %s\n", buf);
59:        fclose(fp);
60:        return 0;
61: }
```

OUTPUT

```
Immediately after opening, position = 0
After reading in abcde, position = 5

The next 5 characters are fghij, and position now = 10

After rewinding, the position is back at 0
and reading starts at the beginning again: abcde
```

16

ANALYSIS This program writes a string, msg, to a file called text.txt. The message consists of the 26 letters of the alphabet, in order. Lines 14 through 18 open text.txt for writing and test to ensure that the file was opened successfully. Lines 20 through 24 write msg to the file using fputs() and check to ensure that the write was successful. Line 26 closes the file with fclose(), completing the process of creating a file for the rest of the program to use.

Lines 30 through 34 open the file again, only this time for reading. Line 35 prints the return value of ftell(). Notice that this position is at the beginning of the file. Line 39 performs a gets() to read five characters. The five characters and the new file position are printed on line 40. Notice that ftell() returns the correct offset. Line 50 calls rewind() to put the pointer back at the beginning of the file, before line 52 prints the file position again. This should confirm for you that rewind() resets the position. An additional read on line 57 further confirms that the program is indeed back at the beginning of the file. Line 59 closes the file before ending the program.

The fseek() Function

More precise control over a stream's position indicator is possible with the fseek() library function. By using fseek(), you can set the position indicator anywhere in the file. The function prototype, in stdio.h, is

```
int fseek(FILE *fp, long offset, int origin);
```

The argument fp is the FILE pointer associated with the file. The distance that the position indicator is to be moved is given by offset in bytes. The argument origin specifies the move's relative starting point. There can be three values for origin, with symbolic constants defined in io.h, as shown in Table 16.2.

TABLE 16.2 Possible origin values for fseek()

Constant	Value	Description
SEEK_SET	0	Moves the indicator offset bytes from the beginning of the file.
SEEK_CUR	1	Moves the indicator offset bytes from its current position.
SEEK_END	2	Moves the indicator offset bytes from the end of the file.

The function fseek() returns 0 if the indicator was successfully moved or nonzero if an error occurred. Listing 16.6 uses fseek() for random file access.

```
1:  /* Random access with fseek(). */
2:
3:   #include <stdlib.h>
4:  #include <stdio.h>
5:
6:  #define MAX 50
7:
8:  int main( void )
9:  {
10:      FILE *fp;
11:      int data, count, array[MAX];
12:      long offset;
13:
14:      /* Initialize the array. */
15:
16:      for (count = 0; count < MAX; count++)
17:          array[count] = count * 10;
18:
19:      /* Open a binary file for writing. */
20:
21:      if ( (fp = fopen("RANDOM.DAT", "wb")) == NULL)
22:      {
23:          fprintf(stderr, "\nError opening file.");
24:          exit(1);
25:      }
26:
27:      /* Write the array to the file, then close it. */
28:
29:      if ( (fwrite(array, sizeof(int), MAX, fp)) != MAX)
30:      {
31:          fprintf(stderr, "\nError writing data to file.");
32:          exit(1);
33:      }
34:
35:      fclose(fp);
36:
37:      /* Open the file for reading. */
38:
39:      if ( (fp = fopen("RANDOM.DAT", "rb")) == NULL)
40:      {
41:          fprintf(stderr, "\nError opening file.");
42:          exit(1);
43:      }
44:
45:      /* Ask user which element to read. Input the element */
46:      /* and display it, quitting when -1 is entered. */
47:
48:      while (1)
```

16

LISTING 16.6 continued

```
49:     {
50:         printf("\nEnter element to read, 0-%d, -1 to quit: ",MAX-1);
51:         scanf("%ld", &offset);
52:
53:         if (offset < 0)
54:             break;
55:         else if (offset > MAX-1)
56:             continue;
57:
58:         /* Move the position indicator to the specified element. */
59:
60:         if ( (fseek(fp, (offset*sizeof(int)), SEEK_SET)) != 0)
61:         {
62:             fprintf(stderr, "\nError using fseek().");
63:             exit(1);
64:         }
65:
66:         /* Read in a single integer. */
67:
68:         fread(&data, sizeof(int), 1, fp);
69:
70:         printf("\nElement %ld has value %d.", offset, data);
71:     }
72:
73:     fclose(fp);
74:     return 0;
75: }
```

INPUT/
OUTPUT

```
Enter element to read, 0-49, -1 to quit: 5

Element 5 has value 50.
Enter element to read, 0-49, -1 to quit: 6

Element 6 has value 60.
Enter element to read, 0-49, -1 to quit: 49

Element 49 has value 490.
Enter element to read, 0-49, -1 to quit: 1

Element 1 has value 10.
Enter element to read, 0-49, -1 to quit: 0

Element 0 has value 0.
Enter element to read, 0-49, -1 to quit: -1
```

ANALYSIS Lines 14 through 35 are similar to Listing 16.5. Lines 16 and 17 initialize an array called data with 50 type int values. The value stored in each array element is equal to 10 times the index. Then the array is written to a binary file called RANDOM.DAT. You know it is binary because the file was opened with mode "wb" on line 21.

Line 39 reopens the file in binary read mode before going into an infinite `while` loop. The `while` loop prompts the user to enter the number of the array element that he wants to read. Notice that lines 53 through 56 check that the entered element is within the range of the file. Does C let you read an element that is beyond the end of the file? Yes. Like going beyond the end of an array with values, C also lets you read beyond the end of a file. If you do read beyond the end (or before the beginning), your results are unpredictable. It's always best to check what you're doing (as lines 53 through 56 do in this listing).

After you have input the element to find, line 60 jumps to the appropriate offset with a call to `fseek()`. Because `SEEK_SET` is being used, the seek is done from the beginning of the file. Notice that the distance into the file is not just *offset*, but *offset* multiplied by the size of the elements being read. Line 68 then reads the value, and line 70 prints it.

Detecting the End of a File

Sometimes you know exactly how long a file is, so there's no need to be able to detect the file's end. For example, if you used `fwrite()` to save a 100-element integer array, you know the file is 200 bytes long (assuming 2-byte integers). At other times, however, you don't know how long the file is, but you still want to read data from the file, starting at the beginning and proceeding to the end. There are two ways to detect end-of-file.

When reading from a text-mode file character-by-character, you can look for the end-of-file character. The symbolic constant `EOF` is defined in stdio.h as `-1`, a value never used by a "real" character. When a character input function reads `EOF` from a text-mode stream, you can be sure that you've reached the end of the file. For example, you could write the following:

```
while ( (c = fgetc( fp )) != EOF )
```

With a binary-mode stream, you can't detect the end-of-file by looking for –1, because a byte of data from a binary stream could have that value, which would result in premature end of input. Instead, you can use the library function `feof()`, which can be used for both binary- and text-mode files:

```
int feof(FILE *fp);
```

The argument `fp` is the `FILE` pointer returned by `fopen()` when the file was opened. The function `feof()` returns 0 if the end of file `fp` hasn't been reached, or a nonzero value if end-of-file has been reached. If a call to `feof()` detects end-of-file, no further read operations are permitted until a `rewind()` has been done, `fseek()` is called, or the file is closed and reopened.

Listing 16.7 demonstrates the use of feof(). When you're prompted for a filename, enter the name of any text file—one of your C source files, for example, or a header file such as stdio.h. Just be sure that the file is in the current directory, or else enter a path as part of the filename. The program reads the file one line at a time, displaying each line on stdout, until feof() detects end-of-file.

INPUT **LISTING 16.7** feof.c. Using feof() to detect the end of a file

```
1:  /* Detecting end-of-file. */
2:  #include <stdlib.h>
3:  #include <stdio.h>
4:
5:  #define BUFSIZE 100
6:
7:  int main( void )
8:  {
9:      char buf[BUFSIZE];
10:     char filename[60];
11:     FILE *fp;
12:
13:     puts("Enter name of text file to display: ");
14:     gets(filename);
15:
16:     /* Open the file for reading. */
17:     if ( (fp = fopen(filename, "r")) == NULL)
18:     {
19:         fprintf(stderr, "Error opening file.");
20:         exit(1);
21:     }
22:
23:     /* If end of file not reached, read a line and display it. */
24:
25:     while ( !feof(fp) )
26:     {
27:         fgets(buf, BUFSIZE, fp);
28:         printf("%s",buf);
29:     }
30:
31:     fclose(fp);
32:     return 0;
33: }
```

INPUT/ OUTPUT
```
Enter name of text file to display:
hello.c
#include <stdio.h>
int main( void )
{
    printf("Hello, world.");
    return(0);
}
```

ANALYSIS The while loop in this program (lines 25 through 29) is typical of a while used in more complex programs that do sequential processing. As long as the end of the file hasn't been reached, the code within the while statement (lines 27 and 28) continues to execute repeatedly. When the call to feof() returns a nonzero value, the loop ends, the file is closed, and the program ends.

Do	Don't
DO use either rewind() or fseek(fp, SEEK_SET, 0) to reset the file position to the beginning of the file.	**DON'T** read beyond the end of a file or before the beginning of a file. Avoid this by checking your position.
DO use feof() to check for the end of the file when working with binary files.	**DON'T** use EOF with binary files.

16

File Management Functions

The term *file management* refers to dealing with existing files—not reading from or writing to them—but deleting, renaming, and copying them. The C standard library contains functions for deleting and renaming files, and you can also write your own file-copying program.

Deleting a File

To delete a file, you use the library function remove(). Its prototype is in stdio.h, as follows:

```
int remove( const char *filename );
```

The variable *filename is a pointer to the name of the file to be deleted. (See the section on filenames earlier in today's lessons.) The specified file must not be open. If the file exists, it is deleted (just as if you used the DEL command from the DOS prompt, Windows Command prompt, or the rm command in UNIX), and remove() returns 0. If the file doesn't exist, if it's read-only, if you don't have sufficient access rights, or if some other error occurs, remove() returns -1.

Listing 16.8 demonstrates the use of remove(). Be careful: If you remove() a file, it's gone forever.

INPUT **LISTING 16.8** remove.c. Using the remove() function to delete a disk file

```
1:  /* Demonstrates the remove() function. */
2:
3:  #include <stdio.h>
```

LISTING 16.8   continued

```
4:
5:  int main( void )
6:  {
7:      char filename[80];
8:
9:      printf("Enter the filename to delete: ");
10:     gets(filename);
11:
12:     if ( remove(filename) == 0)
13:         printf("The file %s has been deleted.\n", filename);
14:     else
15:         fprintf(stderr, "Error deleting the file %s.\n", filename);
16:     return 0;
17: }
```

**INPUT/
OUTPUT**

```
Enter the filename to delete: *.bak
Error deleting the file *.bak.
Enter the filename to delete: list1414.bak
The file list1414.bak has been deleted.
```

ANALYSIS   This program prompts the user on line 9 for the name of the file to be deleted.
Line 12 then calls remove() to delete the entered file. If the return value is 0, the
file was removed, and a message is displayed stating this fact. If the return value is not
zero, an error occurred, and the file was not removed.

Tip   It is always a good idea to verify the user really wants to delete a file.

Renaming a File

The rename() function changes the name of an existing disk file. The function prototype,
in stdio.h, is as follows:

```
int rename( const char *oldname, const char *newname );
```

The filenames pointed to by *oldname* and *newname* follow the rules given earlier in this
chapter. The only restriction is that both names must refer to the same disk drive; you
can't rename a file to a different disk drive. The function rename() returns 0 on success,
or -1 if an error occurs. Errors can be caused by the following conditions (among others)

- The file *oldname* does not exist.
- A file with the name *newname* already exists.
- You try to rename to another disk.

Listing 16.9 demonstrates the use of rename().

INPUT **LISTING 16.9** renameit.c. Using rename() to change the name of a disk file

```
1:  /* Using rename() to change a filename. */
2:
3:  #include <stdio.h>
4:
5:  int main( void )
6:  {
7:      char oldname[80], newname[80];
8:
9:      printf("Enter current filename: ");
10:     gets(oldname);
11:     printf("Enter new name for file: ");
12:     gets(newname);
13:
14:     if ( rename( oldname, newname ) == 0 )
15:         printf("%s has been renamed %s.\n", oldname, newname);
16:     else
17:         fprintf(stderr, "An error has occurred renaming %s.\n", oldname);
18:     return 0;
19: }
```

INPUT/ OUTPUT

```
Enter current filename: list1609.c
Enter new name for file: renameit.c
list1609.c has been renamed renameit.c.
```

ANALYSIS Listing 16.9 shows how powerful C can be. With only 18 lines of code, this program replaces an operating system command, and it's a very friendly function.
Line 9 prompts for the name of the file to be renamed. Line 11 prompts for the new filename. The call to the rename() function is wrapped in an if statement on line 14. The
if statement checks to ensure that the renaming of the file was carried out correctly. If
so, line 15 prints an affirmative message; otherwise, line 17 prints a message stating that
there was an error.

Copying a File

It's frequently necessary to make a copy of a file—an exact duplicate with a different
name (or with the same name but in a different drive or directory). In DOS, you do this
with the COPY command, and other operating systems have equivalents. How do you copy
a file in C? There's no library function, so you need to write your own.

This might sound a bit complicated, but it's really quite simple thanks to C's use of
streams for input and output. Here are the steps you follow:

1. Open the source file for reading in binary mode. (Using binary mode ensures that the function can copy all sorts of files, not just text files.)

2. Open the destination file for writing in binary mode.

3. Read a character from the source file. Remember, when a file is first opened, the pointer is at the start of the file, so there's no need to position the file pointer explicitly.

4. If the function feof() indicates that you've reached the end of the source file, you're finished and can close both files and return to the calling program.

5. If you haven't reached end-of-file, write the character to the destination file, and then loop back to step 3.

Listing 16.10 contains a function, copy_file(), that is passed the names of the source and destination files and then performs the copy operation just as the preceding steps outlined. If there's an error opening either file, the function doesn't attempt the copy operation and returns -1 to the calling program. When the copy operation is complete, the program closes both files and returns 0.

INPUT   **LISTING 16.10**   copyit.c. A function that copies a file

```
 1:  /* Copying a file. */
 2:
 3:  #include <stdio.h>
 4:
 5:  int file_copy( char *oldname, char *newname );
 6:
 7:  int main( void )
 8:  {
 9:      char source[80], destination[80];
10:
11:      /* Get the source and destination names. */
12:
13:      printf("\nEnter source file: ");
14:      gets(source);
15:      printf("\nEnter destination file: ");
16:      gets(destination);
17:
18:      if ( file_copy( source, destination ) == 0 )
19:          puts("Copy operation successful");
20:      else
21:          fprintf(stderr, "Error during copy operation");
22:      return 0;
23:  }
24:  int file_copy( char *oldname, char *newname )
25:  {
26:      FILE *fold, *fnew;
```

LISTING 16.10   continued

```
27:     int c;
28:
29:     /* Open the source file for reading in binary mode. */
30:
31:     if ( ( fold = fopen( oldname, "rb" ) ) == NULL )
32:         return -1;
33:
34:     /* Open the destination file for writing in binary mode. */
35:
36:     if ( ( fnew = fopen( newname, "wb" ) ) == NULL  )
37:     {
38:         fclose ( fold );
39:         return -1;
40:     }
41:
42:     /* Read one byte at a time from the source; if end of file */
43:     /* has not been reached, write the byte to the */
44:     /* destination. */
45:
46:     while (1)
47:     {
48:         c = fgetc( fold );
49:
50:         if ( !feof( fold ) )
51:             fputc( c, fnew );
52:         else
53:             break;
54:     }
55:
56:     fclose ( fnew );
57:     fclose ( fold );
58:
59:     return 0;
60: }
```

16

INPUT/
OUTPUT

```
Enter source file: list1610.c

Enter destination file: tmpfile.c
Copy operation successful
```

ANALYSIS   The function copy_file() works perfectly well, letting you copy anything from a small text file to a huge program file. It does have limitations, however. If the destination file already exists, the function deletes it without asking. A good programming exercise for you is to modify copy_file() to check whether the destination file already exists, and then query the user as to whether the old file should be overwritten.

main() in Listing 16.10 should look very familiar. It's nearly identical to the main() in Listing 16.9, with the exception of line 14. Instead of rename(), this function uses copy(). Because C doesn't have a copy function, lines 24 through 60 create a copy function. Lines 31 and 32 open the source file, fold, in binary read mode. Lines 36 through 40 open the destination file, fnew, in binary write mode. Notice that line 38 closes the source file if there is an error opening the destination file. The while loop in lines 46 through 54 does the actual copying of the file. Line 48 gets a character from the source file, fold. Line 50 checks to see whether the end-of-file marker was read. If the end of the file has been reached, a break statement is executed in order to get out of the while loop. If the end of the file has not been reached, the character is written to the destination file, fnew. Lines 56 and 57 close the two files before returning to main().

Using Temporary Files

Some programs make use of one or more temporary files during execution. A temporary file is a file that is created by the program, used for some purpose during program execution, and then deleted before the program terminates. When you create a temporary file, you don't really care what its name is, because it gets deleted. All that is necessary is that you use a name that isn't already in use for another file. The C standard library includes a function tmpnam() that creates a valid filename that doesn't conflict with any existing file. Its prototype in stdio.h is as follows:

```
char *tmpnam(char *s);
```

The argument s must be a pointer to a buffer large enough to hold the filename. You can also pass a null pointer (NULL), in which case the temporary name is stored in a buffer internal to tmpnam(), and the function returns a pointer to that buffer. Listing 16.11 demonstrates both methods of using tmpnam() to create temporary filenames.

INPUT   **LISTING 16.11** tempname.c. Using tmpnam() to create temporary filenames

```
1:  /* Demonstration of temporary filenames. */
2:
3:  #include <stdio.h>
4:
5:  int main( void )
6:  {
7:      char buffer[10], *c;
8:
9:      /* Get a temporary name in the defined buffer. */
10:
11:     tmpnam(buffer);
12:
```

LISTING 16.11   continued

```
13:      /* Get another name, this time in the function's */
14:      /* internal buffer. */
15:
16:      c = tmpnam(NULL);
17:
18:      /* Display the names. */
19:      printf("Temporary name 1: %s", buffer);
20:      printf("\nTemporary name 2: %s\n", c);
21: return 0;
22: }
```

OUTPUT Temporary name 1: \s3us.
Temporary name 2: \s3us.1

Note

The temporary names created in your system will probably be different from these.

ANALYSIS This program only generates and prints the temporary names; it doesn't actually create any files. Line 11 stores a temporary name in the character array, `buffer`. Line 16 assigns the character pointer to the name returned by `tmpnam()` to `c`. Your program must use the generated name to open the temporary file and then delete the file before program execution terminates. The following code fragment illustrates this:

```
char tempname[80];
FILE *tmpfile;
tmpnam(tempname);
tmpfile = fopen(tempname, "w");   /* Use appropriate mode */
fclose(tmpfile);
remove(tempname);
```

Do	**Don't**
DO remember to remove temporary files that you create. They aren't deleted automatically.	**DON'T** remove a file that you might need again.

Summary

In today's lessons, you learned how C programs can use disk files. C treats a disk file like a stream (a sequence of characters), just like the predefined streams you learned about on Day 14. A stream associated with a disk file must be opened before it can be used, and it must be closed after use. A disk file stream can be opened in either text or binary mode.

After a disk file has been opened, you can read data from the file into your program, write data from the program to the file, or both. There is three general types of file I/O: formatted, character, and direct. Each type of I/O is best used for certain types of data storage and retrieval tasks.

Each open disk file has a file position indicator associated with it. This indicator specifies the position in the file, measured as the number of bytes from the start of the file, where subsequent read and write operations occur. With some types of file access, the position indicator is updated automatically, and you don't have to be concerned with it. For random file access, the C standard library provides functions for manipulating the position indicator.

Finally, C provides some rudimentary file management functions, letting you delete and rename disk files. Today you developed your own function for copying a file.

Q&A

Q Can I use drives and paths with filenames when using `remove()`, `rename()`, `fopen()`, and the other file functions?

A Yes. You can use a full filename with a path and a drive or just the filename by itself. If you use the filename by itself, the function looks for the file in the current directory. Remember, when using a backslash (\), you need to use the escape sequence. Also remember that UNIX uses the forward slash (/) as a directory separator.

Q Can I read beyond the end of a file?

A Yes. You can also read before the beginning of a file. Results from such reads can be disastrous. Reading files is just like working with arrays. You're looking at offsets within memory. If you're using `fseek()`, you should check to make sure that you don't go beyond the end of the file.

Q What happens if I don't close a file?

A It's good programming practice to close any files you open. By default, the file should be closed when the program exits; however, you should never count on this. If the file isn't closed, you might not be able to access it later, because the operating system will think that the file is already in use.

Q How many files can I open at once?

A This question can't be answered with a simple number. The limitation on the number of files that can be opened is based on variables set within your operating system. On DOS systems, an environment variable called FILES determines the number of files that can be opened (this variable also includes programs that are running). Consult your operating system manuals for more information.

Q Can I read a file sequentially with random-access functions?

A When reading a file sequentially, there is no need to use such functions as fseek(). Because the file pointer is left at the last position it occupied, it is always where you want it for sequential reads. You can use fseek() to read a file sequentially; however, you gain nothing.

16

Workshop

The Workshop provides quiz questions to help you solidify your understanding of the material covered and exercises to provide you with experience in using what you've learned.

Quiz

1. What's the difference between a text-mode stream and a binary-mode stream?
2. What must your program do before it can access a disk file?
3. When you open a file with fopen(), what information must you specify, and what does this function return?
4. What are the three general methods of file access?
5. What are the two general methods of reading a file's information?
6. What is the value of EOF?
7. When is EOF used?
8. How do you detect the end of a file in text and binary modes?
9. What is the file position indicator, and how can you modify it?
10. When a file is first opened, where does the file position indicator point to? (If you're unsure, see Listing 16.5.)

Exercises

1. Write code to close all file streams.
2. Show two different ways to reset the file position pointer to the beginning of the file.

3. **BUG BUSTER:** Is anything wrong with the following code?

```
FILE *fp;
int c;

if ( ( fp = fopen( oldname, "rb" ) ) == NULL )
    return -1;

while (( c = fgetc( fp)) != EOF )
    fprintf( stdout, "%c", c );

fclose ( fp );
```

Because of the many possible solutions, answers are not provided for the following exercises.

4. Write a program that displays a file to the screen.

5. Write a program that opens a file and prints it to the printer (stdprn). The program should print only 55 lines per page.

6. Modify the program in exercise 5 to print headings on each page. The headings should contain the filename and the page number.

7. Write a program that opens a file and counts the number of characters. The program should print the number of characters when finished.

8. Write a program that opens an existing text file and copies it to a new text file with all lowercase letters changed to uppercase and all other characters unchanged.

9. Write a program that opens any disk file, reads it in 128-byte blocks, and displays the contents of each block on-screen in both hexadecimal and ASCII formats.

10. Write a function that opens a new temporary file with a specified mode. All temporary files created by this function should automatically be closed and deleted when the program terminates. (Hint: Use the atexit() library function.)

TYPE & RUN 5

Counting Characters

It's time for another Type & Run. This program, called count_ch, opens the specified text file and counts the number of times each character occurs in it. All the standard keyboard characters are counted, including upper- and lower-case letters, numerals, spaces, and punctuation marks. The results are displayed onscreen. In addition to being a potentially useful program, count_ch illustrates some interesting programming techniques. You can use the operating system's redirection operator (>) to place the output in a file. For example, the command

```
COUNT_CH > RESULTS.TXT
```

runs the program and outputs the results in a file named Results.txt, instead of displaying them onscreen. You can view the output in your text editor or print it.

INPUT   LISTING T&R 5   count_ch.c: A program to count characters in a file

```
1:  /* Counts the number of occurrences
2:     of each character in a file. */
3:  #include <stdio.h>
4:  #include <stdlib.h>
5:  int file_exists(char *filename);
```

```
 6:  int main( void )
 7:  {
 8:      char ch, source[80];
 9:      int index;
10:      long count[127];
11:      FILE *fp;
12:
13:      /* Get the source and destination filenames. */
14:      fprintf(stderr, "\nEnter source file name: ");
15:      gets(source);
16:
17:      /* See that the source file exists. */
18:      if (!file_exists(source))
19:      {
20:          fprintf(stderr, "\n%s does not exist.\n", source);
21:      exit(1);
22:      }
23:      /* Open the file. */
24:      if ((fp = fopen(source, "rb")) == NULL)
25:      {
26:          fprintf(stderr, "\nError opening %s.\n", source);
27:       exit(1);
28:      }
29:      /* Zero the array elements. */
30:      for (index = 31; index < 127 ; index++)
31:          count[index] = 0;
32:
33:      while ( 1 )
34:      {
35:         ch = fgetc(fp);
36:         /* Done if end of file */
37:         if (feof(fp))
38:             break;
39:         /* Count only characters between 32 and 126. */
40:       if (ch > 31 && ch < 127)
41:             count[ch]++;
42:       }
43:      /* Display the results. */
44:      printf("\nChar\t\tCount\n");
45:      for (index = 32; index < 127 ; index++)
46:          printf("[%c]\t%d\n", index, count[index]);
47:     /* Close the file and exit. */
48:     fclose(fp);
49:     return(0);
50: }
51: int file_exists(char *filename)
52: {
53: /* Returns TRUE if filename exists,
54:    FALSE if not. */
```

LISTING T&R 5   continued

```
55:     FILE *fp;
56:     if ((fp = fopen(filename, "r")) == NULL)
57:         return 0;
58:     else
59:     {
60:         fclose(fp);
61:         return 1;
62:     }
63: }
```

ANALYSIS Look first at the function `file_exists()` on lines 51 to 63. Passed a filename as its argument, this function returns TRUE if the file exists and FALSE if it doesn't. Code in the function checks for the file by trying to open it in read mode (line 56). This is a general-purpose function that you can use in other programs.

Next, note how screen messages are displayed with the `fprintf()` function rather than `printf()`, as in line 14, for example. Why is this? Because `printf()` always sends output to stdout, the user won't see any messages if the redirection operator is used to direct program output to a disk file. Using `fprintf()` forces the messages to stderr, which is always the screen.

Finally, observe how the numerical value of each character is used as an index to the results array (lines 40 and 41). For example, the numerical value 32 represents a space, so the array element `count[32]` is used to keep a total of spaces.

When you run this program, you will be prompted to enter a file name:

```
Enter source file name: count_ch.c
```

After entering the file name, a count of the characters will be displayed. The following is the output from entering the count_ch.c listing:

```
Char    Count
[ ]     434
[!]     1
["]     14
[#]     2
[$]     0
[%]     4
[&]     2
[']     0
[(]     29
[)]     29
[*]     24
[+]     6
[,]     11
```

```
[-]      0
[.]      13
[/]      20
[0]      4
[1]      11
[2]      7
[3]      4
[4]      0
[5]      0
[6]      1
[7]      4
[8]      1
[9]      0
[:]      1
[;]      27
[<]      5
[=]      10
[>]      3
[?]      0
[@]      0
[A]      1
[B]      0
[C]      5
[D]      2
[E]      6
[F]      3
[G]      1
[H]      0
[I]      2
[J]      0
[K]      0
[L]      7
[M]      0
[N]      2
[O]      1
[P]      0
[Q]      0
[R]      2
[S]      2
[T]      1
[U]      3
[V]      0
[W]      0
[X]      0
[Y]      0
[Z]      1
[[]      6
[\]      11
[]]      6
[^]      0
[_]      3
```

```
[`]     0
[a]     26
[b]     5
[c]     35
[d]     25
[e]     100
[f]     50
[g]     4
[h]     23
[i]     62
[j]     0
[k]     1
[l]     27
[m]     9
[n]     69
[o]     40
[p]     18
[q]     0
[r]     51
[s]     43
[t]     59
[u]     25
[v]     1
[w]     2
[x]     19
[y]     3
[z]     0
[{]     6
[|]     0
[}]     6
[~]     0
```

DAY 17

Manipulating Strings

Text data, which C stores in strings, is an important part of many programs. So far, you have learned how a C program stores strings and how you can input and output strings. C offers a variety of functions for other types of string manipulations as well. Today you will learn

- How to determine the length of a string
- How to copy and join strings
- Functions that compare strings
- How to search strings
- How to convert strings
- How to test characters

Determining String Length

You should remember from earlier lessons that, in C programs, a string is a sequence of characters, with its beginning indicated by a pointer and its end marked by the null character \0. At times, you need to know the length of a string—the number of characters it contains. This length is obtained with the library function strlen(). Its prototype, in string.h, is

```
size_t strlen(char *str);
```

You might be puzzling over the size_t return type. This type is defined in string.h as unsigned, so the function strlen() returns an unsigned integer. The size_t type is used with many of the string functions. Just remember that it means unsigned.

The argument passed to strlen is a pointer to the string whose length you want to know. The function strlen() returns the number of characters between str and the next null character, not counting the null character. Listing 17.1 demonstrates strlen().

LISTING 17.1   strlen.c. Using the strlen() function to determine the length of a string

```
 1:  /* Using the strlen() function. */
 2:
 3:  #include <stdio.h>
 4:  #include <string.h>
 5:
 6:  int main( void )
 7:  {
 8:      size_t length;
 9:      char buf[80];
10:
11:      while (1)
12:      {
13:          puts("\nEnter a line of text, a blank line to exit.");
14:          gets(buf);
15:
16:          length = strlen(buf);
17:
18:          if (length != 0)
19:              printf("\nThat line is %u characters long.", length);
20:          else
21:              break;
22:      }
23:      return 0;
24: }
```

INPUT/
OUTPUT

```
Enter a line of text, a blank line to exit.
Just do it!

That line is 11 characters long.
Enter a line of text, a blank line to exit.
```

This program does little more than demonstrate the use of `strlen()`. Lines 13 and 14 display a message and get a string called `buf`. Line 16 uses `strlen()` to assign the length of `buf` to the variable `length`. Line 18 checks whether the string was blank by checking for a length of `0`. If the string is not blank, line 19 prints the string's size.

Copying Strings

The C library has two functions for copying strings. Because of the way C handles strings, you can't simply assign one string to another, as you can in some other computer languages. You must copy the source string from its location in memory to the memory location of the destination string. The string-copying functions are `strcpy()` and `strncpy()`. These functions require the header file string.h.

17

The `strcpy()` Function

The library function `strcpy()` copies an entire string to another memory location. Its prototype is as follows:

```
char *strcpy( char *destination, const char *source );
```

The function `strcpy()` copies the string (including the terminating null character `\0`) pointed to by `source` to the location pointed to by `destination`. The return value is a pointer to the new string, `destination`.

When using `strcpy()`, you must first allocate storage space for the destination string. The function has no way of knowing whether `destination` points to allocated space. If space hasn't been allocated, the function overwrites `strlen(source)` bytes of memory, starting at `destination`. This can cause unpredictable problems. The use of `strcpy()` is illustrated in Listing 17.2.

Note | When a program uses `malloc()` to allocate memory, as Listing 17.2 does, good programming practice requires the use of the `free()` function to free up the memory when the program is finished with it. You'll learn about `free()` on Day 20, "Working with Memory."

LISTING 17.2 strcpy.c. Before using `strcpy()`, you must allocate storage space for the destination string

```
1:  /* Demonstrates strcpy(). */
2:  #include <stdlib.h>
3:  #include <stdio.h>
```

LISTING 17.2   continued

```
 4:   #include <string.h>
 5:
 6:   char source[] = "The source string.";
 7:
 8:   int main( void )
 9:   {
10:       char dest1[80];
11:       char *dest2, *dest3;
12:
13:       printf("\nsource: %s", source );
14:
15:       /* Copy to dest1 is okay because dest1 points to */
16:       /* 80 bytes of allocated space. */
17:
18:       strcpy(dest1, source);
19:       printf("\ndest1:  %s", dest1);
20:
21:       /* To copy to dest2 you must allocate space. */
22:
23:       dest2 = (char *)malloc(strlen(source) +1);
24:       strcpy(dest2, source);
25:       printf("\ndest2:  %s\n", dest2);
26:
27:       /* Copying without allocating destination space is a no-no. */
28:       /* The following could cause serious problems. */
29:
30:       /* strcpy(dest3, source); */
31:       return 0;
32:   }
```

OUTPUT

```
source: The source string.
dest1:  The source string.
dest2:  The source string.
```

ANALYSIS This program demonstrates copying strings both to character arrays such as dest1 (declared on line 10) and to character pointers such as dest2 (declared along with dest3 on line 11). Line 13 prints the original source string. This string is then copied to dest1 with strcpy() on line 18. Line 24 copies source to dest2. Both dest1 and dest2 are printed to show that the function was successful. Notice that line 23 allocates the appropriate amount of space for dest2 with the malloc() function. If you copy a string to a character pointer that hasn't been allocated memory, you get unpredictable results.

The `strncpy()` Function

The `strncpy()` function is similar to `strcpy()`, except that `strncpy()` lets you specify how many characters to copy. Its prototype is

```
char *strncpy(char *destination, const char *source, size_t n);
```

The arguments `destination` and `source` are pointers to the destination and source strings. The function copies, at most, the first n characters of `source` to `destination`. If `source` is shorter than n characters, enough null characters are added at the end of `source` to make a total of n characters copied to `destination`. If `source` is longer than n characters, no terminating `\0` is added to `destination`. The function's return value is `destination`.

Listing 17.3 demonstrates the use of `strncpy()`.

LISTING 17.3   strncpy.c. The `strncpy()` function

```
 1:  /* Using the strncpy() function. */
 2:
 3:  #include <stdio.h>
 4:  #include <string.h>
 5:
 6:  char dest[] = ".........................";
 7:  char source[] = "abcdefghijklmnopqrstuvwxyz";
 8:
 9:  int main( void )
10:  {
11:      size_t n;
12:
13:      while (1)
14:      {
15:          puts("Enter the number of characters to copy (1-26)");
16:          scanf("%d", &n);
17:
18:          if (n > 0 && n< 27)
19:              break;
20:      }
21:
22:      printf("\nBefore strncpy destination = %s", dest);
23:
24:      strncpy(dest, source, n);
25:
26:      printf("\nAfter strncpy destination = %s\n", dest);
27:      return 0;
28:  }
```

17

Enter the number of characters to copy (1-26)
15

Before strncpy destination = ...
After strncpy destination = abcdefghijklmno..........

In addition to demonstrating the strncpy() function, this program also illustrates an effective way to ensure that only correct information is entered by the user. Lines 13–20 contain a while loop that prompts the user for a number from 1–26. The loop continues until a valid value is entered, so the program can't continue until the user enters a valid value. When a number between 1 and 26 is entered, line 22 prints the original value of dest, line 24 copies the number of characters specified by the user from source to dest, and line 26 prints the final value of dest.

> **Caution**
>
> Be sure that the number of characters copied doesn't exceed the allocated size of the destination. Also, be aware that strncpy() does not add a null terminator.

The strdup() Function

There is another string copying function worth mentioning. The strdup() function is similar to strcpy(), except that strdup() performs its own memory allocation for the destination string with a call to malloc(). In effect, it does what you did in Listing 17.2, allocating space with malloc() and then calling strcpy().

You should note that strdup() is not an ANSI-standard function. It is included with many compilers including the Microsoft, Borland, and Symantec C libraries, but it might not be present (or it might be different) in other C compilers.

The prototype for strdup() is

char *strdup(char *source);

The argument source is a pointer to the source string. The function returns a pointer to the destination string—the space allocated by malloc()—or NULL if the needed memory can't be allocated. Listing 17.4 demonstrates the use of strdup().

LISTING 17.4 strdup.c. Using strdup() to copy a string with automatic memory allocation

```
1:  /* The non-ANSI strdup() function. */
2:  #include <stdlib.h>
```

LISTING 17.4   continued

```
 3:  #include <stdio.h>
 4:  #include <string.h>
 5:
 6:  char source[] = "The source string.";
 7:
 8:  int main( void )
 9:  {
10:      char *dest;
11:
12:      if ( (dest = strdup(source)) == NULL)
13:      {
14:          fprintf(stderr, "Error allocating memory.");
15:          exit(1);
16:      }
17:
18:      printf("The destination = %s\n", dest);
19:      return 0;
20:  }
```

OUTPUT The destination = The source string.

ANALYSIS In this listing, strdup() allocates the appropriate memory for dest. It then makes a copy of the passed string, source. Line 18 prints the duplicated string.

17

Concatenating Strings

If you're not familiar with the term *concatenation*, you might be asking, "What is it?" and "Is it legal?" Well, it means to join two strings—to tack one string onto the end of another—and, in most states, it is legal. The C standard library contains two string concatenation functions—strcat() and strncat()—both of which require the header file string.h.

Using the strcat() Function

The prototype of strcat() is

```
char *strcat(char *str1, const char *str2);
```

The function appends a copy of str2 onto the end of str1, moving the terminating null character to the end of the new string. You must allocate enough space for str1 to hold the resulting string. The return value of strcat() is a pointer to str1. Listing 17.5 demonstrates strcat().

LISTING 17.5   strcat.c. Using `strcat()` to concatenate strings

```
1:  /* The strcat() function. */
2:
3:  #include <stdio.h>
4:  #include <string.h>
5:
6:  char str1[27] = "a";
7:  char str2[2];
8:
9:  int main( void )
10: {
11:     int n;
12:
13:     /* Put a null character at the end of str2[]. */
14:
15:     str2[1] = '\0';
16:
17:     for (n = 98; n< 123; n++)
18:     {
19:         str2[0] = n;
20:         strcat(str1, str2);
21:         puts(str1);
22:     }
23:      return 0;
24: }
```

OUTPUT

```
ab
abc
abcd
abcde
abcdef
abcdefg
abcdefgh
abcdefghi
abcdefghij
abcdefghijk
abcdefghijkl
abcdefghijklm
abcdefghijklmn
abcdefghijklmno
abcdefghijklmnop
abcdefghijklmnopq
abcdefghijklmnopqr
abcdefghijklmnopqrs
abcdefghijklmnopqrst
abcdefghijklmnopqrstu
abcdefghijklmnopqrstuv
```

```
abcdefghijklmnopqrstuvw
abcdefghijklmnopqrstuvwx
abcdefghijklmnopqrstuvwxy
abcdefghijklmnopqrstuvwxyz
```

ANALYSIS The ASCII codes for the letters b–z are 98–122. This program uses these ASCII codes in its demonstration of strcat(). The for loop on lines 17–22 assigns these values in turn to str2[0]. Because str2[1] is already the null character (line 15), the effect is to assign the strings "b", "c", and so on to str2. Each of these strings is concatenated with str1 (line 20), and then str1 is displayed on-screen (line 21).

Using the strncat() Function

The library function strncat() also performs string concatenation, but it lets you specify how many characters of the source string are appended to the end of the destination string. The prototype is

```
char *strncat(char *str1, const char *str2, size_t n);
```

If str2 contains more than n characters, the first n characters are appended to the end of str1. If str2 contains fewer than n characters, all of str2 is appended to the end of str1. In either case, a terminating null character is added at the end of the resulting string. You must allocate enough space for str1 to hold the resulting string. The function returns a pointer to str1. Listing 17.6 uses strncat() to produce the same output as Listing 17.5.

LISTING 17.6   strncat.c. Using the strncat() function to concatenate strings

```c
 1:  /* The strncat() function. */
 2:
 3:  #include <stdio.h>
 4:  #include <string.h>
 5:
 6:  char str2[] = "abcdefghijklmnopqrstuvwxyz";
 7:
 8:  int main( void )
 9:  {
10:      char str1[27];
11:      int n;
12:
13:      for (n=1; n< 27; n++)
14:      {
15:          strcpy(str1, "");
16:          strncat(str1, str2, n);
17:          puts(str1);
18:      }
19:      return 0;
20: }
```

OUTPUT
```
a
ab
abc
abcd
abcde
abcdef
abcdefg
abcdefgh
abcdefghi
abcdefghij
abcdefghijk
abcdefghijkl
abcdefghijklm
abcdefghijklmn
abcdefghijklmno
abcdefghijklmnop
abcdefghijklmnopq
abcdefghijklmnopqr
abcdefghijklmnopqrs
abcdefghijklmnopqrst
abcdefghijklmnopqrstu
abcdefghijklmnopqrstuv
abcdefghijklmnopqrstuvw
abcdefghijklmnopqrstuvwx
abcdefghijklmnopqrstuvwxy
abcdefghijklmnopqrstuvwxyz
```

ANALYSIS You might wonder about the purpose of line 15, `strcpy(str1, "");`. This line copies to `str1` an empty string consisting of only a single null character. The result is that the first character in `str1`—`str1[0]`—is set equal to `0` (the null character). The same thing could have been accomplished with the statements `str1[0] = 0;` or `str1[0] = '\0';`.

Comparing Strings

Strings are compared to determine whether they are equal or unequal. If they are unequal, one string is "greater than" or "less than" the other. Determinations of "greater" and "less" are made with the ASCII codes of the characters. In the case of letters, this is equivalent to alphabetical order, with the one seemingly strange exception that all upper-case letters are "less than" the lowercase letters. This is true because the uppercase letters have ASCII codes 65–90 for A–Z, while lowercase a–z are represented by 97–122. Thus, `"ZEBRA"` would be considered to be less than `"apple"` evaluating by these C functions.

The ANSI C library contains functions for two types of string comparisons: comparing two entire strings and comparing a certain number of characters in two strings.

Comparing Two Entire Strings

The function strcmp() compares two strings, character by character. Its prototype is

```
int strcmp(const char *str1, const char *str2);
```

The arguments str1 and str2 are pointers to the strings being compared. The function's return values are given in Table 17.1. You should notice that both strings are past as constants because neither will be changed. Listing 17.7 demonstrates strcmp().

TABLE 17.1 The values returned by strcmp()

Return Value	Meaning
< 0	str1 is less than str2.
0	str1 is equal to str2.
> 0	str1 is greater than str2.

17

LISTING 17.7 strcmp.c. Using strcmp() to compare strings

```
 1:  /* The strcmp() function. */
 2:
 3:  #include <stdio.h>
 4:  #include <string.h>
 5:
 6:  int main( void )
 7:  {
 8:      char str1[80], str2[80];
 9:      int x;
10:
11:      while (1)
12:      {
13:
14:          /* Input two strings. */
15:
16:          printf("\n\nInput the first string, a blank to exit: ");
17:          gets(str1);
18:
19:          if ( strlen(str1) == 0 )
20:              break;
21:
22:          printf("\nInput the second string: ");
23:          gets(str2);
24:
25:          /* Compare them and display the result. */
26:
27:          x = strcmp(str1, str2);
```

LISTING 17.7.   continued

```
28:
29:          printf("\nstrcmp(%s,%s) returns %d", str1, str2, x);
30:     }
31:     return 0;
32: }
```

OUTPUT

Input the first string, a blank to exit: **First string**

Input the second string: **Second string**

strcmp(First string,Second string) returns -1

Input the first string, a blank to exit: **test string**

Input the second string: **test string**

strcmp(test string,test string) returns 0

Input the first string, a blank to exit: **zebra**

Input the second string: **aardvark**

strcmp(zebra,aardvark) returns 1

Input the first string, a blank to exit:

Note

On some UNIX systems, string comparison functions don't necessarily return
-1 when the strings aren't the same. They will, however, always return a
nonzero value for unequal strings.

The ANSI Standard only states that the return value will be less than, equal
to, or greater than zero.

ANALYSIS   This program demonstrates strcmp(), prompting the user for two strings (lines 16, 17, 22, and 23) and displaying the result returned by strcmp() on line 29. Experiment with this program to get a feel for how strcmp() compares strings. Try entering two strings that are identical except for case, such as Smith and SMITH. You learn that strcmp() is case-sensitive, meaning that the program considers uppercase and lowercase letters to be different.

Comparing Partial Strings

The library function strncmp() compares a specified number of characters of one string to another string. Its prototype is

```
int strncmp(const char *str1, const char *str2, size_t n);
```

The function strncmp() compares n characters of str2 to str1. The comparison proceeds until n characters have been compared or the end of str1 has been reached. The method of comparison and return values are the same as for strcmp(). The comparison is case-sensitive. Listing 17.8 demonstrates strncmp().

LISTING **17.8**   strncmp.c. Comparing parts of strings with strncmp()

```
1:  /* The strncmp() function. */
2:
3:  #include <stdio.h>
4:  #include <string.h>
5:
6:  char str1[] = "The first string.";
7:  char str2[] = "The second string.";
8:
9:  int main( void )
10: {
11:     size_t n, x;
12:
13:     puts(str1);
14:     puts(str2);
15:
16:     while (1)
17:     {
18:         puts("\n\nEnter number of characters to compare, 0 to exit.");
19:         scanf("%d", &n);
20:
21:         if (n <= 0)
22:             break;
23:
24:         x = strncmp(str1, str2, n);
25:
26:         printf("\nComparing %d characters, strncmp() returns %d.", n, x);
27:     }
28:     return 0;
29: }
```

17

**INPUT/
OUTPUT**

```
The first string.
The second string.

Enter number of characters to compare, 0 to exit.
3

Comparing 3 characters, strncmp() returns 0.

Enter number of characters to compare, 0 to exit.
6

Comparing 6 characters, strncmp() returns -1.

Enter number of characters to compare, 0 to exit.
0
```

ANALYSIS This program compares two strings defined on lines 6 and 7. Lines 13 and 14 print the strings to the screen so that the user can see what they are. The program executes a while loop on lines 16–27 so that multiple compares can be done. If the user asks to compare zero characters on lines 18 and 19, the program breaks on line 22; otherwise, a strncmp() executes on line 24, and the result is printed on line 26.

Comparing Two Strings While Ignoring Case

Unfortunately, the ANSI C library doesn't include any functions for case-insensitive string comparison. Fortunately, most C compilers provide their own "in-house" functions for this task. Symantec uses the function strcmpl(). Microsoft uses a function called _stricmp(). Borland has two functions—strcmpi() and stricmp(). Check your library reference manual to determine which function is appropriate for your compiler. When you use a function that isn't case-sensitive, the strings Smith and SMITH compare as equal. Modify line 27 in Listing 17.7 to use the appropriate case-insensitive compare function for your compiler, and try the program again.

Searching Strings

The C library contains a number of functions that search strings. To put it another way, these functions determine whether one string occurs within another string and, if so, where. You can choose from six string searching functions, all of which require the header file string.h:

- strchr()
- strrchr()
- strcspn()

- strspn()
- strpbrk()
- strstr()

The strchr() Function

The strchr() function finds the first occurrence of a specified character in a string. The prototype is

```
char *strchr(constchar *str, int ch);
```

The function strchr() searches str from left to right until the character ch is found or the terminating null character is found. If ch is found, a pointer to it is returned. If not, NULL is returned.

When strchr() finds the character, it returns a pointer to that character. Knowing that str is a pointer to the first character in the string, you can obtain the position of the found character by subtracting str from the pointer value returned by strchr(). Listing 17.9 illustrates this. Remember that the first character in a string is at position 0. Like many of C's string functions, strchr() is case-sensitive and will, therefore, report that the character "F" isn't found in the string "raffle".

LISTING 17.9   strchr.c. Using strchr() to search a string for a single character

```
1:   /* Searching for a single character with strchr(). */
2:
3:   #include <stdio.h>
4:   #include <string.h>
5:
6:   int main( void )
7:   {
8:       char *loc, buf[80];
9:       int ch;
10:
11:      /* Input the string and the character. */
12:
13:      printf("Enter the string to be searched: ");
14:      gets(buf);
15:      printf("Enter the character to search for: ");
16:      ch = getchar();
17:
18:      /* Perform the search. */
19:
20:      loc = strchr(buf, ch);
21:
22:      if ( loc == NULL )
```

17

LISTING **17.9**   continued

```
23:         printf("The character %c was not found.", ch);
24:     else
25:         printf("The character %c was found at position %d.\n",
26:                 ch, loc-buf);
27:     return 0;
28: }
```

INPUT/
OUTPUT

```
Enter the string to be searched: How now Brown Cow?
Enter the character to search for: C
The character C was found at position 14.
```

ANALYSIS   This program uses strchr() on line 20 to search for a character within a string.
strchr() returns a pointer to the location where the character is first found or
NULL if the character isn't found. Line 22 checks whether the value of loc is NULL and
prints an appropriate message. As described in the section "The strchr() Function," the
position of the character within the string is determined by subtracting the string pointer
from the value returned by the function.

The strchr() Function

The library function strrchr() is identical to strchr(), except that it searches a string
for the last occurrence of a specified character in a string. Its prototype is

```
char *strrchr(const char *str, int ch);
```

The function strrchr() returns a pointer to the last occurrence of ch in str and NULL if
it finds no match. To see how this function works, modify line 20 in Listing 17.9 to use
strrchr() instead of strchr().

The strcspn() Function

The library function strcspn() searches one string for the first occurrence of any of the
characters in a second string. Its prototype is

```
size_t strcspn(const char *str1, const char *str2);
```

The function strcspn() starts searching at the first character of str1, looking for any of
the individual characters contained in str2. This is important to remember. The function
doesn't look for the string str2, but only the characters it contains. If the function finds a
match, it returns the offset from the beginning of str1 where the matching character is
located. If it finds no match, strcspn() returns the value of strlen(str1). This indicates that the first match was the null character terminating the string. Listing 17.10
shows you how to use strcspn().

LISTING 17.10   strcspn.c. Searching for a set of characters with strcspn()

```
 1:  /* Searching with strcspn(). */
 2:
 3:  #include <stdio.h>
 4:  #include <string.h>
 5:
 6:  int main( void )
 7:  {
 8:      char  buf1[80], buf2[80];
 9:      size_t loc;
10:
11:      /* Input the strings. */
12:
13:      printf("Enter the string to be searched: ");
14:      gets(buf1);
15:      printf("Enter the string containing target characters: ");
16:      gets(buf2);
17:
18:      /* Perform the search. */
19:
20:      loc = strcspn(buf1, buf2);
21:
22:      if ( loc ==  strlen(buf1) )
23:          printf("No match was found.");
24:      else
25:          printf("The first match was found at position %d.\n", loc);
26:      return0;
27: }
```

**INPUT/
OUTPUT**
```
Enter the string to be searched: How now Brown Cow?
Enter the string containing target characters: Cat
The first match was found at position 14.
```

ANALYSIS   This listing is similar to Listing 17.9. Instead of searching for the first occurrence
of a single character, it searches for the first occurrence of any of the characters
entered in the second string. The program calls strcspn() on line 20 with buf1 and
buf2. If any of the characters in buf2 are in buf1, strcspn() returns the offset from the
beginning of buf1 to the location of the first occurrence. Line 22 checks the return value
to determine whether it is NULL. If the value is NULL, no characters were found and an
appropriate message is displayed on line 23. If a value was found, a message is displayed
stating the character's position in the string.

The `strspn()` Function

This function is related to the previous one, `strcspn()`, as the following paragraph explains. Its prototype is

```
size_t strspn(const char *str1, const char *str2);
```

The function `strspn()` searches `str1`, comparing it character by character with the characters contained in `str2`. It returns the position of the first character in `str1` that doesn't match a character in `str2`. In other words, `strspn()` returns the length of the initial segment of `str1` that consists entirely of characters found in `str2`. The return is 0 if no characters match. Listing 17.11 demonstrates `strspn()`.

LISTING 17.11   strspn.c. Searching for the first nonmatching character with `strspn()`

```
 1:  /* Searching with strspn(). */
 2:
 3:  #include <stdio.h>
 4:  #include <string.h>
 5:
 6:  int main( void )
 7:  {
 8:      char  buf1[80], buf2[80];
 9:      size_t loc;
10:
11:      /* Input the strings. */
12:
13:      printf("Enter the string to be searched: ");
14:      gets(buf1);
15:      printf("Enter the string containing target characters: ");
16:      gets(buf2);
17:
18:      /* Perform the search. */
19:
20:      loc = strspn(buf1, buf2);
21:
22:      if ( loc ==  0 )
23:          printf("No match was found.\n");
24:      else
25:          printf("Characters match up to position %d.\n", loc-1);
26:      return 0;
27: }
```

OUTPUT

```
Enter the string to be searched: How now Brown Cow?
Enter the string containing target characters: How now what?
Characters match up to position 7.
```

ANALYSIS This program is similar to the previous example, except that it calls `strspn()` instead of `strcspn()` on line 20. The function returns the offset into `buf1` where the first character that is not in `buf2` is found. Lines 22–25 evaluate the return value and print an appropriate message.

The `strpbrk()` Function

The library function `strpbrk()` is similar to `strcspn()`, searching one string for the first occurrence of any character contained in another string. It differs in that it doesn't include the terminating null characters in the search. The function prototype is

```
char *strpbrk( const char *str1, const char *str2);
```

The function `strpbrk()` returns a pointer to the first character in `str1` that matches any of the characters in `str2`. If it doesn't find a match, the function returns NULL. As previously explained for the function `strchr()`, you can obtain the offset of the first match in `str1` by subtracting the pointer `str1` from the pointer returned by `strpbrk()` (if it isn't NULL, of course). For example, replace `strcspn()` on line 20 of Listing 17.10 with `strpbrk()`.

The `strstr()` Function

The final and, perhaps, most useful C string searching function is `strstr()`. This function searches for the first occurrence of one string within another, and it searches for the entire string, not just for individual characters within the string. Its prototype is

```
char *strstr(const char *str1, const char *str2);
```

The function `strstr()` returns a pointer to the first occurrence of `str2` within `str1`. If it finds no match, the function returns NULL. If the length of `str2` is 0, the function returns `str1`. When `strstr()` finds a match, you can obtain the offset of `str2` within `str1` by pointer subtraction, as explained earlier for `strchr()`. The matching procedure that `strstr()` uses is case-sensitive. Listing 17.12 demonstrates how to use `strstr()`.

LISTING 17.12 strstr.c. Using `strstr()` to search for one string within another

```
1:  /* Searching with strstr(). */
2:
3:  #include <stdio.h>
4:  #include <string.h>
5:
6:  int main( void )
7:  {
8:      char *loc, buf1[80], buf2[80];
9:
```

17

LISTING **17.12**   continued

```
10:      /* Input the strings. */
11:
12:      printf("Enter the string to be searched: ");
13:      gets(buf1);
14:      printf("Enter the target string: ");
15:      gets(buf2);
16:
17:      /* Perform the search. */
18:
19:      loc = strstr(buf1, buf2);
20:
21:      if ( loc ==  NULL )
22:          printf("No match was found.\n");
23:      else
24:          printf("%s was found at position %d.\n", buf2, loc-buf1);
25:      return 0;
26: }
```

INPUT/
OUTPUT

```
Enter the string to be searched: How now brown cow?
Enter the target string: cow
Cow was found at position 14.
```

ANALYSIS   This function provides an alternative way to search a string. This time you can search for an entire string within another string. Lines 12–15 prompt for two strings. Line 19 uses strstr() to search for the second string, buf2, within the first string, buf1. A pointer to the first occurrence is returned, or NULL is returned if the string isn't found. Lines 21–24 evaluate the returned value, loc, and print an appropriate message.

Do	**Don't**
DO remember that for many of the string functions, there are equivalent functions that let you specify a number of characters to manipulate. The functions that allow specification of the number of characters are usually named strn*xxx*(), where *xxx* is specific to the function.	DON'T forget that C is case-sensitive. A and a are different.

String Conversions

Many C libraries contain two functions that change the case of characters within a string. These functions aren't ANSI standard and, therefore, might differ or not even exist in your compiler. Because they can be quite useful, they are included here. Their proto-types, in string.h, are as follows for the Microsoft C compiler (if you use a different com-piler, they should be similar):

```
char *strlwr(char *str);
char *strupr(char *str);
```

The function `strlwr()` converts all the letter characters in `str` from uppercase to lower-case; `strupr()` does the reverse, converting all the characters in `str` to uppercase. Nonletter characters aren't affected. Both functions return `str`. Note that neither function actually creates a new string, but both modify the existing string in place. Listing 17.13 demonstrates these functions. Remember that to compile a program that uses non-ANSI functions, you might need to tell your compiler not to enforce the ANSI standards.

17

LISTING 17.13   upper.c. Converting the case of characters in a string with `strlwr()` and `strupr()`

```
 1:  /* The character conversion functions strlwr() and strupr(). */
 2:
 3:  #include <stdio.h>
 4:  #include <string.h>
 5:
 6:  int main( void )
 7:  {
 8:      char buf[80];
 9:
10:      while (1)
11:      {
12:          puts("Enter a line of text, a blank to exit.");
13:          gets(buf);
14:
15:          if ( strlen(buf) == 0 )
16:              break;
17:
18:          puts(strlwr(buf));
19:          puts(strupr(buf));
20:      }
21:      return 0;
22: }
```

Enter a line of text, a blank to exit.
Bradley L. Jones

bradley l. jones
BRADLEY L. JONES
Enter a line of text, a blank to exit.

ANALYSIS This listing prompts for a string on line 12. It then checks to ensure that the string isn't blank (line 15). Line 18 prints the string after converting it to lowercase. Line 19 prints the string in all uppercase.

These functions are a part of the Dev-C++, Symantec, Microsoft, and Borland C libraries. You need to check the Library Reference for your compiler before using these functions. If portability is a concern, you should avoid using non-ANSI functions such as these.

Miscellaneous String Functions

This section covers a few string functions that don't fall into any other category. They all require the header file string.h. The functions covered are

- `strrev()`
- `strset()`
- strnset()

The `strrev()` Function

The function `strrev()` reverses the order of all the characters in a string. Its prototype is

`char *strrev(char *str);`

The order of all characters in `str` is reversed, with the terminating null character remaining at the end. The `strrev()` function is not defined in the ANSI standard. As stated before, this means that it may not be supported in all compilers, or that it may be supported differently.

The function returns `str`. After `strset()` and `strnset()` are defined in the next section, `strrev()` is demonstrated in Listing 17.14.

The `strset()` and `strnset()` Functions

Like the previous function, `strset()`, and `strnset()` aren't part of the ANSI C standard library. These functions change all characters (`strset()`) or a specified number of characters (`strnset()`) in a string to a specified character. The prototypes are

```
char *strset(char *str, int ch);
char *strnset(char *str, int ch, size_t n);
```

The function strset() changes all the characters in str to ch except the terminating null character. The function strnset() changes the first n characters of str to ch. If n >= strlen(str), strnset() changes all the characters in str. Listing 17.14 demonstrates both functions.

LISTING 17.14   strings.c. A demonstration of strrev(), strnset(), and strset()

```
1:  /* Demonstrates strrev(), strset(), and strnset(). */
2:  #include <stdio.h>
3:  #include <string.h>
4:
5:  char str[] = "This is the test string.";
6:
7:  int main( void )
8:  {
9:      printf("\nThe original string: %s", str);
10:     printf("\nCalling strrev(): %s", strrev(str));
11:     printf("\nCalling strrev() again: %s", strrev(str));
12:     printf("\nCalling strnset(): %s", strnset(str, '!', 5));
13:     printf("\nCalling strset(): %s", strset(str, '!'));
14:     return 0;
15: }
```

17

OUTPUT
```
The original string: This is the test string.
Calling strrev(): .gnirts tset eht si sihT
Calling strrev() again: This is the test string.
Calling strnset(): !!!!!is the test string.
Calling strset(): !!!!!!!!!!!!!!!!!!!!!!!!!
```

ANALYSIS This program demonstrates the three different string functions. The demonstrations are done by printing the value of a string, str. Line 9 prints the string normally. Line 10 prints the string after it has been reversed with strrev(). Line 11 reverses it back to its original state. Line 12 uses the strnset() function to set the first five characters of str to exclamation marks. To finish the program, line 13 changes the entire string to exclamation marks.

Although these functions aren't a part of the ANSI standard, they are included in the Dev-C++, Symantec, Microsoft, and Borland C compiler function libraries. You should check your compiler's Library Reference manual to determine whether your compiler supports these functions.

String-to-Number Conversions

Sometimes, you will need to convert the string representation of a number to an actual numeric variable. For example, the string "123" can be converted to a type int variable with the value 123. Four functions can be used to convert a string to a number. They are explained in the following paragraphs, and their prototypes are in stdlib.h.

Converting Strings To Integers

The library function atoi() converts a string to an integer. The prototype is

```
int atoi(const char *ptr);
```

The function atoi() converts the string pointed to by ptr to an integer. Besides digits, the string can contain leading whitespace and a + or – sign. Conversion starts at the beginning of the string and proceeds until an unconvertible character (for example, a letter or punctuation mark) is encountered. The resulting integer is returned to the calling program. If it finds no convertible characters, atoi() returns 0. Table 17.2 lists some examples.

TABLE 17.2   String-to-number conversions with atoi()

String	Value Returned by atoi()
"157"	157
"-1.6"	-1
"+50x"	50
"twelve"	0
"x506"	0

The first example is straightforward. In the second example, you might be confused about why the ".6" didn't translate. Remember that this is a string-to-integer conversion. The floating point portion of a number is dropped.

The third example is also straightforward; the function understands the plus sign and considers it a part of the number. The fourth example uses "twelve". The atoi() function can't translate words; it sees only characters. Because the string didn't start with a number, atoi() returns 0. This is also true of the last example.

Converting Strings to Longs

The library function atol() works exactly like atoi(), except that it returns a type long. The function prototype is

```
long atol(const char *ptr);
```

The values returned by atol() would be the same as shown for atoi() in Table 17.2, except that each return value would be a type long instead of a type int.

Converting Strings to Long Longs

Just like the atoi() and atoll() functions, the atoll function converts a string value to a long long value. The prototype for the atoll() function is

```
long long atoll(const char *ptr);
```

Converting Strings to Floating Point Numeric Values

The function atof() converts a string to a type double. The prototype is

```
double atof(const char *str);
```

The argument str points to the string to be converted. This string can contain leading whitespace and a + or – character. The number can contain the digits 0–9, the decimal point, and the exponent indicator E or e. If there are no convertible characters, atof() returns 0. Table 17.3 lists some examples of using atof().

TABLE 17.3 String-to-number conversions with atof()

String	Value Returned by atof()
"12"	12.000000
"-0.123"	-0.123000
"123E+3"	123000.000000
"123.1e-5"	0.001231

Listing 17.15 illustrates the use of atof(). It lets you enter your own strings for conversion.

LISTING 17.15 atof.c. Using atof() to convert strings to type double numeric variables

```
1:  /* Demonstration of atof(). */
2:
3:  #include <string.h>
4:  #include <stdio.h>
5:  #include <stdlib.h>
6:
7:  int main( void )
8:  {
9:      char buf[80];
10:     double d;
11:
```

LISTING 17.15 continued

```
12:    while (1)
13:    {
14:        printf("\nEnter the string to convert (blank to exit):    ");
15:        gets(buf);
16:
17:        if ( strlen(buf) == 0 )
18:            break;
19:
20:        d = atof( buf );
21:
22:        printf("The converted value is %f.", d);
23:    }
24:    return 0;
25: }
```

INPUT/ OUTPUT

```
Enter the string to convert (blank to exit):    1009.12
The converted value is 1009.120000.
Enter the string to convert (blank to exit):    abc
The converted value is 0.000000.
Enter the string to convert (blank to exit):    3
The converted value is 3.000000.
Enter the string to convert (blank to exit):
```

ANALYSIS The while loop on lines 12–23 lets you keep running the program until you enter a blank line. Lines 14 and 15 prompt for the value. Line 17 checks whether a blank line is entered. If it is, the program breaks out of the while loop and ends. Line 20 calls atof(), converting the value entered (buf) to a type double, d. Line 22 prints the final result.

Character Test Functions

The header file ctype.h contains the prototypes for a number of functions that test characters, returning TRUE or FALSE depending on whether the character meets a certain condition. For example, is it a letter or is it a numeral? The is*xxxx*() functions are actually macros, defined in ctype.h. You learn about macros on Day 21, "Advanced Compiler Use." At that time, you might want to look at the definitions in ctype.h to see how they work. For now, you only need to see how they're used.

The is*xxxx*() macros all have the same prototype.

```
int isxxxx(int ch);
```

In the preceding line, ch is the character being tested. The return value is TRUE (nonzero) if the condition is met, or FALSE (zero) if it isn't. Table 17.4 lists the complete set of isxxxx() macros.

TABLE 17.4 The isxxxx() macros

Macro	Action
isalnum()	Returns TRUE if ch is a letter or a digit.
isalpha()	Returns TRUE if ch is a letter.
isblank()	Returns TRUE if ch is blank
iscntrl()	Returns TRUE if ch is a control character.
isdigit()	Returns TRUE if ch is a digit.
isgraph()	Returns TRUE if ch is a printing character (other than a space).
islower()	Returns TRUE if ch is a lowercase letter.
isprint()	Returns TRUE if ch is a printing character (including a space).
ispunct()	Returns TRUE if ch is a punctuation character.
isspace()	Returns TRUE if ch is a whitespace character (space, tab, vertical tab, line feed, form feed, or carriage return).
isupper()	Returns TRUE if ch is an uppercase letter.
isxdigit()	Returns TRUE if ch is a hexadecimal digit (0–9, a–f, A–F).

17

You can do many interesting things with the character-test macros. One example is the function get_int() in Listing 17.16. This function inputs an integer from stdin and returns it as a type int variable. The function skips over leading whitespace and returns 0 if the first nonspace character isn't a numeric character.

LISTING 17.16 getint.c. Using the isxxxx() macros to implement a function that inputs an integer

```
1:  /* Using character test macros to create an integer */
2:  /* input function. */
3:
4:  #include <stdio.h>
5:  #include <ctype.h>
6:
7:  int get_int(void);
8:
9:  int main( void )
10: {
11:     int x;
```

LISTING 17.16 continued

```
12:      x = get_int();
13:
14:      printf("You entered %d.\n", x);
15: }
16:
17: int get_int(void)
18: {
19:      int ch, i, sign = 1;
20:
21:      /* Skip over any leading white space. */
22:
23:      while ( isspace(ch = getchar()) )
24:          ;
25:
26:      /* If the first character is nonnumeric, unget */
27:      /* the character and return 0. */
28:
29:      if (ch != '-' && ch != '+' && !isdigit(ch) && ch != EOF)
30:      {
31:          ungetc(ch, stdin);
32:          return 0;
33:      }
34:
35:      /* If the first character is a minus sign, set */
36:      /* sign accordingly. */
37:
38:      if (ch == '-')
39:          sign = -1;
40:
41:      /* If the first character was a plus or minus sign, */
42:      /* get the next character. */
43:
44:      if (ch == '+' || ch == '-')
45:          ch = getchar();
46:
47:      /* Read characters until a nondigit is input. Assign */
48:      /* values, multiplied by proper power of 10, to i. */
49:
50:      for (i = 0; isdigit(ch); ch = getchar() )
51:          i = 10 * i + (ch - '0');
52:
53:      /* Make result negative if sign is negative. */
54:
55:      i *= sign;
56:
57:      /* If EOF was not encountered, a nondigit character */
58:      /* must have been read in, so unget it. */
59:
```

LISTING 17.16   continued

```
60:      if (ch != EOF)
61:          ungetc(ch, stdin);
62:
63:      /* Return the input value. */
64:
65:      return i;
66: }
```

INPUT/
OUTPUT

```
-100
You entered -100.
abc3.145
You entered 0.
9 9 9
You entered 9.
2.5
You entered 2.
```

17

ANALYSIS This program uses the library function ungetc() on lines 31 and 61, which you learned about on Day 14, "Working with the Screen, Printer, and Keyboard." Remember that this function "ungets," or returns, a character to the specified stream. This returned character is the first one input the next time the program reads a character from that stream. This is necessary because when the function get_int() reads a nonnumeric character from stdin, you want to put that character back, in case the program needs to read it later.

In this program, main() is simple. An integer variable, x, is declared (line 11), assigned the value of the get_int() function (line 12), and printed to the screen (line 14). The get_int() function makes up the rest of the program.

The get_int() function isn't so simple. To remove leading whitespace that might be entered, line 23 loops with a while command. The isspace() macro tests a character, ch, obtained with the getchar() function. If ch is a space, another character is retrieved, until a nonwhitespace character is received. Line 29 checks whether the character is one that can be used. Line 29 could be read, "If the character input isn't a negative sign, a plus sign, a digit, or the end of the file(s)." If this is true, ungetc() is used on line 31 to put the character back, and the function returns to main(). If the character is usable, execution continues.

Lines 38–45 handle the sign of the number. Line 38 checks whether the character entered is a negative sign. If it is, a variable (sign) is set to -1. sign is used to make the final number either positive or negative (line 55). Because positive numbers are the default, after you have taken care of the negative sign, you are almost ready to continue. If a sign is entered, the program must get another character. Lines 44 and 45 take care of this.

The heart of the function is the `for` loop on lines 50 and 51, which continues to get characters as long as the characters gotten are digits. Line 51 might be a little confusing at first. This line takes the individual character entered and turns it into a number. Subtracting the character `'0'` from your number changes a character number to a real number. (Remember the ASCII values.) When the correct numerical value is obtained, the numbers are multiplied by the proper power of 10. The `for` loop continues until a nondigit number is entered. At that point, line 55 applies the sign to the number, making it complete.

Before returning, the program needs to do a little cleanup. If the last number wasn't the end of file, it needs to be put back (in case it's needed elsewhere). Line 61 does this before line 65 returns.

Do	**Don't**
DO take advantage of the string functions that are available.	**DON'T** use non-ANSI functions if you plan to port your application to other platforms.
	DON'T confuse characters with numbers. It's easy to forget that the character "1" isn't the same thing as the number 1.

ANSI Support for Uppercase and Lowercase

While the `strlwr()` and `strupr()` functions will convert a string to lowercase or uppercase, they are not a part of the ANSI standard. The ANSI standard does, however, define two macros for converting information to uppercase or lowercase. Along with the `isxxxx()` macros there are two ANSI defined macros for changing a character's case — `toupper()` and `tolower()`. The use of these macros can be seen in Listing 17.17.

LISTING 17.17   upper2.c. Converting the case of characters in a string with `tolower()` and `toupper()`

```
1:  /* The character conversion functions strlwr() and strupr(). */
2: #include <ctype.h>
3: #include <stdio.h>
4: #include <string.h>
5:
6: int main( void )
7: {
8:     char buf[80];
9:     int  ctr;
```

LISTING 17.17   continued

```
10:
11:     while (1)
12:     {
13:         puts("\nEnter a line of text, a blank to exit.");
14:         gets(buf);
15:
16:         if ( strlen(buf) == 0 )
17:             break;
18:
19:         for ( ctr = 0; ctr< strlen(buf); ctr++)
20:         {
21:             printf("%c", tolower(buf[ctr]));
22:         }
23:
24:         printf("\n");
25:         for ( ctr = 0; ctr< strlen(buf); ctr++)
26:         {
27:             printf("%c", toupper(buf[ctr]));
28:         }
29:         printf("\n");
30:     }
31:     return 0;
32: }
```

INPUT/ OUTPUT	Enter a line of text, a blank to exit.

```
Enter a line of text, a blank to exit.
My aun't name is Carolyn C.
my aun't name is carolyn c.
MY AUN'T NAME IS CAROLYN C.Enter a line of text, a blank to exit.
```

ANALYSIS   This listing prompts for a string on line 13 and uses gets() in line 14 to obtain it. It then checks to ensure that the string isn't blank (line 16). Because the toupper and tolower macros work with individual characters, this listing displays the information in buf differently than the way Listing 17.14 did. You can see in line 19 that a for loop is used to cycle through the characters. Each is then converted.

Note

> Where possible you should use the toupper() and tolower() macros rather than the strupr() and strlwr() non-ANSI functions. You can create your own functions using toupper() and tolower(). Your functions would then be ANSI compliant.

17

Summary

Today's lesson showed the various ways you use C to manipulate strings. Using C standard library functions (and possibly some non-ANSI, compiler-specific functions as well), you can copy, concatenate, compare, and search strings. These are all necessary tasks in most programming projects. The standard library also contains functions for converting the case of characters in strings and for converting strings to numbers. Finally, C provides a variety of character-test functions or, more accurately, macros that perform a variety of tests on individual characters. By using these macros to test characters, you can create your own custom input functions.

Q&A

Q How do I know whether a function is ANSI compatible?

A Most compilers have a Library Function Reference manual or section. This manual or section of a manual lists all the compiler's library functions and how to use them. Usually, the manual includes information on the compatibility of the function. Sometimes, the descriptions state not only whether the function is ANSI-compatible, but also whether it is compatible with DOS, UNIX, Windows, C++, or OS/2. (Most compilers tell you only what is relevant to their compiler.)

Q Are all the available string functions presented in today's lessons?

A No. However, the string functions presented today should cover virtually all your needs. Consult your compiler's Library Reference to see what other functions are available.

Q Does `strcat()` ignore trailing spaces when doing a concatenation?

A No. `strcat()` looks at a space as just another character.

Q Can I convert numbers to strings?

A Yes. You can write a function similar to the one in Listing 17.16, or you can check your Library Reference for available functions. Some functions available include `itoa()`, `ltoa()`, and `ultoa()`. `sprint(f)` can also be used.

Workshop

The Workshop provides quiz questions to help you solidify your understanding of the material covered and exercises to provide you with experience in using what you've learned.

Quiz

1. What is the length of a string, and how can the length be determined?

2. Before copying a string, what must you be sure to do?

3. What does the term *concatenate* mean?

4. When comparing strings, what is meant by "One string is greater than another string"?

5. What is the difference between strcmp() and strncmp()?

6. What is the difference between strcmp() and strcmpi()?

7. What values does isascii() test for?

8. Using Table 17.4, which macros would return TRUE for var?

   ```
   int var = 1;
   ```

9. Using Table 17.4, which macros would return TRUE for x?

   ```
   char x = 65;
   ```

10. What are the character-test functions used for?

Exercises

1. What values do the test functions return?

2. What would the atoi() function return if passed the following values?

   a. "65"

   b. "81.23"

   c. "-34.2"

   d. "ten"

   e. "+12hundred"

   f. "negative100"

3. What would the atof() function return if passed the following?

   a. "65"

   b. "81.23"

   c. "-34.2"

   d. "ten"

   e. "+12hundred"

   f. "1e+3"

17

4. **BUG BUSTER:** Is anything wrong with the following?

```
char *string1, string2;
string1 = "Hello World";
strcpy( string2, string1);
printf( "%s %s", string1, string2 );
```

Because of the many possible solutions, answers aren't provided for the following exercises.

5. Write a program that prompts for the user's last name, first name, and middle name individually. Then store the name in a new string as first initial, period, space, middle initial, period, space, last name. For example, if Bradley, Lee, and Jones are entered, store B. L. Jones. Display the new name to the screen.

6. Write a program to prove your answers to quiz questions 8 and 9.

7. The function strstr() finds the first occurrence of one string within another, and it is case-sensitive. Write a function that performs the same task without case-sensitivity.

8. Write a function that determines the number of times one string occurs within another.

9. Write a program that searches a text file for occurrences of a user-specified target string and then reports the line numbers where the target is found. For example, if you search one of your C source code files for the string "printf()", the program should list all the lines where the printf() function is called by the program.

10. Listing 17.16 demonstrates a function that inputs an integer from stdin. Write a function get_float() that inputs a floating-point value from stdin.

DAY 18

Getting More from Functions

As you know by now, functions are central to C programming. Today you will learn more ways to use functions in your programs, including

- Passing pointers as arguments to functions
- Passing type void pointers as arguments
- Using functions with a variable number of arguments
- Returning a pointer from a function

Some of these topics have been mentioned earlier in this book, but today's lesson provides more detailed information.

Passing Pointers to Functions

The default method of passing an argument to a function is by value. *Passing by value* means that the function is passed a copy of the argument's value. This method has three steps:

1. The argument expression is evaluated.

2. The result is copied onto the *stack,* a temporary storage area in memory.

3. The function retrieves the argument's value from the stack.

The main point is that if a variable is passed as the argument, code in the function cannot modify the value of the variable. Figure 18.1 illustrates passing an argument by value. In this case, the argument is a simple type `int` variable, but the principle is the same for other variable types and more complex expressions.

FIGURE 18.1

Passing an argument by value. The function can't modify the original argument variable.

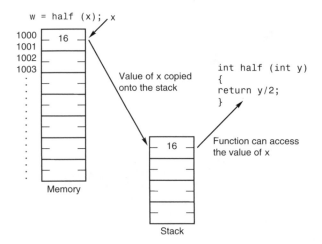

When a variable is passed to a function by value, the function has access to the variable's value but not to the original copy of the variable. As a result, the code in the function can't modify the original variable. This is the main reason why passing by value is the default method of passing arguments: Data outside a function is protected from inadvertent modification.

There is another way to pass an argument to a function. Passing arguments by value is possible with the basic data types (`char`, `short`, `int`, `long`, `long long`, `float`, `double`, and `long double`) and structures. The alternative method is to pass a pointer to the argument variable rather than the value of the variable itself. This method of passing an argument is called *passing by reference*. Because the function has the address of the actual variable, the function can modify the variable's value.

As you learned on Day 9, "Understanding Pointers," passing by reference is the only way to pass an array to a function; passing an array by value is not possible. With other data types, however, you can use either method. If your program uses large structures, passing them by value might cause your program to run out of stack space. Aside from this consideration, passing an argument by reference instead of by value offers an advantage as well as a disadvantage:

- The advantage of passing by reference is that the function can modify the value of the argument variable.
- The disadvantage of passing by reference is that the function can modify the value of the argument variable.

"What?" you might be saying. "An advantage that's also a disadvantage?" Yes. It all depends on the specific situation. If your program requires that a function modify an argument variable, passing by reference is an advantage. If there is no such need, it is a disadvantage because of the possibility of inadvertent modifications.

You might be wondering why you don't use the function's return value to modify the argument variable. You can do this, of course, as shown in the following example:

```
x = half(x);

float half(float y)
{
    return y/2;
}
```

Remember, however, that a function can return only a single value. By passing one or more arguments by reference, you enable a function to "return" more than one value to the calling program. Figure 18.2 illustrates passing by reference for a single argument.

FIGURE 18.2

Passing by reference enables the function to modify the original argument's variable.

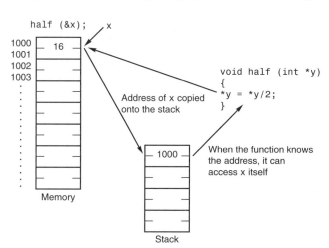

18

The function used in Figure 18.2 is not a good example of a real program in which you would use passing by reference, but it does illustrate the concept. When you pass by reference, you must ensure that the function definition and prototype reflect the fact that the argument passed to the function is a pointer. Within the body of the function, you must also use the indirection operator to access the variable(s) passed by reference.

Listing 18.1 demonstrates passing by reference and the default passing by value. Its output clearly shows that a variable passed by value can't be changed by the function, whereas a variable passed by reference can be changed. Of course, a function doesn't need to modify a variable passed by reference. In such a case, there's no reason to pass by reference.

INPUT   **LISTING 18.1**   args.c. Passing by value and passing by reference

```
1:   /* Passing arguments by value and by reference. */
2:
3:   #include <stdio.h>
4:
5:   void by_value(int a, int b, int c);
6:   void by_ref(int *a, int *b, int *c);
7:
8:   int main( void )
9:   {
10:      int x = 2, y = 4, z = 6;
11:
12:      printf("\nBefore calling by_value(), x = %d, y = %d, z = %d.",
13:          x, y, z);
14:
15:      by_value(x, y, z);
16:
17:      printf("\nAfter calling by_value(), x = %d, y = %d, z = %d.",
18:           x, y, z);
19:
20:      by_ref(&x, &y, &z);
21:      printf("\nAfter calling by_ref(), x = %d, y = %d, z = %d.\n",
22:           x, y, z);
23:      return 0;
24: }
25:
26: void by_value(int a, int b, int c)
27: {
28:     a = 0;
29:     b = 0;
30:     c = 0;
31: }
32:
33: void by_ref(int *a, int *b, int *c)
```

LISTING 18.1 continued

```
34: {
35:     *a = 0;
36:     *b = 0;
37:     *c = 0;
38: }
```

OUTPUT

```
Before calling by_value(), x = 2, y = 4, z = 6.
After calling by_value(), x = 2, y = 4, z = 6.
After calling by_ref(), x = 0, y = 0, z = 0.
```

ANALYSIS This program demonstrates the difference between passing variables by value and passing them by reference. Lines 5 and 6 contain prototypes for the two functions called in the program. In line 5 notice that the by_value() function takes three type int arguments. In contrast, line 6 defines _by_ref() because it takes three pointers to type int variables as arguments. The function headers for these two functions on lines 26 and 33 follow the same format as the prototypes. The bodies of the two functions are similar, but not identical. Both functions assign 0 to the three variables passed to them. In the by_value() function, 0 is assigned directly to the variables. In the by_ref() function, pointers are used, so the variables must be dereferenced before the assignment is made.

Each function is called once by main(). First, the three variables to be passed are assigned values other than 0 on line 10. Line 12 prints these values to the screen. Line 15 calls the first of the two functions, by_value(). Line 17 prints the three variables again. Notice that they are not changed. The by_value() function receives the variables by value and, therefore, can't change their original content. Line 20 calls by_ref(), and line 22 prints the values again. This time, the values have all changed to 0. Passing the variables by reference gives by_ref() access to the actual contents of the variables.

You can write a function that receives some arguments by reference and others by value. Just remember to keep them straight inside the function, using the indirection operator (*) to dereference arguments passed by reference.

Do	**DON'T**
DO pass variables by value if you don't want the original value altered.	**DON'T** pass large amounts of data by value if it isn't necessary. You can run out of stack space.
DO remember to use the indirection operator to dereference the variable passed by reference to a function.	**DON'T** forget that a variable passed by reference should be a pointer.

18

Type `void` Pointers

You've seen the `void` keyword used in a function declaration to specify that the function either doesn't take arguments or doesn't return a value. The `void` keyword can also be used to create a generic pointer—a pointer that can point to any type of data object. For example, the statement

```
void *ptr;
```

declares `ptr` as a generic pointer. `ptr` points to something; you just haven't yet specified what.

The most common use for type `void` pointers is in declaring function parameters. You might want to create a function that can handle different types of arguments. You can pass it a type `int` one time, a type `float` the next time, and so on. By declaring that the function takes a `void` pointer as an argument, you don't restrict it to accepting only a single data type. If you declare the function to take a `void` pointer as an argument, you can pass the function a pointer to anything.

Here's a simple example: You want to write a function that accepts a numeric variable as an argument and divides it by two, returning the answer in the argument variable. Thus, if the variable `val` holds the value 4, after a call to `half(val)` the variable `val` is equal to 2. Because you want to modify the argument, you pass it by reference. Because you want to use the function with any of C's numeric data types, you declare the function to take a `void` pointer:

```
void half(void *val);
```

Now you can call the function, passing it any pointer as an argument. There's one more thing you need, however. Although you can pass a `void` pointer without knowing what data type it points to, you can't dereference the pointer. Before the code in the function can do anything with the pointer, it must know the data type. You do this with a *typecast*, which is nothing more than a way of telling the program to treat this `void` pointer as a pointer to a specific `type`. If `pval` is a `void` pointer, you typecast it as follows:

```
(type *)pval
```

Here, `type` is the appropriate data type. To tell the program that `pval` is a pointer to type `int`, write

```
(int *)pval
```

To dereference the pointer—that is, to access the `int` that `pval` points to—write

```
*(int *)pval
```

Typecasts are covered in more detail on Day 20, "Working with Memory." Getting back to the original topic (passing a void pointer to a function), you can see that to use the pointer, the function must know the data type to which it points. In the case of the function you are writing that will divide its argument by two, there are four possibilities for type that will be used: int, long, float, and double. In addition to passing the void pointer to the variable to be divided by two, you must also tell the function which of the four types the void pointer points. You can modify the function definition as follows:

```
void half(void *pval, char type);
```

Based on the argument type, the function casts the void pointer pval to the appropriate type. Then the pointer can be dereferenced, and the value of the pointed-to variable can be used. The final version of the half() function is shown in Listing 18.2.

INPUT

LISTING 18.2 typecast.c. Using a void pointer to pass different data types to a function

```
1:  /* Using type void pointers. */
2:
3:  #include <stdio.h>
4:
5:  void half(void *pval, char type);
6:
7:  int main( void )
8:  {
9:      /* Initialize one variable of each type. */
10:
11:     int i = 20;
12:     long l = 100000;
13:     float f = 12.456;
14:     double d = 123.044444;
15:
16:     /* Display their initial values. */
17:
18:     printf("\n%d", i);
19:     printf("\n%ld", l);
20:     printf("\n%f", f);
21:     printf("\n%lf\n\n", d);
22:
23:     /* Call half() for each variable. */
24:
25:     half(&i, 'i');
26:     half(&l, 'l');
27:     half(&d, 'd');
28:     half(&f, 'f');
29:
30:     /* Display their new values. */
31:     printf("\n%d", i);
```

18

LISTING 18.2 continued

```
32:     printf("\n%ld", l);
33:     printf("\n%f", f);
34:     printf("\n%lf\n", d);
35:     return 0;
36: }
37:
38: void half(void *pval, char type)
39: {
40:     /* Depending on the value of type, cast the */
41:     /* pointer val appropriately and divide by 2. */
42:
43:     switch (type)
44:     {
45:         case 'i':
46:             {
47:             *((int *)pval) /= 2;
48:             break;
49:             }
50:         case 'l':
51:             {
52:             *((long *)pval) /= 2;
53:             break;
54:             }
55:         case 'f':
56:             {
57:             *((float *)pval) /= 2;
58:             break;
59:             }
60:         case 'd':
61:             {
62:             *((double *)pval) /= 2;
63:             break;
64:             }
65:     }
66: }
```

OUTPUT

```
20
100000
12.456000
123.044444


10
50000
6.228000
61.522222
```

ANALYSIS   As implemented in this listing, the function `half()` on lines 38–66 includes no error checking (for example, if an invalid type argument is passed). This is because, in a real program, you wouldn't use a function to perform a task as simple as dividing a value by two. This is an illustrative example only.

You might think that the need to pass the type of the pointed-to variable would make the function less flexible. The function would be more general if it didn't need to know the type of the pointed-to data object, but that's not the way C works. You must always cast a `void` pointer to a specific type before you dereference it. By taking this approach, you write only one function. If you don't make use of a `void` pointer, you need to write four separate functions—one for each data type.

When you need a function that can deal with different data types, you can often write a macro to take the place of the function. The example just presented—in which the task performed by the function is relatively simple—would be a good candidate for a macro. (Day 21, "Advanced Compiler Use," covers macros.)

Do	**Don't**
DO cast a `void` pointer when you use the value it points to.	**DON'T** try to increment or decrement a `void` pointer.

18

Using Functions That Have a Variable Number of Arguments

You have used several library functions, such as `printf()` and `scanf()`, that take a variable number of arguments. You can write your own functions that take a variable argument list. Programs that have functions with variable argument lists must include the header file stdarg.h.

When you declare a function that takes a variable argument list, you first list the fixed parameters—those that are always present (there must be at least one fixed parameter). You then include an ellipsis (. . .) at the end of the parameter list to indicate that zero or more additional arguments are passed to the function. During this discussion, please remember the distinction between a parameter and an argument, as explained on Day 5, "Functions: The Basics."

How does the function know how many arguments have been passed to it on a specific call? You tell it. One of the fixed parameters informs the function of the total number of arguments. For example, when you use the `printf()` function, the number of conversion specifiers in the format string tells the function how many additional arguments to expect. More directly, one of the function's fixed arguments can be the number of additional arguments. The example you'll see in a moment uses this approach, but first you need to look at the tools that C provides for dealing with a variable argument list.

The function must also know the type of each argument in the variable list. In the case of `printf()`, the conversion specifiers indicate the type of each argument. In other cases, such as the following example, all arguments in the variable list are of the same type, so there's no problem. To create a function that accepts different types in the variable argument list, you must devise a method of passing information about the argument types. For example, you could use a character code, as was done in the function `half()` in Listing 18.2.

The tools for using a variable argument list are defined in stdarg.h. These tools are used within the function to retrieve the arguments in the variable list. They are as follows:

`va_list`	A pointer data type.
`va_start()`	A macro used to initialize the argument list.
`va_arg()`	A macro used to retrieve each argument, in turn, from the variable list.
`va_end()`	A macro used to "clean up" when all arguments have been retrieved.

We've outlined how these macros are used in a function, and then included an example. When the function is called, the code in the function must follow these steps to access its arguments:

1. Declare a pointer variable of type `va_list`. This pointer is used to access the individual arguments. It is common practice, although certainly not required, to call this variable `arg_ptr`.

2. Call the macro `va_start()`, passing it the pointer `arg_ptr` as well as the name of the last fixed argument. The macro `va_start()` has no return value; it initializes the pointer `arg_ptr` to point at the first argument in the variable list.

3. To retrieve each argument, call `va_arg()`, passing it the pointer `arg_ptr` and the data type of the next argument. The return value of `va_arg()` is the value of the next argument. If the function has received n arguments in the variable list, call `va_arg()` n times to retrieve the arguments in the order listed in the function call.

4. When all the arguments in the variable list have been retrieved, call `va_end()`, passing it the pointer `arg_ptr`. In some implementations, this macro performs no action, but in others, it performs necessary clean-up actions. You should get in the habit of calling `va_end()` in case you use a C implementation that requires it.

Now for that example: The function average() in Listing 18.3 calculates the arithmetic average of a list of integers. This program passes the function a single fixed argument, indicating the number of additional arguments followed by the list of numbers.

INPUT   **LISTING 18.3**   vary.c. Using a variable-size argument list

```
1:  /* Functions with a variable argument list. */
2:
3:  #include <stdio.h>
4:  #include <stdarg.h>
5:
6:  float average(int num, ...);
7:
8:  int main( void )
9:  {
10:     float x;
11:
12:     x = average(10, 1, 2, 3, 4, 5, 6, 7, 8, 9, 10);
13:     printf("\nThe first average is %f.", x);
14:     x = average(5, 121, 206, 76, 31, 5);
15:     printf("\nThe second average is %f.\n", x);
16:     return 0;
17: }
18:
19: float average(int num, ...)
20: {
21:     /* Declare a variable of type va_list. */
22:
23:     va_list arg_ptr;
24:     int count, total = 0;
25:
26:     /* Initialize the argument pointer. */
27:
28:     va_start(arg_ptr, num);
29:
30:     /* Retrieve each argument in the variable list. */
31:
32:     for (count = 0; count < num; count++)
33:         total += va_arg( arg_ptr, int );
34:
35:     /* Perform clean up. */
36:
37:     va_end(arg_ptr);
38:
39:     /* Divide the total by the number of values to get the */
40:     /* average. Cast the total to type float so the value */
41:     /* returned is type float. */
42:
43:     return ((float)total/num);
44: }
```

18

OUTPUT
```
The first average is 5.500000.
The second average is 87.800000.
```

ANALYSIS The function `average()` is first called on line 19. The first argument passed, the only fixed argument, specifies the number of values in the variable argument list. In the function, as each argument in the variable list is retrieved on lines 32–33, it is added to the variable `total`. After all arguments have been retrieved, line 43 casts `total` as type `float` and then divides `total` by `num` to obtain the average.

Two other things should be pointed out in this listing. Line 28 calls `va_start()` to initialize the argument list. This must be done before the values are retrieved. Line 37 calls `va_end()` to "clean up," because the function is done with the values. You should use both of these functions in your programs whenever you write a function with a variable number of arguments.

Strictly speaking, a function that accepts a variable number of arguments doesn't need to have a fixed parameter informing it of the number of arguments being passed. For example, you could mark the end of the argument list with a special value not used elsewhere. This method places limitations on the arguments that can be passed, however, so it's best avoided.

Functions That Return a Pointer

On previous day's lessons you have seen several functions from the C standard library whose return value is a pointer. You can write your own functions that return a pointer. As you might expect, the indirection operator (`*`) is used in both the function declaration and the function definition. The general form of the declaration is

```
type *func(parameter_list);
```

This statement declares a function `func()` that returns a pointer to `type`. Here are two concrete examples:

```
double *func1(parameter_list);
struct address *func2(parameter_list);
```

The first line declares a function that returns a pointer to type `double`. The second line declares a function that returns a pointer to type `address` (which you assume is a user-defined structure).

Don't confuse a function that returns a pointer with a pointer to a function. If you include an additional pair of parentheses in the declaration, you declare a pointer to a function, as shown in these two examples:

```
double (*func)(...);    /* Pointer to a function that returns a double. */
double *func(...);      /* Function that returns a pointer to a double. */
```

Now that you have the declaration format straight, how do you use a function that returns a pointer? There's nothing special about such functions—you use them just as you do any other function, assigning their return value to a variable of the appropriate type (in this case, a pointer). Because the function call is a C expression, you can use it anywhere you would use a pointer of that type.

Listing 18.4 presents a simple example, a function that is passed two arguments and determines which is larger. The listing shows two ways of doing this: one function returns an `int`, and the other returns a pointer to `int`.

INPUT **LISTING 18.4** return.c. Returning a pointer from a function

```
1:  /* Function that returns a pointer. */
2:
3:  #include <stdio.h>
4:
5:  int larger1(int x, int y);
6:  int *larger2(int *x, int *y);
7:
8:  int main( void )
9:  {
10:     int a, b, bigger1, *bigger2;
11:
12:     printf("Enter two integer values: ");
13:     scanf("%d %d", &a, &b);
14:
15:     bigger1 = larger1(a, b);
16:     printf("\nThe larger value is %d.", bigger1);
17:     bigger2 = larger2(&a, &b);
18:     printf("\nThe larger value is %d.\n", *bigger2);
19:     return 0;
20: }
21:
22: int larger1(int x, int y)
23: {
24:     if (y > x)
25:         return y;
26:     return x;
27: }
28:
29: int *larger2(int *x, int *y)
30: {
31:     if (*y > *x)
32:         return y;
33:
34:     return x;
35: }
```

18

OUTPUT

```
Enter two integer values: 1111 3000

The larger value is 3000.
The larger value is 3000.
```

ANALYSIS   This is a relatively easy program to follow. Lines 5 and 6 contain the prototypes for the two functions. The first, `larger1()`, receives two `int` variables and returns an `int`. The second, `larger2()`, receives two pointers to `int` variables and returns a pointer to an `int`. The `main()` function on lines 8–20 is straightforward. Line 10 declares four variables. `a` and `b` hold the two variables to be compared. `bigger1` and `bigger2` hold the return values from the `larger1()` and `larger2()` functions, respectively. Notice that `bigger2` is a pointer to an `int`, and `bigger1` is just an `int`.

Line 15 calls `larger1()` with the two `int`s, `a` and `b`. The value returned from the function is assigned to `bigger1`, which is printed on line 16. Line 17 calls `larger2()` with the address of the two `int`s. The value returned from `larger2()`, a pointer, is assigned to `bigger2`, also a pointer. This value is dereferenced and printed on the following line.

The two comparison functions are very similar. They both compare the two values and return the larger one. The difference between the functions is that `larger2()` works with pointers, whereas `larger1()` does not. In `larger2()` notice that the dereference operator is used in the comparisons, but not in the `return` statements on lines 32 and 34.

In many cases, as in Listing 18.4, it is equally feasible to write a function to return a value or a pointer. Which one you select depends on the specifics of your program— mainly on how you intend to use the return value.

Do	**Don't**
DO use all the elements described in today's lessons when writing functions that have variable arguments. This is true even if your compiler doesn't require all the elements. The elements are `va_list`, `va_start()`, `va_arg()`, and `va_end()`.	**DON'T** confuse pointers to functions with functions that return pointers.

Summary

In today's lesson, you learned some more advanced things your C programs can do with functions. You learned the difference between passing arguments by value and by reference, and how the latter technique enables a function to "return" more than one value to the calling program. You also saw how the `void` type can be used to create a generic pointer that can point to any type of C data object. Type void pointers are most commonly used with functions that can be passed arguments that aren't restricted to a single data type. Remember that a type void pointer must be cast to a specific type before you can dereference it.

Today's lesson also showed you how to use the macros defined in stdarg.h to write a function that accepts a variable number of arguments. Such functions provide considerable programming flexibility. Finally, you saw how to write a function that returns a pointer.

Q&A

Q Is passing pointers as function arguments a common practice in C programming?

A Definitely! In many instances, a function needs to change the value of multiple variables, and there are two ways this can be accomplished. The first is to declare and use global variables. The second is to pass pointers so that the function can modify the data directly. The first option is advisable only if nearly every function will use the variable; otherwise, you should avoid it. (See Day 12, "Understanding Variable Scope.")

Q Is it better to modify a variable by assigning a function's return value to it or by passing a pointer to the variable to the function?

A When you need to modify only one variable with a function, usually it's best to return the value from the function rather than pass a pointer to the function. The logic behind this is simple. By not passing a pointer, you don't run the risk of changing any data that you didn't intend to change, and you keep the function independent of the rest of the code.

18

Workshop

The Workshop provides quiz questions to help you solidify your understanding of the material covered and exercises to provide you with experience in using what you've learned.

Quiz

1. When passing arguments to a function, what's the difference between passing by value and passing by reference?
2. What is a type void pointer?

3. What is one reason you would use a `void` pointer?

4. When using a `void` pointer, what is meant by a typecast, and when must you use it?

5. Can you write a function that takes a variable argument list only, with no fixed arguments?

6. What macros should be used when you write functions with variable argument lists?

7. What value is added to a `void` pointer when it's incremented?

8. Can a function return a pointer?

9. What macro is used to retrieve values from a variable lists of arguments passed to a function?

10. What are the elements that need to be used when using variable argument lists?

Exercises

1. Write the prototype for a function that returns an integer. It should take a pointer to a character array as its argument.

2. Write a prototype for a function called `numbers` that takes three integer arguments. The integers should be passed by reference.

3. Show how you would call the `numbers` function in exercise 2 with the three integers `int1`, `int2`, and `int3`.

4. **BUG BUSTER:** Is anything wrong with the following?

```
void squared(void *nbr)
{
  *nbr *= *nbr;
}
```

5. **BUG BUSTER:** Is anything wrong with the following?

```
float total( int num, ...)
{
  int count, total = 0;
  for ( count = 0; count < num; count++ )
    total += va_arg( arg_ptr, int );
  return ( total );
}
```

Because of the many possible solutions, answers are not provided for the following exercises.

6. Write a function that (a) is passed a variable number of strings as arguments, (b) concatenates the strings, in order, into one longer string, and (c) returns a pointer to the new string to the calling program.

7. Write a function that (a) is passed an array of any numeric data type as an argument, (b) finds the largest and smallest values in the array, and (c) returns pointers to these values to the calling program. (Hint: You need some way to tell the function how many elements are in the array.)

8. Write a function that accepts a string and a character. The function should look for the first occurrence of the character in the string and return a pointer to that location.

18

DAY 19

Exploring the C Function Library

As you've seen throughout this book, much of C's power comes from the functions in the C standard library. In today's lessons, you'll explore some of the functions that don't fit into the subject matter of other days. Today you will learn about

- Mathematical functions
- Functions that deal with time
- Error-handling functions
- Functions for searching and sorting data

Mathematical Functions

The C standard library contains a variety of functions that perform mathematical operations. Prototypes for the mathematical functions are in the header file math.h. The math functions all return a type `double`. For the trigonometric functions, angles are expressed in radians rather than degrees, which you may be more used to. Remember, one radian equals 57.296 degrees, and a full circle (360 degrees) contains 2π radians.

Trigonometric Functions

The trigonometric functions perform calculations that are used in some graphical and engineering applications.

Function	Prototype	Description
acos()	double acos(double x)	Returns the arccosine of its argument. The argument must be in the range -1 $<=$ x $<=$ 1, and the return value is in the range 0 $<=$ acos $<=$ π
asin()	double asin(double x)	Returns the arcsine of its argument. The argument must be in the range -1 $<=$ x $<=$ 1, and the return value is in the range $-\pi/2$ $<=$ asin $<=$ $\pi/2$.
atan()	double atan(double x)	Returns the arctangent of its argument. The return value is in the range $-\pi/2$ $<=$ atan $<=$ $\pi/2$.
atan2()	double atan2(double x, double y)	Returns the arctangent of x/y. The value returned is in the range $-\pi$ $<=$ atan2 $<=$ π.
cos()	double cos(double x)	Returns the cosine of its argument.
sin()	double sin(double x)	Returns the sine of its argument.
tan()	double tan(double x)	Returns the tangent of its argument.

Exponential and Logarithmic Functions

The exponential and logarithmic functions are needed for certain types of mathematical calculations.

Function	Prototype	Description
exp()	double exp(double x)	Returns the natural exponent of its argument, that is, e^x where e equals 2.7182818284590452354.
log()	double log(double x)	Returns the natural logarithm of its argument. The argument must be greater than 0.

Function	Prototype	Description
log10()	double log10(double x)	Returns the base-10 logarithm of its argument. The argument must be greater than 0.
frexp()	double frexp(double x, int *y)	The function calculates the normalized fraction representing the value x. The function's return value r is a fraction in the range 0.5 <= r <= 1.0. The function assigns to y an integer exponent such that x = r * 2^y. If the value passed to the function is 0, both r and y are 0.
ldexp()	double ldexp(double x, int y)	Returns x * 2^y.

Hyperbolic Functions

The hyperbolic functions perform hyperbolic trigonometric calculations.

Function	Prototype	Description
cosh()	double cosh(double x)	Returns the hyperbolic cosine of its argument.
sinh()	double sinh(double x)	Returns the hyperbolic sine of its argument.
tanh()	double tanh(double x)	Returns the hyperbolic tangent of its argument.

Other Mathematical Functions

The standard C library contains the following miscellaneous mathematical functions:

Function	Prototype	Description
sqrt()	double sqrt(double x)	Returns the square root of its argument. The argument must be zero or greater.
ceil()	double ceil(double x)	Returns the smallest integer not less than its argument. For example, ceil(4.5) returns 5.0, and ceil(-4.5) returns -4.0. Although ceil() returns an integer value, it is returned as a type double.

19

Function	Prototype	Description
abs()	int abs(int x)	Return the absolute labs()long labs(long x) value of their arguments.
floor()	double floor(double x)	Returns the largest integer not greater than its argument. For example, floor(4.5) returns 4.0, and floor(-4.5) returns -5.0.
modf()	double modf(double x, double *y)	Splits x into integral and fractional parts, each with the same sign as x. The fractional part is returned by the function, and the integral part is assigned to *y.
pow()	double pow(double x, double y)	Returns x^y. An error occurs if x == 0 and y <= 0, or if x < 0 and y is not an integer.
fmod()	double fmod(double x, double y)	Returns the floating-point remainder of x/y, with the same sign as x. The function returns 0 if x == 0.

A Demonstration of the Math Functions

An entire book could be filled with programs demonstrating all of the math functions. Listing 19.1 contains a single program that demonstrates several of these functions.

INPUT   **LISTING 19.1**   math.c. Using the C library math functions

```
1:  /* Demonstrates some of C's math functions */
2:
3:  #include <stdio.h>
4:  #include <math.h>
5:
6:  int main( void )
7:  {
8:
9:      double x;
10:
11:     printf("Enter a number: ");
12:     scanf( "%lf", &x);
13:
14:     printf("\n\nOriginal value: %lf", x);
15:
```

LISTING 19.1 continued

```
16:     printf("\nCeil: %lf", ceil(x));
17:     printf("\nFloor: %lf", floor(x));
18:     if( x >= 0 )
19:         printf("\nSquare root: %lf", sqrt(x) );
20:     else
21:         printf("\nNegative number" );
22:
23:     printf("\nCosine: %lf\n", cos(x));
24:     return 0;
25: }
```

INPUT/
OUTPUT

```
Enter a number: 100.95


Original value: 100.950000
Ceil: 101.000000
Floor: 100.000000
Square root: 10.047388
Cosine: 0.913482
```

ANALYSIS   This listing uses just a few of the math functions that are available in the C standard library. Line 12 inputs a number from the user, which is then printed. Next this value is passed to four of the C library math functions—ceil(), floor(), sqrt(), and cos(). Notice that sqrt() is called only if the number isn't negative because, by definition, negative numbers don't have square roots. You can add any of the other math functions to a program such as this to test its functionality.

Dealing with Time

The C library contains several functions that let your program work with times. In C, the term *times* refers to dates as well as times. The function prototypes and the definition of the structure used by many of the time functions are in the header file time.h.

Representing Time

The C time functions represent time in two ways. The more basic method is the number of seconds elapsed since midnight on January 1, 1970. Negative values are used to represent times before that date. These time values are stored as type long integers. In time.h, the symbols time_t and clock_t are both defined with a typedef statement as long. These symbols are used in the time function prototypes rather than long.

The second method represents a time broken down into its components: year, month, day, and so on. For this kind of time representation, the time functions use a structure tm, defined in time.h as follows:

19

```
struct tm {
  int tm_sec;     // seconds after the minute - [0,59]
  int tm_min;     // minutes after the hour - [0,59]
  int tm_hour;    // hours since midnight - [0,23]
  int tm_mday;    // day of the month - [1,31]
  int tm_mon;     // months since January - [0,11]
  int tm_year;    // years since 1900
  int tm_wday;    // days since Sunday - [0,6]
  int tm_yday;    // days since January 1 - [0,365]
  int tm_isdst;   // daylight savings time flag
};
```

The Time Functions

This section describes the various C library functions that deal with time. Remember that the term *time* refers to the date as well as hours, minutes, and seconds. A demonstration program follows the descriptions.

Obtaining the Current Time

To obtain the current time as set on your system's internal clock, use the time() function. The prototype is

```
time_t time(time_t *timeptr);
```

Remember, time_t is defined in time.h as a synonym for long. The function time() returns the number of seconds elapsed since midnight, January 1, 1970. If it is passed a non-NULL pointer, time() also stores this value in the type time_t variable pointed to by timeptr. Thus, to store the current time in the type time_t variable now, you could write

```
time_t now;
```

```
now = time(0);
```

You also could write

```
time_t now;
time_t *ptr_now = &now;
time(ptr_now);
```

Converting Between Time Representations

Knowing the number of seconds since January 1, 1970, is not often useful. Therefore, C provides the capability to convert time represented as a time_t value to a tm structure, using the localtime() function. A tm structure contains day, month, year, and other time information in a format more appropriate for display and printing. The prototype of this function is

```
struct tm *localtime(time_t *ptr);
```

This function returns a pointer to a static type `tm` structure, so you don't need to declare a type `tm` structure to use—only a pointer to type `tm`. This static structure is reused and overwritten each time `localtime()` is called; if you want to save the value returned, your program must declare a separate type `tm` structure and copy the values from the static structure.

The reverse conversion—from a type `tm` structure to a type `time_t` value—is performed by the function `mktime()`. The prototype is

```
time_t mktime(struct tm *ntime);
```

This function returns the number of seconds between midnight, January 1, 1970, and the time represented by the type `tm` structure pointed to by `ntime`.

Displaying Times

To convert times into formatted strings appropriate for display, use the functions `ctime()` and `asctime()`. Both of these functions return the time as a string with a specific format. They differ because `ctime()` is passed the time as a type `time_t` value, whereas `asctime()` is passed the time as a type `tm` structure. Their prototypes are

```
char *asctime(struct tm *ptr);
char *ctime(time_t *ptr);
```

Both functions return a pointer to a static, null-terminated, 26-character string that gives the time of the function's argument in the following format:

```
Thu Jun 13 10:22:23 1991
```

The time is formatted in 24-hour "military" time. Both functions use a static string, overwriting it each time they're called.

For more control over the format of the time, use the `strftime()` function. This function is passed a time as a type `tm` structure. It formats the time according to a format string. The function prototype is

```
size_t strftime(char *s, size_t max, char *fmt, struct tm *ptr);
```

This function takes the time in the type `tm` structure pointed to by `ptr`, formats it according to the format string `fmt`, and writes the result as a null-terminated string to the memory location pointed to by `s`. The argument `max` should specify the amount of space allocated at `s`. If the resulting string (including the terminating null character) has more than `max` characters, the function returns 0, and the string `s` is invalid. Otherwise, the function returns the number of characters written—`strlen(s)`.

The format string consists of one or more conversion specifiers from Table 19.1.

19

TABLE 19.1 Conversion specifiers that can be used with `strftime()`

Specifier	What It's Replaced By
%a	Abbreviated weekday name.
%A	Full weekday name.
%b	Abbreviated month name.
%B	Full month name.
%c	Date and time representation (for example, 10:41:50 30-Jun-91).
%C	The year as a decimal number from 00 to 99.
%d	Day of month as a decimal number 01 through 31.
%D	Is equivalent to "%m/%d/%y".
%e	The day of the month as a decimal number from 1 to 31.
%F	Is equivalent to "%Y-%m-%d".
%h	The same as "%b", the abbreviated month name.
%H	The hour (24-hour clock) as a decimal number 00 through 23.
%I	The hour (12-hour clock) as a decimal number 00 through 11.
%j	The day of the year as a decimal number 001 through 366.
%m	The month as a decimal number 01 through 12.
%M	The minute as a decimal number 00 through 59.
%p	AM or PM.
%r	The locale's 12 hour clock time.
%R	Is equivalent to "%H:%M".
%S	The second as a decimal number 00 through 59.
%T	Is equivalent to "%H:%M:%S".
%u	The day of week as a decimal number 1 through 7 where 1 is Monday.
%U	The week of the year as a decimal number 00 through 53. Sunday is considered the first day of the week.
%w	The weekday as a decimal number 0 through 6 (Sunday = 0).
%W	The week of the year as a decimal number 00 through 53. Monday is considered the first day of the week.
%x	The date representation (for example, 30-Jun-91).
%X	The time representation (for example, 10:41:50).
%y	The year, without century, as a decimal number 00 through 99.
%Y	The year, with century, as a decimal number.

TABLE 19.1 continued

Specifier	What It's Replaced By
%z	The locale's time zone or abbreviation. If the time zone isn't known, then this would be blank.
%Z	The time zone name if the information is available or blank if not.
%%	A single percent sign %.

Calculating Time Differences

You can calculate the difference, in seconds, between two times with the `difftime()` macro, which subtracts two `time_t` values and returns the difference. The prototype is

```
double difftime(time_t later, time_t earlier);
```

This function subtracts `earlier` from `later` and returns the difference, the number of seconds between the two times. A common use of `difftime()` is to calculate elapsed time, as demonstrated (along with other time operations) in Listing 19.2.

You can determine duration of a different sort using the `clock()` function, which returns the amount of time that has passed since the program started execution, in 1/100-second units. The prototype is

```
clock_t clock(void);
```

To determine the duration of some portion of a program, call `clock()` twice—before and after the process occurs—and subtract the two return values.

Using the Time Functions

Listing 19.2 demonstrates how to use the C library time functions.

INPUT   **LISTING 19.2**   times.c. Using the C library time functions

```
 1:  /* Demonstrates the time functions. */
 2:
 3:  #include <stdio.h>
 4:  #include <time.h>
 5:
 6:  int main( void )
 7:  {
 8:      time_t start, finish, now;
 9:      struct tm *ptr;
10:      char *c, buf1[80];
11:      double duration;
12:
```

19

LISTING 19.2   continued

```
13:        /* Record the time the program starts execution. */
14:
15:        start = time(0);
16:
17:        /* Record the current time, using the alternate method of */
18:        /* calling time(). */
19:
20:        time(&now);
21:
22:        /* Convert the time_t value into a type tm structure. */
23:
24:        ptr = localtime(&now);
25:
26:        /* Create and display a formatted string containing */
27:        /* the current time. */
28:
29:        c = asctime(ptr);
30:        puts(c);
31:        getc(stdin);
32:
33:        /* Now use the strftime() function to create several different */
34:        /* formatted versions of the time. */
35:
36:        strftime(buf1, 80, "This is week %U of the year %Y", ptr);
37:        puts(buf1);
38:        getc(stdin);
39:
40:        strftime(buf1, 80, "Today is %A, %x", ptr);
41:        puts(buf1);
42:        getc(stdin);
43:
44:        strftime(buf1, 80, "It is %M minutes past hour %I.", ptr);
45:        puts(buf1);
46:        getc(stdin);
47:
48:        /* Now get the current time and calculate program duration. */
49:
50:        finish = time(0);
51:        duration = difftime(finish, start);
52:        printf("\nProgram execution time using time() = %f seconds.",
➥duration);
53:
54:        /* Also display program duration in hundredths of seconds */
55:        /* using clock(). */
56:
57:        printf("\nProgram execution time using clock() = %ld hundredths of
➥sec.",
58:             clock());
59:        return 0;
60: }
```

OUTPUT

```
Sun May 19 13:28:53 2002

This is week 20 of the year 2002

Today is Sunday, 05/19/02

It is 28 minutes past hour 01.


Program execution time using time() = 14.000000 seconds.
Program execution time using clock() = 14290 hundredths of sec.
```

ANALYSIS   This program has numerous comment lines, so it should be easy to follow. Because the time functions are being used, the time.h header file is included on line 4. Line 8 declares three variables of type time_t—start, finish, and now. These variables can hold the time as an offset from January 1, 1970, in seconds. Line 9 declares a pointer to a tm structure. The tm structure was described earlier. The rest of the variables have types that should be familiar to you.

The program records its starting time on line 15. This is done with a call to time(). The program then does virtually the same thing in a different way. Instead of using the value returned by the time() function, line 20 passes time() a pointer to the variable now. Line 24 does exactly what the comment on line 22 states: It converts the time_t value of now to a type tm structure. The next few sections of the program print the value of the current time to the screen in various formats. Line 29 uses the asctime() function to assign the information to a character pointer, c. Line 30 prints the formatted information. The program then waits for the user to press Enter.

Lines 36 through 46 use the strftime() function to print the date in three different formats. Using Table 19.1, you should be able to determine what these lines print.

The program then determines the time again on line 50. This is the program-ending time. Line 51 uses this ending time along with the starting time to calculate the program's duration by means of the difftime() function. This value is printed on line 52. The program concludes by printing the program execution time from the clock() function.

19

Error-Handling

The C standard library contains a variety of functions and macros that help you deal with program errors.

The `assert()` Macro

The macro `assert()` can diagnose program bugs. It is defined in assert.h, and its prototype is

```
void assert(int expression);
```

The argument *expression* can be anything you want to test—a variable or any C expression. If *expression* evaluates to TRUE, `assert()` does nothing. If *expression* evaluates to FALSE, `assert()` displays an error message on `stderr` and aborts program execution.

How do you use `assert()`? It is most frequently used to track down program bugs (which are distinct from compilation errors). A bug doesn't prevent a program from compiling, but it causes the program to give incorrect results or to run improperly (locking up, for example). For instance, a financial-analysis program you're writing might occasionally give incorrect answers. You suspect that the problem is caused by the variable `interest_rate` taking on a negative value, which should never happen. To check this, place the statement

```
assert(interest_rate >= 0);
```

at locations in the program where `interest_rate` is used. If the variable ever does become negative, the `assert()` macro alerts you. You can then examine the relevant code to locate the cause of the problem.

To see how `assert()` works, run Listing 19.3. If you enter a nonzero value, the program displays the value and terminates normally. If you enter zero, the `assert()` macro forces abnormal program termination. The exact error message you see will depend on your compiler, but here's a typical example:

```
Assertion failed: x, file list1903.c, line 13
```

Note that, in order for `assert()` to work, your program must be compiled in debug mode. Refer to your compiler documentation for information on enabling debug mode (as explained in a moment). When you later compile the final version in release mode, the `assert()` macros are disabled.

> **INPUT**   **LISTING 19.3**   assert.c. Using the `assert()` macro

```
1:  /* The assert() macro. */
2:
3:  #include <stdio.h>
4:  #include <assert.h>
5:
6:  int main( void )
7:  {
```

LISTING 19.3 continued

```
 8:      int x;
 9:
10:      printf("\nEnter an integer value: ");
11:      scanf("%d", &x);
12:
13:      assert(x >= 0);
14:
15:      printf("You entered %d.\n", x);
16:      return 0;
17: }
```

INPUT/
OUTPUT

```
Enter an integer value: 10
You entered 10.
Enter an integer value: -1

Assertion failed: x, file list1903.c, line 13

Abnormal program termination
```

Your error message might differ, depending on your system and compiler, but the general idea is the same. For example, the Dev-C++ compiler included on the CD generates the following output when –1 is entered:

INPUT/
OUTPUT

```
Enter an integer value: -1
c:\assert.c:13: failed assertion 'x >= 0'
```

```
This application has requested the Runtime to terminate it in an unusual
way.
Please contact the application's support team for more information.
```

19

ANALYSIS Run this program to see that the error message displayed by assert() on line 13 includes the expression whose test failed, the name of the file, and the line number where the assert() is located.

The action of assert() depends on another macro named NDEBUG (which stands for "no debugging"). If the macro NDEBUG isn't defined (the default), assert() is active. If NDE-BUG is defined, assert() is turned off and has no effect. If you place assert() in various program locations to help with debugging and then solve the problem, you can define NDEBUG to turn assert() off. This is much easier than going through the program and removing the assert() statements (only to discover later that you want to use them again). To define the macro NDEBUG, use the #define directive. You can demonstrate this by adding the line

```
#define NDEBUG
```

to Listing 19.3, on line 2. Now the program prints the value entered and then terminates normally, even if you enter -1.

Note that NDEBUG doesn't need to be defined as anything in particular, as long as it's included in a #define directive. You'll learn more about the #define directive on Day 21, "Advanced Compiler Use."

The errno.h Header File

The header file errno.h defines several macros used to define and document runtime errors. These macros are used in conjunction with the perror() function, described in the next section.

The errno.h definitions include an external integer named errno. Many of the C library functions assign a value to this variable if an error occurs during function execution. The file errno.h also defines a group of symbolic constants for these errors, listed in Table 19.2.

TABLE 19.2   The symbolic error constants defined in errno.h

Name	Value	Message and Meaning
E2BIG	1000	Argument list too long (list length exceeds 128 bytes).
EACCES	5	Permission denied (for example, trying to write to a file opened for read only).
EBADF	6	Bad file descriptor.
EDOM	1002	Math argument out of domain (an argument passed to a math function is outside the allowable range).
EEXIST	80	File exists.
EMFILE	4	Too many open files.
ENOENT	2	No such file or directory.
ENOEXEC	1001	Exec format error.
ENOMEM	8	Not enough core (for example, not enough memory to execute the exec() function).
ENOPATH	3	Path not found.
ERANGE	1003	Result out of range (for example, result returned by a math function is too large or too small for the return data type).

You can use errno two ways. Some functions signal, by means of their return values, that an error has occurred. If this happens, you can test the value of errno to determine the nature of the error and take appropriate action. Otherwise, when you have no specific indication that an error occurred, you can test errno. If it's nonzero, an error has occurred, and the specific value of errno indicates the nature of the error. Be sure to reset errno to zero after handling the error. The next section explains perror(), and then Listing 19.4 illustrates the use of errno.

The perror() Function

The perror() function is another of C's error-handling tools. When called, perror() displays a message on stderr describing the most recent error that occurred during a library function call or system call. The prototype, in stdio.h, is

```
void perror(const char *msg);
```

The argument msg points to an optional, user-defined message. This message is printed first, followed by a colon and the implementation-defined message that describes the most recent error. If you call perror() when no error has occurred, the message displayed is no error.

A call to perror() does nothing to deal with the error condition. It's up to the program to take action. The action might consist of prompting the user to do something such as terminate the program. The action the program takes can be determined by testing the value of errno and by the nature of the error. Note that a program need not include the header file errno.h to use the external variable errno. That header file is required only if your program uses the symbolic error constants listed in Table 19.2. Listing 19.4 illustrates the use of perror() and errno for handling runtime errors.

INPUT

LISTING 19.4 perror.c. Using perror() and errno to deal with runtime errors

19

```
1:  /* Demonstration of error handling with perror() and errno. */
2:
3:  #include <stdio.h>
4:  #include <stdlib.h>
5:  #include <errno.h>
6:
7:  int main( void )
8:  {
9:      FILE *fp;
10:     char filename[80];
11:
12:     printf("Enter filename: ");
13:     gets(filename);
14:
15:     if (( fp = fopen(filename, "r")) == NULL)
16:     {
17:         perror("You goofed!");
```

LISTING 19.4 continued

```
18:        printf("errno = %d.\n", errno);
19:        exit(1);
20:    }
21:    else
22:    {
23:        puts("File opened for reading.");
24:        fclose(fp);
25:    }
26:    return 0;
27: }
```

OUTPUT

```
Enter file name: perror.c
File opened for reading.

Enter file name: notafile.xxx
You goofed!: No such file or directory
errno = 2.
```

ANALYSIS This program prints one of two messages based on whether a file can be opened for reading. Line 15 tries to open a file. If the file opens, the else part of the if loop executes, printing the following message:

```
File opened for reading.
```

If there is an error when the file is opened, such as the file not existing, lines 17–19 of the if loop execute. Line 17 calls the perror() function with the string "You goofed!". The error number is then printed. The result of entering a file that does not exist is

```
You goofed!: No such file or directory.
errno = 2
```

Do	Don't
DO check for possible errors in your programs. Never assume that everything is okay.	**DON'T** include the errno.h header file if you aren't going to use the symbolic error constants listed in Table 19.2.

Searching and Sorting

Among the most common tasks that programs perform are searching and sorting data. The C standard library contains general-purpose functions that you can use for each task.

Searching with `bsearch()`

The library function `bsearch()` performs a binary search of a data array, looking for an array element that matches a key. To use `bsearch()`, the array must be sorted into ascending order. Also, the program must provide the comparison function used by `bsearch()` to determine whether one data item is greater than, less than, or equal to another item. The prototype of `bsearch()` is in stdlib.h:

```
void *bsearch(const void *key, const void *base, size_t num, size_t width,
int (*cmp)(const void *element1, const void *element2));
```

This is a fairly complex prototype, so go through it carefully. The argument `key` is a pointer to the data item being searched for, and `base` is a pointer to the first element of the array being searched. Both are declared as type `void` pointers, so they can point to any of C's data objects. The `const` modifiers simply indicate that the values being passed are constants that won't be changed by the functions.

The argument `num` is the number of elements in the array, and `width` is the size (in bytes) of each element. The type specifier `size_t` refers to the data type returned by the `sizeof()` operator, which is `unsigned`. The `sizeof()` operator is usually used to obtain the values for `num` and `width`.

The final argument, `cmp`, is a pointer to the comparison function. This can be a user-written function or, when searching string data, it can be the library function `strcmp()`. The comparison function must meet the following two criteria:

- It is passed pointers to two data items.
- It returns a type `int` as follows:
    - < 0 Element 1 is less than element 2.
    - 0 Element 1 is equal to element 2.
    - > 0 Element 1 is greater than element 2.

The return value of `bsearch()` is a type `void` pointer. The function returns a pointer to the first array element it finds that matches the key, or `NULL` if no match is found. You must cast the returned pointer to the proper type before using it.

The `sizeof()` operator can provide the `num` and `width` arguments as follows. If `array[]` is the array to be searched, the statement

```
sizeof(array[0]);
```

returns the value of `width`—the size (in bytes) of one array element. Because the expression `sizeof(array)` returns the size, in bytes, of the entire array, the following statement obtains the value of `num`, the number of elements in the array:

```
sizeof(array)/sizeof(array[0])
```

19

The binary search algorithm is very efficient; it can search a large array quickly. Its operation is dependent on the array elements being arranged in ascending order. Here's how the algorithm works:

1. The key is compared to the element at the middle of the array. If there's a match, the search is done. Otherwise, the key must be either less than or greater than the array element.

2. If the key is less than the array element, the matching element, if any, must be located in the first half of the array. Likewise, if the key is greater than the array element, the matching element must be located in the second half of the array.

3. The search is restricted to the appropriate half of the array, and then the algorithm returns to step 1.

You can see that each comparison performed by a binary search eliminates half of the array being searched. For example, a 1,000-element array can be searched with only 10 comparisons, and a 16,000-element array can be searched with only 14 comparisons. In general, a binary search requires n comparisons to search an array of 2^n elements.

Sorting with `qsort()`

The library function qsort() is an implementation of the quicksort algorithm, invented by C.A.R. Hoare. This function sorts an array into order. Usually the result is in ascending order, but qsort() can be used for descending order as well. The function prototype, defined in stdlib.h, is

```
void qsort(void *base, size_t num, size_t size,
int (*cmp)(const void *element1, const void *element2));
```

The argument base points at the first element in the array, num is the number of elements in the array, and size is the size (in bytes) of one array element. The argument cmp is a pointer to a comparison function. The rules for the comparison function are the same as for the comparison function used by bsearch(), described in the preceding section: You often use the same comparison function for both bsearch() and qsort(). The function qsort() has no return value.

Searching and Sorting: Two Demonstrations

Listing 19.5 demonstrates the use of qsort() and bsearch(). The program sorts and searches an array of values. Note that the non-ANSI function getch() is used. If your compiler doesn't support it, you should replace it with the ANSI standard function getchar().

INPUT   LISTING 19.5   sort.c. Using the qsort() and bsearch() functions with values

```
1: /* Using qsort() and bsearch() with values.*/
2:
3: #include <stdio.h>
4: #include <stdlib.h>
5:
6: #define MAX 20
7:
8: int intcmp(const void *v1, const void *v2);
9:
10: int main( void )
11: {
12:     int arr[MAX], count, key, *ptr;
13:
14:     /* Enter some integers from the user. */
15:
16:     printf("Enter %d integer values; press Enter after each.\n", MAX);
17:
18:     for (count = 0; count < MAX; count++)
19:         scanf("%d", &arr[count]);
20:
21:     puts("Press Enter to sort the values.");
22:     getc(stdin);
23:
24:     /* Sort the array into ascending order. */
25:
26:     qsort(arr, MAX, sizeof(arr[0]), intcmp);
27:
28:     /* Display the sorted array. */
29:
30:     for (count = 0; count < MAX; count++)
31:         printf("\narr[%d] = %d.", count, arr[count]);
32:
33:     puts("\nPress Enter to continue.");
34:     getc(stdin);
35:
36:     /* Enter a search key. */
37:
38:     printf("Enter a value to search for: ");
39:     scanf("%d", &key);
40:
41:     /* Perform the search. */
42:
43:     ptr = (int *)bsearch(&key, arr, MAX, sizeof(arr[0]),intcmp);
44:
45:     if ( ptr != NULL )
46:         printf("%d found at arr[%d].", key, (ptr - arr));
47:     else
48:         printf("%d not found.", key);
```

19

LISTING 19.5 continued

```
49:        return 0;
50: }
51:
52: int intcmp(const void *v1, const void *v2)
53: {
54:        return (*(int *)v1 - *(int *)v2);
55: }
```

INPUT/
OUTPUT

```
Enter 20 integer values; press Enter after each.
45
12
999
1000
321
123
2300
954
1968
12
2
1999
1776
1812
1456
1
9999
3
76
200
Press Enter to sort the values.

arr[0] = 1.
arr[1] = 2.
arr[2] = 3.
arr[3] = 12.
arr[4] = 12.
arr[5] = 45.
arr[6] = 76.
arr[7] = 123.
arr[8] = 200.
arr[9] = 321.
arr[10] = 954.
arr[11] = 999.
arr[12] = 1000.
arr[13] = 1456.
arr[14] = 1776.
arr[15] = 1812.
arr[16] = 1968.
```

```
arr[17] = 1999.
arr[18] = 2300.
arr[19] = 9999.
Press Enter to continue.

Enter a value to search for:
1776
1776 found at arr[14]
```

ANALYSIS Listing 19.5 incorporates everything described previously about sorting and searching. This program lets you enter up to MAX values (20 in this case). It sorts the values and prints them in order. Then it lets you enter a value to search for in the array. A printed message states the search's status.

Familiar code is used to obtain the values for the array on lines 18 and 19. Line 26 contains the call to qsort() to sort the array. The first argument is a pointer to the array's first element. This is followed by MAX, the number of elements in the array. The size of the first element is then provided so that qsort() knows the width of each item. The call is finished with the argument for the sort function, intcmp.

The function intcmp() is defined on lines 52–55. It returns the difference of the two values passed to it. This might seem too simple at first, but remember what values the comparison function is supposed to return. If the elements are equal, 0 should be returned. If element one is greater than element two, a positive number should be returned. If element one is less than element two, a negative number should be returned. This is exactly what intcmp() does.

The searching is done with bsearch(). Notice that its arguments are virtually the same as those of qsort(). The difference is that the first argument of bsearch() is the key to be searched for. bsearch() returns a pointer to the location of the found key or NULL if the key isn't found. On line 43, ptr is assigned the returned value of bsearch(). ptr is used in the if loop on lines 45–48 to print the status of the search.

Listing 19.6 has the same functionality as Listing 19.5; however, Listing 19.6 sorts and searches strings.

19

INPUT **LISTING 19.6** strsort.c. Using qsort() and bsearch() with strings

```
1:  /* Using qsort() and bsearch() with strings. */
2:
3:  #include <stdio.h>
4:  #include <stdlib.h>
5:  #include <string.h>
6:
7:  #define MAX 20
```

LISTING **19.6**   continued

```
8:
9:  int comp(const void *s1, const void *s2);
10:
11: int main( void )
12: {
13:     char *data[MAX], buf[80], *ptr, *key, **key1;
14:     int count;
15:
16:     /* Input a list of words. */
17:
18:     printf("Enter %d words, pressing Enter after each.\n",MAX);
19:
20:     for (count = 0; count < MAX; count++)
21:     {
22:         printf("Word %d: ", count+1);
23:         gets(buf);
24:         data[count] = malloc(strlen(buf)+1);
25:         strcpy(data[count], buf);
26:     }
27:
28:     /* Sort the words (actually, sort the pointers). */
29:
30:     qsort(data, MAX, sizeof(data[0]), comp);
31:
32:     /* Display the sorted words. */
33:
34:     for (count = 0; count < MAX; count++)
35:         printf("\n%d: %s", count+1, data[count]);
36:
37:     /* Get a search key. */
38:
39:     printf("\n\nEnter a search key: ");
40:     gets(buf);
41:
42:     /* Perform the search. First, make key1 a pointer */
43:     /* to the pointer to the search key.*/
44:
45:     key = buf;
46:     key1 = &key;
47:     ptr = bsearch(key1, data, MAX, sizeof(data[0]), comp);
48:
49:     if (ptr != NULL)
50:         printf("%s found.\n", buf);
51:     else
52:         printf("%s not found.\n", buf);
53:     return 0;
54: }
55:
56: int comp(const void *s1, const void *s2)
```

LISTING 19.6   continued

```
57: {
58:     return (strcmp(*(char **)s1, *(char **)s2));
59: }
```

INPUT/
OUTPUT

```
Enter 20 words, pressing Enter after each.
Word 1: apple
Word 2: orange
Word 3: grapefruit
Word 4: peach
Word 5: plum
Word 6: pear
Word 7: cherries
Word 8: banana
Word 9: lime
Word 10: lemon
Word 11: tangerine
Word 12: star
Word 13: watermelon
Word 14: cantaloupe
Word 15: musk melon
Word 16: strawberry
Word 17: blackberry
Word 18: blueberry
Word 19: grape
Word 20: cranberry

1: apple
2: banana
3: blackberry
4: blueberry
5: cantaloupe
6: cherries
7: cranberry
8: grape
9: grapefruit
10: lemon
11: lime
12: musk melon
13: orange
14: peach
15: pear
16: plum
17: star
18: strawberry
19: tangerine
20: watermelon

Enter a search key: orange
orange found.
```

19

ANALYSIS A couple of points about Listing 19.6 bear mentioning. This program makes use of an array of pointers to strings, a technique introduced on Day 15, "Pointers: Beyond the Basics." As you saw in that chapter, you can "sort" the strings by sorting the array of pointers. However, this method requires a modification in the comparison function. This function is passed pointers to the two items in the array that are compared. However, you want the array of pointers sorted based not on the values of the pointers themselves but on the values of the strings they point to.

Because of this, you must use a comparison function that is passed pointers to pointers. Each argument to comp() is a pointer to an array element, and because each element is itself a pointer (to a string), the argument is, therefore, a pointer to a pointer. Within the function itself, you dereference the pointers so that the return value of comp() depends on the values of the strings pointed to.

The fact that the arguments passed to comp() are pointers to pointers creates another problem. You store the search key in buf[], and you also know that the name of an array (buf in this case) is a pointer to the array. However, you need to pass not buf itself, but a pointer to buf. The problem is that buf is a pointer constant, not a pointer variable. buf itself has no address in memory; it's a symbol that evaluates to the address of the array. Because of this, you can't create a pointer that points to buf by using the address-of operator in front of buf, as in &buf.

What to do? First, create a pointer variable and assign the value of buf to it. In the program, this pointer variable has the name key. Because key is a pointer variable, it has an address, and you can create a pointer that contains that address—in this case, key1. When you finally call bsearch(), the first argument is key1, a pointer to a pointer to the key string. The function bsearch() passes that argument on to comp(), and everything works properly.

Do	**Don't**
DO check out your compiler's documentation or the ANSI documentation to see the other standard functions you can use.	DON'T forget to put your search array into ascending order before using bsearch().

Summary

Today you explored some of the more useful functions supplied in the C function library. There are functions that perform mathematical calculations, deal with time, and assist your program with error handling. The functions for sorting and searching data are particularly useful; they can save you considerable time when you're writing your programs.

Q&A

Q Why do nearly all of the math functions return `doubles`?

A The answer to this question is to achieve precision, not consistency. A `double` is more precise than the other variable types; therefore, your answers are more accurate. On Day 20, "Working with Memory," you will learn the specifics of casting variables and variable promotion. These topics are also applicable to precision.

Q Are `bsearch()` and `qsort()` the only ways in C to sort and search?

A These two functions are provided in the standard library; however, you don't have to use them. Many computer-programming textbooks teach you how to write your own searching and sorting programs. C contains all the commands you need to write your own. You can purchase especially written searching and sorting routines. The biggest benefits of `bsearch()` and `qsort()` are that they are already written, and they are provided with any ANSI-compatible compiler.

Q Do the math functions validate bad data?

A Never assume that data entered is correct. Always validate user-entered data. For example, if you pass a negative value to `sqrt()`, the function generates an error. If you're formatting the output, you probably don't want this error displayed as it is. Remove the `if` statement in Listing 19.1 and enter a negative number to see what I mean.

19

Workshop

The Workshop provides quiz questions to help you solidify your understanding of the material covered and exercises to provide you with experience in using what you've learned.

Quiz

1. What is the return data type for all of C's mathematical functions?

2. What C variable type is `time_t` equivalent to?

3. What are the differences between the `time()` function and the `clock()` function?

4. When you call the `perror()` function, what does it do to correct an existing error condition?

5. Before you search an array with bsearch(), what must you do?

6. Using bsearch(), how many comparisons would be required to find an element if the array had 16,000 items?

7. Using bsearch(), how many comparisons would be required to find an element if an array had only 10 items?

8. Using bsearch(), how many comparisons would be required to find an element if an array had 2 million items?

9. What values must a comparison function for bsearch() and qsort() return?

10. What does bsearch() return if it can't find an element in an array?

Exercises

1. Write a call to bsearch(). The array to be searched is called names, and the values are characters. The comparison function is called comp_names(). Assume that all the names are the same size.

2. **BUG BUSTER:** What is wrong with the following program?

```
#include <stdio.h>
#include <stdlib.h>
int main( void )
{
    int values[10], count, key, *ptr;

    printf("Enter values");
    for( ctr = 0; ctr < 10; ctr++ )
        scanf( "%d", &values[ctr] );

    qsort(values, 10, compare_function());
}
```

3. **BUG BUSTER:** Is anything wrong with the following compare function?

```
int intcmp( int element1, int element2)
{
    if ( element 1 > element 2 )
        return -1;
    else if ( element 1 < element2 )
        return 1;
    else
        return 0;
}
```

Answers are not provided for the following exercises:

4. **ON YOUR OWN:** Modify Listing 19.1 so that the sqrt() function works with negative numbers. Do this by taking the absolute value of x.

5. **ON YOUR OWN:** Write a program that consists of a menu that performs various math functions. Use as many of the math functions as you can.

6. **ON YOUR OWN:** Using the time functions discussed in this chapter, write a function that causes the program to pause for approximately five seconds.

7. **ON YOUR OWN:** Add the assert() function to the program in exercise 4. The program should print a message if a negative value is entered.

8. **ON YOUR OWN:** Write a program that accepts 30 names and sorts them using qsort(). The program should print the sorted names.

9. **ON YOUR OWN:** Modify the program in exercise 8 so that if the user enters QUIT, the program stops accepting input and sorts the entered values.

10. **ON YOUR OWN:** Refer to Day 15 for a "brute-force" method of sorting an array of pointers to strings based on the string values. Write a program that measures the time required to sort a large array of pointers with that method and then compares that time with the time required to perform the same sort with the library function qsort().

19

TYPE & RUN 6

Calculating Mortgage Payments

This Type & Run is called "Mortgage," and as the name suggests, it can calculate the payments on a mortgage or any other type of loan. When you run this program, it prompts you for the following three pieces of information:

- Amount: How much you're borrowing (also called the principal).

- Annual interest rate: The amount of interest charged per year. You need to enter the actual rate, so for 8[171] percent you enter 8.5. Do not adjust for the actual numerical value (0.085 in this case), because the program does this for you.

- The loan duration, or term, in months: This is the number of months over which you will be paying off the loan.

After you type in and run this program, you'll be able to calculate payments on mortgages and other types of loans.

INPUT   **LISTING T&R 6**   mortgage.c. The mortgage calculator

```
1:  /* Calculates loan/mortgage payments. */
2:
3:  #include <stdio.h>
4:  #include <math.h>
5:  #include <stdlib.h>
6:
7:   int main( void )
8:  {
9:     float principal, rate, payment;
10:    int term;
11:    char ch;
12:
13:    while (1)
14:    {
15:       /* Get loan data */
16:       puts("\nEnter the loan amount: ");
17:       scanf("%f", &principal);
18:       puts("\nEnter the annual interest rate: ");
19:       scanf("%f", &rate);
20:       /* Adjust for percent. */
21:       rate /= 100;
22:       /* Adjust for monthly interest rate. */
23:       rate /= 12;
24:
25:       puts("\nEnter the loan duration in months: ");
26:       scanf("%d", &term);
27:       payment = (principal * rate) / (1 - pow((1 + rate), -term));
28:       printf("Your monthly payment will be $%.2f.\n", payment);
29:
30:       puts("Do another (y or n)?");
31:       do
32:       {
33:       ch = getchar();
34:       } while (ch != 'n' && ch != 'y');
35:
36:       if (ch == 'n')
37:           break;
38:    }
39:    return 0;
40: }
```

ANALYSIS   This program assumes a standard loan, such as a typical fixed-rate car or home loan. The payment is calculated using the following standard financial formula:

payment = (*P* * *R*) / (1 - (1 + *R*)^(-*T*))

P is the principal, *R* is the interest rate, and *T* is the term. Note that the ^ symbol means "to the power of." In this formula, it is essential that the term and the rate be expressed in the same time units. Thus, if the loan term is expressed in months, the interest rate must be in months also. Because loans typically have rates expressed as annual rates, line 23 divides the annual rate by 12 to obtain the monthly interest rate. The actual payment calculation is performed on line 27, and line 28 displays the answer.

DAY **20**

Working with Memory

Today's lesson covers some of the more advanced aspects of managing memory within your C programs. Today you will learn

- About type conversions
- How to allocate and free memory storage
- How to manipulate memory blocks
- How to manipulate individual bits

Type Conversions

All of C's data objects have a specific type. A numeric variable can be an `int` or a `float`, a pointer can be a pointer to a `double` or `char`, and so on. Programs often require that different types be combined in expressions and statements. What happens in such cases? Sometimes C automatically handles the different types, so you don't need to be concerned. Other times, you must explicitly convert one data type to another to avoid erroneous results. You've seen this on earlier days' lessons when you had to convert or cast a type `void` pointer to a specific type before using it. In this and other situations, you need a clear understanding of when explicit type conversions are necessary and what types of errors can result when the proper conversion isn't applied. The following sections cover C's automatic and explicit type conversions.

Automatic Type Conversions

As the name implies, automatic type conversions are performed automatically by the C compiler without any action on your part. However, you should be aware of what's going on so that you can understand how C evaluates expressions.

Note | Automatic type conversion is often referred to as *implicit* conversions.

Type Promotion in Expressions

When a C expression is evaluated, the resulting value has a particular data type. If all the components in the expression have the same type, the resulting type is that type as well. For example, if x and y are both type int, the following expression is type int also:

```
x + y
```

What if the components of an expression have different types? In that case, the expression has the same type as its most comprehensive component. From least-comprehensive to most-comprehensive, the numerical data types are

```
char
short
int
long
long long
float
double
long double
```

Thus, an expression containing an int and a char evaluates to type int, an expression containing a long and a float evaluates to type float, and so on.

When creating expressions, the compiler uses two variables or values at a time. For example, if you have the expression:

```
Y + X * 2
```

the compiler would first use the operand, X and the operand 2. Once in completes it would use the resulting value and the operand Y.

Within expressions, individual operands are promoted as necessary to match the associated operands in the expression. Operands are promoted, in pairs, for each binary operator in the expression. Of course, promotion isn't needed if both operands are the same type. If they aren't, promotion follows these rules:

- If either operand is a `long double`, the other operand is promoted to type `long double`.
- If either operand is a `double`, the other operand is promoted to type `double`.
- If either operand is a `float`, the other operand is promoted to type `float`.
- If either operand is a `long`, the other operand is converted to type `long`.

For example, if x is an `int` and y is a `float`, evaluating the expression x/y causes x to be promoted to type `float` before the expression is evaluated. This doesn't mean that the type of variable x is changed. It means that a type `float` copy of x is created and used in the expression evaluation. The value of the expression is, as you just learned, type `float`. Likewise, if x is a type `double` and y is a type `float`, y will be promoted to `double`.

Conversion by Assignment

Promotions also occur with the assignment operator. The expression on the right side of an assignment statement is always promoted to the type of the data object on the left side of the assignment operator. Note that this might cause a "demotion" rather than a promotion. If f is a type `float` and i is a type `int`, i is promoted to type `float` in this assignment statement:

```
f = i;
```

In contrast, the assignment statement

```
i = f;
```

causes f to be demoted to type `int`. Its fractional part is lost on assignment to i. Remember that f itself isn't changed at all; promotion affects only a copy of the value. Thus, after the following statements are executed

```
float f = 1.23;
int i;
i = f;
```

the variable i has the value 1, and f still has the value 1.23. As this example illustrates, the fractional part is lost when a floating-point number is converted to an integer type.

20

Note Most compilers will give a warning if a variable is demoted without explicitly asking for it to be.

You should be aware that when an integer type is converted to a floating-point type, the resulting floating-point value might not exactly match the integer value. This is because the floating-point format used internally by the computer can't accurately represent every possible integer number. For example, the following code could result in a display of 2.999995 instead of 3:

```
float f;
int i = 3;
f = i;
printf("%f", f);
```

In most cases, any loss of accuracy caused by this would be insignificant. To be sure, however, keep integer values in type short, int, long, or long long variables.

Explicit Conversions Using Typecasts

A *typecast* uses the cast operator to explicitly control type conversions in your program. A typecast consists of a type name, in parentheses, before an expression. Casts can be performed on arithmetic expressions and pointers. The result is that the expression is converted to the type specified by the cast. In this manner, you can control the type of expressions in your program rather than relying on C's automatic conversions.

Casting Arithmetic Expressions

Casting an arithmetic expression tells the compiler to represent the value of the expression in a certain way. In effect, a cast is similar to a promotion, which was discussed earlier. However, a cast is under your control, not the compiler's. For example, if i is a type int, the expression

```
(float)i
```

casts i to type float. In other words, the program makes an internal copy of the value of i in floating-point format.

When would you use a typecast with an arithmetic expression? The most common use is to avoid losing the fractional part of the answer in an integer division. Listing 20.1 illustrates this. You should compile and run this program.

INPUT

LISTING 20.1 casting.c. When one integer is divided by another, any fractional part of the answer is lost

```
1:  #include <stdio.h>
2:
3:  int main( void )
4:  {
5:      int i1 = 100, i2 = 40;
6:      float f1;
7:
8:      f1 = i1/i2;
9:      printf("%lf\n", f1);
10:     return 0;
11: }
```

OUTPUT 2.000000

ANALYSIS The answer displayed by the program is 2.000000, but 100/40 evaluates to 2.5. What happened? The expression i1/i2 on line 8 contains two type int variables. Following the rules explained earlier today, you should be able to determine that the value of the expression i1/i2 is type int itself. This is because the two operands are both of type int. As such, the result can represent only whole numbers, so the fractional part of the answer is lost.

You might think that assigning the result of i1/i2 to a type float variable promotes it to type float. This is correct, but now it's too late; the fractional part of the answer is already gone.

To avoid this sort of inaccuracy, you must cast one of the type int variables to type float. If one of the variables is cast to type float, the previous rules tell you that the other variable is promoted automatically to type float, and the value of the expression is also type float. The fractional part of the answer is thus preserved. To demonstrate this, change line 8 in the source code so that the assignment statement reads as follows:

```
f1 = (float)i1/i2;
```

The program will then display the correct answer.

20

Note

In more complex expressions, you might want to cast more than one value.

Casting Pointers

You have already been introduced to the casting of pointers. As you saw on Day 18, "Getting More from Functions," a type void pointer is a generic pointer; it can point to anything. Before you can use a void pointer, you must cast it to the proper type. Note that you don't need to cast a pointer in order to assign a value to it or to compare it with NULL. However, you must cast it before dereferencing it or performing pointer arithmetic with it. For more details on casting void pointers, review Day 18.

Do	Don't
DO use a cast to promote or demote variable values when necessary.	DON'T use a cast just to prevent a compiler warning. You might find that using a cast gets rid of a warning, but before removing the warning this way, be sure you understand why you're getting the warning.

Allocating Memory Storage Space

The C library contains functions for allocating memory storage space at runtime, a process called *dynamic memory allocation*. This technique can have significant advantages over explicitly allocating memory in the program source code by declaring variables, structures, and arrays. This latter method, called *static memory allocation,* requires you to know, when you're writing the program, exactly how much memory you need. Dynamic memory allocation enables the program to react, while it's executing, to demands for memory, such as user input. All the functions for handling dynamic memory allocation require the header file stdlib.h; with some compilers, malloc.h is required as well. Note that all allocation functions return a type void pointer. As you learned on Day 18, a type void pointer must be cast to the appropriate type before being used.

Before we move on to the details, a few words are in order about memory allocation. What exactly does it mean? Each computer has a certain amount of memory (random access memory, or RAM) installed. This amount varies from system to system. When you run a program, whether a word processor, a graphics program, or a C program you wrote yourself, the program is loaded from disk into the computer's memory. The memory space the program occupies includes the program code, as well as space for all the program's static data—that is, data items that are declared in the source code. The memory left over is what's available for allocation using the functions in this section.

How much memory is available for allocation? It all depends. If you're running a large program on a system with only a modest amount of memory installed, the amount of free memory will be small. Conversely, when a small program is running on a multi-megabyte system, plenty of memory will be available. This means that your programs can't make any assumptions about memory availability. When a memory allocation function is called, you must check its return value to ensure that the memory was allocated successfully. In addition, your programs must be able to gracefully handle the situation when a memory allocation request fails. Later today, you'll learn a technique for determining exactly how much memory is available.

Also note that your operating system might have an effect on memory availability. Some operating systems make only a portion of physical RAM available. DOS 6.x and earlier versions fall into this category. Even if your system has multiple megabytes of RAM, a DOS program will have direct access to only the first 640 KB. (Special techniques can be used to access the other memory, but these are beyond the scope of this book.) In contrast, UNIX usually will make all physical RAM available to a program. To complicate matters further, some operating systems, such as Windows and OS/2, provide virtual memory that permits storage space on the hard disk to be allocated as if it were RAM. In this situation, the amount of memory available to a program includes not only the RAM installed, but also the virtual-memory space on the hard disk.

For the most part, these operating system differences in memory allocation should be transparent to you. If you use one of the C functions to allocate memory, the call either succeeds or fails, and you don't need to worry about the details of what's happening.

Allocating Memory with the `malloc()` Function

In lessons on earlier days, you learned how to use the `malloc()` library function to allocate storage space for strings. The `malloc()` function isn't limited to allocating memory for strings, of course; it can allocate space for any storage need. This function allocates memory by the byte. Recall that `malloc()`'s prototype is

```
void *malloc(size_t num);
```

The argument `size_t` is defined in stdlib.h as `unsigned`. The `malloc()` function allocates *num* bytes of storage space and returns a pointer to the first byte. This function returns `NULL` if the requested storage space couldn't be allocated or if *num* == 0. Review the section called "The `malloc()` Function" on Day 10, "Working with Characters and Strings," if you're still a bit unclear on its operation.

Listing 20.2 shows you how to use `malloc()` to determine the amount of free memory available in your system. This program works fine under DOS, or in a DOS box under older versions of Windows. Be warned, however, that you might get strange results on systems such as newer Windows versions, OS/2, and UNIX, which use hard disk space to provide "virtual" memory. The program might take a very long time to exhaust available memory.

20

Caution

If you are running an operating system that allows multiple programs to be running at once, then you will want to quit all other programs before running listing 20.2. If you use all of the memory in your system, your system can lock up or do other unpredictable things.

INPUT

LISTING 20.2   malloc.c. Using `malloc()` to determine how much memory is free

```
1:  /* Using malloc() to determine free memory.*/
2:
3:  #include <stdio.h>
4:  #include <stdlib.h>
5:
6:  /* Definition of a structure that is
7:      1024 bytes (1 kilobyte) in size.) */
8:
9:  struct kilo {
10:     struct kilo *next;
11:     char dummy[1020];
12: };
13:
14: int FreeMem(void);
15:
16: int main( void )
17: {
18:
19:     printf("You have %d kilobytes free.\n", FreeMem());
20:     return 0;
21: }
22:
23: int FreeMem(void)
24: {
25:     /*Returns the number of kilobytes (1024 bytes)
26:     of free memory. */
27:
28:     long counter;
29:     struct kilo *head, *current, *nextone;
30:
31:     current = head = (struct kilo*) malloc(sizeof(struct kilo));
32:
33:     if (head == NULL)
34:         return 0;        /*No memory available.*/
35:
36:     counter = 0;
37:     do
38:     {
39:         counter++;
```

LISTING 20.2 continued

```
40:        current->next = (struct kilo*) malloc(sizeof(struct kilo));
41:        current = current->next;
42:        printf("\r%d", counter);
43:    } while (current != NULL);
44:
45:    /* Now counter holds the number of type kilo
46:       structures we were able to allocate. We
47:       must free them all before returning. */
48:
49:    current = head;
50:    do
51:    {
52:        nextone = current->next;
53:        free(current);
54:        current = nextone;
55:    } while (nextone != NULL);
56:
57:    return counter;
58: }
```

INPUT   You have 60 kilobytes free.

ANALYSIS   Listing 20.2 operates in a brute-force manner. It simply loops, allocating blocks of memory, until the `malloc()` function returns `NULL`, indicating that no more memory is available. On a system with a lot of memory it may take several minutes to complete. Line 42 includes a print statement that displays the counter so you can see that the program is actually doing something.

The amount of available memory is then equal to the number of blocks allocated multiplied by the block size. The function then frees all the allocated blocks and returns the number of blocks allocated to the calling program. By making each block one kilobyte, the returned value indicates directly the number of kilobytes of free memory. As you may know, a kilobyte is not exactly one thousand bytes, but rather 1024 bytes (2 to the 10th power). We obtain a 1024-byte item by defining a structure, which we cleverly named `kilo`, which contains a 1020-byte array plus a 4-byte pointer.

The function `FreeMem()` uses the technique of linked lists, which was covered in more detail on Day 15, "Pointers: Beyond the Basics." In brief, a linked list consists of structures that contain a pointer to their own type (in addition to other data members). There is also a head pointer that points to the first item in the list (the variable `head`, a pointer to type `kilo`). The first item in the list points to the second, the second points to the third, and so on. The last item in the list is identified by a `NULL` pointer member. See Day 15 for more information.

20

Allocating Memory with the `calloc()` Function

The `calloc()` function also allocates memory. Rather than allocating a group of bytes as `malloc()` does, `calloc()` allocates a group of objects. The function prototype is

```
void *calloc(size_t num, size_t size);
```

Remember that `size_t` is a synonym for `unsigned` on most compilers. The argument *num* is the number of objects to allocate, and *size* is the size (in bytes) of each object. If allocation is successful, all the allocated memory is cleared (set to 0), and the function returns a pointer to the first byte. If allocation fails or if either `num` or `size` is 0, the function returns `NULL`.

Listing 20.3 illustrates the use of `calloc()`.

LISTING 20.3   calloc.c. Using the `calloc()` function to allocate memory storage space dynamically

```
1:  /* Demonstrates calloc(). */
2:
3:  #include <stdlib.h>
4:  #include <stdio.h>
5:
6:  int main( void )
7:  {
8:      unsigned long num;
9:      int *ptr;
10:
11:     printf("Enter the number of type int to allocate: ");
12:     scanf("%ld", &num);
13:
14:     ptr = (int*)calloc(num, sizeof(long long));
15:
16:     if (ptr != NULL)
17:         puts("Memory allocation was successful.");
18:     else
19:         puts("Memory allocation failed.");
20:     return 0;
21: }
```

```
Enter the number of type int to allocate: 100
Memory allocation was successful.
Enter the number of type int to allocate: 99999999
Memory allocation failed.
```

This program prompts for a value on lines 11 and 12. This number determines how much space the program will attempt to allocate. The program attempts to allocate enough memory (line 14) to hold the specified number of `long long` variables. If the allocation fails, the return value from `calloc()` is NULL; otherwise, it's a pointer to the allocated memory. In the case of this program, the return value from `calloc()` is placed in the int pointer, `ptr`. An if statement on lines 16–19 checks the status of the allocation based on `ptr`'s value and prints an appropriate message.

Enter different values and see how much memory can be successfully allocated. The maximum amount depends, to some extent, on your system configuration. Some systems can allocate space for 25,000 occurrences of type `long long`, whereas 30,000 fails. Remember that the size of an `long long` depends on your system. On a system with several hundred megabytes of memory, you may be required to enter a very, very large number to get the allocation to fail.

Allocating More Memory with the `realloc()` Function

The `realloc()` function changes the size of a block of memory that was previously allocated with `malloc()` or `calloc()`. The function prototype is

```
void *realloc(void *ptr, size_t size);
```

The `ptr` argument is a pointer to the original block of memory. The new size, in bytes, is specified by `size`. There are several possible outcomes with `realloc()`:

- If sufficient space exists to expand the memory block pointed to by `ptr`, the additional memory is allocated and the function returns `ptr`.

- If sufficient space does not exist to expand the current block in its current location, a new block of the size for `size` is allocated, and existing data is copied from the old block to the beginning of the new block. The old block is freed, and the function returns a pointer to the new block.

- If the `ptr` argument is NULL, the function acts like `malloc()`, allocating a block of `size` bytes and returning a pointer to it.

- If the argument size is 0, the memory that `ptr` points to is freed, and the function returns NULL.

- If memory is insufficient for the reallocation (either expanding the old block or allocating a new one), the function returns NULL, and the original block is unchanged.

Listing 20.4 demonstrates the use of `realloc()`.

20

LISTING 20.4 realloc.c. Using realloc() to increase the size of a block of
dynamically allocated memory

INPUT

```
 1:  /* Using realloc() to change memory allocation. */
 2:
 3:  #include <stdio.h>
 4:  #include <stdlib.h>
 5:  #include <string.h>
 6:
 7:  int main( void )
 8:  {
 9:      char buf[80], *message;
10:
11:      /* Input a string. */
12:
13:      puts("Enter a line of text.");
14:      gets(buf);
15:
16:      /* Allocate the initial block and copy the string to it. */
17:
18:      message = realloc(NULL, strlen(buf)+1);
19:      strcpy(message, buf);
20:
21:      /* Display the message. */
22:
23:      puts(message);
24:
25:      /* Get another string from the user. */
26:
27:      puts("Enter another line of text.");
28:      gets(buf);
29:
30:      /* Increase the allocation, then concatenate the string to it. */
31:
32:      message = realloc(message,(strlen(message) + strlen(buf)+1));
33:      strcat(message, buf);
34:
35:      /* Display the new message. */
36:      puts(message);
37:      return 0;
38:  }
```

OUTPUT

```
Enter a line of text.
This is the first line of text.
This is the first line of text.
Enter another line of text.
This is the second line of text.
This is the first line of text.This is the second line of text.
```

ANALYSIS This program gets an input string on line 14, reading it into an array of characters called buf. The string is then copied into a memory location pointed to by message (line 19). message was allocated using realloc() on line 18. realloc() was called even though there was no previous allocation. By passing NULL as the first parameter, realloc() knows that this is a first allocation.

Line 28 gets a second string in the buf buffer. This string is concatenated to the string already held in message. Because message is just big enough to hold the first string, it needs to be reallocated to make room to hold both the first and second strings. This is exactly what line 32 does. The program concludes by printing the final concatenated string.

Releasing Memory with the `free()` Function

When you allocate memory with either malloc() or calloc(), it is taken from the dynamic memory pool that is available to your program. This pool is sometimes called the *heap,* and it is finite—it has a limit. When your program finishes using a particular block of dynamically allocated memory, you should deallocate, or free, the memory to make it available for future use. To free memory that was allocated dynamically, use free(). Its prototype is

```
void free(void *ptr);
```

The free() function releases the memory pointed to by ptr. This memory must have been allocated with malloc(), calloc(), or realloc(). If ptr is NULL, free() does nothing. Listing 20.5 demonstrates the free() function. (It was also used in Listing 20.2.)

INPUT **LISTING 20.5** free.c. Using free() to release previously allocated dynamic memory

```
1:  /* Using free() to release allocated dynamic memory. */
2:
3:  #include <stdio.h>
4:  #include <stdlib.h>
5:  #include <string.h>
6:
7:  #define BLOCKSIZE 3000000
8:
9:  int main( void )
10: {
11:     void *ptr1, *ptr2;
12:
13:     /* Allocate one block. */
14:
```

20

LISTING 20.5 continued

```
15:     ptr1 = malloc(BLOCKSIZE);
16:
17:     if (ptr1 != NULL)
18:         printf("\nFirst allocation of %d bytes successful.",BLOCKSIZE);
19:     else
20:     {
21:         printf("\nAttempt to allocate %d bytes failed.\n",BLOCKSIZE);
22:         exit(1);
23:     }
24:
25:     /* Try to allocate another block. */
26:
27:     ptr2 = malloc(BLOCKSIZE);
28:
29:     if (ptr2 != NULL)
30:     {
31:         /* If allocation successful, print message and exit. */
32:
33:         printf("\nSecond allocation of %d bytes successful.\n",
34:                 BLOCKSIZE);
35:         exit(0);
36:     }
37:
38:     /* If not successful, free the first block and try again.*/
39:
40:     printf("\nSecond attempt to allocate %d bytes failed.",BLOCKSIZE);
41:     free(ptr1);
42:     printf("\nFreeing first block.");
43:
44:     ptr2 = malloc(BLOCKSIZE);
45:
46:     if (ptr2 != NULL)
47:         printf("\nAfter free(), allocation of %d bytes successful.\n",
48:                 BLOCKSIZE);
49:     return 0;
50: }
```

OUTPUT First allocation of 3000000 bytes successful.
Second allocation of 3000000 bytes successful.

ANALYSIS This program tries to dynamically allocate two blocks of memory. It uses the defined constant BLOCKSIZE to determine how much to allocate. Line 15 does the first allocation using malloc(). Lines 17 through 23 check the status of the allocation by determining whether the return value was equal to NULL. A message is displayed, stating the status of the allocation. If the allocation failed, the program exits. Line 27 tries to allocate a second block of memory, again checking to see whether the allocation was successful (lines 29through 36). If the second allocation was successful, a call to exit()

ends the program. If it was not successful, a message states that the attempt to allocate memory failed. The first block is then freed with `free()` (line 41), and a new attempt is made to allocate the second block.

You might need to modify the value of the symbolic constant `BLOCKSIZE`. On some systems, the value of `3000000` produces the following program output:

```
First allocation of 3000000 bytes successful.
Second attempt to allocate 3000000 bytes failed.
Freeing first block.
After free(), allocation of 300000 bytes successful.
```

On systems with virtual memory, of course, allocation will almost always succeed.

Do	**Don't**
DO free allocated memory when you're done with it.	**DON'T** assume that a call to `malloc()`, `calloc()`, or `realloc()` was successful. In other words, always check to see that the memory was indeed allocated.

Manipulating Memory Blocks

So far today, you've seen how to allocate and free blocks of memory. The C library also contains functions that can be used to manipulate blocks of memory—setting all bytes in a block to a specified value, copying, and moving information from one location to another.

Initializing Memory with the `memset()` Function

To set all the bytes in a block of memory to a particular value, use `memset()`. The function prototype is

```
void *memset(void *dest, int c, size_t count);
```

The argument `dest` points to the block of memory. `c` is the value to set, and `count` is the number of bytes, starting at `dest`, to be set. Note that while `c` is a type `int`, it is treated as a type `char`. In other words, only the low-order byte is used, and you can specify values of `c` only in the range `0` through `255`.

Use `memset()` to initialize a block of memory to a specified value. Because this function can use only a type `char` as the initialization value, it is not useful for working with blocks of data types other than type `char`, except when you want to initialize to `0`. In other words, it wouldn't be efficient to use `memset()` to initialize an array of type `int` to

20

the value 99, but you could initialize all array elements to the value 0. memset() will be demonstrated in Listing 20.6.

Copying Memory with the `memcpy()` Function

memcpy() copies bytes of data between memory blocks, sometimes called *buffers*. This function doesn't care about the type of data being copied—it simply makes an exact byte-for-byte copy. The function prototype is

```
void *memcpy(void *dest, void *src, size_t count);
```

The arguments dest and src point to the destination and source memory blocks, respectively. count specifies the number of bytes to be copied. The return value is dest. If the two blocks of memory overlap, the function might not operate properly—some of the data in src might be overwritten before being copied. Use the memmove() function, discussed next, to handle overlapping memory blocks. memcpy() will be demonstrated in Listing 20.6.

Moving Memory with the `memmove()` Function

memmove() is very much like memcpy(), copying a specified number of bytes from one memory block to another. It's more flexible, however, because it can handle overlapping memory blocks properly. Because memmove() can do everything memcpy() can do (with the added flexibility of dealing with overlapping blocks), you rarely, if ever, have a reason to use memcpy(). The prototype is

```
void *memmove(void *dest, void *src, size_t count);
```

dest and src point to the destination and source memory blocks, and count specifies the number of bytes to be copied. The return value is dest. If the blocks overlap, this function ensures that the source data in the overlapped region is copied before being overwritten. Listing 20.6 demonstrates memset(), memcpy(), and memmove().

INPUT **LISTING 20.6**   mem.c. A demonstration of memset(), memcpy(), and memmove()

```
1:  /* Demonstrating memset(), memcpy(), and memmove(). */
2:
3:  #include <stdio.h>
4:  #include <string.h>
4:
5:  char message1[60] = "Four score and seven years ago ...";
6:  char message2[60] = "abcdefghijklmnopqrstuvwxyz";
7:  char temp[60];
8:
```

LISTING 20.6 continued

```
 9:  int main( void )
10: {
11:     printf("\nmessage1[] before memset():\t%s", message1);
12:     memset(message1 + 5, '@', 10);
13:     printf("\nmessage1[] after memset():\t%s", message1);
14:
15:     strcpy(temp, message2);
16:     printf("\n\nOriginal message: %s", temp);
17:     memcpy(temp + 4, temp + 16, 10);
18:     printf("\nAfter memcpy() without overlap:\t%s", temp);
19:     strcpy(temp, message2);
20:     memcpy(temp + 6, temp + 4, 10);
21:     printf("\nAfter memcpy() with overlap:\t%s", temp);
22:
23:     strcpy(temp, message2);
24:     printf("\n\nOriginal message: %s", temp);
25:     memmove(temp + 4, temp + 16, 10);
26:     printf("\nAfter memmove() without overlap:\t%s", temp);
27:     strcpy(temp, message2);
28:     memmove(temp + 6, temp + 4, 10);
29:     printf("\nAfter memmove() with overlap:\t%s\n", temp);
30:     return 0;
31: }
```

OUTPUT

```
message1[] before memset():     Four score and seven years ago ...
message1[] after memset():      Four @@@@@@@@@@seven years ago ...

Original message: abcdefghijklmnopqrstuvwxyz
After memcpy() without overlap: abcdqrstuvwxyzopqrstuvwxyz
After memcpy() with overlap:    abcdefefefefefefqrstuvwxyz

Original message: abcdefghijklmnopqrstuvwxyz
After memmove() without overlap:        abcdqrstuvwxyzopqrstuvwxyz
After memmove() with overlap:   abcdefefghijklmnqrstuvwxyz
```

ANALYSIS The operation of memset() is straightforward. Note how the pointer notation message1 + 5 is used to specify that memset() is to start setting characters at the sixth character in message1[] (remember, arrays are zero-based). As a result, the sixth through 15th characters in message1[] have been changed to @.

When source and destination do not overlap, memcpy() works fine. The 10 characters of temp[] starting at position 17 (the letters q through z) have been copied to positions 5 though 14, where the letters e through n were originally located. If, however, the source and destination overlap, things are different. When the function tries to copy 10 characters starting at position 4 to position 6, an overlap of 8 positions occurs. You might expect the letters e through n to be copied over the letters g through p. Instead, the letters e and f are repeated five times.

20

If there's no overlap, memmove() works just like memcpy(). With overlap, however, memmove() copies the original source characters to the destination.

Do	**Don't**
DO use memmove() instead of memcpy() in case you're dealing with overlapping memory regions.	**DON'T** try to use memset() to initialize type int, float, or double arrays to any value other than 0.

Working with Bits

As you may know, the most basic unit of computer data storage is the bit. There are times when being able to manipulate individual bits in your C program's data is very useful. C has several tools that let you do this.

The C bitwise operators let you manipulate the individual bits of integer variables. Remember, a *bit* is the smallest possible unit of data storage, and it can have only one of two values: 0 or 1. The bitwise operators can be used only with integer types: char, int, and long. Before continuing with this section, you should be familiar with binary notation—the way the computer internally stores integers. If you need to review binary notation, refer to Appendix C, "Working with Binary and Hexadecimal Numbers."

The bitwise operators are most frequently used when your C program interacts directly with your system's hardware—a topic that is beyond the scope of this book. They do have other uses, however, which we will introduce.

The Shift Operators

Two shift operators shift the bits in an integer variable by a specified number of positions. The << operator shifts bits to the left, and the >> operator shifts bits to the right. The syntax for these binary operators is

x << n

and

x >> n

Each operator shifts the bits in x by n positions in the specified direction. For a right shift, zeros are placed in the n high-order bits of the variable; for a left shift, zeros are placed in the n low-order bits of the variable. Here are a few examples:

Binary 00001100 (decimal 12) right-shifted by 2 evaluates to binary 00000011 (decimal 3).

Binary 00001100 (decimal 12) left-shifted by 3 evaluates to binary 01100000 (decimal 96).

Binary 00001100 (decimal 12) right-shifted by 3 evaluates to binary 00000001 (decimal 1).

Binary 00110000 (decimal 48) left-shifted by 3 evaluates to binary 10000000 (decimal 128).

Under certain circumstances, the shift operators can be used to multiply and divide an integer variable by a power of 2. Left-shifting an integer by n places has the same effect as multiplying it by 2^n, and right-shifting an integer has the same effect as dividing it by 2^n. The results of a left-shift multiplication are accurate only if there is no overflow—that is, if no bits are "lost" by being shifted out of the high-order positions. A right-shift division is an integer division, in which any fractional part of the result is lost. For example, if you right-shift the value 5 (binary 00000101) by one place, intending to divide by 2, the result is 2 (binary 00000010) instead of the correct 2.5, because the fractional part (the .5) is lost. Listing 20.7 demonstrates the shift operators.

INPUT   **LISTING 20.7**   shiftit.c. Using the shift operators

```
1:  /* Demonstrating the shift operators. */
2:
3:  #include <stdio.h>
4:
5:  int main( void )
6:  {
7:      unsigned int y, x = 255;
8:      int count;
9:
10:     printf("Decimal\t\tshift left by\tresult\n");
11:
12:     for (count = 1; count < 8; count++)
13:     {
14:         y = x << count;
15:         printf("%d\t\t%d\t\t%d\n", x, count, y);
16:     }
17:     printf("\n\nDecimal\t\tshift right by\tresult\n");
18:
19:     for (count = 1; count < 8; count++)
20:     {
21:         y = x >> count;
22:         printf("%d\t\t%d\t\t%d\n", x, count, y);
23:     }
24:     return 0;
25: }
```

20

```
Decimal         shift left by    result
255             1                254
255             2                252
255             3                248
255             4                240
255             5                224
255             6                192
255             7                128
Decimal         shift right by   result
255             1                127
255             2                63
255             3                31
255             4                15
255             5                7
255             6                3
255             7                1
```

The Bitwise Logical Operators

Three bitwise logical operators are used to manipulate individual bits in an integer data type, as shown in Table 20.1. These operators have names similar to the TRUE/FALSE logical operators you learned about in earlier chapters, but their operations differ.

TABLE 20.1 The bitwise logical operators

Operator	Action
&	AND
|	Inclusive OR
^	Exclusive OR

These are all binary operators, setting bits in the result to 1 or 0 depending on the bits in the operands. They operate as follows:

- Bitwise AND sets a bit in the result to 1 only if the corresponding bits in both operands are 1; otherwise, the bit is set to 0. The AND operator is used to turn off, or clear, one or more bits in a value.

- Bitwise inclusive OR sets a bit in the result to 0 only if the corresponding bits in both operands are 0; otherwise, the bit is set to 1. The OR operator is used to turn on, or set, one or more bits in a value.

- Bitwise exclusive OR sets a bit in the result to 1 if the corresponding bits in the operands are different (if one is 1 and the other is 0); otherwise, the bit is set to 0.

The following are examples of how these operators work:

Operation	Example
AND	11110000
	& 01010101
	- - - - - - - - - -
	01010000
Inclusive OR	11110000
	| 01010101
	- - - - - - - - - -
	11110101
Exclusive OR	11110000
	^ 01010101
	- - - - - - - - - -
	10100101

You just read that bitwise AND and bitwise inclusive OR can be used to clear or set, respectively, specified bits in an integer value. Here's what that means. Suppose you have a type char variable, and you want to ensure that the bits in positions 0 and 4 are cleared (that is, equal to 0) and that the other bits stay at their original values. If you AND the variable with a second value that has the binary value 11101110, you'll obtain the desired result. Here's how this works:

In each position where the second value has a 1, the result will have the same value, 0 or 1, as was present in that position in the original variable:

```
0 & 1 == 0
1 & 1 == 1
```

In each position where the second value has a 0, the result will have a 0 regardless of the value that was present in that position in the original variable:

```
0 & 0 == 0
1 & 0 == 0
```

Setting bits with OR works in a similar way. In each position where the second value has a 1, the result will have a 1, and in each position where the second value has a 0, the result will be unchanged:

```
0 | 1 == 1
1 | 1 == 1
0 | 0 == 0
1 | 0 == 1
```

20

The Complement Operator

The final bitwise operator we will cover is the complement operator, ~. This is a unary operator. Its action is to reverse every bit in its operand, changing all 0s to 1s, and vice versa. For example, ~254 (binary 11111110) evaluates to 1 (binary 00000001).

All the examples in this section have used type char variables containing 8 bits. For larger variables, such as type int and type long, things work exactly the same.

Bit Fields in Structures

The final bit-related topic is the use of bit fields in structures. On Day 11, "Implementing Structures, Unions, and TypeDefs," you learned how to define your own data structures, customizing them to fit your program's data needs. By using bit fields, you can accomplish even greater customization and save memory space as well.

A *bit field* is a structure member that contains a specified number of bits. You can declare a bit field to contain one bit, two bits, or whatever number of bits are required to hold the data stored in the field. What advantage does this provide?

Suppose that you're programming an employee database program that keeps records on your company's employees. Many of the items of information that the database stores are of the yes/no variety, such as "Is the employee enrolled in the dental plan?" or "Did the employee graduate from college?" Each piece of yes/no information can be stored in a single bit, with 1 representing yes and 0 representing no.

Using C's standard data types, the smallest type you could use in a structure is a type char. You could indeed use a type char structure member to hold yes/no data, but seven of the char's eight bits would be wasted space. By using bit fields, you can store eight yes/no values in a single char.

Bit fields aren't limited to yes/no values. Continuing with this database example, imagine that your firm has three different health insurance plans. Your database needs to store data about the plan in which each employee is enrolled (if any). You could use 0 to represent no health insurance and use the values 1, 2, and 3 to represent the three plans. A bit field containing two bits is sufficient, because two binary bits can represent values of 0 through 3. Likewise, a bit field containing three bits could hold values in the range 0 through 7, four bits could hold values in the range 0 through 15, and so on.

Bit fields are named and accessed in the same way as regular structure members. All bit fields have type unsigned int, and you specify the size of the field (in bits) by following the member name with a colon and the number of bits. To define a structure with a one-bit member named dental, another one-bit member named college, and a two-bit member named health, you write the following:

```
struct emp_data
{
  unsigned dental     : 1;
  unsigned college    : 1;
  unsigned health     : 2;
  ...
};
```

The ellipsis (...) indicates space for other structure members. The members can be bit fields or fields made up of regular data types. Note that bit fields must be placed first in the structure definition, before any nonbit field structure members. To access the bit fields, use the structure member operator just as you do with any structure member. For the example, you can expand the structure definition to something more useful:

```
struct emp_data
{
  unsigned dental     : 1;
  unsigned college    : 1;
  unsigned health     : 2;
  char fname[20];
  char lname[20];
  char ssnumber[10];
};
```

You can then declare an array of structures:

```
struct emp_data workers[100];
```

To assign values to the first array element, write something like this:

```
workers[0].dental = 1;
workers[0].college = 0;
workers[0].health = 2;
strcpy(workers[0].fname, "Mildred");
```

Your code would be clearer, of course, if you used symbolic constants YES and NO with values of 1 and 0 when working with one-bit fields. In any case, you treat each bit field as a small, unsigned integer with the given number of bits. The range of values that can be assigned to a bit field with n bits is from 0 to 2^{n-1}. If you try to assign an out-of-range value to a bit field, the compiler won't report an error, but you will get unpredictable results.

20

Do	Don't
DO use defined constants YES and NO or TRUE and FALSE when working with bits. These are much easier to read and understand than 1 and 0.	**DON'T** define a bit field that takes 8 or 16 bits. These are the same as other available variables such as type char or int.

Summary

Today's lesson covered a variety of C programming topics. You learned how to allocate, reallocate, and free memory at runtime, and you saw commands that give you flexibility in allocating storage space for program data. You also saw how and when to use type-casts with variables and pointers. Forgetting about typecasts, or using them improperly, is a common cause of hard-to-find program bugs, so this is a topic worth reviewing. You also learned how to use the memset(), memcpy(), and memmove() functions to manipulate blocks of memory. Finally, you saw the ways in which you can manipulate and use individual bits in your programs.

Q&A

Q   What's the advantage of dynamic memory allocation? What can't I just declare the storage space I need in my source code?

A If you declare all your data storage in your source code, the amount of memory available to your program is fixed. You have to know ahead of time, when you write the program, how much memory will be needed. Dynamic memory allocation lets your program control the amount of memory used to suit the current conditions and user input. The program can use as much memory as it needs, up to the limit of what's available in the computer.

Q   Why would I ever need to free memory?

A When you're first learning to use C, your programs aren't very big. As your programs grow, their use of memory also grows. You should try to write your programs to use memory as efficiently as possible. When you're done with memory, you should release it. If you write programs that work in a multitasking environment, other applications might need memory that you aren't using. While some systems will automatically return memory when a program ends, not all systems do.

Q   What happens if I reuse a string without calling realloc()?

A You don't need to call realloc() if the string you're using was allocated enough room. Call realloc() when your current string isn't big enough. Remember, the C compiler lets you do almost anything, even things you shouldn't! You can over-write one string with a bigger string as long as the new string's length is equal to or smaller than the original string's allocated space. However, if the new string is bigger, you will also overwrite whatever came after the string in memory. This could be nothing, or it could be vital data. If you need a bigger allocated section of memory, call realloc().

Q **What's the advantage of the `memset()`, `memcpy()`, and `memmove()` functions? Why can't I just use a loop with an assignment statement to initialize or copy memory?**

A You can use a loop with an assignment statement to initialize memory in some cases. In fact, sometimes this is the only way to do it—for example, setting all elements of a type `float` array to the value `1.23`. In other situations, however, the memory will not have been assigned to an array or list, and the `mem...()` functions are your only choice. There are also times when a loop and assignment statement work, but the `mem...()` functions are simpler and faster.

Q **When would I use the shift operators and the bitwise logical operators?**

A The most common use for these operators is when a program is interacting directly with the computer hardware—a task that often requires specific bit patterns to be generated and interpreted. This topic is beyond the scope of this book. Even if you never need to manipulate hardware directly, you can use the shift operators, in certain circumstances, to divide or multiply integer values by powers of two.

Q **Do I really gain that much by using bit fields?**

A Yes, you can gain quite a bit with bit fields. (Pun intended!) Consider a circumstance similar to the example in this chapter in which a file contains information from a survey. People are asked to answer TRUE or FALSE to the questions asked. If you ask 100 questions of 10,000 people and store each answer as a type `char` as T or F, you will need 10,000 × 100 bytes of storage (because a character is 1 byte). This is 1 million bytes of storage. If you use bit fields instead and allocate one bit for each answer, you will need 10,000 × 100 bits. Because 1 byte holds 8 bits, this amounts to 130,000 bytes of data, which is significantly less than 1 million bytes.

Workshop

The Workshop provides quiz questions to help you solidify your understanding of the material covered and exercises to provide you with experience in using what you've learned.

Quiz

1. What is the difference between the `malloc()` and `calloc()` memory-allocation functions?

2. What is the most common reason for using a typecast with a numeric variable?

3. What variable type do the following expressions evaluate to? Assume that c is a type `char` variable, i is a type `int` variable, l is a type `long` variable, and f is a

a. (c + i + 1)

b. (i + 32)

c. (c + 'A')

d. (i + 32.0)

e. (100 + 1.0)

4. What is meant by dynamically allocating memory?

5. What is the difference between the `memcpy()` function and the `memmove()` function?

6. Imagine that your program uses a structure that must (as one of its members) store the day of the week as a value between 1 and 7. What's the most memory-efficient way to do so?

7. What is the smallest amount of memory in which the current date can be stored? (Hint: month/day/year—think of year as an offset from 1900.)

8. What does `10010010 << 4` evaluate to?

9. What does `10010010 >> 4` evaluate to?

10. Describe the difference between the results of the following two expressions:

```
(01010101 ^ 11111111 )
( ~01010101 )
```

Exercises

1. Write a `malloc()` command that allocates memory for 1,000 `longs`.

2. Write a `calloc()` command that allocates memory for 1,000 `longs`.

3. Assume that you have declared an array as follows:

```
float data[1000];
```

Show two ways to initialize all elements of the array to 0. Use a loop and an assignment statement for one method, and the `memset()` function for the other.

4. **BUG BUSTER:** Is anything wrong with the following code?

```
void func()
{
  int number1 = 100, number2 = 3;
  float answer;
  answer = number1 / number2;
  printf("%d/%d = %lf", number1, number2, answer)
}
```

5. **BUG BUSTER:** What, if anything, is wrong with the following code?

```
void *p;
p = (float*) malloc(sizeof(float));
*p = 1.23;
```

6. **BUG BUSTER:** Is the following structure allowed?

```
struct quiz_answers
{
  char student_name[15];
  unsigned answer1   : 1;
  unsigned answer2   : 1;
  unsigned answer3   : 1;
  unsigned answer4   : 1;
  unsigned answer5   : 1;
}
```

Answers are not provided for the following exercises:

7. Write a program that uses each of the bitwise logical operators. The program should apply the bitwise operator to a number and then reapply it to the result. You should observe the output to be sure you understand what's going on.

8. Write a program that displays the binary value of a number. For instance, if the user enters 3, the program should display 00000011. (Hint: You will need to use the bitwise operators.)

20

DAY 21

Advanced Compiler Use

Today is the last day of your 21 days of C. At this time, you have actually learned nearly all the key topics you need to know about programming with the C language syntax. Today you will cover some additional features of C. Today you will learn

- Programming with multiple source-code files
- Using the C preprocessor
- Using command-line arguments

Programming with Multiple Source-Code Files

Until now, all your C programs have consisted of a single source-code file, (not counting the header files, of course). A single source-code file is often all you need, particularly for small programs, but you can also divide the source code for a single program among two or more files, a practice called *modular programming*. Why would you want to do this? The following sections explain.

Advantages of Modular Programming

The primary reason to use modular programming is closely related to structured programming and its reliance on functions. As you become a more experienced programmer, you develop more general-purpose functions that you can use, not only in the program for which they were originally written, but in other programs as well. For example, you might write a collection of general-purpose functions for displaying information onscreen. By keeping these functions in a separate file, you can use them again in different programs that also display information onscreen. When you write a program that consists of multiple source-code files, each source file is called a *module*.

Modular Programming Techniques

A C program can have only one `main()` function. The module that contains the `main()` function is called the *main module,* and other modules are called *secondary modules*. A separate header file is usually associated with each secondary module (you'll learn why later in today). For now, look at a few simple examples that illustrate the basics of multiple module programming. Listings 21.1, 21.2, and 21.3 show the main module, the secondary module, and the header file, respectively, for a program that inputs a number from the user and displays its square.

INPUT   **LISTING 21.1**   list2101.c: the main module

```
 1:  /* Inputs a number and displays its square. */
 2:
 3:  #include <stdio.h>
 4:  #include "calc.h"
 5:
 6:  int main( void )
 7:  {
 8:      int x;
 9:
10:      printf("Enter an integer value: ");
11:      scanf("%d", &x);
12:      printf("\nThe square of %d is %ld.\n", x, sqr(x));
13:      return 0;
14: }
```

INPUT   **LISTING 21.2**   calc.c: the secondary module

```
 1:  /* Module containing calculation functions. */
 2:
 3:  #include "calc.h"
 4:
```

LISTING 21.2 continued

```
5:  long sqr(int x)
6:  {
7:     return ((long)x * x);
8:  }
```

INPUT   **LISTING 21.3**   calc.h: the header file for calc.c

```
1:  /* calc.h: header file for calc.c. */
2:
3:  long sqr(int x);
4:
5:  /* end of calc.h */
```

INPUT/   Enter an integer value: **100**
OUTPUT
             The square of 100 is 10000.

ANALYSIS   Let's look at the components of these three files in greater detail. The header file, calc.h, contains the prototype for the sqr() function in calc.c. Because any module that uses sqr() needs to know sqr()'s prototype, the module must include calc.h.

The secondary module file, calc.c, contains the definition of the sqr() function. The #include directive is used to include the header file, calc.h. Note that the header filename is enclosed in quotation marks rather than angle brackets. (You'll learn the reason for this later today.)

The main module, list2101.c, contains the main() function. This module also includes the header file, calc.h.

After you use your editor to create these three files, how do you compile and link the final executable program? Your compiler controls this for you. At the command line, enter

```
xxx list2101.c calc.c
```

where *xxx* is your compiler's command. This directs the compiler's components to perform the following tasks:

1. Compile list2101.c, creating list2101.obj (or list2101.o on a UNIX system). If it encounters any errors, the compiler displays descriptive error messages.

2. Compile calc.c, creating calc.obj (or calc.o on a UNIX system). Again, error messages appear if necessary.

21

3. Link list2101.obj, calc.obj, and any needed functions from the standard library to create the final executable program list2101.exe.

If you are using an integrated development environment, you can often create a project that takes care of compiling multiple source files for you. For example, if you are using the Dev-C++ compiler that came with this book, you can compile the previous listings using the following steps:

1. Open Dev-C++

2. Select File | New Project. You will be presented with the dialog box presented in Figure 21.1.

3. Select C project and then click on Console Application. You will be presented with the New Project Name dialog as shown in Figure 21.2.

4. Enter the name of your project such as, List2101. You will be asked to save this file.

5. The IDE will be opened with an untitled C file in it as shown in Figure 21.3. You can either type the code for one of the files into this or you can simply close the file. If you enter the code, you'll want to save the file. You can then enter the other two source files by selecting Project | Add Source File.

6. If you already created the source files, then you can add them to the project you just created. Do this by selecting Project | Add to project. You can then select the three files. These will be added to the IDE.

7. Compile the project the same way you've been compiling your source files before.

For more on compiling projects with Dev-C++, see the help files.

FIGURE 21.1

Dev-C++ New Project Dialog.

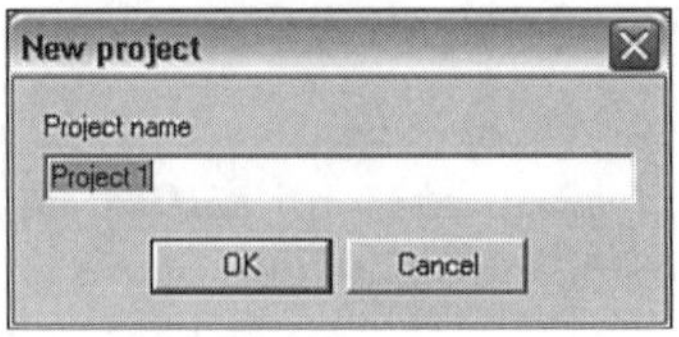

FIGURE 21.2

Dev-C++ New Project Name.

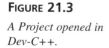

FIGURE 21.3

A Project opened in Dev-C++.

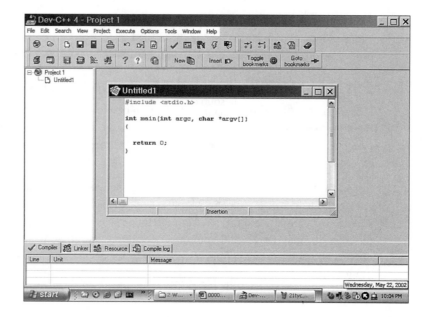

Module Components

As you can see, the mechanics of compiling and linking a multiple-module program are quite simple. The only real question is what to put in each file. This section gives you some general guidelines.

The secondary module should contain general utility functions—that is, functions that you might want to use in other programs. A common practice is to create one secondary module for each type of function—for example, keyboard.c for your keyboard functions, screen.c for your screen display functions, and so on. To compile and link more than two modules, list all source files on the command line:

```
tcc mainmod.c screen.c keyboard.c
```

The main module should contain main(), of course, and any other functions that are program-specific (meaning that they have no general utility).

There is usually one header file for each secondary module. Each file has the same name as the associated module, with an .h extension. In the header file, put

- Prototypes for functions in the secondary module
- #define directives for any symbolic constants and macros used in the module
- Definitions of any structures or external variables used in the module

21

Because this header file might be included in more than one source file, you want to prevent portions of it from compiling more than once. You can do this by using the preprocessor directives for conditional compilation (discussed later in this chapter).

External Variables and Modular Programming

In many cases, the only data communication between the main module and the secondary module is through arguments passed to and returned from the functions. In this case, you don't need to take special steps regarding data visibility; but what about an external variable that needs to be visible in both modules?

Recall from Day 12, "Understanding Variable Scope," that an external variable is one declared outside of any function. An external variable is visible throughout the entire source code file in which it is declared. However, it is not automatically visible in other modules. To make it visible, you must declare the variable in each module, using the extern keyword. For example, if you have an external variable declared in the main module as

```
float interest_rate;
```

you make interest_rate visible in a secondary module by including the following declaration in that module (outside of any function):

```
extern float interest_rate;
```

The extern keyword tells the compiler that the original declaration of interest_rate (the one that set aside storage space for it) is located elsewhere, but that the variable should be made visible in this module. All extern variables have static duration and are visible to all functions in the module. Figure 21.4 illustrates the use of the extern keyword in a multiple-module program.

 Caution   If you use extern declarations and then don't actually declare the variable elsewhere, you will get an error. This error will occur either when you link the final program or at run time.

In Figure 21.4, the variable x is visible throughout all three modules. In contrast, y is visible only in the main module and secondary module 1.

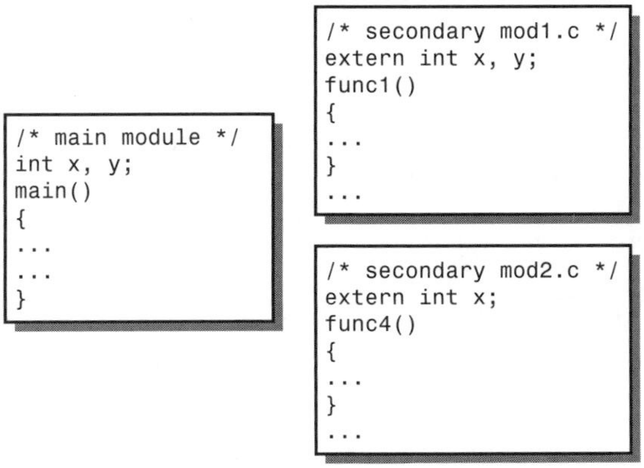

FIGURE 21.4

Using the extern *keyword to make an external variable visible across modules.*

```
/* main module */
int x, y;
main()
{
...
...
}
```

```
/* secondary mod1.c */
extern int x, y;
func1()
{
...
}
...
```

```
/* secondary mod2.c */
extern int x;
func4()
{
...
}
...
```

Using .obj Files

After you've written and thoroughly debugged a secondary module, you don't need to recompile it every time you use it in a program. After you have the object file for the module code, all you need to do is link it with each program that uses the functions in the module.

When you compile a program, the compiler creates an object file that has the same name as the C source code file and an .obj extension (or an .o extension on UNIX systems). For example, suppose you're developing a module called keyboard.c and compiling it, along with the main module database.c, using the following command:

```
tcc database.c keyboard.c
```

The keyboard.obj file is also on your disk. After you know that the functions in keyboard.c work properly, you can stop compiling it every time you recompile database.c (or any other program that uses it), linking the existing object file instead. To do this, use the command

```
tcc database.c keyboard.obj
```

The compiler then compiles database.c and links the resulting object file database.obj with keyboard.obj to create the final executable file database.exe. This saves time, because the compiler doesn't have to recompile the code in keyboard.c. However, if you modify the code in keyboard.c, you must recompile it. In addition, if you modify a header file, you must recompile all the modules that use it.

21

Do	**Don't**
DO create generic functions in their own source files. This way, they can be linked into any other programs that need them.	**DON'T** try to compile multiple source files together if more than one module contains a main() function. You can have only one main(). (You can only have one function of any name.) **DON'T** always use the C source files when compiling multiple files together. If you compile a source file into an object file, recompile only when the file changes. This saves a great deal of time.

Using the Make Utility

Almost all C compilers come with a make utility that can simplify and speed the task of working with multiple source-code files. This utility, which is usually called nmake.exe, lets you write a *make file,* so called because it defines the dependencies between your various program components. What does dependency mean?

Imagine a project that has a main module named program.c and a secondary module named second.c. There are also two header files, program.h and second.h. The program.c includes both of the header files, whereas second.c includes only second.h. Code in program.c calls functions in second.c.

program.c is dependent on the two header files because it includes them both. If you make a change to either header file, you must recompile program.c so that it will include those changes. In contrast, second.c is dependent on second.h but not on program.h. If you change program.h, there is no need to recompile second.c—you can just link the existing object file second.obj that was created when second.c was last compiled.

A make file describes the dependencies such as those just discussed that exist in your project. Each time you edit one or more of your source code files, you use the nmake utility to "run" the make file. This utility examines the time and date stamps on the source code and object files and, based on the dependencies you have defined, instructs the compiler to recompile only those files that are dependent on the modified file(s). The result is that no unnecessary compilation is done, and you can work at the maximum efficiency.

For projects that involve one or two source code files, it usually isn't worth the trouble of defining a make file. For larger projects, however, it's a real benefit. Refer to your compiler documentation for information on how to use its nmake utility.

The C Preprocessor

The preprocessor is a part of all C compiler packages. When you compile a C program, the preprocessor is the first compiler component that processes your program. In most C compilers, the preprocessor is part of the compiler program. When you run the compiler, it automatically runs the preprocessor.

The preprocessor changes your source code based on instructions, or *preprocessor directives,* in the source code. The output of the preprocessor is a modified source code file that is then used as the input for the next compilation step. Normally you never see this file, because the compiler deletes it after it's used. However, later today, you'll learn how to look at this intermediate file. First, you need to learn about the preprocessor directives, all of which begin with the # symbol.

The `#define` Preprocessor Directive

The `#define` preprocessor directive has two uses: creating symbolic constants and creating macros.

Simple Substitution Macros Using `#define`

You learned about substitution macros on Day 3, "Storing Information: Variables and Constants," although the term used to describe them in that chapter was *symbolic constants*. You create a substitution macro by using #define to replace text with other text. For example, to replace text1 with text2, you write

```
#define text1 text2
```

This directive causes the preprocessor to go through the entire source code file, replacing every occurrence of text1 with text2. The only exception occurs if text1 is found within double quotation marks, in which case no change is made.

The most frequent use for substitution macros is to create symbolic constants, as explained on Day 3. For example, if your program contains the following lines:

```
#define MAX 1000
x = y * MAX;
z = MAX - 12;
```

during preprocessing, the source code is changed to read as follows:

```
x = y * 1000;
z = 1000 - 12;
```

The effect is the same as using your editor's search-and-replace feature in order to change every occurrence of MAX to 1000. Your original source code file isn't changed, of course. Instead, a temporary copy is created with the changes. Note that #define isn't limited to creating symbolic numeric constants. For example, you can write

21

```
#define ZINGBOFFLE printf
ZINGBOFFLE("Hello, world.");
```

although there is little reason to do so. You should also be aware that some authors refer to symbolic constants defined with #define as being macros themselves. (Symbolic constants are also called *manifest constants*.) However, in this book, the word *macro* is reserved for the type of construction described next.

Creating Function Macros with #define

You can use the #define directive also to create function macros. A *function macro* is a type of shorthand, using something simple to represent something more complicated. The reason for the "function" name is that this type of macro can accept arguments, just like a real C function does. One advantage of function macros is that their arguments aren't type sensitive. Therefore, you can pass any numeric variable type to a function macro that expects a numeric argument.

Let's look at an example. The preprocessor directive

```
#define HALFOF(value) ((value)/2)
```

defines a macro named HALFOF that takes a parameter named value. Whenever the preprocessor encounters the text HALFOF(value) in the source code, it replaces it with the definition text and inserts the argument as needed. Thus, the source code line

```
result = HALFOF(10);
```

is replaced by this line:

```
result = ((10)/2);
```

Likewise, the program line

```
printf("%f", HALFOF(x[1] + y[2]));
```

is replaced by this line:

```
printf("%f", ((x[1] + y[2])/2));
```

A macro can have more than one parameter, and each parameter can be used more than once in the replacement text. For example, the following macro, which calculates the average of five values, has five parameters:

```
#define AVG5(v, w, x, y, z) (((v)+(w)+(x)+(y)+(z))/5)
```

The following macro, in which the conditional operator determines the larger of two values, also uses each of its parameters twice. (You learned about the conditional operator on Day 4, "Statements, Expressions, and Operators.")

```
#define LARGER(x, y) ((x) > (y) ? (x) : (y))
```

A macro can have as many parameters as needed, but all the parameters in the list must be used in the substitution string. For example, the macro definition

```
#define ADD(x, y, z) ((x) + (y))
```

is invalid, because the parameter z is not used in the substitution string. Also, when you invoke the macro, you must pass it the correct number of arguments.

When you write a macro definition, the opening parenthesis must immediately follow the macro name; there can be no white space. The opening parenthesis tells the preprocessor that a function macro is being defined and that this isn't a simple symbolic constant type substitution. Look at the following definition:

```
#define SUM (x, y, z) ((x)+(y)+(z))
```

Because of the space between SUM and (, the preprocessor treats this like a simple substitution macro. Every occurrence of SUM in the source code is replaced with (x, y, z) ((x)+(y)+(z)), clearly not what you wanted.

Also note that in the substitution string, each parameter is enclosed in parentheses. This is necessary to avoid unwanted side effects when passing expressions as arguments to the macro. Look at the following example of a macro defined without parentheses:

```
#define SQUARE(x) x*x
```

If you invoke this macro with a simple variable as an argument, there's no problem. But what if you pass an expression as an argument?

```
result = SQUARE(x + y);
```

The resulting macro expansion is as follows, which doesn't give the proper result:

```
result = x + y * x + y;
```

If you use parentheses, you can avoid the problem, as shown in this example:

```
#define SQUARE(x) (x)*(x)
```

This definition expands to the following line, which does give the proper result:

```
result = (x + y)*(x + y);
```

You can obtain additional flexibility in macro definitions by using the *stringizing operator* (#) (sometimes called the *string-literal operator*). When a macro parameter is preceded by # in the substitution string, the argument is converted into a quoted string when the macro is expanded. Thus, if you define a macro as

```
#define OUT(x) printf(#x)
```

21

and you invoke it with the statement

```
OUT(Hello Mom);
```

it expands to this statement:

```
printf("Hello Mom");
```

The conversion performed by the stringizing operator takes special characters into account. Thus, if a character in the argument normally requires an escape character, the # operator inserts a backslash before the character. Continuing with the example, the invocation

```
OUT("Hello Mom");
```

expands to

```
printf("\"Hello Mom\"");
```

The # operator is demonstrated in Listing 21.4. First, you need to look at one other operator used in macros, the *concatenation operator* (##). This operator concatenates, or joins, two strings in the macro expansion. It doesn't include quotation marks or special treatment of escape characters. Its main use is to create sequences of C source code. For example, if you define and invoke a macro as

```
#define CHOP(x) func ## x
salad = CHOP(3)(q, w);
```

the macro invoked in the second line is expanded to

```
salad = func3 (q, w);
```

You can see that, by using the ## operator, you determine which function is called. You have actually modified the C source code.

Listing 21.4 shows an example of one way to use the # operator.

LISTING 21.4   preproc.c. Using the # operator in macro expansion

```
 1:  /* Demonstrates the # operator in macro expansion. */
 2:
 3:  #include <stdio.h>
 4:
 5:  #define OUT(x) printf(#x " is equal to %d.\n", x)
 6:
 7:  int main( void )
 8:  {
 9:     int value = 123;
10:     OUT(value);
```

LISTING 21.4 continued

```
11:    return 0;
12: }
```

 OUTPUT   `value is equal to 123.`

ANALYSIS   By using the # operator on line 5, the call to the macro expands with the variable name `value` as a quoted string passed to the `printf()` function. After expansion on line 9, the macro `OUT` looks like this:

```
printf("value" " is equal to %d.",  value );
```

Macros Versus Functions

You have seen that function macros can be used in place of real functions, at least in situations where the resulting code is relatively short. Function macros can extend beyond one line, but they usually become impractical beyond a few lines. When you can use either a function or a macro, which should you use? It's a trade-off between program speed and program size.

A macro's definition is expanded into the code each time the macro is encountered in the source code. If your program invokes a macro 100 times, 100 copies of the expanded macro code are in the final program. In contrast, a function's code exists only as a single copy. Therefore, in terms of program size, the better choice is a true function.

When a program calls a function, a certain amount of processing overhead is required in order to pass execution to the function code and then return execution to the calling program. There is no processing overhead in "calling" a macro, because the code is right there in the program. In terms of speed, a function macro has the advantage.

These size/speed considerations aren't usually of much concern to the beginning programmer. Only with large, time-critical applications do they become important.

Viewing Macro Expansion

At times, you might want to see what your expanded macros look like, particularly when they aren't working properly. To see the expanded macros, you instruct the compiler to create a file that includes macro expansion after the compiler's first pass through the code. You might not be able to do this if your C compiler uses an Integrated Development Environment (IDE); you might have to work from the command prompt. Most compilers have a flag that should be set during compilation. This flag is passed to the compiler as a command-line parameter.

21

For example, to precompile a program named program.c with the Microsoft compiler, you would enter

```
cl /E program.c
```

On a UNIX compiler, you would enter

```
cc -E program.c
```

The preprocessor makes the first pass through your source code. All header files are included, #define macros are expanded, and other preprocessor directives are carried out. Depending on your compiler, the output goes either to stdout (that is, the screen) or to a disk file with the program name and a special extension. The Microsoft compiler sends the preprocessed output to stdout. Unfortunately, it's not at all useful to have the processed code whip by on your screen! You can use the redirection command to send this output to a file, as in this example:

```
cl /E program.c > program.pre
```

You can then load the file into your editor for printing or viewing.

Do	Don't
DO use #defines, especially for symbolic constants. Symbolic constants make your code much easier to read. Examples of things to put into defined constants are colors, true/false, yes/no, the keyboard keys, and maximum values. Symbolic constants are used throughout this book.	**DON'T** overuse macro functions. Use them where needed, but be sure they are a better choice than a normal function.

Using the #include Directive

You have already learned how to use the #include preprocessor directive to include header files in your program. When it encounters an #include directive, the preprocessor reads the specified file and inserts it at the location of the directive. You can't use the * or ? wildcards to read in a group of files with one #include directive. You can, however, nest #include directives. In other words, an included file can contain #include directives, which can contain #include directives, and so on. Most compilers limit the number of levels deep that you can nest, but if the compiler supports the ANSI standard, then you usually can nest up to 15 levels.

There are two ways to specify the filename for an #include directive. If the filename is enclosed in angle brackets, such as #include <stdio.h> (as you have seen throughout this book), the preprocessor first looks for the file in the standard directory. If the file isn't found, or no standard directory is specified, the preprocessor looks for the file in the current directory.

"What is the standard directory?" you might be asking. In DOS, it's the directory or directories specified by the DOS INCLUDE environment variable. Your DOS documentation contains complete information on the DOS environment. To summarize, however, you set an environment variable with a SET command (usually, but not necessarily, in your autoexec.bat file). Most compilers automatically set the INCLUDE variable in the autoexec.bat file when the compiler is installed.

The second method of specifying the file to be included is enclosing the filename in double quotation marks: #include "myfile.h". In this case, the preprocessor doesn't search the standard directories; instead, it looks in the directory containing the source code file being compiled. Generally speaking, header files that you write should be kept in the same directory as the C source code files, and they are included by using double quotation marks. The standard directory is reserved for header files supplied with your compiler.

Using #if, #elif, #else, and #endif

These four preprocessor directives control conditional compilation. The term *conditional compilation* means that blocks of C source code are compiled only if certain conditions are met. In many ways, the #if family of preprocessor directives operates like the C language's if statement. The difference is that if controls whether certain statements are executed, whereas #if controls whether they are compiled.

The structure of an #if block is as follows:

```
#if condition_1
  statement_block_1
#elif condition_2
  statement_block_2
  ...
#elif condition_n
  statement_block_n
#else
  default_statement_block
#endif
```

21

The test expression that #if uses can be almost any expression that evaluates to a constant. You can't use the sizeof() operator, typecasts, or the float type. Most often you use #if to test symbolic constants created with the #define directive.

Each *statement_block* consists of one or more C statements of any type, including pre-processor directives. They don't need to be enclosed in braces, although they can be.

The #if and #endif directives are required, but #elif and #else are optional. You can have as many #elif directives as you want, but only one #else. When the compiler reaches an #if directive, it tests the associated condition. If it evaluates to TRUE (nonzero), the statements following the #if are compiled. If it evaluates to FALSE (zero), the compiler tests, in order, the conditions associated with each #elif directive. The statements associated with the first TRUE #elif are compiled. If none of the conditions evaluates as TRUE, the statements following the #else directive are compiled.

Note that, at most, a single block of statements within the #if...#endif construction is compiled. If the compiler finds no #else directive, it might not compile any statements.

The possible uses of these conditional compilation directives are limited only by your imagination. Here's one example. Suppose you're writing a program that uses a great deal of country-specific information. This information is contained in a header file for each country. When you compile the program for use in different countries, you can use an #if...#endif construction as follows:

```
#if ENGLAND == 1
#include "england.h"
#elif FRANCE == 1
#include "france.h"
#elif ITALY == 1
#include "italy.h"
#else
#include "usa.h"
#endif
```

Then, by using #define to define the appropriate symbolic constant, you can control which header file is included during compilation.

Using #if...#endif to Help Debug

Another common use of #if...#endif is to include conditional debugging code in the program. You could define a DEBUG symbolic constant set to either 1 or 0. Throughout the program, you can insert debugging code as follows:

```
#if DEBUG == 1
  debugging code here
#endif
```

During program development, if you define DEBUG as 1, the debugging code is included to help track down any bugs. After the program is working properly, you can redefine DEBUG as 0 and recompile the program without the debugging code.

The `defined()` operator is useful when you write conditional compilation directives. This operator tests to see whether a particular name is defined. Thus, the expression

```
defined( NAME )
```

evaluates to `TRUE` or `FALSE`, depending on whether `NAME` is defined. By using `defined()`, you can control compilation, based on previous definitions, without regard to the specific value of a name. Referring to the previous debugging code example, you could rewrite the `#if...#endif` section as follows:

```
#if defined( DEBUG )
  debugging code here
#endif
```

You can also use `defined()` to assign a definition to a name only if it hasn't been previously defined. Use the `NOT` operator (`!`) as follows:

```
#if !defined( TRUE )      /* if TRUE is not defined. */
#define TRUE 1
#endif
```

Notice that the `defined()` operator doesn't require that a name be defined as anything in particular. For example, after the following program line, the name `RED` is defined, but not as anything in particular:

```
#define RED
```

Even so, the expression `defined( RED )` still evaluates as `TRUE`. Of course, occurrences of `RED` in the source code are removed and not replaced with anything, so you must use caution.

Avoiding Multiple Inclusions of Header Files

As programs grow, or as you use header files more often, you run the risk of accidentally including a header file more than once. This can cause the compiler to balk in confusion. Using the directives that you've learned, you can easily avoid this problem. Look at the example shown in Listing 21.5.

INPUT   **LISTING 21.5**   prog.h. Using preprocessor directives with header files

```
1:  /* prog.h - A header file with a check to prevent multiple includes! */
2:
3:  #if defined( prog_h )
4:  /* the file has been included already */
5:  #else
6:  #define prog_h
7:
```

21

LISTING 21.5   continued

```
 8:  /* Header file information goes here... */
 9:
10:
11:
12: #endif
```

 ANALYSIS   Examine what this header file does. On line 3, it checks whether prog_h is defined. Notice that prog_h is similar to the name of the header file. If prog_h is defined, a comment is included on line 4, and the program looks for the #endif at the end of the header file. This means that nothing more is done.

How does prog_h get defined? It is defined on line 6. The first time this header is included, the preprocessor checks whether prog_h is defined. It won't be, so control goes to the #else statement. The first thing done after the #else is to define prog_h so that any other inclusions of this file skip the body of the file. Lines 7 through 11 can contain any number of commands or declarations.

> **Tip**
>
> You should include preprocessor directive checks as shown in listing 21.5 with all of the header files you create. This will prevent them from being included multiple times.

The #undef Directive

The #undef directive is the opposite of #define—it removes the definition from a name. Here's an example:

```
#define DEBUG 1
   /* In this section of the program, occurrences of DEBUG    */
   /* are replaced with 1, and the expression defined( DEBUG ) */
   /* evaluates to TRUE. *.
#undef DEBUG
   /* In this section of the program, occurrences of DEBUG   */
   /* are not replaced, and the expression defined( DEBUG )  */
   /* evaluates to FALSE. */
```

You can use #undef and #define to create a name that is defined only in parts of your source code. You can use this in combination with the #if directive, as explained earlier, for more control over conditional compilations.

Predefined Macros

Most compilers have a number of predefined macros. The most useful of these are __DATE__, __TIME__, __LINE__, and __FILE__. Notice that each of these are preceded and followed by double underscores. This is done to prevent you from redefining them, on the theory that programmers are unlikely to create their own definitions with leading and trailing underscores.

These macros work just like the macros described earlier in this chapter. When the pre-compiler encounters one of these macros, it replaces the macro with the macro's code. __DATE__ and __TIME__ are replaced with the current date and time. This is the date and time the source file is precompiled. This can be useful information as you're working with different versions of a program. By having a program display its compilation date and time, you can tell whether you're running the latest version of the program or an earlier one.

The other two macros are even more valuable. __LINE__ is replaced by the current source-file line number. __FILE__ is replaced with the current source-code filename. These two macros are best used when you're trying to debug a program or deal with errors. Consider the following printf() statement:

```
31:
32: printf( "Program %s: (%d) Error opening file ", __FILE__, __LINE__ );
33:
```

If these lines were part of a program called myprog.c, they would print

```
Program myprog.c: (32) Error opening file
```

This might not seem important at this point, but as your programs grow and spread across multiple source files, finding errors becomes more difficult. Using __LINE__ and __FILE__ makes debugging much easier.

Do	Don't

DO use the __LINE__ and __FILE__ macros to make your error messages more helpful.
 	
DO put parentheses around the value to be passed to a macro. This prevents errors. For example, use this:
 	
`#define CUBE(x)    (x)*(x)*(x)`
 	
instead of this:
 	
`#define CUBE(x)    x*x*x`
	DON'T forget the #endif when using the #if statement.

21

Using Command-Line Arguments

Your C program can access arguments passed to the program on the command line. This refers to information entered after the program name when you start the program. If you start a program named progname from the C:\> prompt, for example, you could enter

```
C:\>progname smith jones
```

The two command-line arguments smith and jones can be retrieved by the program during execution. You can think of this information as arguments passed to the program's main() function. Such command-line arguments permit information to be passed to the program at startup rather than during execution, which can be convenient at times. You can pass as many command-line arguments as you like. Note that command-line arguments can be retrieved only within main(). To do so, declare main() as follows:

```
main(int argc, char *argv[])
{
    /* Statements go here */
}
```

The first parameter, argc, is an integer giving the number of command-line arguments available. This value is always at least 1, because the program name is counted as the first argument. The parameter argv[] is an array of pointers to strings. The valid subscripts for this array are 0 through argc - 1. The pointer argv[0] points to the program name (including path information), argv[1] points to the first argument that follows the program name, and so on. Note that the names argc and argv[] aren't required—you can use any valid C variable names you like to receive the command-line arguments. However, these two names are traditionally used for this purpose, so you should probably stick with them.

The command line is divided into discrete arguments by any whitespace. If you need to pass an argument that includes a space, enclose the entire argument in double quotation marks. For example, if you enter

```
C:>progname smith "and jones"
```

smith is the first argument (pointed to by argv[1]); and jones is the second (pointed to by argv[2]). Listing 21.6 demonstrates how to access command-line arguments in your programs.

INPUT   **LISTING 21.6**   args.c. Passing command-line arguments to main()

```
1:  /* Accessing command-line arguments. */
2:
3:  #include <stdio.h>
```

LISTING 21.6   continued

```
 4:
 5:  int main(int argc, char *argv[])
 6:  {
 7:      int count;
 8:
 9:      printf("Program name: %s\n", argv[0]);
10:
11:      if (argc > 1)
12:      {
13:          for (count = 1; count < argc; count++)
14:              printf("Argument %d: %s\n", count, argv[count]);
15:      }
16:      else
17:          puts("No command line arguments entered.");
18:      return 0;
19:  }
```

OUTPUT

```
list21_6
Program name: C:\LIST2106.EXE
No command line arguments entered.

list2106 first second "3 4"
Program name: C:\LIST21_6.EXE
Argument 1: first
Argument 2: second
Argument 3: 3 4
```

ANALYSIS   This program does no more than print the command-line parameters entered by the user. Notice that line 5 uses the argc and argv parameters shown previously. Line 9 prints the one command-line parameter that you always have, the program name. Notice this is argv[0]. Line 11 checks to see whether there is more than one command-line parameter. Why more than one and not more than zero? Because there is always at least one—the program name. If there are additional arguments, a for loop prints each to the screen (lines 13 and 14). Otherwise, an appropriate message is printed (line 17).

Command-line arguments generally fall into two categories: those that are required because the program can't operate without them, and those that are optional, such as flags that instruct the program to act in a certain way. For example, imagine a program that sorts the data in a file. If you write the program to receive the input filename from the command line, the name is required information. If the user forgets to enter the input filename on the command line, the program must somehow deal with the situation. The program could also look for the argument /r, which signals a reverse-order sort. This argument isn't required; the program looks for it and behaves one way if it's found and another way if it isn't.

21

Note

Graphical IDEs will usually allow you to enter command line arguments into a dialog box. For example, the Dev-C++ compiler included on the CD of this book will allow you to enter command line arguments by selecting the parameter button on the compilation dialog. Figure 21.5 shows the dialog after the parameter button has been pressed.

FIGURE 21.5

The parameters button.

Do	DON'T
DO use argc and argv as the variable names for the command-line arguments for main(). Most C programmers are familiar with these names.	**DON'T** assume that users will enter the correct number of command-line parameters. Check to be sure they did; and if not, display a message explaining the arguments they should enter.

Summary

Today you covered some of the more advanced programming tools available with C compilers. You learned how to write a program that has source code divided among multiple files or modules. This practice, called modular programming, makes it easy to reuse general-purpose functions in more than one program. You saw how you can use preprocessor directives to create function macros, for conditional compilation, and other tasks. Finally, you saw that the compiler provides some function macros for you.

Q&A

Q When compiling multiple files, how does the compiler know which filename to use for the executable file?

A You might think the compiler uses the name of the file containing the `main()` function; however, this isn't usually the case. When compiling from the command line, the first file listed is used to determine the name. For example, if you compiled the following with Borland's Turbo C, the executable would be called FILE1.EXE:

```
tcc file1.c main.c prog.c
```

Q Do header files need to have an .h extension?

A No. You can give a header file any name you want. It is standard practice to use the .h extension.

Q When including header files, can I use an explicit path?

A Yes. If you want to state the path where a file to be included is, you can. In such a case, you put the name of the include file between quotation marks.

Q Are all the predefined macros and preprocessor directives presented in today's lesson?

A No. The predefined macros and directives presented in today's lesson are ones common to most compilers. However, most compilers also have additional macros and constants.

Q Is the following header also acceptable when using `main()` with command-line parameters?

```
main( int argc, char **argv);
```

A You can probably answer this one on your own. This declaration uses a pointer to a character pointer instead of a pointer to a character array. Because an array is a pointer, this definition is virtually the same as the one presented in this chapter. This declaration is also commonly used. (See Day 8, "Using Numeric Arrays," and Day 10, "Working with Characters and Strings," for more details.)

Workshop

The Workshop provides quiz questions to help you solidify your understanding of the material covered and exercises to provide you with experience in using what you've learned.

21

Quiz

1. What does the term *modular programming* mean?

2. In modular programming, what is the main module?

3. When you define a macro, why should each argument be enclosed in parentheses?

4. What are the pros and cons of using a macro in place of a regular function?

5. What does the `defined()` operator do?

6. What must always be used if `#if` is used?

7. What extension do compiled C files have? (Assume that they have not been linked.)

8. What does `#include` do?

9. What is the difference between this line of code:

   `#include <myfile.h>`

   and the following line of code

   `#include "myfile.h"`

10. What is `__DATE__` used for?

11. What does `argv[0]` point to?

Exercises

Because many solutions are possible for the following exercises, answers are not provided.

1. Use your compiler to compile multiple source files into a single executable file. (You can use Listings 21.1, 21.2, and 21.3 or your own listings.)

2. Write an error routine that receives an error number, line number, and module name. The routine should print a formatted error message and then exit the program. Use the predefined macros for the line number and module name. (Pass the line number and module name from the location where the error occurs.) Here's a possible example of a formatted error:

   `module.c (Line ##): Error number ##`

3. Modify exercise 2 to make the error message more descriptive. Create a text file with your editor that contains an error number and message. Call this file ERRORS.TXT. It could contain information such as the following:

   ```
   1     Error number 1
   2     Error number 2
   90    Error opening file
   100   Error reading file
   ```

Have your error routine search this file and display the appropriate error message based on a number passed to it.

4. Some header files might be included more than once when you're writing a modular program. Use preprocessor directives to write the skeleton of a header file that compiles only the first time it is encountered during compilation.

5. Write a program that takes two filenames as command-line parameters. The program should copy the first file into the second file. (See Day 16, "Using Disk Files," if you need help working with files.)

6. This is the last exercise of the book (not counting the bonus week), and its content is up to you. Select a programming task of interest to you that also meets a real need you have. For example, you could write programs to catalog your compact disc collection, keep track of your checkbook, or calculate financial figures related to a planned house purchase. There's no substitute for tackling a real-world programming problem in order to sharpen your programming skills and help you remember all the things you learned in this book.

21

WEEK 3

In Review

You have finished your third and final week of learning how to program in C (but don't forget the bonus week!). You started the week covering such advanced topics as pointers and disk files. In the middle of the week, you saw a few of the many functions contained in most C compilers' libraries of functions. You ended the week by discovering the odds and ends needed to get the most from your compiler and the C language. The following program pulls together many of these topics.

15

16

17

18

19

20

21

Note The numbers to the left of the line numbers indicate the day that covers the concept presented on that line. If you're confused by the line, refer to the referenced day for more information.

LISTING R3.1   week3.c. Week 3's review listing

```
 1: /* Program Name:  week3.c                           */
 2: /* Program to keep track of names and phone numbers. */
 3:
 4: /* Information is written to a disk file specified    */
 5: /* with a command-line parameter.                     */
 6:
 7: #include <stdlib.h>
 8: #include <stdio.h>
 9: #include <time.h>
10: #include <string.h>
11:
12: /*** defined constants ***/
13: #define YES    1
14: #define NO     0
15: #define REC_LENGTH  54
16:
17: /*** variables ***/
18:
19: struct record {
20:    char fname[15+1];            /* first name + NULL    */
21:    char lname[20+1];            /* last name + NULL     */
22:    char mname[10+1];            /* middle name + NULL   */
23:    char phone[9+1];             /* phone number + NULL  */
24: } rec;
25:
26: /*** function prototypes ***/
27:
28: int  main(int argc, ch ar *argv[]);
29: void display_usage(char *filename);
30: int  display_menu(void);
31: void get_data(FILE *fp, char *progname, char *filename);
32: void display_report(FILE *fp);
33: int  continue_function(void);
34: int  look_up( FILE *fp );
35:
36: /* start of program */
37:
38: int main(int argc, ch ar *argv[])
39: {
40:    FILE *fp;
41:    int  cont = YES;
42:
```

CH 19
CH 18

CH 21

CH 21
CH 16

LISTING R3.1   continued

```
CH 21    43:     if( argc < 2 )
         44:     {
         45:         display_usage("WEEK3");
         46:         exit(1);
         47:     }
         48:
         49:     /* Open file. */
CH 16    50:     if ((fp = fopen( argv[1], "a+")) == NULL)
         51:     {
         52:         fprintf( stderr, "%s(%d)—Error opening file %s",
         53:                             argv[0],__LINE__, argv[1]);
         54:         exit(1);
         55:     }
         56:
         57:     while( cont == YES )
         58:     {
         59:         switch( display_menu() )
         60:         {
CH 18    61:           case '1': get_data(fp, argv[0], argv[1]); /* Day 18*/
         62:                     break;
         63:           case '2': display_report(fp);
         64:                     break;
         65:           case '3': look_up(fp);
         66:                     break;
         67:           case '4': printf("\n\nThank you for using this program!\n");
         68:                     cont = NO;
         69:                     break;
         70:           default:  printf("\n\nInvalid choice, Please select 1 to 4!");
         71:                     break;
         72:         }
         73:     }
CH 16    74:     fclose(fp);         /* close file */
         75:     return(0);
         76: }
         77:
         78: /* display_menu() */
         79:
         80: int display_menu(void)
         81: {
         82:     char ch, buf[20];
         83:
         84:     printf( "\n");
         85:     printf( "\n      MENU");
         86:     printf( "\n    ========\n");
         87:     printf( "\n1.  Enter names");
         88:     printf( "\n2.  Print report");
         89:     printf( "\n3.  Look up number");
         90:     printf( "\n4.  Quit");
         91:     printf( "\n\nEnter Selection ==> ");
         92:     gets(buf);
         93:     ch = *buf;
```

LISTING R3.1   continued

```
94:      return(ch);
95: }
96:
97: /****************************************************
98:   Function:  get_data()
99: ****************************************************/
100:
101: void get_data(FILE *fp, char *progname, char *filename)
102: {
103:    int cont = YES;
104:
105:    while( cont == YES )
106:    {
107:       printf("\n\nPlease enter information: " );
108:
109:       printf("\n\nEnter first name: ");
110:       gets(rec.fname);
111:       printf("\nEnter middle name: ");
112:       gets(rec.mname);
113:       printf("\nEnter last name: ");
114:       gets(rec.lname);
115:       printf("\nEnter phone in 123-4567 format: ");
116:       gets(rec.phone);
117:
118:       if (fseek( fp, 0, SEEK_END ) == 0)
119:          if( fwrite(&rec, 1, sizeof(rec), fp) != sizeof(rec))
120:          {
121:             fprintf( stderr, "%s(%d) Error writing to file %s",
122:                              progname,__LINE__, filename);
123:             exit(2);
124:          }
125:       cont = continue_function();
126:    }
127: }
128:
129: /****************************************************
130: Function:  display_report()
131: Purpose:    To print out the formatted names and numbers
132:             of people in the file.
133: ****************************************************/
134:
135: void display_report(FILE *fp)
136: {
137:    time_t rtime;
138:    int num_of_recs = 0;
139:
140:    time(&rtime);
141:
142:    fprintf(stdout, "\n\nRun Time: %s", ctime( &rtime));
143:    fprintf(stdout, "\nPhone number report\n");
144:
```

LISTING R3.1 continued

```
145:      if(fseek( fp, 0, SEEK_SET ) == 0)
146:      {
147:         fread(&rec, 1, sizeof(rec), fp);
148:         while(!feof(fp))
149:         {
150:            fprintf(stdout,"\n\t%s, %s %c %s", rec.lname,
151:                                      rec.fname, rec.mname[0],
152:                                      rec.phone);
153:            num_of_recs++;
154:            fread(&rec, 1, sizeof(rec), fp);
155:         }
156:         fprintf(stdout, "\n\nTotal number of records: %d",
157:                 num_of_recs);
158:         fprintf(stdout, "\n\n* * * End of Report * * *");
159:      }
160:      else
161:         fprintf( stderr, "\n\n*** ERROR WITH REPORT ***\n");
162: }
163:
164: /**************************************************
165:  *  Function:  continue_function()
166:  **************************************************/
167:
168: int continue_function( void )
169: {
170:     char ch, buf[20];
171:     do
172:     {
173:        printf("\n\nDo you wish to enter another? (Y)es/(N)o ");
174:        gets(buf);
175:        ch = *buf;
176:     } while( strchr( "NnYy", ch) == NULL );
177:
178:     if(ch == 'n' || ch == 'N')
179:        return(NO);
180:     else
181:        return(YES);
182: }
183:
184: /*****************************************************************
185:  *  Function:  display_usage()
186:  *****************************************************************/
187:
188: void display_usage( char *filename )
189: {
190:     printf("\n\nUSAGE: %s filename", filename );
191:     printf("\n\n   where filename is a file to store people\'s names");
192:     printf("\n      and phone numbers.\n\n");
193: }
194:
195: /*********************************************
```

LISTING R3.1   continued

```
196: *  Function:  look_up()
197: *  Returns:   Number of names matched
198: *************************************************/
199:
200: int look_up( FILE *fp )
201: {
202:     char tmp_lname[20+1];
203:     int  ctr = 0;
204:
205:     fprintf(stdout, "\n\nPlease enter last name to be found: ");
206:     gets(tmp_lname);
207:
208:     if( strlen(tmp_lname) != 0 )
209:     {
210:        if (fseek( fp, 0, SEEK_SET ) == 0)
211:        {
212:           fread(&rec, 1, sizeof(rec), fp);
213:           while( !feof(fp))
214:           {
215:              if( strcmp(rec.lname, tmp_lname) == 0 )
216:              /* if matched */
217:              {
218:                 fprintf(stdout, "\n%s %s %s - %s", rec.fname,
219:                                                    rec.mname,
220:                                                    rec.lname,
221:                                                    rec.phone);
222:                 ctr++;
223:              }
224:              fread(&rec, 1, sizeof(rec), fp);
225:           }
226:        }
227:        fprintf( stdout, "\n\n%d names matched.", ctr );
228:     }
229:     else
230:     {
231:         fprintf( stdout, "\nNo name entered." );
232:     }
233:     return(ctr);
234: }
```

CH 17 (208), CH 16 (210), CH 16 (212), CH 17 (215)

ANALYSIS This program is similar in some respects to the programs presented in Week 1 in Review and Week 2 in Review. Fewer data items are tracked, but additional program capabilities have been added. week3.c lets the user keep track of names and phone numbers of friends, business contacts, and so on. As written, the program tracks only first name, last name, middle name, and phone number. It would be a simple matter to have the program record additional information, and you might want to try this as an exercise. The major difference between this program and the earlier review programs is that there is no limit to the number of people who can be entered into the program. This is because a disk file is used for data storage.

When you start the program, you enter the name of the data file on the command line. `main()` starts on line 38 with the `argc` and `argv` arguments required to get the command-line parameters. You learned about this on Day 21, "Advanced Compiler Use." Line 43 checks the value of `argc` to see how many parameters were entered on the command line. If `argc` is less than 2, only one parameter was entered (the command to run the program), which means that the user didn't specify a data filename. In this case, the program calls `display_usage()` with `argv[0]` as an argument. `argv[0]`, the first parameter entered on the command line, is the name of the program.

The `display_usage()` function is on lines 188 through 193. Whenever you write a program that takes command-line arguments, it's a good idea to include a function similar to `display_usage()` that tells the user how to use the program. Why doesn't the function just hard-code the name of the program (week3) instead of using the command-line argument? The answer is simple. When you obtain the program name from the command line, you don't have to worry if the user renames the program; the usage description is always accurate.

Most of the new concepts in this program come from Day 16, "Using Disk Files." Line 40 declares a file pointer `fp` that is used throughout the program to access the data file. Line 50 tries to open this file with a mode of `"a+"` (remember, `argv[1]` is the second item listed on the command line—the data filename). The `"a+"` mode is used because you want to be able to add to the file as well as read any records that already exist. If the file open operation fails, lines 52 and 53 display an error message before line 54 exits the program. Notice that the error message contains descriptive information. Also notice that `__LINE__`, covered on Day 21, indicates the line number where the error occurred.

If the file is opened successfully, a menu is displayed. When the user chooses to exit the program, line 74 closes the file with `fclose()` before the program returns control to the operating system. Other menu options enable the user to enter a record, display all records, or search for a particular person.

In the `get_data()` function, there are a few significant changes. Line 101 contains the function header. The function now accepts three pointers. The first pointer is the most important: It is the handle for the file to be written to. Lines 105 through 126 contain a `while` loop that continues to get data until the user wants to quit. Lines 107 to 116 prompt for the data in the same format that the program in Week 2 in Review did. Line 118 calls `fseek()` to set the pointer in the disk file to the end to write the new information. Notice that this program doesn't do anything if the seek fails. A complete program would handle such a failure, but I omitted it here to keep the program from getting too long. Line 119 writes the data to the disk file with a call to `fwrite()`.

The report feature in this program also has changed. One feature typical of most "real-world" reports is the inclusion of the current date and time at the top of the report. On line 137, the variable `rtime` is declared. This variable is passed to `time()` and then displayed using the `ctime()` function. These time functions were presented on Day 19, "Exploring the C Function Library."

Before the program can start printing the records in the file, it needs to reposition the file pointer at the beginning of the file. This is done on line 145 with another call to `fseek()`. after the file pointer is positioned, records can be read one after the other. Line 147 does the first read. If the read is successful, the program begins a `while` loop that continues until the end of the file is reached (when `feof()` returns a nonzero value). If the end of the file hasn't been reached, line 150 prints the information, line 153 counts the record, and line 154 tries to read the next record. You should notice that functions are used without checking their return values in order to keep the program a reasonable length. To protect the program from errors, the function calls should contain checks to ensure that no errors occurred.

One function in the program is new. Lines 200–234 contain the function `look_up()`, which searches the disk file for all records that contain a certain last name. Lines 205 and 206 prompt for the name to be found and store it in a local variable called `tmp_lname`. If `tmp_lname` isn't blank (line 208), the file pointer is set to the beginning of the file. Each record is then read. Using `strcmp()` (line 215), the record's last name is compared to `tmp_lname`. If the names match, the record is printed (lines 218–222). This continues until the end of the file is reached. Again, you should notice that not all the functions have their return values checked. You should always check return values.

You should be able to modify this program to create your own files that can store any information. Using the functions you learned during Week 3, along with the other functions in the C library, you should be able to create a program to do just about anything you want.

BONUS WEEK

At a Glance

You have finished learning C in 21 days. By now you should feel comfortable with the C programming language. Additionally, you should feel comfortable creating your own programs.

Where You're Going

Most people who learn C also want to understand other programming languages. This bonus week covers three additional programming languages—C++, Java, and C#. Although the next few days don't provide comprehensive coverage, they will give you an understanding of what these languages are. They will also give you enough information to be able to build fully functioning small-scale projects using these languages.

During the next few days, you will find that C++, Java, and C# are very similar to C. You'll also learn a little on how they differ from C. Bonus Day 1, "Object-Oriented Programming Languages," gives you an overview of object-oriented programming as well as a high-level perspective on C++, Java, and C#. Most important, you'll learn the key constructs for doing object-oriented programming.

Bonus Days 2 and 3 will cover C++. C++ is the most popular object-oriented language and is very similar to C. In fact, C++ is a superset of C. Odds are that the compiler on which you learned to program C also compiles C++ programs. You'll learn more about C++ in the next few days.

BD1

BD2

BD3

BD4

BD5

BD6

BD7

Bonus Days 4 through 6 cover Java. Java is also very similar to C and C++. Java has become very popular in the last few years because of its portability and because of its ties to the Web. In just the few days presented during this bonus week, you will learn to create simple applets and applications. You'll start learning details about Java starting on Bonus Day 4, "The Java Programming Language."

Finally, you will finish the bonus week with a quick look at one of the newest languages for doing object-oriented programming, C#.

Bonus Week

Bonus Day 1

Object-Oriented Programming Languages

In the past 21 days, you have learned to program in C. C is considered a procedural programming language. You will now learn about object-oriented programming languages and OOP (object-oriented programming). Today you will learn

- The difference between an object-oriented language and a procedural language
- The most common object-oriented languages and their constructs
- The high-level differences when comparing C to C++, Java, and C# (pronounced C-Sharp)
- To write your first Java application

Procedural and Object-Oriented Languages

C is generally considered to be a procedural language. This was discussed on Day 1, "Getting Started with C." A procedural language is one that starts at the beginning and executes each line, one after another. Program flow might switch to other parts of the code listing; however, this switch is based on redirection from the previous line of code. In a procedural language, program design is based on the use of procedures or functions.

Over the past couple of decades, several object-oriented languages have been developed; the most commonly used ones are C++ and Java. As the name implies, an object-oriented language makes use of objects. You'll learn more about objects throughout today's lesson; but, defined briefly, an object is an independent and reusable section of software code that can perform a specific task and store specified data related to that task. Object-oriented languages can also use procedures, but they have additional features for defining and using objects.

Why were object-oriented languages developed? The main reason is the increasing complexity of programs. Despite the power of procedural languages such as C, they were not well suited for creation and maintenance of large complex applications. A large program, such as a word processor or spreadsheet, was difficult to maintain, modify, and debug when it was written in a procedural language. Object-oriented languages were developed mainly as a solution to this problem.

Although C can be used to create object-oriented programs, the object-oriented features that make this possible are not built into the language. This makes C difficult to use in this manner. Languages such as C++ and Java have been created specifically to make object-oriented programming easier. Before you look at some details of C++, Java, and C#, you need to understand what makes a language object oriented.

Note

> Object-oriented programming is often simply referred to as OOP. The OOP acronym is now very common.

Note

> Although C++ is an object-oriented language, it can be used to write procedure code—although this is not recommended!

The Object-Oriented Constructs

You have already learned that an object-oriented language works with objects. What exactly are these objects? There are three key features that help to define the objects of an object-oriented programming language. It is the implementation of these features that make a language object oriented. These constructs are

- Polymorphism
- Encapsulation
- Inheritance

Some people also consider reuse as the fourth feature that helps define an object-oriented programming language. Reuse is simply the capability to use the same code easily in multiple programs without substantial rewriting. If you effectively implement the three key features, you will automatically obtain reuse.

 Note

> One of the reasons developers prefer an OOP language to a procedural language, such as C, is the factor of reuse. Although you can reuse functions and libraries in C, this does not give the power provided by the reuse of classes and templates. You'll learn about classes in Bonus Day 3, "Working with C++ Classes and Objects."

Adapting with Polymorphism

The first trait of an object-oriented programming language is polymorphism. *Poly* means many and *morph* means form. A polymorphic program is one that can take many forms. In other words, the program is able to adapt automatically. Consider an example. If you were asked to draw a circle, what facts would you need to know? If you were given the center point and a point on the circle, you'd be able to draw the circle. Additionally, if you were given three points that were on the circle, you'd be able to draw it. If you were given the radius and the center point, you'd have a third way of drawing a circle. Figure B1.1 illustrates these methods for drawing a circle.

If you are writing a C program to draw a circle, you could include three different functions in order to adapt to the different ways a user might want to draw a circle. You could also create three uniquely named functions such as

```
draw_circle_with_points(int x1, int y1, int x2, int y2, int x3, int y3);

draw_circle_with_radius(int ctrX, int ctrY, long radius);

draw_circle_with_center_and_point(int ctrX, int ctrY, int x1, int y1);
```

FIGURE B1.1

*Different parameters
for drawing a circle.*

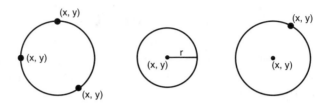

Worse, you could call these draw_circle(), draw_circle2(), and draw_circle3().
This is not very practical. Take a look at Listing B1.1. You will notice something odd
about this listing which draws two squares. You should notice that there is more than one
square() function. Squares are being used because the code is simpler than that for cir-
cles.

LISTING B1.1   square.cpp. Multiple square functions

```
1: /* A C listing with something odd -  */
2: /*   using a square() function twice */
3: #include <stdio.h>
4: #include <stdlib.h>
5:
6: /* square function - the first one! */
7: void square( int topleftX, int topleftY, long width )
8: {
9:     int xctr = 0;
10:     int yctr = 0;
11:     // This listing assumes bottom values are greater than top values
12:
13:     for ( xctr = 0; xctr < width; xctr++)
14:     {
15:         printf("\n");
16:
17:         for ( yctr = 0; yctr < width; yctr++ )
18:         {
19:             printf("*");
20:         }
21:     }
22: }
23:
24: /* square function - the second one! */
25: void square( int topleftX, int topleftY, int bottomleftX, int bottomleftY)
26: {
27:     int xctr = 0;
28:     int yctr = 0;
29:
30:     // This listing assumes bottom values are greater than top values
31:
32:     for ( xctr = 0; xctr < bottomleftX - topleftX; xctr++)
```

LISTING B1.1 continued

```
33:     {
34:         printf("\n");
35:
36:         for ( yctr = 0; yctr < bottomleftY - topleftY; yctr++ )
37:         {
38:             printf("*");
39:         }
40:     }
41: }
42:
43: int main(int argc, char* argv[])
44: {
45:     int   pt_x1 = 0, pt_y1 = 0;
46:     int   pt_x2 = 5, pt_y2 = 5;
47:     int   pt_x3 = 0, pt_y3 = 0;
48:     long  side = 4;
49:
50:     // Call the square function two different ways
51:     square( pt_x1, pt_y1, pt_x2, pt_y2);
52:
53:     printf("\n\n");   //put blank lines between squares
54:
55:     square( pt_x3, pt_y3, side);
56:
57:     return 0;
58: }
```

OUTPUT
```
*****
*****
*****
*****
*****


****
****
****
****
```

ANALYSIS If you try to compile this listing as C, it will generate an error. If you compile it as a C++ program, it will work. As you can see, this listing has two functions with the same name (see lines 7 and 25). You can also see in lines 51 and 55 that the square() function is called in two different ways. You learned earlier in this book that this is not correct in a C program. In an object-oriented program, this is acceptable. This is polymorphism in action. When the square function is called, the program determines which is the appropriate one to use. With a C++ program, the programmer does not need to worry about which is correct.

Caution

Listing B1.1 is a C listing that incorporates a feature of C++. If you are using a C++ compiler (such as Microsoft's Visual C++ or Borland's C++) to compile your programs, the above listing will compile and run. If you are using an older C compiler, you might get errors because function overloading isn't a supported C feature. Additionally, if you have the ANSI C flag set on your compiler so that only ANSI C code will compile, the previous listing will not work because this is actually an ANSI C++ feature.

Polymorphism can go beyond the use just demonstrated. In fact, what has just been presented is also called function or method overloading. The key to polymorphism is that your programs can adapt to what is sent to you. Polymorphism makes your program and code much more reusable.

Note

There are other more appropriate examples of polymorphism that are beyond the scope of this book. These advanced usages of polymorphism involve having objects change their types in order to be treated as something different. For example, you can create an object that is a person and an object that is a client. Using polymorphism you'd be able to use a client type as if it were a person type. Again, this use of polymorphism is beyond the scope of this book.

Encapsulating it All

A second characteristic of an object-oriented programming language is encapsulation. Encapsulation enables you to create objects that are self-contained.

Note

When combined with polymorphism, encapsulation enables you to create objects that are self-sufficient, and, therefore, easy to reuse.

Encapsulation enables you to create black box functionality. Black box functionality means that the person using your code doesn't need to know how it works. Instead, he only needs to know how to call the functionality and what results he will get in return. Consider the circle example shown earlier. If you want to display a circle, all that matters is that you know how to call the circle routines. An even better example is illustrated in Figure B1.2.

Figure B1.2

Encapsulation provides black box functionality.

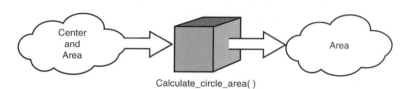

Area = Calculate_circle_area(center_x, center_y, radius);

Center and Area → Calculate_circle_area( ) → Area

As you can see, the `calculate_circle_area()` routine is a black box. You don't need to know how it works in order to use it. All you need to know is what parameters it takes and what value you'll get in return. The following code might be a part of the `calculate_circle_area()` routine:

```
...
...
PI = 3.14;
area = PI * r * r;
...
...
```

This is not a complete listing. Notice that this routine simply sets `PI` equal to `3.14` in line 3. In line 4, this value is used to calculate the area. Because this value is encapsulated, you can actually make a change to the value of PI and not affect any of the programs that call this routine. You could change PI to `3.14159` in line 3 and all the programs that call this routine will still work. You might be thinking that regular C functions can be used to encapsulate functionality in this way, and you are correct. However the encapsulation possible with an object-oriented language goes even further.

Encapsulating Your Data

In addition to encapsulating functionality, you can also encapsulate data. Consider the circle routine mentioned earlier. To store information about a circle, all you need to know is the center point and the radius. As you learned in the earlier discussion, a user might ask that you draw a circle by using three points that are located on the circle, or he might ask that you draw it by using the center point and one point on the circle. Within your black box, you can store the center point and the radius. You don't have to tell the user that you are storing the radius or the center point; however, you might end up using these pieces of data when you implement functionality for your routines. Regardless of what information users provide, you'll be able to use the circle routine by keeping track of just the radius and the center point. For example, a function to determine a circle's area, `calculate_circle_area()`, can use the radius and center point rather than any other data without telling the user.

By encapsulating data and functionality, you create black box functionality. You have created an object that not only stores the circle's data (its center point and radius) but that also knows how to draw the circle onscreen. The benefit is that you can reuse these black boxes without having to know how their internals work. This level of reuse also enables you to change the implementation of the functionality without having to change any of the calling programs.

 Note On Bonus Day 3, "Working with C++ Classes and Objects," you will learn about classes and objects. Classes enable you to encapsulate data and functionality in an object-oriented programming language such as C++, Java, or C#.

Pulling from the Past with Inheritance

The third characteristic of an object-oriented programming language is inheritance. Inheritance is the capability to create new objects that expand the characteristics of existing objects. Consider the square functionality discussed earlier. A square object can contain the following information:

- Top-left corner point
- Length of side
- The character with which to draw the square
- A function to return the area of the square

If you know the top-left corner and the length of the side, you can draw the square. A function to return the area of the square can be encapsulated within the square object as well.

Using inheritance, you can extend the square into a cube object. Actually, the cube object inherits from the square object. All of the characteristics of the square object become a part of the cube. The cube object modifies the existing area function to return the area of the cube instead of the area of the square; however, everything else can be used directly from the square object. A person using the cube object doesn't really need to know the square is involved (see Figure B1.3).

OOP in Action

To help illustrate the three object-oriented programming concepts, a small C++ program is presented in Listing B1.2. This listing is provided to help you see that a C++ listing does not look exactly like a C listing. During the next few days, the code in this listing will become clearer.

FIGURE B1.3

A cube inherits parts of a square.

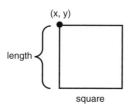

(x, y)

length

square

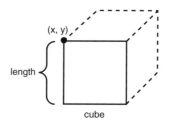

(x, y)

length

cube

Area of square = length * length

Area of cube = Area of square * length

BD1

LISTING B1.2   cube.cpp. C++ OOP in action

```cpp
1: // A C++ program with square and cube classes
2: #include <iostream.h>
3:
4: // Simple square class
5: class square {
6:    public:
7:       square();
8:       square(int);
9:       int length;
10:       long area();
11:       int draw();
12: };
13:
14: //simple cube class inheriting from the square class
15: class cube: public square {
16:    public:
17:       cube( int );
18:       long area();
19: };
20:
21: //constructor for square
22: square::square()
23: {
24:       length = 4;
25: }
26:
27: //overloaded constructor for square
28: square::square( int init_length )
29: {
30:       length = init_length;
31: }
32:
33: //square class' area function
34: long square::area( void )
35: {
36:       return((long) length * length);
37: }
```

LISTING B1.2   continued

```
38:
39: //square class' draw function
40: int square::draw()
41: {
42:    int ctr1 = 0;
43:    int ctr2 = 0;
44:
45:    for (ctr1 = 0; ctr1 < length; ctr1++ )
46:    {
47:       cout << "\n";  /* new line */
48:       for ( ctr2 = 0; ctr2 < length; ctr2++)
49:       {
50:           cout << "*";
51:       }
52:    }
53:    cout << "\n";
54:
55:    return 0;
56: }
57:
58: //cube class' constructor
59: cube::cube( int init_length)
60: {
61:    length = init_length;
62: }
63:
64: //cube class' area function
65: long cube::area()
66: {
67:    return((long) length * length * length);
68: }
69:
70: int main()
71: {
72:    square square1;
73:    square1.length = 5;
74:    square square2(3);
75:    square square3;
76:    cube cube1(4);
77:
78:    cout << "\nDraw square 1 with area of " << square1.area() << "\n";
79:    square1.draw();
80:
81:    cout <<"\nDraw square 2 with area of " << square2.area() << "\n";
82:    square2.draw();
83:
84:    cout << "\nDraw square 3 with area of " << square3.area() << "\n";
85:    square3.draw();
86:
```

BD1

LISTING B1.2   continued

```
87:     cout << "\nDraw cube 1 with area of " << cube1.area() << "\n";
88:     cube1.draw();  //Actually uses square's draw function
89:
90:     return 0;
91: }
```

OUTPUT

```
Draw square 1 with area of 25

*****
*****
*****
*****
*****

Draw square 2 with area of 9

***
***
***

Draw square 3 with area of 16

****
****
****
****

Draw cube 1 with area of 64

****
****
****
****
```

> **Note**   The cout object in C++ is used for printing. You will learn about cout in tomorrow's lesson.

ANALYSIS   This is not the best-written C++ program; however, it does illustrate the differences between C++ and C in a relatively few lines of code. Later in today's lesson, you will see that Java also uses very similar concepts to these. In the next few days, you'll learn ways to improve this listing. Tomorrow you will also learn more about printing in C++ with the cout object. You can see that this object is used a number of times in this listing.

Polymorphism, encapsulation, and inheritance are all a part of this listing. A class called square is defined in lines 5 to 12. The details of this class will be discussed on Bonus Day 3. For now, notice that the declaration contains both functions (lines 7, 8, 10, and 11) and data (line 9). This enables all the features of a square to be encapsulated into one place. You can see in lines 22 and 28 that there are two different ways of setting up the square class. Inheritance is also illustrated in the listing. The cube class inherits from the square class as you can see in line 15. Finally, you can see that reuse is also a feature of this listing. The cube declaration reuses the square functionality. Additionally, the cube and square declarations have been written to where they could easily be reused in other listings. This will all be clearer after Bonus Day 3 when you cover C++ classes and objects.

The Relationship of C++ to C

C++ is a superset of C. This means that all the features of C are available in C++. All the features of C++ are not, however, available in C. If you look back at Listing B1.2, you should be able to determine what most of the code does. Only a few of the constructs will be new to you.

C++ was created in order to have a programming language that is easier to use with the object-oriented constructs. Keywords such as class and template are added to make creating objects and reusable code easier. Additionally, keywords such as try and catch are added to make finding and preventing errors easier. All these changes helped to create a language that is much more powerful as well as reusable.

C++ Programs

Just like C, C++ is used for more than creating executable programs. The most common types of programs created with C++ are presented in Table B1.1.

TABLE B1.1   C++ program types

Program Type	Description
executables	Programs that can be run by an operating system
libraries	Routines created to link to other programs being created
dynamic linked libraries	Routines created that can reside in memory and be linked to other programs at runtime
controls	Routines created that can be used in the creation of other programs

The Java Programming Language

You might not believe it, but the Java language was first conceived as a way to program a device called Star7 (*7) that could control household appliances. The originators of Java, a company called Sun Microsystems, were looking into the future to a time when a house's appliances—its video cassette recorder, furnace, stereo, refrigerator, and so on— would all be connected to a network and controlled by a central computer. What characteristics would such a language require? Here are the most important ones:

- It should be architecture neutral. This is just a fancy way of saying that the operation of the language does not depend on the hardware it is running on.

- It should be robust. Programs written in Java need to be highly resistant to crashes.

- It should be object oriented. The advantages of the object-oriented approach greatly reduce the chance of unforeseen errors. Plus, they can make fixing errors easier should they occur.

- It needs to be safe. Being designed for networked computing, Java needs to be safe from possible attack by viruses.

- It must combine power with simplicity. Java should not limit the programmer in any way, but also it must not be confusing and hard to learn.

None of these individual features is new. What is new is the attempt to combine them all in a single programming language. It was soon realized that the power of this new language gave it many uses beyond the programming of appliances. Now, hundreds of thousands of developers have chosen Java as their language of choice.

The Relationship of Java to C and C++

When you start looking at Java code, a lot of it will be familiar. This is to be expected because Java is based on the C++ language—and, as you learned earlier today, C++ is based on C. However, there are significant differences between the Java:C++ relationship and the C++:C relationship.

C++, you will recall, is a superset of C. This means that C++ includes all parts of C and then adds on a bunch of new stuff (mainly the object-oriented features). Okay, that sounds reasonable. Is Java then C++ with still more features added?

No. In fact, it is most accurate to think of Java as C++ with some features removed. This might sound strange, but it really makes a lot of sense. C++ is an extremely powerful and flexible language, and it lets you do just about anything you want in just about any way you want. With that flexibility comes danger and complexity, which go against the desired characteristics of Java. Thus, Java can be thought of as C++ without those features that cause unnecessary complexity, jeopardize security, interfere with hardware independence, and so on.

Another difference between C++ and Java is this: although C++ permits you to use object-oriented programming, Java *requires* that you do. You are assured that the advantages of object-oriented programming are present throughout the entire program.

What about C#? C# is a newer language that is based on C and C++. Like Java, using object-oriented programming concepts is not optional, rather it is required. Like Java, C# removes some of the dangers and complexities of C++ while adding in simpler support for OOP.

Java's Platform Independence

When Java was first introduced, perhaps the one thing that was most exciting for programmers was its promised platform independence. In theory, you could write a single Java program and have it execute without modification on a PC, a Macintosh, a Sun workstation, or any other computer platform supported by Java. This was a truly major advance. How does Java's platform independence work?

When you write a program, in C or Java or whatever, you use the English-like statements and keywords of the specific language. A computer, however, cannot directly understand your program. A computer's central processing unit, or CPU, understands only the specific binary instructions it was designed to work with. The CPU, therefore, must translate your program, from your programming language into the binary instructions that are readable. When you compile a C program, this is exactly what you are doing—translating source code to binary code.

Unfortunately, different computers use different CPUs. Although the general principles behind all CPUs are the same, they differ in the details. This means that the binary code must be generated for a specific CPU. A Macintosh will not understand binary code created for a PC, and vice versa.

Java's solution to this problem is as follows. When a Java program is compiled, it is not translated all the way to binary instructions but rather to bytecode. Bytecode can be thought of as an intermediate step between source code and binary code. The important factor is that bytecode has no CPU-specific elements in it. In other words, it is still generic and platform independent.

Each different platform, or type of computer, has its own Java interpreter. This interpreter is specifically designed to translate Java bytecode into the CPU-specific binary instructions required for this particular system. The interpreter is called the Java Virtual Machine (JVM), and the process of translating the bytecode to binary instructions is done as the program is executing. Hence, when you write a Java program, you can distribute the same compiled bytecode for use on any system that has a Java Virtual Machine.

| Caution | Although Java is supposed to be platform independent, things have not worked out that way. It is still a lot better than any other language, but a variety of factors have resulted in Java not having the complete platform independence that was intended. |

BD1

Packages

Code reuse is a strong point of any object-oriented language, and inheritance is perhaps the main mechanism by which reusability is accomplished. Java takes this one step further with packages (sometimes also called class libraries). A Java package streamlines and simplifies the reuse of classes (objects). A package is in many ways like a library or applications programming interface (API) in other languages.

Packages also help to manage name spaces. The idea of a name space is related to the fact that two different classes might have the same name. Because a Java program is likely to use at least several packages—some that are part of the Java language, others from third-party firms, and some you create yourself—the possibility exists for confusion between same-name classes. In Java, each package defines a separate name space, and a class name needs to be unique only within its own name space. In other words, a class is identified by both its package (name space) and its name.

Java Applets Versus Applications

Java was designed to write to different types of programs. An application is a full-fledged program designed to run on its own, just like the programs you have been creating in C. An applet is a special kind of program designed to be distributed over the Internet and executed in a browser. For the most part, there is not much difference in writing applications or applets, except that applets are a bit simpler because the browser in which they execute performs some of the tasks that a Java application must do for itself.

Java's Class Libraries

Java is more than just a programming language. When you install a Java development tool you also get a comprehensive set of classes that are ready for you to use. Java's class libraries are similar to the function library that is part of C and to the class libraries that are provided with C++ compilers. For most of the commonly needed program functions, such as screen display, networking, or Internet access, you are likely to find the functionality you need already built and tested in one of Java's class libraries. Whichever Java development tool you use, it will have documentation on the details of its class libraries.

Saying `Hello, World` with Java

Way back on Day 1, you were introduced to C programming by writing the traditional first C program, `Hello, World`! Tomorrow, you'll learn how to say `Hello, World` with C++. Now it's Java's turn. Listing B1.3 shows the Java code for `Hello, World`!

LISTING B1.3   hello.java. A Java version of `Hello, World`!

```
1:  public class HelloWorld
2:  {
3:      public static void main(String args[])
4:      {
5:          Say("Hello, world!");
6:      }
7:      private static void Say(String message)
8:      {
9:          System.out.println(message);
10:     }
11: }
```

OUTPUT `Hello, World!`

ANALYSIS This program is very simple, but is actually a bit more complex than it needs to be in order to show you a Java function (called a method). Line 1 starts the definition of the program `HelloWorld`. Note that the program is defined as a class. This is an example of how Java requires all aspects of a program to use object-oriented techniques. Line 3 starts the definition of the `main()` function, which is a required part of all Java applications just as in C (but a Java applet does not require a `main()` function, as you'll learn in the subsequent chapter). When a Java application runs, execution begins in the `main()` function. The code on line 5 calls the `Say()` function, passing it the argument `"Hello, World!"` Then the closing brace on line 6 marks the end of the `main()` function.

The function `Say()` is defined on lines 7 to 10. In many ways, this looks like a C function, doesn't it? Note that the function argument is type `String`, which is one of the predefined objects in Java's class libraries. Line 9 does the actual work of printing the text on the screen. `System.out` is another one of Java's predefined objects, corresponding to the `stdout` stream in C and the `cout` object in C++. Calling the `println` method of the `System.out` object displays the specific text onscreen.

This sample program is a Java console program, which works with text input and output only. Where you see the output depends on the details of the Java development tool you are using. If you are using a command line Java, the output appears on that command line. If you are using one of the graphical Java development environments, you'll see the output in a window labeled Java Console.

Do	Don't
DO consider learning C++ or Java if you need to write large, complex programs.	DON'T abandon C, because it is very useful for many types of small-to-medium sized programming projects.

The C# Programming Language

Released to the public in June 2000, C#—pronounced See Sharp—has not been around for very long. C# is a new language created by Microsoft and submitted for standardization to ECMA.

C# was created to remove a lot of the problems that other programming languages had. It was intended to be a language that could be used going into the future. You'll see that C# looks a lot like C, C++, and Java. Listing B1.4 presents a simple C# program. On the seventh bonus day you will be introduced to C#.

LISTING B1.4   sample.cs. A simple C# program

```
 1:  // app.cs - A sample C# application
 2:  //----------------------------------------------
 3:
 4:  using System;
 5:
 6:  class sample
 7:  {
 8:      public static void Main()
 9:      {
10:          //Declare variables
11:
12:          int radius = 4;
13:          const double PI = 3.14159;
14:          double area;
15:
16:          //Do calculation
17:
18:          area = PI * radius * radius;
19:
20:          //Print the results
21:
22:          Console.WriteLine("Radius = {0}, PI = {1}", radius, PI );
23:          Console.WriteLine("The area is {0}", area);
24:      }
25:  }
```

OUTPUT
```
Radius = 4, PI = 3.14159
The area is 50.3344
```

Summary

Today you covered the basics of object-oriented programming (OOP). You learned about objects and the concepts that make up an object-oriented programming language—polymorphism, inheritance, encapsulation, and reuse. You have also seen that the basics of the C++ programming language are exactly the same as the C programming language. Additionally, you learned that Java is just another evolution of the C and C++ programming languages. Over the next six bonus days, you will learn even more details on C++, Java, and C#.

Q&A

Q Why learn C if C++, Java, or C# does so much more?

A The object-oriented constructs are a little more complicated to use. For the beginner, C is an easy place to start because it is procedural, and thus it is easy to follow the flow of the code. Because C++, Java, and C# are based on C, a lot of what you have already learned will carry over if you move to one of these object-oriented languages. If you are planning large and complex programs and want to have the capability to reuse code and functionality, you should consider C++ or Java. If you are using Microsoft .NET, you can consider C# as well as C++ and Java. If you are going to be maintaining existing code, there is a good chance you'll need to learn C because there is a large amount of legacy C code in use.

Q How important is it to understand the object-oriented concepts?

A It is essential. You must understand these concepts if you are to effectively use the powerful tools of object-oriented programming languages. Don't worry if you don't completely understand encapsulation, inheritance, and polymorphism right away. As you work with C++, Java or C#, things will become clearer.

Workshop

The Workshop provides quiz questions to help you solidify your understanding of the material covered and exercises to provide you with experience in using what you've learned. Answers to the quiz are provided in Appendix F.

Quiz

1. What are the characteristics of an object-oriented programming language?

2. A function can be defined more than once with different parameters. This is an example of what?

3. What keywords are in C but not in C++?

4. Can C be used to do object-oriented programming?

5. Does Java include all the features found in C++?

6. Can you write a procedural program in C++ or Java?

7. The `printf()` function is used to print in C. What command is used to print in C++?

8. What command is used to print in Java?

9. What command is used to print in C#?

Exercises

1. Review your C compiler to determine whether it will also compile C++. If so, change the compiler option on your compiler to compile for C++ rather than C (if necessary). Recompile a couple of your C programs written earlier in this book.

Note

> The compilers included with this book will work with the C++ programs.

BONUS WEEK

BONUS DAY 2

The C++ Programming Language

C++ is the best known and most used of the object-oriented programming languages. Yesterday, you learned the basic characteristics of an object-oriented language. You also learned a few of the characteristics of C++ that make it different from C. Today, you will dive directly into the C++ programming language. Today you will

- Write your first C++ program
- Discover the similarities between C and C++ data types and operators
- Learn the specifics of overloading functions
- Understand inline functions
- Learn the C++ keywords

Hello C++ World!

In Day 1, you saw your first C program. This program is presented again in Listing B2.1.

LISTING B2.1   hello.c. The C Hello World program

```
1:    #include <stdio.h>
2:
3:    int main( void )
4:    {
5:       printf( "Hello World!\n");
6:       return 0;
7:    }
```

OUTPUT   Hello World!

This listing should seem simple to you now. Your first C++ listing is just as simple. Listing B2.2 presents the near equivalent of the C Hello World listing written in C++.

LISTING B2.2   hello.cpp. The C++ Hello World program

```
1:    #include <iostream.h>
2:
3:    int main( void )
4:    {
5:       cout << "Hello C++ World!\n";
6:       return 0;
7:    }
```

OUTPUT   Hello C++ World!

ANALYSIS   You can see that there are only a few differences between the C++ listing and the C listing presented in B2.1. The first difference occurs in line 1. In C++, you are working with a different set of libraries and routines. Instead of including and linking to standard C functions, you will link to C++ object-oriented functions and values. In line 1, you are linking to the iostream.h header file, instead of stdio.h. The iostream.h file contains the necessary values to help you perform input and output in C++.

In line 5, you see the second big change. Instead of using a function and parenthesis, you are using cout to send the text to the output device. cout is an object that takes care of output for you. Rather than passing values to the cout object, you redirect values to it. The redirection operator (<<) is used to redirect values to cout. In this case, you can see that Hello C++ World! is being redirected to this object. As with C statements, a semi-colon ends C++ statement.

Note   Tomorrow, you will learn more about objects and classes.

Printing in C++

In your C listings, you used a number of functions to print such as puts() and printf(). Although you can use these C functions in a C++ listing, you really should not. Functions such as these are not object-oriented, nor are they as optimal as the C++ alternatives.

BD2

As you saw in Listing B2.2, when printing in a C++ program, you should use the cout object. The cout object enables you to send output to the standard output device. As stated before, you do not use cout in the same way you use a function in C. Rather, you redirect values to cout, and it, in turn, sends them to the standard output device.

One of the benefits of cout is that it is object-oriented. The cout object encapsulates printing functionality. When using printf(), you had to specify the data types of variables being printed. With the cout object, you do not. It adapts to handle what you send it. Listing B2.3 helps to illustrate this.

LISTING B2.3   cout.cpp. Printing with cout

```
 1: //Using cout with different data types
 2: #include <iostream.h>
 3:
 4: int main(int argc, char* argv[])
 5: {
 6:     int   an_int = 123;
 7:     long  a_long = 987654321;
 8:     float a_float = (float) 123.456;
 9:     char  a_char = 'A';
10:     char *a_string = "A String";
11:     bool  a_boolean = true;
12:
13:     cout << "\n";
14:     cout << "an int:   "<< an_int    << '\n';
15:     cout << "a long:   "<< a_long    << '\n';
16:     cout << "a float:  "<< a_float   << '\n';
17:     cout << "a char:   "<< a_char    << '\n';
18:     cout << "a string: "<< a_string  << '\n';
19:     cout << "a bool:   "<< a_boolean << '\n';
20:
21:     return 0;
22: }
```

an int: 123
a long: 987654321
a float: 123.456
a char: A
a string: A String
a bool: 1

ANALYSIS A number of different data types are used to declare a number of variables in lines 6–11. In lines 14–19, you see cout being used with each of these variables being redirected. As you can see by the output, all are printed.

> **Note** cout requires that the iostream.h header file be included.

Understanding the C++ Keywords

All the keywords within the C programming language work in C++. Remember, C++ is a superset of C. Everything in a C program will work in a C++ program. This does not, however, mean that you should use everything you can in a C program in your C++ programs!

In addition to the C keywords, C++ adds several additional keywords. A list of the commonly used ANSI standard C++ keywords is presented in the list which follows. Note that the C++ keywords that are not considered a part of C are in bold text. As you can see, all the familiar C keywords are available. Additionally, the functionality of the C keywords is exactly what you have already learned!

Some of the common C++ keywords

break	case	**catch**	**class**
const	continue	**delete**	do
double	else	float	for
goto	if	**inline**	int
long	**namespace**	**new**	**operator**
private	**protected**	**public**	static
struct	switch	**throw**	**try**
union	void	while	

> **Note** Words in bold are ANSI C++ keywords not a part of the ANSI C language.

The C++ Data Types

In Day 3, "Storing Information: Variables and Constants," you learned about the C data types. The same data types are all available in C++. In addition to the data types presented in Day 3, there are two additional data types commonly used in C++. The first is the bool data type. A bool is a Boolean number that is stored in a single byte. The value of a bool is either True or False.

BD2

Note Remember that False is considered 0 and True is considered any other number.

In addition, C++ adds the capability to package data in a format called a class. Classes define objects in C++. Classes will be covered in detail in tomorrow's lesson.

Declaring Variables in C++

Another difference you'll find in C++ is tied to the declaration of variables. In C, you are only allowed to declare a variable at the beginning of any block. The most common place to declare a variable in C is at the beginning of a function; however, it is also possible to declare a variable in other locations as long as it is at the start of a block.

In C++, you can declare a variable at any time. This means that you can wait to declare a variable until you are ready to use it. After they are declared, basic variables will stay in scope until the current block ends. Listing B2.4 illustrates this capability to declare a variable at any point.

LISTING B2.4   vars.cpp. Declaring variables in locations other than the beginning of a block

```
 1:   //Showing variable declarations the C++ way
 2:   #include <iostream.h>
 3:
 4:   int main(int argc, char* argv[])
 5:   {
 6:       char a_char = 'x';
 7:
 8:       for (int ctr = 1; ctr < 10; ctr++ )
 9:       {
10:           cout << "\nLine: " << ctr << " - printing the char: " << a_char;
11:       }
```

LISTING B2.4 continued

```
12:
13:      char *just_for_fun = "Just For Fun!!!";
14:
15:      cout << "\n\njust_for_fun = " << just_for_fun << "\n";
16:
17:      return 0;
18:  }
```

OUTPUT
```
Line: 1 - printing the char: x
Line: 2 - printing the char: x
Line: 3 - printing the char: x
Line: 4 - printing the char: x
Line: 5 - printing the char: x
Line: 6 - printing the char: x
Line: 7 - printing the char: x
Line: 8 - printing the char: x
Line: 9 - printing the char: x

just_for_fun = Just For Fun!!!
```

ANALYSIS As you can see, this is a pretty straightforward listing. Line 8, where the ctr variable is being declared, should be of particular interest. In a pure C program, this listing would generate an error. In C, you would be required to declare ctr earlier, at the beginning of the function. Declaring a variable at the beginning of a looping structure, as shown in Listing B2.4, is very common in C++. In C++, you can declare a variable when you are ready to use it.

As a second example, line 13 also declares a variable, just_for_fun. This is obviously not at the beginning of a block, nor is it at the beginning of the main() function. As you can see, this variable is perfectly valid in C++ and prints its contents using the cout object in the next line.

Be careful about declaring variables in the middle of a function. Although C++ allows you to declare variables anywhere, if declare your variables at the beginning of a block, you make it easier for others to find and understand them. This, in turn makes it easier to debug the program.

DO	**DON'T**
DO declare variables at the beginning of blocks rather than in the middle in order to make your programs easier to follow.	**DON'T** forget that local variables take precedence over global variables if the same name is used.

Doing Operations in C++

The operators available in C++ are virtually the same as those available in C++. This means that everything you have already learned regarding operators applies.

C++ adds one additional operator that is used for error handling. This operator is the throw operator. It is beyond the scope of this book to go into details on how the throw operator and exception handling work within C++. Understand that the throw operator enables you to better handle errors in C++.

Working with Functions in C++

Yesterday, you were shown an example of overloading functions in C++. You saw that a function's name can be used more than once. In the following sections, you will learn the specifics of overloading functions within C++. You will also learn about a few other features of C++ that relate to functions, including

- Using default values for function parameters
- Using inline functions

Overloading Functions

Overloading functions is the simplest form of polymorphism supported by C++. As you saw yesterday, C++ does not complain if you use the same function name more than once. The capability to reuse a function name enables you to create programs that are adaptive and, thus, smarter. By creating a function that can be called in multiple ways, you are providing the user of the function with options. Consider the examples used yesterday. In the square listing, you learned that a person can draw a square in multiple ways. Whether the square function was called with two points or with a point and the width, the square was drawn.

In order for a C++ compiler to support the polymorphic nature of overloading functions, there are a few rules you must follow. You allow a function to accept different parameters by declaring and defining multiple instances of the function. Each unique instance must have at least one parameter that is different from the other instances. This difference must be in the data type. Consider the following two function calls for a function called rectangle:

```
int rectangle( int topleftx, int toplefty, int width, int length );

int rectangle( int topleftx, int toplefty, int bottomrightx, int
          bottomright y );
```

Although this seems to show two different ways to call a rectangle function, it is not. Trying to overload the rectangle function with the above two declarations will generate an error. Although the parameters being passed seem to be different—a point is being passed instead of the width and length—, the compiler won't see these as different. Rather, the compiler will see two calls to rectangle that both have four arguments that are all type int values.

If you change the second declaration to

```
int rectangle( int topleftx, int toplefty, long bottomrightx, long
               bottomright y );
```

the compiler will then be able to tell the difference between the two. One will receive long values— the other, integers. Additionally, the following is another rectangle function that can also be defined:

```
int rectangle( int topleftx, int toplefty );
```

This function is different from the others because it only has two parameters. This is enough to enable the compiler to differentiate it from the others. You do, however, need to be cautious with this third function, as you'll see in the next section.

Creating Default Function Parameter Values

In addition to being able to overload functions, you can also set default values for function parameters. This allows a function to adapt if a parameter is omitted. It also enables you to set up some values, even if the user didn't supply them. Consider the rectangle example presented in Listing B2.5.

LISTING B2.5   rect.cpp. Using default values for function parameters

```
 1: //Using default parameters
 2: #include <iostream.h>
 3:
 4: // Function prototype with default parameters
 5: void rectangle (int width = 3, int length = 3, char draw_char = 'X');
 6:
 7: int main(int argc, char* argv[])
 8: {
 9:     cout << "\nrectangle( 8, 2, \'*\' );\n";
10:     rectangle( 8, 2, '*' );
11:
12:     cout << "\nrectangle( 4, 5 );\n";
13:     rectangle( 4, 5 );
14:
15:     cout << "\nrectangle( 2 );\n";
16:     rectangle( 2 );
```

LISTING B2.5   continued

```
17:
18:     cout << "\nrectangle( );\n";
19:     rectangle( );
20:
21:     return 0;
22: }
23:
24: void rectangle ( int width, int length, char draw_char )
25: {
26:    int ctr1 = 0;
27:    int ctr2 = 0;
28:
29:    for (ctr1 = 0; ctr1 < length; ctr1++ )
30:    {
31:        cout << "\n";
32:        for ( ctr2 = 0; ctr2 < width; ctr2++)
33:        {
34:            cout << draw_char;
35:        }
36:    }
37:    cout << "\n";
38: }
```

BD2

OUTPUT

```
rectangle( 8, 2, '*' );

********
********

rectangle( 4, 5 );

XXXX
XXXX
XXXX
XXXX
XXXX

rectangle( 2 );

XX
XX
XX

rectangle( );

XXX
XXX
XXX
```

ANALYSIS As you can see in this listing, there is only one `rectangle()` declaration and function being used. This function differs from previous examples by using default values. The function prototype in line 5 contains values being assigned to each of the parameters. These values are considered default values.

In line 10, you see that the `rectangle()` function is called in the normal way with each of its three parameters being passed. In line 13, however, you see that the `draw_char` value has been left off. In the output, you can see that the rectangle is still drawn using an `'X'`. The `'X'` character is the default value set in line 5. In lines 16 and 19, the rectangle function is called again, each time with one less parameter. In each case, the default parameters are pulled from the prototype in line 5.

When using default values, it is always assumed that the values presented are valid from the left to the right. For example, using the `rectangle()` function above, you cannot pass a display character without passing a width and length. The following would generate bad results:

```
rectangle( '*' );
```

This call to `rectangle()` uses the ASCII value of `'*'` for the width rather than for the display character. Using the `rectangle()` function declared in line 5 of Listing B2.5, the first parameter of the rectangle function is always the width, the second is always the length, and the third is the display character. You might believe that the following

```
rectangle ( , , '*');
```

would fix this problem; however, this will generate an error. You must pass actual parameters.

> **Tip**
>
> You should place values that will probably be defaulted as far to the right in the argument list as possible.

Inline Functions

Inline functions are also a feature of C++ that is not available in C. An inline function is like any other function. The difference lies in how the compiler treats the function. By declaring a function as inline, you are making a request to the compiler. You are requesting that the compiler replace all calls to the inline function with a copy of the code within the inline function.

Inline functions are used simply for speed. Each time you call a function, a little bit of time is used to go to and return from the function. By declaring a function as inline, you don't spend this time going to and from the function because the function's code is placed directly in the listing. The tradeoff for this speed is program size. The code for the function is duplicated in each place it is called. This means if you call an inline function 15 times, there will be 15 copies of the function's code in your listing. Listing B2.6 presents a listing using inline functions.

LISTING B2.6   inline.cpp. Using an inline function

BD2

```
1: //Using inline functions
2: #include <iostream.h>
3:
4: inline long square( long value )
5: {
6:     return (value * value );
7: }
8:
9: inline long halve( long value )
10: {
11:     return (value / 2);
12: }
13:
14: int main(int argc, char* argv[])
15: {
16:     long nbr;
17:
18:     cout <<"\nEnter a number: ";
19:     cin >> nbr;
20:
21:     cout <<"\n\nSquared: " << square(nbr);
22:     cout <<"\nHalved: "  << halve(nbr);
23:
24:     cout <<"\nHalf the square: ";
25:     cout << halve(square(nbr));
26:
27:     cout << "\n\nDone!";
28:
29:     return 0;
30: }
```

OUTPUT

```
Enter a number: 16

Squared: 256
Halved: 8
Half the square: 128

Done!
```

This listing is pretty straightforward. A number is entered by the user. The program uses the C++ input object, cin, to retrieve this number. The cin object does just the opposite of the cout object you learned a little bit about earlier. You can redirect input into a variable from the cin object. In this case, you are directing a value into the nbr variable. After it is obtained, the value is squared, halved, and then the squared value is halved. Each of these values is printed out.

An inline function is declared and defined in line 4 of the listing, as well as in line 9. Other than the use of the keyword, inline, inline functions are declared just as any other function is declared. As stated before, the inline specifier is a request to the compiler to place the code of these functions inline. If the request is honored, the code is duplicated. Listing B2.7 shows roughly what the resulting code looks like if the inline request is honored.

Note

Listing B2.7 shows how inline functions affect the code. The compiler also expands out the includes, drops the comments, compresses white space, and more.

LISTING B2.7   Resulting code if inline request is honored

```
 1: //Using inline functions
 2: #include <iostream.h>
 3:
 4: int main(int argc, char* argv[])
 5: {
 6:     long nbr;
 7:
 8:     cout <<"\nEnter a number: ";
 9:     cin >> nbr;
10:
11:     cout <<"\n\nSquared: " << (nbr * nbr);
12:     cout <<"\nHalved: "  << (nbr/2);
13:
14:     cout <<"\nHalf the square: ";
15:     cout << ((nbr * nbr)/2);
16:
17:     cout << "\n\nDone!";
18:
19:     return 0;
20: }
```

Figure B2.1

Inline functions verses regular functions.

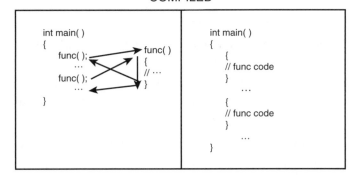

ORIGINAL

```
int main( )
{
    func( );
        ...
    func( );
        ...
}
inline func( ) {// func code}
```

COMPILED

Without inline specifier

With inline specifier

BD2

 Caution

Specifying a function as inline does not guarantee that it will actually be inline. This is only a request to the compiler.

 Tip

You should keep inline functions small and concise. If a function is more than a line or two of code, it probably should not be inline.

Summary

Today, you covered the basics of C++ programming. More specifically, you learned which operators and keywords are a part of C++, but are not a part of the C language. These operators and keywords make up the building blocks of C++. In tomorrow's lesson, you'll learn how to start building the core part of a C++ program—a class.

Q&A

Q **Are functions the only thing that can be overloaded?**

A No. Operators can also be overloaded in C++. It is beyond the scope of this book to explain operator overloading. You'll learn tomorrow that operator overloading is common when working with classes.

Q **How are Boolean values (type `bool` variables) different from the values stored in a bit?**

A Boolean values are stored in a single byte as either `True` or `False`. Only one Boolean value can be stored in a single byte. A bit can also be `true` or `false` (set as being `0` or `1`). There can be more than one bit in a single byte. In an 8-bit byte, an 8-bit value can be stored; however, only one bool value can be stored.

Q **Today's lesson covered overloading functions and using inline functions. What are member functions?**

A Member functions are also a feature of C++ that are not available in C. Member functions are a part of a class. Classes and member functions will both be covered in detail in tomorrow's lesson.

Q **Can I use `printf()` and `fprintf()` in my C++ programs?**

A Although you can use C functions in your C++ listings, it is not recommended. The `cout` class is much more streamlined than the bulky `printf()` functions. This combined with the object-oriented nature of the `cout` object make it a much more appropriate choice. If you use `printf()`, you are moving away from creating an object-oriented program.

Q **What are a few recommended books to read to learn more about C++?**

A This book does not try to teach everything you need to know about C++. To learn more, you can purchase a number of other books, including *Sams Teach Yourself C++ in 21 Days* by Jesse Liberty.

Workshop

The Workshop provides quiz questions to help you solidify your understanding of the material covered and exercises to provide you with experience in using what you've learned. Answers to the quiz are provided in Appendix F.

Quiz

1. What C++ object is available for printing?

2. When should you use `printf()` in a C++ program?

3. What values can be stored in the `bool` data type?

4. What is the difference between declaring variables in C++ versus C?

5. What operator(s) are available in C++ that are not available in C?

6. What is the difference between using default values and using function overloading?

7. Which of the following function declarations can be overlaid with each other?

   ```
   int triangle( int angle, int side1, int side2);

   int triangle(int side1, int side2, int side 3);

   int triangle(int side1, int side 2, int angle);
   ```

8. Declare a function called triangle that receives three parameters: `side1`, `side2`, and `side3`. Each of these should be of type `int`. Set each of the sides to have a default value of `0`.

9. True or False: An inline function is a function that is replicated into the code within a listing.

Exercises

1. Write a program that calculates the area of a box. Allow the user to enter the height, width, and length of the box.

2. Modify the program in exercise 1 to calculate the cost of shipping the box. Assume that the cost is based solely on the number of cubic units of the box. If the box is under 100 cubic units, the cost is $5. If it is over 100 and less than 1000 units, it is $10. If it is over 1000 units, it is $20. Create the function to use a default value of $20.

3. Specify the function that calculates the area of the box to be inline.

BD2

BONUS WEEK

BONUS DAY **3**

Working with C++ Classes and Objects

Yesterday you were told that classes were the key to object-oriented programming and thus C++ programming. Today you will cover a lot of ground with C++. Specifically, today you will learn

- What a class is
- What objects are
- How to instantiate an object
- How functions and data are used within classes
- When to use constructors and destructors
- How to work with classes as data members
- About inheritance and how to apply it
- What to do to learn even more about C++

Working with Complex Data in C++

You have learned that there are a number of different data types that can be used to store information. You've seen that a type `int` variable can be used to track simple numbers. A `char` can be used to track individual characters. A character array can be used to track a string.

In the real world, you encounter many different objects, such as a person's name, a shape, an invoice, an electronic book, a checkbook transaction, and so on. The simple data types provided in C and in C++ don't effectively track all these complex objects. You learned that structures are a way of tracking these more complex data objects. You can use structures to create your own user-defined data types. With structures you can create data types to track complex data such as a name, a rectangle, an invoice, or a checkbook transaction. For example, you can track the time using the following structure:

```
struct time
{
    int hours;
    int minutes;
    int seconds;
};
```

With this time structure, you can declare a number of time variables to use in your programs. For example, you can create a program to store a start time and an end time as shown in Listing B3.1.

LISTING B3.1   endtime.cpp. Using a time structure

```
 1: //Program using a time structure
 2: //
 3: #include <iostream.h>
 4:
 5: struct time {
 6:     int hours;
 7:     int minutes;
 8:     int seconds;
 9: };
10:
11: void print_time(struct time tm);
12:
13: int main(int argc, char* argv[])
14: {
15:     struct time start_time;
16:     struct time end_time;
17:
```

LISTING B3.1 continued

```
18:        start_time.hours = 8;
19:        start_time.minutes = 15;
20:        start_time.seconds = 20;
21:
22:        end_time.hours = 10;
23:        end_time.minutes = 11;
24:        end_time.seconds = 12;
25:
26:        cout << "\nStart time:   ";
27:        print_time(start_time);
28:        cout << "\n\nEnd time:   ";
29:        print_time(end_time);
30:
31:        return 0;
32: }
33:
34: // Print a time structure in h:m:s format
35: //-------------------------------------------
36: void print_time(struct time tm)
37: {
38:        cout << tm.hours << ":" << tm.minutes << ":" << tm.seconds;
39: }
```

BD3

OUTPUT

```
Start time:   8:15:20

End time:   10:11:12
```

ANALYSIS Listing B3.1 presents a simple structure in lines 5–9 that holds the time in hours, minutes, and seconds. In lines 15 and 16 two structures are declared as start_time and end_time. The data members of each of these time structures are initialized in lines 18–24. The time values are then printed out in the function display_time(), which is prototyped in line 11 and defined in lines 36–39.

Using Functions with Structures

Listing B3.1 uses a structure to create a time data element. There are a number of functions you can associate with the time structure. You have already seen a simple function called display_time(). The following are additional functions that can be directly associated with the time structure:

add_hour()

add_minute()

add_second()

The functionality of these routines should be obvious. The add_hour() function simply adds to the hours value in the structure, the add_minute() adds to the minutes data member, and the add_second() adds to the seconds data member. Listing B3.2 illustrates the use of these three simple functions with the start and end time structures.

LISTING **B3.2**   time2.cpp. Using the add... functions with the time structure

```
 1: // Program using a time structure with additional functions
 2: // for adding time.
 3: //
 4: #include <iostream.h>
 5:
 6: struct time {
 7:     int hours;
 8:     int minutes;
 9:     int seconds;
10: };
11:
12: void print_time(struct time tm);
13: void add_hour(struct time *tm);
14: void add_minute(struct time *tm);
15: void add_second(struct time *tm);
16:
17: int main(int argc, char* argv[])
18: {
19:     struct time start_time = {7, 15, 20};
20:     struct time end_time = {10, 20, 30};
21:
22:     // Print initial times
23:     cout << "\nStart time:   ";
24:     print_time(start_time);
25:     cout << "\nEnd time:   ";
26:     print_time(end_time);
27:
28:     // Add 1 hour, 1 minute, and 1 second to end time
29:     add_hour(&end_time);
30:     add_minute(&end_time);
31:     add_second(&end_time);
32:
33:     // Print final times
34:     cout << "\n\nStart time:   ";
35:     print_time(start_time);
36:     cout << "\nNew end time:   ";
37:     print_time(end_time);
38:
39:     return 0;
40: }
41:
42: // Print a time structure in h:m:s format
```

LISTING B3.2   continued

```cpp
43: //------------------------------------------
44: void print_time(struct time tm)
45: {
46:     cout << tm.hours << ":" << tm.minutes << ":" << tm.seconds;
47: }
48:
49: // Add 1 to the number of hours
50: //----------------------------
51: void add_hour(struct time *tm)
52: {
53:     tm->hours += 1;
54:     while (tm->hours >= 24 )
55:     {
56:         tm->hours -= 24;
57:     }
58: }
59:
60: // Add 1 to the number of minutes
61: //----------------------------
62: void add_minute(struct time *tm)
63: {
64:     tm->minutes += 1;
65:     while (tm->minutes >= 60)
66:     {
67:         add_hour(tm);
68:         tm->minutes -= 60;
69:     }
70: }
71:
72: // Add 1 to the number of seconds
73: //----------------------------
74: void add_second(struct time *tm)
75: {
76:     tm->seconds += 1;
77:     while (tm->seconds >= 60)
78:     {
79:         add_minute(tm);
80:         tm->seconds -= 60;
81:     }
82: }
```

BD3

OUTPUT

```
Start time:  7:10:15
End time:  11:20:30

Start time:  7:10:15
New end time:  12:21:31
```

ANALYSIS   As you can see, Listing B3.2 differs from Listing B3.1 in a couple of ways. The first is that the three add... functions have been added to the listing. The prototypes are provided in lines 13–15, and the actual functions are in lines 59–82. In lines 29, 30, and 31, the main() function passes the address of the end_time structure to each of the add... functions. The add... functions then add the appropriate value to the structure's member variables.

A little bit of additional functionality has been added to this listing. Each of the add... functions includes a few lines of code that check if the value is large enough to increment the larger time unit. For example, 60 seconds equals one minute. When the seconds hit 60, the add_minute() function is called, and the minutes are reset. Similar logic is applied to the hours and minutes functions as well.

Note

> You also see that the values for the structures are initialized differently in this listing. Rather than initializing each data member individually, the initial values are placed in the structures as they are declared (see lines 19 and 20). This can be done in both C and C++.

Tip

> If you are uncomfortable with the way Listing B3.2 is using pointers, you should review Days 9 and 11 that cover the use of pointers.

Using Member Functions

In Bonus Day 1, you learned about the features of an object-oriented language. One of these features is encapsulation. In Bonus Day 1, you learned that encapsulation describes the capability to create objects that are self-contained. In C++, you can actually make the time structure more self-contained by associating the functions that have been created in Listing B3.2 with the time structure itself. Just as you have the member data variables (hours, minutes, and seconds), you can also have member functions. These member functions can be part of your structure in the same way as the data members. Listing B3.3 presents a similar Listing to B3.2; however, in this listing add_hour(), add_minute(), add_second(), and display_time() are all member functions of the time structure.

LISTING B3.3   time3.cpp. Using member functions in the time structure

```
1: // Program using a time structure with member functions
2: //
3: #include <iostream.h>
4:
```

```
 5: struct time {
 6:     // Data Members:
 7:     int hours;
 8:     int minutes;
 9:     int seconds;
10:
11:     // Member Functions:
12:     void print_time(void);
13:     void add_hour(void);
14:     void add_minute(void);
15:     void add_second(void);
16: };
17:
18: int main(int argc, char* argv[])
19: {
20:     struct time start_time = {7, 15, 20};
21:     struct time end_time = {10, 20, 30};
22:
23:     // Print initial times
24:     cout << "\nStart time:  ";
25:     start_time.print_time();
26:     cout << "\nEnd time:  ";
27:     end_time.print_time();
28:
29:     // Add 1 hour, 1 minute, and 1 second to end time
30:     end_time.add_hour();
31:     end_time.add_minute();
32:     end_time.add_second();
33:
34:     // Print final times
35:     cout << "\n\nStart time:  ";
36:     start_time.print_time();
37:     cout << "\nNew end time:  ";
38:     end_time.print_time();
39:
40:     return 0;
41: }
42:
43: // Print a time structure in h:m:s format
44: //----------------------------------------
45: void time::print_time(void)
46: {
47:     cout << hours << ":" << minutes << ":" << seconds;
48: }
49:
50: // Add 1 to the number of hours
51: //----------------------------
52: void time::add_hour(void)
53: {
```

BD3

LISTING B3.3   continued

```
54:        hours += 1;
55:        while (hours >= 24 )
56:        {
57:            hours -= 24;
58:        }
59: }
60:
61: // Add 1 to the number of minutes
62: //-------------------------------
63: void time::add_minute(void)
64: {
65:        minutes += 1;
66:        while (minutes >= 60)
67:        {
68:            add_hour();
69:            minutes -= 60;
70:        }
71: }
72:
73: // Add 1 to the number of seconds
74: //-------------------------------
75: void time::add_second(void)
76: {
77:        seconds += 1;
78:        while (seconds >= 60)
79:        {
80:            add_minute();
81:            seconds -= 60;
82:        }
83: }
```

OUTPUT

```
Start time:  7:10:15
End time:   11:20:30

Start time:  8:11:16
New end time: 12:21:31
```

ANALYSIS   Although this listing is different from the previous listing, it accomplishes the same end results. This listing is, however, more object oriented. Looking at lines 5–16, you see that the time structure has been defined. In this example, in lines 12–15 of the time structure, you can see that the add... functions and the print_time() function have been declared. Note that these are inside of the structure. It is this internal declaration that makes these functions members of the time structure, just as the data members in lines 7–9 are members of the time structure.

In lines 20–24, you can see that this new listing starts out in the same way as the previous listing does. In line 25, you see the first real difference—the use of one of the member functions. As you can see in line 25, member functions are used in the same way as data members. The member operator (.) is used to access the function in the same format as a data member. Remember, to access a data member in a structure, you use the format

`structure_name.data_member_name`

Accessing a member function is done the same way:

`structure_name.member_function_name([passed_values])`

You might wonder why the structure name isn't passed to the `add...` and `print_time()` functions. Each member function is associated with a specific declaration of the structure, just as the data members are. When using the member function, you will generally be specifying which `time` structure you're using. For example, in line 25, you are calling the `print_time()` function within the `start_time` `time` structure. In line 27, you are calling the `print_time()` function in the `end_time` `time` structure. Because you know which declaration of the structure you are using, you don't need to pass the structure's address.

BD3

You'll notice that in the actual `add...` functions, you also don't need to specify which structure is being used (see line 68). Because there is a specific instance of the structure being called, the compiler assumes that you are using the same structure. This is the same reason the data members don't need to be preceded by the structure name as well.

Defining Member Functions

Because more than one structure could have member functions with the same name, you need to associate the member functions with the structure when you are defining them. As you can see in Listing B3.3, this is accomplished by using a slightly different format for the function headers when defining the functions. In line 52, you can see the `add_hour()` function header. As you can see, the structure name followed by two colons is used before the actual function name. This additional code associates the function to the structure.

The general structure for defining a member function is

```
return_value class_name::member_function_name( parameters )
{
    // function body
}
```

Remember, you need to include the structure name in this way because you could have multiple structures with the same member function names. For example, you could have a birthday structure and an anniversary structure, which both have month, day, and year values called `month`, `day`, and `year`. Each of these structures could also have similarly named functions such as a `display_date()` function. By including the structure name in the function definition (as is done in Listing B3.3), you can associate the appropriate function definition with the correct structure.

 Note
> Just like the data members, the function members can only be used in the context of the structure. If you try to use a member function outside of another member function from the same structure, you must include the structure name. If you don't use the structure name, you will get an error.

Using Classes

Although you may not have realized it, you have already been using classes in your C++ programs. A structure is a specialized form of a class. You'll learn more about this in a few minutes.

`class` is another keyword that is available in C++. Like the `struct` keyword, the `class` keyword enables you to create your own user-defined data types. You create a class in the same way as you create a structure. Earlier you created a new data type called `time`, which was a structure. The `time` structure could have been declared as follows instead:

```
class time {
    int hours;
    int minutes;
    int seconds;
};
```

Now instead of being defined as a structure, the `time` data type is defined as a class. This only required that you use the `class` keyword instead of the `struct` keyword. In addition to the data values, the member functions added in Listing B3.3 can also be declared as part of the `time` class.

Unlike declaring a structure, using a class to declare objects doesn't require you to include the `class` keyword. The class name is all you need. This is, in essence, equivalent to having declared a structure with a `typedef`. To declare the `end_time` and `start_time` data elements with the `time` structure, you do the following:

```
struct time start_time;
struct time end_time;
```

Using a class, you do the following:

```
time start_time;
time end_time;
```

This is pretty straightforward. You should note that when you use a class to declare a new data item, you are actually declaring an object. In other words, in C++ an *object* is simply a declared data item created by using a class. Both `start_time` and `end_time` are objects created using the `time` class.

Remember, although a structure is a specialized type of class, there are differences. Before looking at what is different in Listing B3.3 using classes instead of structures, first look at the key difference between classes and structures. This difference lies in the default method to access data in a structure versus the default method in a class.

BD3

Note You use a class to create an object. When you use a class to create an object, you are *instantiating* the class. Instantiation is simply creating an instance of a class.

Controlling Access to Data in a Class

Within a class—and hence a structure—you can determine which routines have access to data by using one of three additional keywords that are a part of C++. These keywords are:

- `public`
- `private`
- `protected`

By default, the members of a class are `private`. This includes both the data members and the member functions. For structures, the default access is `public`. This difference is significant.

Public Data

If data is declared as `public`, it is accessible not only by member functions within the class or structure, but also by any external source within your program. If you have a structure such as

```
struct name {
    string firstname;
    string lastname;
    string formatted_name();
}
```

you can access all of these members because they are public by default. This means that we can access any of these three structure members in the following way:

obj_name.firstname

obj_name.lastname

obj_name.formatted_name()

with *obj_name* being the name of the variable (object) that was declared using the name structure. Because these are public, you can call any of these three members from any-where in your program.

Creating Private Data

Structures are public by default, and classes are private by default. Private members of a class cannot be accessed from anywhere in your programs. They are private. This means they can only be accessed by member functions within the class.

If you declared a class such as the following:

```
class name {
    string firstname;
    string lastname;
    string formatted_name();
}
```

by default all of the members are private. You cannot access firstname or lastname except from member functions within the name class. This means that only the member function formatted_name() has access to these two variables. The following code would result in an error:

```
class name {
    string firstname;
    string lastname;
    string formatted_name();
};

int main(int argc, char* argv[])
{
    name myName

    myName.firstname = "Bradley"    //Error, data is private
    ...
    ...
    return 0;
}
```

The error in this code is due to the fact that myName contains only private data members. Only other members within the object would be able to use the three members.

Tip Whenever possible, you should declare the data members of your class as private instead of public. You can use member functions to access data.

Declaring Protected Data

The third access modifier is protected. Protected data members are treated differently than public and private ones. The protected keyword will be covered in more detail later today after you learn about inheritance.

Setting the Access Type on Class Data

You now know that structures have public data by default and that normal classes have private members by default. What do you do if you want to change these access modes? This is simple. You use the public, private, and protected keywords in your programs' classes. Listing B3.4 rewrites Listing B3.3 explicitly using the public and private keywords.

BD3

LISTING B3.4 access.cpp. Declaring, defining, and using private and public data

---

```cpp
1: // Controlling data access to data members and member functions
2: #include <iostream.h>
3:
4: class time {
5:
6: private:
7:    // Data Members:
8:    int hours;
9:    int minutes;
10:    int seconds;
11:
12: public:
13:    // Member Functions:
14:    void init( int h, int m, int s);
15:    void print_time(void);
16:    void add_hour(void);
17:    void add_minute(void);
18:    void add_second(void);
19: };
20:
21: int main(int argc, char* argv[])
22: {
23:     time start_time;
24:     time end_time;
25:
```

LISTING B3.4   continued

```
26:        start_time.init(7, 15, 20);
27:        end_time.init(10, 20, 30);
28:
29:        // Print initial times
30:        cout << "\nStart time:   ";
31:        start_time.print_time();
32:        cout << "\nEnd time:   ";
33:        end_time.print_time();
34:
35:        // Add 1 hour, 1 minute, and 1 second to end time
36:        end_time.add_hour();
37:        end_time.add_minute();
38:        end_time.add_second();
39:
40:        // Print final times
41:        cout << "\n\nStart time:   ";
42:        start_time.print_time();
43:        cout << "\nNew end time:   ";
44:        end_time.print_time();
45:
46:        return 0;
47: }
48:
49: // Print a time structure in h:m:s format
50: //----------------------------------------
51: void time::print_time(void)
52: {
53:        cout << hours << ":" << minutes << ":" << seconds;
54: }
55:
56: // Add 1 to the number of hours
57: //-----------------------------
58: void time::add_hour(void)
59: {
60:        hours += 1;
61:        while (hours >= 24 )
62:        {
63:            hours -= 24;
64:        }
65: }
66:
67: // Add 1 to the number of minutes
68: //-------------------------------
69: void time::add_minute(void)
70: {
71:        minutes += 1;
72:        while (minutes >= 60)
73:        {
74:            add_hour();
```

LISTING B3.4 continued

```
75:            minutes -= 60;
76:       }
77: }
78:
79: // Add 1 to the number of seconds
80: //-------------------------------
81: void time::add_second(void)
82: {
83:    seconds += 1;
84:    while (seconds >= 60)
85:    {
86:        add_minute();
87:        seconds -= 60;
88:    }
89: }
90:
91: // Initialize data member values
92: //-------------------------------
93: void time::init(int h, int m, int s)
94: {
95:    hours = h;
96:    minutes = m;
97:    seconds = s;
98: }
```

BD3

OUTPUT
```
Start time:  7:15:20
End time:  10:20:30

Start time:  7:15:20
New end time:  11:21:31
```

ANALYSIS You can see that the access to the members of the time class is being controlled in this listing. In line 6, the private keyword is being used to explicitly create private values. In this listing, the data members—hours, minutes, and seconds—are all private. This means that only the member functions of the time class can access these private data members. The public keyword is being used in line 12 to declare public values. The member functions init(), display_time(), and the add... functions are all public.

You should notice that a new member function has been included in line 14 of the time class. This function, called init(), is included in order to set the initial values of the private data members. Because the data members are declared as private, you can only access them by using a member function within the class. You cannot set the values from the main() function of this listing, as you did in Listing B3.3.

The init() function is called in lines 26 and 27. As you can see, this function sets the values of the data members in the time class. Looking at the function definition in lines 91–98, you see that the function simply sets the hours, minutes, and seconds values in the class to those passed to the initialization function.

To fully understand the access keywords, add the following between lines 27 and 29:

```
time.hour = 5;
```

When you execute the listing with this line, you'll get an error. The reason for the error is because hour is a private member of the time class, and private members can only be accessed from member functions within the class.

Creating Access Member Functions

If you set up your member data variables to be private, how do you access them? Listing B3.4 doesn't have an easy way to get the value of hours, minutes, or seconds. How should you set these values individually, and how would you access them? The title of this section gives away the answer to this question. To access the data, you simply set up access member functions.

An access member function is a public member function with the sole purpose of setting or getting a data member within the class. Generally, these functions will be a few lines in length. Listing B3.5 presents the time structure with access functions added. To cut down the size of the listing, the add... functions have been removed.

LISTING B3.5   property.cpp. Using access member functions

```
 1: // Using access functions
 2: #include <iostream.h>
 3:
 4: class time {
 5:
 6: private:
 7:    int   hours;
 8:    int   minutes;
 9:    int   seconds;
10:
11: public:
12:    void init( int h, int m, int s);
13:    void print_time(void);
14:
15:    void set_hours( int h);
16:    void set_minutes( int m );
17:    void set_seconds( int s );
```

LISTING B3.5 continued

```
18:
19:     int  get_hours( void );
20:     int  get_minutes( void );
21:     int  get_seconds( void );
22: };
23:
24: int main(int argc, char* argv[])
25: {
26:     time myTime;
27:
28:     myTime.init(11, 43, 20);
29:
30:     //print the initialized time
31:     cout << "\nMy time is:  ";
32:     myTime.print_time();
33:
34:     //reset the time data members individually
35:     cout << "\n\nResetting time to 3:12:30...\n";
36:
37:     myTime.set_hours( 3 );
38:     myTime.set_minutes(12);
39:     myTime.set_seconds (30);
40:
41:     //print the time data members individually
42:     cout << "\nThe hours are now:   " << myTime.get_hours();
43:     cout << "\nThe minutes are now: " << myTime.get_minutes();
44:     cout << "\nThe seconds are now: " << myTime.get_seconds();
45:
46:     return 0;
47: }
48:
49: // Print a time structure in h:m:s format
50: //--------------------------------------
51: void time::print_time(void)
52: {
53:     cout << hours << ":" << minutes << ":" << seconds;
54: }
55:
56: // Initialize data member values
57: //------------------------------
58: void time::init(int h, int m, int s)
59: {
60:     hours = h;
61:     minutes = m;
62:     seconds = s;
63: }
64:
65: // Access functions
66: //-----------------
```

LISTING B3.5 continued

```
67: int time::get_hours()
68: {
69:     return hours;
70: }
71: int time::get_minutes()
72: {
73:     return minutes;
74: }
75: int time::get_seconds()
76: {
77:     return seconds;
78: }
79: void time::set_hours( int h )
80: {
81:     hours = h;
82: }
83: void time::set_minutes( int m )
84: {
85:     minutes = m;
86: }
87: void time::set_seconds( int s )
88: {
89:     seconds = s;
90: }
```

OUTPUT

```
My time is:  11:43:20

Resetting time to 3:12:30...

The hours are now:   3
The minutes are now: 12
The seconds are now: 30Press
```

ANALYSIS This listing has cut out some of the member functions from the time class. Six new member functions have been added. Within the class, you can see that the first three in lines 15–17 each set a data member's value. In lines 19–21 the second three are presented. Each of these returns a value from one of the data members. The definitions for these functions are in lines 67–90.

So why would you create the private data members and use access member functions if doing so adds so much more code? It seems like simply making the data all public would be the easiest solution.

Although adding member functions seems like a lot of additional work, it actually enables you to encapsulate your program's functionality. It also gives you the capability to make changes to the class's data members without having to change all of the programs that use your class. Consider an example of how using access functions can help you. In the time structure, the hours, minutes, and seconds have all been stored in integer data variables. You can change your class so that these are all stored in character variables. A character variable can be used to save a numeric value that is much higher than 60. Because 60 is the biggest value you are storing, characters will work fine.

What change would you make in order to implement such a change? If you are accessing the integer data members directly from all your programs, you must ensure that all your programs now pass a character value instead of an integer. If you are using access functions, you can still pass in integer values. Your access functions are all that need to change. They can simply convert the integer to a character and visa versa. This enables you to continue using your existing programs without changing them at all!

Changing from an integer value to a character is a simplistic example. Consider a second example. You might have a rectangle class that stores the top-right point for the rectangle, as well as the rectangle's width and length. You can decide to make a change to your class and store the top-right and bottom-left points and not store the width and length. Such a change would generally cause you to rewrite all the programs using the rectangle. By using access functions, you can continue to access the class the same way. You simply need to make the appropriate translation in the access member functions so that two points are used.

BD3

Do	Don't
DO use classes instead of structures if member functions are going to be included.	**DON'T** declare anything public that doesn't need to be.
DO use access functions when possible instead of directly accessing data members of a class.	

Structures Versus Classes

It bears repeating that although structures and classes are very similar, there is a difference. By default, the data members of a structure are public, which means they are accessible outside of the structure's member functions. The default access control for a class is private. This means that by default, only the class's member functions can access the private members.

Housekeeping with Classes

Earlier, you learned that to initially set data values into the class, an `init()` function was called. C++ actually provides a mechanism in which you can initialize objects created with a class at the time they are created. Additionally, a mechanism is in place to do clean-up at the end of the life of an object. This clean-up is done at the time the object is destroyed. To help in these situations, C++ provides constructors and destructors.

Starting with Constructors

A constructor is a specialized member function within a class. The name of the constructor is the same as the name of a class. By default, C++ provides a constructor that sets up a class. You can, however, create your own constructor. If you do, the default work done by the compiler will be overridden.

Because a constructor is executed at the time a class is being created, it is perfect for initializing any data members and for making any allocations you need for a class.

Ending with Destructors

A destructor is also a specialized member function within a class. The destructor has the same name as the class; however, the destructor also has a tilde (~) before its name. A destructor is executed as an object is being destroyed. An object is destroyed when it goes out of scope. For the `time` class, the destructor is called `~time()`.

A destructor gives you the opportunity to do clean-up. For example, consider a class that dynamically allocates memory when an object is created from it. A constructor can be used to do the dynamic allocation. The destructor can be used to free the memory.

Using Constructors and Destructors

Listing B3.6 presents an example of using a constructor and a destructor with a class. This example dynamically allocates memory in the constructor and releases it in the destructor. Messages are printed in order for you to see when these member functions are called. You should note that two new keywords are presented to do the memory allocation.

LISTING B3.6   const.cpp. Using constructors and destructors

```
1: //Using constructors and destructors
2: #include <iostream.h>
3:
4: class value {
```

LISTING B3.6 continued

```
 5: private:
 6:     int val;
 7: public:
 8:     int get_value();
 9:     value(int nbr = 99);
10:     ~value();
11: };
12:
13: int main(int argc, char* argv[])
14: {
15:     cout << "\nGetting ready to declare myValue...";
16:
17:     value myValue;
18:
19:     cout <<"\nmyValue is now declared...";
20:
21:     cout <<"\n\nPrinting myValue: " << myValue.get_value();
22:
23:     cout << "\n\nEnding program.";
24:
25:     return 0;
26: }
27:
28: int value::get_value()
29: {
30:     return val;
31: }
32:
33: // Contructor for value class
34: //--------------------------
35: value::value( int nbr )
36: {
37:     // Do initializations.
38:     val = nbr;
39:     cout << "\n...In the constructor...\n";
40: }
41:
42: // Destructor for value class
43: //--------------------------
44: value::~value()
45: {
46:     // No real logic here for this class
47:     cout << "\n...In the destructor...\n";
48: }
```

BD3

OUTPUT

```
Getting ready to declare myValue...
...In the constructor...

myValue is now declared...

Printing myValue: 99

Ending program.
...In the destructor...
```

ANALYSIS Listing B3.6 creates a simple class called `value` that stores an integer value. A single private data member is simply an integer that holds a value. In lines 9–10, you see the constructor and destructor member functions that are a part of this class. You also can see that a C++ feature you learned about in Day 22 is also being used—default parameters. The `value` constructor uses a default parameter. If the `value` constructor is called without the `nbr` parameter, the value `99` will be the default.

> **Note**
>
> Remember that default values can be used with any function in C++. Using them in constructors is a common practice. This helps to ensure that you have a value to use.

In lines 35–40, you see the constructor's definition. This function is called whenever the value class is used to create an object. You can see that this constructor simply assigns the parameter that is passed to the object to the `val` data member (see line 38). A message is then printed out so you can see that the constructor has been entered.

In lines 44–48, you see the `value` class's destructor definition. For the `value` class, there is really no need to declare a destructor. The default destructor suffices. This destructor is created for the purpose of printing a message (line 47) stating that the destructor has been entered. If you review the output from this listing, you will find it interesting that the destructor is executed after the `Ending program` message is displayed near the end of the `main()` function. The destructor is called when the object is destroyed. In this case, the object is destroyed when the `main()` function ends.

Function Overloading Revisited

Yesterday you learned about function overloading. Function overloading can be used in a number of ways with classes. Specifically, you will find it very valuable to overload a class's constructor. Consider the constructor for a `date` class. You could create a number of constructors that enable you to set up objects by using any number of different formats:

- Three numeric values for month, day, year such as 1, 21, and 2001
- A single string value such as "January, 21, 2001"
- A string and two numeric values such as "January", 21, and 2001

For a class to be as useful as possible, try to create constructors and functions that can be called in as many ways as possible.

Review of the OOP Constructs in C++

On the first Bonus Day, you learned that C++ is an object-oriented programming language. You also learned that there were three features characteristic of an object-oriented language. These are

- Polymorphism
- Encapsulation
- Inheritance

BD3

You have already covered how C++ can implement polymorphism and encapsulation. You learned that one of the primary ways C++ implements polymorphism is by function overloading. By overloading your functions, you can create routines that can react to different parameters. You learned that by overloading constructors you can create objects that use different parameters for initializing. For example, in yesterday's lesson there was a discussion on creating date objects. Such an object can be constructed in a variety of different formats, including text such as "December 25, 2001", three numbers such as 12, 25, 2001, or a combination of text and numbers such as "December", 25, 2001. By overloading an object's constructor, you can create a function with the capability to work with any of these scenarios.

Note The more common use of polymorphism allows objects to be used as if they were different types. Showing this use of polymorphism is beyond the scope of this book.

Encapsulation was also covered. Yesterday's lesson taught you how to encapsulate information and functionality into a C++ class. Using such a class, you learned that you can instantiate objects that contain both data and functions.

The final characteristic of an object-oriented language is inheritance. In some of the following sections, you will learn the very basics of single inheritance. Before learning this, you should first look at the idea of using classes as data members within other classes.

Using Classes as Data Members

When you learned about structures and looping constructs in C, you also learned about nesting. You learned that nesting was simply placing one statement or block inside of another. Like everything else you learned in C, nesting also applies to C++.

When all is said and done, a class is simply another data structure. Because you can use data structures inside of a class, it is given that you should, therefore, be able to use a class inside of another class. Indeed, you can. Consider a class that simply stores a point:

```
class point
{
  private:
      int x;
      int y;
  public:
      int get_x();
      int get_y();
      void set_x(int val);
      void set_y(int val);
      point();
      point(int valx, int valy);
};
```

The guts of this class will be presented as an exercise at the end of today's lesson. For now, you can see that this class stores an x and a y value for a point. It also contains access functions for getting and setting each of these values. Finally, it contains two constructors: one that takes no parameters, and a second one that takes an x and a y value.

If you want to create a line class, you can use the point class as a data member. A line class can be declared as follows:

```
class line
{
  private:
      point start;
      point end;
  public:
      point get_start();
      point get_end();
      void set_start(point val);
      void set_end(point val);
      point();
};
```

As you can see, this class uses points in the same way as the point class, presented earlier, uses integers. A starting point and an ending point make up a line. The line class defines two point objects as its data members. Access functions get and set these points. The point objects are used just as any other data member.

Accessing Classes in Classes

You access a class within a class in the same way you would access a nested structure. Remember that you are accessing data members. To access the x value of the starting point in a line object called line1, you use

```
line1.start.x
```

You access the y value of the ending point in the same line object by using the following:

```
Line1.end.y
```

Inheriting in C++

Although C++ offers the capability to nest classes within other classes, C++ also offers a more powerful feature. This is the third feature of an object-oriented language: inheritance.

BD3

Inheritance is the capability to create new classes by building upon existing classes. Consider an example. There are people in the world. Every person in the world can be characterized by a number of features. Characteristics that describe every person include

- a name
- an age
- the country lived in
- other miscellaneous features

Now consider an employee at a company. Not every person is an employee at a company; however, every employee at a company can be considered a person. An employee has all the features of a person listed above, plus additional characteristics such as

- the name of a company where work is performed
- a salary
- other miscellaneous features

Consider a student. A student is not an employee; however, a student is a person. A student, too, has all the characteristics of a person, plus a few additional characteristics such as

- a student ID
- a school
- other miscellaneous features

In programming terms, it is said that an employee inherits the characteristics of a person. Additionally, a student inherits the characteristics of a person. Figure B3.1 illustrates the relationship between these three potential classes.

If you create classes to store a persons, employees, and students, you can make a couple of additional statements. You can say that

- Person is a base class.
- Employee and student are subclasses.
- There is no relationship between employee and student, although they use—descend from—the same base class.

A *base class* is simply a class that is inherited from by another class.

A *subclass* is simply a class that *inherits* from another class.

FIGURE B3.1

The relationship between the person, student, and employee classes.

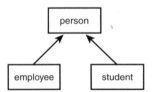

Building a Base Class for Inheritance

The best way to understand the power of inheritance is to see it in action. Before you can inherit, you need a base class from which to inherit. You can build a base class just as you built classes earlier today. The base class for today's example is the person class. Listing B3.7 presents a base class, as well as some code to see it in use.

LISTING B3.7   base.cpp. The person class set up to be used as a base class

```
1: #include <iostream.h>
2: #include <string.h>
3:
4: #define MAX_LEN 81
5:
6: class person {
```

LISTING B3.7 continued

```
 7: protected:
 8:     char fname[MAX_LEN];
 9:     char lname[MAX_LEN];
10:     int  age;
11: public:
12:     void set_fname(char fn[] ) { strcpy(fname, fn); };
13:     void set_lname(char ln[] ) { strcpy(lname, ln); };
14:     void set_age( int a ) { age = a ; };
15:     char *get_name(char *fullname);
16:     int  get_age( void ) { return age; };
17:     person(char fn[] = "blank", char ln[] = "blank");
18: };
19:
20: person::person( char fn[], char ln[] )
21: {
22:     strcpy(fname, fn);
23:     strcpy(lname, ln);
24:     age = -1;
25: }
26:
27: char *person::get_name(char fullname[])
28: {
29:     strcpy(fullname, fname);
30:     strcat(fullname, " ");
31:     strcat(fullname, lname);
32:
33:     return fullname;
34: }
35:
36: int main(int argc, char* argv[])
37: {
38:     char full[MAX_LEN + MAX_LEN];
39:
40:     person brad("Bradley", "Jones");
41:     brad.set_age(21);
42:
43:     person blank;
44:
45:     cout << "\nPerson brad:  " << brad.get_name(full);
46:     cout << "\n        age:  " << brad.get_age();
47:
48:     cout << "\nPerson blank: " << blank.get_name(full);
49:     cout << "\n        age: " << blank.get_age();
50:     cout << "\n";
51:
52:     return 0;
53: }
```

BD3

OUTPUT
```
Person brad:  Bradley Jones
         age:  21
Person blank: blank blank
         age: -1
```

ANALYSIS Listing B3.7 presents a relatively simple class called person. Additionally, in lines 36–53, a main() routine is provided that instantiates two person objects. An object called brad is instantiated in line 40. This object is constructed with values. The age for the brad object is also set in the following line to a nice wishful 21. In line 43, a second object called blank is instantiated. The blank object uses all default values in its construction. In the output, you can see that all the default values are printed.

In looking at the base class in lines 6–34, note a few new items. Many of the public member functions of the person class have their code directly after the declaration. For example, in line 12, the set_fname() function has the code—a simple call to the string copy function—right after its declaration. This is equivalent to declaring an inline function. When a routine is short, it is easier and clearer to simply declare it inline within the class. If a member function is a bit longer, such as get_name() in line 15, it is best to declare it outside the class definition. The get_name() function is declared in lines 27–34.

This listing has a few other items that you were not presented with in earlier listings. In line 2, the string.h header file is included. This was for the string copy and string catenation functions used within the listing. In line 4, a constant was defined for the maximum length being used.

> **Caution**
>
> You should note that there is no error checking in this listing. There is nothing that prevents a name from being longer than 81 characters. Such error-checking logic has been left out of these examples to help keep them short.

The Protected Access Data Modifier

The most important change you should notice in Listing B3.7 is in line 7. The keyword protected is being used. You should have expected the keyword private to be used. As you learned yesterday, using private keeps other parts of a listing from accessing data members or values. If you are going to implement inheritance, you may want to let these private values be accessed directly by the classes that inherit from this base class. To do this, you use the protected keyword. The protected keyword will only let the current class and classes that inherit the current class access the values.

Inheriting from a Base Class

Now that you have a base class, you are ready to inherit from it. Listing B3.8 presents an employee class that inherits from the person class you just created. The employee is a subclass of person.

 Note To help you out, the bold lines in Listing B3.8 point out what has been added to the code from Listing B3.7.

LISTING B3.8 employee.cpp. Inheriting from the person class

```
 1: // Inheritance illustrated
 2: #include <iostream.h>
 3: #include <string.h>
 4:
 5: #define MAX_LEN 81
 6:
 7: class person {
 8: protected:
 9:     char fname[MAX_LEN];
10:     char lname[MAX_LEN];
11:     int  age;
12: public:
13:     void set_fname(char fn[] ) { strcpy(fname, fn); };
14:     void set_lname(char ln[] ) { strcpy(lname, ln); };
15:     void set_age( int a ) { age = a ; };
16:     char *get_name(char *fullname);
17:     int  get_age( void ) { return age; };
18:     person(char fn[] = "blank", char ln[] = "blank");
19: };
20:
21: class employee : public person {
22: protected:
23:     long salary;
24: public:
25:     void set_salary(long sal) { salary = sal; };
26:     long get_salary() { return salary; };
27:     employee(char fn[] = "eblank", char ln[] = "eblank");
28: };
29:
30: person::person( char fn[], char ln[] )
31: {
32:     strcpy(fname, fn);
33:     strcpy(lname, ln);
34:     age = -1;
```

BD3

LISTING B3.8 continued

```
35: }
36:
37: char *person::get_name(char fullname[])
38: {
39:     strcpy(fullname, fname);
40:     strcat(fullname, " ");
41:     strcat(fullname, lname);
42:
43:     return fullname;
44: }
45:
46: employee::employee( char fn[], char ln[] ) : person(fn, ln)
47: {
48:     salary = 0;
49: }
50:
51:
52: int main(int argc, char* argv[])
53: {
54:     char full[MAX_LEN + MAX_LEN];
55:
56:     person brad("Bradley", "Jones");
57:     brad.set_age(21);
58:
59:     person blank;
60:
61:     cout << "\nPerson brad:  " << brad.get_name(full);
62:     cout << "\n        age:  " << brad.get_age();
63:
64:     cout << "\nPerson blank: " << blank.get_name(full);
65:     cout << "\n         age: " << blank.get_age();
66:     cout << "\n";
67:
68:     employee kyle( "Kyle", "Rinne" );
69:     kyle.set_salary( 50000 );
70:     kyle.set_age(32);
71:
72:     cout << "\nEmployee kyle: " << kyle.get_name(full);
73:     cout << "\n          age: " << kyle.get_age();
74:     cout << "\n       salary: " << kyle.get_salary();
75:     cout << "\n\n";
76:
77:     return 0;
78: }
```

OUTPUT

```
Person brad:  Bradley Jones
         age:  21
Person blank: blank blank
         age:  -1

Employee kyle: Kyle Rinne
         age:  32
      salary:  50000
```

ANALYSIS Much of this listing is the same as the previous listing. You can see that the per-son class has been declared just as it was in Listing B3.7. The new code has been bolded to make it easier for you to see where the changes are.

In line 21 you see the first real changes. One of these is the declaration for the employee class. This declaration is presented as

```
class employee : public person {
```

Just as in a regular class, the employee definition starts off with the keyword class followed by the name of the new class—employee, in this case. What is new is the colon and the text which follows. The colon indicates that employee is a subclass. The name of the base class to which employee is a subclass is then presented—person, in this case. The public keyword provides access to the components of the person class to the employee class. If you were creating a subclass called student, you would start the definition off with

```
class student : public person {
```

Additionally, if you were going to use employee as a base class to create a new class called temp_employee, you would start the definition off with

```
class temp_employee : public employee {
```

The temp_employee inherits from employee. You should note that because employee inherits from person, temp_employee also has access to the person members and features. Figure B3.1 illustrates these inheritance structures.

Looking back at Listing B3.8, you can see that the declaration for the employee class is relatively short. The employee class is short in this case because it also contains everything in the person class. Only those things that are new or different are added to this class. In this case, that means a single data member called salary, two access functions for salary, and a constructor.

Implementing the Subclass Constructor

In lines 46–50 you see the employee class's constructor. Again, you should notice that this constructor is different from the person class's constructor. The first part of the constructor's header is the same:

```
employee::employee( char fn[], char ln[])
```

The `employee` constructor accepts a first name and a last name. In line 27, you can see that if the first or last name is left off, the default value of `eblank` is passed to the function.

When constructing an `employee`, you are actually creating a `person` and then constructing the `employee`. When the constructor for the employee class is called, a call to the constructor of the base class, `person`, is made first. After the person constructor has executed, the subclass's constructor is executed. The object isn't considered constructed until both constructors are executed successfully. Listing B3.9 will help illustrate this later in today's lesson.

In Listing B3.8, you want to pass the values sent to the `employee` constructor through to the `person` constructor. To do this, you add the values to the end of the constructor's header line, as shown in line 46. As you can see in line 46, the first name and last name values are sent to the `person` constructor.

In line 48, the `employee` constructor initializes `salary` value to 0. When this is completed, the first name and last name will be set to the values set when the `employee` object is instantiated, or `eblank` if nothing is passed. The age will be set to [ms]1 as initialized in the `person` constructor, and the `salary` will be initialized to 0.

Using the Subclass

In line 68 of Listing B3.8, an employee object called `kyle` is instantiated. In this case `"Kyle"` and `"Rinne"` are passed to the constructor of the class. In line 69, the `set_salary()` member function of the `employee` class is called. In line 70, you can see that the `set_age()` member function can also be used. Even though `set_age()` is a part of `person`, it is declared as public, so the subclass, `employee`, can use the function as if it were its own. In lines 72–74, you can see that the access functions can be used to print out the appropriate values as well.

Constructors and Destructors Revisited

Previously, it was stated that constructors for subclasses still call the base class's constructor. The same is true of destructors. For destructors, first the subclass is called and then the base class. Using the `employee` class, the `employee` destructor code is executed first, and then the `person` destructor code is executed. Listing B4.3 is a short listing that illustrates this order by printing a simple message in each of the functions. You can review this code and its output.

LISTING B3.9   order.cpp. Constructor and destructor order of operation with inheritance

```
1: #include <iostream.h>
2:
3: class base {
4: protected:
5:     int  Bval;
6: public:
7:     void set_Bval(int x) { Bval = x; };
8:     int  get_Bval(int x) { return Bval; };
9:     base( int x = -99 );
10:     ~base();              //destrutor
11: };
12:
13: class sub : public base {
14: protected:
15:     int Sval;
16: public:
17:     void set_Sval( int x ) { Sval = x; };
18:     int  get_Sval() { return Sval; };
19:     sub( int x = -22 );
20:     ~sub();               // destructor
21: };
22:
23: base::base( int x )
24: {
25:     Bval = x;
26:     cout << "\n B >> in base class constructor...";
27: }
28:
29: base::~base()
30: {
31:     cout << "\n B >> ...in base class destructor";
32: }
33:
34: sub::sub( int x ) : base ( -1 )
35: {
36:     cout << "\n S >> in sub class constructor...";
37: }
38:
39: sub::~sub()
40: {
41:     cout << "\n S >> ...in sub class destructor";
42: }
43:
44: int main(int argc, char* argv[])
45: {
46:     cout << "\n . >> Instantiating a sub class...\n";
47:
48:     sub sub1;
```

BD3

LISTING B3.9 continued

```
49:
50:    cout << "\n . >> ...sub class instantiated...";
51:    cout << "\n . >> ...ending program...\n";
52:
53:    return 0;
54: }
```

```
. >> Instantiating a sub class...

B >> in base class constructor...
S >> in sub class constructor...
. >> ...sub class instantiated...
. >> ...ending program...

S >> ...in sub class destructor
B >> ...in base class destructor
```

> **Tip**
>
> Review the output of Listing B3.9 and make sure you understand it. Knowing the order in which code is executed can save you a lot of time when trying to hunt down errors in code and code logic.

A Caution on What You've Learned About C++

In the last couple of days, you have learned quite a bit about C++ and object-oriented programming. You have, however, only just begun to scratch the surface of what is available in C++. There are a lot of features of C++ you haven't covered, including, but not limited to

- multiple inheritance
- templates
- RTTI (Run-Time Type Information)
- friend functions
- nonpublic inheritance
- overriding versus overloading
- overloading operators

Each of these features offers additional functionality to your C++ programs and can help to extend the capability to reuse your C++ code. Because each of these features help in reuse, they are all typically used in real world C++ programs. It is beyond the scope of this book to cover all these here. However, with what has been covered here, you are primed to start using C++.

Where to Go to Learn More

You have learned the foundation of C++. To learn more, you should consider looking at a book that covers all the features of C++. This could include another *Sams Teach Yourself* book such as *Sams Teach Yourself C++ in 21 Days* by Jesse Liberty, or a more advanced book such as *C++ Unleashed*.

Summary

Today you covered the core concepts that make C++ an object-oriented language. You learned about classes and the objects that can be instantiated with them. You learned about data members and member functions. Additionally, you learned how to create and use constructors and destructors.

BD3

A lot of material was covered today; however, if you move deeper into C++, understanding today's material will be crucial. The object is the center of object-oriented programming. Today you learned how to encapsulate information into an object. You also saw how to make an object more polymorphic by using function overloading.

As today's lesson progressed, you reviewed the object-oriented constructs implemented in C++. You then saw how classes can be used as data members within other classes. After a quick listing, you jumped into single inheritance, where you saw how to use base classes and subclasses. In learning about inheritance, you also learned about the order in which constructors and destructors are executed in derived classes. Finally, today's lessons ended by providing a caution that you have just begun the journey into C++.

In tomorrow's lesson, you get to change focus, although only slightly. Starting tomorrow, you move into a primer on another object-oriented language, Java.

Q&A

Q **If a structure can do everything a class can, why not use classes for everything—or use structures for everything?**

A Generally a structure is used if you are using only data member values. If you are including member functions, it is recommended that you use a class instead of a structure.

Q Can I use member functions in structures in my C programs?

A No. Remember that C++ structures are a specialized type of class. Member functions are a part of a class. C does not have a class construct, so you shouldn't try to use classes, nor should you try to use member functions.

Q Can I write full-fledged C++ programs using what is covered in this book?

A You can write complete C++ programs using what was learned in the lessons in this book; however, you have only learned a few of the basics of C++. If you try to update or modify existing C++ programs, you may find that they are much more complex than any you saw here.

Q Can you inherit from more than one base class?

A Yes. In C++ you can inherit from multiple base classes. Just as you inherited from both your mother and your father, a class can have multiple parents. The new subclass, then, has characteristics of both of the base classes. It is beyond the scope of this book to go into more detail on this.

Workshop

The Workshop provides quiz questions to help you solidify your understanding of the material covered and exercises to provide you with experience in using what you've learned. Answers to the quiz are provided in Appendix F.

Quiz

1. What is the difference between a structure and a class in C++?
2. Can you assign values to a class?
3. What is an object?
4. What does it mean when you instantiate a class?
5. Which object-oriented programming characteristics do classes use?
6. Where within your programs can you access a private data member of a class?
7. Where within your programs can you access a public data member of a class?
8. When is a constructor executed?
9. When is a destructor executed?
10. How is using a class as a data member different from using other types of data?
11. If a guppy inherits from a fish class, the guppy is said to be the
    a. base class
    b. subclass
    c. Neither the base class nor the subclass

12. If a guppy inherits from a `fish` class, then the `fish` is said to be the

    a. base class

    b. subclass

    c. Neither the base class nor the subclass

13. What would be the header line for the declaration of the guppy class used in quiz question 4?

14. Which executes first, a base class's constructor or the sub class's constructor?

15. Which executes first, a base class's destructor or the sub class's destructor?

Exercises

1. Create a class that will hold a point. Call the class point. This should contain an x value and a y value that are both private. Use data access members.

2. Create a class for a circle. The data members can be the circle's center point and the circle's radius. Use the point class from exercise 1 to create the point's center data member.

3. Create a constructor for the circle class in exercise 2. Use zeros as default parameters for the point's center. Use 1 as the default radius.

4. Create a public member function that returns the circle's circumference.

5. Write the code for the point class presented at the beginning of today's lesson.

6. Write the code for the line class presented at the beginning of today's lesson.

7. Rewrite the code for the `line` class so that it inherits the point class and extends it by also storing a length.

8. Rewrite Listing B4.3 to work for the `student` class instead of the `employee` class.

BD3

BONUS DAY 4

Java Language Fundamentals

Java was designed to avoid many of the pitfalls of C and C++, while retaining their strengths and adding new capabilities. If you recently learned C, Java may seem a little strange, but many programmers prefer it over all other programming languages. Today, you will start your Java mini-course. You will learn

- Basic components of a Java program
- Java keywords and identifiers
- Data types for numbers and strings
- Text input and output
- Java operators and program flow control

Structure of a Java Program

As you learned on Bonus Day 1, Java programs come in two types. *Applets* are small- to medium-sized programs that are designed to be distributed and used on the World Wide Web, typically as part of a Web page. *Stand alone applications* are programs that run on their own, just like the C programs you have seen throughout this book. Java can be used in a number of ways. Java applets use to receive a lot of attention because of all the hype surrounding the Web. Java can also be used to create components, server-side Web applications, and enterprise-level objects. Most importantly, Java is useful for creating stand-alone applications. In this brief introduction to Java, you will concentrate on using Java for stand-alone applications, as that is more directly comparable to the uses of C and C++ you have seen elsewhere in this book.

Java Program Essentials

At the most simple level, a Java program consists of two parts, one contained within the other. As with just about everything else in Java, a program is a class and is defined as follows:

```
public class ProgramName
{

}
```

All the code that makes up the program is placed within the braces, and the entire source code file is saved on disk with an extension of java. A program called *ProgramName* would be stored as *ProgramName*.java. The second essential part of a Java program is the main function. When you execute a Java program, execution starts in main just as it does in C and C++. Here's what main looks like:

```
public class ProgramName {

    public static void main (String args[])
    {

    }
}
```

You'll note that main takes an argument called args[]. This is the way that command line arguments are passed to a Java program. Unlike C, you don't have an integer argc variable stating how many values were provided. Instead, you use args.length.

Working with Imports

Almost every Java program, except the simplest, must use the import statement to have access to classes that the program uses. You must use import with classes that are part of Java, as well as with classes you have written. import statements are placed at the start of a Java source code file, before the class definition. You can import classes individually, as in this example that imports the class someClass from the package my.package:

```
import my.package.someClass;
```

You can also use the * wildcard to import all classes in a package:

```
import java.io.*;
```

This line imports all classes in the `java.io` package. Packages that are part of Java have names starting with java. If your program makes reference to a class without having imported it, the compiler generates an error. A Java program can have as many `import` statement as it needs.

 Note A package is simply a file that contains classes. Using the wildcard character, you can include all of the classes from the file.

Methods

In Java, a *method* is essentially the same thing as a function in C or C++. Methods are so named simply because Java is a completely object-oriented language and, by convention, objects have methods, not functions. You saw an example of a method in the `Hello, World` example presented on Bonus Day 1, "Object-Oriented Programming Languages." In a Java program, most of the code is in methods.

BD4

Comments

No programming language is complete without the capability to add comments to the source code. Java has three comment styles. One is just like a C comment; anything between `/*` and `*/` is a comment and is ignored by the compiler:

```
/* This is
all
one
        big
comment */
```

The second style is the same as C++; anything after `//` on a line is a comment:

```
// This is a comment.
X = 5; //This is also a comment.
```

Java's third comment style is used for automatic generation of documentation. It is like the C comment style with the addition of an extra asterisk:

```
/** This comment will be included in class documentation
    created by the Javadoc tool. */
```

With this style of comment, you can us a program called Javadoc to generate documentation from your program. The use of Javadoc is beyond the scope of this book, but you need to know about this comment style in case you run across it in Java code.

Java Keywords

Like all programming languages, Java has a set of *keywords* that are the core of the language. You cannot use keywords as identifiers, such as variable names, in your programs. Java has more keywords than C (Java has about 50 keywords), but still that is a manageable number. A few of the keywords are not actually used yet, but have been reserved for possible future use. Table B4.1 lists the Java keywords, organizing them by category. Of course, you do not yet know what most of these keywords mean. You'll learn about most of them, however, in this and the next two bonus days.

TABLE B4.1 Java language keywords

Category	Keywords
Built-in data types	boolean
	byte
	char
	double
	float
	int
	long
	short
	strictfp
	widefp
	void
Used in expressions	new
	this
	super
Used in selection statements	break
	case
	default
	else
	if
	switch
Used in iteration statements	continue
	do
	for
	while
Used in other statements	catch
	finally
	return
	synchronized
	throw

TABLE B4.1 continued

Category	Keywords
Declaration modifiers	abstract
	final
	private
	protected
	public
	static
Used with classes and methods	class
	extends
	implements
	import
	instanceof
	interface
	native
	package
	throws
	transient
	volatile
Reserved for future use	const
	goto

BD4

Java Identifiers

An *identifier* is a name that you supply for a variable, class, or other program element. Java is very flexible when it comes to identifiers. They can be any length and can contain letters, the underscore character, the dollar sign character, and the digits 0 through 9 (although the first character of an identifier cannot be a digit). By letters, Java does not mean only the 26 characters of the English alphabet, but all the thousands of characters from various languages that are represented in the Unicode character set. To be specific, all Unicode characters above hex value 00C0 can be used in a Java identifier. Here are some examples:

```
interestRate
$_9
ø9ú
```

As with any language, you cannot use keywords as identifiers. Also, it is wise programming practice to use identifiers that describe the item they refer to. In the list above, the first identifier adheres to this rule. The other two, although perfectly legal, break the rule and should be avoided.

Caution Java identifiers and keywords are all case-sensitive, just as with C and C++, so you need to use care when typing. A set of guidelines for identifier names has been developed, and by following it you reduce the chance of errors. These guidelines are not mandatory, however, we recommend them.

Class and interface namesare descriptive nouns with the first letter of each word in uppercase. Examples are `BarGraph` and `AddressList`. Interfaces are sometimes named with the `able` suffix, as in `Sortable` or `Mailable`.

Object and variable names are nouns or noun phrases with the first letter in lowercase and subsequent words uppercase. Examples are `interestRate` and `marchReport`.

Method names are verbs or verb phrases with the first letter in lowercase and subsequent words in uppercase. Examples are `calculateAverage` and `clearAllData`.

Constant names are all uppercase with words separated by an underscore. Examples are `MAXIMUM_COUNT` and `OLD_INTEREST_RATE`.

Data Types

Java data types come in two flavors. The nonobject data types are called the *primitive* data types. These will be familiar to you from your experience with C and C++, although there are some differences in Java. There is another object type for storage and manipulation of strings (text), called `String`. Each of these types will be covered in turn.

The Primitive Data Types

Java has eight built-in data types that are called *primitive types* because they are not objects. Their names are `boolean`, `char`, `byte`, `short`, `int`, `long`, `float`, and `double`. The primitive data types can be separated based on the type of data they can hold.

True/False Data

Use the `boolean` data type to hold true/false, yes/no data. A type `boolean` variable can hold only the two values `true` and `false`. Unlike other programming languages, which use the numerical value `0` for false and `-1` for true, the Java `boolean` type is not based on numbers.

Integer Numeric Data

Java has four primitive types to hold integer numeric data—that is, numbers with no fractional part. The four types—`byte`, `short`, `int`, and `long`—differ in the amount of memory they take up and in the range of values they can hold. When you need to store an integer value, select one of these primitive types based on the largest and smallest values the variable will be required to hold. All these types are signed, which means they can hold negative or positive numbers. Table B4.2 provides the details on the integer data types.

 Note

Note that the size of each of the primitive types is the same on all platforms. This is different from C and C++, where the size of the data types may vary between platforms.

TABLE B4.2 Java's primitive integer data types

Integer data type	Size	Range of values
byte	1 byte (8 bits)	−128 to 127
short	2 bytes (16 bits)	−32,768 to 32,767
int	4 bytes (32 bits)	−2,147,483,688 to 2,147,483,647
long	8 bytes (64 bits)	-9.22×10^{18} to 9.22×10^{18} (approximate range)

BD4

Floating Point Numeric Data

For floating point numbers—numbers with a fractional part—Java offers two primitive types. Type double is the one you should use in most circumstances. It takes 8 bytes of memory, and permits an accuracy of 14 to 15 decimal places, while permitting a huge range of -1.7×10^{308} to 1.7×10^{308}, more than enough for any imaginable need.

The second floating point type, float, is provided primarily for compatibility with the many existing data files that use this format. Type float is stored in 4 bytes of memory and is significantly less flexible than type double, offering accuracy of only 6–7 decimal places and a range of -3.4×10^{38} to 3.4×10^{38}.

Character Data

Java has a single primitive data type called char used to store printable characters. It is 2 bytes in size and is intended to hold the unsigned values 0 to 65,535 that represent the Unicode character set. Although, technically, a type char holds a numeric value, you should never use it for numbers.

Do	Don't
DO: Use the primitive numerical data type appropriate for the range of values your data will have to hold.	**DON'T**: Use type float in your programs unless you need it for compatibility with existing data files.

Constants

A constant is a data item whose value cannot change as the program is executing. Any of Java's primitive data types can be used as constants. To create a constant, use the `final` keyword in the declaration:

```
final double INTEREST_RATE = 0.05;
final int MAXIMUM_COUNT = 200;
```

Declaring and Initializing Variables

To create a variable of a specified primitive type, use the type name followed by one or more variable names.

```
double f;
int counter;
byte b1, b2, b3;
```

You have the option of initializing a variable at the same time it is declared. Simply follow the variable name with the assignment operator (=) and the desired initial value:

```
double f=1.23;
int counter=0;
byte b1, b2=13, b3;
```

The initial value must be appropriate for the data type. Either of the following initializations will cause an error—the first because the value 2000 is too large for type `byte`, and the second because type `int` cannot hold a fractional value.

```
byte b1=2000;
int counter=1.23;
```

Variable Scope

In Java, variables and other program elements, such as methods and objects, have a scope. An item's scope determines where in the program it can be accessed. Scope is determined by the use of certain keywords in the item's declaration and the location of the declaration. If an item is declared inside a method, its access is limited to that method, and no keywords are applicable. However, for items declared outside a method, access can be controlled as described here:

- The `private` keyword. The item is accessible only within the class where it is declared.
- No keyword. The item is accessible in all classes that are in the same package.
- The `protected` keyword. The item is accessible in all classes that are in the same package, as well as in subclasses based on the class.
- The `public` keyword. The item is accessible anywhere the class is accessible.

The following code sample provides some examples. The comments in the code explain what's going on.

```
Public class MyClass {

    private int count;     // Accessible only in this class.
    long averageWeight;    // Accessible in other classes in the same package.
    protected boolean paymentReceived; // Accessible in other classes in the
                                       // same package and in subclasses.
    public double sumOfPayments;       // Accessible anywhere the MyClass
                                       // class is accessible.

    public void someMethod ()     // This method can be called from
    {                             // anywhere the class is accessible.

        short temporaryTotal; // Accessible only within someMethod.

    }

    private void anotherMethod ()     // This method can be called
    {                                 // only from within  the class.

        short temporaryTotal; // Accessible only within anotherMethod.
                              // Totally separate from the same name
                              // variable in someMethod.
    }
```

BD4

Storing String Data

You may remember that both C and C++ store strings (text) in arrays of characters. Java has significantly improved the way a program stores strings, providing the String class for this purpose. This approach offers the significant advantages of object-oriented programming, and it also simplifies the programmer's task. This is because a String object does a lot more than simply store string data—it also has an assortment of methods that perform various actions on the stored data.

Working with Strings

As you do with the primitive data types, you must declare a String object before you can use it. Declaring a string is done in the same manner as declaring any other data type:

```
String lastName;
```

After you have a String variable, you assign data to it using the assignment operator:

```
lastName = "Smith";
```

You can combine the declaration and assignment in one line, if desired:

```
String lastName = "Smith";
```

To combine strings, a process known as *concatenation*, use the + operator. Java knows you are working with strings and not numbers, so it knows to concatenate the strings rather than trying to perform addition. Here are a few examples:

```
String fullName, firstName, lastName;
firstName = "Peter";
lastName = "Aitken";
fullName = firstName + " " + lastName;
```

The result of these operations are to place "Peter Aitken" within `fullName`.

String literals are written as you see above—text enclosed in double quotation marks. As in C and C++, certain characters are represented by escape codes. The Java escape codes are presented in Table B4.3

TABLE B4.3   Java character escape codes

Escape code	Character represented
\b	backspace
\t	tab
\n	new line
\f	form feed
\r	carriage return
\"	double quotation mark
\'	single quotation mark
\\	backslash

String Methods

The `String` object has a variety of methods that you use to work with string data. One method you will find valuable is `length()`. The `length()` method returns the number of characters in a string:

```
MyString = "Java programming";
n = MyString.length();
//n now equals 16.
```

Note that the result of calling the `length()` method is 16. Unlike C and C++, a null character is not counted.

Other methods let you modify a string, perform string comparisons, extract characters from strings, and more. You should be able to find more details on the `String` class and its methods in the documentation that came with whatever Java development tool you are using.

The program in Listing B4.1 demonstrates some of the methods of the `String` class.

LISTING B4.1　StringTest.Java demonstrates some uses of the String class

```
 1:  import java.lang.System;
 2:  import java.lang.String;
 3:
 4:  public class StringTest {
 5:
 6:      public static void main(String args[]) {
 7:
 8:      String s1 = "Teach Yourself C in 21 Days";
 9:
10:      System.out.println("The original string: " + s1);
11:      System.out.println("Converted to uppercase: " + s1.toUpperCase());
12:      System.out.println("Converted to lowercase: " + s1.toLowerCase());
13:      System.out.println("The first Y is at position " + s1.indexOf('Y'));
14:      System.out.println("Replacing 'e' with '!': "+s1.replace('e', '!'));
15:      System.out.println("This string has " + s1.length()+" characters.");
16:      }
17:  }
```

OUTPUT
```
The original string: Teach Yourself C in 21 Days
Converted to uppercase: TEACH YOURSELF C IN 21 DAYS
Converted to lowercase: teach yourself c in 21 days
The first Y is at position 6.
Replacing 'e' with '!': T!ach Yours!lf C in 21 Days
This string has 27 characters.
The original string is unchanged: Teach Yourself C in 21 Days
```

BD4

ANALYSIS　This is a simple program. Lines 1–6 should be familiar to you, performing the necessary imports, defining the program class, and defining the main method. Within main, line 8 declares an instance of the String class and initializes it. Then, the remaining code uses some of the methods of the String class to manipulate the string and display the results on screen. It's important to note that methods of the String class do not modify the original string, but rather they return a new string with the changes.

Input and Output

The most basic Java applications are called *console* applications because their input and output consist entirely of text input from the keyboard and output to the screen. Java has plenty of graphic capabilities, implemented in the Abstract Windowing Toolkit (AWT) or the Swing class library, but coverage of that topic is beyond the scope of this brief introduction. Console input/output is all you'll need to get started with Java.

Outputting text to the screen is done with the println method of the System.out class. You saw this method used in the Hello, World example from Bonus Day 1. The syntax is simple:

```
System.out.println("This text will be displayed on the screen.");
System.out.println(s); // Assumes s is a String object.
```

Text input is a bit more complicated. Although there is a `System.in` object that can be used for keyboard input, on its own it is suitable only for single characters. To input a line of text, which is usually what you need to do, you must use a couple of higher-level classes called `BufferedReader` and `InutStreamReader`. Rather than trying to explain the details, I'll just tell you the required steps:

1. Import java.lang.System, java.io.InputStreamReader, and java.io.BufferedReader.
2. Declare a variable of type `BufferedReader`.
3. Initialize the variable created in step 2 as follows (assuming the variable is named kb):

   ```
   kb = new BufferedReader(new InputStreamReader(System.in));
   ```
4. Call the object's `readLine` method to input a line of text from the keyboard.

The sample program in Listing B4.2 shows how this is done.

LISTING B4.2 InputOutputTest.java demonstrates console I/O

```
 1: import java.lang.System;
 2: import java.io.InputStreamReader;
 3: import java.io.BufferedReader;
 4: import java.io.IOException;
 5:
 6: public class InputOutputTest {
 7:
 8:     public static void main(String args[]) throws IOException {
 9:         // Set up to read lines from the keyboard.
10:         BufferedReader kb;
11:         String s1;
12:
13:         kb = new BufferedReader(new InputStreamReader(System.in));
14:         System.out.println("Enter a line of text: ");
15:         s1 = kb.readLine();
16:         System.out.println("You entered " + s1);
17:
18:     }
19: }
```

OUTPUT
```
Enter a line of text: Java programming
You entered Java programming
```

ANALYSIS Lines 1–4 of this program import the required Java classes. Line 6 defines the class InputOutputTest, representing the test program. The throws IOException part of this line is a reference to Java's error-handling mechanisms, which will be covered on Bonus Day 6. Line 10 declares a variable of type `BufferedReader`. I called this variable `kb` because it will be used for keyboard input. Line 11 declares a variable of type `String`, used in Java to hold text data (covered earlier today). Line 13 initializes `kb` so it is ready for use. Line 14 displays a prompt on the screen. Line 15 reads a line of text from the keyboard and stores it in `s1`. Finally, line 16 displays the entered text on the screen.

There are more details of console input/output in Java, but the above techniques will serve for the Java programs to be presented here.

Arrays

As in C and C++, a Java array is an indexed method of storing data. Each element in an array has the same name, and each is distinguished from the others by a numerical index. For example, if you create an array called `MyArray`, and specify that it contains 100 type `int` variables, you would have `MyArray[0]`, `MyArray[1]`, up to `MyArray[99]`. An array can hold either primitive data types or objects. There are two steps to creating an array in Java. First, you must declare an identifier to reference the array. The syntax is

```
type ArrayIdentifier [];
```

Type is the name of a class or a primitive data type, and *ArrayIdentifier* is the name of the array. The empty brackets are what sets an array declaration apart from a regular variable declaration. The second step creates the actual array and sets the array identifier to reference it:

```
ArrayIdentifier = new type [elements];
```

Type is the data type of the array and must be the same type as used in the identifier declaration. *Elements* is the number of elements in the array. The two steps for creating a Java array can be combined in a single line of code:

```
type ArrayIdentifier = new type [elements];
```

If an array is a primitive data type or the `String` type, you can start using it without any further steps.

```
String Names = new String [50];
int Numbers = new int [100];
...
Names[1] = "Peter";
Names[2] = "John";
Numbers[1] = 2;
Numbers[2] = Numbers[1] + 5;
```

BD4

If, however, the array is of an object type, you must explicitly initialize each element of the array with a reference to an object:

```
MyClass ClassArray = new MyClass [10];
for (int i=0; i<10; i++) {
    ClassArray[i] = new MyClass; }
```

Java arrays can have more than one dimension. Multidimensional arrays are created by using one set of brackets for each dimension, with the same syntax as described above for a one-dimensional arrays:

```
int twoDimensionalArray [][] = new int[10][5];
byte fourDimensionalArray [][][][];
fourDimensionalArray = new byte[4][4][5][5];
```

 Caution Java arrays start with element 0, and not element 1 as you might think. Thus, an array with 100 elements has elements [0] through [99], and trying to use element [100] does not work. If you want an *n* element array with elements [1] through [*n*]–for example, days[1] through days[365] to refer to the days of the year—your only choice is to create an array 1 element larger than needed and ignore element [0].

Operators

An *operator* is a symbol that performs some operation on data, such as adding and subtracting. You have already met the assignment operator (=), which is used to assign values. For the most part, operators in Java are identical to those in C and C++. Java has the standard arithmetic operators for addition (+), subtraction (-), multiplication (*), division (/), and modulus (%). And, like C and C++, Java offers the unary increment (++) and decrement (--) operators which, respectively, increase and decrease an integer value by 1. Rounding out the mathematical operators are the assignment with operators +=, -=, *=, and /=, which provide a shorthand for operating on the contents of variables. For example:

```
x += 5 ; // Same as x = x + 5;
y *= 1.5; // Same as y = y * 1.5;
```

Java's comparison operators are also the same as those in C and C++: equal to (==), not equal to (!=), greater than (>), greater than or equal t0 (>=), less than (<), less than or equal to (<=).

Finally, Java's logical operators are also the same as you have learned before: NOT (!), AND (&&), and OR (||).

This has been a very brief explanation of Java's operators. For more details you can turn back to Day 4,"Statements, Expressions and Operators," to review C's operators.

Flow Control

Flow control refers to controlling which parts of your code execute, when they execute, and how many times they execute. Flow control statements are essential so your program can react to user input, different data conditions, and other factors.

 Note   Java uses braces {} to enclose the code in a class or a method. Braces are also used to create compound statements (a block, just as in C or C++). Any group of two or more Java statement within braces is a compound statement, and it is treated as a unit for execution purposes.

if...else

The `if` control structure executes just like in C and C++. A Java statement is executed only if a condition is true. Optionally, the `else` clause executes a second statement if the condition is false. Remember, a statement can be a single simple statement or a compound statement (in braces) containing multiple simple statements. The syntax is

```
if (condition) statement1 else statement2;
```

Condition is an expression that evaluates to true or false. `statement1` is executed if *condition* is true; `statement2` is executed if *condition* is false. You can simply omit the `else` clause if there are no statements to be executed or *condition* is false:

```
if (condition) statement1;
```

`if...else` structures can be nested as required to test multiple conditions:

```
if (condition1) {
    if (condition2)
        statement1;
    else
        statement2;
    }
else
  statement3;
```

You can also stack `if` statements to test multiple conditions:

```
if (condition1)
    statement1;
else if (condition2)
```

BD4

```
    statement2;
else if (condition3)
    statement3;
else
statement4;
```

while and do...while

The while and do...while structures execute a statement repeatedly as long as a specified condition is true. The syntax for while is:

```
while (condition)
    statement;
```

The syntax for do...while is as follows:

```
do
    statement;
while (condition)
```

The main difference between these two structures is that while checks *condition* first, before executing the statement(s), so that if *condition* is initially false, the statements will not be executed at all. In contrast, do...while does not check *condition* until the statement(s) have been executed once, so you are guaranteed at least one execution. As you can see, both of these statements are like their C counterparts.

switch

You use the switch construct to compare an expression against several test values, executing the code that is associated with the matching value. The syntax is

```
switch (expression) {
    case test1:
        statementblock1;
    case test2:
        statementblock2;
    case test3:
        statementblock3;
    default:
        statementblock4;
}
```

If *expression* equals *test1*, *statement1* is executed, and so on. If there is no match, the statement following the default keyword is executed. The default keyword is optional. If omitted, and there is no match, none of the statements in the switch construct are executed. If there is more than one match, only the first one matters. Note that each statement block in a switch construct should end with a break statement to prevent execution from "falling through" to the next section. Here's an example of switch:

```
switch(numberOfSiblings) {
    case 0:
        System.out.println("An only child, I see.");
        break;
    case 1:
        System.out.println("The typical family!");
        break;
    case 2:
        System.out.println("Three kids can be a handful.");
        break;
    default:
        System.out.println("It must have been crowded at your house!.");
}
```

Suppose the `break` statement were omitted from the `case 0:` block. Then, when the expression is equal to 0, the code under `case 0:` would be executed followed by the code under `case 1:`. In other words, when `switch` finds a match, it starts executing code at the matching `case` statement and continues until it finds a `break` statement or reaches the end of the `switch` construct. Again, this functionality matches C and C++.

for

The `for` construct is used to execute a block of statements a specified number of times. The syntax is

```
for (variable = initial value; expression1; expression2)
{
    statementblock;
}
```

variable is any numeric variable, and *expression1* is a Boolean (true/false) expression. Here's how a `for` construct works when execution reaches it:

1. *variable* is set equal to initial value.

2. *expression1* is evaluated. If true, `statementblock` is executed. If false, exit the `for` construct.

3. Evaluate *expression2*.

4. Return to step 2.

Most frequently, the `for` construct is used to "count" from one value to another. This loop counts up from 0 to 100 and displays the values on the screen:

```
for (i = 0; i < 101; i++)
{
    System.out.println(i);
}
```

The variable used in the loop can be one declared earlier, or it can be declared as part of the loop. In this example, the loop counts down from 100 to 50 by twos:

```
for (int i = 100; i >= 50; i -= 2)
{
}
```

You can count by fractional values too, as long as the data type of the variable is appropriate:

```
for (double d = 0.0; d < .99; d += 0.01)
{
```

Summary

You learned a lot about the basics of Java today. You encountered a lot of material, but it should have been easy to understand because Java is so similar to C and C++ in the areas we covered today. Now that you know the fundamentals of Java program structure, keywords, identifiers, variables, arrays, operators, and flow control, you are ready to move on to the really interesting parts of Java covered in the next two days' lessons.

Q&A

Q Is Java identical to C and C++ in the basics of data types, operators, and flow control?

A Almost, but not quite. There are a few differences, but knowing something about C and/or C++ will certainly give you a "leg up" when learning Java.

Q How does Java differ from C and C++ in the way text data is stored?

A Both C and C++ use an array of characters to store text (strings). In contrast Java uses the String class. Because it is a class rather than a simple array, String offers significantly more power and flexibility for working with text.

Q What is a console program? Is this all Java can do?

A A console program is one whose input and output involve only text displayed on the screen or typed in by the user. Java is also capable of very sophisticated windows and graphics, but console I/O is sufficient for showing you the fundamentals of the language.

Workshop

The Workshop provides quiz questions to help you solidify your understanding of the material covered, and exercises to provide you with experience in using what you've learned. Answers to the quiz are provided in Appendix F.

Quiz

1. What Java primitive data type can hold the largest range of integer values?

2. Does Java support functions?

3. What Java construct would you use to execute a block of statements repeatedly as long as a certain condition is true?

4. What does the `import` statement do?

5. How do you create a comment in Java?

6. What's wrong with this code?
   ```
   int count;
   Count = 0;
   ```

7. What data types can be used in Java arrays?

Exercise

1. Install and work with a java compiler. Compile and execute the listings presented in today's lessons.

BD4

BONUS DAY 5

Working with Java Classes and Methods

Classes are to Java programming as feet are to walking—you cannot take a single step without them. A large part of your Java programming effort will be devoted to creating your own classes to perform the custom tasks that your application requires. Today you will learn

- How to define a class
- How to create class properties and methods
- How to define packages
- How to use inheritance

Defining a Class

A class definition has several parts, some of which are optional. You have already seen the basics of defining a class when you created the demo programs on Bonus Day 4. In Java, everything—including a program—is a class. However, most Java classes are not programs but are used in programs, and there are additional details to the class definition. The following is the most basic syntax for a class definition:

```
class className
{

}
```

That's pretty simple. In fact, it looks exactly like a program class definition (there generally will be no `main()` method, however). The `class` keyword is required to identify a class definition. The `className` is an identifier for the class created using the Java identifier rules described on Bonus Day 4. This is the name you'll use to refer to the class in your programs.

Few class definitions are so simple, however, so there will usually be additional elements in the definition. The full syntax for a class definition, with optional elements in brackets, is

```
[modifiers] class className [extends SuperClassName]
{
}
```

The modifiers control two things about the class. One is its *privacy*, which determines the scope of the class (you learned about scope on Bonus Day 4). Privacy keywords for class definitions are listed in Table B5.1. Most classes you create will be `public`.

TABLE B5.1 Privacy keywords for class definitions

Keyword	Description
public	Class accessible to everyone
private	Class accessible to no one
[no keyword]	Class accessible throughout its package
protected	Class accessible throughout its package and within subclasses

The second thing controlled by the modifiers has to do with inheritance. You can use one (but not both) of the following keywords:

- `Abstract`. You can inherit from this class (use it as a superclass), but you cannot create instances of the class. Use abstract when you create a class that is designed as a template for other classes, but you cannot use it on its own.

- `Final`. You can create instances of the class, but it cannot be used as a superclass (another class cannot inherit from this class) .

The optional extends *superClassName* clause is used when you are using inheritance—in other words, when the new class is based on an existing class. The class you are inheriting from can be a class you created or a class that is part of Java, as long as the class was not created using the final keyword. When you create a class based on a superclass, the new class automatically inherits all the superclass's methods and properties. Inheritance will be covered in more detail later today.

Caution A class, like a Java program, requires that you include all the classes and packages utilized by the code in that class. The include statements come just before the class definition in the source code file.

Specifying the Class Package

Every class that you create in Java is part of a package. To specify which package, use the package keyword in your class definition file. This statement should be the very first one in the file, before any include statements:

```
package PackageName;
```

If you omit a package specification, the class will be put in a default, no-name package. This is not a good idea. You should create packages containing related classes, which will help you keep track of things. Then, when another source code file needs the class, you can use the import statement to import the entire package or one or more specific classes from the package.

Creating Class Properties

A *property* is a chunk of data, or information, associated with a class. For example, if you created a class called Circle to represent a circle, it would probably have a property called Radius for the circle's radius. A property of a class is nothing more than a variable declared inside the class and made available outside the class. You learned the basics of Java variables and how to declare them on Bonus Day 4. A variable that is to serve as a property must be declared at the start of the class definition, outside any methods:

```
public class circle
{
  public double radius;
  public int anotherProperty;
  public byte yetAnotherProperty;
  public MyClass anObjectProperty; // MyClass is a programmer-defined class.
  public String oneLastProperty;

  // Other class code goes here.
}
```

BD5

Note

> Just as with C++ member variables, you should make property variables private and create two function to access it—one to get its value and one to set is value.

A Simple Demonstration

Before continuing with the details of class definitions, it is a good idea to see how to create and use a simple class. This Java project will have two files. One, SimpleClass.java, will define a very simple class that does nothing more than provide two properties, one to store a number and the other to store some text. The second file, ClassBasicsDemo.java, is a program that makes use of SimpeClass. The source code for these two files is shown in Listings B5.1 and B5.2.

LISTING B5.1   Code in SimpleClass.java

```
1:  import java.lang.String;
2:
3:  public class SimpleClass {
4:
5:      public double data;
6:      public String text;
7:  }
```

LISTING B5.2   Code in ClassBasicsDemo.java

```
 1: public class ClassBasicsDemo {
 2:    public static void main(String args[])
 3:    {
 4:      SimpleClass MyClass;
 5:
 6:      MyClass = new SimpleClass();
 7:      MyClass.data = 1.2345;
 8:      MyClass.text = "A class act.";
 9:      System.out.print("The number stored in MyClass is ");
10:      System.out.println(MyClass.data);
11:      System.out.print("The text stored in MyClass is ");
12:      System.out.println(MyClass.text);
13:    }
14: }
```

OUTPUT

```
The number stored in MyClass is 1.2345
The text stored in MyClass is A class act
```

ANALYSIS Let's look at SimpleClass.java first. Line 1 imports the String class, necessary because the class you are creating makes use of String. Line 3 is the class definition, indicating that this class does not inherit from any other class and that it has public visibility. Lines 5 and 6 declare the two variables that are the class's properties.

ClassBasicsDemo.java is a bit more complicated. Line 1 of course is the class definition, and line 2 defines the main method that is required in any Java stand-alone program. Line 4 declares a variable of type SimpleClass—in other words, a variable that can hold a reference to an instance of SimpleClass. Then, line 6 uses the new keyword to actually create an instance of SimpleClass and assign the reference to the variable MyClass. Lines 7 and 8 assign data to the object properties using the standard syntax *objectname.propertyname*. Finally, lines 9 through 12 display the property values on the screen.

Note   You might be wondering why the program ClassBasicsDemo did not use the include statement to reference the class SimpleClass. That's because the two files are part of the same Java project. If SimpleClass had been compiled as part of a separate package, the include statement would be required.

Class Methods

Although some classes contain only properties, most classes contain one or more methods. A method is simply a Java function. It is a separate section of code that has a name, can be passed arguments, and can return a value to the calling program. In Java, as in all languages, methods (functions) are used to isolate sections of code that perform a specific task. The syntax for creating a method is

```
privacyKeyword type methodName (argument1, argument2, ...)
{
    ...
}
```

The *privacyKeyword* determines where the method can be called from. Use public to make the method callable from outside the class the method is in (this is what you'll usually use). Use private to restrict the method to being called by code within the class.

The type keyword specifies the return type of the method—in other words, the type of the data returned by the method to the caller. It can be an object type, such as String, or one of Java's primitive types.

BD5

The *methodName* is the method's name, which you'll use to call it. It is constructed using the rules for Java identifiers that were presented on Bonus Day 4.

A method can take any number of arguments. For each argument, the method declaration includes the type of the argument and the argument identifier. For example, here is a declaration for a method that takes two type int arguments and returns a type long:

```
public long SomeMethod (int arg1, int arg2)
{
    ...
}
```

If a method takes no arguments, use an empty set of parentheses after the method name. When you call a method, the arguments passed must match the number and type of arguments in the method definition.

To return a value from a method, use the return statement inside the method as follows:

```
return expression;
```

Expression is any Java expression that evaluates to a value of the same type as the method's declared return type. When execution reaches a return statement the expression is evaluated, and the method terminates. A method can have more than one return statement in it, but only the first one that execution reaches has any effect.

Note Some methods do not return a value to the calling program. To create such a method, use void as the return type in the method definition. Then use return, by itself, to terminate the method. Lacking a return statement, a type void method terminates when execution reaches the closing brace.

A Method Demonstration

The following program demonstrates a class with methods. In fact, this class has nothing but methods, lacking any properties! The definition of the class ClassWithMethods is shown in Listing B5.3, and the sample program that uses this class, MethodsDemo, is shown in Listing B5.4.

LISTING B5.3 Source code for ClassWithMethods.java

```
1:  import java.lang.String;
2:
3:  public class ClassWithMethods {
4:
```

LISTING B5.3   continued

```
 5:     public void displayText(String message, boolean newline) {
 6:     // Displays message on the console, moving to
 7:     // the start of a new line after message only
 8:     // if newline is true.
 9:     if (newline)
10:         System.out.println(message);
11:     else
12:         System.out.print(message);
13:     }
14:
15:     public double halfOf(double value) {
16:     // Returns half of its argument.
17:     return value / 2;
18:     }
19:
20:     public long sumOf(long value1, long value2) {
21:     // Returns the sum of its arguments.
22:     long result;
23:     result = value1 + value2;
24:     return result;
25:     }
26: }
```

LISTING B5.4   MethodsDemo.java demonstrates using class methods

```
 1: import java.lang.Double;
 2: import java.lang.Long;
 3:
 4: public class MethodsDemo {
 5:   public static void main(String args[]) {
 6:     ClassWithMethods The_Class;
 7:     String temp;
 8:     double d;
 9:     long l;
10:
11:     The_Class = new ClassWithMethods();
12:     The_Class.displayText("Using ClassWithMethods:", true);
13:     The_Class.displayText("Half of 99 is ", false);
14:     d = The_Class.halfOf(99);
15:     temp = Double.toString(d);
16:     The_Class.displayText(temp, true);
17:     The_Class.displayText("The sum of 12345 and 997766 is ", false);
18:     l = The_Class.sumOf(12345, 997766);
19:     temp = Long.toString(l);
20:     The_Class.displayText(temp, true);
21:   }
22: }
```

BD5

OUTPUT

```
Using ClassWithMethods:
Half of 99 is 49.5
The sum of 12345 and 997766 is 1010111
```

ANALYSIS   In ClassWithMethods.java, line 1 imports the required String class, and line 3 is the class definition. Lines 5 to 12 define the method displayText, which takes one type String and one type boolean argument. It has no return value. Code in the method tests the value of the newline argument. If it is true, System.out.println is used to display the message on the screen and then start a new line. If newline is false, System.out.print is used to display the message without starting a new line.

Lines 15 to 18 define the method halfOf. This method takes one type double argument and returns a type double. There is only one line of code in the method. It divides the argument by 2 and returns the resulting value.

Lines 20 to 24 define the method sumOf, which takes two type long arguments and also returns a type long. Line 22 declares a variable to hold the temporary result, and line 23 performs the calculation. Then line 24 terminates the method and returns the result to the caller.

Now let's look at MethodsDemo.java. Lines 1 and 2 import two classes that will be used in the program (explained below). Lines 4 and 5 are the program class and main method definitions, as you have seen before. Line 6 declares a variable of type ClassWithMethods, and lines 7 to 9 declare several primitive type variables the program will use. Line 11 creates an instance of ClassWithMethods. Now the program can get to work.

Lines 12 and 13 use the displayText method to display two messages on the console. A new line is started after the first message, but not after the second. Line 14 uses the halfOf method to calculate half of the value 99, assigning the return value to the variable d. Line 15 makes use of the toString method of Java's Double class to convert the numerical value d into a string, which is stored in temp. Line 16 displays this string on the console.

Lines 17 to 20 are essentially a repeat of lines 13 to 16 except that the sumOf method is called and the Long.toString method is used to convert the numerical value to text.

Tip

Java has a set of classes corresponding to the primitive numeric data types; these classes are called Boolean, Character, Integer, Long, Float, and Double. Each of these classes has some useful methods, such as the toString method used in the previous listing to create a string representation of a numeric value. These classes can be very useful, and you can find out more in your Java documentation.

Overloading Methods

You learned on Bonus Day 1 that one of the features of object-oriented programming is the technique of overloading. This technique lets you create two or more methods (functions) that have the same name, but differ in the number and/or type of arguments. When you call the method, Java automatically uses the correct ones based on the arguments you pass.

To demonstrate, I created a class with three methods called sumOf, each of which returns the sum of its arguments. One method takes two arguments, one takes three arguments, and the other takes four arguments. This class is called Overloaded, and its code is presented in Listing B5.5. The program OverloadDemo, in Listing B5.6, demonstrates the overloaded methods.

LISTING B5.5   Overloaded.java. The Overloaded class has an overloaded method

```
 1:  public class Overloaded {
 2:
 3:      public double sumOf(double v1, double v2) {
 4:            return v1 + v2;
 5:      }
 6:
 7:      public double sumOf(double v1, double v2, double v3) {
 8:            return v1 + v2 + v3;
 9:      }
10:
11:      public double sumOf(double v1, double v2, double v3, double v4) {
12:            return v1 + v2 + v3 + v4;
13:      }
14:  }
```

BD5

LISTING B5.6   OverloadDemo.java. Demonstration of the overloaded methods in the class Overloaded

```
 1:  import java.lang.String;
 2:  import java.lang.Double;
 3:
 4:  public class OverloadDemo
 5:  {
 6:      public static void main(String args[])
 7:      {
 8:        Overloaded MyClass;
 9:        double d;
10:
11:        MyClass = new Overloaded();
```

LISTING B5.6   continued

```
12:            System.out.println("Adding two numbers: ");
13:            System.out.print("  The sum of 1.4 and 6.7 is ");
14:            d = MyClass.sumOf(1.4, 6.7);
15:            System.out.println(Double.toString(d));
16:            System.out.println("Adding three numbers: ");
17:            System.out.print("  The sum of 1.4, 6.7, and 12.2 is ");
18:            d = MyClass.sumOf(1.4, 6.7, 12.2);
19:            System.out.println(Double.toString(d));
20:            System.out.println("Adding four numbers: ");
21:            System.out.print("  The sum of 1.4, 6.7, 12.2, and -4.1 is ");
22:            d = MyClass.sumOf(1.4, 6.7, 12.2, -4.1);
23:            System.out.println(Double.toString(d));
24:        }
25:  }
```

OUTPUT

```
Adding two numbers:
The sum of 1.4 and 6.7 is 8.1.
Adding three numbers:
The sum of 1.4, 6.7, and 12.2 is 20.299999999999997
Adding 4 numbers:
The sum of 1.4, 6.7, 12.2, and -4.1 is 16.199999999999997
```

ANALYSIS   In the first listing, the code for the class Overloaded is quite simple. Lines 3 to 5 define one sumOf method, taking two type double arguments. Lines 7 to 9 and 11 to 13 define the other two sumOf methods, one taking three and the other taking four type double arguments. Within each method, the code simply adds the arguments together and returns the result.

Lines 1 and 2 of OverloadDemo import two Java classes the program uses. Lines 8 and 9 declare the two variables that are required, and line 11 creates an instance of the Overloaded class. Lines 12–13 display some explanatory text on the console. Line 14 uses the sumOf method to add two numbers, and line 15 displays the result on the screen. Lines 16 to 19 and 20 to 23 repeat the same process for three and four numbers, respectively.

 Caution   In the output from this example, note that the second and third answers are not perfectly accurate. This occurs because the way in which a computer stores floating point numbers makes it impossible to accurately represent certain values. The very minor loss in accuracy that results is meaningless for most applications.

Class Constructors

Every class has a special method called a *constructor*. Just like in C++, a class's constructor is called automatically when a new instance of the class is created. You put code in the constructor to perform any initialization steps that are required by the class. Some simple classes do not need a constructor, so it is omitted, but most classes beyond really simple ones will use a constructor.

The syntax for a constructor is as follows:

```
ClassName (ParameterList)
{
}
```

As you can see, the name of a constructor method is always identical to the name of the class it is in. The *ParameterList* is an optional list of parameters that is passed to the constructor. The list has the same syntax as the method arguments covered earlier today. If the constructor takes no arguments, use a set of empty parentheses.

Listing B5.7 presents an example of a class with a constructor. The class `circle` has a property called `radius`, and you want to ensure that the value is always defined by setting it in the constructor. Listing B5.7 shows the code for circle.java.

LISTING B5.7 circle.java. The class `circle` has a constructor

```
1:  public class circle {
2:
3:      public double radius;
4:
5:      circle (double r) {
6:          radius = r;
7:      }
8:  }
```

BD5

The short program in Listing B5.8 demonstrates how the constructor is used.

LISTING B5.8 UseCircle.java. Creating a new `circle` object calls the constructor

```
1:  import java.lang.String;
2:  import java.lang.Double;
3:
4:  public class ConstructorDemo {
5:      public static void main(String args[]) {
6:
7:          circle c1;
8:          c1 = new circle(1.25);
```

LISTING B5.8 continued

```
 9:          System.out.println("The circle's radius is "
10:                          + Double.toString(c1.radius));
11:     }
12:  }
```

OUTPUT   The circle's radius is 1.25

ANALYSIS   The first listing defines a class named `circle`. Line 1 is the class definition, and line 3 declares a property named `radius`. The constructor is in lines 5 to 7. You can see that the constructor is declared to take one type `double` argument. When the constructor is called, the value passed in the argument `r` is assigned to the property `radius`.

The second listing shows how the constructor is used. Lines 1 to 5 should be familiar to you. Line 7 declares a variable of type `circle`. Line 8 uses the `new` keyword to create an instance of the class `circle`. When the instance is created, the constructor is called and is passed the argument `1.25` that is specified. Lines 9 and 10 demonstrates that the value is indeed stored in the `radius` property by displaying it on the screen.

Java is very careful about matching the arguments passed to a constructor and the parameters declared as part of the constructor. If they do not match in number and type, the program will not compile. If a class has no constructor at all or has a constructor defined with no parameters, use empty parentheses when creating an instance of the class:

```
MyObject = new ClassName();
```

Like any method, a class constructor can be overloaded. This can be useful when there are different ways of initializing the object. Remember, overloaded methods have the same name, but you can identify them by their parameters. To demonstrate, modify the previous example so that the `circle` class has another property, `name`, used to hold a text description of the object. You'll add two more constructors to the class to permit three ways of initializing it:

- Pass no arguments. `Radius` is set to `0`, and `name` is set to `"Unnamed"`.
- Pass one numeric argument. Radius is set to the argument value, and name is set to `"Unnamed"`.
- Pass one numeric and one string argument. Both `radius` and `name` are initialized.

Listings B5.9 and B5.10 show the source code for the new class and demonstration program.

LISTING B5.9 circle2.java. A class with an overloaded constructor

```
1:   import java.lang.String;
2:
3:   public class circle {
4:
5:       public double radius;
6:       public String name;
7:
8:       circle () {
9:         radius = 0;
10:        name = "Unnamed";
11:      }
12:
13:      circle (double r) {
14:        radius = r;
15:        name = "Unnamed";
16:      }
17:
18:      circle (double r, String n) {
19:        radius = r;
20:        name = n;
21:      }
22:   }
```

LISTING B5.10 UseCircle2.java. Demonstrating the use of overloaded constructors

```
1:  import java.lang.String;
2:  import java.lang.Double;
3:
4:  public class ConstructorDemo {
5:    public static void main(String args[]) {
6:
7:      circle c1;
8:      circle c2;
9:      circle c3;
10:
11:     c1 = new circle();
12:     c2 = new circle(99.99);
13:     c3 = new circle(0.001, "Harold");
14:     System.out.println("For c1:");
15:     System.out.println("  The radius is " + Double.toString(c1.radius));
16:     System.out.println("  The name is " + c1.name);
17:     System.out.println("For c2:");
18:     System.out.println("  The radius is " + Double.toString(c2.radius));
19:     System.out.println("  The name is " + c2.name);
20:     System.out.println("For c3:");
21:     System.out.println("  The radius is " + Double.toString(c3.radius));
```

BD5

LISTING **B5.10**   continued

```
22:   System.out.println("  The name is " + c3.name);
23:   }
24: }
```

OUTPUT

```
For c1:
    The radius is 0.0
    The name is Unnamed
For c2:
    The radius is 99.99
    The name is Unnamed
For c3:
    The radius is 0.0010
    The name is Harold
```

ANALYSIS   In the code for the circle class, lines 5 and 6 declare the class's two properties. Lines 8 to 11 define a constructor that takes no arguments, and the code here initializes the two properties to their default values. Lines 13 to 16 define a constructor that takes a single type double argument, and code in this constructor initializes the radius property to this value and the name property to the default value. Lines 18 to 21 define a third constructor, this time taking two arguments—one type double and one type String. Code in this constructor uses the argument values to initialize the class's two properties.

The demonstration program in Listing B5.10 creates three instances of the circle class. Lines 7 to 9 declare the variables that will hold the object references. Line 11 creates a new instance passing no arguments, so the class's first constructor will be called. Lines 12 and 13 create other instances of the class, passing one and two arguments respectively. The remaining lines of code display the property values of the three circle objects so you can see that the values were initialized properly.

Using Inheritance

Inheritance is one of the most powerful features of Java and other object-oriented programming languages. Inheritance lets you create a new class not from scratch, but based on an existing class. When you do this, the new or *child* class automatically has, or inherits, all the properties and methods of the original or *parent* class (sometimes called the *superclass*). Then, you can add new properties and methods to the child class, or you can create replacements for properties and methods from the parent class.

Let's look at a hypothetical example. Suppose you are writing a program to perform financial calculations. You have a class that performs just about all the needed calculations—car payments, mortgages, and so forth—but omits one thing that you want to include in your program, lease payments. Do you need to start from scratch and create a totally new class containing all the needed features? Not with inheritance you don't! Simply create a child class based on the existing class, and add a method to perform the desired lease calculations.

To create a child class, use the `extends` keyword in the class definition:

```
public class ChildClassName extends ParentClassName {
    ...
}
```

> **Caution**
>
> Remember, you cannot inherit from a class that was created using the `final` keyword. Final classes cannot serve as parent classes.

Consider an example demonstrating inheritance. Suppose you have created a class called `ListOfNumbers` that keeps track of certain statistics of a list of numbers: namely, the number of values in the list and the sum of all the values. The class also has a method that permits you to add a number to the list. Note that the individual values in the list are not saved, just the count and the sum. This class is called `ListOfNumbers`, and its code is presented in Listing B5.11.

LISTING B5.11 Lists.java. The class `ListOfNumbers` maintains the count and total of values added to it

```
1:  public class ListOfNumbers {
2:
3:      protected int icount;
4:      protected double itotal;
5:
6:      //Constructor.
7:      ListOfNumbers() {
8:          icount = 0;
9:          itotal = 0;
10:     }
11:
12:     public void Add(double x) {
13:         icount++;
14:         itotal += x;
15:     }
16:
17:     public int count() {
18:         return icount;
19:     }
20:
```

BD5

LISTING B5.11   continued

```
21:      public double total() {
22:            return itotal;
23:      }
24:  }
```

 Lines 3 and 4 declare two variables to hold the class's properties. Note that these are declared with the `protected` keyword so they are not visible outside the class except in subclasses. These properties are made available outside the class by methods. Lines 7 to 10 are the class constructor that initializes both of the class properties to `0`. Lines 12 to 15 define the `Add` method that is called to add a value to the list. Code in this method updates the `icount` and `itotal` properties with the new value. Lines 17 to 19 define a method called `count`, which does nothing more than return the value of the `icount` property. Lines 21 to 23 do the same thing for the `itotal` property.

Note

This class introduces the powerful technique of making a class's properties private or protected, and then accessing them via class methods. This technique has many uses, including (as in this case) making a property read-only. Because the class has a method to read the property, but none to set it, a program that uses the class can read the value of `icount` and `itotal`, but it cannot change these values directly.

After you have written and tested the class `ListOfNumbers`, you realize that you need a class that implements a similar list but has one more feature: the capability to obtain the average of all the values that have been added to the list. Rather than rewrite the source code for `ListOfNumbers`, you can simply create a subclass based on `ListOfNumbers`, adding the needed functionality. The source code for this class, called `BetterListOfNumbers`, is shown in Listing B5.12.

LISTING B5.12   Better.java. The class `BetterListOfNumbers` is based on the `ListOfNumbers` class

```
1:  class BetterListOfNumbers extends ListOfNumbers {
2:
3:      public double average() {
4:          if (icount > 0)
5:            return itotal / icount;
6:          else
7:            return 0;
8:      }
9:  }
```

ANALYSIS Line 1 opens the class definition. By using the extends keyword with the name of the class ListOfNumbers, this line indicates that BetterListOfNumbers will be a subclass of (that is, will inherit from) the class ListOfNumbers. Lines 3 to 8 define the one new method for this class, called average. Code in this method tests the value of the property icount. If this is greater than 0 (at least one value has been added to the list), the average is calculated and returned. If icount is 0 (no values have been added to the list), 0 is returned. Note that the variables icount and itotal are declared in ListOfNumbers but are available in BetterListOfNumbers because they were declared with the protected keyword.

The program NumberList, shown in Listing B5.13, demonstrates these two classes.

LISTING B5.13 NumberList.java. NumberList demonstrates the classes ListOfNumbers and BetterListOfNumbers

```
 1:  public class NumberList {
 2:
 3:    public static void main(String args[]) {
 4:
 5:      ListOfNumbers MyList = new ListOfNumbers();
 6:      BetterListOfNumbers MyBetterList = new BetterListOfNumbers();
 7:
 8:      MyList.Add(4);
 9:      MyList.Add(8);
10:      MyList.Add(9.6);
11:      MyBetterList.Add(4);
12:      MyBetterList.Add(8);
13:      MyBetterList.Add(9.6);
14:
15:      System.out.println("From class ListOfNumbers:");
16:      System.out.print("Total = ");
17:      System.out.println(MyList.total());
18:      System.out.print("Count = ");
19:      System.out.println(MyList.count());
20:      System.out.println("From class BetterListOfNumbers:");
21:      System.out.print("Total = ");
22:      System.out.println(MyBetterList.total());
23:      System.out.print("Count = ");
24:      System.out.println(MyBetterList.count());
25:      System.out.print("Average = ");
26:      System.out.println(MyBetterList.average());
27:    }
28:  }
```

BD5

OUTPUT
```
From class ListOfNumbers:
Total = 21.6
Count = 3
From class BetterListOfNumbers:
Total = 21.6
Count = 3
Average = 7.2
```

ANALYSIS   Line 5 declares a variable of type ListOfNumbers and also uses the new keyword to create a new instance of the class. Line 6 does the same for the class BetterListOfNumbers. Lines 8 to 10 use the add method to add three values to the ListOfNumbers object. Lines 11 to 13 add the same three values to the BetterListOfNumbers object. The remaining code displays the property values from the two objects. As you can see, the BetterListOfNumbers object has all the properties and methods of its parent class, as well as its own additional method, average.

Summary

Classes are at the heart of Java programming, and today you have learned the fundamentals of creating and using classes in a Java program. A class is an independent software component that can have properties (which hold data) and methods (which perform actions). You saw that Java classes you create will be placed in a package with related classes. You also learned that a Java file must use the import keyword in order to use classes that are not a part of its project. Finally, you saw how the very powerful, object-oriented technique of inheritance is used, permitting a new class to be created based on an existing class.

Q&A

Q How is a Java class that is a stand alone program different from a class that is not itself a program?

A To be a program, a class must include a main method. This is where execution starts when the program runs. Other classes do not have main.

Q What are the two main components that make up Java classes?

A One major component of Java classes is properties. A class property is used to store data. The other main component is the method. A method contains code that performs some action.

Q When you overload a method, the methods have the same name. How does Java tell overloaded methods apart?

A Although overloaded methods do have the same name, they must differ in the number and/or data type of their arguments. When a program calls an overloaded method, Java can tell which one to call based on the number and type of arguments passed.

Q How are Java methods different from functions in C and C++?

A There are no important differences between Java methods and C/C++ functions. However in Java a method must be inside a class.

Workshop

The Workshop provides quiz questions to help you solidify your understanding of the material covered, and exercises to provide you with experience in using what you've learned. Answers to the quiz are provided in Appendix F.

Quiz

1. What name should you assign to a class constructor method?
2. When and where would you use the `extends` keyword?
3. Do all Java methods return a value to the caller?
4. Can a class constructor be overloaded?
5. When is a constructor method called?
6. Can you use any Java class as the parent class for inheritance?
7. What Java keyword is used to prevent a class from being inherited?
8. Can an object be created from an abstract class?

BD5

BONUS WEEK

BONUS DAY **6**

More Java Techniques

Java is a full-featured and powerful language. You learned the most important basics of Java during the previous two days. There is a lot more to learn about Java; however, only some of the more important aspects of the language will be covered. Today you will learn

- How to use exceptions to deal with run-time errors
- The basics of reading and writing files
- How to use graphics with Java
- How to program Java applets

Working with Java Exceptions

No matter how skillful a programmer you are, you cannot guarantee that your program will never encounter an error condition. Various circumstances out of your control, such as user input, hardware failures, and network outages can cause errors. A properly written program handles errors gracefully, which means that it does not crash or cause data loss when an error occurs. Proper error handling will also prevent an application from bringing the entire system down when an error occurs.

In Java, an error is referred to as an *exception*. When an error occurs, the program is *throwing an exception*. Different errors cause different types of exceptions to be thrown. Java defines a variety of exception classes corresponding to just about any error situation you can imagine.

Java provides keywords specifically for working with exceptions. These are `try` and `catch`. In broad terms, Java error handling works like this:

1. Use the `try` keyword to identify blocks of code where particular exceptions are likely to occur.

2. Use the `catch` keyword to identify code that will be executed should an exception occur within a specific `try` block. A block of code identified with a `catch` keyword is an exception handler. There will be a separate `catch` block for each type of exception you expect.

3. If an error occurs in a `try` block, an exception of the type corresponding to the error is thrown or generated.

4. The exception generated in (3) is compared with the `catch` blocks following the try block. If a match is found, the code in that `catch` block is executed.

If an exception does not occur, the code in the catch blocks is not executed. The following shows an example of how try and catch statements are laid out:

```
try {
    // Code that may generate an exception
    // is placed here.
}
catch (ExceptionType1 e) {
    // Code to handle the error corresponding to
    // ExceptionType1 goes here.
}
catch (ExceptionType2 e) {
    // Code to handle the error corresponding to
    // ExceptionType2 goes here.
}
```

Some classes that are part of Java are designed to throw exceptions, and code that uses these classes must use `try` and `catch` appropriately, or the Java compiler will not accept the code. You are given a warning when this happens, and you can correct the code as needed. A powerful feature of Java exceptions is that they can be thrown "up" the hierarchy of methods. In other words, if method A calls method B, then method B can either deal with any exceptions it generates, or it can throw them "up" to method A for handling.

Java exceptions are a complex topic. You will see some details of how they are used in the section on file input/output.

Reading and Writing Files

Java has a complete set of classes for all types of file input and output. Covering all the details is well beyond the scope of this chapter, so I will limit coverage to basic text input and output.

Reading Text Files

Reading from text files is done with the FileReader and BufferedReader classes, part of the java.io package. When you create an instance of the FileReader class, you pass it the name (including path, if required) of the file you want to read:

```
FileReader inFile = new FileReader(filename);
```

Then you use the reference to the FileReader object to create an instance of Bufferedreader:

```
BufferedReader buff = new Bufferedreader(inFile);
```

Now you are ready to read text from the file using the readLine method. This method reads a single line of text and returns it as a type String. If the end of the file has been reached, it returns the special value null. By repeatedly calling readLine until it returns null, you can read the entire contents of a text file a line at a time.

Because file manipulations are full of possibilities for error, you must use Java's error handling to catch exceptions. You'll see how this is done in the sample program in Listing B6.1. Be sure to change the filename in line 6 as required.

LISTING B6.1 reading.c. Reading text from a file a line at a time

BD6

```
 1: import java.io.*;
 2: public class ReadTextFile {
 3:   public static void main(String args[]) {
 4:     String s;
 5:     try {
 6:       FileReader inFile = new FileReader("c:\\test.txt");
 7:       BufferedReader buff = new BufferedReader(inFile);
 8:       boolean endOfFile = false;
 9:       while (!endOfFile) {
10:         s = buff.readLine();
11:         if (s == null)
12:           endOfFile = true;
13:         else
```

LISTING B6.1   continued

```
14:              System.out.println(s);
15:          }
16:          buff.close();
17:      }
18:      catch (IOException e) {
19:          System.out.println("An error occurred: " + e.toString());
20:      }
21:  }
22: }
```

OUTPUT   (if the file does not exist):

```
An error occurred: java.io.FileNotFoundException: c:\test.txt
```

```
(The system cannot find the file specified)
```

OUTPUT   (if the file exists):

```
This is a test file.
It contains 3 lines of text.
This is the last line.
```

Note

> In today's lesson, we use file path names based on Windows and DOS. If you are using Unix or a different operating systems, you will want to use the appropriate file format. For example, unix machines tend to use a forward slash instead of a backslash.

ANALYSIS   Your output will depend on the contents of the file you select, of course. Lines 1 to 4 should be familiar to you by now and do not require any explanation. Line 5 starts a try block, marking the code where Java should look for exceptions. Line 6 creates a type FileReader object, associating it with the file c:\test.txt. Note the use of \\ to represent a single backslash in the filename, because \ is one of Java's escape characters. Line 7 creates a BufferedReader object associated with the FileReader object just created. Line 8 creates a type Boolean variable to serve as the end of file flag. Line 9 sets up a while loop that will repeat as long as endOfFile is false. Line 10 reads a line of text from the file. Lines 11 to 15 test the value of the input. If it is null, endOfFile is set to true, thus ending the loop. Otherwise the input text is displayed on the screen. Finally, line 16 closes the file. Line 17 marks the end of the try block.

Lines 18 to 20 are the catch block that is executed if the code in the try block throws an exception of type IOException. This code displays the error message shown in the first output above.

Writing Text Files

To write text to a file, use the `FileWriter` class. The syntax for creating a `FileWriter` object is

```
FileWriter outFile = new FileWriter(filename, append);
```

Filename is the name (including path, if required) of the file. The optional *append* applies only if *filename* already exists. Set *append* to `true` if the new data is to be appended to the file, `false` to overwrite the file. Then, create a `BufferedWriter` object based on the `FileWriter` object:

```
BufferedWriter buff = new BufferedWriter(outFile);
```

Now you can use the `BufferedWriter` object's `write` method to output text to the file:

```
buff.write(text);
```

Text is a type `String` containing the text to output. New lines are not started automatically. If you want the text to start on a new line, put the new line character (`\n`) at the start of the text. The program in Listing B6.2 demonstrates writing text to a file.

LISTING B6.2   writing.java. Writing text to a file

```
 1: import java.lang.System;import java.io.*;
 2:
 3: public class WriteTextFile {
 4:   public static void main(String args[]) {
 5:     String s;
 6:     BufferedReader kb;
 7:     boolean fileError = false;
 8:
 9:     kb = new BufferedReader(new InputStreamReader(System.in));
10:     try {
11:       FileWriter outFile = new FileWriter("c:\\output.txt");
12:       BufferedWriter buff = new BufferedWriter(outFile);
13:       System.out.println("Enter lines of text to put in the file.");
14:       System.out.println("Enter a blank line when done.");
15:       boolean done = false;
16:       while (!done) {
17:         s = kb.readLine();
18:         if (s.length() > 0 ) {
19:           s = s + "\n";
20:           buff.write(s);
21:         }
22:         else
23:           done = true;
24:       }
25:       buff.close();
```

BD6

LISTING B6.2   continued

```
26:      }
27:      catch (IOException e) {
28:          System.out.println("Error: " + e.toString());
29:          fileError = true;
30:      }
31:      if (!fileError)
32:          System.out.println("File successfully written.");
33:      else
34:          System.out.println("An error occurred - file not written.");
35:  }
36: }
```

OUTPUT   (if an error occurs, writing to a: with no diskette inserted):

```
Error: java.io.FileNotFoundException: a:\output.txt(The device is not
ready)
An error occurred - file not written.
```

OUTPUT   (if no error occurs):

```
Enter lines of text to put in the file.
Enter a blank line when done.
This is line 1.
This is line 2.
This is the last line.
File successfully written.
```

ANALYSIS   Lines 1 to 5 should need no explanation. Lines 6 and 9 set up a BufferedReader object to read lines of text from the keyboard. This technique was covered on Bonus Day 5. Line 10 opens the try block where exceptions may occur. Lines 11 and 12 set up the FileWriter and BufferedWriter objects that will be used to write text to the file. This code creates a file named output.txt in the root folder on drive C:. Be sure to change this name if you want to.

Lines 13 and 14 display instructions to the user. Line 15 sets up a boolean done flag. Line 16 starts a while loop that will execute as long as the done flag is false. Line 17 reads a line of text from the keyboard, and line 18 checks the length of the text. If the length is not 0 (some text was entered), a new line character is added to the end of the text (line 19), and the text is written to the file (line 20). If the length is 0, indicating a blank line was entered, the done flag is set to true which terminates the loop.

Lines 27 to 30 are the catch block for this code. If an exception is caught, the error message is displayed and the fileError variable is set to true. If no exception occurs, of course, this code is not executed at all.

Finally, lines 31 to 35 display one of two farewell messages depending on whether the fileError flag is true or false.

Doing Graphics and Windows

Any modern programming language must have support for graphics. Using Java for console applications, as we have been doing, is fine for a learner just starting out, but almost any real-world program is going to require windows, menus, dialog boxes, and other screen elements. The developers of Java approached this problem by creating the Abstract Window Toolkit (AWT). The AWT is perhaps the most complex part of Java, and entire books have been devoted just to the AWT. Only a brief look will be provided here. You can explore other sources of information if you want to go further.

 Note

There are other libraries within Java as well, libraries such as Swing. Covering all the libraries is beyond the scope of this book.

Creating Windowing Applications

Screen windows in a Java program are based on the Frame class. Any application that will use screen windows will have a declaration like this:

```
public class MyWindowingApplication extends Frame {
}
```

The Frame class provides most of the basic window functionality that you need, such as a title bar, a border, the capability to be resized, and so forth. You can add the additional elements that are specific to your program. To see how easy it is, the program in Listing B6.3 creates a window and displays a message in it.

LISTING B6.3   window.java. A Java program to display a message in a window

BD6

```
 1: import java.awt.*;
 2:
 3: public class AWT_Test1 extends Frame {
 4:
 5:    // Constructor.
 6:    public AWT_Test1(String title) {
 7:        super(title);
 8:        Label lbl = new Label("Hello from Java", Label.CENTER);
 9:        lbl.setFont(new Font("Helvetica", Font.PLAIN, 16));
10:        add("Center", lbl);
11:    }
```

LISTING B6.3   continued

```
12:
13:    public static void main(String args[]) {
14:        AWT_Test1 Test = new AWT_Test1("A Java Window");
15:        Test.resize(350,250);
16:        Test.show();
17:    }
18: }
```

OUTPUT   (see Figure B6.1)

FIGURE B6.1

The output of the program in Listing B6.3.

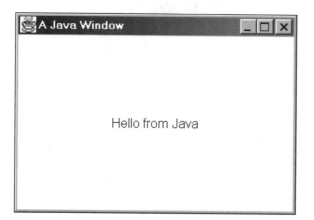

ANALYSIS   Line 1 of this program imports the classes in the AWT. Line 3 declares the class (program) AWT_Test1 to be a subclass of Frame. Lines 6 through 10 form the class constructor, which is declared to take one type String argument that is the window's title. Line 7 uses the super keyword to pass the title to the superclass constructor—in other words, the constructor method of the Frame class (see the sidebar for more on super). Other code in the constructor creates a new label object with the text "Hello from Java" (line 8), defines the font and font size for the label (line 9), and adds the label at the center of the window (line 10).

In the main method, line 14 creates a variable named Test and initializes it with a new instance of the class AWT_Test1. Creating a new instance calls the class constructor (lines 6 through 10), passing it the string "A Java window" which is then passed up to the superclass constructor, as described above. Line 15 sets the window size to 350×250 pixels. Finally, line 16 displays the window onscreen.

You can see that Java AWT graphics are completely object based, which is in perfect keeping with the object-oriented nature of Java itself.

Note   Within a subclass, you use the super keyword to call methods belonging to the superclass. Thus, the line super.SomeMethod(); calls the method named SomeMethod in the superclass. Using super by itself calls the superclass's constructor. The only place you can do this is on the first line in the subclass's constructor. Note that the superclass's constructor will automatically be called from the subclass's constructor, but by using super you can specify the arguments to be passed.

Drawing Shapes and Lines

The Java AWT has many classes that are used for creating both two-dimensional and three-dimensional shapes. The classes for drawing shapes are found in the java.awt.geom. package. Basically, there is a class for each type of shape: rectangle, line, ellipse, and so on. The general procedure for creating and displaying such shapes is as follows:

1. Create a window (Frame) as was explained in the previous demonstration program.

2. Create an instance of each type of shape you want to draw: lines, rectangles, ellipses, and so forth. Set the properties to provide the desired shape characteristics, such as location, size, and color.

3. Create a class that is based on the Canvas class. In this class create a paint method that contains the code to draw the shapes. The paint method is automatically called by the operating system when the screen display needs updating.

4. Create an instance of the class defined in step 3 and place it on the frame created in step 1.

You can see that the steps for creating the shapes are separate from the steps for displaying them on the screen. I realize that this is a rather complex topic. Because I cannot go into the details at length, it is best to use a demonstration program. The code in Listing B6.4 creates a window and draws several simple shapes on it.

BD6

LISTING B6.4   Drawing.java. Using the Java AWT to draw shapes onscreen

```
1:  import java.awt.*;
2:  import java.awt.geom.*;
3:
4:  public class DrawingTest extends Frame {
5:      Shape shapes[] = new Shape[4];
6:      public DrawingTest (String title) {
7:          super(title);
8:          setSize(500, 400);
```

LISTING B6.4   continued

```
 9:            drawShapes();
10:            add("Center", new MyCanvas());
11:        }
12:        public static void main(String args[]) {
13:            DrawingTest app = new DrawingTest("Drawing test");
14:            app.show();
15:        }
16:        void drawShapes () {
17:          shapes[0] = new Rectangle2D.Double(12.0,12.0, 98.0, 120.0);
18:          shapes[1] = new Ellipse2D.Double(150.0, 150.0,90.0,30.0);
19:          shapes[2] = new RoundRectangle2D.Double(200.0, 25,
20:                      235.0, 250.0, 50.0, 100.0);
21:          GeneralPath path = new GeneralPath(new Line2D.Double(100.0,
22:                      350.0, 150.0, 300.0));
23:          path.append(new Line2D.Double(150.0, 300.0,
24:                      200.0, 350.0), true);
25:          path.append(new Line2D.Double(200.0, 350.0,
26:                      250.0, 300.0), true);
27:          path.append(new Line2D.Double(250.0, 300.0,
28:                      300.0, 350.0), true);
29:          shapes[3] = path;
30:        }
31:
32:        class MyCanvas extends Canvas {
33:          public void paint(Graphics graphics) {
34:              Graphics2D gr = (Graphics2D) graphics;
35:              for (int i=0; i<4; i++)
36:                  gr.draw(shapes[i]);
37:          }
38:        }
39:    }
```

OUTPUT   See Figure B6.2.

ANALYSIS   Lines 1 and 2 import the required AWT classes. Line 4 defines the program as a subclass of Frame, required to display a screen window. Line 5 declares an array of type Shape that is an AWT class for drawing shapes.

Lines 6 to 11 make up the class constructor and are executed when the program is instantiated. Line 7 uses the super keyword to pass the program title to the Frame superclass. Line 8 sets the window size to be 500 pixels wide and 400 pixels high. Line 9 calls the drawShapes method (defined later) to create the shapes, and line 10 creates an instance of MyCanvas (also defined later) and adds it, centered, to the window.

FIGURE B6.2

Graphics output created by the program in Listing B6.4.

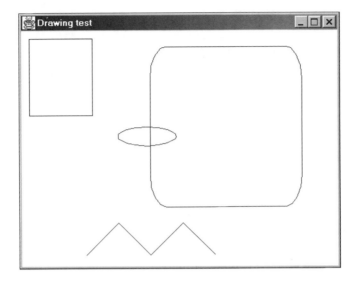

Lines 12 to 15 are the main method that is executed when the program is run. Code here is quite simple, because most of the work of the program is done elsewhere. Line 13 creates an instance of the program, which causes the constructor in lines 6 to 11 to be executed. Line 14 makes the program visible on the screen.

The drawShapes method in lines 16 to 30 does the job of creating the shapes. Lines 17 to 19 create three different shapes and assign them to elements 0, 1, and 2 of the shapes[] array that was declared earlier. Line 21 creates a GeneralPath object, which is used to combine several individual drawing elements into a single shape. In this statement, a line is added as the first element of the path. Then lines 23 to 28 add three more lines to the path, and line 29 assigns the resulting drawing object to element 3 of the shapes[] array. Note that this code only creates the shapes but does not display them.

Lines 22 to 38 define the class MyCanvas, which is a subclass of the AWT class Canvas. As the name implies, this class provides a surface on which you can draw. An instance of MyCanvas was placed in the program's window on line 10, so it is all ready for use. Lines 33 to 37 define the paint method (actually you are replacing the Canvas class's own paint method). This method is automatically called whenever the window needs refreshing, such as when the program first starts, or if it is restored after being minimized. The code in this method creates an instance of the Graphics2D class and then loops through the shapes[] array using the draw method to draw each shape.

BD6

Do	Don't
DO learn about the classes available in the AWT in order to program graphics effectively.	**DON'T** forget that creating a shape and actually drawing it are two different steps.

Using Buttons and Pop-Up Windows

Although drawing graphics shapes is often useful, more often a Java program must use predefined screen elements such as buttons, menus, text boxes, and the like. The AWT provides a full range of classes for all the screen elements that you see used in windowing applications. In addition, Java provides the capability to detect user events, such as when the user clicks on a menu command or a button. It then allows you to react appropriately. Later, a program will be presented that demonstrates a few of these capabilities, but first you need some more background information.

Layout Managers in Java

When you create a window that contains a variety of elements, such as buttons, labels, and text boxes, you, of course, want to arrange these elements within the window in a neat and attractive manner—one that makes sense with respect to the program's functionality. Some programming languages, such as Visual Basic, let the programmer precisely position window elements both by dragging them around during program design and by setting their locations and sizes numerically. The developers of Java did not choose this approach because Java programs are designed to run on such a wide variety of platforms with widely different display hardware. Some other approach to window layout was needed.

The approach that they developed uses a tool called a *layout manager*. When you create a window or any other container that can hold visual elements, you associate a layout manager with it. Then, as buttons and other elements are added to the container, the layout manager controls how they are arranged within the container. Because this happens when the program is running, information about the specific display hardware is available to the layout manager, and it can arrange the elements appropriately for the current display.

The Java AWT has five basic layout managers. The default, FlowLayout, arranges elements left-to-right, top-to-bottom. The other managers are called GridLayout, BorderLayout, CardLayout, and GridBagLayout. The layout managers are classes, as is just about everything else in Java, so you must create an instance of the one you want to use:

```
FlowLayout lm = new FlowLayout();
```

Next, the layout manager object is associated with the container object using the setLayout method, typically in the constructor:

```
setLayout(lm);
```

You'll see how this is done in detail in the next demonstration program.

Handling Events

To deal with user events, such as the user clicking a button or any other component, Java uses the action method. The syntax for this method is as follows:

```
public boolean action(Event evt, Object arg) {
    }
```

The first argument is an Event object that represents the event that occurred. The second argument depends on the identity of the component that receives the event, as explained in Table B6.1.

TABLE B6.1   Action method object arguments for different components

Component	Argument type	Argument data
Button	String	The button's label.
Check box	Boolean	Always true.
Radio button	Boolean	Always true.
Choice menu	String	The label of the selected item.
Text field	String	The field's text.

The action method is called every time a related user event occurs. Code in the method must make use of the arguments to determine what component received the action and then direct execution appropriately. The method should return true if code in the method has handled the event, or false if the event has not been handled and needs to be passed up the object hierarchy for handling elsewhere.

Working with Controls and Events

Now that you've read a little about controls and events, it is time to look at a demonstration. The next program uses buttons, a layout manager, pop-up windows, and user events. The program displays a main window that contains two buttons. Click one of the buttons to display a second pop-up window, then click the Close button in the pop-up window to close it. Finally, click the second button in the main window to end the program. Listing B6.5 is the PopUpWindow class, and Listing B6.6 presents the main program.

BD6

LISTING B6.5 The PopUpWindow class is defined in PopUpWindow.java

```
1:   import java.awt.*;
2:
3:   class PopUpWindow extends Frame {
4:
5:     FlowLayout lm = new FlowLayout(FlowLayout.CENTER);
6:
7:     public PopUpWindow(String title) {
8:         super(title);
9:         setSize(300, 100);
10:        setLayout(lm);
11:        Button b = new Button("Close");
12:        add(b);
13:     }
14:
15:     public boolean action(Event evt, Object arg) {
16:         hide();
17:         return true;
18:     }
19:   }
```

ANALYSIS Line 3 defines the class PopUpWindow as a subclass of Frame. Line 5 creates a FlowLayout object using the CENTER argument, which specifies that the layout manager must center components in the window as much as possible. Lines 7 to 13 form the class constructor that receives a type String argument specifying the window title. Line 8 uses the super keyword to pass the window title to the superclass. Line 8 defines the pop-up window's size, and line 10 specifies that the previously created layout manager should be used when arranging components. Lines 11 and 12 create a new Button object with the caption "Close", and add it to the window.

Lines 15 to 18 define an event handler method for the class. Because there is only one possible event for this class—the user clicking the Close button—there is no need to write code to determine which event occurred. This event handler simply calls the hide method to hide the window and then returns true indicating the event has been handled within the method.

LISTING B6.6 This program PopUpDemo.java demonstrates the PopUpWindow class and user events

```
1:   import java.lang.System.*;
2:   import java.awt.*;
3:
4:   public class PopUpWindowDemo extends Frame {
5:
6:     Button open, quit;
```

LISTING B6.6   continued

```
7:      Frame popup = new PopUpWindow("I am a popup window");
8:      FlowLayout lm = new FlowLayout(FlowLayout.CENTER);
9:
10:     public PopUpWindowDemo (String title) {
11:         super(title);
12:         setLayout(lm);
13:         setSize(400, 250);
14:         open = new Button("Show pop-up window");
15:         add(open);
16:         quit = new Button("Quit program");
17:         add(quit);
18:     }
19:     public static void main(String args[]) {
20:         PopUpWindowDemo app = new PopUpWindowDemo ("Pop-up window demo");
21:         app.show();
22:     }
23:
24:     public boolean action(Event evt, Object arg) {
25:         if (evt.target instanceof Button) {
26:             String label = (String)arg;
27:             if (label.equals("Show pop-up window")) {
28:                 if (!popup.isShowing())
29:                     popup.show();
30:             }
31:             else {
32:                 System.exit(0);
33:             }
34:         }
35:         return true;
36:     }
37: }
```

OUTPUT   (See Figure B6.3.)

BD6

FIGURE B6.3

The output of the pop-up window demonstration program.

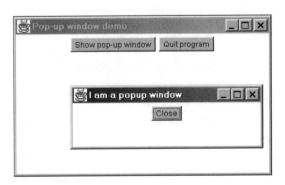

ANALYSIS The first 4 lines of the program should require no explanation. Line 6 creates two type Button variables that will be used to refer to the program's two buttons. Line 7 creates an instance of the PopUpWindow class, passing it the text to be displayed as the window title. When this line is executed the pop-up window is created, and its constructor is executed, but the window is not displayed yet. Line 8 creates a layout manager object to use when adding components to the main window.

Lines 10 to 18 are the constructor method for the program. Line 11 uses super to pass the window title to the superclass. Line 12 associates the layout manager (that was created in line 8) with this class's window. Line 13 sets the initial window size. Lines 14 to 17 create two buttons (labeled "Show pop-up window" and "Quit program") and add them to the window.

Lines 19 to 22 are the program's main method. This method is made up of only two lines of code. Line 20 creates an instance of the program, and line 21 makes it visible on the screen.

Lines 24 to 36 are the action method for this program. First, line 25 checks to see if whatever event happened occurred to a Button object. If so, line 26 retrieves the label on the button that was clicked and puts it in the variable label. If the label indicates that the "Show pop-up window" button was clicked, the code in line 28 checks whether the pop-up window is already displayed. If so, it does nothing. If not, line 29 displays the pop-up window. If the Quit button was clicked, line 35 exits the program.

You can see that in a relatively small program, Java lets you implement fairly sophisticated programming including push buttons, windows, and event detection. There is a lot more to the Java AWT, and I hope this brief sampling has whetted your appetite for more!

Programming Java Applets

So far, the discussion of Java to programming has focused on stand-alone applications. Another use of Java, a very popular use in fact, is to program *applets*, small programs that are designed to be deployed on the World Wide Web and run in a Web browser such as Netscape Navigator or Microsoft Internet Explorer. A Java applet is designed to be part of a Web page. When you "surf" to a Web site that uses Java applets, the applets simply appear in the browser as part of the page. Applets can be used for a wide variety of tasks such as displaying animations, performing calculations, or just about anything the programmer can think up.

Differences Between Applets and Applications

For the most part, programming a Java applet is no different from programming a stand-alone application. In fact, it is possible to write a Java program that is both an application and an applet. The differences between applet and application program can be summed up as follows:

- For security reasons, applets cannot access files. It is obvious that you would not want a Web page snooping around on your hard disk, uploading your personal financial information, or deleting essential system files.

- An applet does not need a main method. Because the execution of an applet is controlled by the browser it is running in, there is no need for main. If a program is designed to be both applet and application, it will have a main, but this method will be ignored when the program is running as an applet.

- Applet programming is a little simpler than application programming because the browser that the applet runs in takes care of some details, such as sizing and position the program window—things that a stand-alone application has to do for itself.

- Console input/output is meaningless for an applet.

Understanding the Structure of an Applet

To get started with applets, look at Listing B6.7. This is not a real applet, but rather the bare skeleton of an applet. The analysis that follows explains the various parts.

LISTING **B6.7** applet.java. The skeleton of a Java applet

```
 1:  import java.applet.Applet;
 2:
 3:  public class AppletTest extends Applet {
 4:
 5:      public void init() {}
 6:
 7:      public void start() {}
 8:
 9:      public void stop() {}
10:
11:      public void destroy() {}
12:
13:      public void paint() {}
14:  }
```

BD6

ANALYSIS   Line 1: All applets must import java.applet.Applet in addition to any other classes they need.

Line 3: Applets must be declared as subclasses of the Java class `Applet`. This class contains most of the "behind-the-scenes" machinery that makes applets work.

Line 5: The `init` method is the first thing called when an applet is run. It is an applet's equivalent to a constructor method.

Line 7: The `start` method is called immediately after the `init` method. In many ways, it is equivalent to the `main` method in stand-alone applications.

Line 9: The `stop` method is called when the applet is being terminated. It is always called before the `destroy` method.

Line 11: The `destroy` method is the last method called when the applet is shutting down.

Line 13: The `paint` method is called when the applet's screen display requires updating. You put the code that draws the applet's visual interface here.

One important thing to note about these methods is that you never call them directly yourself. They are automatically called, when and if needed, by the browser in which the applet is running. You put code in these methods, as required by the applet, to perform initialization steps and to clean up upon termination. Some simpler applets will use only one or two of these methods; more complex applets might use all of them.

Putting an Applet on a Web Page

Most modern Web browsers support Java, but there are still some older browsers in use that do not. Also, even with a browser that does support Java applets, this support might be turned off for various reasons. Fortunately, a browser that does not have Java support will simply ignore an applet included in a Web page.

To include an applet on a Web page you use the `<APPLET>` tag in the page's HTML. The syntax is

```
<APPLET Name = AppletClassName
Code = FullPathToApplet
WIDTH = w
HEIGHT = h
ALT=text>
</APPLET>
```

AppletClassName is the name of the class file (appletname.class) created when you compile the applet. *FullPathToApplet* is the full path to the .class file. The *w* and *h* values specify the size of the applet window, in pixels. *Text* is text that will be displayed only if the browser does not support Java. This is optional, but a good idea. A Web page can have multiple applet on it, each defined by its own `<APPLET>` tag. Here is an example of a real `<APPLET>` tag:

```
<applet
   name="AppletTest"
   code="AppletTest" codebase="file:/C:/WINDOWS/jws/AppletTest"
   width="200"
   height="100"
   align="Top"
   alt="If you had a java-enabled browser, you would see an applet here."
>
</applet>
```

Using an Applet

Applets are wonderfully fascinating programming topics, and you'll find many books on Java that devote themselves entirely to applets. To close off this third day of Java programming, here's a sample Java applet that shows you the fundamentals. This program displays text in the browser window, and when the user clicks the text the color changes. Listing B6.8 shows the HTML code used to display this applet. Listing B6.9 shows the applet code itself. To load this applet, you must edit the <APPLET> tag so it correctly points to the folder where you have placed AppletTest.class.

LISTING B6.8   AppletTest.html. The HTML code to display the AppletTest applet

```
<html>
<body>
Here is the applet:
<applet
   name="AppletTest"
   code="AppletTest" codebase="file:/C:/WINDOWS/jws/AppletTest"
   width="400"
   height="100"
   align="Top"
   alt="If you had a java-enabled browser, you would see an applet here."
>
</applet>
</body>
</html>
```

BD6

LISTING B6.9   AppletTest.java. A simple Java applet

```
1:   import java.applet.Applet;
2:   import java.awt.*;
3:
4:   public class AppletTest extends Applet {
5:     Font f = new Font("TimesRoman", Font.BOLD, 36);
6:     boolean useRed = true;
7:
```

LISTING B6.9 continued

```
 8:    public void paint(Graphics screen) {
 9:        screen.setFont(f);
10:        if (useRed)
11:            screen.setColor(Color.red);
12:        else
13:            screen.setColor(Color.blue);
14:        screen.drawString("This is an applet!", 5, 30);
15:    }
16:
17:    public boolean mouseDown(Event evt, int x, int y) {
18:        useRed = !useRed;
19:        repaint();
20:        return true;
21:    }
22: }
```

OUTPUT (See Figure B6.4.)

FIGURE B6.4

The AppletTest applet running in Microsoft Internet Explorer.

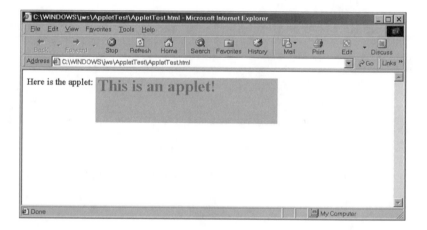

ANALYSIS Lines 1 and 2 import the required classes, which in this case are the Applet class and the AWT classes. Line 4 defines the application as a subclass of Applet. Line 5 creates a new Font object with Times Roman font in 36 point boldface. Line 6 sets up a type Boolean which will control the color used for the text display.

Lines 8 through 15 are the paint method, which is automatically called by the Applet superclass as needed. Line 9 specifies that the font created in line 5 will be used for the text display. Line 10 tests the value of the useRed flag. If it is true, in line 11, the screen's color is set to red. If it is false, line 13 sets the screen's color to blue. Finally line 14 uses the drawstring method to display the text.

Lines 17 through 20 define a method that will respond to mouse events—in this case, specifically to the mouse being clicked over the applet. The code in this method simply toggles the useRed flag from true to false or from false to true, and then it calls the repaint method. Repaint is a method of the Applet superclass. One of the things it does is call theAppletTest object's paint method to redisplay the text in the new color.

> **Caution**
>
> <APPLET> is one of many tags used by HTML, or hypertext markup language, to create Web pages. You'll need to learn a bit about HTML to effectively create Web pages, although some Web design tools do most of the work of generating tags for you.

Summary

Today you wrapped up your introduction to Java. It differs from C and C++ in that it requires your programs to be object-oriented. This makes it a little trickier to learn. After you get started, however, you'll see that Java really makes a lot of programming tasks easier. It also reduces the effort required for debugging and maintaining the program down the road. In addition, with applets, your Java expertise can be extended to the Web. In tomorrow's final bonus day, you'll learn about one of the newest programming languages, C#.

Q&A

Q How does Java handle runtime errors?

A In Java, errors are called exceptions. Any section of code that may generate an exception should be enclosed in a try block. Every try block must be accompanied by one or more catch blocks to deal with the exceptions that may have occurred (been thrown) in that code.

Q Do you have to use exception handling in your Java programs?

A It depends. Some Java classes are defined to require exception handling when the classes are used, for example the classes that relate to file input and output (where the possibilities of exceptions occurring are high). In other situations, exception handling is not absolutely required, but as with any programming language it's always a good idea to include code to permit your programs to deal with runtime errors gracefully.

BD6

Q When creating a window with components in Java, how do you control the placement of the various window elements?

A You do not control the placement of elements directly. Rather you assign a layout manager to the window, and the layout manager arranges the elements according to its rules.

Q When you create a graphical element, such as a line or a rectangle, does it automatically appear on the screen?

A No. Creating a drawing object is totally separate from displaying it on the screen. After creating the object, you must use one of the AWT's drawing methods to actually display the element.

Q What are the main differences between a Java applet and an application?

A An applet has no `main` method; rather execution begins with the `init` and `start` methods. Also, an applet cannot read or write disk files.

Workshop

The Workshop provides quiz questions to help you solidify your understanding of the material covered, and exercises to provide you with experience in using what you've learned. Answers to the quiz are provided in Appendix F.

Quiz

1. Does every `try` block need an accompanying `catch` block?

2. Does the `BufferedWriter` object's `write` method automatically start a new line when writing text to a file?

3. What class are all Java applets based on?

4. When creating a window-based application, what method do you call to make the program visible on the screen?

5. How does a Java application respond to user events?

6. Can a Java applet have a `main` method?

7. What two methods are called, and in what order, when an applet begins execution?

8. What is the very last method called when an applet terminates?

BONUS WEEK

BONUS DAY 7

The C# Programming Language

You've learned C, you took a quick look at C++, and then you explored a bit of Java. Today is a brief introduction to yet another object oriented language that gets part of its roots from C and C++. Today you will learn about C# (pronounced "*See-Sharp*"). You will also

- Learn why C# is a great programming language to use
- Discover the steps in the Program Development Cycle
- Understand how to write, compile, and run your first C# program
- Explore error messages generated by the compiler and linker
- Review the types of applications that can be created with C#

What Is C#?

Released to the public in June 2000, C# has not been around for very long. C# is a new language created by Microsoft and standardized by ECMA, a standards organization. This new language was created by a team of people at

Microsoft led by Anders Hejlsberg . Interestingly, Hejlsberg is a Microsoft Distinguished Engineer who has created other products and languages, including Borland Turbo C++ and Borland Delphi. With C#, the focus was on taking what was right about existing languages and adding improvements to make something better.

 Note   The C# ECMA standards will be known as ECMA-334.

C# is a powerful and flexible programming language. Like all programming languages, it can be used to create a variety of applications. Your potential with C# is limited only by your imagination. The language does not place constraints on what you can do. C# has already been used for projects as diverse as dynamic Web sites, development tools, and even compilers.

Like C++ and Java, C# was created as an object-oriented programming (OOP) language. Other programming languages include object-oriented features, but very few are fully object-oriented. Even more than being object-oriented, C# was created with the idea of creating components and working on the Web. Later in today's lesson you will understand how C# compares to some of these other programming languages. You'll also learn what types of applications can be created.

Why C#?

Many people believed that there was no need for a new programming language. Java, C++, Perl, Microsoft Visual Basic, and other existing languages were believed to offer all the functionality needed.

Like Java, C# is a language derived from C and C++, but it was created from the ground up. Microsoft started with what worked in C and C++ and included new features that would make these languages easier to use. Many of these features are very similar to what can be found in Java. Ultimately, Microsoft had a number of objectives when building the language. These objectives can be summarized in the claims made about C#:

- C# is simple.
- C# is modern.
- C# is object-oriented.

In addition to these reasons, there are others for using C#:

- C# is powerful and flexible.
- C# is a language of few words.

- C# is modular.
- C# will be popular.

C# Is Simple

C# removes some of the complexities and pitfalls of languages such as C++, including the removal of macros, templates, multiple inheritance, and virtual base classes. These are all areas that cause either confusion or potential problems for C++ developers. If you are learning C# as your first language, rest assured—these are topics you won't have to spend time learning!

C# is simple for many to learn because it is based on C and C++. If you are familiar with C and C++—or even Java—you will find C# very familiar in many aspects. Statements, expressions, operators, and other functions are taken directly from C and C++, but improvements make the language simpler. Some of the improvements include eliminating redundancies. Other areas of improvement include additional syntax changes. For example, C++ has three operators for working with members: ::, ., and ->. Knowing when to use each of these three symbols can be very confusing in C++. In C#, these are all replaced with a single symbol—the "dot" operator. For newer programmers, this and many other features eliminate a lot of confusion.

C# Is Modern

What makes a modern language? Features such as exception handling, garbage collection, extensible data types, and code security are features that are expected in a modern language. C# contains all of these.

Note

> As you learned on day 9, pointers are an integral part of C. They are also the most confusing part of languages like C and C++. C# removes much of the complexity and trouble caused by pointers. In C#, there are automatic features that take care of working with data types and pointers. A feature called garbage collection occurs automatically. Garbage collection makes sure that pointers and memory are freed when they are no longer needed.

C# Is Object-Oriented

The keys to an object-oriented language are encapsulation, inheritance, and polymorphism. You learned about these concepts when covering C++ and Java. C# supports all of these as well. Remember, *encapsulation* is the placing of functionality into a single package. *Inheritance* is a structured way of extending existing code and functionality into new programs and packages. *Polymorphism* is the capability of adapting to what needs to be done.

BD7

C# Is Powerful and Flexible

As mentioned before, with C# you are limited only by your imagination. The language places no constraints on what can be done. C# can be used for projects as diverse as creating word processors, graphics, spreadsheets, and even compilers for other languages.

C# makes it easy to create classes, objects, and other components that can be packaged and reused easily. Additionally, it has been created with the Internet in mind. Additionally, the use of attributes makes it possible to expand the functionality of the language without the need to change the language.

C# Is a Language of Few Words

C# is a language that uses a limited number of words. C# contains only a handful of keywords, which serve as the base on which the language's functionality is built. Table B7.1 lists the C# keywords. You'll see that many of these keywords are the same as those used in C. There are, however, a number of additional keywords within C#.

TABLE B7.1 The C# Keywords

abstract	as	base	bool	break
byte	case	catch	char	checked
class	const	continue	decimal	default
delegate	do	double	else	enum
event	explicit	extern	false	finally
fixed	float	for	foreach	
goto	if	implicit	in	int
interface	internal	is	lock	long
namespace	new	null	object	operator
out	override	params	private	protected
public	readonly	ref	return	sbyte
sealed		short	sizeof	stackalloc
static	string	struct	switch	this
throw	true	try	typeof	uint
ulong	unchecked	unsafe	ushort	using
virtual	void	while		

Note There are a few other reserved words used in C# programs. While not keywords, they should be treated as though they were. Specifically, get, set, and value.

C# Is Modular

Like Java, C# code is written in chunks called classes, which contain routines called *member methods*. These classes and methods can be reused in other applications or programs. By passing pieces of information to the classes and methods, you can create useful, reusable code.

C# Will Be Popular

C# is one of the newest programming languages. At the time this book was written, C# was gaining popularity; however, its future was still unknown. It is a good bet that C# will become a very popular language for a number of reasons. One of the key reasons is Microsoft and the promises of .NET.

Microsoft wants C# to be popular. Although a company cannot make a product be popular, it can help. Not long ago, Microsoft suffered the abysmal failure of the Microsoft Bob operating system. Although Microsoft wanted Bob to be popular, it failed.

C# stands a better chance of success than Microsoft Bob. I don't know whether people at Microsoft actually used Bob in their daily jobs. C#, however, *is* being used by Microsoft. Many of its products have already had portions rewritten in C#. By using it, Microsoft helps validate the capabilities of C# to meet the needs of programmers.

Microsoft .NET is another reason why C# stands a chance to succeed. .NET is a change in the way the creation and implementation of applications is done. Although virtually any programming language can be used with .NET, C# is proving to be the language of choice.

C# will also be popular for all the features mentioned earlier: simplicity, object-orientation, modularity, flexibility, and conciseness.

C# Versus Other Programming Languages

BD7

Perhaps you're wondering about the differences between C# and languages like C++ and Java. You might also be wondering whether C# is worth learning.

Note

> The top questions on Internet discussion forums related to .NET are
> - What is the difference between Java and C#?
> - Isn't C# just a Java clone?
> - What is the difference between C# and C++?
> - Which should I learn, Visual Basic.NET or C#?

Microsoft says that C# brings the power of C++ with the ease of Visual Basic. C# does bring a lot of power, but is it as easy as Visual Basic? It might not be as easy as Visual Basic 6, but it is as easy as Visual Basic .NET (version 7), which was rewritten from the ground up. The end result is that Visual Basic is really no easier than programming C#. In fact, you can actually write many programs with less code using C#.

Although C# removes some of the features of C++ that cause programmers a lot of grief, no power or functionality was really lost. Some of the programming errors that are easy to create in C++ can be totally avoided in C#. This can save you hours or even days in finishing your programs.

Types of C# Programs

It is worth knowing what types of applications you can create with C#. There are a number of types you can build:

- **Console applications.** Console applications run from the command line. Throughout this book you will create console applications, which are primarily character- or text-based and therefore remain relatively simple to understand.
- **Windows applications.** You can also create Windows applications that take advantage of the graphical user interface (GUI) provided by Microsoft Windows.
- **Web Services.** Web services are routines that can be called across the Web.
- **Web Form / ASP.NET applications.** ASP.NET applications are executed on a Web server and generate dynamic Web pages.

In addition to these types of applications, C# can be used to do a lot of other things, including creating libraries, creating controls, and more.

Creating a C# Program

There are a few editors available for C#. Microsoft has added C# capabilities to its Visual Studio product which includes Visual C# .NET. This is the most predominant editor available. If you don't have Visual Studio .NET, however, you can still do C# programming.

There are also other editors available for C#. Like Visual Studio .NET, many of these enable you to do all the steps of the development cycle without leaving the editor. More importantly, most of these color-code the text you enter. This makes it much easier to find possible mistakes. Many editors will even help you by given you information on what you need to enter and giving you a robust help system.

If you don't have a C# editor, don't fret. Most computer systems include a program that can be used as an editor. If you're using Microsoft Windows, you can use either Notepad or WordPad as your editor.

As you will learn later, unlike C, C++, and Java, a C# compiler is available free of charge. Because of this, you can start programming C# programs without spending any money!

Naming Your Source Files

Although not explicitly stated, you have seen that C programs tend to have a .c extension. C++ programs generally have a .cpp extension. Java programs have a .java extension. For your C# programs, you'll want to include a .cs extension. Although you could give your source file any name and extension, .cs is recognized as the appropriate extension to use.

Executing a C# Program

It is important to understand a little bit about how a C# program executes. C# programs are different from programs you could create with other programming languages.

C# programs are created to run on the Common Language Runtime (CLR). This means that if you create a C# executable program and try to run it on a machine that doesn't have the CLR or a compatible runtime, it won't execute.

The benefit of creating programs for a runtime environment is portability. In languages such as C and C++, if you wanted to create a program that could run on different platforms or operating systems, you had to compile different executable programs. For example, if you wrote a C application and you wanted to run it on a Linux machine and a Windows machine, you would have to create two executable programs—one on a Linux machine and one on a Windows machine. With C#, you create only one executable program, and it runs on either machine.

BD7

NEW TERM If you want your program to execute as fast as possible, you want to create a true executable. With programs such as C and C++, the compiler creates a file that can be executed with no further effort.

With C#, you use a compiler that does not produce machine language. Instead it produces an Intermediate Language (IL) file. Because this isn't directly executable by the computer, you need something more to happen to translate or further compile the program for the computer. The CLR or a compatible C# runtime does this final compile just as it is needed.

One of the first things the CLR does with an IL file is a final compile of the program. In this process, the CLR converts the code from the portable, IL code to a language (machine language) that the computer can understand and run. The CLR actually compiles only the parts of the program that are being used. This saves time. Additionally, after a portion of your IL file has been given a true compile on a machine, it never needs to be compiled again, because the final compiled portion of the program is saved and used the next time that portion of the program is executed.

Note

> Because the runtime needs to compile the IL file, it takes a little more time to run a program the first time than it does to run a fully compiled language such as C++. After the first time a program is completely executed, the time difference disappears because the fully compiled version will be used from that point. You also have the ability to have this compilation done when you install the program.

 New Term The last minute compiling of a C# program is called Just In Time compiling or *jitting*.

Compiling C# Source Code

To create the IL file, you use the C# compiler. You typically use the `csc` command to run the compiler, followed by the name of the source file. For example, to compile a source file called radius.cs, you type the following at the command line:

```
csc radius.cs
```

If you're using a graphical development environment, compiling is even simpler. In most graphical environments, you can compile a program by selecting the compile icon or selecting the appropriate option from the menu. After the code is compiled, selecting the run icon or selecting the appropriate option from the menus executes the program. You should check your compiler's manuals for specifics on compiling and running a program.

NEW TERM After you compile, you have an IL file. If you look at a list of the files in the directory or folder in which you compiled, you should find a new file that has the same name as your source file, but with an .exe (rather than a .cs) extension. The file with the .exe extension is your "compiled" program (called an *assembly*). This program is ready to run on the CLR. The assembly file contains all the information that the common runtime needs to know to execute the program.

After your program is a compiled IL file, you can run it by entering its name at the command-line prompt or just as you would run any other program. The program will not run, however, unless you have the Microsoft .NET Runtime installed. If you don't have the runtime installed you will get errors.

The C# Compiler and the .NET Runtime

Before compiling your C# programs, you'll need to get a copy of a C# compiler. You also learned in the previous section that you need a .NET Runtime. The Microsoft .NET Framework includes a runtime as well as a C# compiler. At the time of this book's writing, the .NET Framework could be downloaded free from the Microsoft Web site.

Your First C# Program

Listing B7.1 illustrates a simple C# program. This demonstration uses a program named hello.cs, which does nothing more than display the words Hello, World! On the screen. This program is the traditional program used to introduce people to programming. It is also a good one for you to use to learn.

LISTING 1.1 hello.cs. A simple C# program

```
1:  class Hello
2:  {
3:      public static void Main()
4:      {
5:          System.Console.WriteLine("Hello, World!");
6:      }
7:  }
```

As you can see in line 1, C# programs are enclosed in a class. This keeps in line with being an object-oriented language. You can also see that like C and the other languages, a Main() method is used as the primary entry point to a program. One difference from C is the fact that the Main() method starts with a capital letter instead of a lower case letter. Like C, C# is case-sensitive, so this is an important distinction.

BD7

Displaying Basic Information

It is beyond the scope of a single day's lessons to teach you a lot about C#. To give you a small look at C#, two methods will be presented. These are methods for displaying information. Two routines for displaying basic information are

- `System.Console.WriteLine()`
- `System.Console.Write()`

These routines print information to the screen. Both print information in the same manner, with only one small difference. The `WriteLine()` routine writes information to a new line. This is similar to the `puts()` function in C. The `Write()` routine does not start a new line when information is written. This is similar to the `printf()` function in C.

The information you want displayed on the screen is written between the parentheses. If you are printing text, you include the text between the parentheses and within double quotes. For example, the following prints the text `"Hello World"`:

```
System.Console.WriteLine("Hello World");
```

This prints `Hello World` on the screen. The following examples illustrate other text being printed:

```
System.Console.WriteLine("This is a line of text");
System.Console.WriteLine("This is a second line of text");
```

If you execute these consecutively, you see the following displayed:

```
This is a line of text
This is a second line of text
```

Now consider the following two lines. If these execute consecutively, what do you see printed?

```
System.Console.WriteLine("Hello ");
System.Console.WriteLine("World!");
```

If you guessed that these would print

```
Hello World!
```

you are not correct! Those lines print the following:

```
Hello
World!
```

Notice that each word is on a separate line. If you execute the two lines using the `Write()` routine instead, you get the results you want:

```
Hello World!
```

As you can see, the difference between the two routines is that `WriteLine()` automatically goes to a new line after the text is displayed, whereas `Write()` does not. Listing B7.3 shows the two routines in action.

LISTING B7.3   display.cs—Using `WriteLine()` and `Write()`

```
 1:  // display.cs - printing with WriteLine and Write
 2:  // — — — — — — — — — — — — — — — — — — — — — — — —·
 3:
 4:  class display
 5:  {
 6:      public static void Main()
 7:      {
 8:          System.Console.WriteLine("First WriteLine Line");
 9:          System.Console.WriteLine("Second WriteLine Line");
10:
11:          System.Console.Write("First Write Line");
12:          System.Console.Write("Second Write Line");
13:
14:          // Passing parameters
15:          System.Console.WriteLine("\nWriteLine: Parameter = {0}", 123 );
16:
17:          System.Console.Write("Write: Parameters = {0} and {1}", 456, 789);
18:      }
19:  }
```

OUTPUT
```
First WriteLine Line
Second WriteLine Line
First Write LineSecond Write Line
WriteLine: Parameter = 123
Write: Parameters = 456 and 789
```

ANALYSIS   This listing uses the `System.Console.WriteLine()` routine on lines 8 and 9 to print two pieces of text. You can see from the output that each of these print on a separate line. Lines 11 and 12 show the `System.Console.Write()` routine. These two lines print on the same line. There is not a return line feed after printing. Lines 15 and 17 show each of these routines with the use of a parameter. You should notice that the parameters are not implemented the same as in C. With C and `printf()` you used a percentage sign to indicate a parameter. In C# you include a parameter value between braces. You should also notice that the parameters in C# are numbered. Parameters are not simply applied in order like in C and `printf()`. Rather, the first parameter is applied to `{0}`, the second to `{1}`.

BD7

Note Like in C programming, counting in C# starts with zero, not one.

Consider another example of printing in C#:

```
System.Console.Write("Value 1 is {0} and value 2 is {1}", 123, "Brad");
```

This prints

```
Value 1 is 123 and value 2 is Brad
```

You should notice that unlike C, you also don't need to worry about what types the parameters are. Although a number and a string were both printed, the parameters were identified in the same way. The language takes care of the rest. Like in C, there are modifiers that can be used if you want to format or change the way data is presented.

Note There is another important thing to know about `WriteLine()` and `Write()`. These methods are a part of the .NET Framework. The .NET Framework is used with any of the .NET programming languages. This includes Visual Basic .NET.

C# and the Web

In addition to standard applications, you can also create Web applications using C#. It is beyond the scope of this single day's lesson to show you everything about C#; however, Listing B7.4 illustrates the use of C# in a Web application. In this listing, C# is being used with ASP.NET to create a simple "hello world" Web application. To run this application, you will need a server that supports ASP.NET.

LISTING B7.4 hello.aspx. A "hello world" ASP.NET application using C#

```
 1:  <script runat="server" language="C#">
 2:     void doClick(object sender, EventArgs e) {
 3:         MyLabel.Text = "Hello, world! (C# ASP.NET in action!)";
 4:     }
 5:  </script>
 6:  <html>
 7:     <head><title>Hello World C# ASP.NET App</title></head>
 8:     <body>
 9:         <P>C# Web application...</P>
10:         <form runat="server">
```

LISTING B7.4 continued

```
11:             <asp:button runat="server" text="Say Hello"
12:                onclick="doClick" />
13:             <p>
14:             <asp:label runat="server" text="" id="MyLabel" />
15:          </form>
16:       </body>
17:    </html>
```

OUTPUT Figure B7.1 shows the hello.aspx program when the web page is first displayed. When you click the button, you see the result shown in Figure B7.2.

FIGURE B7.1

The initial output of the Hello.aspx program.

FIGURE B7.2

The output after selecting the button and running the C# code.

ANALYSIS This is a relatively short program with only a small amount of functionality. This is also a Web program that requires a server that supports ASP.NET. This would include Microsoft's Internet Information Server.

When you first run this program, you get a Web page as shown in Figure B7.1. If you look at the code in lines 6 to 17, you'll see what looks like standard HTML to display a

BD7

form. Lines 10, 11, and 14 contain an extra ASP.NET command—runat="server".
Otherwise, this is straight HTML. C# is used in lines 1 to 4 within an ASP.NET script.
This script is called when the button on the form is clicked. As you can see, the script
identifies the language as C# in line 1. In line 3 all the work is done. A line of text is
assigned to the label on the form.

This is not complex C# code; however, it could be. Instead of simply assigning a value to
a label, you could do any C# programming you need to do for your program. The idea
here was to show how simple it is to start using C# with a Web application.

Summary

At the beginning of today's lesson you learned what C# has to offer, including its power,
its flexibility, and its object orientation. You also learned that C# is considered simple
and modern.

Today you explored the various steps involved in writing a C# program. You also took a
quick look at a simple C# application. You followed this by getting a closer look at how
C# can display information with Write() and WriteLine(). Overall you should have
noticed that a lot of the C# syntax comes from C.

The last section of today's lesson took you to the Web. You saw a simple "hello world"
application that used C# with ASP.NET.

Q&A

Q If I wanted to learn C#, what would be a good book?

A If you have enjoyed this book, you should also enjoy *Sams Teach Yourself C# in 21
Days* (ISBN 0-672-32071-1).

Q Will a C# program run on any machine?

A No. A C# program will run only on machines that have the Common Language
Runtime (CLR) installed. If you copy the executable program to a machine that
does not contain the CLR, you get an error. On versions of Windows without the
CLR, you usually are told that a DLL file is missing.

Q If I want to give people a program I wrote, which files do I need to give them?

A One of the nice things about C# is that it is a compiled language. This means that
after the source code is compiled, you have an executable program. If you want to
give the hello program to all your friends with computers, you can. You give them
the executable program, hello.exe. They don't need the source file, hello.cs, and
they don't need to own a C# compiler. They do need to use a computer system that
has a C# runtime, such as the Common Language Runtime from Microsoft.

Q Where can I get a C# compiler?

A A C# compiler is a part of the Microsoft .NET Framework. You can download the framework from Microsoft's Web site (www.Microsoft.com).

Workshop

The Workshop provides quiz questions to help you solidify your understanding of the material covered and exercises to provide you with experience in using what you've learned. Answers to the quiz are provided in Appendix F.

Quiz

1. Give three reasons why C# is a great choice of programming language.

2. What do IL and CLR stand for?

3. What are the steps in the Program Development Cycle?

4. What command do you need to enter to compile a program called my_prog.cs with your compiler?

5. What extension should you use for your C# source files?

6. Is filename.txt a valid name for a C# source file?

7. If you execute a program that you have compiled and it doesn't work as you expected, what should you do?

8. What is machine language?

9. What two statements can be used to write information in C# programs?

Exercises

1. Use your text editor to look at the EXE file created by Listing B7.1. Does the EXE file look like the source file? (Don't save this file when you exit the editor.)

2. Enter and compile the following program. What does this program do?

```
1:  class AClass
2:  {
3:      static void Main()
4:      {
5:          int x,y;
6:          for ( x = 0; x < 10; x++, System.Console.Write( "\n" ) )
7:              for ( y = 0; y < 10; y++ )
8:                  System.Console.Write( "X" );
9:      }
10: }
```

BD7

WEEK 4

Bonus Week in Review

BD1

BD2

BD3

BD4

BD5

BD6

BD7

You've now finished this book! With the completion of the bonus week you have actually gone beyond teaching yourself C and have also learned about C++, Java, and C#.

More important than having learned about C++, Java and C#, you have learned about object-oriented programming. On Bonus Day 1, you saw that the promise of an OOP is the capability to reuse code. You also learned that an object-oriented programming language is characterized by polymorphism, encapsulation, and inheritance.

On the second and third bonus days, you learned about C++. You learned that a class is the basic construct used by C++ to create objects. Not only did you learn to define classes, but you also learned to create objects using a class. In addition to classes, you learned about a number of other features in C++. You learned about

- Inline functions—Functions that have their bodies copied to each call so that their code appears inline

- Function overloading—The reuse of a function name with different parameters

- Default parameters—Setting values that are used if a value is not passed to a function

- Member functions—Functions that are part of a class

- Constructors—A function that is called when an object is created using a class

- Destructors—A function that is called when an object is destroyed

In days four, five, and six of the bonus week, you learned about Java. In Bonus Day 4, you learned about the basic components of a Java program, as well as about the keywords, identifiers, program flow, and data types. In Bonus Day 5 you learned how to define classes, objects, and packages in Java. You learned that a class is an independent software component that can have properties (which hold data) and methods (which perform actions).

In Bonus Day 5, you also learned that a Java file must use the `import` keyword in order to use classes that are not a part of its project. Day 5 ended with an introduction to using the very powerful, object-oriented technique of inheritance, permitting new classes to be created based on existing classes.

On Day 6 you wrapped up your Java primer. You saw how to use exceptions to deal with runtime errors; you learned to read and write files and how to do graphics with Java. Your day ended with a discussion and an example of using Java applets.

You finished the bonus week with a quick look at C# on Day 7. You learned why this newest of the languages is destined to be popular. You also saw a couple of simple C# programs.

Your experiences in the bonus week give you an idea of what it takes to program in C++, Java or C#. These primers presented you with enough information to get started writing your own programs and applets.

APPENDIX A

ASCII Character Chart

Dec	Hex	ASCII	Dec	Hex	ASCII
0	00	null	32	20	space
1	01	☺	33	21	!
2	02	☻	34	22	"
3	03	♥	35	23	#
4	04	♦	36	24	$
5	05	♣	37	25	%
6	06	♠	38	26	&
7	07	•	39	27	'
8	08	◘	40	28	(
9	09	○	41	29	)
10	0A	◙	42	2A	*
11	0B	♂	43	2B	+
12	0C	♀	44	2C	'
13	0D	♪	45	2D	-
14	0E	♫	46	2E	.
15	0F	☼	47	2F	/
16	10	►	48	30	0
17	11	◄	49	31	1
18	12	↕	50	32	2
19	13	‼	51	33	3
20	14	¶	52	34	4
21	15	§	53	35	5
22	16	▬	54	36	6
23	17	↨	55	37	7
24	18	↑	56	38	8
25	19	↓	57	39	9
26	1A	→	58	3A	:
27	1B	←	59	3B	;
28	1C	∟	60	3C	<
29	1D	↔	61	3D	=
30	1E	▲	62	3E	>
31	1F	▼	63	3F	?

A

Dec	Hex	ASCII
64	40	@
65	41	A
66	42	B
67	43	C
68	44	D
69	45	E
70	46	F
71	47	G
72	48	H
73	49	I
74	4A	J
75	4B	K
76	4C	L
77	4D	M
78	4E	N
79	4F	O
80	50	P
81	51	Q
82	52	R
83	53	S
84	54	T
85	55	U
86	56	V
87	57	W
88	58	X
89	59	Y
90	5A	Z
91	5B	[
92	5C	\
93	5D	]
94	5E	^
95	5F	–

Dec	Hex	ASCII
96	60	`
97	61	a
98	62	b
99	63	c
100	64	d
101	65	e
102	66	f
103	67	g
104	68	h
105	69	i
106	6A	j
107	6B	k
108	6C	l
109	6D	m
110	6E	n
111	6F	o
112	70	p
113	71	q
114	72	r
115	73	s
116	74	t
117	75	u
118	76	v
119	77	w
120	78	x
121	79	y
122	7A	z
123	7B	{
124	7C	¦
125	7D	}
126	7E	~
127	7F	Δ

Dec	Hex	ASCII		Dec	Hex	ASCII
128	80	Ç		161	A1	í
129	81	ü		162	A2	ó
130	82	é		163	A3	ú
131	83	â		164	A4	ñ
132	84	ä		165	A5	Ñ
133	85	à		166	A6	ª
134	86	å		167	A7	º
135	87	ç		168	A8	¿
136	88	ê		169	A9	⌐
137	89	ë		170	AA	¬
138	8A	è		171	AB	½
139	8B	ï		172	AC	¼
140	8C	î		173	AD	¡
141	8D	ì		174	AE	«
142	8E	Ä		175	AF	»
143	8F	Å		176	B0	▪
144	90	É		177	B1	▪
145	91	æ		178	B2	▪
146	92	Æ		179	B3	│
147	93	ô		180	B4	┤
148	94	ö		181	B5	╡
149	95	ò		182	B6	╢
150	96	û		183	B7	╖
151	97	ù		184	B8	╕
152	98	ÿ		185	B9	╣
153	99	Ö		186	BA	║
154	9A	Ü		187	BB	╗
155	9B	¢		188	BC	╝
156	9C	£		189	BD	╜
157	9D	¥		190	BE	╛
158	9E	₧		191	BF	┐
159	9F	ƒ		192	C0	└
160	A0	á		193	C1	┴

A

Dec	Hex	ASCII	Dec	Hex	ASCII
194	C2	┬	227	E3	π
195	C3	├	228	E4	Σ
196	C4	─	229	E5	σ
197	C5	+	230	E6	μ
198	C6	╞	231	E7	γ
199	C7	╟	232	E8	Φ
200	C8	╚	233	E9	θ
201	C9	╔	234	EA	Ω
202	CA	╩	235	EB	δ
203	CB	╦	236	EC	∞
204	CC	╠	237	ED	$\varnothing$
205	CD	=	238	EE	$\in$
206	CE	╬	239	EF	$\cap$
207	CF	╧	240	F0	$\equiv$
208	D0	╨	241	F1	$\pm$
209	D1	╤	242	F2	$\geq$
210	D2	╥	243	F3	$\leq$
211	D3	╙	244	F4	$\lceil$
212	D4	╘	245	F5	$\rfloor$
213	D5	╒	246	F6	$\div$
214	D6	╓	247	F7	$\approx$
215	D7	╫	248	F8	$\circ$
216	D8	╪	249	F9	$\bullet$
217	D9	┘	250	FA	·
218	DA	┌	251	FB	$\sqrt{}$
219	DB	█	252	FC	^{n}
220	DC	▄	253	FD	^{2}
221	DD	▌	254	FE	■
222	DE	▐	255	FF	
223	DF	▀			
224	E0	α			
225	E1	β			
226	E2	Γ			

APPENDIX **B**

C/C++ Reserved Words

The identifiers listed in Table B.1 are reserved and keywords for C. You shouldn't use them for any other purpose in a C program. They are allowed, of course, within double quotation marks.

Also included is a list of words that aren't reserved in C but are C++ reserved words. These C++ reserved words aren't described here, but if there's a chance your C programs might eventually be ported to C++, you need to avoid these words as well.

TABLE B.1 Reserved C keywords

Keyword	Description
asm	Keyword that denotes inline assembly language code.
auto	The default storage class. Means to create the variable on entry to the block and destroy it on exit from the block.
break	Command that exits for, while, switch, and do...while statements unconditionally.
case	Command used within the switch statement.
char	The simplest C data type.

TABLE B.1 continued

Keyword	Description
const	Data modifier that prevents a variable from being changed. See `volatile`.
continue	Command that resets a `for`, `while`, or `do...while` statement to the next iteration.
default	Command used within the `switch` statement to catch any instances not specified with a `case` statement.
do	Looping command used in conjunction with the `while` statement. The loop will always execute at least once.
double	Data type that can hold double-precision floating-point values.
else	Statement signaling alternative statements to be executed when an `if` statement evaluates to FALSE.
enum	Data type that allows variables to be declared that accept only certain values.
extern	Data modifier indicating that a variable will be declared in another area of the program.
float	Data type used for floating-point numbers.
for	Looping command that contains initialization, incrementation, and conditional sections.
goto	Command that causes a jump to a predefined label.
if	Command used to change program flow based on a TRUE/FALSE decision.
inline	Used to declare a function as inline. Inline functions are may be copied into the listing rather than being called like a regular function.
int	Data type used to hold integer values.
long	Data type used to hold larger integer values than `int`.
register	Storage modifier that specifies that a variable should be stored in a register if possible.
restrict	An access modifier used with pointers.
return	Command that causes program flow to exit from the current function and return to the calling function. It can also be used to return a single value.
short	Data type used to hold integers. It isn't commonly used, and it's the same size as an `int` on most computers.
signed	Modifier used to signify that a variable can have both positive and negative values. See `unsigned`.
sizeof	Operator that returns the size of the item in bytes.
static	Modifier used to signify that the compiler should retain the variable's value.
struct	Keyword used to combine C variables of any data type into a group.

TABLE B.1 continued

Keyword	Description
switch	Command used to change program flow in a multitude of directions. Used in conjunction with the case statement.
typedef	Modifier used to create new names for existing variable and function types.
union	Keyword used to allow multiple variables to share the same memory space.
unsigned	Modifier used to signify that a variable will contain only positive values. See signed.
void	Keyword used to signify either that a function doesn't return anything or that a pointer being used is considered generic or able to point to any data type.
volatile	Modifier that signifies that a variable can be changed. See const.
while	Looping statement that executes a section of code as long as a condition remains TRUE.
_Bool	A type large enough to store a value of 0 or 1.
_Complex	Support for complex types. It is not required that that _Complex be supported.
_Imaginary	Support for imaginary types. It is not required that that _Imaginary be supported.

In addition to the preceding keywords, the following are C++ reserved words:

catch	new	template
class	operator	this
delete	private	throw
except	protected	try
finally	public	virtual
friend		

B

APPENDIX C

Working with Binary and Hexadecimal Numbers

As a computer programmer, you might sometimes be required to work with numbers expressed in binary and hexadecimal notation. This appendix explains what these systems are and how they work. To help you understand, let's first review the common decimal number system.

The Decimal Number System

The decimal system is the base-10 system that you use every day. A number in this system—for example, 342—is expressed as powers of 10. The first digit (counting from the right) gives 10 to the 0 power, the second digit gives 10 to the 1 power, and so on. Any number to the 0 power equals 1, and any number to the 1 power equals itself. Thus, continuing with the example of 342, you have:

3        $3 \times 10^2 = 3 \times 100 = 300$

4        $4 \times 10^1 = 4 \times 10 = 40$

2        $2 \times 10^0 = 2 \times 1 = 2$

         Sum = 342

The base-10 system requires 10 different digits, 0 through 9. The following rules apply to base 10 and to any other base number system:

- A number is represented as powers of the system's base.
- The system of base n requires n different digits.

Now let's look at the other number systems.

The Binary System

The binary number system is base 2 and therefore requires only two digits, 0 and 1. The binary system is useful for computer programmers, because it can be used to represent the digital on/off method in which computer chips and memory work. Here's an example of a binary number and its representation in the decimal notation you're more familiar with, writing 1011 vertically:

1        $1 \times 2^3 = 1 \times 8 = 8$

0        $0 \times 2^2 = 0 \times 4 = 0$

1        $1 \times 2^1 = 1 \times 2 = 2$

1        $1 \times 2^0 = 1 \times 1 = 1$

         Sum = 11 (decimal)

Binary has one shortcoming: It's cumbersome for representing large numbers.

The Hexadecimal System

The hexadecimal system is base 16. Therefore, it requires 16 digits. The digits 0 through 9 are used, along with the letters A through F, which represent the decimal values 10 through 15. Here is an example of a hexadecimal number and its decimal equivalent:

2        $2 \times 16^2 = 2 \times 256 = 512$

D $13 \times 16^1 = 13 \times 16 = 208$

A $10 \times 16^0 = 10 \times 1 = 10$

         Sum = 730 (decimal)

The hexadecimal system (often called the hex system) is useful in computer work because it's based on powers of 2. Each digit in the hex system is equivalent to a four-digit binary number, and each two-digit hex number is equivalent to an eight-digit binary number. Table C.1 shows some hex/decimal/binary equivalents.

TABLE C.1 Hexadecimal numbers and their decimal and binary equivalents

Hexadecimal Digit	Decimal Equivalent	Binary Equivalent
0	0	0000
1	1	0001
2	2	0010
3	3	0011
4	4	0100
5	5	0101
6	6	0110
7	7	0111
8	8	1000
9	9	1001
A	10	1010
B	11	1011
C	12	1100
D	13	1101
E	14	1110
F	15	1111
10	16	10000
F0	240	11110000
FF	255	11111111

C

APPENDIX D

Portability Issues

The term *portability* refers to the ease with which a program's source code can be moved from one platform to another. Can the program you wrote for your PC be compiled on a UNIX workstation? How about a Macintosh? One of the major reasons people choose C as their programming language is its portability. C is potentially one of the most portable programming languages.

Why *potentially*? Most C compilers provide *extensions*, which are extra features that can be very useful but that aren't part of the C standard. If you try to port to another platform a program that uses compiler extensions, you will almost surely run into problems and have to recode parts of the program. If you're sure that your program will never be moved to another platform, you can use your compiler's extensions freely. However, if portability could be an issue, you need to tread more carefully. This appendix outlines the issues you need to consider.

The ANSI Standard

Portability doesn't happen by accident. It occurs when you adhere to a set of standards adhered to by other programmers and other compilers. For this reason, it's wise to choose a compiler that follows the standards for C programming set by the American National Standards Institute (ANSI). The ANSI committee sets standards for many areas, including other programming languages. Almost all C compilers provide the option of adhering to the ANSI standard.

The ANSI Keywords

The C language contains relatively few keywords. A *keyword* is a word that is reserved for a program command. The keywords were listed on Day 1 as well as in Appendix B.

Most compilers provide additional reserved words as well. Examples of compiler-specific keywords are near and huge. Although several compilers might use the same compiler-specific keywords, there is no guarantee that those keywords will be portable to every ANSI standard compiler.

Case Sensitivity

Case sensitivity is an important issue in programming languages. Unlike some languages that ignore case, C is case-sensitive. This means that a variable named a is different than a variable named **A**. Listing D.1 illustrates the difference.

INPUT   **LISTING D.1**   listD01.c. Case sensitivity

```
1:  /*=========================================================*
2:   * Program: listD01.c                                      *
3:   * Book:    Teach Yourself C in 21 Days                    *
4:   * Purpose: This program demonstrates case sensitivity     *
5:   *=========================================================*/
6:  #include <stdio.h>
7:  int main(void)
8:  {
9:     int    var1 = 1,
10:           var2 = 2;
11:    char   VAR1 = 'A',
12:           VAR2 = 'B';
13:    float  Var1 = 3.3,
14:           Var2 = 4.4;
15:    int    xyz  = 100,
16:           XYZ  = 500;
17:
18:    printf( "\n\nPrint the values of the variables...\n" );
19:
20:    printf( "\nThe integer values:   var1 = %d, var2 = %d",
21:            var1, var2 );
22:    printf( "\nThe character values: VAR1 = %c, VAR2 = %c",
23:            VAR1, VAR2 );
24:    printf( "\nThe float values:     Var1 = %f, Var2 = %f",
25:            Var1, Var2 );
26:    printf( "\nThe other integers:   xyz = %d, XYZ = %d",
27:            xyz, XYZ );
```

LISTING D.1   continued

```
28:
29:    printf( "\n\nDone printing the values!\n" );
30:
31:    return 0;
32:  }
```

OUTPUT

```
Print the values of the variables...

The integer values:     var1 = 1, var2 = 2
The character values:   VAR1 = A, VAR2 = B
The float values:       Var1 = 3.300000, Var2 = 4.400000
The other integers:     xyz = 100, XYZ = 500

Done printing the values!
```

ANALYSIS   This program uses several variables with the same names. In lines 9 and 10, var1 and var2 are defined as integer values. In lines 11 and 12, the same variable names are used with different cases. This time VAR1 and VAR2 are all-uppercase. In lines 13 and 14, a third set of declarations is made with the same names, but with another different case. This time, Var1 and Var2 are declared as float values. In each of these three sets of declarations, values are placed in the variables so that they can be printed later. The printing for these three sets of declarations occurs in lines 20 through 25. As you can see, the values placed in the variables are retained, and each value is printed.

Lines 15 and 16 declare two variables of the same type—integers—and the same names. The only difference between these two variables is that one is uppercase and the other is not. Each of these variables has its own value, which is printed in lines 26 and 27.

Although it's possible to use only case to differentiate variables, this isn't a practice to enter into lightly. Not all computer systems that have C compilers available are case-sensitive. Because of this, code might not be portable if only case is used to differentiate variables. For portable code, you always should ensure that variables are differentiated by something other than the case of the variable name.

Case sensitivity can cause problems in more than just the compiler. It also can cause problems with the linker. The compiler might be able to differentiate between variables with only case differences, but the linker might not.

Most compilers and linkers let you set a flag to cause case to be ignored. You should check your compiler to determine the flag that needs to be set. When you recompile a listing with variables differentiated by case only, you should get an error similar to the following one. Of course, var1 would be whatever variable you're using.

D

```
listD01.c:
Error listD01.c 16: Multiple declaration for 'var1' in function main
*** 1 errors in Compile ***
```

Portable Characters

Characters within the computer are represented as numbers. On an IBM PC or compatible, the letter A is represented by the number 65, and the letter a is represented by the number 97. These numbers come from the ASCII character set table (which can be found in Appendix A).

If you're writing portable programs, you can't assume that the ASCII table is the character translation table being used. A different table might be used on a different computer system. In other words, on a mainframe, character 65 might not be A.

 Caution You must be careful when using character numerics. Character numerics might not be portable.

Two general rules apply to how a character set is to be defined. The first rule restricting the character set is that the size of a character's value can't be larger than the size of the char type. In an 8-bit system, 255 is the maximum value that can be stored in a single char variable. Because of this, you wouldn't have a character with a value greater than 255. If you're working on a machine with a 16-bit character, 65,535 is the maximum value for a character.

The second rule restricting the character set is that each character must be represented by a positive number. The portable characters within the ASCII character set are those from 1 to 127. The values from 128 to 255 aren't guaranteed to be portable. These extended characters can't be guaranteed because a signed character has only 127 positive values.

Guaranteeing ANSI Compatibility

The predefined constant __STDC__ is used to help guarantee ANSI compatibility. When the listing is compiled with ANSI compatibility set on, this constant is defined—generally as 1. It is undefined when ANSI compatibility isn't on.

Virtually every compiler gives you the option to compile with ANSI enforced. This is usually done either by setting a switch within the IDE (Integrated Development Environment) or by passing an additional parameter on the command line when compiling. By setting the ANSI on, you help ensure that the program will be portable to other compilers and platforms.

To compile a program using Borland's C++ command line, you would enter the following on the command line:

```
BCC -A program.c
```

If you're compiling with a Microsoft compiler, you would enter

```
CL /Ze program.c
```

Note

> Most compilers with Integrated Development Environments (IDEs) provide an ANSI option. By selecting the ANSI option, you are virtually guaranteed ANSI compatibility.

The compiler then provides additional error checking to ensure that ANSI rules are met. In some cases, there are errors and warnings that are no longer checked. An example is prototype checking. Most compilers display warnings if a function isn't prototyped before it is used; however, the ANSI standards don't require this. Because ANSI doesn't require the prototypes, you might not receive the required prototype warnings.

Avoiding the ANSI Standard

There are several reasons why you wouldn't want to compile your program with ANSI compatibility on. The most common reason involves taking advantage of your compiler's added features. Many features, such as special screen-handling functions, either aren't covered within the ANSI standard or might be compiler-specific. If you decide to use these compiler-specific features, you won't want the ANSI flag set. In addition, if you use these features, you might eliminate the portability of your program. Later in this appendix, you'll see a way around this limitation.

Do	Don't
DO use more than just case to differentiate variable names.	DON'T assume numeric values for characters.

Using Portable Numeric Variables

The numeric values that can be stored in a specific variable type might not be consistent across compilers. Only a few rules are defined within the ANSI standard regarding the numeric values that can be stored in each variable type. On Day 3, "Storing Data:

Variables and Constants," Table 3.1 presented the values typically stored in IBM-compatible PCs. However, these values aren't guaranteed.

The following rules apply to variable types:

- A character (char) is the smallest data type. A character variable (type char) will be one byte.

- A short variable (type short) will be smaller than or equal to an integer variable (type int).

- An integer variable (type int) will be smaller than or equal to the size of a long variable (type long).

- An unsigned integer variable (type unsigned) is equal to the size of a signed integer variable (type int).

- A float variable (type float) will be less than or equal to the size of a double variable (type double).

Listing D.2 presents a commonly used way to print the size of the variables based on the machine on which the program is compiled.

INPUT   **LISTING D.2**   Printing the size of the data types

```
 1:   /*=============================================================*
 2:    * Program: listD02.c                                         *
 3:    * Book:    Teach Yourself C in 21 Days                       *
 4:    * Purpose: This program prints the sizes of the variable     *
 5:    *          types of the machine the program is compiled on   *
 6:    *=============================================================*/
 7:   #include <stdio.h>
 8:   int main(void)
 9:   {
10:     printf( "\nVariable Type Sizes" );
11:     printf( "\n=========================" );
12:     printf( "\nchar          %d", sizeof(char) );
13:     printf( "\nshort         %d", sizeof(short) );
14:     printf( "\nint           %d", sizeof(int) );
15:     printf( "\nfloat         %d", sizeof(float) );
16:     printf( "\ndouble        %d", sizeof(double) );
17:
18:     printf( "\n\nunsigned char   %d", sizeof(unsigned char) );
19:     printf( "\nunsigned short  %d", sizeof(unsigned short) );
20:     printf( "\nunsigned int    %d\n", sizeof(unsigned int) );
21:
22:     return 0;
23:   }
```

OUTPUT

```
Variable Type Sizes
===========================
char             1
short            2
int              2
float            4
double           8

unsigned char    1
unsigned short   2
unsigned int     2
```

ANALYSIS As you can see, the sizeof() operator is used to print the size in bytes of each variable type. The output shown is based on the program's being compiled on a 16-bit IBM-compatible PC with a 16-bit compiler. If compiled on a different machine or with a different compiler, the sizes might be different. For example, a 32-bit compiler on a 32-bit machine might yield four bytes rather than two for the size of an integer.

Maximum and Minimum Values

If different machines have variable types that are different sizes, how do you know what values can be stored? It depends on the number of bytes that make up the data type and whether the variable is signed or unsigned. On Day 3, "Storing Information: Variables and Constants," Table 3.2 shows the different values you can store based on the number of bytes. The maximum and minimum values that can be stored for integral types, such as integers, are based on the bits. For floating values, such as floats and doubles, larger values can be stored at the cost of precision. Table D.1 shows both integral-variable and floating-decimal values.

TABLE D.1 Possible values based on byte size

Number of Bytes	Unsigned Maximum	Signed Minimum	Signed Maximum
		Integral Types	
1	255	−128	127
2	65,535	−32,768	32,767
4	4,294,967,295	−2,147,483,648	2,147,438,647
8		1.844674×E19	

D

TABLE D.1 continued

Number of Bytes	Unsigned Maximum	Signed Minimum	Signed Maximum
Floating Decimal Sizes			
4*		3.4 E–38	3.4 E38
8**		1.7 E–308	1.7 E308
10***		3.4 E–4932	1.1 E4932

*Precision taken to 7 digits.
**Precision taken to 15 digits.
***Precision taken to 19 digits.

Knowing the maximum value based on the number of bytes and variable type is good; however, as you saw earlier, you don't always know the number of bytes in a portable program. In addition, you can't be completely sure of the level of precision used in floating-point numbers. Because of this, you must be careful about what numbers you assign to variables. For example, assigning the value of 3,000 to an integer variable is a safe assignment, but what about assigning 100,000? If it's an unsigned integer on a 16-bit machine, you'll get unusual results because the maximum value is 65,535. If a 4-byte integer is being used, assigning 100,000 would be okay.

 Caution

You aren't guaranteed that the values in Table D.1 are the same for every compiler. Each compiler might choose a slightly different number. This is especially true with the floating-point numbers, which can have different levels of precision. Tables D.2 and D.3 provide a compatible way of using these numbers.

ANSI has standardized a set of defined constants that are to be included in the header files limits.h and float.h. These constants define the number of bits within a variable type. In addition, they define the minimum and maximum values. Table D.2 lists the values defined in limits.h. These values apply to the integral data types. The values in float.h contain the values for the floating-point types.

TABLE D.2 The ANSI-defined constants within limits.h

Constant	Value
CHAR_BIT	Character variable's number of bits.
CHAR_MIN	Character variable's minimum value (signed).
CHAR_MAX	Character variable's maximum value (signed).

TABLE D.2 continued

Constant	Value
SCHAR_MIN	Signed character variable's minimum value.
SCHAR_MAX	Signed character variable's maximum value.
UCHAR_MAX	Unsigned character's maximum value.
INT_MIN	Integer variable's minimum value.
INT_MAX	Integer variable's maximum value.
UINT_MAX	Unsigned integer variable's maximum value.
SHRT_MIN	Short variable's minimum value.
SHRT_MAX	Short variable's maximum value.
USHRT_MAX	Unsigned short variable's maximum value.
LONG_MIN	Long variable's minimum value.
LONG_MAX	Long variable's maximum value.
ULONG_MAX	Unsigned long variable's maximum value.
LLONG_MAX	Long long variable's maximum length.
ULLONG_MAX	Unsigned long long variable's maximum length.

D

TABLE D.3 The ANSI-defined constants within float.h

Constant	Value
FLT_DIG	Precision digits in a variable of type float.
DBL_DIG	Precision digits in a variable of type double.
LDBL_DIG	Precision digits in a variable of type long double.
FLT_MAX	Float variable's maximum value.
FLT_MAX_10_EXP	Float variable's exponent maximum value (base 10).
FLT_MAX_EXP	Float variable's exponent maximum value (base 2).
FLT_MIN	Float variable's minimum value.
FLT_MIN_10_EXP	Float variable's exponent minimum value (base 10).
FLT_MIN_EXP	Float variable's exponent minimum value (base 2).
DBL_MAX	Double variable's maximum value.
DBL_MAX_10_EXP	Double variable's exponent maximum value (base 10).
DBL_MAX_EXP	Double variable's exponent maximum value (base 2).
DBL_MIN	Double variable's minimum value.
DBL_MIN_10_EXP	Double variable's exponent minimum value (base 10).

TABLE D.3   continued

Constant	Value
DBL_MIN_EXP	Double variable's exponent minimum value (base 2).
LDBL_MAX	Long double variable's maximum value.
LDBL_MAX_10_DBL	Long double variable's exponent maximum value (base 10).
LDBL_MAX_EXP	Long double variable's exponent maximum value (base 2).
LDBL_MIN	Long double variable's minimum value.
LDBL_MIN_10_EXP	Long double variable's exponent minimum value (base 10).
LDBL_MIN_EXP	Long double variable's exponent minimum value (base 2).

The values in Tables D.2 and D.3 can be used when storing numbers. Ensuring that a number is above or equal to the minimum constant and less than or equal to the maximum constant ensures that the listing will be portable. Listing D.3 prints the values stored in the ANSI-defined constants, and Listing D.4 demonstrates the use of some of these constants. The output may be slightly different depending on the compiler used.

INPUT   **LISTING D.3**   Printing the values stored in the ANSI-defined constants

```
 1:   /*========================================================*
 2:    * Program:   listD03.c                                   *
 3:    * Book:      Teach Yourself C in 21 Days                 *
 4:    * Purpose:   Display of defined constants.               *
 5:    *========================================================*/
 6:   #include <stdio.h>
 7:   #include <float.h>
 8:   #include <limits.h>
 9:
10:   int main( void )
11:   {
12:       printf( "\n CHAR_BIT        %d ", CHAR_BIT );
13:       printf( "\n CHAR_MIN        %d ", CHAR_MIN );
14:       printf( "\n CHAR_MAX        %d ", CHAR_MAX );
15:       printf( "\n SCHAR_MIN       %d ", SCHAR_MIN );
16:       printf( "\n SCHAR_MAX       %d ", SCHAR_MAX );
17:       printf( "\n UCHAR_MAX       %d ", UCHAR_MAX );
18:       printf( "\n SHRT_MIN        %d ", SHRT_MIN );
19:       printf( "\n SHRT_MAX        %d ", SHRT_MAX );
20:       printf( "\n USHRT_MAX       %d ", USHRT_MAX );
21:       printf( "\n INT_MIN         %d ", INT_MIN );
22:       printf( "\n INT_MAX         %d ", INT_MAX );
23:       printf( "\n UINT_MAX        %ld ", UINT_MAX );
24:       printf( "\n LONG_MIN        %ld ", LONG_MIN );
25:       printf( "\n LONG_MAX        %ld ", LONG_MAX );
```

LISTING D.3   continued

```
26:        printf( "\n ULONG_MAX        %e ", ULONG_MAX );
27:        printf( "\n FLT_DIG          %d ", FLT_DIG );
28:        printf( "\n DBL_DIG          %d ", DBL_DIG );
29:        printf( "\n LDBL_DIG         %d ", LDBL_DIG );
30:        printf( "\n FLT_MAX          %e ", FLT_MAX );
31:        printf( "\n FLT_MIN          %e ", FLT_MIN );
32:        printf( "\n DBL_MAX          %e ", DBL_MAX );
33:        printf( "\n DBL_MIN          %e \n", DBL_MIN );
34:
35:        return(0);
36:    }
```

OUTPUT

```
CHAR_BIT        8
CHAR_MIN        -128
CHAR_MAX        127
SCHAR_MIN       -128
SCHAR_MAX       127
UCHAR_MAX       255
SHRT_MIN        -32768
SHRT_MAX        32767
USHRT_MAX       65535
INT_MIN         -2147483648
INT_MAX         2147483647
UINT_MAX        -1
LONG_MIN        -2147483648
LONG_MAX        2147483647
ULONG_MAX       8.121967e-298
FLT_DIG         6
DBL_DIG         15
LDBL_DIG        15
FLT_MAX         3.402823e+038
FLT_MIN         1.175494e-038
DBL_MAX         1.797693e+308
DBL_MIN         2.225074e-308
```

D

Note   Output values will vary from compiler to compiler; therefore, your output may differ from the output shown here for Listing D.3.

ANALYSIS   Listing D.3 is straightforward. The program consists of `printf()` function calls. Each function call prints a different defined constant. You'll notice the conversion character used (in this case, `%d`) depends on the type of value being printed. This listing provides a synopsis of what values your compiler used. You could also have looked in the float.h and limits.h header files to see whether these values had been defined. This program should make determining the constant values easier.

LISTING D.4   Using the ANSI-defined constants

```
 1:   /*==============================================================*
 2:    * Program: listD04.c                                          *
 3:    * Book:    Teach Yourself C in 21 Days                        *
 4:    *                                                             *
 5:    * Purpose: To use maximum and minimum constants.             *
 6:    * Note:    Not all valid characters are displayable to the   *
 7:    *          screen!                                            *
 8:    *==============================================================*/
 9:
10:   #include <float.h>
11:   #include <limits.h>
12:   #include <stdio.h>
13:
14:   int main( void )
15:   {
16:       unsigned char ch;
17:       int  i;
18:
19:       printf( "Enter a numeric value.");
20:       printf( "\nThis value will be translated to a character.");
21:       printf( "\n\n==> " );
22:
23:       scanf("%d", &i);
24:
25:       while( i < 0 || i > UCHAR_MAX )
26:       {
27:           printf("\n\nNot a valid value for a character.");
28:           printf("\nEnter a value from 0 to %d ==> ", UCHAR_MAX);
29:
30:           scanf("%d", &i);
31:       }
32:       ch = (char) i;
33:
34:       printf("\n\n%d is character %c\n", ch, ch );
35:
36:       return(0);
37:   }
```

```
Enter a numeric value.
This value will be translated to a character.

==> 5000


Not a valid value for a character.
Enter a value from 0 to 255 ==> 69


69 is character E
```

ANALYSIS Listing D.4 shows the UCHAR_MAX constant in action. The first new items you should notice are the includes in lines 10 and 11. As stated earlier, these two include files contain the defined constants. If you're questioning the need for float.h to be included in line 10, you're doing well. Because none of the decimal point constants are being used, the float.h header file isn't needed. Line 11, however, is needed. This is the header file that contains the definition of UCHAR_MAX that is used later in the listing.

Lines 16 and 17 declare the variables that will be used by the listing. An unsigned character, ch, is used along with an integer variable, i. When the variables are declared, several print statements are issued to prompt the user for a number. Notice that this number is entered into an integer. Because an integer is usually capable of holding a larger number, it is used for the input. If a character variable were used, a number that was too large would wrap to a number that fits a character variable. This can easily be seen by changing the i in line 23 to ch.

Line 25 uses the defined constant to see whether the entered number is greater than the maximum for an unsigned character. We are comparing to the maximum for an unsigned character rather than an integer because the program's purpose is to print a character, not an integer. If the entered value isn't valid for a character—or, more specifically, for an unsigned character—the user is told the proper values that can be entered (line 28) and is asked to enter a valid value.

Line 32 casts the integer to a character value. In a more complex program, you might find that switching to the character variable is easier than continuing with the integer. This can help to prevent reallocating a value that isn't valid for a character into the integer variable. For this program, the line that prints the resulting character, line 34, could just as easily have used i rather than ch.

Classifying Numbers

In several instances, you'll want to know information about a variable. For instance, you might want to know whether the information is numeric, a control character, an uppercase character, or any of nearly a dozen different classifications. There are two different ways to check some of these classifications. Consider Listing D.5, which demonstrates one way of determining whether a value stored in a character is a letter of the alphabet.

INPUT   **LISTING D.5**   Is the character a letter of the alphabet

```
1:  /*========================================================*
2:   * Program: listD05.c
3:   * Purpose: This program may not be portable due to the  *
4:   *          way it uses character values.                *
5:   *========================================================*/
```

LISTING D.5 continued

```
 6:  #include <stdio.h>
 7:  int main(void)
 8:  {
 9:    unsigned char x = 0;
10:    char trash[256];                 /* used to remove extra keys */
11:    while( x != 'Q' && x != 'q' )
12:    {
13:      printf( "\n\nEnter a character (Q to quit) ==> " );
14:
15:      x = getchar();
16:
17:      if( x >= 'A' && x <= 'Z')
18:      {
19:        printf( "\n\n%c is a letter of the alphabet!", x );
20:        printf("\n%c is an uppercase letter!", x );
21:      }
22:      else
23:      {
24:        if( x >= 'a' && x <= 'z')
25:        {
26:          printf( "\n\n%c is a letter of the alphabet!", x );
27:          printf("\n%c is a lowercase letter!", x );
28:        }
29:        else
30:        {
31:          printf( "\n\n%c is not a letter of the alphabet!", x );
32:        }
33:      }
34:      gets(trash); /* eliminates enter key */
35:    }
36:    printf("\n\nThank you for playing!\n");
37:    return 0;
38:  }
```

OUTPUT

```
Enter a character (Q to quit) ==> A

A is a letter of the alphabet!
A is an uppercase letter!

Enter a character (Q to quit) ==> f

f is a letter of the alphabet!
f is a lowercase letter!

Enter a character (Q to quit) ==> 1

1 is not a letter of the alphabet!
```

```
Enter a character (Q to quit) ==> *

* is not a letter of the alphabet!

Enter a character (Q to quit) ==> q

q is a letter of the alphabet!
q is a lowercase letter!

Thank you for playing!
```

ANALYSIS This program checks to see whether a letter is between the uppercase letter A and the uppercase letter Z. In addition, it checks to see whether it is between the lowercase a and the lowercase z. If x is between one of these two ranges, you would think you could assume that the letter is alphabetic. This is a bad assumption! There is no standard for the order in which characters are stored. If you're using the ASCII character set, you can get away with using the character ranges; however, your program isn't guaranteed portability. To guarantee portability, you should use a character-classification function.

There are several character-classification functions. Each is listed in Table D.4 with what it checks for. These functions return 0 if the given character doesn't meet its check; otherwise, they return a value other than 0.

TABLE D.4   Character-classification functions

Function	Description
isalnum()	Checks to see whether the character is alphanumeric.
isalpha()	Checks to see whether the character is alphabetic.
iscntrl()	Checks to see whether the character is a control character.
isdigit()	Checks to see whether the character is a decimal digit.
isgraph()	Checks to see whether the character is printable (space is an exception).
islower()	Checks to see whether the character is lowercase.
isprint()	Checks to see whether the character is printable.
ispunct()	Checks to see whether the character is a punctuation character.
isspace()	Checks to see whether the character is a whitespace character.
isupper()	Checks to see whether the character is uppercase.
isxdigit()	Checks to see whether the character is a hexadecimal digit.

With the exception of an equality check, you should never compare the values of two different characters. For example, you could check to see whether the value of a character variable is equal to `'A'`, but you wouldn't want to check to see whether the value of a character is greater than `'A'`.

```
if( X > 'A' )     /* NOT PORTABLE!! */
...
if( X == 'A' )    /* PORTABLE */
...
```

Listing D.6 is a rewrite of Listing D.5. Instead of using range checks, the appropriate character classification values are used. Listing D.6 is a much more portable program.

INPUT   **LISTING D.6**   Using character-classification functions

```
 1:  /*==============================================================*
 2:   * Program: listD06.c                                           *
 3:   * Book:    Teach Yourself C in 21 Days                         *
 4:   * Purpose: This program is an alternative approach to          *
 5:   *          the same task accomplished in Listing D.5.          *
 6:   *          This program has a higher degree of portability!    *
 7:   *==============================================================*/
 8:  #include <ctype.h>
 9:
10:  int main(void)
11:  {
12:    unsigned char x = 0;
13:    char trash[256];              /* use to flush extra keys */
14:    while( x != 'Q' && x != 'q' )
15:    {
16:       printf( "\n\nEnter a character (Q to quit) ==> " );
17:
18:       x = getchar();
19:
20:       if( isalpha(x) )
21:       {
22:          printf( "\n\n%c is a letter of the alphabet!", x );
23:          if( isupper(x) )
24:          {
25:             printf("\n%c is an uppercase letter!", x );
26:          }
27:          else
28:          {
29:             printf("\n%c is a lowercase letter!", x );
30:          }
31:       }
32:       else
33:       {
34:          printf( "\n\n%c is not a letter of the alphabet!", x );
35:       }
36:       gets(trash);   /* get extra keys */
```

LISTING D.6 continued

```
37:    }
38:    printf("\n\nThank you for playing!\n");
39:    return(0);
40: }
```

INPUT/
OUTPUT

```
Enter a character (Q to quit) ==> z

z is a letter of the alphabet!
z is a lowercase letter!

Enter a character (Q to quit) ==> T

T is a letter of the alphabet!
T is an uppercase letter!

Enter a character (Q to quit) ==> #

# is not a letter of the alphabet!

Enter a character (Q to quit) ==> 7

7 is not a letter of the alphabet!

Enter a character (Q to quit) ==> Q

Q is a letter of the alphabet!
Q is an uppercase letter!

Thank you for playing!
```

ANALYSIS The outcome should look virtually identical to that for Listing D.5—assuming you ran the program with the same values. This time, instead of using range checks, the character-classification functions were used. Notice that line 8 includes the ctype.h header file. When this is included, the classification functions are ready to go. Line 20 uses the isalpha() function to ensure that the character entered is a letter of the alphabet. If it is, a message is printed in line 22 stating that fact. Line 23 then checks to see whether the character is uppercase with the isupper() function. If x is an uppercase character, a message is printed in line 25; otherwise, the message in line 29 is printed. If the letter isn't a letter of the alphabet, a message is printed in line 34. Because the while loop starts in line 14, the program continues until Q or q is pressed. You might think line 14 detracts from the portability of this program, but that is incorrect. Remember that equality checks for characters are portable, and inequality checks aren't portable. "Not equal to" and "equal to" are both equality checks.

D

Do	**Don't**
DO use the character classification functions when possible.	**DON'T** use numeric values when determining maximums for variables. Use the defined constants if you're writing a portable program.
DO remember that `"!="` is considered an equality check.	

Converting a Character's Case: A Portability Example

A common practice in programming is to convert the case of a character. Many people write a function similar to the following:

```
char conv_to_upper( char x )
{
    if( x >= 'a' && x <= 'z' )
    {
        x -= 32;
    }
    return( x )
}
```

As you saw earlier, the `if` statement might not be portable. The following is an update function with the `if` statement updated to the portable functions presented in the preceding section:

```
char conv_to_upper( char x )
{
    if( isalpha( x ) && islower( x ) )
    {
        x -= 32;
    }
    return( x )
}
```

This example is better than the previous listing in terms of portability; however, it still isn't completely portable. This function makes the assumption that the uppercase letters are a numeric value that is 32 less than the lowercase letters. This is true if the ASCII character set is used. In the ASCII character set, `'A'` + 32 equals `'a'`; however, this isn't necessarily true on every system. This is especially untrue on non-ASCII character systems.

Two ANSI standard functions take care of switching the case of a character. The `toupper()` function converts a lowercase character to uppercase; the `lowercase()` function converts an uppercase character to lowercase. The previous function would look as follows when rewritten:

```
toupper();
```

As you can see, this is a function that already exists. In addition, this function is defined by ANSI standards, so it should be portable.

Portable Structures and Unions

When using structures and unions, care must also be exercised if portability is a concern. Word alignment and the order in which members are stored are two areas of incompatibility that can occur when working with these constructs.

Word Alignment

Word alignment is an important factor in the portability of a structure. Word alignment is the aligning of data on a word boundary. A *word* is a set number of bytes. A word usually is equivalent to the size of the processor on the computer being used. For example, an IBM 16-bit PC generally has a two-byte word. Two bytes equals 16 bits.

An example will make this easy to understand. Consider the following structure. Using two-byte integers and one-byte characters, determine how many bytes of storage are needed to store the structure.

```
struct struct_tag {
   int   x;     /* ints will be 2 bytes */
   char  a;     /* chars are 1 byte */
   int   y;
   char  b;
   int   z;
} sample = { 100, 'A', 200, 'B', 300);
```

Adding up the integers and the characters, you might come up with eight bytes for the amount of storage. This answer could be true. It also could be wrong! If word alignment is on, this structure will take 10 bytes of storage. Figures D.1 and D.2 illustrate how the structure would be stored in memory.

FIGURE D.1

Word alignment is off.

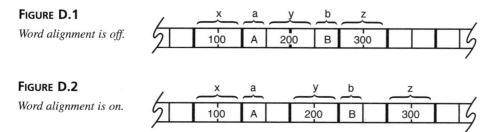

FIGURE D.2

Word alignment is on.

D

A program can't assume that the word alignment will be the same or that it will be on or off. The members could be aligned on every two bytes, four bytes, or eight bytes. You can't assume that you know.

Reading and Writing Structures

When reading or writing structures, you must be cautious. It's best to never use a literal constant for the size of a structure or union. If you're reading or writing structures to a file, the file probably won't be portable. This means you need to concentrate only on making the program portable. The program then needs to read and write the data files specific to the machine compiled on. The following is an example of a `read` statement that would be portable:

```
fread( &the_struct, sizeof( the_struct ), 1, filepointer );
```

As you can see, the `sizeof` command is used instead of a literal. Regardless of whether byte alignment is on or off, the correct number of bytes should be read.

Structure Order

When you create a structure, you might assume that the members will be stored in the order in which they are listed. There isn't a standard stating that a certain order must be followed. Because of this, you can't make assumptions about the order of information within a structure.

Preprocessor Directives

On Day 21, "Advanced Compiler Use," you learned about several preprocessor directives you can use. Several preprocessor directives have been defined in the ANSI standards. You use two of these all the time: `#include` and `#define`. Several other preprocessor directives are in the ANSI standards. The additional preprocessor directives available under the ANSI guidelines are listed in Table D.5.

TABLE D.5 ANSI standard preprocessor directives

#define	#if
#elif	#ifdef
#else	#ifndef
#endif	#include
#error	#pragma

Using Predefined Constants

Every compiler comes with predefined constants. A majority of these are typically compiler-specific. This means that they probably won't be portable from one compiler to the next. However, several predefined constants are defined in the ANSI standards. The following are some of these constants:

Constant	Description
__DATE__	This is replaced by the date at the time the program is compiled. The date is in the form of a literal string (text enclosed in double quotes). The format is `"Mmm DD, YYYY"`. For example, January 1, 1998, would be `"Jan 1, 1998"`.
__FILE__	This is replaced with the name of the source file at the time of compilation. This will be in the form of a literal string.
__LINE__	This will be replaced with the number of the line on which __LINE__ appears in the source code. This will be a numeric decimal value.
__STDC__	This literal will be defined as 1 if the source file is compiled with the ANSI Standard. If the source file wasn't compiled with the ANSI flag set, this value will be undefined.
__TIME__	This is replaced with the time that the program is compiled. This time is in the form of a literal string (text enclosed in double quotes). The format is `"HH:MM:SS"`. An example would be `"12:15:03"`.

D

Using Non-ANSI Features in Portable Programs

A program can use constants and other commands that aren't ANSI-defined and still be portable. You accomplish this by ensuring that the constants are used only if compiled with a compiler that supports the features used. Most compilers provide defined constants that you can use to identify themselves. By setting up areas of the code that are supportive for each of the compilers, you can create a portable program. Listing D.7 demonstrates how this can be done.

INPUT   **LISTING D.7**   A portable program with compiler specifics

```
1:  /*========================================================*
2:   * Program: listD07.c                                     *
3:   * Purpose: This program demonstrates using defined       *
4:   *          constants for creating a portable program.    *
5:   * Note:    This program gets different results with      *
```

LISTING D.7 continued

```
 6:  *            different compilers.                            *
 7:  *=========================================================*/
 8:  #include <stdio.h>
 9:  #ifdef _WINDOWS
10:
11:  #define STRING "DOING A WINDOWS PROGRAM!\n"
12:
13:  #else
14:
15:  #define STRING "NOT DOING A WINDOWS PROGRAM\n"
16:
17:  #endif
18:
19:  int main(void)
20:  {
21:     printf( "\n\n") ;
22:     printf( STRING );
23:
24:  #ifdef _MSC_VER
25:
26:     printf( "\n\nUsing a Microsoft compiler!" );
27:     printf( "\n   Your Compiler version is %s\n", _MSC_VER );
28:
29:  #endif
30:
31:  #ifdef __TURBOC__
32:
33:     printf( "\n\nUsing the Turbo C compiler!" );
34:     printf( "\n   Your compiler version is %x\n", __TURBOC__ );
35:
36:  #endif
37:
38:  #ifdef __BORLANDC__
39:
40:     printf( "\n\nUsing a Borland compiler!\n" );
41:
42:  #endif
43:
44:     return(0);
45:  }
```

OUTPUT Here's the output you'll see when you run the program using a Turbo C for DOS 3.0 compiler:

```
NOT DOING A WINDOWS PROGRAM

Using the Turbo C compiler!
   Your compiler version is 300
```

Here's the output you'll see when you run the program using a Borland C++ compiler under DOS:

```
NOT DOING A WINDOWS PROGRAM

Using a Borland compiler!
```

Here's the output you'll see when you run the program using a Microsoft compiler under DOS:

```
NOT DOING A WINDOWS PROGRAM

Using a Microsoft compiler!
   Your compiler version is >>
```

ANALYSIS   This program takes advantage of defined constants to determine information about the compiler being used. In line 9, the `#ifdef` preprocessor directive is used. This directive checks to see whether the following constant has been defined. If the constant has been defined, the statements following the `#ifdef` are executed until an `#endif` preprocessor directive is reached. In the case of line 9, a determination of whether _WINDOWS has been defined is made. An appropriate message is applied to the constant STRING. Line 22 then prints this string, which states whether or not this listing has been compiled as a Windows program.

Line 24 checks to see whether _MSC_VER has been defined. _MSC_VER is a constant that contains the version number of a Microsoft compiler. If a compiler other than a Microsoft compiler is used, this constant won't be defined. If a Microsoft compiler is used, this will be defined with the version number of the compiler. Line 27 will print this compiler version number after line 26 prints a message stating that a Microsoft compiler was used.

Lines 31 through 36 and lines 38 through 42 operate in similar manners. They check to see whether Borland's Turbo C or Borland's professional compiler were used. The appropriate message is printed based on these constants.

As you can see, this program determines which compiler is being used by checking the defined constants. The object of the program—to print a message stating which compiler is being used—is the same regardless of which compiler is used. If you're aware of the systems that you will be porting, you can put compiler-specific commands into the code. If you do use compiler-specific commands, you should ensure that the appropriate code is provided for each compiler.

ANSI Standard Header Files

Several header files that can be included are set by the ANSI standards. It's good to know which header files are ANSI standard, because these can be used in creating portable programs. Appendix E, "Common C Functions," contains the ANSI header files along with a list of their functions.

Summary

This appendix exposed you to a great deal of material. This information centered around portability. C is one of the most portable languages—if not the most portable language. Portability doesn't happen by accident. ANSI standards have been created to ensure that C programs can be ported from one compiler to another and from one computer system to another. You should consider several areas when writing portable code. These areas include variable case, choosing which character set to use, using portable numerics, ensuring variable sizes, comparing characters, using structures and unions, and using preprocessor directives and preprocessor constants. This appendix ended with a discussion of how to incorporate compiler specifics into a portable program.

Q&A

Q How do you write portable graphics programs?

A ANSI doesn't define any real standards for programming graphics. Graphics programming is more machine dependent than other programming areas, so it can be somewhat difficult to write portable graphics programs.

If you decide to write graphics functions, one option is to wrap the graphics routines into a function that gets called the same way. This function can then be swapped out when you change platforms.

Q Should you always worry about portability?

A No, it's not always necessary to consider portability. Some programs that you write will be used only by you on your system. In addition, some programs won't be ported to a different computer system. Because of this, some nonportable functions, such as `system()`, can be used that wouldn't be used in portable programs.

Q Are comments portable if they are done with `//` instead of `/*` and `*/`? ISO/IEC 9899:1999

A If the ISO/IEC 9899:1999 standard is being followed (the newest ANSI C standard), forward slashes are allowed. Older ANSI versions did not support the forward slash comments; however, many compilers did.

Workshop

The Workshop provides quiz questions to help you solidify your understanding of the material covered and exercises to provide you with experience in using what you've learned.

Quiz

1. Which is more important: efficiency or maintainability?

2. What is the numeric value of the letter a?

3. What is guaranteed to be the largest unsigned character value on your system?

4. What does ANSI stand for?

5. Are the following variable names valid in the same C program?

   ```
   int lastname,

   LASTNAME,

   LastName,

   Lastname;
   ```

6. What does `isalpha()` do?

7. What does `isdigit()` do?

8. Why would you want to use functions such as `isalpha()` and `isdigit()`?

9. Can structures be written to disk without worrying about portability?

10. Can `__TIME__` be used in a `printf()` statement to print the current time in a program? Here's an example:

    ```
    printf( "The Current Time is: %s", __TIME__ );
    ```

Exercises

1. **BUG BUSTER:** What, if anything, is wrong with the following function?

   ```
   void Print_error( char *msg )
   {
       static int ctr = 0,
                  CTR = 0;
       printf("\n" );
       for( ctr = 0; ctr < 60; ctr++ )
       {
           printf("*");
       }
       printf( "\nError %d, %s - %d: %s.\n", CTR,
               __FILE__, __LINE__, msg );
       for( ctr = 0; ctr < 60; ctr++ )
       {
   ```

D

```
        printf("*");
    }
}
```

2. Write a function that verifies that a character is a vowel.

3. Write a function that returns 0 if it receives a character that isn't a letter of the alphabet, 1 if it is an uppercase letter, and 2 if it is a lowercase letter. Keep the function as portable as possible.

4. **ON YOUR OWN:** Understand your compiler. Determine what flags must be set to ignore variable case, allow for byte alignment, and guarantee ANSI compatibility.

5. Is the following code portable?

```c
void list_a_file( char *file_name )
{
    system("TYPE " file_name );
}
```

6. Is the following code portable?

```c
int to_upper( int x )
{
    if( x >= 'a' && x <= 'z' )
    {
        toupper( x );
    }
    return( x );
}
```

APPENDIX E

Common C Functions

This appendix lists the function prototypes contained in each of the header files supplied with most C compilers. Functions that have an asterisk after them were covered in this book.

The functions are listed alphabetically. Following each name and header file is the complete prototype. Notice that the header file prototypes use a notation different from that used in this book. For each parameter a function takes, only the type is given in the prototype; no parameter name is included. Here are two examples:

```
int func1(int, int *);
int func1(int x, int *y);
```

Both declarations specify two parameters—the first a type `int`, and the second a pointer to type `int`. As far as the compiler is concerned, these two declarations are equivalent.

TABLE E.1 Common C functions listed in alphabetical order

Function	Header File	Function Prototype
abort*	stdlib.h	void abort(void);
abs	stdlib.h	int abs(int);
acos*	math.h	double acos(double);
asctime*	time.h	char *asctime(const struct tm *);
asin*	math.h	double asin(double);
assert*	assert.h	void assert(int);
atan*	math.h	double atan(double);
atan2*	math.h	double atan2(double, double);
atexit*	stdlib.h	int atexit(void (*)(void));
atof*	stdlib.h	double atof(const char *);
atof*	math.h	double atof(const char *);
atoi*	stdlib.h	int atoi(const char *);
atol*	stdlib.h	long atol(const char *);
bsearch*	stdlib.h	void *bsearch(const void *, const void *, size_t, size_t, int(*) (const void *, const void *));
calloc*	stdlib.h	void *calloc(size_t, size_t);
ceil*	math.h	double ceil(double);
clearerr	stdio.h	void clearerr(FILE *);
clock*	time.h	clock_t clock(void);
cos*	math.h	double cos(double);
cosh*	math.h	double cosh(double);
ctime*	time.h	char *ctime(const time_t *);
difftime	time.h	double difftime(time_t, time_t);
div	stdlib.h	div_t div(int, int);
exit*	stdlib.h	void exit(int);
exp*	math.h	double exp(double);
fabs*	math.h	double fabs(double);
fclose*	stdio.h	int fclose(FILE *);
fcloseall*	stdio.h	int fcloseall(void);
feof*	stdio.h	int feof(FILE *);
fflush*	stdio.h	int fflush(FILE *);

TABLE E.1   continued

Function	Header File	Function Prototype
fgetc*	stdio.h	int fgetc(FILE *);
fgetpos	stdio.h	int fgetpos(FILE *, fpos_t *);
fgets*	stdio.h	char *fgets(char *, int, FILE *);
floor*	math.h	double floor(double);
flushall*	stdio.h	int flushall(void);
fmod*	math.h	double fmod(double, double);
fopen*	stdio.h	FILE *fopen(const char *, const char *);
fprintf*	stdio.h	int fprintf(FILE *, const char *, ...);
fputc*	stdio.h	int fputc(int, FILE *);
fputs*	stdio.h	int fputs(const char *, FILE *);
fread*	stdio.h	size_t fread(void *, size_t, size_t, FILE *);
free*	stdlib.h	void free(void *);
freopen	stdio.h	FILE *freopen(const char *, const char *, FILE *);
frexp*	math.h	double frexp(double, int *);
fscanf*	stdio.h	int fscanf(FILE *, const char *, ...);
fseek*	stdio.h	int fseek(FILE *, long, int);
fsetpos	stdio.h	int fsetpos(FILE *, const fpos_t *);
ftell*	stdio.h	long ftell(FILE *);
fwrite*	stdio.h	size_t fwrite(const void *, size_t, size_t, FILE *);
getc*	stdio.h	int getc(FILE *);
getch*	stdio.h	int getch(void);
getchar*	stdio.h	int getchar(void);
getche*	stdio.h	int getche(void);
getenv	stdlib.h	char *getenv(const char *);
gets*	stdio.h	char *gets(char *);
gmtime	time.h	struct tm *gmtime(const time_t *);
isalnum*	ctype.h	int isalnum(int);
isalpha*	ctype.h	int isalpha(int);
isascii*	ctype.h	int isascii(int);
iscntrl*	ctype.h	int iscntrl(int);

E

TABLE E.1 continued

Function	Header File	Function Prototype
isdigit*	ctype.h	int isdigit(int);
isgraph*	ctype.h	int isgraph(int);
islower*	ctype.h	int islower(int);
isprint*	ctype.h	int isprint(int);
ispunct*	ctype.h	int ispunct(int);
isspace*	ctype.h	int isspace(int);
isupper*	ctype.h	int isupper(int);
isxdigit*	ctype.h	int isxdigit(int);
labs	stdlib.h	long int labs(long int);
ldexp	math.h	double ldexp(double, int);
ldiv	stdlib.h	ldiv_t div(long int, long int);
localtime*	time.h	struct tm *localtime(const time_t *);
log*	math.h	double log(double);
log10*	math.h	double log10(double);
malloc*	stdlib.h	void *malloc(size_t);
mblen	stdlib.h	int mblen(const char *, size_t);
mbstowcs	stdlib.h	size_t mbstowcs(wchar_t *, const char *, size_t);
mbtowc	stdlib.h	int mbtowc(wchar_t *, const char *, size_t);
memchr	string.h	void *memchr(const void *, int, size_t);
memcmp	string.h	int memcmp(const void *, const void *, size_t);
memcpy	string.h	void *memcpy(void *, const void *, size_t);
memmove	string.h	void *memmove(void *, const void*, size_t);
memset	string.h	void *memset(void *, int, size_t);
mktime*	time.h	time_t mktime(struct tm *);
modf	math.h	double modf(double, double *);
perror*	stdio.h	void perror(const char *);
pow*	math.h	double pow(double, double);
printf*	stdio.h	int printf(const char *, ...);
putc*	stdio.h	int putc(int, FILE *);

TABLE E.1 continued

Function	Header File	Function Prototype
putchar*	stdio.h	int putchar(int);
puts*	stdio.h	int puts(const char *);
qsort*	stdlib.h	void qsort(void*, size_t, size_t, int (*)(const void*, const void *));
rand	stdlib.h	int rand(void);
realloc*	stdlib.h	void *realloc(void *, size_t);
remove*	stdio.h	int remove(const char *);
rename*	stdio.h	int rename(const char *, const char *);
rewind*	stdio.h	void rewind(FILE *);
scanf*	stdio.h	int scanf(const char *, ...);
setbuf	stdio.h	void setbuf(FILE *, char *);
setvbuf	stdio.h	int setvbuf(FILE *, char *, int, size_t);
sin*	math.h	double sin(double);
sinh*	math.h	double sinh(double);
sleep*	time.h	void sleep(time_t);
sprintf	stdio.h	int sprintf(char *, const char *, ...);
sqrt*	math.h	double sqrt(double);
srand	stdlib.h	void srand(unsigned);
sscanf	stdio.h	int sscanf(const char *, const char *, ...);
strcat*	string.h	char *strcat(char *,const char *);
strchr*	string.h	char *strchr(const char *, int);
strcmp*	string.h	int strcmp(const char *, const char *);
strcmpl*	string.h	int strcmpl(const char *, const char *);
strcpy*	string.h	char *strcpy(char *, const char *);
strcspn*	string.h	size_t strcspn(const char *, const char *);
strdup*	string.h	char *strdup(const char *);
strerror	string.h	char *strerror(int);
strftime*	time.h	size_t strftime(char *, size_t, const char *, const struct tm *);
strlen*	string.h	size_t strlen(const char *);
strlwr*	string.h	char *strlwr(char *);
strncat*	string.h	char *strncat(char *, const char *, size_t);

E

TABLE E.1   continued

Function	Header File	Function Prototype
strncmp*	string.h	int strncmp(const char *, const char *, size_t);
strncpy*	string.h	char *strncpy(char *, const char *, size_t);
strnset*	string.h	char *strnset(char *, int, size_t);
strpbrk*	string.h	char *strpbrk(const char *, const char *);
strrchr*	string.h	char *strrchr(const char *, int);
strspn*	string.h	size_t strspn(const char *, const char *);
strstr*	string.h	char *strstr(const char *, const char *);
strtod	stdlib.h	double strtod(const char *, char **);
strtok	string.h	char *strtok(char *, const char*);
strtol	stdlib.h	long strtol(const char *, char **, int);
strtoul	stdlib.h	unsigned long strtoul(const char*, char **, int);
strupr*	string.h	char *strupr(char *);
system*	stdlib.h	int system(const char *);
tan*	math.h	double tan(double);
tanh*	math.h	double tanh(double);
time*	time.h	time_t time(time_t *);
tmpfile	stdio.h	FILE *tmpfile(void);
tmpnam*	stdio.h	char *tmpnam(char *);
tolower	ctype.h	int tolower(int);
toupper	ctype.h	int toupper(int);
ungetc*	stdio.h	int ungetc(int, FILE *);
va_arg*	stdarg.h	(type) va_arg(va_list, (type));
va_end*	stdarg.h	void va_end(va_list);
va_start*	stdarg.h	void va_start(va_list, lastfix);
vfprintf	stdio.h	int vfprintf(FILE *, constchar *, ...);
vprintf	stdio.h	int vprintf(FILE*, constchar *, ...);
vsprintf	stdio.h	int vsprintf(char *, constchar *, ...);
wcstombs	stdlib.h	size_t wcstombs(char *, const wchar_t *, size_t);
wctomb	stdlib.h	int wctomb(char *, wchar_t);

APPENDIX F

Answers

This appendix lists the answers for the quizzes and exercise sections at the end of each day's lesson. Note that for many of the exercises, more than one solution is possible. In most cases, only one of many possible answers is listed. In other cases, you'll see additional information to help you solve the exercise.

Answers for Day 1

Quiz

1. C is powerful, popular, and portable.

2. The compiler translates C source code into machine-language instructions that your computer can understand.

3. Editing, compiling, linking, and testing.

4. The answer to this question depends on your compiler. Consult your compiler's manuals.

5. The answer to this question depends on your compiler. Consult your compiler's manuals.

6. The appropriate extension for C source files is .C (or .c).

Note: C++ uses the extension .CPP. You can write and compile your C programs with a .CPP extension, but it's more appropriate to use a .C extension.

7. FILENAME.TXT would compile. However, it's more appropriate to use a .C extension rather than .TXT.

8. You should make changes to the source code to correct the problems. You should then recompile and relink. After relinking, you should run the program again to see whether your corrections fixed the program.

9. Machine language is made up of digital or binary instructions that the computer can understand. Because the computer can't understand C source code, a compiler translates source code to machine code, also called object code.

10. The linker combines the object code from your program with the object code from the function library and creates an executable file.

Exercises

1. When you look at the object file, you see many unusual characters and other gibberish. Mixed in with the gibberish, you also see pieces of the source file.

2. This program calculates the area of a circle. It prompts the user for the radius and then displays the area.

3. This program prints a 10×10 block made of the character X. A similar program is covered on Day 6, "Basic Program Control."

4. This program generates a compiler error. You should get a message similar to the following:

```
Error: ch1ex4.c: Declaration terminated incorrectly
```

This error is caused by the semicolon at the end of line 3. If you remove the semicolon, this program should compile and link correctly.

5. This program compiles OK, but it generates a linker error. You should get a message similar to the following:

```
Error: Undefined symbol _do_it in module...
```

This error occurs because the linker can't find a function called do_it. To fix this program, change do_it to printf.

6. Rather than printing a 10×10 block filled with the character X, the program now prints a 10×10 block of smiley faces.

Answers for Day 2

Quiz

1. A block.

2. The main() function.

3. You use program comments to make notations about the program's structure and operation. Any text between /* and */ is a program comment and is ignored by the compiler. Additionally, you can use single line comments. Any text on the same line following two forward slashes (//) is considered a comment.

4. A function is an independent section of program code that performs a certain task and has been assigned a name. By using a function's name, a program can execute the code in the function.

5. A user-defined function is created by the programmer. A library function is supplied with the C compiler.

6. An #include directive instructs the compiler to add the code from another file into your source code during the compilation process.

7. Comments shouldn't be nested. Although some compilers let you to do this, others don't. To keep your code portable, you shouldn't nest comments.

8. Yes. Comments can be as long as needed. A comment can start with /* and won't end until a */ is encountered.

9. An include file is also known as a header file.

10. An include file is a separate disk file that contains information needed by the compiler to use various functions.

Exercises

1. Remember, only the main() function is required in C programs. The following is the smallest possible program, but it doesn't do anything:

```
void main(void)
{
}
```

This also could be written

```
void main(void){}
```

2.   a. Statements are on lines 8, 9, 10, 12, 20, and 21.

     b. The only variable definition is on line 18.

     c. The only function prototype (for display_line()) is on line 4.

F

    d. The function definition for `display_line()` is on lines 16 through 22.

    e. Comments are on lines 1, 15, and 23.

3. A comment is any text included between `/*` and `*/`. Examples include the following:

```
/* This is a comment */
/*???*/
/*
This is a
     third comment */
```

You can also use single-line comments which is any text after to forward slashes.

4. This program prints the alphabet in all capital letters. You should understand this program better after you finish Day 10, "Characters and Strings."

The output is

```
ABCDEFGHIJKLMNOPQRSTUVWXYZ
```

5. This program counts and prints the number of characters and spaces you enter. This program also will be clearer after you finish Day 10.

Answers for Day 3

Quiz

1. An integer variable can hold a whole number (a number without a fractional part), and a floating-point variable can hold a real number (a number with a fractional part).

2. A type `double` variable has a greater range than type `float` (it can hold larger and smaller values). A type `double` variable also is more precise than type `float`.

3.   a. The size of a `char` is one byte.

    b. The size of a `short` is less than or equal to the size of an `int`.

    c. The size of an `int` is less than or equal to the size of a `long`.

    d. The size of an `unsigned` is equal to the size of an `int`.

    e. The size of a `float` is less than or equal to the size of a `double`.

4. The names of symbolic constants make your source code easier to read. They also make it much easier to change the constant's value.

5.   a. `#define MAXIMUM 100`

    b. `const int MAXIMUM = 100;`

6. Letters, numerals, and underscores.

7. Names of variables and constants should describe the data being stored. Variable names should be in lowercase, and constant names should be in uppercase.

8. Symbolic constants are symbols that represent literal constants.

9. If it's an unsigned int that is 2 bytes long, the minimum value it can hold is 0. If it is signed, –32,768 is the minimum.

Exercises

1. a. Because a person's age can be considered a whole number, and a person can't be a negative age, an unsigned int is suggested.

    b. unsigned int

    c. float

    d. If your expectations for yearly salary aren't very high, a simple unsigned int variable would work. If you feel you have the potential to go above $65,535, you probably should use a long. (Have faith in yourself; use a long.)

    e. float. (Don't forget the decimal places for the cents.)

    f. Because the highest grade will always be 100, it is a constant. Use either const int or a #define statement.

    g. float. (If you're going to use only whole numbers, use either int or long.)

    h. Definitely a signed field. Either int, long, or float. See answer 1.d.

    i. double

2. Answers for exercises 2 and 3 are combined here.

    Remember, a variable name should be representative of the value it holds. A variable declaration is the statement that initially creates the variable. The declaration might or might not initialize the variable to a value. You can use any name for a variable, except the C keywords.

    a. unsigned int age;

    b. unsigned int weight;

    c. float radius = 3;

    d. long annual_salary;

    e. float cost = 29.95;

    f. const int max_grade = 100; or #define MAX_GRADE 100

    g. float temperature;

    h. long net_worth = -30000;

    i. double star_distance;

F

3. See answer 2.

4. The valid variable names are b, c, e, g, h, i, and j.

Notice that j is correct; however, it isn't wise to use variable names that are this long. (Besides, who would want to type them?) Most compilers wouldn't look at this entire name. Instead, they would look only at the first 31 characters or so.

The following are invalid:

a. You can't start a variable name with a number.

d. You can't use a pound sign (#) in a variable name.

f. You can't use a hyphen (-) in a variable name.

Answers for Day 4

Quiz

1. It is an assignment statement that instructs the computer to add 5 and 8, assigning the result to the variable x.

2. An expression is anything that evaluates to a numerical value.

3. The relative precedence of the operators.

4. After the first statement, the value of a is 10, and the value of x is 11. After the second statement, both a and x have the value 11. (The statements must be executed separately.)

5. 1

6. 19

7. (5 + 3) * 8 / (2 + 2)

8. 0

9. See the section "Operator Precedence Revisited" near the end of this chapter. It shows the C operators and their precedence.

a. < has higher precedence than == does.

b. * has higher precedence than +.does.

c. != and == have the same precedence, so they are evaluated left-to-right.

d. >= has the same precedence as >. Use parentheses if you need to use more than one relational operator in a single statement or expression.

10. The compound assignment operators let you combine a binary mathematical operation with an assignment operation, thus providing a shorthand notation. The compound operators presented in this chapter are +=, -=, /=, *=, and %=.

Exercises

1. This listing should have worked, even though it is poorly structured. The purpose of this listing is to demonstrate that whitespace is irrelevant to how the program runs. You should use whitespace to make your programs readable.

2. The following is a better way to structure the listing from exercise 1:

```c
#include <stdio.h>

int x, y;

int main( void )
{
    printf("\nEnter two numbers ");
    scanf( "%d %d",&x,&y);
    printf("\n\n%d is bigger\n",(x>y)?x:y);
    return 0;
}
```

This listing asks for two numbers, x and y, and then prints whichever one is bigger.

3. The only changes needed in Listing 4.1 are the following:

```c
16:     printf("\n%d    %d", a++, ++b);
17:     printf("\n%d    %d", a++, ++b);
18:     printf("\n%d    %d", a++, ++b);
19:     printf("\n%d    %d", a++, ++b);
20:     printf("\n%d    %d", a++, ++b);
```

4. The following code fragment is just one of many possible answers. It checks to see if x is greater than or equal to 1 and less than or equal to 20. If these two conditions are met, x is assigned to y. If these conditions are not met, x is not assigned to y; therefore, y remains the same.

```c
if ((x >= 1) && (x <= 20))
    y = x;
```

5. The code is as follows:

```c
y = ((x >= 1) && (x <= 20)) ? x : y;
```

Again, if the statement is TRUE, x is assigned to y; otherwise, y is assigned to itself, thus having no effect.

6. The code is as follows:

```c
if (x < 1 && x > 10 )
    statement;
```

7.   a. 7

  b. 0

  c. 9

  d. 1 (true)

  e. 5

F

8.   a. TRUE

      b. TRUE

      c. TRUE. Notice that there is a single equals sign, making the if an assignment instead of a relation.

      d. TRUE

9. The following is one possible answer:

```
if( age < 21 )
    printf( "You are not an adult" );
else if( age >= 65 )
        printf( "You are a senior citizen!");
        else
            printf( "You are an adult" );
```

10. This program has four problems. The first is on line 3. The assignment statement should end with a semicolon, not a colon. The second problem is the semicolon at the end of the if statement on line 6. The third problem is a common one: The assignment operator (=) is used rather than the relational operator (==) in the if statement. The final problem is the word otherwise on line 8. This should be else. Here is the corrected code:

```
/* a program with problems... */
#include <stdio.h>
int x = 1;
int main( void )
{
    if( x == 1)
        printf(" x equals 1" );
    else
        printf(" x does not equal 1");
    return 0;
}
```

Answers for Day 5

Quiz

1. Yes! (Well, OK, this is a trick question, but you had better answer "yes" if you want to become a good C programmer.)

2. Structured programming takes a complex programming problem and breaks it into a number of simpler tasks that are easier to handle one at a time.

3. After you've broken your program into a number of simpler tasks, you can write a function to perform each task.

4. The first line of a function definition must be the function header. It contains the function's name, its return type, and its parameter list.

5. A function can return either one value or no values. The value can be of any of the C variable types. On Day 18, "Getting More from Functions," you'll see how to get more values back from a function.

6. A function that returns nothing should be type `void`.

7. A function definition is the complete function, including the header and all the function's statements. The definition determines what actions take place when the function executes. The prototype is a single line, identical to the function header, but it ends with a semicolon. The prototype informs the compiler of the function's name, return type, and parameter list.

8. A local variable is declared within a function.

9. Local variables are independent from other variables in the program.

10. `main()` should be the first function in your listing.

Exercises

1. `float do_it(char a, char b, char c)`

   Add a semicolon to the end, and you have the function prototype. As a function header, it should be followed by the function's statements enclosed in braces.

2. `void print_a_number( int a_number )`

   This is a `void` function. As in exercise 1, to create the prototype, add a semicolon to the end. In an actual program, the header is followed by the function's statements.

3. a. `int`

   b. `long`

4. There are two problems. First, the `print_msg()` function is declared as a `void`; however, it returns a value. The `return` statement should be removed. The second problem is on the fifth line. The call to `print_msg()` passes a parameter (a string). The prototype states that this function has a `void` parameter list and, therefore, shouldn't be passed anything. The following is the corrected listing:

```
#include <stdio.h>
void print_msg (void);
int main( void )
{
    print_msg();
    return 0;
}
```

F

```
void print_msg(void)
{
    puts( "This is a message to print" );
}
```

5. There should not be a semicolon at the end of the function header.

6. Only the larger_of() function needs to be changed:

```
21: int larger_of( int a, int b)
22: {
23:     int save;
24:
25:     if (a > b)
26:         save = a;
27:     else
28:         save = b;
29:
30:     return save;
31: }
```

7. The following assumes that the two values are integers and an integer is returned:

```
int product( int x, int y )
{
    return (x * y);
}
```

8. The following listing checks the second value passed to verify that it is not 0. Division by zero causes an error. You should never assume that the values passed are correct.

```
int divide_em( int a, int b )
{
    int answer = 0;

    if( b == 0 )
        answer = 0;
    else
        answer = a/b;

    return answer;
}
```

9. Although the following code uses main(), it could use any function. Lines 9, 10, and 11 show the calls to the two functions. Lines 13 through 16 print the values. To run this listing, you need to include the code from exercises 7 and 8 after line 19.

```
1:  #include <stdio.h>
2:
3:  int main( void )
4:  {
```

```
5:     int number1 = 10,
6:         number2 = 5;
7:     int x, y, z;
8:
9:     x = product( number1, number2 );
10:    y = divide_em( number1, number2 );
11:    z = divide_em( number1, 0 );
12:
13:     printf( "\nnumber1 is %d and number2 is %d", number1, number2 );
14:     printf( "\nnumber1 * number2 is %d", x );
15:     printf( "\nnumber1 / number2 is %d", y );
16:     printf( "\nnumber1 / 0 is %d", z );
17:
18:     return 0;
19: }
```

10. The code is as follows:

```
/* Averages five float values entered by the user. */

#include <stdio.h>

float v, w, x, y, z, answer;

float average(float a, float b, float c, float d, float e);

int main( void )
{
    puts("Enter five numbers:");
    scanf("%f%f%f%f%f", &v, &w, &x, &y, &z);

    answer = average(v, w, x, y, z);

    printf("The average is %f.\n", answer);

    return 0;
}

float average( float a, float b, float c, float d, float e)
{
    return ((a+b+c+d+e)/5);
}
```

F

11. The following is the answer using type int variables. It can run only with values less than or equal to 9. To use values larger than 9, you need to change the values to type long.

```
/* this is a program with a recursive function */

#include <stdio.h>

int three_powered( int power );
```

```
int main( void )
{
    int a = 4;
    int b = 9;

    printf( "\n3 to the power of %d is %d", a,
    three_powered(a) );
    printf( "\n3 to the power of %d is %d\n", b,
    three_powered(b) );

    return 0;
}

int three_powered( int power )
{

    if ( power < 1 )
        return( 1 );
    else
        return( 3 * three_powered( power - 1 ));
}
```

Answers for Day 6

Quiz

1. The first index value of an array in C is 0.

2. A for statement contains initializing and increment expressions as parts of the command.

3. A do...while contains the while statement at the end and always executes the loop at least once.

4. Yes, a while statement can accomplish the same task as a for statement, but you need to do two additional things. You must initialize any variables before starting the while command, and you need to increment any variables as a part of the while loop.

5. You can't overlap the loops. The nested loop must be entirely inside the outer loop.

6. Yes, a while statement can be nested in a do...while loop. You can nest any command within any other command.

7. The four parts of a for statement are the initializer, the condition, the increment, and the statement(s).

8. The two parts of a while statement are the condition and the statement(s).

9. The two parts of a do...while statement are the condition and the statement(s).

Exercises

1. `long array[50];`

2. Notice that in the following answer, the 50th element is indexed to `49`. Remember that arrays start at `0`.

   `array[49] = 123.456;`

3. When the statement is complete, x equals `100`.

4. When the statement is complete, `ctr` equals 11. (`ctr` starts at 2 and is incremented by 3 while it is less than `10`.)

5. The inner loop prints five `X`s. The outer loop prints the inner loop 10 times. This totals 50 `X`s.

6. The code is as follows:

   ```
   int x;
   for( x = 1; x <= 100; x += 3) ;
   ```

7. The code is as follows:

   ```
   int x = 1;
   while( x <= 100 )
       x += 3;
   ```

8. The code is as follows:

   ```
   int ctr = 1;
   do
   {
       ctr += 3;
   } while( ctr < 100 );
   ```

9. This program never ends. `record` is initialized to `0`. The `while` loop then checks to see whether `record` is less than `100`. `0` is less than `100`, so the loop executes, thus printing the two statements. The loop then checks the condition again. `0` is still, and always will be, less than `100`, so the loop continues. Within the brackets, `record` needs to be incremented. You should add the following line after the second `printf()` function call:

   `record++;`

10. Using a defined constant is common in looping; you'll see examples similar to this code fragment in Weeks 2 and 3. The problem with this fragment is simple. The semicolon doesn't belong at the end of the `for` statement. This is a common bug.

F

Answers for Day 7

Quiz

1. There are two differences between puts() and printf():

   printf() can print variable parameters.

   puts() automatically adds a newline character to the end of the string it prints.

2. You should include the stdio.h header file when using printf().

3. a. \\ prints a backslash.

    b. \b prints a backspace.

    c. \n prints a newline.

    d. \t prints a tab.

    e. \a (for "alert") sounds the beep.

4. a. %s for a character string

    b. %d for a signed decimal integer

    c. %f for a decimal floating-point number

5. a. b prints the literal character b.

    b. \b prints a backspace character.

    c. \ looks at the next character to determine an escape character (see Table 7.1).

    d. \\ prints a single backslash.

Exercises

1. puts() automatically adds the newline; printf() does not. The code is as follows:

```
printf( "\n" );
puts( " " );
```

2. The code is as follows:

```
char c1, c2;
int d1;
scanf( "%c %ud %c", &c1, &d1, &c2 );
```

3. Your answer might vary:

```
#include <stdio.h>
int x;

int main( void )
{
    puts( "Enter an integer value" );
```

```
    scanf( "%d", &x );

    printf( "\nThe value entered is %d\n", x );

    return 0;
}
```

4. It's typical to edit a program to allow only specific values to be accepted. The following is one way to accomplish this exercise:

```
#include <stdio.h>
int x;

int main( void )
{
    puts( "Enter an even integer value" );
    scanf( "%d", &x );
    while( x % 2 != 0)
    {
        printf( "\n%d is not even, Please enter an even \
        number: ", x );
        scanf( "%d", &x );
    }
    printf( "\nThe value entered is %d\n", x );

    return 0;
}
```

5. The code is as follows:

```
#include <stdio.h>
int array[6], x, number;

int main( void )
{
    /* loop 6 times or until the last entered element is 99 */
    for( x = 0; x < 6 && number != 99; x++ )
    {
        puts( "Enter an even integer value, or 99 to quit" );
        scanf( "%d", &number );
        while( number % 2 == 1 && number != 99)
        {
            printf( "\n%d is not even, Please enter an even \
                    number: ", number);
            scanf( "%d", &number );
        }
        array[x] = number;
    }
    /* now print them out... */
    for( x = 0; x < 6 && array[x] != 99; x++ )
    {
        printf( "\nThe value entered is %d", array[x] );
```

F

```
        }

        return 0;
    }
```

6. The previous answers already are executable programs. The only change that needs to be made is in the final `printf()`. To print each value separated by a tab, change the `printf()` statement to the following:

```
printf( "%d\t", array[x]);
```

7. You can't have quotes within quotes. To print quotes within quotes, you must use the escape character `\"`. Additionally, you must include a single slash at the end of the first line in order to have the text continued to the second line. The following is the corrected version:

```
printf( "Jack said, \"Peter Piper picked a peck of pickled \
peppers.\"");
```

8. This listing has three errors. The first is the lack of quotes in the `printf()` statement. The second is the missing address-of operator in the `answer` variable in the `scanf()`. The final error is also in the `scanf()` statement. Instead of `"%f"`, it should have `"%d"`, because `answer` is a type `int` variable, not a type `float`. The following is corrected:

```
int get_1_or_2( void )
{
    int answer = 0;

    while( answer < 1 || answer > 2 )
    {
        printf("Enter 1 for Yes, 2 for No ");      /* corrected */

        scanf( "%d", &answer );                     /* corrected */
    }
    return answer;
}
```

9. Here is the completed `print_report()` function for Listing 7.1:

```
void print_report( void )
{
    printf( "\nSAMPLE REPORT" );
    printf( "\n\nSequence\tMeaning" );
    printf( "\n=========\t=======" );
    printf( "\n\\a\t\tBell (alert)" );
    printf( "\n\\b\t\tBackspace" );
    printf( "\n\\f\t\tForm feed" );
    printf( "\n\\n\t\tNew line" );
    printf( "\n\\r\t\tCarriage Return" );
    printf( "\n\\t\t\tHorizontal tab" );
```

```
        printf( "\n\\v\t\tVertical tab" );
        printf( "\n\\\\\\t\tBackslash" );
        printf( "\n\\\?\t\tQuestion mark" );
        printf( "\n\\\'\t\tSingle quote" );
        printf( "\n\\\"\t\tDouble quote" );
        printf( "\n...\t\t...");
    }
```

10. The code is as follows:

```
/* Inputs two floating-point values and */
/* displays their product. */

#include <stdio.h>

float x, y;

int main( void )
{
    puts("Enter two values: ");
    scanf("%f %f", &x, &y);
    printf("\nThe product is %f\n", x * y);
    return 0;
}
```

11. The following program prompts for 10 integers and displays their sum:

```
/* Input 10 integers and display their sum. */

#include <stdio.h>

int count, temp;
long total = 0;       /* Use type long to ensure we don't */
/* exceed the maximum for type int. */

int main( void )
{
    for (count = 1; count <=10; count++)
    {
        printf("Enter integer # %d: ", count);
        scanf("%d", &temp);
        total += temp;
    }

    printf("\n\nThe total is %d\n", total);

    return 0;
}
```

12. The code is as follows:

```
/* Inputs integers and stores them in an array, stopping */
/* when a zero is entered. Finds and displays the array's */
```

F

```c
/* largest and smallest values */
#include <stdio.h>

#define MAX 100

int array[MAX];
int count = -1, maximum, minimum, num_entered, temp;

int main( void )
{
    puts("Enter integer values one per line.");
    puts("Enter 0 when finished.");

    /* Input the values */

    do
    {
        scanf("%d", &temp);
        array[++count] = temp;
    } while ( count < (MAX-1) && temp != 0 );

    num_entered = count;

    /* Find the largest and smallest. */
    /* First set maximum to a very small value, */
    /* and minimum to a very large value. */

    maximum = -32000;
    minimum = 32000;

    for (count = 0; count <= num_entered && array[count] != 0; count++)
    {
        if (array[count] > maximum)
        maximum = array[count];

        if (array[count] < minimum )
            minimum = array[count];
    }

    printf("\nThe maximum value is %d", maximum);
    printf("\nThe minimum value is %d\n", minimum);

    return 0;
}
```

Answers for Day 8

Quiz

1. All of them, but one at a time. A given array can contain only a single data type.

2. 0. Regardless of the size of an array, all C arrays start with subscript 0.

3. $n-1$

4. The program compiles and runs, but it produces unpredictable results.

5. In the declaration statement, follow the array name with one set of brackets for each dimension. Each set of brackets contains the number of elements in the corresponding dimension.

6. 240. This is determined by multiplying 2×3×5×8.

7. array[0][0][1][1]

8. `sizeof(xyz) / sizeof(long)`

Exercises

1. `int one[1000], two[1000], three[1000];`

2. `int array[10] = { 1, 1, 1, 1, 1, 1, 1, 1, 1, 1 };`

3. This exercise can be solved in numerous ways. The first way is to initialize the array when it's declared:

   ```
   int eightyeight[88] = {88,88,88,88,88,88,88,...,88};
   ```

   However, this approach requires that you to place 88 88s between the braces (instead of using ..., as I did). I don't recommend this method for initializing such a large array. The following is a better method:

   ```
   int eightyeight[88];
   int x;

   for ( x = 0; x < 88; x++ )
       eightyeight[x] = 88;
   ```

4. The code is as follows:

   ```
   int stuff[12][10];
   int sub1, sub2;

   for( sub1 = 0; sub1 < 12; sub1++ )
       for( sub2 = 0; sub2 < 10; sub2++ )
           stuff[sub1][sub2] = 0;
   ```

5. Be careful with this fragment. The bug presented here is easy to create. Notice that the array is 10×3 but is initialized as a 3×10 array.

F

To describe this differently, the left subscript is declared as 10, but the `for` loop uses x as the left subscript. x is incremented with three values. The right subscript is declared as 3, but the second `for` loop uses y as the right subscript. y is incremented with 10 values. This can cause unpredictable results. You can fix this program in one of two ways. The first way is to switch x and y in the line that does the initialization:

```
int x, y;
int array[10][3];
int main( void )
{
   for ( x = 0; x < 3; x++ )
      for ( y = 0; y < 10; y++ )
         array[y][x] = 0;           /* changed */

   return 0;
}
```

The second way (which is recommended) is to switch the values in the `for` loops:

```
int x, y;
int array[10][3];
int main( void )
{
   for ( x = 0; x < 10; x++ )      /* changed */
      for ( y = 0; y < 3; y++ )    /* changed */
         array[x][y] = 0;

   return 0;
}
```

6. This, I hope, was an easy bug to bust. This program initializes an element in the array that is out of bounds. If you have an array with 10 elements, their subscripts are 0 to 9. This program initializes elements with subscripts 1 through 10. You can't initialize `array[10]`, because it doesn't exist. The `for` statement should be changed to one of the following examples:

   ```
   for( x = 1; x <=9; x++ )  /* initializes 9 of the 10 elements */
   ```

   ```
   for( x = 0; x <= 9; x++ )
   ```

   Note that x <= 9 is the same as x < 10. Either is appropriate; x < 10 is more common.

7. The following is one of many possible answers:

   ```
   /* Using two-dimensional arrays and rand() */

   #include <stdio.h>
   #include <stdlib.h>

   /* Declare the array */
   ```

```
int array[5][4];
int a, b;

int main( void )
{
   for ( a = 0; a < 5; a++ )
   {
      for ( b = 0; b < 4; b++ )
      {
         array[a][b] = rand();
      }
   }

   /* Now print the array elements */

   for ( a = 0; a < 5; a++ )
   {
      for ( b = 0; b < 4; b++ )
      {
         printf( "%d\t", array[a][b] );
      }
      printf( "\n" );    /* go to a new line */
   }

   return 0;
}
```

8. The following is one of many possible answers:

```
/* random.c: using a single-dimensional array */

#include <stdio.h>
#include <stdlib.h>
/* Declare a single-dimensional array with 1000 elements */

int random[1000];
int a, b, c;
long total = 0;

int main( void )
{
   /* Fill the array with random numbers. The C library */
   /* function rand() returns a random number. Use one */
   /* for loop for each array subscript. */

   for (a = 0; a < 1000; a++)
   {
      random[a] = rand();
      total += random[a];
   }
   printf("\n\nAverage is: %ld\n",total/1000);
   /* Now display the array elements 10 at a time */
```

F

```
    for (a = 0; a < 1000; a++)
    {
       printf("\nrandom[%d] = ", a);
       printf("%d", random[a]);

       if ( a % 10 == 0 && a > 0 )
       {
           printf("\nPress Enter to continue, CTRL-C to quit.");
           getchar();
       }
    }
    return 0;
}           /* end of main() */
```

9. The following are two solutions. The first initializes the array at the time it is
   declared, and the second initializes it in a for loop.

   Answer 1:

```
#include <stdio.h>

/* Declare a single-dimensional array */

int elements[10] = { 0, 1, 2, 3, 4, 5, 6, 7, 8, 9 };
int idx;

int main( void )
{
   for (idx = 0; idx < 10; idx++)
   {
      printf( "\nelements[%d] = %d ", idx, elements[idx] );
   }
   return 0;
}           /* end of main() */
```

   Answer 2:

```
#include <stdio.h>

/* Declare a single-dimensional array */

int elements[10];
int idx;

int main( void )
{
   for (idx = 0; idx < 10; idx++)
      elements[idx] = idx ;

   for (idx = 0; idx < 10; idx++)
      printf( "\nelements[%d] = %d ", idx, elements[idx] );

   return 0;
}
```

10. The following is one of many possible answers:

```c
#include <stdio.h>

/* Declare a single-dimensional array */

int elements[10] = { 0, 1, 2, 3, 4, 5, 6, 7, 8, 9 };
int new_array[10];
int idx;

int main( void )
{
   for (idx = 0; idx < 10; idx++)
   {
      new_array[idx] = elements[idx] + 10 ;
   }

   for (idx = 0; idx < 10; idx++)
   {
      printf( "\nelements[%d] = %d \tnew_array[%d] = %d",
      idx, elements[idx], idx, new_array[idx] );
   }
   return 0;
}
```

Answers for Day 9

Quiz

1. The address-of operator is the & sign.

2. The indirection operator * is used. When you precede the name of a pointer by *, it refers to the variable pointed to.

3. A pointer is a variable that contains the address of another variable.

4. Indirection is the act of accessing the contents of a variable by using a pointer to the variable.

5. They are stored in sequential memory locations, with lower array elements at lower addresses.

6. &data[0]

    data

7. One way is to pass the length of the array as a parameter to the function. The second way is to have a special value in the array, such as NULL, signify the array's end.

8. Assignment, indirection, address-of, incrementing, differencing, and comparison.

F

9. Differencing two pointers returns the number of elements in between. In this case, the answer is 1. The actual size of the elements in the array is irrelevant.

10. The answer is still 1.

Exercises

1. `char *char_ptr;`

2. The following declares a pointer to `cost` and then assigns the address of `cost` (`&cost`) to it:

   ```
   int *p_cost;
   p_cost = &cost;
   ```

3. Direct access: `cost = 100;`

   Indirect access: `*p_cost = 100;`

4. `printf( "Pointer value: %d, points at value: %d", p_cost, *p_cost);`

5. `float *variable = &radius;`

6. The code is as follows:

   ```
   data[2] = 100;
   *(data + 2) = 100;
   ```

7. This code also includes the answer for exercise 8:

   ```
   #include <stdio.h>

   #define MAX1 5
   #define MAX2 8

   int array1[MAX1] = { 1, 2, 3, 4, 5 };
   int array2[MAX2] = { 1, 2, 3, 4, 5, 6, 7, 8 };
   int total;

   int sumarrays(int x1[], int len_x1, int x2[], int len_x2);

   int main( void )
   {
       total = sumarrays(array1, MAX1, array2, MAX2);
       printf("The total is %d\n", total);

       return 0;
   }

   int sumarrays(int x1[], int len_x1, int x2[], int len_x2)
   {

       int total = 0, count = 0;
   ```

```
    for (count = 0; count < len_x1; count++)
       total += x1[count];

    for (count = 0; count < len_x2; count++)
       total += x2[count];

    return total;
}
```

8. See the answer for exercise 7.

9. The following is just one possible answer:

```
#include <stdio.h>

#define SIZE 10

/* function prototypes */
void addarrays( int [], int []);

int main( void )
{
   int a[SIZE] = {1, 1, 1, 1, 1, 1, 1, 1, 1, 1};
   int b[SIZE] = {9, 8, 7, 6, 5, 4, 3, 2, 1, 0};

   addarrays(a, b);

   return 0;
}

void addarrays( int first[], int second[])
{
    int total[SIZE];
    int *ptr_total = &total[0];
    int ctr = 0;

    for (ctr = 0; ctr < SIZE; ctr ++ )
    {
       total[ctr] = first[ctr] + second[ctr];
       printf("%d + %d = %d\n", first[ctr], second[ctr], total[ctr]);
    }
}
```

Answers for Day 10

Quiz

1. The values in the ASCII character set range from 0 to 255. From 0 to 127 is the standard ASCII character set, and 128 to 255 is the extended ASCII character set.

2. As the character's ASCII code.

3. A string is a sequence of characters terminated by the null character.

4. A sequence of one or more characters enclosed in double quotation marks.

5. To hold the string's terminating null character.

6. As a sequence of ASCII values corresponding to the quoted characters, followed by 0 (the ASCII code for the null character).

7. a. 97
    b. 65
    c. 57
    d. 32
    e. 206
    f. 6

8. a. I
    b. a space
    c. c
    d. a
    e. n
    f. NUL
    g. ☻

9. a. 9 bytes. (Actually, the variable is a pointer to a string, and the string requires 9 bytes of memory—8 for the string and 1 for the null terminator.)
    b. 9 bytes
    c. 1 byte
    d. 20 bytes
    e. 20 bytes

10. a. A
    b. A string!
    c. 0 (NULL)
    d. This is beyond the end of the string, so it could have any value.
    e. !
    f. This contains the address of the first element of the string.

Exercises

1. `char letter = '$';`

2. `char array[18] = "Pointers are fun!";`

3. `char *array = "Pointers are fun!";`

4. The code is as follows:

```
char *ptr;
ptr = malloc(81);
gets(ptr);
```

5. The following is just one possible answer. A complete program is provided:

```
#include <stdio.h>

#define SIZE 10

/* function prototypes */
void copyarrays( int [], int []);

int main( void )
{
    int ctr=0;
    int a[SIZE] = {1, 2, 3, 4, 5, 6, 7, 8, 9, 10};
    int b[SIZE];

    /* values before copy */
    for (ctr = 0; ctr < SIZE; ctr ++ )
    {
        printf( "a[%d] = %d, b[%d] = %d\n",
                ctr, a[ctr], ctr, b[ctr]);
    }

    copyarrays(a, b);

    /* values after copy */
    for (ctr = 0; ctr < SIZE; ctr ++ )
    {
        printf( "a[%d] = %d, b[%d] = %d\n",
                ctr, a[ctr], ctr, b[ctr]);
    }

    return 0;
}

void copyarrays( int orig[], int newone[])
{
    int ctr = 0;

    for (ctr = 0; ctr < SIZE; ctr ++ )
```

F

```
        {
            newone[ctr] = orig[ctr];
        }
    }
```

6. The following is one of many possible answers:

```
#include <stdio.h>
#include <string.h>

/* function prototypes */
char * compare_strings( char *, char *);

int main( void )
{
    char *a = "Hello";
    char *b = "World!";
    char *longer;

    longer = compare_strings(a, b);

    printf( "The longer string is: %s\n", longer );

    return 0;
}

char * compare_strings( char * first, char * second)
{
    int x, y;

    x = strlen(first);
    y = strlen(second);

    if( x > y)
        return(first);
    else
        return(second);
}
```

7. This exercise was on your own!

8. a_string is declared as an array of 10 characters, but it's initialized with a string larger than 10 characters. a_string needs to be bigger.

9. If the intent of this line of code is to initialize a string, it is wrong. You should use either char *quote or char quote[100].

10. No.

11. Yes. Although you can assign one pointer to another, you can't assign one array to another. You should change the assignment to a string-copying command such as strcpy().

Answers for Day 11

Quiz

1. The data items in an array must all be of the same type. A structure can contain data items of different types.

2. The structure member operator is a period. It is used to access members of a structure.

3. `struct`

4. A structure tag is tied to a template of a structure and is not an actual variable. A structure instance is an allocated structure that can hold data.

5. These statements define a structure and declare an instance called `myaddress`. This instance is then initialized. The structure member `myaddress.name` is initialized to the string `"Bradley Jones"`, `yaddress.add1` is initialized to `"RTSoftware"`, `myaddress.add2` is initialized to `"P.O. Box 1213"`, `myaddress.city` is initialized to `"Carmel"`, `myaddress.state` is initialized to `"IN"`, and `myaddress.zip` is initialized to `"46032-1213"`.

6. `word myWord;`

7. The following statement changes `ptr` to point to the second array element:
   ```
   ptr++;
   ```

Exercises

1. The code is as follows:
   ```
   struct time {
       int hours;
       int minutes;
       int seconds;
   } ;
   ```

2. The code is as follows:
   ```
   struct data {
       int value1;
       float value2;
       float value3;

   } info ;
   ```

3. `info.value1 = 100;`

4. The code is as follows:
   ```
   struct data *ptr;
   ptr = &info;
   ```

F

5. The code is as follows:

```
ptr->value2 = 5.5;
(*ptr).value2 = 5.5;
```

6. The code is as follows:

```
struct data {
    char name[21];
    struct data *ptr;
};
```

7. The code is as follows:

```
typedef struct {
    char address1[31];
    char address2[31];
    char city[11];
    char state[3];
    char zip[11];
} RECORD;
```

8. The following uses the values from quiz question 5 for the initialization:

```
RECORD myaddress = {"RTSoftware",
                    "P.O. Box 1213",
                    "Carmel", "IN", "46032-1213" };
```

9. This code fragment has two problems. The first is that the structure should contain a tag. The second is the way sign is initialized. The initialization values should be in braces. Here is the corrected code:

```
struct zodiac {
    char zodiac_sign[21];
    int month;
} sign = {"Leo", 8};
```

10. The union declaration has only one problem. Only one variable in a union can be used at a time. This is also true of initializing the union. Only the first member of the union can be initialized. Here is the correct initialization:

```
/* setting up a union */
union data{
    char a_word[4];
    long a_number;
}generic_variable = { "WOW" };
```

Answers for Day 12

Quiz

1. The scope of a variable refers to the extent to which different parts of a program have access to the variable, or where the variable is visible.

2. A variable with local storage class is visible only in the function where it is defined. A variable with external storage class is visible throughout the program.

3. Defining a variable in a function makes it local; defining a variable outside of any function makes it external.

4. Automatic (the default) or static. An automatic variable is created each time the function is called and is destroyed when the function ends. A static local variable persists and retains its value between calls to the function.

5. An automatic variable is initialized every time the function is called. A static variable is initialized only the first time the function is called.

6. False. When declaring register variables, you're making a request. There is no guarantee that the compiler will honor the request.

7. An uninitialized global variable is automatically initialized to 0; however, it's best to initialize variables explicitly.

8. An uninitialized local variable isn't automatically initialized; it could contain anything. You should never use an uninitialized local variable.

9. Because the variable count is now local to the block, the printf() no longer has access to a variable called count. The compiler gives you an error.

10. If the value needs to be remembered, it should be declared as static. For example, if the variable were called vari, the declaration would be

    ```
    static int vari;
    ```

11. The extern keyword is used as a storage-class modifier. It indicates that the variable has been declared somewhere else in the program.

12. The static keyword is used as a storage-class modifier. It tells the compiler to retain the value of a variable or function for the duration of a program. Within a function, the variable keeps its value between function calls.

Exercises

1. register int x = 0;

2. The code is as follows:

```
/* Illustrates variable scope. */
#include <stdio.h>

void print_value(int x);

int main( void )
{
    int x = 999;

    printf("%d", x);
    print_value( x );
```

F

```
        return 0;
    }

    void print_value( int x)
    {
        printf("%d", x);
    }
```

3. Because you're declaring var as a global, you don't need to pass it as a parameter.

```
    /* Using a global variable */
    #include <stdio.h>

    int var = 99;

    void print_value(void);

    int main( void )
    {
        print_value();
        return 0;
    }

    void print_value(void)
    {
        printf( "The value is %d\n", var );
    }
```

4. Yes, you need to pass the variable var in order to print it in a different function.

```
    /* Using a local variable*/
    #include <stdio.h>

    void print_value(int var);

    int main( void )
    {
        int var = 99;
        print_value(  var );

        return 0;
    }

    void print_value(int var)
    {
        printf( "The value is %d\n", var );
    }
```

5. Yes, a program can have a local and global variable with the same name. In such cases, active local variables take precedence.

```
    /* Using a global */
    #include <stdio.h>
```

```
int var = 99;

void print_func(void);

int main( void )
{
    int var = 77;
    printf( "Printing in function with local and global:");
    printf( "\nThe Value of var is %d", var );
    print_func( );

    return 0;
}
void print_func( void )
{
    printf( "\nPrinting in function  only global:");
    printf( "\nThe value of var is %d\n", var );
}
```

6. There is only one problem with a_sample_function(). Variables can be declared at the beginning of any block, so the declarations of crtl and star are fine. The other variable, ctr2, is not declared at the beginning of a block; it needs to be. The following is the corrected function within a complete program.

Note: If you're using a C++ compiler instead of a C compiler, the listing with a bug might run and compile. C++ has different rules concerning where variables can be declared. However, you should still follow the rules for C, even if your compiler lets you get away with something different.

```
#include <stdio.h>

void a_sample_function( );
int main( void )
{
    a_sample_function();
    return 0;
}

void a_sample_function( void )
{
    int ctr1;

    for ( ctr1 = 0; ctr1 < 25; ctr1++ )
        printf( "*" );

    puts( "\nThis is a sample function" );
    {
        char star = '*';
        int ctr2;      /* fix */
        puts( "\nIt has a problem\n" );
```

```
        for ( ctr2 = 0; ctr2 < 25; ctr2++ )
        {
            printf( "%c", star);
        }
    }
}
```

7. This program actually works properly, but it could be better. First of all, there is no need to initialize the variable x to 1, because it's initialized to 0 in the for statement. Also, declaring the variable tally to be static is pointless because, within the main() function, static keywords have no effect.

8. What is the value of star? What is the value of dash? These two variables are never initialized. Because they are both local variables, each could contain any value. Note that, although this program compiles with no errors or warnings, there is still a problem.

   There is a second issue that should be brought up about this program. The variable ctr is declared as global, but it's only used in print_function(). This isn't a good assignment. The program would be better if ctr were a local variable in print_function().

9. This program prints the following pattern forever. See exercise 10.

   X==X==X==X==X==X==X==X==X==X==X==X==X==X==X==X==X==X==...

10. This program poses a problem because of the global scope of ctr. Both main() and print_letter2() use ctr in loops at the same time. Because print_letter2() changes the value, the for loop in main() never completes. This could be fixed in a number of ways. One way is to use two different counter variables. A second way is to change the scope of the counter variable ctr. It could be declared in both main() and print_letter2() as a local variable.

    An additional comment on letter1 and letter2. Because each of these is used in only one function, they should be declared as local. Here is the corrected listing:

```
#include <stdio.h>
void print_letter2(void);              /* function prototype */

int main( void )
{
    char letter1 = 'X';
    int ctr;

    for( ctr = 0; ctr < 10; ctr++ )
    {
        printf( "%c", letter1 );
        print_letter2();
    }
```

```
        return 0;
    }

    void print_letter2(void)
    {
        char letter2 = '=';
        int ctr;                    /* this is a local variable */
                                    /* it is different from ctr in main() */
        for( ctr = 0; ctr < 2; ctr++ )
            printf( "%c", letter2 );
    }
```

Answers for Day 13

Quiz

1. Never. (Unless you are very careful.)

2. When a `break` statement is encountered, execution immediately exits the `for`, `do...while`, or `while` loop that contains the `break`. When a `continue` statement is encountered, the next iteration of the enclosing loop begins immediately.

3. An infinite loop executes forever. You create one by writing a `for`, `do...while`, or `while` loop with a test condition that is always true.

4. Execution terminates when the program reaches the end of `main()` or the `exit()` function is called.

5. The expression in a `switch` statement can evaluate to a `long`, `int`, or `char` value.

6. The `default` statement is a case in a `switch` statement. When the expression in the `switch` statement evaluates to a value that doesn't have a matching case, control goes to the default case.

7. The `exit()` function causes the program to end. A value can be passed to the `exit()` function. This value is returned to the operating system.

8. The `system()` function executes a command at the operating system level.

Exercises

1. `continue;`

2. `break;`

3. For a DOS system, the answer would be
   `system("dir");`

4. This code fragment is correct. You don't need a `break` statement after the `printf()` for `'N'`, because the `switch` statement ends anyway.

F

5. You might think that the `default` needs to go at the bottom of the `switch` statement, but this isn't true. The `default` can go anywhere. There is a problem, however. There should be a `break` statement at the end of the `default` case.

6. The code is as follows:

```c
if( choice == 1 )
    printf("You answered 1");
else if( choice == 2 )
        printf( "You answered 2");
    else
        printf( "You did not choose 1 or 2");
```

7. The code is as follows:

```c
do {
    /* any C statements */
} while ( 1 );
```

Answers for Day 14

Quiz

1. A stream is a sequence of bytes. A C program uses streams for all input and output.

2.   a. A printer is an output device.

   b. A keyboard is an input device.

   c. A modem is both an input and an output device.

   d. A monitor is an output device. (Although a touch screen would be an input device and an output device.)

   e. A disk drive can be both an input and an output device.

3. All C compilers support three predefined streams: `stdin` (the keyboard), `stdout` (the screen), and `stderr` (the screen). Some compilers, also support `stdprn` (the printer), and `stdaux` (the serial port COM1). Note that the Macintosh doesn't support the `stdprn` function.

4.   a. `stdout`

   b. `stdout`

   c. `stdin`

   d. `stdin`

   e. `fprintf()` can use any output stream. Of the five standard streams, it can use `stdout`, `stderr`, `stdprn`, and `stdaux`.

5. Buffered input is sent to the program only when the user presses Enter. Unbuffered input is sent one character at a time, as soon as each key is pressed.

6. Echoed input automatically sends each character to `stdout` as it is received; unechoed input does not.

7. You can "unget" only one character between reads. The `EOF` character can't be put back into the input stream with `unget()`.

8. With the newline character, which corresponds to the user's pressing Enter.

9.   a. Valid

       b. Valid

       c. Valid

       d. Not valid. There is not an identifier of q.

       e. Valid

       f. Valid

10. `stderr` can't be redirected; it always prints to the screen. `stdout` can be redirected to somewhere other than the screen.

Exercises

1. `printf( "Hello World" );`

2. `fprintf( stdout, "Hello World" );`

   `puts( "Hello World");`

3. `fprintf( stdaux, "Hello Auxiliary Port" );`

4. The code is as follows:
   ```
   char buffer[31];
   scanf( "%30[^*]", buffer );
   ```

5. The code is as follows:
   ```
   printf( "Jack asked, \"What is a backslash\?\"\nJill said, \
   \"It is \'\\\'\"");
   ```

6. Hint: Use an array of 26 integers. To count each character, increment the appropriate array element for each character read.

7. Hint: Get a string at a time, and then print a formatted line number followed by a tab and the string. Second Hint: Check out the Print_It program in Type & Run 1!

F

Answers for Day 15

Quiz

1. The code is as follows:
   ```
   float x;
   float *px = &x;
   float **ppx = &px;
   ```

2. The error is that the statement uses a single indirection operator and, as a result, assigns the value 100 to px instead of to x. The statement should be written with a double indirection operator:

   ```
   **ppx = 100;
   ```

3. array is an array with two elements. Each of these elements is itself an array that contains three elements. Each of these elements is an array that contains four type int variables.

4. array[0][0] is a pointer to the first four-element array of type int.

5. The first and third comparisons are true; the second is not true.

6. `void func1(char *p[]);`

7. It has no way of knowing. This value must be passed to the function as another argument.

8. A pointer to a function is a variable that holds the address where the function is stored in memory.

9. `char (*ptr)(char *x[]);`

10. If you omit the parentheses surrounding *ptr, the line is a prototype of a function that returns a pointer to type char.

11. The structure must contain a pointer to the same type of structure.

12. It means that the linked list is empty.

13. Each element in the list contains a pointer that identifies the next element in the list. The first element in the list is identified by the head pointer.

14.   a. var1 is a pointer to an integer.

      b. var2 is an integer.

      c. var3 is a pointer to a pointer to an integer.

15.   a. a is an array of 36 (3×12) integers.

      b. b is a pointer to an array of 12 integers.

      c. c is an array of 12 pointers to integers.

16.   a. z is an array of 10 pointers to characters.

       b. y is a function that takes an integer (field) as an argument and returns a
          pointer to a character.

       c. x is a pointer to a function that takes an integer (field) as an argument and
          returns a character.

Exercises

1. `float (*func)(int field);`

2. `int (*menu_option[10])(char *title);`

   An array of function pointers can be used in conjunction with a menuing system.
   The number selected from a menu could correspond to the array index for the
   function pointer. For example, the function pointed to by the fifth element of the
   array would be executed if item 5 were selected from the menu.

3. `char *ptrs[10];`

4. ptr is declared as an array of 12 pointers to integers, not a pointer to an array of 12
   integers. The correct code is

   ```
   int x[3][12];
   int (*ptr)[12];

   ptr = x;
   ```

5. The following is one of many possible solutions:

   ```
   struct friend {
       char name[35+1];
       char street1[30+1];
       char street2[30+1];
       char city[15+1];
       char state[2+1];
       char zipcode[9+1];
       struct friend *next;
   }
   ```

Answers for Day 16

Quiz

1. A text-mode stream automatically performs translation between the newline character (\n), which C uses to mark the end of a line, and the carriage-return linefeed
   character pair that DOS uses to mark the end of a line. In contrast, a binary-mode
   stream performs no translations. All bytes are input and output without modification.

F

2. Open the file using the `fopen()` library function.

3. When using `fopen()`, you must specify the name of the disk file to open and the mode to open it in. The function `fopen()` returns a pointer to type `FILE`; this pointer is used in subsequent file access functions to refer to the specific file.

4. Formatted, character, and direct.

5. Sequential and random.

6. `EOF` is the end-of-file flag. It is a symbolic constant equal to `-1`.

7. `EOF` is used with text files to determine when the end of the file has been reached.

8. In binary mode, you must use the `feof()` function. In text mode, you can look for the `EOF` character or use `feof()`.

9. The file position indicator indicates the position in a given file where the next read or write operation will occur. You can modify the file position indicator with `rewind()` and `fseek()`.

10. The file position indicator points to the first character of the file, or offset `0`. The one exception is if you open an existing file in append mode, in which case the position indicator points to the end of the file.

Exercises

1. `fcloseall();`

2. `rewind(fp);` and `fseek(fp, 0, SEEK_SET);`

3. You can't use the `EOF` check with a binary file. You should use the `feof()` function instead.

Answers for Day 17

Quiz

1. The length of a string is the number of characters between the start of the string and the terminating null character (not counting the null character). You can determine the length of a string using the `strlen()` function.

2. You must be sure to allocate sufficient storage space for the new string.

3. *Concatenate* means to join two strings, appending one string to the end of another.

4. When you compare strings, "greater than" means that one string's ASCII values are larger than the other string's ASCII values.

5. `strcmp()` compares two entire strings. `strncmp()` compares only a specified number of characters within the string.

6. `strcmp()` compares two strings, considering the case of the letters. (For example, `'A'` and `'a'` are different.) `strcmpi()` ignores case. (For example, `'A'` and `'a'` are the same.)

7. `isascii()` checks the value passed to see whether it's a standard ASCII character between 0 and 127. It doesn't check for extended ASCII characters.

8. `isascii()` and `iscntrl()` both return TRUE; all others return FALSE. Remember, these macros look at the character value.

9. 65 is equivalent to the ASCII character A. The following macros return TRUE: `isalnum()`, `isalpha()`, `isascii()`, `isgraph()`, `isprint()`, and `isupper()`.

10. The character-test functions determine whether a particular character meets a certain condition, such as whether it is a letter, punctuation mark, or something else.

Exercises

1. TRUE (1) or FALSE (0)

2.   a. 65
      b. 81
      c. −34
      d. 0
      e. 12
      f. 0

3.   a. 65.000000
      b. 81.230000
      c. −34.200000
      d. 0.000000
      e. 12.000000
      f. 1000.000000

4. `string2` wasn't allocated space before it was used. There is no way to know where `strcpy()` copies the value of `string1`.

F

Answers for Day 18

Quiz

1. Passing by value means that the function receives a copy of the value of the argument variable. Passing by reference means that the function receives the address of the argument variable. The difference is that passing by reference allows the function to modify the original variable, whereas passing by value does not.

2. A type `void` pointer can point to any type of C data object (in other words, it's a generic pointer).

3. By using a `void` pointer, you can create a generic pointer that can point to any object. The most common use of a `void` pointer is to declare function parameters. You can create a function that can handle different types of arguments.

4. A typecast provides information about the type of the data object that the `void` pointer is pointing to at the moment. You must cast a `void` pointer before dereferencing it.

5. A function that takes a variable argument list must be passed at least one fixed argument. This is done to inform the function of the number of arguments being passed each time it is called.

6. `va_start()` should be used to initialize the argument list. `va_arg()` should be used to retrieve the arguments. `va_end()` should be used to clean up after all the arguments have been retrieved.

7. Trick question! `void` pointers can't be incremented, because the compiler wouldn't know what value to add.

8. A function can return a pointer to any of the C variable types. A function can also return a pointer to such storage areas as arrays, structures, and unions.

9. `va_arg()`

10. The elements are `va_list`, `va_start()`, `va_arg()`, and `va_end()`.

Exercises

1. `int function( char array[] );`

2. `int numbers( int *nbr1, int *nbr2, int *nbr3);`

3. The code is as follows:
```
int number1 = 1, number2 = 2, number3 = 3;
numbers( &number1, &number2, &number3);
```

4. Although the code might look confusing, it is correct. This function takes the value being pointed to by `nbr` and multiplies it by itself.

5. When using variable parameter lists, you should use all the macro tools. This includes `va_list`, `va_start()`, `va_arg()`, and `va_end()`. See Listing 18.3 for the correct way to use variable parameter lists.

Answers for Day 19

Quiz

1. Type `double`.

2. On most compilers, it's equivalent to a `long`; however, this isn't guaranteed. Check the TIME.H file with your compiler or your reference manual to find out what variable type your compiler uses.

3. The `time()` function returns the number of seconds that have elapsed since midnight, January 1, 1970. The `clock()` function returns the number of 1/100 seconds that have elapsed since the program began execution.

4. Nothing. It simply displays a message that describes the error.

5. Sort the array into ascending order.

6. 14

7. 4

8. 21

9. `0` if the values are equal, `>0` if the value of element 1 is greater than element 2, and `<0` if the value of element 1 is less than element 2.

10. `NULL`

Exercises

1. The code is as follows:
```
bsearch( myname, names, (sizeof(names)/sizeof(names[0]))),
sizeof(names[0]), comp_names);
```

2. There are three problems. First, the field width isn't provided in the call to `qsort()`. Second, the parentheses shouldn't be added to the end of the function name in the call to `qsort()`. Third, the program is missing its comparison function. `qsort()` uses `compare_function()`, which isn't defined in the program.

3. The compare function returns the wrong values. It should return a positive number if `element1` is greater than `element2` and a negative number if `element1` is less than `element2`.

F

Answers for Day 20

Quiz

1. `malloc()` allocates a specified number of bytes of memory, whereas `calloc()` allocates sufficient memory for a specified number of data objects of a certain size. `calloc()` also sets the bytes of memory to 0, whereas `malloc()` doesn't initialize them to any specific value.

2. To preserve the fractional part of the answer when dividing one integer by another and assigning the result to a floating-point variable.

3.   a. `long`

     b. `int`

     c. `char`

     d. `float`

     e. `float`

4. Dynamically allocated memory is allocated at runtime—while the program is executing. Dynamic memory allocation lets you allocate exactly as much memory as is needed, only when it is needed.

5. `memmove()` works properly when the source and destination memory regions overlap, whereas `memcpy()` does not. If the source and destination regions don't overlap, the two functions are identical.

6. By defining a bit field member with a size of 3 bits. Because 2^3 equals 8, such a field is sufficient to hold values 1 through 7.

7. 2 bytes. Using bit fields, you could declare a structure as follows:
```
struct date
{
  unsigned month : 4;
  unsigned day   : 5;
  unsigned year  : 7;
}
```
   This structure stores the date in 2 bytes (16 bits). The 4-bit `month` field can hold values from 0 to 15, sufficient for holding 12 months. Likewise, the 5-bit `day` field can hold values from 0 to 31, and the 7-bit `year` field can hold values from 0 to 127. We assume that the year value will be added to 1900 to allow year values from 1900 to 2027.

8. 00100000

9. 00001001

10. These two expressions evaluate to the same result. Using exclusive OR with 11111111 is the same as using the complement operator: Each bit in the original value is reversed.

Exercises

1. The code is as follows:

```
long *ptr;
ptr = malloc( 1000 * sizeof(long));
```

2. The code is as follows:

```
long *ptr;
ptr = calloc( 1000, sizeof(long));
```

3. Using a loop and assignment statement:

```
int count;
for (count = 0; count < 1000; count++)
data[count] = 0;
```

Using the memset() function:

```
memset(data, 0, 1000 * sizeof(float));
```

4. This code will compile and run without error; however, the results will be incorrect. Because number1 and number2 are both integers, the result of their division will be an integer, thus losing any fractional part of the answer. In order to get the correct answer, you need to cast the expression to type float:

```
answer = (float) number1/number2;
```

5. Because p is a type void pointer, it must be cast to the proper type before being used in an assignment statement. The third line should be as follows:

```
*(float*)p = 1.23;
```

6. No. When using bit fields, you must place them within a structure first. The following is correct:

```
struct quiz_answers
{
  unsigned answer1    : 1;
  unsigned answer2    : 1;
  unsigned answer3    : 1;
  unsigned answer4    : 1;
  unsigned answer5    : 1;
  char student_name[15];
}
```

F

Answers for Day 21

Quiz

1. *Modular programming* refers to the program development method that breaks a program into multiple source-code files.

2. The main module contains the `main()` function.

3. To avoid unwanted side effects by ensuring that complex expressions passed as arguments to the macro are fully evaluated first.

4. Compared to a function, a macro results in faster program execution but larger program size.

5. The `defined()` operator tests to see whether a particular name is defined, returning `TRUE` if the name is defined and `FALSE` if it isn't.

6. You must use `#endif`.

7. Compiled source files become object files with an .OBJ extension.

8. `#include` copies the contents of another file into the current file.

9. An `#include` statement with double quotes looks in the current directory for the include file. An `include` statement with <> searches the standard directory for the include file.

10. `__DATE__` is used to place into the program the date that the program was compiled.

A string containing the name of the current program, including path information.

Answers for Bonus Day 1

Quiz

1. An OOP language is characterized by

   Polymorphism

   Encapsulation

   Inheritance

   Reuse

2. Polymorphism

3. None. All of the C commands can be used in a C++ program.

4. C can be used to do object oriented programming; however, it would be very complex. C++ and Java both have object-oriented features built into them. If you are going to do object-oriented programming, you are much better off using C++ or Java.

5. No. Java can be thought of as C++ minus those features that cause unnecessary complexity and the likelihood of errors.

6. For C++ the answer is yes—you have the option of using either procedural or object-oriented techniques (or both) in a program. With Java, the answer is no. Java requires the use of object-oriented techniques.

7. `cout`

8. `System.out.println()`

9. `System.Console.WriteLine()`

Answers for Bonus Day 2

Quiz

1. True or False

2. You should never use `printf()` in a C++ program.

3. bool

4. Variables in C++ can be declared at any point within a listing.

5. `throw`

6. Default values enable you to create a single function that can take a multiple number of parameters. Overloading functions allows you to create different functions that take different data types or different numbers of parameters.

7. All three of these have the same number of parameters with the same data types; therefore, none of these functions can be overlaid with each other.

8. `int triangle( int side1 = 0, int side2 = 0, int side 3 = 0 );`

   This is a bit of a trick question. The definition of the inline function is true. The compiler does not do this for every function specified as inline. The compiler may choose to ignore the inline specifier if it doesn't believe the resulting code will be more efficient.

F

Answers for Bonus Day 3

Quiz

1. A structure is a special form of the class in C++. The structure's members are public by default. A class' members are private by default. Note that, if you are using member functions, you should use a class instead of a structure.

2. A class is only a definition, so you cannot assign values to it. You can use it to create an object. The object can have values assigned to it.

3. An object is a variable that has been created using a class.

4. To instantiate a class means to create an object using the class.

5. Classes have characteristics from all three object-oriented features. Classes illustrate encapsulation because they contain all the data and functionality in a single construct. Polymorphism can be seen in the fact that classes can have overlaid functions including their constructors. Inheritance is also a feature of classes. Bonus Day 4 will illustrate inheritance in more detail.

6. A private data member can only be accessed from other data members within a class.

7. A public data member can be accessed directly from any part when the object is in scope.

8. A constructor is executed when an object is instantiated.

9. A destructor is executed when an object is destroyed.

10. A class isn't different from using other types of data as a data member. You can use a class just as you can use an integer, character, structure, or any other data type.

11.   a. base class

        b. subclass

        c. neither the base class nor the subclass

    The guppy is the subclass.

12.   a. base class

        b. subclass

        c. neither the base class nor the subclass

    The fish is the base class.

13. `class guppy : public fish {`

14. The base class constructor executes first.

15. The subclass destructor executes first.

Answers for Bonus Day 4

Quiz

1. Type `long`.

2. Yes, but they are called *methods*.

3. Either `while` or `do...while`.

4 You use `import` to make other classes available in your Java program.

5. There are three Java comment styles:

   - Anything between `/*` and `*/` is a comment.

   - Anything on a line after `//` is a comment.

   - Anything between `/**` and `*/` is a comment.

6. Java identifiers are case-sensitive, so `count` and `Count` refers to two different things.

7. Any type—there are no restrictions on data type in Java arrays.

Answers for Bonus Day 5

Quiz

1. You have no choice in the matter. Constructor method always have the same name as the class they are in.

2. Use `extends` in the first line of a class definition to specify the parent class that the new class will inherit from.

3. No. If the return type of a method is declared as `void`, the method does not return a value.

4. Yes, as long as the different constructor methods all have a different number and/or type of arguments.

5. When an instance of the class is created.

6. No. If a class was created with the `final` keyword, it cannot be used as a parent class.

7. The `final` keyword is used to prevent a class from being inherited from.

8. No, an abstract class cannot be used to instantiate an object. You can, however, inherit from it.

F

Answers for Bonus Day 6

Quiz

1. Yes. The Java compiler will not permit a `try` without a following `catch`.

2. No. You must add the new line character `\n` to the string if you want to start a new line.

3. On `java.applet.Applet`.

4. Use the `show` method to display an application.

5. There are several techniques for responding to user events, but the most important one uses the `action` method, which is called automatically when an event such as a mouse click occurs.

6. Yes, but it is ignored when the applet runs.

7. The methods `init` and `start` are called, in that order.

8. The `destroy` method.

Answers for Bonus Day 7

Quiz

1. • C# is simple.

    • C# is modern.

    • C# is object-oriented.

    • C# is powerful and flexible.

    • C# is a language of few words.

    • C# is modular.

    • C# will be popular.

2. IL stands for Intermediate Language. CLR stands for Common Language Runtime.

3. a. Create the source file.

    b. Compile the program.

    c. Execute the program.

4. `csc my_prog.cs`

5. `.cs`

6. Yes; however, it is not recommended.

7. You should review the code to verify that you didn't create a logic error.

8. It is the language that a computer can understand.

9. `Write()` and `WriteLine()`.

Exercises

1. The listing should look like mumbled and jumbled text. It could include weird characters and more.

2. The program prints out a block of X's:

```
XXXXXXXXXX
XXXXXXXXXX
XXXXXXXXXX
XXXXXXXXXX
XXXXXXXXXX
XXXXXXXXXX
XXXXXXXXXX
XXXXXXXXXX
XXXXXXXXXX
XXXXXXXXXX
```

F

APPENDIX G

Getting Started with Dev-C++

You will find a copy of Dev-C++ on the CD that comes with this book. While this is a C++ compiler, it can also be used to create C programs. In this appendix you will learn

- What Dev-C++ is
- How to install Dev-C++
- How to enter, compile, and run a program in Dev-C++

Caution   Note that Bloodshed Dev-C++ is Windows program. If you are not running
Windows 95 or later, you will not be able to use this program. See the document files that come with the compiler for more information.

What is Dev-C++

Bloodshed Dev-C++ is an Integrated Development Environment (IDE) that can be used to create and compile C or C++ programs. Dev-C++ is included on the CD that came with this book.

Dev-C++ has many tools, like a Setup Creator, automatically DLL generation, Project Templates, Icon Library and much more. To learn more about each of these tools, you should consult the help files that come with the tool.

In order to use Dev-C++, you need a system that has Windows 95 or later (98, 2000, NT, etc.). Additionally, you need a system with at least 8 megabytes of RAM, 30 megabytes of hard disk space and at least a 100MHz processor. To get better performance, it is recommended that you actually have at least 32 megabytes of ram, 45 megabytes of hard disk space and a 233MHz or faster processor.

Installing Dev-C++ on Microsoft Windows

Dev-C++ is included on the CD that came with this book. When you insert the CD, if you have autorun enabled, you will be greeted with the CD's menu. Select "Launch Dev-C++ Installer" to start the installation process for Dev-C++. This will be located in a Compiler Center section of the CD.

If autorun is not enabled, you will need to run the setup program directly from the CD. You can run the Dev-C++ setup program by selecting and running the Setup.EXE program in the Dev-C++ directory on the CD. If your CD drive is D, you would run D:\Dev-C++\Setup.EXE.

Regardless of whether you select to install Dev-C++ using the CD's menus or by executing the setup program directly, when the program runs, you will first be greeted with the licensing agreement (Figure G.1).

Dev-C++ is distributed under the standard GNU licensing agreement. If you are unfamiliar with the GNU licensing agreement, then you can read the information presented in the dialog displayed in Figure G.1.

FIGURE G.1

The Dev-C++ License agreement.

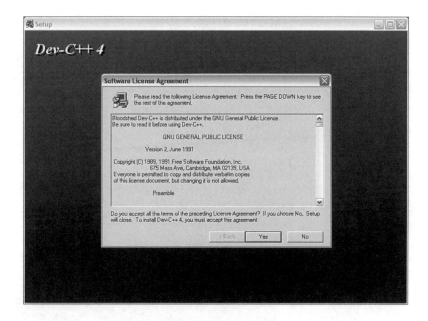

To move beyond this screen, press the Yes button. This will present you with the dialog presented in Figure G.2.

FIGURE G.2

The Setup Type dialog.

G

From the dialog presented in Figure G.02 you can select the type of setup you would like. If you are unsure, then you should use the typical setup. From this dialog, you can also change where Dev-C++ is installed. By default the program will be installed into a directory called Dev-C++ on your C: drive. If you'd like it installed somewhere else, select the browse button and enter a new directory. Once you are satisfied with your selections, press the Next button to continue.

Note   You can also select the Compact or Custom install options. Compact will allow you to install the fewest options, thus taking up the least amount of space. Selecting Custom will give you additional control over what is installed.

After selecting the setup type, the installation will start (see Figure G.3).

FIGURE G.3

Installing the Dev-C++ files.

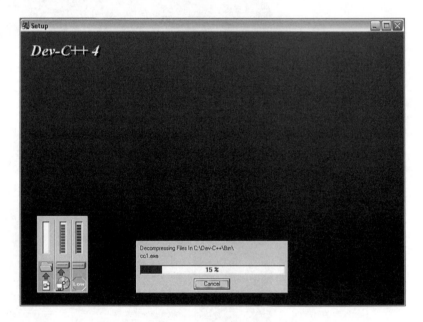

Once all the files are copied, the setup program will add Dev-C++ to your start up menu. You will then be prompted with one final dialog (Figure G.4). From this dialog you can choose to review the readme file and to launch the program. Alternatively, you can simply select Finish to end the setup. You will then be able to run the program from the Start menu in Windows.

The Dev-C++ Programs

The Dev-C++ installation will place a number of links on your Windows Start menu. The following links are placed under the Dev-C++ menu option:

- Debugger
- Dev-C++
- Dev-C++ help file
- GDB Debugger help
- License
- ReadMe
- Standard Template Library guide
- Tutorial

This book is about programming in C, not about using the Dev-C++ development environment. To find out more about each of the above options, you should review the Dev-C++ Help files and tutorial. The following sections will, however, show you the basics of compiling a C program with Dev-C++.

 Tip

Start with the Dev-C++ help file rather than the Tutorial if you are interested in learning more about Dev-C++.

Using Dev-C++

You can use Dev-C++ to create both C and C++ programs. You run the development environment by selecting Program Files, Dev-C++, Dev-C++. This will launch the Dev-C++ IDE. When you run the program, you will be placed into the IDE as shown in Figure G.4.

While Dev-C++ is generally setup to use project files, you can also use it to enter a single C source file. A project file is used to create an application that can contain multiple files. For most of the applications you create in this book, you only need to enter a single source file at a time.

Customizing Dev-C++ for C Programming

Before learning to enter and run a program, there are a few options you should consider setting. You only need to set these options once.

G

FIGURE G.4

*The initial Dev-C++
IDE.*

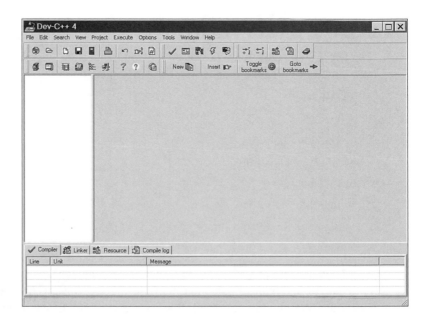

To set the compiler to use the ANSI C standard, select "Compiler options" from the Options menu. This will present you with the dialog shown in Figure G.5.

FIGURE G.5

*The Compiler options
dialog.*

From this dialog you should chose the C/C++ Compiler tab. This will present the dialog in Figure G.6.

In this dialog you should first check the "Support all ANSI C programs" option. This will allow the compiler to recognize ANSI standard commands. You should also go ahead and check "Attempt to support some aspects of traditional C compilers." For more on what these options do, you can check the help files that came with the compiler.

FIGURE G.6

The C/C++ options dialog.

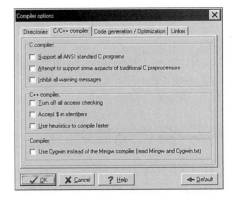

You should note that the Dev-C++ compiler supports the ANSI standards prior to ANSI C-99 (ISO/IEC 9899:1999). This means that the most recent ANSI standard is not recognized by this version of Dev-C++. This includes the support of single line comments. Single line comments will give you an error if the "Support all ANSI C programs" option is selected. If you want to support single line comments, you should not select this option. Consult the help files in Dev-C++ to see what other features are not supported.

Entering and Compiling with Dev-C++

You do not need to use projects in Dev-C++ with the listings presented in this book. Rather, you can enter and compile each listing individually. Listing G.1 presents a small program that can be entered and compiled as an example.

LISTING G.1   Sample.c – Sample program

```
 1:  // Sample.c
 2:  #include <stdlib.h>
 3:
 4:  int main( void )
 5:  {
 6:       printf("Dev-C++ Sample Program at work!");
 7:
 8:       system("PAUSE");
 9:       return 0;
10:  }
```

Note   Don't enter the line numbers or colons. These are for reference only.

G

To enter and compile the Sample.c program in Listing G.1, follow these steps:

1. **Create a new source file.**

   With Dev-C++ open, select "New Source file" from the File menu option. Dev-C++ will automatically create a source file and place some code into it. Figure G.7 shows this dialog with the default code.

FIGURE G.7

The default source file.

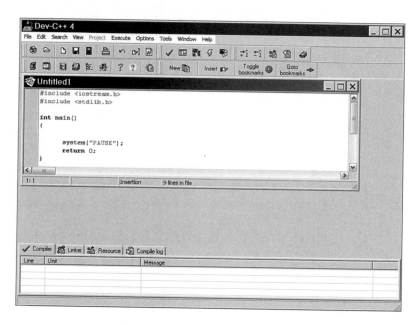

2. **Enter the source file.**

   As shown in Figure G.8, replace the code in the dialog with the code from Listing G.1 above. You will enter listings from this book in the same manner. You should note that line 6 of this listing prints out a simple message. Line 8 is added to cause the program to pause until you press a key. Without this line, when you execute the program you would not see the results because they would be displayed and removed too fast. More will be said on this later.

3. **Save the source file.**

   Once you have entered the source code, you need to save it. Dev-C++ gives the file a default name of Untitled followed by a number. To save your program and give it a more useful name, select "Save unit as" from the File menu. You will be prompted with a standard save dialog as shown in Figure G.9.

FIGURE G.8

Entering your own source code.

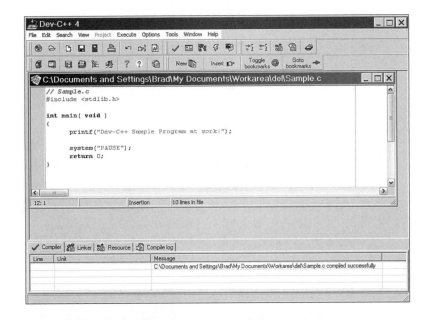

FIGURE G.9

The Save unit as dialog.

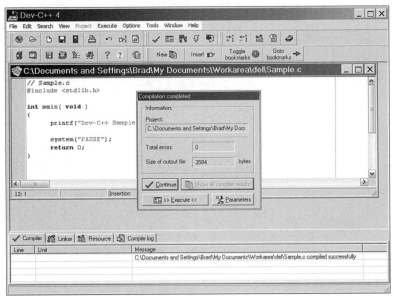

G

In this dialog you can name your file. You can also change the directory in which you save the file. Before saving the file, you should change the "Save source as" option to "C source file". This will insure that a .c extension is used rather than a

.cpp (C++) extension. Save the sample file as Sample. By selecting the C source file option, a .c extension will automatically be added. Once you have saved the file, the dialog will reflect the new name that you have given the file. You can then use the disk icon to save the file.

 Note   You can actually use the disk icon or the menu options interchangeably.

Compiling a Dev-C++ Program

Once you've entered and saved your C program, you need to compile it. To compile in Dev-C++, you select Compile from the Execute menu option. Alternatively you can select the check mark icon or Ctrl+F9. When you compile the program, a dialog will be displayed indicating whether there were any errors (see Figure G.10) .

FIGURE G.10

Compiling your program.

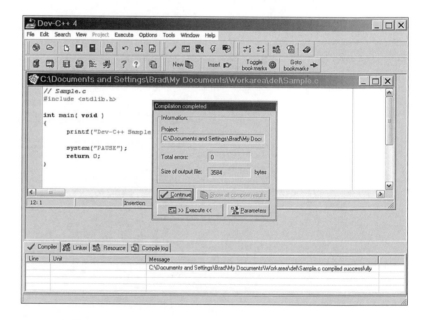

As you can see in Figure G.10, the Total errors box indicates no errors. If this is not zero, there were errors. These errors will be listed at the bottom of the screen. If you received any errors when you entered the listing, make sure that you entered the listing exactly as displayed. Also make sure you didn't include the line numbers and colons.

If you press Continue, you will be returned to the editor.

Running a Program Created with Dev-C++

From the dialog presented in Figure G.10, you can also run the program. You do this by selecting the Execute button. If the program is a DOS program—as the one in Listing G.1 is—a DOS windows will be opened and the program will be ran. When the program ends, the DOS window will automatically be closed. Figure G.11 presents the Sample.c program being executed by pressing the Execute button. If the dialog presented in chapter Figure G.10 is already closed, you can run the program by either pressing the F9 key or by selecting Run from the Execute menu option.

FIGURE G.11

Executing your program from the Dev-C++ IDE.

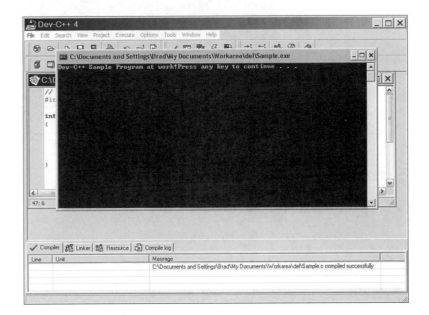

The system("PAUSE") command in line 8 prompts you to press a key before the program will end. In most of the programs you create in this book, there will not be a pause command. This means that you may not notice the program run. This is because the DOS window will open, the program will run, and then the DOS window will immediately close. To get around this, you can open a DOS window yourself. A DOS window can be opened by selecting Command Prompt from the Accessories menu option on the Program Options menu from the Start menu of Windows. Once you have opened a Command Prompt window, you can change to the directory you saved your program. Once there, type the name of the program with no extension to run it. Figure G.12 presents the Sample program running in a Command Prompt window.

G

FIGURE G.12

Executing your program from a Command Prompt.

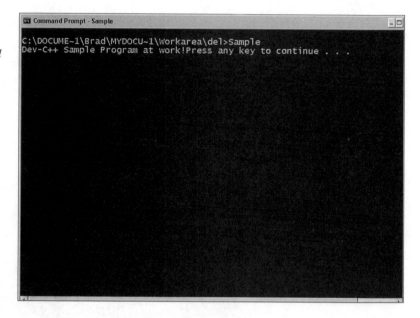

Summary

After reading this appendix, you should be able to install and use the Dev-C++ compiler. Dev-C++ has a number of features that were not covered in this appendix. For more information on using the IDE, consult the help and other files that came with it.

Note

Note that the Help files included with Dev-C++ include an FAQ (Frequently Asked Questions) list. This list includes questions along with answers to many common problems you may run into.

INDEX

Symbols

C

How can we make this index more useful? Email us at indexes@samspublishing.com

Q-R

qsort() function, 550

quicksort algorithm, 550

quotation marks

    format strings, 148

radians, trigonometric functions, 533

RAM, 42, 570. *See also* memory

    address, 196

random file access

    versus sequential, 457

        fseek() function, 460, 463

        ftell()/rewind() functions, 458-460

random.c, 185

reading

    strings, 237

        gets() function, 237-241

        scanf() function, 241-243

    structures, portability, 816

    text files, 745-746

reading file data, 445

readLine method, 745

realloc() function, 575-577

rectangles, nested structures of, 254

recursion

    calling functions, 116-118

    indirect, 116

redirecting input/output, 368-370

redirection command, 606

redirection operator (<<), 650

register keywords, 295

register variables, 295

registers, 295

relational operators, 71

    evaluating, 78

    precedence, 80

remove() function, 465

rename() function, 466

renaming files, 466-467

reserved words, 9, 789, 791

return keyword, 111

return statements, 100, 111-112

    of functions, 102

return types, of functions, writing, 105

reusing code, OOP, 631

rewind() function, 458-460

Ritchie, Dennis, 7

running programs, 35

S

samples. *See* listings

scanf() function, 32, 157, 160-161, 241-243

    arguments, 161

    listing, 242-243

scanf() function, 356-358

    arguments, 350-352

    conversion specifiers, 350-352

    handling extra characters, 352-355

    precision modifiers, 352

scope, 286-288

    external compared to external static, 295

    external variables, 289

    function parameters, 294

screen output, 358

    character output functions, 358-360

        fputc() function, 360

        putc() function, 360

        putchar() function, 358-360

    formatted output functions, 361-368

    string output functions, 360-361

searching library functions

    bsearch, 549

    example, 550-553, 556

searching strings, 494

    strchr() function, 495

    strcspn() function, 496

How can we make this index more useful? Email us at indexes@samspublishing.com

Bradley L. Jones

Learn the skills and concepts to master C# programming in just 21 days

Apply your C# knowledge in the real world

SAMS
Teach Yourself

C#

in 21 Days

SAMS

Sams Teach Yourself C# in 21 Days

Bradley L. Jones

0-672-32071-1

$39.99 USA/$59.95 CAN

SAMS Teach Yourself in 21 Days

Sams Teach Yourself in 21 Days *teaches you all the skills you need to master the basics and then moves on to the more advanced features and concepts. This series is designed for the way you learn. Go chapter by chapter through the step-by-step lessons or just choose those lessons that interest you the most.*

Sams Teach Yourself C++ in 21 Days, Fourth Edition
0-672-32072-X
Jesse Liberty
$34.99US / $52.95CAN

Other Sams Teach Yourself in 21 Days Titles

Sams Teach Yourself Object Oriented Programming in 21 Days
0-672-32109-2
Anthony Sintes
$39.99US / $62.99CAN

Sams Teach Yourself XML in 21 Days
0-672-32093-2
Devan Shepherd
$39.99US / $62.99CAN

Sams Teach Yourself Perl in 21 Days, Second Edition
0-672-32035-5
Laura Lemay and
Richard Colburn
$34.99US / $52.95CAN

Sams Teach Yourself SQL in 21 Days
0-672-32451-2
Ron Plew and Ryan
Stephens
$39.99US / $62.99CAN

Sams Teach Yourself J2EE in 21 Days
0-672-32384-2
Martin Bond, et. al.
$49.99US / $77/99CAN

Sams Teach Yourself Java 2 in 21 Days, Third Edition
0-672-32370-2
Laura Lemay and
Rogers Cadenhead
$34.99US / $52.95CAN

SAMS

www.samspublishing.com

All prices are subject to change.

What's on the CD-ROM

The companion CD-ROM contains all of the source code for the examples developed in the book, DJGPP (a DOS-based C/C++ compiler), and Dev-C++ (a Windows-based C/C++ compiler).

Windows Installation Instructions

1. Insert the disc into your CD-ROM drive.
2. From the Windows desktop, double-click the My Computer icon.
3. Double-click the icon representing your CD-ROM drive.
4. Double-click on `start.exe`. Follow the on-screen prompts to access the CD-ROM information.

> **Note**
> If you have the AutoPlay feature enabled, `start.exe` will be launched automatically whenever you insert the disc into your CD-ROM drive.

By opening this package, you are also agreeing to be bound by the following agreement:

You may not copy or redistribute the entire CD-ROM as a whole. Copying and redistribution of individual software programs on the CD-ROM is governed by terms set by individual copyright holders.

The installer and code from the author(s) are copyrighted by the publisher and the author(s). Individual programs and other items on the CD-ROM are copyrighted or are under an Open Source license by their various authors or other copyright holders.

This software is sold as-is without warranty of any kind, either expressed or implied, including but not limited to the implied warranties of merchantability and fitness for a particular purpose. Neither the publisher nor its dealers or distributors assumes any liability for any alleged or actual damages arising from the use of this program. (Some states do not allow for the exclusion of implied warranties, so the exclusion may not apply to you.)

NOTE: This CD-ROM uses long and mixed-case filenames requiring the use of a protected-mode CD-ROM Driver.